COMPETING VISIONS

COMPETING VISIONS
A History of California

Robert W. Cherny
San Francisco State University

Richard Griswold del Castillo
San Diego State University

Gretchen Lemke-Santangelo
Saint Mary's College of California

Houghton Mifflin Company
Boston   New York

Publisher: Charles Hartford
Sponsoring Editor: Jeffrey Greene
Editorial Assistant: Kisha Mitchell
Senior Project Editor: Bob Greiner
Editorial Assistant: Robert Woo
Manufacturing Coordinator: Renee Ostrowski
Senior Marketing Manager: Sandra McGuire

Printed in the U.S.A.

Library of Congress Catalog Number: 2004112828

ISBN: 0-395-95964-0

3456789-QUF-11 10 09 08 07

Contents

5 | California and the Crisis of the Union, 1850–1870   124

6 | California in the Gilded Age, 1870–1900   159

7 | California in the Progressive Era, 1895–1920   194

8 | California Between the Wars, 1919–1941   231

9 | World War II and the Great Transformation 266

10 | Postwar California: Prosperity and Discontent in the Golden State 301

11 | Contested Visions: Activism and Politics, 1964–1970   337

12 | Era of Limits   373

13 | California Enters the New Millennium 409

Preface

The decision to write this textbook grew out of our experience teaching California history to an increasingly diverse student population. Our classrooms contain an exciting mix of students from a myriad of ethnic, multiethnic, international, gender, and socioeconomic backgrounds. Their levels of academic readiness also differ, and nearly all are products of a visual, rather than print-oriented, culture. In light of this diversity, we, as educators, needed a text geared toward varied learning styles and academic skill levels—one that would stress reading comprehension, critical thinking, and the synthesis and integration of knowledge. Just as important, we needed a more inclusive text that reflected the history of all of our students—one designed to foster active identification with the past, civic engagement, an appreciation of diversity, and cross-cultural communication and understanding. Thus, we wrote this text for our students and ourselves, and with the hope that our colleagues would find it equally useful.

Themes

Three major themes, which run throughout the thirteen chapters, highlight continuity over time and provide a common, unifying thread for the narrative. They are also crafted to enhance students' global and cross-cultural awareness. The first, California and its relationship to its region, the nation, and the world, places California within a national, and often global, context. The state, although frequently depicted as a trendsetter or "place apart," has always been influenced by outside demographic, environmental, political, cultural, and economic forces. Its first people came from diverse cultural and linguistic backgrounds, and developed complex trade networks that facilitated cultural and economic exchange far beyond the state's current boundaries. Later, as part of Spain's global empire, California and its people were subject to new influences and pressures. In turn, Mexico's war for independence and America's war with Mexico profoundly altered the state's cultural, economic, political, and environmental landscape. More recently, California's integration into the Pacific Rim economy has created a new set of challenges and prospects. Once again, the state is in dynamic interaction with other geographic entities.

A second theme is cultural richness and diversity. Here we focus on how demographic diversity has created a broad range of cultural expression. Beginning with California's first people, cultural diversity has been an integral part of the human landscape. Wave after wave of migrants and immigrants, the emergence of ethnic enclaves, and the birth of numerous subcultures have added additional layers of richness, and at times produced interesting cultural fusions. As a consequence, the state's cuisine, music, art, architecture, folklore, cinema, theater, dance, and public spaces all carry the imprint of its incredibly diverse and increasingly complex mixture of ethnic and national groups.

Such diversity has also led to competing visions of the "California Dream," the text's third and final theme. Since at least 1769, Californians have been at odds over the allocation of cultural, economic, and political power. The dream, synonymous with opportunity, not only placed individuals and groups in competition, but also carried different meanings for different people. To some, for example, the state's natural resources represented an opportunity for industrial expansion and monetary advancement. To others, California's natural endowment represented the opportunity to maintain an older, more traditional way of life, a font of physical and spiritual renewal, or a fragile and irreplaceable part of the planet's life support system. In social terms, many equated opportunity with toleration and inclusion, while others saw opportunity in discrimination and exclusion. Politically, many Californians linked opportunity to the progressive or liberal traditions that encouraged a stronger role for government in allocating resources and guiding growth and expansion. Others, however, equated "big government" with the erosion of individual opportunity and initiative.

Consistent with these themes, we have chosen to emphasize some topics more than others. In developing the history of state politics, most chapters stress political challenges from the powerless and disfranchised, and the competing visions of a diverse electorate. The state's natural resources, and conflicts over their allocation and exploitation, also figure prominently in the text. Finally, the experience and contributions of California's multiethnic and multinational constituents are integral to every chapter.

Approach

To enhance learning among a diverse student population we crafted a text with a chronological and narrative format. This approach, while offering the advantages of clarity and coherence, also reflects a renewed emphasis on synthesis and the big picture among historians and educators. Moreover, the sequential framework helps students follow, connect, and integrate historical knowledge—the foundation of learning to think historically. Within the general narrative we added several other learning aids. Each chapter opens with a vignette about a specific individual whose experience illuminates important developments of the period. This feature, representing the personal side of history, is designed to promote active engagement with the past and a sense of human agency—the sense that all Californians shape the state's history, present, and future. Every chapter also includes a list of significant dates and events, and a series of study questions intended to enhance reader comprehension and promote critical thinking and debate.

Similarly, many of the photograph and illustration captions ask students to look critically at what they are seeing. Concise chapter introductions and summaries reinforce reading comprehension, and synthesize and integrate the material. Suggested readings at the end of each chapter encourage more in-depth research into topics of special interest.

Our individual interests as practicing historians shaped our choices as we constructed the text. Richard Griswold del Castillo, professor of Chicana and Chicano studies at San Diego State University, wrote chapters one through four. He teaches courses in Chicano history and the Mexican/United States borderlands. His research focuses on the nineteenth-century Southwest, and Mexican American community history and civil rights struggles. The first chapter, devoted to the history of California's indigenous people, emphasizes the diversity and complexity of California Indian cultures. Subsequent chapters relate the history of the first Euro-Americans and mestizos who came north to colonize California, stressing the influence of Indian peoples on the culture and economy of the missions, presidios, and pueblos. These chapters present new perspectives on the ways in which the Indians resisted colonial subjugation, as well as the cultural fusion that took place before the American era. They also emphasize the ways in which the emerging Californio culture was a vital and adaptive response to the new environment. The chapter on the Mexican War and Gold Rush reflects the influence of thirty years of new scholarship that challenges the older "triumphalist" vision of American progress and prosperity. The conflicts among Indian, Spanish-Mexican, and Anglo-American cultures, and an assessment of what was gained and lost in the American conquest of California are important features of this chapter.

Robert W. Cherny, professor of history at San Francisco State University, teaches courses on U.S. history between the Civil War and World War II as well as courses on the history of California. His research focuses on American politics between the Civil War and World War I, and politics and labor in California and the West from the Civil War to World War II. His chapters, five through eight, trace the state's history from about 1850 until World War II. There is a special effort to explain economic cycles and their relation to the state's economic development and diversification. Other major topics include the experiences of an increasingly diverse population that included not only the descendants of the first peoples and the Californios but also migrants from other parts of North America, Europe, Latin America, and Asia; changing gender roles for men and women; political development, including political responses to ethnic diversity and to economic issues; and the relation of cultural expression to all these other patterns. There is also attention to urbanization, especially the development of San Francisco in the late nineteenth century and Los Angeles in the early twentieth century.

Gretchen Lemke-Santangelo, professor of history at Saint Mary's College of California and author of chapters nine through twelve, teaches courses in California and U.S. history, African American history, the history of American women, and U.S. environmental history. Her research focuses on African American migration, twentieth-century movements for social change, and urban poverty. Her chapters, beginning with World War II and concluding in the late 1980s, cover standard material on population growth, economic expansion, natural resources, environmental degradation, public policy, and major political figures and legislation. However, there are many features that depart from the traditional narrative. Racial tensions and discrimination are covered in each chapter, but with an emphasis on civil rights activism and protest. Rather than being portrayed as passive victims, Mexican Americans, African Americans, Asian Americans, and Indians are represented as active agents of social, political, and cultural change. Gender also receives significant attention, including in-depth coverage of women's status and activism, and the emergence of gay, lesbian, and transgender communities and institutions. Her discussion of politics extends to neglected social movements such as the welfare rights, disability rights, eco-feminist, environmental justice, and AIDS action initiatives, along with more familiar ethnic power, antiwar, New Left, countercultural, gay pride, and women's movements. Similarly, discussion of economic policy and expansion are balanced with coverage of labor activism, employment and wage discrimination, class tensions and stratification, capital and white flight, access to social services and affordable housing, and competing liberal and conservative economic visions.

Chapter thirteen, jointly written by all the authors and Joshua Paddison, now a Ph.D. candidate in history at UCLA, covers contemporary issues and events—many of which unfolded as we wrote: the recent economic recession, energy deregulation and crisis, the unfolding Enron scandal, the impact of 9/11, the recall of Governor Gray Davis, and the election of Arnold Schwarzenegger. The chapter also covers the state's increasing integration into the global economy through the North American Free Trade Agreement and Pacific Rim trade, the erosion of California's infrastructure (including public schools), the declining affordability of housing and health care, immigration policy and anti-immigrant hostility, increasing demographic diversity, and recent cultural trends.

Teaching Aids

A computerized test bank prepared by Professor Emily Rader of El Camino College and Jacqueline Braitman of the University of California at Los Angeles contains multiple-choice and essay questions.

Acknowledgments

The authors wish to thank the attentive, insightful, and creative staff at Houghton Mifflin. Jeff Greene, ever patient, supportive, and generous with his time, shepherded the manuscript through its conceptualization to its actual production. Thank you for having faith in our vision. Bob Greiner and Robert Woo, along with Susan Holtz and Patti Isaacs, as well as others in the Houghton Mifflin team, did a masterful job during production. Thank you for your creative insights and tact.

Joshua Paddison provided crucial assistance with the development of chapter thirteen.

Several of our California history colleagues carefully read and commented on three separate drafts of the manuscript. Their knowledge of the subject and attention to detail make it a far more balanced, accessible, and meaningful text. We extend our deepest thanks to these readers:

Daniel Lewis, *California State Polytechnic University, Pomona*
Nancy J. Taniguchi, *California State University, Stanislaus*
John Putman, *San Diego State University*
Dian Self, *American River College*
E. A. Schwartz, *California State University, San Marcos*
Ernesto S. Sweeney, *Loyola Marymount University, Los Angeles*
Edie Sparks, *University of the Pacific*
Nancy Quam-Wickham, *California State University, Long Beach*
Denise S. Spooner, *California State University, Northridge*
Carolle J. Carter, *San José State University*
Joseph A. Pitti, *California State University, Sacramento*

In addition to the formal readers, several individuals and institutions offered invaluable support and assistance as we moved through the writing and revision process. Gretchen Lemke-Santangelo would especially like to thank Saint Mary's College Office of Faculty Development, Anthony Santangelo, and Anna Marie Daniels. Robert Cherny would like to thank the students who served as his research assistants over the course of this project, including Michael Lumish, Jennifer Choi, Ann Wilson, and Peter Gray.

Richard Griswold del Castillo
Robert W. Cherny
Gretchen Lemke-Santangelo

COMPETING VISIONS

1

California's Origins: The Land and the People, Before Spanish Settlement

Main Topics

▌ Diversity: Origins of California and Its Native Peoples

▌ Cycles of Life: The Food Quest, Spirituality, and Rituals

▌ A Closer Look: Six Regional Peoples

▌ Significance: The Importance of California Natives and Other North American Native Peoples in Non-Indian History

▌ Summary

"In the beginning on the water that was everywhere, a downy feather swirled and swirled upon a tiny fleck of foam."

If you were a Yuki Indian child living in what is now Mendocino County in 13,000 BCE, you might have listened enraptured as an elder began to tell this story of creation, one version of many that existed among the earliest of North American cultures.

"Listen closely to the feather," the elder might have intoned, "and you will hear the singing of Taikomol, the creator of the world, whose name means He-who-goes-alone. Swirling and singing, swirling and singing, Taikomol rose up from the water and became a man—but he was not alone. Hanging from his body was another god, the god Coyote, the selfish one of death and pain. With Coyote at his side, Taikomol made a

CHAPTER 1	California's Origins: The Land and the People, Before Spanish Settlement
CENOZOIC PERIOD, 66 MILLION YEARS BCE	Warm-blooded animals populate North America
MIOCENE PERIOD, 23 MILLION YEARS BCE	Creation of the Sierra Nevada mountains
PLEISTOCENE PERIOD, 2 MILLION YEARS BCE	Cooling and ice age create valleys and present-day coastline of California
13,000 BCE	Estimate of first human settlement in California
900 BCE	Corn, beans, and squash enter Colorado River region from Mexico
100 BCE–700 CE	Introduction of pottery in California
1542 CE	Juan Rodriguez Cabrillo explores California coast
1602 CE	Sebastián Vizcaíno discovers Monterey Bay
1769 CE	First Euro-Americans settle in California

basket from parts of his own body. Reaching deep into the basket he drew forth a ball of mud, which he molded with pine pitch to make the earth. Jealous Coyote clung to Taikomol as he traveled over the new earth four times from north to south, fastening its four corners with a sky made from the skins of four whales. This earth is good, Taikomol thought, and so he wanted to share all he had created. Reaching deep again into his basket he found sticks of wood, and placed them in a protected place, a kind of house. Through the night Taikomol was swirling and singing over this house, with Coyote hovering at his side and peeking sharply into the dwelling with his jealousy growing. When dawn broke the darkness, the sticks walked as people into the morning.

"Taikomol was filled with joy at his creation and wanted people to live forever, but jealous Coyote wanted them to die. When the first son died and was buried, Taikomol offered to bring him back to life, but Coyote said that the dead should remain dead. The other gods agreed, and for that reason people do not come to life again after they die."

As the elder finished, your young eyes might have shone as you repeated softly to yourself, "For that reason people do not come to life again after they die." Creative stories such as this one, passed on through the generations, reflect the very diversity of California itself, distinctive from its beginnings in its geographic formations, climate, variety and plenitude of flora and fauna, and the multiplicity of its Indian peoples. The earliest human history of this region shows that in California no single generalization could ever capture reality; it has always been an unusual locale where, because of its lush environment, a large population of diverse peoples could live together and thrive.

Questions to Consider

▌ What factors explain California's distinctiveness as a place, and how did those factors affect the characteristics of its first settlers?

▌ What important characteristics did the first settlers share, and what were some salient differences?

▌ How did the many achievements of the native peoples contribute to the non-Indian history of the North American continent?

Diversity: Origins of California and Its Native Peoples

The land that the Yukis believe was created by Taikomol was located at that time at about the same latitude as twenty-first-century Cuba. It later became known as California. Sixty million years ago, ocean waves lapped the western side of the Sierra Nevada mountains, which were then merely well-worn hills. These hills allowed the winds to carry torrential tropical rains eastward, where the ocean's moisture created a tropical forest with great varieties of exotic plants and animals. In some places, the annual rainfall exceeded fifty inches. This area is now known as the Great Basin, and includes the present-day states of Nevada, Arizona, and Utah. In Cenozoic California (sixty-six million years ago), the great dinosaurs that had once ranged over the land had already mysteriously disappeared and warm-blooded mammals such as lions, giant sloths, and camels roamed the land.

Forty-three million years later the earth began to move upward, thrust by tremendous volcanic pressures in its crust (Miocene period, twenty-three million years ago). A series of earthquakes thrust up solid rock formations, including the Sierra Nevada range—pushed ten thousand feet up in the air—and the coastal mountain ranges. These mountains were massive enough to cut off the flow of rainstorms that had been watering the Great Basin. To the east of these mountains a desert began to develop. Mount Lassen and other now-extinct volcanoes erupted, darkening the skies and layering the earth with a rich ash. Mount Shasta, Mount Whitney, and scores of other enormous peaks reached their present altitudes. Simultaneously the climate began to cool around the world, perhaps

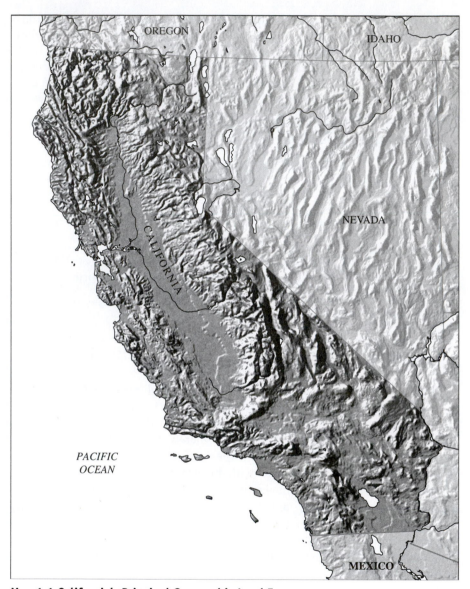

Map 1.1 California's Principal Geographic Land Forms

Source: Map taken from Robert F. Heizer, ed., *Handbook of North American Indians: California,* William C. Sturtevant, series ed. (Washington, D.C.: Smithsonian Institution Press, 1978), p. ix.

because a chain of volcanoes between North and South America filled in the Panama lowlands and stopped water circulation between the Pacific and Atlantic Oceans. Or perhaps because of the uplift of the great Himalayan Mountain Ranges, which changed airflow patterns.

This cooling continued for the next few million years (the late Pleistocene period). Enormous glaciers crept slowly south, carrying with them billions of tons of rock and earth, leveling mountains and filling in valleys. Death Valley, the lowest spot in North America (282 feet below sea level), was born of the upward and downward movement of the earth's crust and, between glacier movements, was filled with fresh water. The glaciers cut through the mountains, creating the beautiful Yosemite Valley. As the polar caps grew, the ocean froze and retreated, exposing new land, including millions of acres of valleys and hills west of the mountains, which are now the San Joaquin Valley and Southern California.

The retreating water also created a new coastline. The San Francisco, Monterey, and San Diego harbors appeared. About a hundred thousand years ago, a narrow land bridge connecting the Asian continent with North America was exposed. Animals began to find their way across: The horse, then merely a few feet tall, and the camel wandered north and west from North America into China, and then Africa, where their evolution and eventual domestication changed human history. From Asia to North America came new animals such as the bison and mammoth, followed by human beings.

Most American scientists believe that these humans came as part of a larger migration of people who crossed the Bering Strait from Asia, followed the big game animals south, and reached the southern tip of South America within ten thousand years—perhaps in some cases using oceangoing canoes to travel down the Pacific Coast. Despite the general agreement among American scientists about the Asian origin of these people, European experts are more skeptical of the certainty of the evidence of a Bering Strait crossing, and native people themselves have different versions of their origins. There is a noticeable absence of accounts of migration from a land of ice and snow in the traditional stories of the American Indian peoples. The Hopis, for example, tell of traveling to the north from their warm lands until they reached a land of "perpetual snow." Some tribes believe that the earth was prepared for them by the gods and that humans did not migrate to their land but were suddenly created there. Still others have no primal origin legend at all but only stories of migration from the east—not the north.

Although radiocarbon tests of human remains located on Santa Rosa Island off the coast of Santa Barbara indicate that these first families arrived thirty thousand years ago, these data are also under scrutiny. A number of scholars of Native American history have seriously questioned the dating of human settlement, noting unexplained evidence that could mean human beings lived in North America much earlier. Indeed, anthropologists and archeologists are debating the radiocarbon tests that show evidence of humans in the area as far back as 30,000 BCE.

The native peoples in California were scattered and they spoke more than one hundred different languages. Nowhere else in North America, outside of Central Mexico, did so many Indian groups congregate in such density with so much diversity. After almost fifty years of scientific scholarship and debate most historians and anthropologists concede that perhaps as many as three hundred thousand people lived in California before the first European settlement.

Anthropologists have generally classified these first inhabitants into six groups, based on their common root languages, with their linguistic origins suggesting their movement from different geographic regions. The first, and largest, were the Penutian-speaking peoples, living in numerous bands and clans mostly in central and northern California. They were most closely related to the Indian peoples of the Pacific Northwest and may have arrived by moving down the coast, by boat or on foot. Next were the Hokan-speaking peoples, scattered throughout the state as far north as Shasta County and as far south as San Diego. They appear to have migrated from the Southwest—present-day Arizona and New Mexico. The Uto-Aztecan–speaking people lived along the Kern River and in the Mojave and Colorado Deserts as well as in the Los Angeles basin, and seem to have traveled from the Southwest or perhaps mainland Mexico. Smaller groups included Athabascan-speaking people living in extreme northern California, who probably entered from Alaska, and the Algic-stock peoples, including the Yiot and Yurok Indians, who lived along the northern coast in Humboldt County. The Algic-stock languages are related to those of the Algonquians in the eastern part of the United States. A small group of Yukian-speaking peoples lived in northern Mendocino County; their language is unique to California and has no relation to any other in North America. They were split into four groups, geographically separated from each other, and each speaking a different dialect of their language. Their origins are uncertain.

At first these various Indians lived in bands, small groups of two or three extended families, whose membership was voluntary and changing. But as the population increased, they began to form lineages, or larger permanent groupings of families who were forbidden to intermarry because they claimed a common ancestor. Clans developed next, formed by amalgamating several biologically related lineages. Some of the coastal native peoples eventually created larger social and political systems, organizing what could be called towns. The Chumash people, for example, who lived in what later became Santa Barbara and Ventura and on the coastal islands, had large governments and complex social systems. All of the one hundred or so California language groups—which anthropologists call tribelets or village communities—had distinct territorial and spiritual identities, group histories, and destinies.

Politically, the California natives developed two kinds of government, both with a headman assisted by a governing council. The first kind of government included a lineage group who all traced their descent from a common ancestor, while the second was a band of individuals who were not all related by blood. The lineage-based governments had more institutionalized forms of political decision making, with a stable council and headman. In the band-based government, decisions were made by the headman and council as needs arose. Like the Chumash, the Gabrielino/Tongva people (also in southern California) seem to have evolved complex political governing systems that were able to govern large villages with many different clans and lineages, but anthropologists are not certain as to their exact form of government. Everywhere in California, before the Spanish arrived, Native American government often mixed spiritual with secular authority.

All of these systems grew out of this land of tremendous contrasts: lush valleys and grasslands teeming with game and edible plants; formidable mountains whose deep snows made life nearly impossible in the winters; vast deserts with little water and ferocious heat in the summer; and finally, a coastal littoral whose mild climate and multitudes of fish and wildlife invited settlement. Although its first inhabitants found the desert climates cooler and fresh water more plentiful, Californians today share with them the area's impressive environmental diversity, unique in the United States. In one day a person can drive from a foggy seashore beach through lush irrigated valleys, past snow-covered mountains, and into a blistering arid desert.

In the twenty-first century we find that the southwestern part of the state, including the Los Angeles, San Gabriel, and San Fernando Valleys, has a relatively arid, semi-Mediterranean climate, with large variations in rainfall from the mountains to the coastal plains. The mild climate has attracted millions of residents and, although the southern mountain ranges surrounding the coastal littoral are high enough (6000–11,000 feet) to have snow in the winter, providing some natural springs and rivers, this is not enough water for the burgeoning population. Water is imported to the south from northern California's rivers as well as from the Colorado River, and the large population has caused water and air pollution, not to mention the decimation of native plants and animals.

North of Santa Barbara, along the California coast, the climate changes as the Coast Range, whose hills and mountains are between 1000 and 5000 feet high, trap the offshore breezes and prevent the reduction of inland heat. The north central coastal mountains and valleys have their own unique environment, cooler than southern California, with more precipitation. Summers are generally overcast and foggy, while winter skies are brilliant, with the rainy season beginning sometime after January. Here one can find some of the most beautiful coastal scenery in California. North from Santa Barbara lies Morro Bay, which is guarded by an impressive rock sentry. Further north along the coast is Big Sur, with its breathtaking ocean vistas, waterfalls, and towering redwoods. Just north of Big Sur, Monterey Bay is one of the richest aquatic wildlife regions in the world. Inland from here are rolling hills with oak trees, grasslands, and fertile alluvial valleys, the largest of which is Salinas Valley.

Further north is San Francisco Bay, one of the most impressive natural harbors in the world, covering more than 400 square miles. Its entrance—the Golden Gate—is so narrow that the bay is really more like an inland sea, surrounded by low-lying hills rich in vegetation. The extensiveness of the bay and its connection with the Sacramento and San Joaquin Rivers make water transportation of prime importance. Today it is possible for oceangoing cargo ships to dock at Sacramento or Stockton. The bay gives easy access to the fertile Sonoma and Santa Clara Valleys. The climate in this region of California is always cool, and much wetter than southern California. North from here the terrain changes. From the Russian River to the Oregon border, the coast is rugged, with steep cliffs that hug the ocean. Frequent storms lash the beaches and there are few harbors, the most notable being Humboldt Bay. This region has redwood and pine forests, interspersed with woodland grass and small valleys.

East of this northern coastal region a tableland—interspersed with mountain ranges and the majestic snowcapped peaks of Mount Lassen and Mount

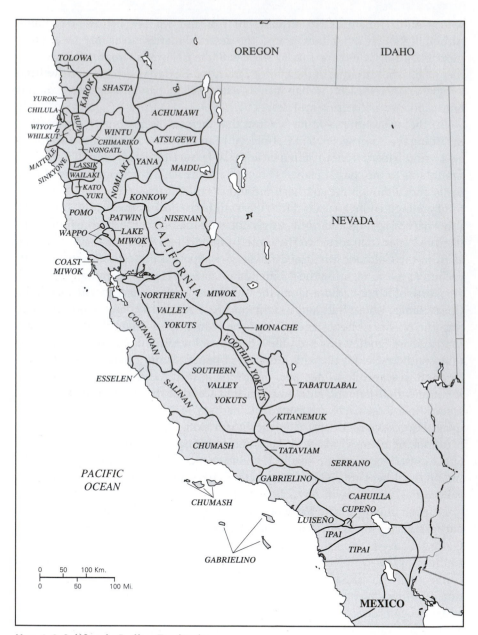

Map 1.2 California Indian Territories

Shasta—provides evidence of a prehistoric volcanic past. Between forests of pine and fir that cover the mountain ranges are the flatlands—the product of ancient lava flows, with an elevation between three thousand and five thousand feet, covered with sagebrush and junipers. Rain and snow define the seasons; lakes and rivers are plentiful.

The most mountainous region of California is the Sierra Nevada, a range running some four hundred miles from Mount Lassen in the north to the Tejon Pass in the south. Mount Whitney (14,494 feet in elevation), one of the tallest mountains in the continental United States, resides here with other peaks nearly as high. The Sierra mountains include the awe-inspiring Yosemite Valley and Sequoia National Park, along with breathtaking waterfalls, rapidly flowing mountain streams and rivers, and the largest freshwater lake in the state, Lake Tahoe. The Sierras provide much of the water that the entire state depends upon. On average, over fifty inches of rain are captured in the mountain snowfall each winter, providing year-round water for the Kern, Yosemite, San Joaquin, Sacramento, Tuolume, Stanislaus, and other rivers. The discovery of gold here in 1848 changed California forever.

South and east of the Sierras lies a vast desert that harbors a rich diversity of plant and animal life. Sage, cacti, and grasses survive the fierce heat of the desert summer, while juniper and piñon trees grow on the higher plateaus. After a brief rainy season in March or April the desert explodes in wildflowers, some seeds of which can lie dormant for years. The desert region has the lowest point in the United States—Death Valley (282 feet below sea level)—as well as several lakes of historical importance, notably Mono and Owens Lakes. Imperial and Coachella Valleys in the southern desert are of prime importance today as agricultural centers, thanks to irrigation. The huge Salton Sea receives the runoff of excess irrigation water from the Imperial Valley. It was created in the early 1900s by a temporary rechanneling of the Colorado River, and today its salinity is greater than that of seawater.

The 450-mile-long Central Valley lies between the Sierra Nevada and the coastal mountains and is on average 50 miles wide. The valley is drained by the San Joaquin River in the south and the Sacramento River in the north, both fed by numerous tributaries flowing from the Sierras. The two great rivers meet near Sacramento and form a delta region. The temperate weather, richness of the soil, and increased availability of irrigation have made this region invaluable farmland. Although this is a major difference from the times of California's first peoples, they, too, experienced a land of many contrasts—contrasts that have led some to say that there are many Californias.

Cycles of Life: The Food Quest, Spirituality, and Rituals

The Food Quest

Imagine bright sunshine and deep blue skies framing a spry old woman as she leads her granddaughter along the path that winds through the fertile hills of the San Joaquin Valley around 3000 BCE. Spying something in the brush, the elder woman stops and kneels, as does the girl, looking carefully at the delicate green plant her grandmother is grasping in strong, sure hands. "In digging wild potatoes we never take the mother plant. We just select the babies that have no flowers, just leaves. We are thinning out the area so that more will grow next year." The girl nods as they set about collecting the flowerless young plants. As their baskets fill her mind drifts to other harvestings the two have shared, of wild onions, tobacco, and various bulbs. She breathes deeply of the clear air, remembering the late summer and early autumn times when it was acrid with the smell of the burnings done annually in the chaparral. Those fires cleared space for the young growth needed for making baskets, and increased the places where edible and medicinal plants could be produced. The girl thinks ahead to when she will help her grandmother broadcast the seeds of grain-yielding grasses and green annuals between trees so they will be able to survive the drought.

This image, based on a twentieth-century Yokut description of how the tribe's ancestors passed along knowledge of their natural environment, gives us some idea of how the early peoples managed their environment and dealt with the depletion of larger game that accompanied the population increase of those times. As thousands of years of hunting and gathering gave way to a greater dependence on a variety of grass plants, acorns, and marine life as dietary supplements, the California Indians developed techniques of cultivation, propagation, and preparation to increase their food supply. The burnings this young girl recalls are the early incarnations of a tradition described to anthropologist Florence Shipek by elders of the Kumeyaay peoples of San Diego County in the 1960s. The elders also reported planting and hybridizing oak tree cuttings to produce more acorns.

While they worked, these two women might have looked across the hills toward the stand of oak trees near their village, grown from such cuttings. Oak trees then, as in the twenty-first century, could be found throughout California as well as the greater Southwest and northern Mexico. The indigenous peoples of Alta and Baja California developed the techniques that made the highly nutritious fruit of those trees—acorns—into a staple food. Each mature tree of the seven different species of oak could produce up to five hundred pounds of acorns annually, but these nuts could only be gathered for a few weeks each year.

To pass the time as they pick greens, the elder reviews with her grandchild how acorns must be leached of their bitter tannic acids to make them edible. She rejects the method of immersing the acorns in mud near a streambed for several months, for there are all sorts of risks involved in leaving anything on its own like that. She prefers to shell the acorns and grind them into a meal, pouring water over it until the acid leaches out through coiled baskets. Stone or sand basins were also used for the leaching process, a process that was probably an original innovation of the California Indians. The young girl thought of how her mother, taught by her grandmother, organized the long hours of work required by their small family for several weeks to produce the acorn meal. Later, the meal could be boiled into mush or baked into cakes. In a good season, they could gather enough acorns to make meal that would last them until the next gathering. She feels grateful for those bountiful years.

As the sun sinks lower and the sky turns to pinks and purples, the two women might spot the girl's father and brother near the oak trees, returning from a trade journey to the coast. The pair would be laden with fish and game received in exchange for acorns, trading as the Wiot peoples did near present-day Eureka.

Trade patterns revolved around the need for food. One of the most important and pervasive items of trade was obsidian, black volcanic glass stone used to make arrow and spear points. Crystal salt, gathered from the Owens Valley and the Colorado River or distilled from seawater, was also commonly traded. The peoples in San Diego traded acorn meal for melons grown by the Yuman (Quechan) Indians. Abalone shells from the Pacific Ocean have been found in middens (refuse heaps) on the eastern side of Baja California, indicating a trade in shells between the western coastal communities and those further inland.

The stories the two men would surely bring back from their trip might well include tales highlighting the religious significance that the mountains, lakes, rivers, and other natural features had for them. They believed that the land was given to them by the gods and their ancestors, with boundaries established through tradition and warfare. They not only traveled for survival, they also made spiritual journeys. Their concept of the land differed from that of the Europeans both in its relation to the spiritual, and in their belief that land was for the use of families and clans as groups—not as individuals.

Almost every native group had occasion to travel within its territory and occasionally outside it to obtain needed foods or implements, just as this imaginary family did. Given the diversity of California Indian language groups, lineages, bands, clans, and towns, generalizations about them as a whole are difficult to make. We can say that, unlike the peoples living along the Colorado River and further east, they did not develop maize agriculture. Those more eastern tribes cultivated maize, corn, beans, and squash once these plants had spread north from central Mexico after 900 BCE. For the California Indians, however, lush flora and fauna were available to those living near the coast and in the north, so there was no need to develop farming. And in any case, especially in the south, scant rainfall made agriculture without irrigation problematic. Almost all the western groups had territories that crossed two or more ecological food zones, enabling them to draw from different regions in different seasons and thus not remain wholly dependent on any one food source.

California's various Indians were also similar in that they were perhaps the most omnivorous peoples in the Americas, eating practically everything that was not poisonous. Besides acorns, fish, and game, they ate insects, shellfish, grasses, lizards, snakes, cactus, and scores of species of wild plants. Baskets, pottery vessels, bows and arrows, harpoons, nets, grinding and cutting stones, and other practical implements that line the shelves of California's museums today are evidence of the importance of food gathering to all of the state's various historical cultures.

The grandmother described earlier could be a distant ancestor of Delfina Cuero's grandmother, who was a San Diego mission Indian. Cuero, born in 1900, tells how she learned about the edible world from her mother in one of the few existing autobiographies of a native Indian in California. She lists scores of plants and animals that were part of her people's diet along the coast of San Diego, saying "I was little and don't remember all, but there was plenty of food here then.

Delfina Cuero, a Kumeyaay Indian woman, was born in Mission Valley, San Diego, in 1900. Her moving autobiography tells of the hardships endured by Indian people and their survival despite urban growth. Her people's traditions survived well into the twentieth century.

We had to hunt for plant food all day to find enough to eat. We ate a lot of cactus plants. We ate a lot of shellfish. There were lots of rabbits there too."

The California Indians actively shaped their natural environment so as to extract its maximum food value. And they passed on their burgeoning environmental management techniques through oral transmission—usually through shamans, or spiritual leaders—from generation to generation. The most common management technique was the use of fire to control brush and tree growth, to create a layer of ash that nourished the seed-bearing grasses of the next season, and to drive game into traps. The annual clearing of brush by fire was an important ecological activity, creating places where grasses could grow and where game could forage. Burning the chaparral regions and grasslands promoted the growth of "burn species" of edible plants and grasses that normally would not flourish in these areas. Frequent burnings in forested areas also prevented the buildup of dense brush whose accidental burning might have large-scale, disastrous results. Environmental historians believe that land management practices—especially burning—were so significant in maintaining a balance among the land, the flora, and the fauna of pre-conquest California that the decline of the Indian population after European settlement produced a change in the natural environment—a change caused by the unchecked growth of brush and chaparral. As estimated by ethnohistorians, perhaps 10 percent of the plants and 30 percent of the animals common in pre-Columbian California have since disappeared, victims of encroaching European plants and animals. Perhaps as much as 90 percent of all flora and fauna present in California today are not native to the region, but have appeared since the arrival of Europeans in North America.

Many native life forms have almost disappeared in twenty-first century California. Before the Spanish, the coastal region hosted thousands of acres of American dune grass and Pacific beach grass. Beginning in the American era these two grasses were gradually replaced by European beach grasses. These grasses trap more sand and create huge sand dunes, which in turn make it harder for other varieties of plants to thrive. Similarly, the coastal prairie regions once contained perennial bunch grasses that have been replaced by varieties of European spreading grasses, including Italian rye grass and wild oats and barley.

Spirituality

Although physical nourishment was a time-consuming enterprise for Indian families like the imaginary Yokuts described earlier, the food quest was balanced in their lives with time spent striving to live in harmony with the hidden forces of nature. Spirits inhabited the world of all native peoples in the Americas; communicating with those spirits occupied a good portion of their lives, especially during changes in season and on special occasions such as coming of age, marriage, and death.

Imagine another dawn breaking in the life of another Indian family, among the Cahuilla. The father has spent some weeks instructing his adolescent son in the correct ways to dance, eat, bathe, and participate in one of the most important spiritual exercises of their community, the *toloache* ceremony. (In some Indian groups, girls also participated in this ritual.)

Gently, the father shakes his boy to wakefulness. "Come, my son—the elders are ready," he says, and the boy shakes off his slumber to hurry outside. There the boy lines up with his friends, all aged ten to fifteen, as the shaman inspects them carefully. "You," he points to one, then another, continuing down the line. "You, and you, and you. Come." The boys are escorted to a ceremonial enclosure, where they will remain for a week while the old people dance all night and prepare the jimsonweed potion called toloache.

Mixing the crushed roots of the poisonous datura—or jimsonweed—with water created a narcotic potion that produced visions in those who drank it. The Indians believed these visions were a means of communicating with the supernatural. Where the toloache cult originated and how it spread is not certain, though some scholars believe it began among the peoples of southern California and diffused north and east, driven by the dislocations caused by the Spanish occupation.

Death can be caused by ingesting toloache; it was only used with great preparation and supervision by the Indians, and drunk perhaps once in a person's life. The process was supervised by the shaman, or religious leader of the tribe, who was also an expert in folk medicine. The shaman (usually male, but sometimes female) was key to the preservation of such rituals as the toloache ceremony. Shamans had power by virtue of an animal that came to them in dreams or visions—bestowed upon them by the Great Spirit so they could help people connect with each other and the natural world. It was believed the shaman could change shapes and become the guardian spirit animal.

When the boys are called forth from their hut into a moonless night a week later, a hush falls upon the watching crowd. The father looks proudly at his son who is standing tall, unblinking; he can tell the boy is ready to drink and become a man. "Tonight and only tonight you taste the toloache that will transport you to the world of the Great Spirit," the shaman intones, holding high a gourd filled with the sacred potion. Each boy drinks, and the drumming and dancing begin. One by one the boys collapse; as they do they are carried with great jubilation back into the hut. The father keeps a strong face to squelch any small anxiety he might have as he gently lays down his son, who is muttering now in the throes of his vision. "Go away, Coyote, go away," the boy cries out suddenly. "I know your tricks and selfish ways." Later he will tell his father, "Coyote tempted me to jump from the highest cliff into the swirling waters below, saying he would catch me. 'Drink more toloache,' he told me, 'it will make you powerful like the shaman, look, like me, I am drinking all the time—come, we will fly!' But I told him no, I know your deceit for my father told me you are self-destructive and a liar. And Coyote howled as he flew away, hanging his head in shame for his weakness. 'You are right, wise boy, do not jump, I cannot catch you, I cannot,' he wailed and faded and I woke up sweating." The boy's father nods wisely as his son finishes describing his vision, for everyone knows Coyote is all of these things, both destructive and regretful.

On the next night and the next, the boys are called out of the hut, taught songs, lore, and correct living. They learn the oral myths passed down through generations—stories with many animals like Coyote who had human personalities and magical powers. And stories that explained to them the meaning of life and recorded the tribe's own history. Coyote was a nearly universal mythic figure who could be the trickster or hero, depending on local interpretations. Among the Maidu, for example, the Coyote and Earthmaker gods were opposed to each other and struggled in the creation of the earth and people. Coyote appeared in many guises: as messenger, transformer, creator, but most often as the divine deceiver of humankind. Often, myths were related to geographical features of tribal territory, such as a mountain peak, lake, or river. Certainly the boys had heard these tales before, as the telling of them was woven into daily life—how the Great Spirit created the world, why death existed, why human society was organized as it was—but now the boys, too, became responsible for keeping this knowledge alive.

An introduction to medicinal lore might also have been included in their training, again supervised by the shaman, who also preserved the tribe's vast knowledge of medicine, spiritual incantations, and the uses of various herbs. Similar to the *curanderos* (herbal faith healers) among the Mexicans, shamans were practitioners of holistic medicine. Using breath and touch in addition to plants and animals, shamans facilitated true cures in the only way thought possible—by bringing the body and the soul into harmony with the natural world. A Chumash

Indian, Fernando Librado, told of many cures that he witnessed after the afflicted one had been given a toloache potion to drink. Once, a man who had been severely beaten and was near death was revived and completely cured within a few days of drinking toloache and being rubbed over with tobacco. Another who was in great pain from broken bones received almost immediate relief and was eventually healed after drinking toloache.

While these specialized cures were needed in serious cases, knowledge of medicinal plants was part of the cultural heritage of all the people. The boys might learn about the many uses of tobacco, grown or traded by almost all the native groups and thought to have curative and spiritual powers when chewed, eaten, or smoked. They might be shown medicinal plants good for treating many common ailments: from sore muscles, headaches, cramps, and nausea, to common colds, rheumatism, cuts, bites, wounds, and sores. Their sisters, in their own coming-of-age rituals, might learn about other plants useful for contraception, menstrual problems, and childbirth. When the Spanish began to occupy California they liberally borrowed from native medicinal lore, using special herbs to treat arrow wounds, as well as wild chamomile and manzanilla for respiratory illnesses. A number of our modern medicines derive from the plants used by the North American Indians.

Once taught the ways of the tribe, the boys eat no meat and drink nothing but cold water for the rest of that month. After this they are men. Sitting by the fire, the young man who saw Coyote in his visions contemplates his future. His father smiles softly, careful that his son does not see his pride as he observes the seriousness on that youthful face. Then he breaks the young man's reverie. "Tomorrow you will join us on the hunt. Today we prepare ourselves in the temescal. Come, help carry the rocks."

Together father and son join the other men of the village placing heated rocks inside the rounded structure made of saplings and covered with grass and hides. This *temescal,* or sweathouse, was another significant part of their spiritual life. Sprinkling water on the rocks, the men gathered inside the steamy hut to chant, sing, smoke, and pray. An hour or two later they would emerge and immediately plunge into cold water, purified for success in undertakings such as hunting and war.

Rituals

> When the sun rises and the stars and the moon go down, then the old man of the house wakens everyone and begins with breakfast which is to eat meat and tortillas (acorn cakes), for we do not have bread. This done, he takes his bow and arrows and leaves the house with vigorous and quick step. . . . His old woman staying at home makes the meal. The son, if he is a man, works with the men.

These words of Pablo Tac, a San Luis Rey mission Indian in the 1820s, offer a glimpse of their daily life before the Spanish arrived. Although generalizations about the diverse Indian communities are difficult to make, each had its own

In 1854 a U.S. expedition led by Lieutenant Colonel William Emory traveled through the desert regions of California and Arizona to survey the international boundary. Along the way artists sketched the region's plants, animals, and inhabitants. Arthur Schott created this picture of a Diegueño family in 1854. Do you see any Spanish or Mexican influence?

regional version of rituals surrounding marriage, morals, and leisure—the activities that gave meaning and purpose to life—all drawn from the sustenance of each of their rich and varied environments.

Common to many of these activities was song of one form or another. Like the initiation rites of the Cahuilla described above, young girls of the Diegueño or Kumeyaay Indians participated in a Wakunish, or womanhood ceremony, at puberty. A bed of hot sand was prepared and the girl placed on top of it, surrounded by dancing and singing members of her village. Following this she returned to her special hut to be instructed in the sacred affairs of the community. A sand painting was used to show the girl her place in the universe, and marriageable girls were tattooed on their chins after a period of fasting.

Song and dance also figured in marriage rituals. Chumash marriage celebrations began with a private ceremony for the family where invited guests brought presents, according to former mission Indian Fernando Librado. Later there was a feast followed by what he called a Jealousy Dance, in which five figures performed a burlesque of a love affair and temptations of other men. Pablo Tac remembered another ritual dance, of the Luiseño people:

> The dancers in this dance can be as many as thirty, more or less. Going out of the house, they turn their faces to the singers and begin to give kicks, but not hard ones, because it is not the time, and when the song is finished the captain of the dancers touching his feet cries, "Hu," and all fall silent.

In some groups boys were married before they were twenty-one, to a suitable bride selected by their parents from outside both the immediate family and the band. The parents gave gifts to the family of the girl, and sometimes the boy went to work for his future in-laws to prove he could provide for the girl. Among some tribelets there was no formal ceremony, merely an agreement among the parents. During the first weeks after the marriage, members of the village visited the new couple to confirm that they were part of the group.

Indian and Spanish morality differed, which was a source of great conflict between them. Though marriage and kinship were usually governed among Indians by strict rules, and patriarchal values held sway, most California Indians did not regard virginity as being of great value; so premarital sex was rarely forbidden, according to the research of historian Albert Hurtado. Adultery and sexual misconduct by women was sometimes punished by payment of indemnities to wronged husbands and by the whipping of errant wives. However, sexual mores among Indian groups varied as greatly as they did between Indians and Europeans, and sweeping generalizations are perilous. In some groups women as well as men could divorce their spouse if mistreated. Prostitution was almost unknown among Indians, Hurtado thinks, because "marital, premarital, and extramarital associations provided sufficient sexual opportunities."

Along with many other natives in the Americas, the California Indians also valued a *berdache* tradition, in which homosexual transvestites were thought to have special mystical powers. Many villages regarded them as a third sex, highly valued as marriage partners because of their strength and spiritual gifts. This acceptance of homosexuality was regarded by Christian missionaries as proof of the Indians' inherent sinfulness.

Many California Indians believed in cremating their dead, another practice that was unacceptable to European Catholics of the time. "Only when everything is burned can his spirit go into the next world and not have to keep coming back after his things," remembers Delfina Cuero. The funeral ceremony of her people, the Kumeyaay, involved cremating the departed along with all their worldly possessions the day after they died. Their bones and ashes were preserved in jars. Gifts were sent from other bands to the family of the deceased, along with "shell money." Tradition dictated that the shell money was then returned to the band who sent it, along with more gifts. A year later the other bands were invited to participate in a mourning ceremony during which everyone sang songs about the eagle and deer all night long, followed by a great feast in the morning. Figurines made of cattails, representing the dead, were burned and food and baskets were given away. Later the visitors returned the original gifts along with more food. Such exchanges served to promote communication and good will among the villages.

Singing was also featured in leisure time activities. Songs that kept local legends, myths, and history alive were memorized and sung, often directed toward the Great Spirit. Each band had one singer who knew all the songs and stories and who taught them to the others. One Luiseño story, the legend of Takwish, was told through 1050 songs that were sung from sunset Friday until sunrise on Sunday. There were probably hundreds of such stories among the California peoples, each encapsulating the "soul" of the people, transmitting their identity and heritage to the next generation.

A popular gambling and guessing game called *peon* was also accompanied by songs. And the Indians participated with great gusto in many other kinds of games that emphasized both competition and community. Men and boys engaged in mock battles with one another using stones instead of arrows, and children played a game of throwing a stick through a rolling hoop. Pablo Tac remembers a ball game resembling modern football that was played with thirty or forty men and women on each side. The idea was to unearth a hidden ball using sticks and then to carry it to the goal while the other team sought to prevent a score. Each game lasted three or four hours.

A Closer Look: Six Regional Peoples

Before the arrival of the Europeans, the varied lives of native Californians reflected the diversity of the land they inhabited. A closer examination of six of the many native groups that spread across this land provides greater insight into their similarities as well as their differences. From the Gabrielino/Tongva peoples of the south to the Shastans of the north, each group's development was inseparably woven into the fabric of their environment.

The Gabrielino/Tongva

The Gabrielino/Tongva peoples migrated to southern California from the greater Southwest sometime after 500 BCE. They lived in more than a hundred villages scattered throughout the area of present-day Los Angeles and Orange Counties, as well as the offshore islands (see Map 1.2). Named for the San Gabriel mission constructed near their villages, or *rancherías* (as the Spanish called them), they were a Cupan-speaking people. Part of the Uto-Aztecan family of languages, Cupan is linguistically related to languages of the Pueblo Indians in New Mexico and the Aztecs of central Mexico.

The Gabrielinos worshiped the god Qua-o-ar, also called Chingichngish. According to what is known through Spanish sources, they believed the earth was created by a divine brother and sister, who formed the first human, Wiyot, a male who was self-generating (he had children without a woman). Wiyot was poisoned by his children, but before he died he vowed to return. As his children were cremating Wiyot, Coyote appeared and said that he wanted to die with his captain. Coyote jumped into the fire, while tearing a piece of meat from Wiyot's stomach and eating it. Soon after that Chingichngish was born, and he then created a new race of people, giving them a body of laws and proscriptions. The reported practice of Gabrielino shamans eating a piece of the flesh of a dead body just prior to its cremation was supposedly a re-creation of the birth of their "all-powerful" god. Eventually Chingichngish was taken up into the heavens, dancing a sacred dance, and he became the stars.

The worship of Chingichngish evolved into a more formalistic religion with special worship places, elaborate ceremonies, and sacrifices to this god as well as to the Sun and Moon, who also had divine status. The Gabrielinos also venerated animals, especially the Eagle, whom they considered to be the soul of a great leader. Their religion was male-centered; only men were allowed primary access to divine powers. The veneration of Chingichngish may have been influenced by Catholicism in a syncretic way, but it is unclear to what degree.

The lengthiest Gabrielino rituals involved deceased tribal members. After a three-day mourning ceremony with dancing and wailing, the dead were cremated along with all their possessions. Each year the family conducted another mourning ceremony in honor of the deceased one, at which the legends of the community were honored. During the eight-day celebration, the longest and most elaborate of the year, newly born children were given their father's names, any remaining possessions of the deceased were burned, and an eagle was ceremonially sacrificed.

Like many California native groups, the Gabrielinos were patrilineal, tracing their descent through the father. Arranged marriages often took place, after which a wife moved into the home of her husband and was then forbidden to visit her family of origin, although they could visit her. Divorce was possible, in which case the families returned the wedding gifts. A wife's infidelity was punishable by death or beating.

Of the tribe's three social classes, leaders and their families were at the top, followed by a middle class of respected families and then by common villagers. Upper- and middle-class families controlled land and marked the boundaries of their possessions with symbolic figures carved on trees or posts, or painted on rocks. Each village had its own autonomous organization dominated by one lineage and ruled by a male leader who passed on his power through his male heir. If no male heir existed a related woman might be selected by the family council.

Occasionally feuds among the various lineages and villages erupted, with villages sometimes allying together to engage in war. Armed and bloody conflicts arose when other tribes trespassed on ranchería lands, when women were taken, or when enemies invoked evil powers. The Gabrielino warriors used heavy wooden clubs, reed armor, and bows and arrows. The whole village took part in battles, with women and children as helpers. Enemy wounded were killed on the field, while captured male warriors were publicly tortured and scalped.

Most of the time, however, peace reigned, fostered by intermarriages and trade within Gabrielino groups and with the Cahuilla, Chumash, and Luiseño. The Gabrielino's main trade item was steatite, a kind of rock from the island of Santa Catalina used to make carvings of sacred animals. They imported acorns, obsidian, and deerskin from the inland territories and exchanged salt, shellfish, and sea otter pelts. They also traded with the Pueblo Indians of what is now Arizona and New Mexico.

The Chumash

The Chumash people settled in villages in central California around 1000 CE, in the area from San Luis Obispo to Malibu, on the coastal Channel Islands—San Miguel, Santa Rosa, Santa Cruz, and Anacapa—and as far inland as the central San Joaquin Valley (see Map 1.2). They became one of the largest language groups in California and were among the native peoples sighted by the European expedition led by Juan Rodriguez Cabrillo in October 1542.

Expert craftsmen, especially in woodworking and basketry, they constructed planked wooden canoes up to thirty feet long that enabled them to fish far out to sea and to visit the offshore islands. Using harpoons with stone points and ropes made out of yucca fiber, they hunted sea otters, seals, swordfish, and whales. Their large carved oak bowls were the envy of the Europeans; their wooden-handled knives and arrows remain marvels of beauty. California Indian basketry in general is noted for its decoration and workmanship, and Chumash baskets were so tightly woven that when waterproofed with asphaltum or tar they could be used to carry and store water, as well as for cooking. The tar came from natural pools, which had oozed into a small lake located in the western region of what is today the Los Angeles basin. The women were responsible for weaving these useful works of art. They also wove fishnets, floor mats, storage baskets, and strainers.

Chumash rock art paintings can be found in caves and on rocks and ledges throughout the Santa Barbara area. Many California native groups drew or inscribed designs and mysterious symbols on rocks, but few of these are as colorful and dramatic as those of the Chumash. The designs are abstract, most probably done in conjunction with the toloache ceremony or with female puberty rites. The drawings may have been meant to sanctify a particularly holy spot—almost all of them are located near water in inaccessible regions, far from the coast.

The permanent villages of the Chumash included well-constructed round homes built of poles and interwoven grass, some up to fifty feet in diameter and able to hold up to seventy persons. Within these homes were beds on wood frames with divisions in between for privacy and a fire pit in the center for cooking. Every village had at least one sweathouse, a number of storehouses, a building used for ceremonies, a cemetery, and a recreation house.

As did many California natives, the Chumash enjoyed a variety of games. A ball game similar to soccer, played with a round wooden ball, was popular with the boys and men. And even females played a hoop game that involved trying to throw a pole through a rolling hoop. Women also gambled alongside men in various games of chance, especially a dice game using walnut shells filled with tar.

Like the Gabrielinos, this tribe was patrilineal and had a definite class system. Those who owned the large canoes and were the heads of large families enjoyed high status. Wealthy family members dressed accordingly, adorned with semi-precious stones and rare bird feathers.

The area in which the Chumash lived was blessed with many resources. Still, they had extensive trade relationships with surrounding communities. In exchange for deerskins, acorns, obsidian, and precious stones, they traded abalone shells, whalebone, wooden bowls, and asphaltum. They were expert at making fishhooks out of shell and these were valuable trade items. Those who lived on the four offshore islands visited the mainland periodically to obtain food and luxuries, sometimes paddling more than forty miles in open sea and bringing with them a variety of marine items such as sea lion bristles (used as needles), whalebones, and pelican feathers.

According to early European accounts, the Chumash were a gentle people. In the 1770s, Governor Pedro Fages wrote that they were "of good disposition, affable, liberal, and friendly toward the Spaniard." Among them punishment was rare and compensation was the modality of justice. Disputes were settled by referees and intertribal wars were fought with restraining ritual and little bloodshed. Their friendly and accepting manner made them good candidates for missionization by the Spanish priests. Within a century, however, epidemics, starvation, and displacement reduced the Chumash to near extinction.

The Costanoans

The Costanoan peoples migrated to Monterey Bay and the southern part of the San Francisco Bay area about 500 CE and lived in more than fifty autonomous, relatively small, permanent villages (see shaded portion of Map 1.2). By the time of their first contact with Europeans they had a population of more than ten thousand, divided into eight language groups and more than thirty different ethnic populations, each with different names and different dialects. Their name derives from the Spanish *costa* (coast), but as was the case with many native California peoples, they did not use this name themselves.

One group of Costanoans may have been the first miners in California, excavating a tunnel near present-day New Almaden to mine cinnabar, a compound based on mercury and used to make colorful paints. Because this was the only deposit of this particular mineral in California, it was a valuable asset and the Costanoans fought with surrounding tribes for the rights to the mine. Indians from as far away as the Pacific Northwest traveled to Costanoan territory to trade for cinnabar.

Like the Chumash, the Costanoans developed boats, but theirs were made of tule reeds and used for fishing in the bays as well as for transportation and trading expeditions. They bartered the products of the bays with the interior Indian groups for piñon nuts, acorns, and decorative stones and shells. Warfare with other groups seems to have been more pronounced among the Costanoan peoples, usually caused by trespassing into their territory. (Territorial boundaries of ethnic groups were well delineated and frequently marked.) In battle the

In 1816 Louis Choris, a Frenchman, painted and sketched more than 100 pictures of California Indian people. These were published in 1822 and provide some of the earliest realistic images of the natives of this region.

Costanoans killed male captives and took women; afterward the decapitated heads of their enemies adorned their villages. Costanoans shared the common religious tradition that included a creation story involving the destruction of the earth by flooding, followed by the rebirth of people. They believed Coyote taught people to hunt and fish, and was the grandfather of Duck Hawk, a god who helped humans by killing monsters and looking after their welfare. They believed in an afterlife in which they went to another land across the sea. On the day of death, the corpse was cremated. During the mourning ceremony members of the immediate family covered themselves with ashes and beat themselves in sorrow, a practice which sometimes resulted in their own deaths. It was forbidden to speak a deceased's name until it had been formally given to another within the tribe.

Grizzly bears were also venerated as representing important animal spirits, and were frequently captured alive and cared for by some tribes. Special shamans dressed in grizzly bear skins and used poisoned claws to kill enemy captives. The Chumash Indian Fernando Librado recalled the ceremonies surrounding the bear medicine man when he was interviewed by anthropologist John P. Harrington in 1914. "To make their bear suits they would first kill a bear and pull its skin off over the head, cutting the paws and skin carefully." Librado remembered that occasionally other Indians would try to kill the bear medicine man (whom they believed to be an evil spirit). But the bear shamans were believed to be protected by the supernatural powers they possessed (they were protected, too, by the many layers of skins they wore).

Costanoan tribal organization was similar to that of the Gabrielino/Tongva and the Chumash. The position of chief was hereditary, but any chief's authority was circumscribed by a strong sense of individual freedom among community members. Their social world revolved around the family of the father and they had large families, perhaps averaging fifteen per household. Wealthier men had more than one wife, which made for complex arrangements. Among some Costanoans there were three designations for children, indicating known parentage: man's son, man's daughter, and woman's child (unknown father). Marriage appears to have been rather informal, and divorce was easily accomplished, with the children going with the wife.

The Miwoks and Yokuts

Other Indian groups lived far from the ocean and European settlement. Two of these groups were the Miwoks and Yokuts. The Miwoks inhabited an area running from the north and east of San Francisco Bay to Sacramento and the foothills of the Sierras; the Yokuts lived in the San Joaquin Valley south of Sacramento. Like other groups these two populations settled in scattered independent villages, the members of each village speaking a different dialect although bound by a probable common ancestry in the ancient past.

In 1769, the Miwok population probably exceeded twenty-five thousand. They were noted for their construction of large round subterranean meetinghouses, sometimes forty to fifty feet in diameter, in which it was possible to assemble the whole village for important ceremonies and crucial discussions. The Sierra Miwoks built conical homes of bark and wood, insulated by several layers to withstand the cold winters. The Miwoks divided all creatures into two types, the water and land descendants, and their social organization and adoption of animal names followed this dualist system. For example, among the Sierra Miwoks, the grizzly bear represented the land and the coyote the water. Individuals were given a personal name according to their relationship to the land or water moieties (sides). The Miwoks had three types of leaders: the chief, who arbitrated disputes and administered punishments; the speaker, who organized everyone for ceremonies and work; and the messengers, who acted as representatives to other groups and as announcers during ritual celebrations. Hunters and gatherers, the Miwoks developed a variety of technologies, including seed beaters, dip nets and seines for fish, specialized traps and snares for small game, and deer runs (fenced areas that trapped prey).

The Yokuts shared the same linguistic origin as the Miwoks and numbered some twenty thousand people who lived in about forty independent groups. In the south the Yokuts lived along the banks of the Kern, Tule, King, and San Joaquin Rivers, and along the shore of Tulare Lake. In this era the San Joaquin Valley was much marshier than it is now and this created a rich aquatic environment. The Yokut way of life therefore revolved around the marshes formed by the many rivers in the valley. The ubiquitous tule plant was used for making everything from baskets to canoes, and it was also used for food. Because their food source was always in one place these Yokuts built permanent villages using large tule mats for construction and they perfected freshwater fishing with specialized nets, floating tule mats, spring traps, and decoys. They ate mussels, turtles, geese, and ducks, along with tule and grass seeds, and supplemented this diet with acorns, which they obtained by trade.

The northern Yokuts also lived along the river edges but they had more access to acorns as a staple food. About eighteen thousand Yokuts lived in the area south of Stockton to Madera. Those features that distinguished them from their southern cousins are few. They built their river villages on mounds to protect against floods and had small tule huts for each family, but they also built larger assembly structures and sweathouses. They raised dogs, primarily, it seems, for their meat, and the puppies were an item of trade as far away as Monterey. These Yokuts had a dualistic family system like that of the Miwoks whose territory bounded them on the north. Among the foothill Yokuts, plural marriages and divorce were common, and a woman's rights were strongly protected by her family.

The Shastans

Finally, in the Klamath and Scott River Valleys of the mountainous regions of northern California and southern Oregon there lived about three thousand Shastan peoples, a collection of groups who shared dialects of the same language. Noted for their many feuds and wars within their own group and with other northern groups such as the Modocs, the Shastans fought in retaliation for past insults and injuries as well as for control of territory. Nevertheless they maintained trade relations with surrounding rancherías in order to obtain baskets, obsidian, beads, and animal skins in exchange for acorn meal, salt, and wolf skins.

The Shastan peoples, too, were patrilineal, with rule by a headman or chief. Often the wife of the chief was an important political spokesperson in resolving conflicts. Settlement of disputes usually required payment in clamshell money, deer skins, or woodpecker scalps to the aggrieved party. The headman also regulated the ownership of hunting and fishing territory, which could be inherited by families.

Harsh winters impelled the Shastans to build sturdy warm dwellings, partially excavated, with solid wood logs and boards as walls and roofs. During the summer months the families lived in temporary camps. They also built large assembly halls for ceremonial purposes, for use as a sweathouse, and for lodging during the winter.

Shastan territory was lush with small game, salmon, trout, eels, and turtles. The women were entrusted with fishing, while the men hunted. Deer meat was a primary food source. They also had a gathering culture, with both men and women seeking acorns and pine nuts. Cultivated tobacco was offered up as a sacrifice to ensure good hunting.

Coyote is a major figure in Shastan belief, as a source of both evil and good. The stories used by the Shastans to pass on their beliefs were preoccupied with the pervasiveness of evil, which had to be combated by manipulation of the spiritual world through the offices of male shamans and female doctors. They seem to have been preoccupied with status, prestige, and the order of society, which made insults and loss of face great evils and resentments a major theme of cultural life.

Significance: The Importance of California Natives and Other North American Native Peoples in Non-Indian History

Beginning in 1769 with the first Spanish settlement and lasting until 1848, when California was transferred to the United States, the California Indians vastly outnumbered the Euro-American population. If history were written emphasizing the most demographically important groups, then, until the discovery of gold, California's history would be primarily that of its native peoples, with small attention given to the Spanish, Mexican, and Anglo immigrants. But history reflects political and cultural power and is usually written by the conquerors.

Spanish, Mexican, and early Anglo American settlers in California were almost uniformly critical of the native peoples. The Spanish had mixed views about the Indians, whom they considered "child-like," "indolent," and given to indulge in "brutal appetites," while paradoxically seeing them as innocent and naturally God's children. Some Mexican settlers, or *pobladores,* viewed the native peoples either as dangerous threats to civilization or as lazy *peones* who needed strong guidance. The Anglos called the California Indians "digger Indians," classifying them as the most primitive of all North American Indian peoples for lack of such rudimentary accomplishments of civilization as farming and pottery. Such negative valuation allowed Euro-Americans to justify taking Indian lands and destroying their societies.

Herbert Howe Bancroft, a famous and influential nineteenth-century California historian, believed that the California Indians were culturally inferior to the whites. Many modern misconceptions about the level of culture attained by the California Indians can be traced to nineteenth-century positivist scholars, notably Lewis Henry Morgan, one of those who conceived of all human cultural evolution as progressing through stages of savagery, barbarism, and finally civilization. These scholars tended to equate "civilization" with the development of agriculture and technology and relegated food-gathering societies to the level of barbarism, not taking into account that human intelligence is also reflected in successful adaptation to an environment. Such beliefs persisted into the 1960s and even later, with historians and anthropologists usually characterizing the California native cultures as "primitive" and "underdeveloped," thus reflecting prejudices that are the product of ignorance as well as ethnocentrism born out of racialist ideologies of the past.

These attitudes make it hard to remember that much of the drama of those years of conquest was played out against a backdrop of the extensive, rich, and diverse native culture that existed across the North American continent. The many groups in California were descendants of natives who had migrated from the east and north, and as such they shared cultural patterns with the larger Indian society. Along with other Indian peoples in North America in 1492, the California Indians developed a culture that fit their natural environment. Few

In 1806 a Russian ship visited San Francisco Bay, and the artist Wilhelm Gottlief Tilesius von Tilenau traveled to Mission in San José, where he sketched a dance that had been arranged for their entertainment. Compare this picture with those shown in the earlier two photos in this chapter. Which ones seem more realistic?

natives in what later became the United States relied entirely on agriculture (those who did were mostly limited to New Mexico and Arizona); most shared an economy based on hunting, gathering, and the selective cultivation of plants. Techniques developed by California Indians for maintaining the ecological balance between the population and the natural world of vegetation and animal life make them the first environmentalists. Their periodic burning of brush areas to stimulate the new growth of food crops, decrease insect pests, manage game, and open new country helped maintain an equilibrium that was severely disturbed by the Europeans and Americans. Not until the late twentieth century would scientists finally realize the wisdom of native management practices.

Until at least the mid-nineteenth century, the most important work force in California was composed of its native peoples. The foundation of the livestock industry and of agriculture depended on native labor, as did the construction of early public and private buildings and the first towns. The physical monuments to the Spanish and Mexican eras, the missions and the ranchos, were built with Indian labor. The native peoples contributed elements of their language to hundreds of place names, such as Shasta, Napa, Tuolomne, Yuba, Tehachapai, Tecate, and Ukiah. They shared their knowledge of the use of medicinal plants with the first Spanish and Mexican settlers, and they helped them defend their small settlements against attacks by other Indians. Elements of Indian culture found their way into the mission system set up by the Spanish. The first *vaqueros,* or cowboys, in California were Indians employed by the missions to manage the cattle, sheep, and goats brought by the Spanish. Native cultures, languages, and identities continue to exist within California, making these first people very much part of the history of the state from the earliest times to the present day.

Summary

During the course of millions of years California evolved into a region of tremendous geographic and natural diversity. The many climates and natural ecosystems helped create the varied ways of life of its hundreds of thousands of first settlers—migrants whose speech derived from six linguistic groups and was expressed in more than a hundred dialects. The lush plants and game that flourished in California sustained this large Indian population, who created innovative ways of nurturing their natural resources.

Despite the multiplicity of their origins and languages, the Indian peoples shared certain values, perhaps reflecting their common origin in prehistoric time. They all managed their natural environment to produce the maximum amount of food, whether by controlled burns, hunting, or scattering of wild seeds. Almost all of them developed techniques for harvesting and grinding acorns into a staple food, and they all traded with other groups. A rich oral tradition of myths, legends, and stories—especially about the character Coyote and the event of the flood—was common to all groups, as was the veneration of animal spirits. Complex ceremonies, songs, and rituals connected them to their natural environment. They all had shamans who organized their spiritual life, and many used jimsonweed or other psychotropic plants as part of their religion, as well as the temescal or sweathouse. Their complex patterns of lineage, relationship, and status, including class systems in some groups, and their relatively small villages, reflected the patterns of all the native peoples on the continent—with the exception of the metropolitan civilizations in central Mexico. Their peaceful and nonwarlike image has some element of truth to it, despite the bloody intertribal warfare that periodically existed. Outside of central Mexico, native peoples rarely engaged in wars of conquest and territorial aggrandizement. The first Californians were neither more nor less sophisticated or warlike than other peoples in North America before the arrival of the Europeans.

A review of some of the most populous indigenous groups in California illustrates their rich heritage and many accomplishments. Their ability to learn how to live with the incredible diversity and richness of California's climate and geography and develop cultures that balanced human and natural resources is an important ideal that seems to be regaining value in the new millennium.

Modern anthropologists evaluate cultures on their own merits, not in terms of a universal model of development that favors European culture, such as the models used by nineteenth-century historians and positivist scholars. Ultimately, the California Indians must be understood on their own terms, not in comparison to other Indians or to European and American notions of civilization. Then, perhaps, we can better appreciate the true diversity of California's past and how that diversity may shape the future.

Suggested Readings

- Fages, Pedro, *A Historical, Political, and Natural Description of California*, trans. by Herbert Ingram Priestley (Berkeley: University of California Press, 1937). An eyewitness account of the native cultures in California, written in 1772.

- Griffin, Paul F., and Robert N. Young, *California: The New Empire State, a Regional Geography* (San Francisco: Fearon Publishers, 1957). A good introduction to the geographic diversity of California.

- Heizer, Robert F., ed., "California," in *Handbook of North American Indians*, William C. Sturtevant, series ed. (Washington, D.C.: Smithsonian Institution Press, 1978). The best overall survey of the complexities and diversities of the California Indians.

- Kroeber Alfred L., *Handbook of the Indians of California* (Washington, D.C.: Bureau of American Ethnology, Bulletin 78, 1925). A landmark study of the indigenous people done by the most respected California anthropologist of the twentieth century.

- Librado, Fernando, *Breath of the Sun: Life in Early California As Told by a Chumash Indian, Fernando Librado, to John P. Harrington*, edited by Travis Hudson (Banning, Calif.: Malki Museum Press; [S.l.]: Ventura County Historical Society, 1979). A glimpse into the daily life of the California Indians during the early 1900s.

- Margolin, Malcolm, ed., *The Way We Lived: California Indian Stories, Songs and Reminiscences* (Berkeley: Heyday Books, 1981). A good collection of the oral tradition.

- Tac, Pablo, *Indian Life and Customs at Mission San Luis Rey* (Mission San Luis Rey, 1958). A rare account of a mission Indian who wanted to be a priest.

2

The Spanish Colonization of California, 1769–1821

Main Topics

▮ The Spanish Conquest and Empire

▮ Demographic and Ethnic Growth of California

▮ Establishing Presidios and Pueblos

▮ Gender Relations in Spanish California

▮ Political Developments in Spanish California

▮ The Importance of the Spanish Era in California

Pablo Tac was a Luiseño Indian born in Mission San Luis Rey in 1822. He came from a family of six children, most of whom had been born at his people's *ranchería* (small settlement) near the mission. In 1832 Father Antonio Peyri chose Pablo and another boy to travel with him to Mexico City to study for the priesthood. They arrived at the College of San Fernando, where Tac lived until 1834, when Father Peyri took both boys to Spain and then to Rome for further education financed by the church. In Rome the older boy died but Tac finished his education, studying humanities, philosophy, and rhetoric. He took his preliminary vows in 1839, intending to return to California as a missionary.

While in the seminary, Tac was asked to prepare a grammatical description of the Luiseño language and a dictionary. In addition to this document he wrote a history of his people and a description of life in the missions. This rare document

CHAPTER 2	The Spanish Colonization of California, 1769–1821
1519	Cortés conquers the Aztecs in central Mexico
1542	Juan Rodríguez Cabrillo discovers San Diego Bay, named San Miguel
1579	Francis Drake lands on California's coast
1602	Sebastián Vizcaíno lands in San Diego Bay and gives it its name
1769	First Spanish expeditions to settle Alta California
1770	Monterey founded by Father Junípero Serra
1775	First major Indian rebellion at Mission San Diego
1775	De Anza expedition brings new settlers to California
1776	Lieutenant José Moraga founds the presidio of San Francisco
1777	Pueblo of San José established
1781	Pueblo of Nuestra Señora la Reina de los Angeles founded
1781	Yuma uprising closes all travel with Arizona
1784	Chumash uprising against the missions
1792	English explorer George Vancouver visits California harbors
1810	Beginning of wars of independence from Spain
1812	Russians build Fort Ross on California coast
1818	Pirate Hippolyte Bouchard sacks Monterey
1822	News of Mexico's independence arrives in California

gives us an interpretation of history through the eyes of a Christianized California Indian, but we should be cautious about relying too much on his memories of his Indian past—they are in the context of his newly found religion and his probable desire to please his European mentors. At the same time, however, some scholars have analyzed his writings in terms of themes of resistance embedded in his narrative.

Tac recalled his people's history of warfare with the Kumeyaay peoples to the south before the Spaniards arrived. They were always at war with tribes that did not speak their language: "Always strife day and night." He described their war practices. "They would surprise the enemy either when they were sleeping or when the men were leaving the house, the women remaining alone; and they would kill the women, old people and children. This done, they burned the camp, fleeing to their homes. . . . In this miserable state they lived until merciful God freed us of these miseries through Father Antonio Peyri, a Catalan, who arrived in our country in the afternoon with seven Spanish soldiers."

Tac related stories about the arrival of the first Spanish in his village and their attempts to speak to the Indian leaders. According to Tac they were told, "What is it that you seek here? Get out of our country!" Tac continued, "It was a great mercy that the Indians did not kill the Spanish when they arrived, and very admirable, because they have never wanted another people to live with them, and until those days there was always fighting."

Tac remembered that the priest appointed native *alcaldes,* who were more proficient in Spanish; each was given a staff of authority. At Mission San Luis Rey there were seven alcaldes. The priest communicated with the Indians through the alcaldes, who in turn carried the news to their villages. The laborers at the mission were accompanied by a Spanish majordomo and the alcaldes, whose purpose was "to hurry them if they are lazy . . . and to punish the guilty or lazy one who leaves his plow and quits the field." And, regarding the priests: "In the Mission of San Luis Rey de Francia the Fernandino Father is like a king. He has his pages, alcaldes, majordomos, musicians, soldiers, gardens, ranchos, livestock, horses by the thousand, cows, bulls by the thousand, oxen, mules, asses, 12,000 lambs, 200 goats, etc."

Pablo Tac died on December 13, 1841, before he could be ordained a priest; he was not yet twenty years old. His written work is the only account of California mission life written by an Indian, and it is also the first literature published by a California Indian.

Pablo Tac's life story dramatizes the major changes that the Indians experienced as they encountered the Euro-American settlers. The goal of the Spanish priests and soldiers was to convert and pacify thousands of native peoples who lived near the California coast. They hoped to make the natives into loyal Spanish Catholic subjects, with the California missions at the core of the Spanish project to settle California. There were some successes, as evidenced in Tac's narrative, but by and large the process of Hispanicization resulted in the introduction of new diseases that decimated the Indian population. However, by introducing the Spanish language, culture, and political system the Europeans added new diversity to an already heterogeneous society. The mixture of cultures would produce a resilient frontier environment—one that prepared California for new challenges.

Questions to Consider

- How and why did the Spanish finally settle Alta California?
- What were the characteristics of the society that they sought to create?
- How can we evaluate the debate over the modern interpretations of the California missions?
- What was the status of women in this colonial society?
- What was the influence of other Europeans on California's history?
- What is the importance of the Spanish era?

The Spanish Conquest and Empire

The Spaniards were the first Europeans to colonize the New World, preceding the English by more than one hundred years. From their first settlements in the Caribbean Islands, Hispaniola, and Cuba, they soon began the exploration and settlement of the American continents. In 1519 Hernan Cortés led an expedition of soldiers from Cuba to confirm rumors of a powerful and wealthy kingdom on the western mainland of present-day Mexico. Cortés led his men in the Spanish conquest of the Aztec empire. The epic adventure took two years and was made possible by the assistance of hundreds of thousands of Indians who resented Aztec tyranny, and by the use of new weapons, and animals (such as the horse and dog), and most importantly by the new diseases brought by the Europeans, such as influenza, smallpox, and a more virulent form of syphilis. By 1521 the Spanish had established a foothold in central Mexico. Almost immediately Cortés began sending out expeditions to find other wealthy kingdoms.

The Spanish consolidation of political, religious, and military power over the former Aztecs, their vassals, and outlying tribes was rapid and quite remarkable. Within fifty years of the conquest—aided by a rapid depopulation of the Indians due to disease and mistreatment—the Spanish constructed an efficient government to exploit the labor and wealth of this land, which they called New Spain. The cultural transformation of this new colony would take hundreds of years, as the Indian population continued to outnumber the Españoles. Gradually a *mestizo*, or mixed, culture emerged with various degrees of mixture between ancient Indian and Spanish Catholic life. The complexity of New Spain's evolution in terms of racial and ethnic identity is a point that scholars are now exploring in great depth.

Political control of this caldron of subjugated people led to the creation of a complex bureaucracy controlled by the Spanish *peninsulares* and assisted by American-born mestizos and *criollos*. At the top was the Spanish king's representative, the viceroy, who was to implement the royal edicts and endless administrative decrees flowing from the Council of the Indies in Spain. Under the viceroy, the military and the church had their complex administrative organizations for the control and conversion of the Indians. The Spaniards occupied all of the positions of power. Soon, converted Indians and the children of the conquest—the mestizos, who were of mixed Indian and Spanish descent—began to serve as lower-level administrators in the army, courts, and town councils. Given the tremendous distances involved, the size and diversity of the indigenous populations, and the relatively small Iberian-born population, the Spanish Empire in the New World was a remarkable achievement—one that lasted more than three hundred years.

Spain's Exploration of the Californias

California was one of the last frontiers to be colonized by the Spanish government, as a result of a change in the dynastic rulers in Spain as well as the perception of threats from other European powers. Hernan Cortés, the conqueror of the Aztecs, was an important leader in the early exploration of Baja California. His initiatives began the process of conquest that would lead to settlement. For almost ten years, while expanding the empire, Cortés labored to build oceangoing vessels on the west coast of Mexico in order to look for *Otro Méjico*—another golden kingdom—and perhaps to discover a northwest passage, a sea route around North America. In 1532 he sent two ships north but they never returned. In 1533 two more ships left and landed on the Baja California peninsula at La Paz, where they encountered rumors of fabulous pearl fisheries further north. Cortés himself set out in 1534, and named the Baja California peninsula—which he thought to be an island—"Santa Cruz." He and his men found some pearls but mostly desert lands and inhospitable Indians. In 1539 he sent Francisco de Ulloa with three vessels to search for new kingdoms further north. Ulloa sailed up the Gulf of California, later renamed the Sea of Cortés, to the mouth of the Colorado River.

The name "California" probably derives from a European adventure novel published in 1500 by the Spaniard Garcí Ordóñez de Montalvo. His book, *Las Sergas de Esplandián* (*The Exploits of Esplandián*), tells the story of a mythical island inhabited by Amazons and ruled by Queen Calafia. Literary scholars regard this book as a justification of the triumph of Spanish imperialism. In the book the Amazons and their queen are dark-skinned women who fight with weapons of gold, the only metal available in their land. To aid in their battles, they trap and domesticate griffins (mythical dragon-like birds) and feed them male captives, as well as their own male children. Queen Calafia, with her Amazons and griffins, appears at the siege of Constantinople and fights on the side of the Moslems.

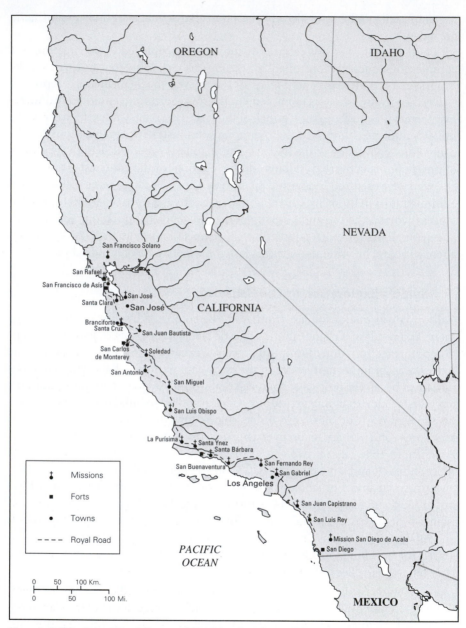

OREGON

IDAHO

NEVADA

CALIFORNIA

San Francisco Solano

San Rafael

San Francisco de Asis

Santa Clara

San José

●San José

Branciforte
Santa Cruz

San Juan Bautista

San Carlos
de Monterey

Soledad

San Antonio

San Miguel

San Luis Obispo

La Purísima

Santa Ynez

Santa Bárbara

San Buenaventura

San Fernando Rey

San Gabriel

Los Angeles

San Juan Capistrano

San Luis Rey

Mission San Diego de Acala

San Diego

MEXICO

PACIFIC
OCEAN

† Missions

■ Forts

● Towns

- - - Royal Road

0   50   100 Km.

0   50   100 Mi.

Map. 2.1 Missions, Presidios, and Pueblos in Alta California During the Mexican Era, 1769–1821

PRO & CONS

SPANISH decision 2 establish A MISSION system

Later on, however, she converts to Christianity, marries a man, and returns with him to her native island of California. The island of Queen Calafia is described in the novel as being "at the right hand of the Indes" and the early explorers, including Cortés, expected to find it within ten days of sailing off the Mexican coast. Thus the name came to be applied to the Baja California peninsula.

While the Spanish explored Baja California before 1540, more than two hundred years passed before Alta California became a Spanish colony. Alta California finally became known to the Western world as a result of the international rivalries of the European powers. Initially, the Spanish king hoped that the exploration of the western coast of the continent north of New Spain would lead to the discovery of a northwest passage. This would enable Spain to outmaneuver its rivals in trade with the Orient. In the late sixteenth century, the Spanish needed a suitable port on the Pacific Coast to provision the valuable Manila galleons as they made their way south to Acapulco laden with riches from the Philippines. In the seventeenth century the Spanish monarchy anxiously tried to prevent other European powers from settling in the vast territories that Spain had claimed. In the east, French explorers and trappers threatened to encroach on present-day Louisiana and Texas. In the northwest, the Russians and British showed interest in expansion. As a result, the Spanish crown slowly moved to finance the exploration and settlement of its remotest frontier possessions, Texas and Alta California. Other considerations motivated new settlement on the frontier, including a desire by the Spanish Catholic church to expand their missionizing endeavors as far north as possible. By the late eighteenth century Baja California had already been colonized with missions and military outposts (called *presidios*) and Alta California seemed to be the next logical step in the conquest of souls.

Early Maritime Exploration and Encounters

In 1542 an expedition led by the Portuguese navigator Juan Rodríguez Cabrillo set sail from Navidad on the northwest coast of Mexico to explore the northern territories. On September 28 he discovered a "very good harbor," which he named San Miguel because it was the feast day of that saint. Anchoring near the mouth of the harbor, which was later renamed San Diego by Sebastián Vizcaíno, Cabrillo's men explored the bay with a small boat. A shore party rowed toward a group of curious Kumeyaay Indians but as the Spanish neared land, most of them ran off. Only three natives remained to inspect the strange newcomers. Cabrillo's men gave these three some gifts, and through hand motions the Indians communicated that they knew of other strange men like them who had been seen inland. This news may have been related to Francisco Vásquez de Coronado's expedition into New Mexico in 1540.

Cabrillo continued north and a group of sailors who went ashore at Catalina Island were met by local Gabrielino men. The women fled to the interior. Later the natives paddled their canoes out to the Spanish ship and received beads and other manufactured items. Leaving Catalina and sailing north along the coast,

Cabrillo named prominent geographical features as he went. North of Point Conception the expedition landed at San Miguel Island (which they named Isla de la Posesión). Cabrillo had an accident and broke his arm, but despite this injury he ordered the crew to continue north. Sailing against the current and the prevailing winds, they reached a point near San Francisco without ever discovering the entrance to the great bay, and finally had to turn back due to bad weather and Cabrillo's failing health. Cabrillo died as they reached San Miguel Island. After burying Cabrillo on the island, the sailors proceeded as far north as the present southern border of Oregon and then, because of severe storms, returned to their home port of Navidad (located near present-day Puerto Vallarta on the west coast of Mexico).

The next European visitor to California was Francis Drake, an English pirate who was later given a royal commission and knighthood for his war against the Spanish. In 1578 Drake's ship, *The Golden Hind,* raided Spanish settlements in Chile and Peru and sailed up the Pacific Coast so heavily laden with treasure that the ship's seams began to leak. On June 17, 1579, they put into a harbor probably somewhere near the present-day San Francisco and stayed five weeks while they repaired the ship. Drake named the area Nova Albion, or New England, because the white cliffs reminded him of the white cliffs of Dover in his homeland. While on land the sailors traded with the native people and Drake wrote brief descriptions of the Indians, probably the Coastal Miwoks.

Following Drake, captains of Manila galleons entered the bays along California's coast seeking fresh water, food, and wood for repairs. The Spanish had begun their conquest of the Philippines in 1564 and immediately began sending treasure ships laden with silks and spices back to Spain via Mexico. As the galleons set sail from Manila to New Spain, they followed currents and prevailing winds, traveling north to Japan and then west. The galleons struck the American coast near Mendocino and then sailed south. The first galleon to sight the California coast took 129 days to make the passage and in the process many of the crew died from scurvy. For the next several hundred years, as regulated by the Spanish crown, a Manila galleon annually passed down the California coast. In 1595 Sebastián Rodríguez Cermeño sailed a galleon along the California coast to map it and to search for possible ports. Landing in Drake's bay, which he named "La Baya de San Francisco," Cermeño stayed a month and traveled inland to trade with the local Miwok Indians for food and supplies. Unfortunately his treasure ship was wrecked in a storm and his men had to build a small launch to return down the coast to Mexico. Because of this disaster the Spanish government forbade galleons from use in further coastal explorations.

An intensification of rivalry over the Asian trade and the need to find ports for the galleons along the Pacific Coast led the king to commission an exploration by Sebastián Vizcaíno, a Basque merchant in Acapulco who had sailed on several galleons but was not a professional sailor. Vizcaíno sailed with three ships from Mexico in 1602 and, because he was sailing against the current and winds, took four months to reach California. He entered the bay named San Miguel by Cabrillo on November 10 and, since the name of his flagship was the *San Diego de Alcalá* and the feast day of this saint was on November 12, he renamed the harbor San Diego. The expedition stayed ten days, during which they refitted their ships, buried crew members who had died from scurvy, set up a tent church, and sent an expedition inland to scout the territory.

Vizcaíno's ships continued north to Catalina Island, and then to a bay he named Monterey, after the Conde de Monterey, Viceroy of Mexico. While anchored in the bay he noted the ideal conditions for a galleon port. It had tall trees for repairs (unlike San Diego) and plenty of game and fish. His exaggerated praise of Monterey as a fine harbor later convinced the Spanish authorities that it should be the main port of a proposed colony. Vizcaíno continued north as far as Cape Mendocino, when storms and the illness of his crew convinced him to turn back. Although Vizcaíno described the potential ports he had explored in California, changes in galleon design, allowing more space for supplies, meant that the treasure ships bypassed California for the next 165 years.

The First California Colony

Alarmed by British and Russian interest in their northern frontier possessions, the Spanish government decided to establish permanent settlements there, in 1769, to secure their claims and block any claims by other powers. The energetic new administrator, the Visitor-General José de Gálvez, was determined to reorganize the northwestern frontier and expand it by settling Alta California. He commissioned two land and two sea expeditions to converge on the harbor of San Diego; all were to be under the command of Captain Gaspar de Portolá, while Father Junípero Serra was to be in charge of the founding of missions. The first contingent arrived on April 11, 1769, when the ship *San Antonio*, commanded by Juan Perez, anchored in San Diego bay. That same day, as remembered in Kumeyaay lore but not noted by the Spanish, an earthquake shook the mountains and the sun was partially eclipsed—portentous signs, perhaps, that the world as they knew it was about to pass away.

A few weeks later a second ship arrived, the *San Carlos*, commanded by Vicente Vila. This early collection of soldiers, sailors, Indians from Baja California, priests, and a doctor brought the colonists to a few more than one hundred. When they arrived most of the sailors were sick with typhus, a debilitating disease transmitted by lice and fleas. Within the next few weeks more than half of the men died on shore in a tent camp. On May 14, the first overland expedition of soldiers arrived at San Diego, commanded by Captain Fernando de Rivera y Moncada. Father Juan Crespí and a contingent of Christianized Indians from the southern missions accompanied the soldiers marching overland up the Baja California peninsula from Loreto. Soon after their arrival the commanders decided to abandon the beach and find a more permanent settlement. Pedro Fages picked the new location, a hill overlooking the bay and the nearby river. This became the site of the first settlement in California, eventually a fortified presidio with a temporary mission located within the walls.

Finally on July 1, 1769, the expedition led by Captain Gaspar de Portolá with Father Junípero Serra arrived. Besides a contingent of soldiers they also brought forty-four Christianized natives from Baja California. As Father Serra celebrated his first mass under an outdoor ramada on July 16, 1769, only 126 of the 219 explorers and settlers who had arrived during the past months remained alive. Those who were left had something to celebrate. A few days before Father Serra's mass, Portolá took a group of soldiers north to establish a settlement in Monterey and the *San Antonio* returned to Mexico for supplies, leaving a group of about forty people in San Diego.

The first report of a Spanish settler's encounter with the native people was written by Miguel Costansó, an engineer and mapmaker: He described his impressions of the Indians when a Spanish expedition set out to find water:

> These Indians (the Kumeyaay) stopped every little while upon some height, watching our men, and showing the fear which the strangers caused them by the very thing they did to hide it. They thrust one point of their bows down in the soil, and grasping it by the other end they danced and whirled about with indescribable velocity. But, as soon as they saw our men draw near, they again withdrew themselves with the same swiftness.

Finally the Spaniards communicated their peaceful intent by burying their own weapons in the dirt and giving gifts of ribbons, glass, and beads. The Kumeyaay then indicated where to find good water, and the Spaniards began walking up the San Diego river valley. They soon reached another Indian village where they met with a warm reception. Later, Costansó wrote that the Kumeyaay "are of haughty temper, daring, covetous, great jesters, and braggarts, although of little valor; they make great boast of their powers and hold the most respect for the most valiant." This evaluation of the character of the local natives presaged the tortured path that Spanish–Indian relations would follow throughout California.

Demographic and Ethnic Growth of California

The demographic and ethnic growth of the new Spanish outpost shows a society composed mainly of unmarried males of diverse ethnicity. Historians have had difficulty determining with certainty who these individuals were. For a decade San Diego was a transient presidio with very few of the soldiers remaining very long—a foreshadowing, perhaps, of the military future for San Diego. The leaders of the founding expedition, Fathers Serra and Vizcaíno and Captain Portolá, were Spaniards. This has led some to suppose that the whole expedition was composed of fair-skinned Spanish conquistadors. Notwithstanding the practical impossibility of determining the ethnicity of the surviving soldiers, there is evidence to suggest that the majority of them were probably of mixed blood—mestizos and mulattos.

The Spanish developed a complex system of classifying various mixtures of European, African, and Indian parentage. A caste system was used to exclude non-Iberians from higher political and economic posts and to create a stratified society along racial and economic lines. On the far northern frontier, however, ethnic distinctions blurred and became more fluid. In California there was a great division between the *gente de razón* (literally, people of reason), meaning those who were Catholic Christians and European in culture, and those *sin razón* (without reason), the nonconverted native people. A great premium was given to those Spaniards who could prove their *limpieza de sangre,* or "purity of blood," meaning there was no intermarriage with Jews, Moors, or other non-Christians in their ancestry. Often people with wealth were able to purchase papers certifying that their bloodlines were pure and European, thus elevating them within the caste system.

Hubert Howe Bancroft, a historian of California's pioneers, thought that most of the settlers in California were "half-breeds." Nevertheless, in the late nineteenth century Americans came to think of the first Spanish-speaking settlers as Spaniards. Los Angeles's founding families, however, are an example of the importance of the non-Spanish-born settlers. Of the eleven male heads of households who were among the founders of Los Angeles in 1781, only two were Iberians; the others were a multiethnic group that was predominantly Indian, mulatto, and mestizo. Historians have found that a large number of Spanish-speaking colonists throughout the Southwest were not Iberian Spaniards at all but rather of mixed blood, *castas,* and Hispanicized Indians, most of whom had migrated from adjacent Mexican frontier provinces. The first evidence we have of the ethnicity of the surviving colonists in the presidio of San Diego, for example, is the Spanish census taken in 1790, which counted 190 persons. Of the ninety-six adults, forty-nine were *españoles* but only three of those had been born in Europe. The rest had probably been "whitened" (on the frontier, people could "pass," depending on their wealth and occupation) to meet Mexico City's requirements that most of the soldiers be *español.* The census listed the balance of the soldiers as mulattos and *colores quebrados* (some African ancestry), mestizos and coyotes (degrees of Indian–Spanish mixture), and *indios.*

Whatever the ethnicity of the settlers and colonists who came to Alta California from Mexico, their numbers grew slowly. *Mestizaje,* or the mixture of races and cultures, began in Mexico with the conquest and continued on the far northern frontier. Soldiers married local Indian women, and female immigrants who came to California were mostly mestizo or mulatto. By 1800, some thirty-one years after the initial settlement in San Diego, the total Spanish-speaking population in California, excluding the mission Indians, priests, and soldiers, was probably about 550 people in about 100 families. This small group lived in three pueblos surrounded by perhaps as many as 30,000 mission Indians. Meanwhile the vast majority of native peoples remained free of the mission system and never accepted Spanish domination.

The Missions

Without a doubt the most important Spanish institutions in Alta California were the missions, for they changed the way of life for thousands of native people and formed the economic backbone of the province. The object of the missions was to convert the natives to Christianity as well as to Hispanicize them, instructing them in the rudiments of the Spanish language and culture. After a period of time, specified in the Law of the Indies as ten years, the missions were to be secularized or disbanded and the mission Indians were to form new towns and be converted into loyal farmers and ranchers. In this way the Spanish hoped to extend their control over all of California. This was the ideal, but in fact, after the ten years, the mission fathers concluded that the Indians were not able to make the transition and they postponed freedom for their charges again and again. The final objective was to turn the Indian people into Christian laborers, who would be loyal to the Spanish crown and capable of defending themselves against intrusions by hostile Indians and foreigners.

Beginning with the first mission at San Diego, Father Junípero Serra labored to found as many missions as possible. Serra was one of a generation of frontier priests who combined extremes of asceticism and self-denial with practical political sense and a fighting spirit. He was born on the Spanish island of Mallorca to poor parents who sent him away to a Franciscan school where, because of his intelligence, he was encouraged to become a priest. When he was only twenty-four years of age he was appointed professor of theology and for five years he taught at distinguished Spanish universities. In 1749 he gave up his prestigious career to travel to Mexico. Arriving in Vera Cruz he insisted on walking the hundreds of miles to Mexico City, an act of willpower and commitment that he repeated many times in his life. Serra worked among the Indians in Mexico as a missionary and an administrator of the College of San Fernando. In 1767 the Jesuits were expelled from the New World and Serra was chosen to administer the missions they had built in Baja California. A few years later, despite being an asthmatic and suffering a chronic leg injury, Serra traveled north to lead the founding of new missions in Alta California. For the rest of his life he suffered from scurvy and from exhaustion due to walking hundreds of miles. He also practiced many mortifications of the flesh, such as wearing shirts with barbs, self-flagellation, and self-burning, in order to purify his spirit.

Father Serra established San Carlos Boromeo, the mission at Monterey, which was later moved to the Carmel River. He also founded the missions of San Antonio de Padua, San Gabriel Arcángel, San Luís Obispo de Tolosa, San Francisco de Asís, San Juan Capistrano, San Buenaventura, and Santa Clara de Asís. After Serra's death in 1784 Father Fermín Francisco de Lasuén labored from 1785 to 1803 to complete the construction of nine more missions. The last one to be established in the Mexican era was founded in 1823, after his death. Together the missions totaled twenty-one, each one about a day's ride apart and strategically located near the coast. Father Lasuén was a gentle and refined man who was wholly devoted to the memory of Father Serra. Besides building new missions Lasuén expanded

An Indian woman at a rancho prepares corn meal (*masa*) for tortillas. The technique for grinding the corn kernels using the stone roller (*mano*) and slab (*metate*) was imported from central Mexico and originated with the indigenous people there.

and rebuilt older mission buildings, and under his diplomatic guidance the mission system prospered, experiencing less conflict with the military and government than had been true under Serra.

The conversion of the Indians was not easy. From the beginning, the natives who were to be missionized were not willing participants in this project. At first the harvest of souls was alarmingly meager. After its founding, a year passed at Mission San Diego before the first convert was made. This was followed by several revolts against the mission *padres* (fathers, or priests). At the missions located near a presidio or a pueblo there were frequent problems between the native people and the soldiers or civilians. The priests often complained of the corrupting influence of Spanish ways. Rapes of Indian women were a frequent source of conflict, causing many of them to flee into the backcountry to get away from the Spaniards. As a result, Serra moved two missions, San Diego and Monterey, farther away from their nearby presidios.

Conversions occurred nevertheless, because the Spanish priests offered food and goods that the native people found valuable. Often the natives came to the missions out of curiosity and were converted without fully understanding the import of their actions. Once baptized, they were called neophytes and were subject to the authority of the padre, who began to regulate their lives to lead them toward becoming a full member of the Christian community. If they ran away, soldiers were sent to hunt them down, bring them back, and to help in their punishment. Sometimes the soldiers seized any Indians they could find—whether they were runaways or not. Once the mission reached a critical mass, having enough neophytes to farm surpluses and raise cattle, the mission became a magnet for those who needed food, and conversion to Christianity was a way to ensure survival.

In this way, the twenty-one missions slowly grew in size and economic importance. During the sixty-five years of their existence, the fathers baptized 79,000 California Indians. The most populous and prosperous of the missions were those in southern California, including San Gabriel and Mission San Luis Rey. The missions produced the bulk of the province's food used to feed the colonists and soldiers. The natives were taught to grow wheat, corn, barley, and other grain crops, to cultivate grapevines and olive orchards, and to raise cattle and other livestock. The mission fathers trained some neophytes as artisans— shoemakers, gunsmiths, carpenters, blacksmiths, and masons. Others learned to weave textiles, make candles, and tan hides. The fathers taught their charges European instruments and music, and Indian choirs and orchestras performed religious music for special masses and fiestas. The mission Indians were responsible for tending the vineyards, fruit orchards, and wheat fields, and for raising thousands of cattle and horses.

The work regime at the California missions followed a strict timetable including morning and evening prayers and the segregation of workers by sex. Workers were overseen by Indian *mayordomos* (overseers) and *alcaldes* (leaders). Neophytes worked six days a week for five to eight hours a day. Roll call was taken at every meal and those shirking their duties were punished by imprisonment or whippings. As Pablo Tac recalled, the Indian mayordomos were there "to hurry them if they are lazy . . . and to punish the guilty or lazy one who leaves his plow and quits the field. . . ." At night, the unmarried women and sometimes the men were locked in dormitories. At some missions, neophytes were allowed to return to their villages for short durations to gather supplemental foods, but they were expected to return for mass and for work when needed.

The padres controlled the allocation of food, rationing it according to their judgment of the economic needs of the mission and those of their charges. An *interrogatorio*, or questionnaire, sent from Mexico City in the early 1800s asked the mission fathers a series of questions, one about the diet of the mission Indians. The answers—while allowing for the padres' desire to make conditions appear favorable—reveal the diversity of the missions. Father Martinez at Mission San Luis Obispo stated that he gave his workers three meals a day: *atole* (a corn gruel) in the morning, *pozole* (a soup of wheat, grains, and meat) at noon, and at night another serving of atole. At Mission San Buenaventura, Father José Señán stated that he gave the Indians one meal a day, "inasmuch as when they work they also eat. . . ." Other missionaries testified that the Indians continued gathering their traditional foods, which supplemented the mission food supply.

Neophyte Resistance

For many native Californians, the missions were not a positive experience. They were coerced into working and staying against their will, fearing punishment if they ran away. The most dreadful consequence of their stay was their exposure to European diseases, which often proved fatal. They had no resistance to chicken-pox, measles, smallpox, and influenza, and deaths mounted with each passing year, even in areas far from Spanish settlements. Venereal disease was especially deadly. Thousands of mission neophytes died from syphilis and gonorrhea and the epidemic spread to non-mission Indians as well. The strict regulations, humiliation, punishments for minor offenses, and rapes of women by soldiers engendered a smoldering resentment of the Spaniards. Often a chief grievance was the lack of food. The strict discipline of the mission fathers and the destruction of the indigenous food sources by cattle, sheep, and horses created levels of starvation at some missions. Conditions were such that the numbers of runaways increased and in some cases there were rebellions.

The first uprising was at Mission San Diego only six years after its founding. On November 4, 1775, around midnight, an estimated one thousand Kumeyaay Indians attacked the mission and burned most of it to the ground, killing Fathers Luis Jayme and Vicente Fuster, who became California's first martyrs. The survivors of the first attack took refuge in an adobe storehouse, where they held off the Indians until dawn. They were finally rescued by a group of loyal neophytes and Baja California Indians. The uprising apparently came at the instigation of two brothers, Carlos and Francisco, both newly baptized neophytes who had been punished for stealing a fish from an old woman. Carlos was the chief of the local ranchería. Resenting their treatment by the padres, they ran away from the mission and began to organize an uprising of the surrounding rancherías. When they learned that about half the presidio garrison had been sent north to San Juan Capistrano, they saw this as their chance to wipe out the Spaniards once and for all. In the Spanish investigation that followed, some accused the resident neophytes of helping the attackers, but they denied it, insisting that they had been forced to go along with the uprising.

In the years that followed, there were other rebellions. In 1781, Quechan (Yuman) Indians attacked the two missions that had been built on the California side of the Colorado River. The attack occurred when Captain Fernando de Rivera y Moncada and a party of colonists bound for California were passing through. Rivera's troops had abused some of the Quechan peoples, and the distribution of gifts was considered inadequate. The natives attacked, destroying both missions and killing four friars, thirty soldiers, and Rivera himself. The massacre ended all further land travel between Mexico and California during the Spanish period.

In 1785, at Mission San Gabriel, a female shaman named Toypurina planned to lead a group of *indios bárbaros* (non-mission Indians) and join with neophytes led by Nicolas José to overthrow the Spanish authorities. Toypurina was accused of being a witch by the Spanish authorities because she claimed to have received revelations from the goddess Chupu that the Indian people would die if they were baptized. In eighteenth-century Mexico, mestiza, Indian, and mulatta women were frequently accused of witchcraft, which was seen as a political crime. The soldiers learned of the planned rebellion, however, and arrested both leaders. Toypurina was banished to Monterey, where she eventually was baptized and married a presidio soldier.

During the Mexican period, a major rebellion took place among the Chumash peoples on the eve of the secularization of the missions, in 1824. The cause of this rebellion was the mistreatment of the neophytes by the soldiers and the strict work regime. Thousands of neophytes allied with *gentiles* (unbaptized Indians) from the interior and took over La Purísima and Santa Ynez missions for more than a month, and briefly occupied Mission Santa Bárbara. After a battle in which the padres tried to prevent needless slaughter, the rebels fled to the interior. Later Father Vicente Sarría, accompanied by troops led by Pablo de la Portilla, convinced remnants of the Santa Bárbara rebels to return.

In October of 1828, with the permission of the priest, Padre Duran, an Indian alcalde named Estanislao led scores of his fellow kinsmen away from Mission San José to the interior to help his community harvest acorns, nuts, and other foods. Once there, Estanislao notified the Spanish authorities that they were in rebellion. He was soon joined by hundreds of other runaways from the northern

Indian artisans produced these images of the stations of the cross at Mission San Fernando about 1800. They worked under the direction of the Spanish priests but still managed to express their local culture. Can you find evidence of this in the image?

missions. Estanislao's success in resisting the Spanish government was undoubtedly due partly to the fact that natives from many different groups could now communicate with each other using a *lingua franca*—Spanish. For a time, Estanislao defeated the expeditions that were sent to subjugate him, until he finally succumbed to Lt. Mariano G. Vallejo's expedition. Eventually Estanislao escaped, returned to Mission San José, and received a pardon for his rebellion. He died a few years later, working as an auxiliary soldier who hunted runaway neophytes. The Estanislao rebellion created tremendous fear among the Spanish settlers in Alta California. As a result of his movement a network to assist runaway mission Indians grew up and Indian raids on settlements from San Gabriel to San José increased.

Historian James Sandos has noted that there were a variety of other forms of resistance to the mission system, ranging from graffiti secretly scrawled on mission walls, to reports of sacred visions urging natives to renounce their Christian baptism. George Harwood Phillips, an expert on California Indian resistance, has noted that the stations of the cross painted by neophytes at Mission San Fernando depicted Indian alcaldes as the tormentors of Christ—a subtle message of protest. Other methods of resistance included running away, abortion, and secret retention of traditional customs, such as the use of the temescal. In a few cases the mission Indians were moved to kill the mission priests, as in the assassination of Father Andrés Quintana at Mission Santa Cruz in 1812.

Evaluation of the California Missions

In the 1980s devoted Catholics intensified a campaign to canonize Father Junípero Serra as a saint. Immediately a debate ensued over the record of the treatment of the natives in the missions. Native American activists, in particular, felt outrage that people wanted to honor the man who, they argued, led in the enslavement, mistreatment, and death of their people. They assembled evidence of mistreatment in the form of oral testimony by native peoples. Tribal councils passed resolutions opposing canonization. And academics wrote position papers buttressed by historical quotes and evidence arguing that Serra should not be honored. The issue of the California Indians' encounter with the Spanish is heated, provoking spirited and emotional defense of Serra by non-Indian scholars and Catholic leaders. Beatification is a long process, and Serra has advanced through the preliminary steps. The uproar over this issue demonstrates that the mission period is still very controversial in the lives of people today.

The treatment of native peoples is a major point of debate about the Spanish colonization of the Americas. A wide range of historians and anthropologists as well as Indian activists agree that the mission system throughout the Southwest, whatever its rationale at the time, resulted in the deaths—nearly all unintentional—of thousands of native Americans. The mission system in California was perhaps the most extensive, long-lived, and destructive of all those established in the Spanish and Mexican frontier. The missions in Texas were abandoned after a short period. The ones in New Mexico provoked a violent, successful rebellion in 1680 that curtailed missionary activities until the Spanish reconquest in 1692. In Arizona the missions were few and scattered. But in California, the twenty-one missions and their *asistencias* (branch missions) significantly changed the economy and lifestyle of those who were mission laborers as well as the way of life of those who lived far from the missions.

The Indian population declined. The natives were concentrated in missions, exposed to new and fatal diseases, and deprived of their traditional foods. The extent of the decimation can only be estimated. In California the missions grew to include about twenty thousand neophytes at their peak. The mission annals from 1769 to 1834 recorded 62,600 deaths but only 29,100 births. Anthropologist Sherburne Cook and historian Albert Hurtado have estimated that the Indian population of California decreased by more than 150,000 during the mission period. In the region where missions were established the decline of the population was more noticeable; almost 75 percent of the native peoples died.

Defenders of the missions point out that the mission fathers did not intend to expose their wards to fatal diseases and that their attitudes toward crime and punishment were a product of the age, not especially cruel for that time. Some martyred friars willingly sacrificed themselves rather than kill natives who attacked them. Father Serra and other priests advocated forgiveness and pardons for those who ran away, although the military frequently exacted their own punishments for this offense. The priests, however, were not saints and even Father Serra was willing to admit that "in the infliction of the punishment . . . there may have been inequalities and excesses on the part of some Fathers." Yet the mission priests' religious devotion to the task of conversion and the spiritual welfare of their flock was beyond question. Their attitudes and beliefs were a product of their historical culture, in which the soul was considered more important than the body and severe punishments were the norm. Taken as a group the mission fathers were not vicious for the times in which they lived. The tragedy was that they were helpless to prevent the deaths of the very Indians they sought to save.

The missions accomplished a great deal in developing the first agricultural economy in California. The first citrus trees, grapevines, corn, beans, wheat, barley, and oats came with the mission fathers. They promoted the raising of livestock, horses, cattle, pigs, goats, and sheep. The mission economy became the backbone for the development of large ranchos in the Mexican era and farms in the American era. The mission fathers trained the Indians to be *vaqueros*—farmers and skilled workers. As a result the Indian work force became crucial to the development of California's economy through much of the nineteenth century.

Nevertheless, we must also consider the missions from the point of view of the native Californians. The mission records themselves help us appreciate their grievances. Large numbers of neophytes ran away from the restrictive controls of the padres—an obvious indication of their dissatisfaction with the mission. By 1817 Mission San Diego had 316 runaways, the second largest number in the system, topped only by Mission San Gabriel, with 595. Running away was often provoked by hunger and by the corporal punishments that were administered by the mayordomos under the direction of the padres. Despite glowing reports of mission prosperity, chronicled by the mission padres, death, disease, and hunger were daily realities of mission life. Deaths from disease were often hastened by malnutrition. Despite the abundance, the neophytes who worked to make it possible were badly fed. The hunger of the Indians was not limited to the missions. The introduction of European livestock and plants soon took over key hunting and gathering grounds and there were severe punishments for poaching. Hunger drove non-mission Indians to seek employment and food by working for the pueblo dwellers and for the presidio garrisons.

Establishing Presidios and Pueblos

Throughout the Western Hemisphere the Spanish king and his advisers laid down the policies and directions that guided conquest and colonization. The underlying premise was that the unsettled lands were the property of the king and that the native peoples were his subjects. Individual Spaniards were not entirely free to explore or settle where they wanted. The settlement of towns and military outposts was subject to approval, planning, and regulation. Guidelines were articulated in a number of decrees and laws, the most influential being the Recopilación de Leyes de las Indias in 1680. However, despite regulations, the frontier settlers often did not follow the laws to the letter.

Captain Gaspar de Portolá, commander of one of the first expeditions sent to colonize California, had specific orders to found a presidio at Monterey Bay. In 1769 he marched north from San Diego into new territory with only twelve

A watercolor drawing of the San Francisco presidio in 1816 by Luis Choris, an artist who accompanied a Russian voyage around the world. The farthest northern presidio in California, San Francisco had yet to develop as a civilian settlement.

Vue du Presidio s. Francisco.

soldiers and a contingent of Baja California Indians. The ship *San Antonio* was to meet them in Monterey with Father Serra and others. As they passed through southern California, the natives were friendly and curious. In July they experienced a violent earthquake near the Santa Ana River and noted the richness of the grasslands in the Los Angeles basin. Portolá's land expedition stayed along the coast but had to cross the coastal range north of San Luis Obispo. They finally saw Monterey Bay, but Portolá did not recognize it from previous descriptions, so he pushed further north. Finally, a group led by Sergeant José Francisco de Ortega, Portolá's scout, stumbled upon San Francisco Bay, viewing it for the first time from a hill. A few months later, in May, Portolá founded the presidio of Monterey, south of San Francisco, and built a wooden stockade and shelters for the troops. Father Serra, who had arrived in Monterey by ship, organized the construction of a mission called San Carlos Borromeo near the presidio and on June 3, 1770, they formally dedicated both structures.

As was true throughout Latin America, the mission and the presidio were the first undertakings in the Spanish colonization of new territories. In California the most immediate need was for more provisions and for reinforcements. Due to diligent lobbying by Father Serra, who returned to Mexico City after the founding of the presidio at Monterey, the government sent other expeditions to California to strengthen the tiny settlements. The new viceroy, Antonio de Bucareli, was receptive to pleas for more support because he had evidence of Russian and British interest in California. In 1773 he issued a *reglamento,* a statement of how the new colony should be administered. This document was later slightly modified and reissued by Felipe de Neve, the newly appointed governor of California. Known as the Neve Reglamento, this document served as the guide for the administration of the colony until the end of the Spanish period (1821). It emphasized the importance of the conversion of the natives and the establishment of missions, of careful planning in laying out towns, of careful record keeping, and of regular supply ships from Mexico. Bucareli suggested the secularization of the missions and foresaw that they would become the center for towns.

The same year that he issued the Reglamento, Bucareli gave permission for Captain Juan Bautista de Anza, an important frontier soldier and explorer, to open a trail between Spanish settlements in southern Arizona and California and ordered him to establish a presidio on San Francisco Bay. The next year Anza succeeded in leading an expedition of twenty soldiers and two hundred livestock over the desert trails from Tucson to the mission at San Gabriel and then north to Monterey. In 1775 Anza led another expedition with more than 240 colonists making the 1500-mile journey, during which eight babies were born and there was only one death—a woman who died in childbirth. Most of the settlers went on to Monterey and a contingent helped establish a new presidio. Unfortunately, due to political conflicts with Lieutenant Governor Fernando Rivera y Moncada, Anza was not able to lead the final expedition to settle San Francisco himself. So, on September 17, 1776, Lieutenant José Moraga and Fathers Francisco Palou and Pedro Cambón founded the presidio and the mission of San Francisco.

The Spanish government decided to found civil towns in California primarily as agricultural centers to provide food for their presidios. The mission fathers had resisted having the presidio depend on the mission for supplies. Three official pueblos were eventually founded in California during the Spanish era: San José de Guadalupe (San José), El Pueblo de Nuestra Señora la Reina de los Angeles del Río de Porciúncula (Los Angeles), and the Villa de Branciforte (Santa Cruz). Following long-established Spanish customs of town planning, the viceroy allowed the settlers certain rights, among them the right to elect a town government to regulate matters of daily life and the right to hold private property or town lots. Each pueblo was given a grant of land to be administered by the local government for the common good. Usually this grant approximated four square leagues, or nearly twenty square miles, a size that included not only a village but also surrounding agricultural lands.

The civil settlements in California were populated by settlers drawn from the local presidios as well as from special colonizing expeditions. In 1777 the California governor, Felipe Neve, authorized fourteen men and their families to leave the presidios of Monterey and San Francisco to found the pueblo of San José. And in 1781 Neve authorized a colonizing expedition of twelve settlers and their families from Sinaloa to settle near Mission San Gabriel in southern California near Yangna, an Indian village. This was the pueblo of Los Angeles, founded on September 4, 1781, by a group composed mostly of mulatto and mestizo families. Branciforte was the last town founded in the Spanish period, and the least successful. In 1796 the government tried to recruit retired soldiers from Mexico to live in the new town, but no one wanted to go north to the forbidding lands of Alta California. Finally the government recruited convicts and their families and forced them to settle the new town, but it did not flourish.

It may seem strange to us today that more Mexican colonists did not go north to California during the Spanish and Mexican periods. This lack of large-scale movement was attributable to a number of factors. First, there was a cultural predisposition to prefer urban life to life in the hinterland. The vast majority of the Mexican population was not free to move about and live where they wanted. Spain and then Mexico tried to control and regulate the movement of people away from the metropolitan center. Second, most people in Mexico had developed deep ties to their extended families and regions and were reluctant to abandon their homes for the dangerous unknown territory to the north. There was widespread ignorance of the resources and climate of the north in addition to stories of Indian attacks, gruesome deaths, and massacres on the northern frontier. Finally, it was not easy to travel to California overland from Mexico. Settlers had to traverse the Sonora and Mojave Deserts, which were controlled by unfriendly Indians. The cost of travel for most Mexicans was prohibitive unless the government subsidized the expedition. Similar barriers worked to prevent a large-scale migration of settlers to other regions north of Mexico.

Spain gave fewer than twenty land grants to individuals during its rule of California—all to ex-soldiers, as a reward for their services. Most of the good land was reserved for the missions, and it was not until the Mexican period (after 1821) that private land grants became common.

The civilian settlers in the three Spanish towns relied primarily on agriculture and stockraising for their living. To assist them in their labors they borrowed Indian neophytes from the nearby missions and also employed local *gentiles,* or unbaptized Indians. The government tried through regulation to limit exploitation and corruption but this was largely ineffective. The employment of mission Indians in the towns was so popular that it seriously threatened the mission fathers' conversion efforts. Without California Indians working in the fields of the town lands, the Spanish pueblos probably would have failed.

Gender Relations in Spanish California

The first expeditions of explorers and settlers to San Diego in 1769 did not include women, but it was evident to Spanish authorities that women would be essential for the long-term success of the colonization effort. Antonia I. Castañeda, Gloria Miranda, Rosaura Sánchez, and others have written about the important role women played in this period of California's history. In general they have reported that Spanish and Mexican women were severely limited by the patriarchal

In 1791 an artist with the Spanish Malaspina expedition sketched this woman, a wife of a soldier at the presidio of Monterey. Her dress indicates an attention to female style and beauty despite the isolation and poverty of the settlement.

values of their society, but they also retained a degree of protection and autonomy. Indian women, however, were more likely to be victims of the early male-oriented exploration and conquest of California than Spanish and Mexican women.

Following their experience in central Mexico, the mission padres sought to eliminate Indian customs and attitudes toward sexuality that conflicted with Catholic doctrine and morals. Accordingly, the priests severely punished women for sexual misconduct. For example, at Mission San Diego, one native woman miscarried, and then was charged with infanticide and forced to endure humiliating punishments. The priests encouraged neophyte women's fertility, since all children were to be born into the Christian faith. At the same time, however, the priests outlawed Indian dances, ceremonies, and songs that were part of their fertility ritual. Women who refused to comply were sometimes accused of being witches.

Males in the secular population, especially the soldiers, often raped Indian women. This became a source of conflict between the Spanish and the native Californians. Rape, as analyzed by historian Antonia Castañeda, was more than a personal act of lust. It also was a means of subjugating the native population and expressing the power of the male colonizer over the colonized, both male and female. It served to humiliate and subjugate the Indian men and families.

A few Spanish colonists settled down and established families with Indian women. Initially, a small number of soldiers married native women at the encouragement of the priests. Castañeda found that, in the 1770s, 37 percent of the Monterey presidio soldiers married local Indian women, but, for the entire period, the intermarriage rate was just 15 percent. In order to reproduce the culture of the mother country, women from Mexico were necessary, and it therefore became a priority to import female colonists.

Non-California Indian women either came with their husbands from Mexico in the various expeditions or alone, as was the case with María Feliciana Arballo, who traveled to California with her two children in the Anza expedition of 1775. Additionally, in 1800 the government sent a group of ten girls and nine boys who were orphans to California, where they were distributed among families already there. The girls, with one exception, were married within a few years. Gloria Miranda has studied women in Spanish Los Angeles. She found that almost all the marriages were arranged, and at a tender age—thirteen was the youngest age at marriage, while the average age in the pueblo was twenty. Very few adult women remained single due to the overall scarcity of women. The more affluent families tended to have lots of children as befitting their means. Ignacio Vicente Ferrer Vallejo, an early settler in Monterey, had thirteen children. His son, Mariano Vallejo, fathered sixteen children, and José María Pico, a soldier in San Diego, fathered ten children.

Spanish colonial society was patriarchal, with the ethic of honor deeply ingrained. A man's honor depended on his ability to control others, in particular the women within the family. The church's doctrines and hierarchy supported notions of male domination and superiority. Yet women were able to carve out niches of respect, in part because, under colonial laws, they had property rights within marriage. The notion of community property for women was part of the Spanish codes. The idea was to protect the honor of a woman and her family of origin within a marriage.

Rosaura Sánchez has studied the narratives of Mexican California women collected by Hubert Howe Bancroft in the 1870s. Several illustrate the ways in which mestiza women in Spanish California related to male authority. One narrative is the story of Apolinaria Lorenzana, a woman who came to California as one of the orphans in 1800. She grew up in San Diego but refused to marry, working instead as a schoolteacher and then as a nurse and teacher at the mission. She earned the nickname "La Beata" (the Pious One) because of her devotion to helping Indians. During the Mexican period, she received two rancho land grants from the governor as a reward for her services. She bought a third rancho and lived an independent life from the revenues. Lorenzana's life reveals her independence, strength of character, and dedication to her work.

Another account is that of Eulalia Pérez, who worked as a *llavera,* or keeper of the keys, at mission San Gabriel. Among other things, Eulalia was in charge of making sure that the girls were locked in at night in their dormitory. She also supervised and directed many of the routines of mission life: the rationing of food, the training of women as weavers, and the catechizing of the neophytes. Eulalia's story shows a complete acceptance of the mission as a humane institution whose primary mission was to teach. Neither Pérez nor Lorenzana was critical of the treatment given to mission Indians but rather they saw themselves as humanizing the process of acculturation.

We also have the story of Eulalia Callis, who was the wife of California governor Pedro Fages. She desperately wanted to leave the desolate California frontier and return to Mexico City. In 1785 she publicly accused her husband of infidelity and filed a petition for legal separation. She refused to accept a compromise mediated by the priests and continued slandering the governor. The authorities arrested her and, because she was a woman, kept her locked up inside Mission San Carlos Borromeo for two months. During that time she began proceedings for a divorce, but before they were completed the couple reconciled. A year later she persuaded Fages to resign and the family returned to Mexico. Contemporary historians see Eulalia's story as evidence of female independence and outrage in the face of patriarchy, but it also reveals that women had the right to divorce, even in colonial New Spain.

Spanish Californian Culture

During the Spanish administration of California the military and the church were the dominant powers enforcing discipline according to the law. Civil culture existed primarily in the towns, where people were freer from authoritarian rules. Spain granted very few private ranchos in this period and so the hacienda lifestyle had not yet developed. Spanish society was decidedly male, primarily governed by the military and the church.

The culture that the Spanish settlers brought with them from central Mexico and the adjacent northern frontier settlement was one that made family the core of society—a family that was, in theory, strictly governed by the father. Many of the families were related by marriage or by *compadrazgo,* godparentage. Thus the idea of family was not limited to the nuclear one—but to an extensive network of individuals scattered throughout the province. In Hispanic cultures godparents frequently acted as surrogate parents and they expected the same respect and obligations from their godchildren as they did from their children. Hospitality was also an important value and fact of life, given the scarcity of the population and the common religion, Catholicism.

Despite the many rules governing behavior, challenges to authority were inevitable. Sexual misconduct by both men and women was punished. In the 1790s Sebastián Alvitre of Los Angeles and Francisco Ávila of San José were punished with sentences of forced work, prison, and exile for fornicating with Indian and married women. The provincial records are full of warnings from officials about the evils and punishments of adultery and sexual impropriety. Likewise the authorities tried, with mixed success, to regulate gambling and the consumption of alcohol.

There were no formal schools in Alta California before 1800, when Governor Borica established the first school. The school was in a public granary in San José and was taught by retired sergeant Manuel Vargas. Funding for the school came from a compulsory tax of thirty-one cents per pupil. Eventually Vargas was lured to teach in San Diego, where the citizens raised 250 dollars for his pay. Several other schools sprang up in San José and Santa Barbara. The primary subject was *La Doctrina Cristiana*—the catechism and doctrine—followed by reading and writing.

By 1820 there were approximately 3270 Spanish and mestizo settlers in California, many of them children from large families. Most of the population growth until this time had been through natural increase rather than immigration. The kind of culture that evolved was one that was deeply influenced by the native Indians. The missionized Indians did almost all the work in constructing the presidios, missions, and public works. Most of the Spanish male adult population consisted of soldiers, priests, or administrators. Intermarriage with native women and with women who came north from Mexico produced many children. The spirit of the culture remained that of a frontier outpost whose survival still depended on the authoritarian institutions of the military and the church.

Political Developments in Spanish California

As noted earlier, the first government in California was a military one, headed in 1769 by Governor Pedro Fages. Power was shared with Father Serra, the father-president of the missions in charge of ecclesiastical affairs. From the start and continuing thereafter, conflicts arose between the two authorities. Serra fought with Fages over where to build the missions and over the sexual misconduct of the soldiers toward Indian women. For the next forty years, clerics occasionally criticized the military government for the lack of protection of the missions or for the misbehavior of soldiers. In 1771 Felipe de Neve became the military governor and he energetically set about founding new pueblos and presidios by recruiting more colonists from Mexico. Accordingly, secular authority within the province became more important. The three pueblos were given forms of self-government, including the right to elect officials and to make local ordinances. Neve ordered that mission Indians be allowed the same rights and that certain prerogatives of the clergy be reduced.

The Spanish town government established in California was a type of local democracy. The system underwent some changes in the Mexican era, but its basic character was that of a Spanish institution. Each male head of household of the pueblo was given a small grant of land from the community lands granted by the king. These landholders had the right to vote in elections, which were held yearly. Historian Michael Gonzalez summarized the town government in Los Angeles in the 1830s. Although changed slightly in structure in the Mexican era, the town government election system reflected the Spanish traditions. At nine in the morning the property-owning *pobladores* were summoned to the plaza by a drumroll. After hearing nomination speeches for the various offices, they voted by a show of hands for electors, called *compromisarios*. These electors then selected the members of the town council, or *ayuntamiento*. These included one *alcalde,* or administrator/judge; two *regidores,* or councilmen; the *sindico,* or town attorney; and an *escribano,* or secretary. During the Spanish era the military governor appointed an additional member, the *comisionado,* in lieu of an alcalde when no literate person was available. The comisionado had veto power over actions taken by the council. Members of the ayuntamiento were limited to two terms in office. The town council met weekly to hear petitions for land, listen to accusations of domestic strife, rule on violations of public ordinances, and decide on action in times of crisis.

In the Spanish era the military government had more control in the town councils than was true in the Mexican period. The exact composition and duties of the members varied from pueblo to pueblo. But essentially the ayuntamiento allowed the Spanish colonists a form of self-government and free expression. Among the missionized Indians, the missionaries allowed the alcaldes to have authority to mediate minor disputes and to exercise some authority as a leader during times of war. The mission fathers relied on the Indian alcaldes as intermediaries whose authority could be countermanded by the padre.

The town records of the pueblos provide a glimpse into the realities of daily life. The pueblo of Los Angeles was the largest of the Spanish towns, with more than 615 settlers in 1820. About a third of the *vecinos* lived in surrounding ranchos and had homes in the pueblo proper. Los Angeles was known as a settlement where there were conflicts between the local officials and the general population. The annals of the Spanish period are full of disputes, complaints, petitions, and grievances directed against the government by the vecinos. Pío Pico remembered that upon his arrival in Los Angeles from San Diego he was ordered by the local alcalde to work on the new aqueduct. But Pico refused because he considered the alcalde a "brutish ignorant man." José Sánchez complained that an alcalde put him in irons because he refused to copy some documents without pay. The pueblo did not have a church until 1822 and, in order to comply with the law of attending mass, one had to travel to Mission San Gabriel. The pobladores built their homes around the plaza area with streets running roughly in a grid pattern. A *zanja madre,* or main irrigation ditch, ran through the center of the town and was used for washing, bathing, and drinking.

Other small civilian settlements, ruled by military officials from the local presidios, appeared in San Diego, Monterey, and San Francisco. Their growth would increase during the Mexican period. The civilian settlers were dependent on the missions for surplus food and skilled and unskilled workers and on the presidios for protection. The church and military authorities sought to control the settlers' lives but with the increase in population and with political changes brought about by independence from Spain this control diminished.

The Wars of Independence in New Spain

In 1810 the colonists living in New Spain began a lengthy rebellion and civil war that eventually resulted in independence in 1821. The precipitating causes of the rebellion in New Spain, soon to be called Mexico, were the exclusion of many *criollos* (the children of Spaniards who were born in the New World) from important political and ecclesiastical posts, and the long-term oppression of the Indian population. In a complex series of events—involving the overthrow of the Spanish government by a French revolutionary army in 1809 and a struggle among the Creoles and Spaniards over who would be the caretaker of royal authority in the Americas—millions of Indians, mulattos, and mestizos came to question the legitimacy of the royal government. Eventually Father Miguel Hidalgo y Costilla, a priest in the small town of Dolores, emerged as the leader of an insurrection. Although he was captured and executed a year later, the rebellion continued with new leaders, lasting more than eleven years and ravaging Mexico's economy and population. In the process California became even more isolated from the central government of Mexico as resources were used by the king to fight both the rebels in the New World and the French in Europe. This lack of resources created an economic crisis throughout the borderlands, which weakened the missions as well as the presidios.

News traveled slowly and the Californians did not learn of the rebellion until 1811. Most clerics were loyal to Spain, since many of them were Spanish peninsulares. The military commanders similarly owed allegiance and their careers to the established monarchy. A few young Californios decided to join the rebellion. In 1811 Francisco María Ruiz, the comandante of the presidio at San Diego, discovered a "seditious" paper being circulated among some of the troops. This was probably propaganda from the Hidalgo rebellion in Mexico. Ruiz found that sixty men had formed a conspiracy to overthrow Spanish authority and he promptly arrested five of the ringleaders, including José María Pico, the father of the future Mexican governor of California, Pío Pico. Two of the San Diego conspirators were eventually released, but three others died in irons within the presidio jail.

Years passed without incident until the fall of 1818 when news came that the French pirate, Hippolyte Bouchard, was working his way down the California coast, ravaging Spanish settlements. He raided Monterey and torched the presidio in November, then sailed down the coast and landed a party at Dana Point to get supplies from Mission San Juan Capistrano. News of an impending attack on San Diego made for sleepless nights, but Bouchard bypassed the harbor. The only result of this agitation was to motivate the government to send more troops and money to San Diego.

The California garrisons remained loyal to Spain, as did the mission fathers. The idea of a social rebellion of Indians led by Creole liberals was anathema to the Spanish-speaking residents of the pueblos. Everyone knew that in California the natives outnumbered the colonists by more than ten to one. There would be no revolution in California, at least not yet.

On April 20, 1822, news of the proclamation of Mexico's independence from Spain arrived by ship in San Diego harbor. Throughout the province, the officers, soldiers, and civilians were required to take oaths of allegiance to the newly independent government. The friars and neophytes were required to take a similar oath. There were no reported protests to this change of allegiance. A few Spanish priests left California, but most stayed. Within a few months the *de razón* (Spanish and mestizo) male population of the province began involving themselves in the politics of the new government. While Mexico's independence seemed to make no apparent immediate difference in the daily lives of the Californios, profound social and economic transformations were on the way that would radically alter the lives of natives and Californios alike.

Foreign Interest in Spanish California

One of the motives for the founding of a Spanish colony in Alta California had been to preempt other European powers from encroaching on the Pacific Coast. During the fifty-eight years of Spanish control, Britain, France, and Russia launched exploration expeditions to the coast of California. These European rivals threatened the Spanish monopoly in the Pacific and were of great concern to the Spanish king and his advisers.

In 1786, the French Comte de la Pérouse visited Monterey for ten days during a voyage around the world. He surveyed the mission system, pronounced it an abject failure, and made notes about the cultural and military weaknesses of the Spanish settlement. This, of course, was to justify and encourage a possible French takeover of Spanish California. Later he published his impressions along with some of the first European sketches of the California natives and countryside.

Another explorer who made known the resources of the Pacific Coast was Alexandro Malaspina, an Italian commissioned by the king of Spain to visit his American possessions and search for the Northwest Passage. Malaspina had artists and scientists on board to report on the local environments and cultures. In 1792 his ships visited Monterey, where he stayed for two weeks making observations on the flora and fauna as well as the local inhabitants.

The English explorer George Vancouver visited California ports three times between 1792 and 1794. He later published his observations about the deficiencies of the Spanish settlements. Secretly, he reported the weaknesses of the Spanish defenses in California to the English king, an indication of England's interest in acquiring this territory.

In 1796, the first American ship, the *Otter*, commanded by Ebenezer Dorr, visited California. Dorr's visit was noticeable mainly because he left behind eleven Australian convicts who had stowed away on his ship. For a year they worked as skilled artisans in Monterey but then the governor sent them by ship to Spain. Following this first visit, other American otter-hunting ships navigated off the coast and illegally traded manufactured goods with the locals.

One of the most memorable foreign visits to California was made by Nikolai Rezanov, a representative of the Russian-American Fur Company. In 1806, he visited San Francisco ostensibly to obtain supplies for the Russian fur outpost at Sitka, but more probably to investigate the fur-trading prospects in California. The California governor was initially opposed to giving aid to the Russians since that would strengthen their colony, which was in territory claimed by Spain. During his stay, Rezanov met and fell in love with Concepción Argüello, sixteen-year-old daughter of the comandante of the presidio at San Francisco. The family agreed to the marriage, with Concepción's approval. The governor also granted permission for a cargo of food to be sent to Sitka. Promising to return after he was granted permission by the czar to marry, Rezanov returned to Russia. Unfortunately, while crossing Siberia on his way to St. Petersburg, he died. Meanwhile, Concepción waited in vain for the return of Count Rezanov; her vigil lasted thirty-five years until she finally received news of Rezanov's death. For the rest of her life she refused all suitors and took on the robes of a *beata*, a holy woman, devoting herself to acts of charity. In later years this tragic love story became the subject of poems and novels, part of Spanish California's romantic past.

Following the Rezanov visit, other Russian ships visited California ports seeking sea otter pelts, sealskins, and provisions. In 1812 the Russian-American Fur Company, after negotiating with the Pomo Indians, built a wooden stockade fort eighteen miles north of Bodega Bay. They called it Fort Rossiya, an archaic name for Russia. (Americans later called it Fort Ross.) The purpose of Fort Rossiya was to provide a base to grow food for the fur-hunting colonies located farther north in Kodiak and Sitka. Eventually the colony grew to more than four hundred, a mixture of Aleuts, Russians, and local Indians, and intermarriages between the Aleuts and the local natives promoted peace. The Russian priests were not very active in trying to convert the Indians. Soon the Russians established a seasonal settlement at Bodega Bay as well.

Through the writings of la Pérouse and Vancouver in addition to the visits of the Russian and American fur hunters, the richness of California's natural resources became more widely known. The recurring observation that the Spanish authorities were not very successful in exploiting this wealth and that their colony was poorly defended and underpopulated was also of great interest. In subsequent decades, after Mexican independence, California's mythic name, as an island of unknown wealth, magnetized the imaginations of increasing numbers of non-Spanish speakers.

The Importance of the Spanish Era in California

The development of California's European-stock settlement after 1821 was a natural outgrowth of customs and tendencies set in motion during the Spanish administration. During the next few decades the surplus of cattle in California's economy and the reliance on Indian labor were the very foundations of Mexican California. This continued into the first decades of the American period. The trading system and large ranching operations that the missions pioneered, especially the labor system involving native peoples, were the basis of the development of the rancho economy in the Mexican era. The Spanish culture was firmly established. The importance of family loyalty and Catholic piety, the competition between *norteños* and *sureños* (northern and southern Californians), community fiestas, and the ethic of gracious hospitality all continued without interruption into the Mexican era.

Unfortunately, so too did the decimation of the native Californians from European diseases. By the end of the mission period, in the 1830s, the Indian population had probably been reduced by as much as 100,000. Spanish cattle and sheep overran traditional food-gathering areas. Whole villages disappeared as the inhabitants were forced to move to find new food-gathering grounds. Indians were killed off or reduced by disease, and those who survived were forced to become neophytes in the missions, or servants in the pueblos or presidios. Thousands of Indians became migrants, drifting between Spanish settlements and their traditional villages.

The most visible remnants of Spain in California today are the rebuilt and reconstructed missions, most of which still serve as houses of worship. As symbols of a distant era they have been romanticized in novels and movies. Most are tourist attractions whose tranquil atmosphere suggests a peaceful, pastoral past. For some, however, they stand as symbols of an oppressive regime that began the destruction of a way of life.

Even though Spanish authority lasted fewer than fifty years, Spain succeeded in transferring her language and culture to Alta California. Place names echo this heritage: La Jolla, Santa Ana, San Joaquin, Sacramento, Sierra Nevada, San Francisco, and many more. The layout of towns, Spanish-style architecture, the patio, the plaza, the rancho, all survive in altered forms as elements in California's built environment. The Spanish introduced European plants and animals that forever changed the flora and fauna of California.

Some elements of Spanish town government and statutory law survive to this day. The lands owned by the municipalities of San Diego, Los Angeles, and San José are based on the generous Spanish government grants to the pueblos. The Spanish law concerning water rights as a communal rather than a private resource continues to influence California's legal history. So too does the Spanish legal doctrine of community property.

Increasingly, the Spanish language is an important second language in California, as Latinos—whose roots extend into Mexico and Latin America—continue with a second chapter in the Spanish colonization project. The language spoken by Father Serra, the presidio soldiers and settlers, as well as many mission Indians can be heard in the streets and fields of California in the twenty-first century. Thus the profound changes begun in 1769 continue to echo into the present.

Suggested Readings

- Bolton, Herbert Eugene. One of the most prolific scholars in Spanish California studies. Students should consult his book-length studies on Father Juan Crespi, De Anza, and especially his translation of Father Francisco Palou's *Historical Memoirs of New California* (New York: Russell & Russell, 1966).

- Castañeda, Antonia I., "Presidarias y Pobladores: Spanish-Mexican Women in Frontier Monterey, Alta California, 1770–1821" (Ph.D. dissertation, Stanford University, 1990). One of the few book-length monographs about Spanish women in this period.

- Cook, Sherburne F., *The Conflict Between the California Indian and White Civilization* (Berkeley and Los Angeles: University of California Press, 1976). An anthropologist who has interpreted a wealth of data to help us understand the dimensions of the conflict.

- Costo, Rupert, and Jeannette H. Costo, *The Missions of California: A Legacy of Genocide* (San Francisco: Indian Historian Press, 1987). A historical attack on the pro-Spanish interpretation of the missions written by California Indian historians.

- Engelhardt, Father Zephyrin, *The Missions and Missionaries of California* (San Francisco: James Barry, 1908–1929). The classic defense of the California missions is this four-volume work by the Franciscan priest, as well as the scholarly writings of Msgr. Francis J. Weber, in his individual histories of the missions.

▌ Geiger, Father Maynard, *The Life and Times of Fray Junípero Serra, O.F.M.; or, The Man Who Never Turned Back, 1713–1784: A Biography* (Washington: Academy of American Franciscan History, 1959). The classic study of Father Serra's labors in California.

▌ Gutiérrez, Ramón A., and Richard J. Orsi, eds., *Contested Eden: California Before the Gold Rush* (Berkeley and Los Angeles: University of California Press, 1998). An anthology of the most recent interpretations of California's history before 1848. New essays on the ecological consequences of conquest.

▌ Monroy, Douglas, *Thrown Among Strangers: The Making of Mexican Culture in Frontier California* (Berkeley and Los Angeles: University of California Press, 1990). A well-written discussion of the California Indian interactions with the Spanish, Mexican, and Anglo frontiers.

▌ Weber, David J., *The Spanish Frontier in North America* (New Haven and London: Yale University Press, 1992). The masterwork by one of the leading borderlands scholars, setting the California experience in a larger context.

3

Mexican California, 1821–1846

Main Topics

▌ A New Political Order

▌ The Rise of the Ranchos

▌ Social Relations in Mexican California

▌ California and the World

▌ Summary

In 1877, a Californio ranchero named José del Carmen Lugo recalled life during the Mexican era for Thomas Savage, one of historian Hubert Howe Bancroft's research assistants. His memory about the work routine provides important details about the reality of rancho life in Mexican California—specifics that contradict the vision of an idyllic, lazy, pastoral existence that has often been depicted in literature and film.

The Californian way of life in my early years was as follows: at eight o'clock in the evening the entire family was occupied in its prayers. In commending themselves to God, they recited the rosary, and other special prayers which each one addressed to the saint of his or her name or devotion. Husband and wife slept in the same room, and nearly always in the same bed. The children—if there were any, and the dwelling had conveniences and separate apartments—slept, the men in the galleries out-side in the open-air, and women in an enclosed quarter of which the parents kept the key, if there was the key, a thing that was not very common.

CHAPTER 3	Mexican California, 1821–1846
1822	Luis Argüello elected as *jefe político,* or governor, of newly independent California
1824	Chumash rebellion against missions ends
1825	José María Echeandía selected as California's governor; unofficial capital in San Diego
1826	Beginning of secularization of the missions; American fur trapper Jedediah Smith enters California
1831	Rebellion against Governor Manuel Victoria by southern Californians (sureños)
1833	José María Padrés and José María Híjar recruit 204 settlers to go to California
1834	Governor José Figueroa continues secularization of the missions
1836	Norteños led by Juan Bautista de Alvarado rebel against Governor Mariano Chico
1838	Civil war: sureños and norteños battle for control of the province
1839	Governor Juan Bautista de Alvarado and the norteños win
1840	John Sutter obtains land grant at junction of Sacramento and American Rivers
1841	Bidwell-Bartleson overland expedition enters California
1842	Governor Manuel Micheltorena appointed; Americans led by Commodore Thomas ap Catesby Jones occupy the port of Monterey
1843	Andrés and Pío Pico obtain grant to Rancho San Onofre y Margarita, largest rancho in California
1846	Donner expedition ends in tragedy

At three o'clock in the morning the entire family was summoned to their prayers. After this, the women betook themselves to the kitchen and other domestic tasks, such as sweeping, cleaning, dusting, and so on. The men went to their labor in the field—some to the cattle, others to look after the horses. The milking of the cattle was done by the men or the Indian servants. Ordinarily some women had charge of the milking, to see that the milk was cleaned and strained. The women and the Indian servants under them made the small, hard, flat cheeses, the cheese proper, butter, curds, and a mixture made to use with beans.

The women's labors last until seven or eight in the morning. After that they were busy cooking, sewing, or washing. The men passed the day in labor in the fields according to the location—some preparing the ground for sowing the seed,

The Lugo family assembled before the family two-story adobe in Los Angeles in 1870. The founder of the family, Francisco Salvador Lugo, came to California in 1774. His son Antonio received several large land grants stretching from San Diego to Sonoma. He was considered the wealthiest man in California during the 1850s. His son Vicente built this adobe in 1854. His wife is in the center of the photo. By the time of this photo the vast Lugo holdings had dwindled to less than 400 acres. Can you point out the Mexican and California influences as well as the American in their dress?

bringing in wood, sowing the seed, reaping, and so on. Some planted cotton, some hemp, some planted both. This was done by those who had facilities for it; they planted and harvested in the things they needed most for the benefit of their families, such as rice, corn, beans, barley, and other grains, squash, watermelons, and cantaloupes.

The lands in the immediate vicinity of Los Angeles were set to fruit trees such as grapes, pears, apples, pomegranates, here and there an olive, cactus fruit, peaches, and other minor fruits. The owners of fields who could not obtain seeds of oranges, lemons, or producing fruits were found at the missions because the Padres selfishly refused to allow them to grow elsewhere than at their missions.

In José del Carmen Lugo's memory, the Mexican era of California's history was one in which industry and labor were transforming the land. Prosperity seemed to be less an automatic result of climate than the result of family and individual efforts. Indeed this was a major change from the Spanish era. The mission no longer had a monopoly on the land and labor. Now private rancheros rather than mission friars shaped the economic and the political destiny of California. To be sure, there was much continuity in everyday life but the older order was passing away and in its place a Californio way of life emerged.

Questions to Consider

- What were the main characteristics of Mexican political life in Alta California?

- How did the creation of the ranchos change the social and economic development of the province?

- How did secularization of the missions affect the California natives?

- To what degree did these changes lead to greater foreign influence?

- What kind of impact did these foreigners have on the Mexican and Indian peoples?

A New Political Order

In the decades following Mexican independence from Spain the European settlers of Alta California became more independent in spirit as they developed a stronger regional identity. They began to call themselves "Californios," Spanish-speaking inheritors of a frontier society that had an intense loyalty to family and to place. Ironically, the landholding Californios of this era owed their prosperity and independent spirit to the policies of the central government of Mexico, whose policies led to the redistribution of the mission lands and the creation of new wealthy families. The Mexican government enacted secularization laws designed to end the Catholic church's tutelage of native people and to create a nation of independent farmers. Under these laws the Christianized natives who had worked for the missions were supposed to be emancipated and given small tracts of land. But the land hunger of the Californios and the failure of the missions to fully assimilate the natives resulted in the former mission Indians becoming a landless, exploited, and homeless class. Upon the departure of the mission padres, most of the neophytes left the missions and soon their lands were declared abandoned and open to petition for a land grant from the government. Ultimately the mission lands passed to the hands of several hundred Californio families who became the new leaders of Alta California. For the native people, who outnumbered the Mexican population, sporadic resistance against the settlers and ranchers continued.

Early Self-Government: Solá and Argüello

With independence from Mexico, California's political situation became much more complicated as a succession of Mexican governors who attempted to administer the affairs of the province provoked conspiracies and rebellions that finally led to a greater local independence and opposition to centralized control.

In many ways the controversies in California during the Mexican era mirrored the struggle going on in Mexico, where the federalists and centralists battled one another over the degree of authority the central government should have. The Californios learned of the liberal ideas flowing from the American and French Revolutions and the Spanish liberal Constitution of 1812—ideas of democracy, secularism, and freedom of expression, all concepts that had been banned under the Spanish regime. These ideas, mixed with strong ties to family, an identification with and loyalty to the region, and a geographic isolation from Mexico City, shaped the distinctive path of Californio politics.

In 1822, with news that Agustín Iturbide had proclaimed himself emperor of Mexico, the last Spanish governor of California, Pablo Vicente de Solá, convened a junta to decide how to proceed. The junta decided to allow the army officers and citizens of the pueblos to vote for electors who, in turn, would choose a representative to the Mexican legislature. Even some mission Indians were allowed to vote. The electors met in Monterey and chose Governor Solá as the delegate, but before he could leave, a commissioner from Mexico City arrived with new instructions. Now, a *diputación,* or provincial legislature, was to be elected by the *ayuntamiento* (town council) and army officers, and this local body was to elect a new governor. Accordingly, a group of Californios elected Luis Argüello, one of their own, as the new governor.

Argüello's two-year term as governor was marked by revolts of the mission Indians at Santa Barbara, Santa Inés, and Purísima Concepción, and by conflict with the mission administrators over the relocation of Mission San Francisco. The Indian rebellion was ultimately put down (see Chapter 2), and Argüello compromised with the church authorities to allow Mission San Francisco to remain where it was and to allow the founding of the last mission, San Francisco Solano, near present-day Sonoma. Finally, in 1824 news came of Iturbide's abdication and the creation of a Mexican Federal Republic governed by a constitution. While this seemed to promise more home rule for the Californios on paper, the immediate consequence, ironically, was to deny the local population the right to elect their own governor.

The Governorship of José María Echeandía

In 1825 the Mexican government selected José María Echeandía as the new governor of the territory of Alta California. Traveling by ship to the port of San Diego, Echeandía decided to remain in the presidio there because he preferred the mild climate compared to that of the designated capital, Monterey. With Echeandía's residence in San Diego, a rivalry developed between north and south. The politicos of the north resented the south's emergence as the de facto seat of government. Nevertheless, for the next few years San Diego was the unofficial capital of the territory and the governor carried out all of his official business there. Occasionally he would venture forth to Los Angeles and even to Monterey for short periods.

For the next five years Governor Echeandía sought to implement policies that reflected the changing direction of the Mexican government. One of those policies was to ensure the loyalty of the former-Spanish subjects to the Mexican Republic. Soon after his arrival, Echeandía ordered the celebration of the first Mexican Independence Day. On September 16, 1825, the presidio fired sixteen cannon shots, Mexican flags were displayed on the presidio fortifications, and a formal ceremony took place in the plaza at 9:30 in the morning. Next, the entire population formed a procession to the church to give thanks, followed by a fiesta hosted by the governor.

The missionary priests, most of whom were Spanish, had refused to take an oath of loyalty to the new Mexican government. On April 28, 1826, the governor met in San Diego with a group of padres and after some discussion the priests agreed to take the oath if it was "compatible with our religion and profession." Finally, all five of the padres of the San Diego district and those in the other missions agreed to take the oath. Several of the older priests returned to Spain to retire. In all of Alta California there were about thirty-six mission priests who were affected by this new change of government.

The Mexican government passed a series of secularization laws that mandated the dismantling of the remnants of Spain's power in Mexico. This meant breaking up the mission system and converting the lands to private property. Echeandía began to implement this secularization of mission lands. On April 28, 1826, he began discussions with the padres to determine how best to carry this out. They suggested that Indians "of good conduct and long service" could form independent towns near the missions. In the spirit of this discussion Echeandía issued a decree of partial emancipation on July 25, 1826. Indians could leave the mission if they had been Christians since childhood or for fifteen years, were married, and had a means of earning a living. They had to apply to the comandante of the local presidio and get a written permit in order to travel from place to place. The proclamation initially applied only to the San Diego, Santa Barbara, and Monterey districts but it was later extended to other missions. Only a very few mission Indians could meet the requirements, and only a small number participated. Governor Echeandía brought his secularization plan before the territorial assembly on July 20, 1830, and it was approved.

Rebellion Against Centralism: Governor Victoria

In 1830 the Mexican central government appointed Lieutenant Colonel Manuel Victoria to succeed Governor Echeandía as the jefe político of Alta California. Before Victoria could assume office, a group of San Diego's most prominent families, in league with other Californios, sought to influence Echeandía to carry out a more-rapid secularization policy, so that they might take possession of the mission lands, properties, herds, and Indian labor. The young reformers included the Bandinis, Carrillos, Vallejos, Picos, and Alvarados—men who were enthusiastic about republicanism and the possibility of obtaining new rancho lands. Echeandía

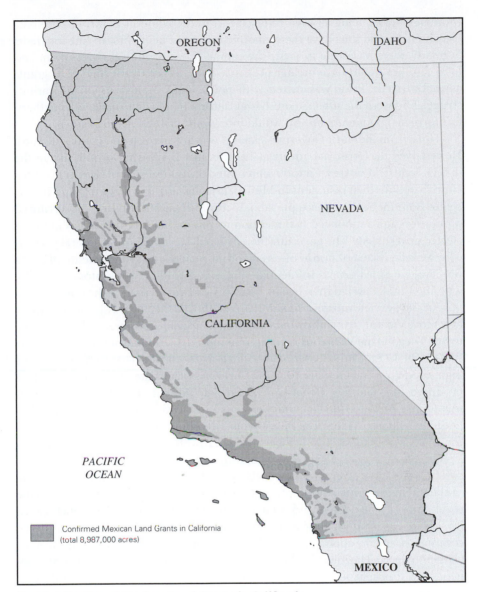

Map 3.1 Confirmed Mexican Land Grants in California

was persuaded to try to carry out the secularization of mission lands before the new governor took over. As soon as Victoria assumed office, however, he over-turned Echeandía's decrees. He represented the centralists, a more-conservative political faction that opposed ideas of liberalism.

One of the themes that developed in the Mexican era—and continues today—was the rivalry between the northern and southern Californians. Each side competed for the location of the customshouse and territorial government. Under Mexico's laws all foreign vessels had to pay duties at the port of entry in

Monterey before being allowed to engage in trade. Whoever controlled the customhouse would thus have the economic benefit of being first in line for trade. Similarly, there was pride in being the capital of the territorial government and local families would have greater influence over decisions affecting land grants as well as trade. Pride was mixed with politics and economics in the various struggles between the *sureños* (southern Californians) and the *norteños* (northern Californians). This competition would intensify in the American period.

Thus, from the start, Governor Victoria was not popular with many sureños. He removed the territorial government from San Diego and went to live in the official capital, Monterey. Victoria represented the centralist, antidemocratic, pro-church factions then resurgent in Mexico. Despite a request from a group of delegates from the San Francisco presidio, Victoria refused to convene the territorial diputación and announced his intention to restore military rule and abolish all elected government. The governor then ordered the execution of several persons who were convicted of minor offenses and suspended the ayuntamiento of Santa Barbara. He exiled several influential norteños, including José Antonio Carrillo, without a trial. Carrillo then began agitating for a revolt against the governor.

For the next few months the sureños secretly and then openly led a movement to remove Victoria from office. Juan Bandini, a Peruvian immigrant who had come to San Diego in the 1820s, was perhaps the most active leader of the anti-Victoria movement. In San Diego, Bandini wrote an eloquent protest against the governor's high-handedness on October 10, 1831. This was perhaps the first protest literature produced in California. Other prominent San Diegans shared Bandini's sentiments. José Antonio Carrillo, who was in exile in Mexico, traveled secretly to San Diego to help plan a rebellion. Pío de Jesús Pico, who later became a Mexican governor of California, was also involved and later wrote an account of the affair.

On November 29, 1831, Pico, Bandini, and Carrillo, with "about a dozen" companions, took over the San Diego presidio and issued a *pronunciamento* (a statement justifying a rebellion). When former governor Echeandía joined the revolt, most of the officers and soldiers of the presidio did too. The rebels called for the removal of Victoria as governor, the separation of military and civil commands, and the appointment of Echeandía as interim governor. The Pronunciamento de San Diego was California's first written declaration of political independence. Probably penned by Juan Bandini, in the florid literary style of the day, it set forth the reasons for people to join the rebellion against Victoria. It accused Victoria of "criminal abuse" and of breaking the law, while claiming that the pronunciamento signers were motivated by "love of country" and "respect for the laws." It listed as grievances the governor's suspension of the government of Santa Barbara, the execution of several people in violation of the procedures of law, and the banishment of several prominent Californios. The document called Victoria a despot.

The Victoria rebellion was ultimately resolved when a military force of sureños from San Diego and Los Angeles met Victoria's small group of only thirty men near Cahuenga Pass in December 1831. After a short skirmish two men were killed and Victoria was wounded. His army retreated to Mission San Gabriel, where he finally agreed to resign his governorship. The next month he traveled to the port of San Diego and on January 17, 1832, he left for Mexico.

Secularization of the Missions: José Figueroa

After the rebellion against Victoria the political struggles among Californios, between families, and between the norteños and sureños complicated things for many months. Agustín Zamorano led a norteño faction that claimed to be the legitimate government of the territory north of Santa Barbara, while Echeandía claimed jurisdiction over the south. Zamorano served until the arrival of José Figueroa, the new governor appointed by Mexico City. Figueroa felt that the sureño Californio leaders were a "clique of conceited and ignorant men." However, the Californios eventually benefited through his implementation of the final secularization of the mission lands.

José Figueroa was a mestizo military officer who had fought alongside José María Morelos and Vicente Guerrero during the Mexican Wars of Independence. He came to California after having served as the military commander in charge of pacifying the local Indians in Sonora and Sinaloa. He proved to be a man who understood the Californios' intense regional pride and need for mission lands.

During the 1830s, the intention of the Mexican government was to convert the California mission properties into Indian pueblos. This policy, which had envisioned free settlements of Hispanicized natives, ultimately was subverted by the local Californios, many of whom regarded the Indians as incapable of self-government or property ownership. The secularization of the mission lands and the emancipation of the neophytes, however, proceeded rapidly under Governor Figueroa, and subsequent Mexican governors completed the legal process.

The secularization of the missions affected about eighteen thousand Christianized natives in California. At the beginning Governor Figueroa took the unusual step of traveling to some of the missions to explain the benefits of emancipation to the natives in person. In San Diego he spoke to 160 families; however, only 10 families agreed to accept their freedom, which was not enough to form a pueblo. So Figueroa appointed Santiago Argüello as the *comisionado*, or commissioner, in charge of Indian properties at San Diego. Eventually enough ex-neophyte families accepted their changed status and established the Indian pueblo of San Dieguito, near the mission. Others near Mission San Luis Rey moved to an already existing native pueblo at Las Flores. And another Indian pueblo grew up in San Pascual, near present-day Escondido. Each of these new pueblos was instructed to select their own *alcalde*, or mayor. Thus, the Kumeyaay Indians, not the Spanish-speaking descendants of the founders of the presidio, elected the first self-government in the San Diego district. Those natives who agreed to live in these pueblos were informally allowed to use the lands they needed for dwellings and agriculture. The remaining ex-mission lands were declared abandoned and thus open to petition for ownership by the Californios.

Many mission Indians did not embrace the idea of living as free farmers. Most left the mission lands and returned to their former lives, thus rejecting further supervision and control by Mexican authorities. Moreover, many had maintained contact with relatives and extended families outside the mission lands, and they wanted to go home. Others, whose villages had disappeared because of disease or war, were now homeless, lacking the protection of the mission padres. Traditional lands that had been the homeland of native peoples were now controlled by rancheros. As a result, thousands of homeless Christianized Indians sought to eke out an existence by hiring themselves out to the Spanish-speaking population as vaqueros, domestic servants, mistresses, and indispensable laborers within the Mexican pueblos and presidios.

By 1834 six missions in California had been secularized and the rest would soon follow. The wealthiest and most populous, Mission San Luis Rey, was administered by Pío Pico. At Mission San Diego there were more than five thousand neophytes and most of them departed after the priests left. An estimated two thousand moved closer to the newly constructed town of San Diego (as yet not officially a pueblo), where they found occasional work as servants and laborers. For the remainder of the Mexican period, the Christianized ex-neophyte native population greatly outnumbered the Mexican mestizo population within the San Diego district. For many Mexican settlers, Indian allegiances were suspect, and frequent raids and rumors of impending attacks always raised suspicions of alliances between the local Indians and the *indios bárbaros*.

During the decade that followed, the Californios petitioned the Mexican government, eager to claim hundreds of ranchos formed out of lands that had been declared "abandoned" by mission administrators. Many of these same administrators ended up owning the very lands they supervised. Who benefited from this era of rancho creation? Rancho grantees were those who, because of political influence or because of long service to the mission or presidio, were in a position to claim the land and the cattle on it. To be successful, individuals had to do more than claim the lands. They also had to have the interest and ability to manage a cattle ranch. Eventually more than seven hundred private land grants were approved by the Mexican government. A portion of the grants went to foreigners— mostly to naturalized American citizens.

Governor Figueroa died before seeing the final result of the Mexican government's secularization laws. These included: (1) the dispossession of the missionized Indians of the lands they had depended upon for food and shelter, (2) the creation of a new floating class of homeless, exploitable Indian laborers, and (3) the birth of a new aristocracy of landed families who increasingly asserted their rights over those of the Mexican governors and the Indians alike.

Rebellion, Revolution, and Home Rule

Governor Manuel Victoria was succeeded by a series of temporary governors who inspired contempt and rebellion. José Castro served briefly as a temporary governor, followed by Nicolás Gutiérrez. Gutiérrez was quickly replaced, in 1835, by Mariano Chico, a representative of the newly emergent centralist faction in Mexico City. The centralists believed in reducing the autonomy of the state government, removing local controls, and substituting that of military authorities from Mexico City. The centralists threatened the new autonomy of the Californio rancheros. The subsequent Californio revolts against the Mexican governors occurred at about the same time as rebellions in the Mexican states of Queretaro, Zacatecas, Yucatán, New Mexico, and Texas. All were sparked by reactions against the centralist ascendancy in Mexico City, which was led by General José Antonio Lopez y Santa Anna. The government's military forces suffered a disastrous defeat in Texas in 1836, leaving them less able to enforce their will on the far-flung northern territories. Accordingly, the Californio rebels escaped punishment at the hands of General Santa Anna.

In 1836 Juan Bautista Alvarado led a norteño rebellion against Chico, calling for California's independence from Mexico until the federal system was restored. In reaction to the prospect of the dominance of Monterey, the sureños in San Diego and Los Angeles joined forces to offer an alternative to Alvarado's rebellion. The San Diego ayuntamiento proclaimed loyalty to the Mexican government, but by early 1837, Alvarado secured Los Angeles' peaceful adherence to his government. San Diego's representatives had no choice but to go along. Many who had been most outspoken against Alvarado exiled themselves to Baja California. Later Alvarado's troops occupied San Diego for two days looking for dissidents, and arrested several San Diegans who had opposed him.

The last effort by the sureños to salvage their regional pride and political influence began in the spring of 1837 when an anti-Alvarado group from San Diego gathered about forty men and persuaded the ayuntamiento to endorse "El Plan de San Diego." This document, written by Juan Bandini, formally recognized the official Mexican government and rejected Alvarado's rebellion. The sureños proposed that they organize a loyalist government to rule the territory, now reorganized as a department, until the Mexican government approved a legitimate governor.

The leaders of "El Plan de San Diego" were Bandini, Santiago E. Argüello, and Pío Pico. Together they traveled north to get the Los Angeles ayuntamiento's endorsement of El Plan. By June 1837, the sureños had assembled an army of about 150 men and were prepared to meet Alvarado on the field of battle to decide who would rule California. The expected struggle did not take place, however. Before any fighting occurred, news from Mexico arrived confirming the establishment of a new centralist government and everyone, including Alvarado, accepted it. In July 1837 Alvarado took an oath to support the constitution and the provincial diputación selected him as governor until a new Mexican appointee arrived.

The civil war between the north and the south continued when the replacement governor, Carlos Carrillo, arrived. Carrillo sided with the sureño faction, named Los Angeles the new capital of the department, and moved the customshouse to

San Diego. Shortly thereafter, Alvarado refused to recognize Carrillo until he was officially ordered to relinquish the governorship. Meanwhile, Alvarado sent representatives to Mexico City to plead his case as the legitimate governor and he prepared to challenge Carrillo with force of arms.

In the spring of 1838, the sureños and norteños assembled for battle near Mission San Buenaventura. About half of the soldiers on the sureño side were from San Diego. They exchanged shots and one person was killed before the southerners were outmaneuvered and retreated to Los Angeles. Remnants of the army, led by Carrillo, continued fleeing to San Diego, where they prepared for a last stand. Before further bloodshed, the two governors met in April 1838 near Mission San Luis Rey. They signed a "treaty" that called on Mexico City to determine who was the legitimate governor. A formal notification arrived in August and, to the bitter disappointment of the sureños, the central government named Alvarado as the legitimate provisional governor. Carrillo left for Mexico.

The final blow to the sureños' political aspirations occurred when Alvarado sent a force to San Diego to round up those who had opposed him. On Christmas Eve, 1838, Alvarado's troops surrounded Bandini's house on the plaza in San Diego during the performance of a traditional *pastorela* (Christmas drama). Bandini was not there but the other leaders were arrested and taken away in chains. A year passed before San Diego's citizens redeemed themselves in the eyes of the new governor, through oaths of loyalty. On February 6, 1839, the main families in San Diego sent Alvarado a letter congratulating him for his appointment as governor. Home rule had been reestablished but the cost had been to inflame familial and regional rivalries.

Alvarado was a native-born northern Californian who, as governor of the territory, led his compatriots in democratic revolutions and protests against Mexico City's high-handed leaders. He championed legislative initiative, public schools, government improvements, and many other projects to improve the economy and political health of the department. He presided over the most momentous economic change in the history of California, the breakup of the mission lands and the distribution of these lands to the native Californians, foreigners, and Indians.

Alvarado was related to another powerful California figure, General Mariano Vallejo. Together they lived through the American takeover of their territory and both authored multivolume histories that remain unpublished and untranslated in the Bancroft library. In 1827 the diputación at Monterey voted to change the name of California to "Moctezuma" in honor of the Aztecs but were overturned by the national government. As a young man, Alvarado and his friends secretly purchased books that were on the Catholic church's Index of Forbidden Books list and for that they were threatened with excommunication. Alvarado, along with many other prominent Californios, had a mistress and several children to whom he gave his name. In his maturity, Alvarado became an alcoholic whose periodic binges were embarrassing, causing him to miss his wedding and his own inauguration as governor, and to panic when the Americans mistakenly invaded Monterey in 1842.

Despite these weaknesses Alvarado was a capable leader and politician who enjoyed the respect of many native Californians. He participated in most of the crucial turning points of the territory's history—the revolts against Nicolás Gutiérrez and then against Micheltorena made Alvarado the longest-termed governor of Mexican California.

Micheltorena and the Catesby Jones Affair

In 1842 Mexico again attempted to impose a non-Californio governor, General Manuel Micheltorena. He arrived with three hundred troops termed *cholos* (meaning low-class mestizos and Indios) by the status-conscious Californios, who accused them of petty thievery and disorder. It is true that many of the troops were unpaid ex-convicts who were encouraged to forage for their sustenance. An additional cause for the disaffection of the norteños was their desire to regain local political power.

During Micheltorena's first year as governor and American naval officer, Commodore Thomas ap Catesby Jones, occupied the port of Monterey on the mistaken notion that war had broken out between Mexico and the United States.

An artist with Commodore Thomas ap Catesby Jones's naval squadron painted this watercolor of Monterey in 1842. The U.S. naval ships are in the harbor and the main street, Calle Principal, depicts the two-story house of the American consul Thomas Larkin. What evidence is there that the painting was done after the American commander learned of his mistake in thinking there was war between Mexico and the United States?

This mistake gave Mexico a preview of the war-like intentions of the United States and made any negotiation over the peaceful acquisition of California by the United States impossible. Jones was the commander of the Pacific squadron, and he had secret orders to occupy Monterey in the event that Mexico decided to cede California to Britain. While in the Peruvian port of Callao he received false information that the United States and Mexico were at war and that the British naval commander in the Pacific was sailing toward California with plans to occupy it. Jones's two ships, the *United States* and the *Cyane,* raced toward California and, on October 18, 1842, entered the harbor at Monterey. The next day Jones demanded the surrender of the town to his troops. Alvarado, the military commander, received the message and reluctantly surrendered, fearing bombardment of the town by the Americans. Jones's men lowered the Mexican flag that flew in front of the governor's house. Later that day, one of Jones's men was reading through the government archives and discovered recent newspapers indicating that there was no war between the two countries. In the meantime the local population had fled the town.

Governor Micheltorena was visiting Los Angeles when he heard the news of the mistaken capture of the capital. Commodore Jones decided to sail to San Pedro to meet with the governor and offer his formal apologies. The governor held a formal dinner in Los Angeles in honor of his guests and apologies flowed with the wine. That night, however, reports of strange ships sighted off the coast led Governor Micheltorena to fear a full-scale American invasion. Daylight, however, brought assurances that it had been a false alarm. After appropriate formalities and typical Californio hospitality, the Americans returned to their ships and sailed away.

A few years later, in 1845, Alvarado and José Castro led a rebellion in Monterey against Micheltorena that resulted in another "battle" at Cahuenga Pass. Though only a mule and a horse were killed, the governor was forced to depart for Mexico. As a compromise between the regional factions, Pío Pico assumed the title of governor and Los Angeles became the capital. José Castro became the military comandante in charge of the northern district, including the customshouse in Monterey.

The last Mexican governor was a *paisano,* a native-born Californio. Pío de Jesús Pico was born in San Gabriel Mission of mixed African and mestizo ancestry. He grew up in San Diego and moved to Los Angeles in the 1830s, where he became important in local politics. During his short tenure as governor he completed the secularization of the missions and confirmed a flurry of land grants to his friends as he saw the approaching threat of the Anglo Americans. As he said in a speech: "They are cultivating farms, establishing vineyards, erecting mills, sawing up lumber, building workshops, and doing a thousand other things which seem natural to them, but which Californians neglect or despise." He was helpless to prevent the American takeover of his beloved land during the U.S-Mexican War. On the eve of that conflict, the Californios continued to be divided into northern and southern factions, and this weakened their ability to respond to a foreign invasion.

The Rise of the Ranchos

A review of the political history of Mexican California shows that Californios increasingly asserted their self-confidence in their ability to control their own society. This was based on the creation of a native California landholding class whose prosperity grew with each season as the cattle and livestock multiplied beyond count. The Mexican government encouraged private landholding, and the land was free for the taking, providing the claimant met the necessary conditions. The newly independent Mexico liberalized the Spanish trade restrictions, opening California to trade with Americans, the British, and Russians. Thus the prosperity of the ranchos during this era was a product of political decisions made in Mexico. An unintended result, however, was the creation of a new spirit of independence and rebellion.

Under Mexican laws the usual way an individual obtained a rancho grant was to file a written petition with the governor of the territory requesting a defined piece of land, described in very general terms and accompanied with a crude map, or *diseño*. If the governor approved, he would order the local officials to investigate the lands to determine whether they were actually vacant and that there were no conflicting interests. The results of the investigation, called the *informe*, were then returned to the governor and, if he approved, a formal grant was made. All of the paperwork attached to the grant was called the *expediente*. However, the grant was not considered final until the territorial assembly approved it. The final act of possession then took place with a formal ceremony involving the local officials.

Mexican officials approved more than seven hundred private land grants following these procedures. One of the largest, Rancho San Onofre y Margarita, was 89,742 acres, granted to Andrés and Pío Pico in 1841. Many of the grants were more modest in size. For example, in 1843 the government granted Rancho La Cañada de los Coches (Glen of the Hogs), which amounted to only 23.39 acres, to Apolinaria Lorenzana, "La Beata." In 1845 Guajome Rancho (Home of the Frog), consisting of 2,219.41 acres, was granted to Andrés and José Manuel, two Luiseño Indians. Women as well as Indians were eligible to receive land grants. Historian Gloria Ricci Lothrop found that fifty-five ranchos—or 13 percent of the total of seven hundred grants—were given to women, many of whom were the sole managers of their estates.

The land itself was not worth much without livestock, but the cattle that roamed virtually wild on the grasslands were usually inherited from the missions as part of the grant. Disputes over the ownership of these herds became matters for the local *juez de campos* (judge of the plains), or for the alcalde. As elsewhere in the Mexican Southwest, brands were registered and periodic rodeos were required to sort out the herds. In the Los Angeles district, for example, rancheros were required by law to have rodeos in January and April and the general public was required to assist in the roundup. During these rodeos the vaqueros sorted out vast herds of cattle that had intermingled on the open range, branding the newborn calves and castrating the young bulls. They were paid with food and the fiesta that followed each day of labor.

The Californio men prided themselves on their horsemanship and had many opportunities to display this talent during these events. It was considered manly to be able to lasso and kill a cow, using a horsehair lariat and long lance, without dismounting from one's horse. Horseracing was a passion, as was the sport of *correr el gallo,* which involved plucking a buried chicken from the ground while galloping at full speed. Many of the vaqueros were Indians who had learned these skills at the missions. The Californios distinguished themselves from these common laborers by their elaborate dress, fine mounts, and, for the very rich, ornate saddle and livery.

As was true throughout all of northern Mexico, cattle raising created a unique culture, with its own vocabulary and independent spirit. The vaqueros taught the American immigrants who entered the Mexican frontier the basic techniques of stock raising in a semi-arid environment. Law, brands, and customs regarding the open range are of Spanish-Mexican origin and much of the mystique of the American cowboy arises from these Mexican roots.

In Mexican California, stock raising was more a way of life than an industry, which it later became under the Americans. The meat of the cattle was of little value, since it had to be eaten immediately, unless preserved as jerky. Instead, the hide and the fat of the animal—the tallow—provided value to the daily life of the settlers and later to the Yankee clipper ships that came to California. If an occasional cow was killed mysteriously it was of no consequence as long as the "California dollar" (the hide) was left behind. Hence the poor had a ready source of food. The Indians who lived on the ranchos farmed small plots and helped raise sheep, goats, pigs, horses, mules, and cattle. They were paid in kind, with foodstuffs and the right to build an adobe or *jacale* (brush) hut on rancho land.

It is probably wrong to characterize the Californio ranchos as similar to the haciendas in mainland Mexico, because they were more informal in their organization. The Indian vaqueros and farmers were not bound by the rules of peonage that prevailed in central Mexico. The Indians who worked on the ranchos were not paid in money but with food, clothing, and shelter. A sense of paternalism prevailed, with the rancheros as the patrons and the Indians as servants and workmen. The Californios sought to create a lifestyle and mystique surrounding their class. While the Mexican government had abolished the system of official ethnic distinctions, known as the *casta* system, the Californios maintained pretensions about their racial purity as *gente de razón* and insisted on deference from the natives. They justified their ownership of the Indian lands by arguing that the Indians had abandoned them and that the Californios had thus inherited the Indians' sovereignty over the land.

The most prominent of the seven hundred families who became landholders in Mexican California emerged as the political leaders in this period, as described earlier. In the far north, Mariano Vallejo, owner of Rancho Petaluma, was the powerful

Pío Pico, his wife, and nieces, probably in the 1850s. Pico was the last Mexican governor and one of the largest rancho owners in California. What evidence is there that Mexican Californios had different attitudes toward race than did most Americans of this era?

comandante of the region, placed there to defend the north from British and Russian encroachments. In Monterey, Juan Bautista de Alvarado and his family periodically controlled local politics. The Santa Barbara district was led by Pablo de la Guerra; Los Angeles by the Pico brothers, Andrés and Pío; and San Diego by Juan Bandini and José Antonio Carrillo. There were other notables who contributed to the Californio legend, and some of them were Anglo Americans who slowly began to discover the richness of the soil and married the Californio daughters.

The expansion of the ranchos, particularly the growing number of cattle and horses, put a severe strain on the native population. The grazing animals consumed vast amounts of grasses, nuts, and roots, which had been staples in the diet of many Indian communities. In order to eat, many began to slaughter the free-ranging cattle and to raid settlements. This in turn provoked reprisals from the rancheros. The end of the mission system freed thousands of Indians from required labor. Many, however, were forced to hire themselves out to the rancheros as vaqueros (cowboys) and farmers. Many worked without wages but at least were able to gain food and shelter for their families. The natives became the mainstay of the Mexican labor force in these years.

Environmental Changes

Environmental historians such as William Preston have noted that the introduction of livestock by the Spanish and Mexicans began to change the ecosystem of the state. The proliferation of cattle and horses led to periodic overgrazing as well as to the creation of well-worn trails on hills and in the valleys. On Santa Catalina Island goats introduced by the Spanish multiplied so greatly that they drove more than forty-eight animal and plant species to extinction. Adding to the pressures on the grasslands, native wild animals began to proliferate, mainly because the Indians who had previously hunted them were now either living on wild cattle or living in the missions or pueblos. Periodic large-scale slaughters of cattle and even horses by the Mexican rancheros led to an explosion in the grizzly bear population, which fed off the carcasses and refuse. Other changes during the Spanish and Mexican eras were wrought by foreign hunting. Otters, fur seals, sea lions, beavers, and minks were increasingly slaughtered by Russian, British, and American hunters. The great demand for their pelts in Europe led to their near decimation. Finally, the introduction of European food crops led to environmental changes. Roughly ten thousand acres of land were under cultivation by 1834, watered by irrigation systems that drew from dammed rivers and creeks. Along with corn, wheat, oats, and other grains came the introduction of European weeds that quickly spread and competed with native plants. California's declining Indian population, due to the introduction of European diseases, led to an increase in wild game and the proliferation of European plants and livestock. This changed the ecosystem, forcing Indians as well as native species to adapt to a new environment.

Social Relations in Mexican California

Political independence from Spain did not radically change the cultural and social patterns of Spanish California. Patriarchy continued to hold sway in social relations and the family continued to be the primary social and political unit. Indians were still at the bottom of the hierarchy. Major changes in the twenty-seven years of Mexican administration included the creation of a landed class that had pretensions of aristocracy and the opening up of California to increased trade with foreigners. Both factors would undermine the older Spanish colonial conventions and ideals.

The Growth of Town Governments

Town governments grew in the Mexican period as former soldiers and their families settled near the presidios where they had once served. Spain had given the civilian population living in Monterey a pueblo government and lands in 1794. Monterey's municipal government was occasionally overshadowed by the territorial government, as in the period from 1839 to 1840, when the centralist governor abolished the local town council. The population surrounding the presidio of Monterey was more numerous, including seven missions and the Spanish villa of Branciforte (Santa Cruz), with a total of about 1600 gente de razón by 1840. By the time of the U.S.-Mexican War about 550 people lived in the town.

San Diego's civilian settlement was located just downhill from the site of the first presidio. By 1834 the town finally had a sufficient population—four hundred people—to qualify for pueblo status, with the right to elect local officials and to obtain a grant of land from the government. This lasted until 1838 when the declining population and political competition with Monterey resulted in the loss of their local government. In 1845, Governor Pío Pico confirmed San Diego's ownership of 48,000 acres of former mission lands, including water rights. It was the largest such concession ever given to a Mexican town in California.

San Francisco also was established as a pueblo government in 1834 after achieving a sufficient number in population, probably about two hundred individuals between the peninsula and Contra Costa. The settlement of Yerba Buena, the nucleus of modern-day San Francisco, grew as town lots were sold by the pueblo government out of its four square leagues of public lands, which had been granted by the Mexican governor. From the beginning the settlers of this new town were multiethnic and multinational, including Americans, Englishmen, Frenchmen, Spaniards, Mexicans, and native Californios. By 1840 Yerba Buena had fifty residents; sixteen of them were foreigners.

In 1835 the military garrison at San Francisco was transferred north and thus Sonoma, another Mexican-era pueblo, was founded. In the town itself there were probably not more than two hundred people, a mixture of Hispanicized mission Indians and former soldiers and their families. Nearby was the Petaluma hacienda of Mariano Vallejo, the comandante whose energetic policies of pacification of the northern Indians through alliances made it possible for more than eighty ranchos to be established.

Mariano Guadalupe Vallejo was born in Monterey on July 4, 1807, and became a professional soldier during the Mexican regime, rising in rank and authority to become comandante-general of California by 1838. Vallejo was in charge of the colonization of the *frontera norte,* the region north of San Pablo Bay and the Sacramento River. Vallejo was skilled at forming lasting alliances with the local Indians, and more than fifty of the presidio soldiers in Sonoma were native California Indians. He was instrumental in helping to organize the town governments of San Francisco and Sonoma. Much of the time he paid for the expenses of the Mexican military out of his own pocket. He opposed the Russian settlement at Fort Ross as well as the growth of Sutter's Fort in Sacramento. Vallejo opposed Governor Juan Bautista Alvarado, who he thought was incompetent and lacking initiative. Partly because of his public dissatisfaction, Micheltorena was sent to replace Alvarado. In 1844 Vallejo disbanded the military forces in Sonoma because he could no longer afford to pay them. Thereafter he supported annexation by the United States even after being imprisoned by the Bear Flag rebels in 1846.

Californianas: Mexican Californian Women

Indian and Mexican women were largely responsible for the growth of a domestic Hispano-Indian culture and society in California. Under Mexican government the established patriarchal forms of life continued. The government and men considered women's reproductive capacities most important for the success of the colony. Accordingly, women were expected to bear large families. Teresa de la Guerra, for example, had twenty-five children; Francisca Benicia Vallejo had sixteen children; and Angustias de la Guerra Ord had eleven children. Unfortunately, infant mortality was quite high, as was death from childbirth. Mexican culture accorded a woman status through her production of children and women were thus valued within the family for their role as childbearers.

In addition to childbearing, women played a key role in the Californio economy. They worked in the domestic production of clothes, soap, candles, and other household items. The wealthier Californianas supervised scores of domestic servants and worked alongside them. Californianas, moreover, were trained to ride horses from an early age. Some of the stereotypes about Mexican patriarchal society have to be modified when considering the female rancheras of California. On small ranchos women and men worked side-by-side in the many labors associated with farming and ranching. Fermina Espinosa, for example, was the owner of Santa Rita rancho. Because her husband was not so inclined, she ran the ranch—riding, roping, and branding—in addition to bearing many children. On Rancho Sal-Si-Puedes, the four daughters of Vicente Ávila dressed like men and rode about the rancho doing the work of livestock raising—in addition to weaving blankets, churning butter, and making cheese.

Historian Rosaura Sanchez has studied many examples of female independence and agency in Mexican California and has warned against overgeneralizing. Women were still subject to male authority. Arranged marriages were the norm, especially among the wealthier classes. Single women were not free to choose their own suitors and elaborate rituals regulated courtship. The first communications of love may have found their way around the watchful eyes of the parents, but their approval was necessary for meetings and marriage. Women were generally considered male possessions to be protected and controlled. Women did have property rights and the right to divorce and file lawsuits against their husbands, but these rights were not commonly exercised.

One story that illustrates the many complexities of women's status in Mexican California is that of Josefa Carrillo, daughter of Joaquin Carrillo of San Diego. In 1829 she eloped with Henry Delano Fitch, an American merchant sea captain, thus becoming one of the first Californianas to marry a foreigner. While the account of this affair has been told a number of times by California historians, the narration she gave in 1875 at the age of sixty-five gives her version of events.

When Captain Henry D. Fitch made a call on the port of San Diego in 1826, he was introduced to Josefa and fell in love. Within a year he requested her hand in marriage and her parents approved. Several years passed before Captain Fitch agreed to become a Catholic and a Mexican citizen so the two could be married. The marriage was scheduled for April 15, 1829, the day after his baptism. Halfway through the marriage ceremony a message arrived from Governor Echeandía

Californio vaqueros roping a steer. Widely praised for their skills as horsemen, the Californios rarely dismounted. Why is the man standing in front of the steer? This painting by the Spanish artist Augusto Ferran was probably done during the Gold Rush.

ordering the rites to cease, because the marriage was in violation of a law prohibiting non-Catholics from marrying Catholics.

Henry and Josefa decided to elope, sailing south and eventually marrying in a Catholic ceremony in Valparaiso, Chile. A year later, Captain Fitch's ship returned to the San Diego harbor and Josefa learned that her father considered the family dishonored by the elopement and had "promised to kill her on sight."

Nevertheless, courageously, and determined to be either reconciled or killed, Josefa went to beg her father's forgiveness. Entering his study, she threw herself on her knees and "in a humble tone begged for pardon, reminding him that if she had disobeyed him it had been only to cast off a hated tyranny [Governor Echeandía] who overturned the laws and customs." Her father responded, saying "I pardon you daughter, you are not to blame if our governors are despots." Josefa and her husband eventually went to Monterey, where Captain Fitch faced charges of forcible abduction, and he was sent to Mission San Gabriel for three months. As a penalty for his crime, he was given a penance of donating a fifty-pound bell to the church at the Los Angeles pueblo and the couple was commanded to hear high mass with lighted candles for three *días festivos,* or special days.

This love story involved family honor, governmental intervention, and paternal power. Josefa threw herself on her father's mercy and cleverly politicized her actions so he could accept her return with honor. She succeeded in manipulating the patriarchal system. The most important part of Josefa's 1875 narration, rendered in the most detail with the greatest passion, was not the interrupted marriage, the elopement, or the trial, but rather her confrontation with her father. Josefa may have been subject to male authority, but she knew how to manipulate it to her advantage.

Mexican–Indian Relations

With the secularization of the missions, thousands of native Californians tried to return to the lives they had once known, fleeing inland and into the foothills to join with remnants of their peoples or with other native groups. They soon found that things had changed, even for tribes far from the missions. Numerous diseases had decimated their numbers, and the ecology of traditional gathering grounds had been forever changed by the grazing of Mexican livestock and the introduction of European plants. The cattle and even horses were tempting targets for hungry natives who had grown used to mission food. Consequently, native groups periodically raided outlying ranchos and military retaliation inevitably followed.

Aside from the mission revolts (see Chapter 2), the most notable periods of Mexican–Indian violence took place in the 1830s in southern California, following secularization. One memorable incident was an Indian attack in 1837 on Rancho Jamul, located east of San Diego, and owned by Doña Eustaquia López, who lived at the rancho with her two unmarried daughters and young son. A band of Kumeyaay assisted by some servants attacked the rancho, killing the foreman, his son, and several others. The Indians carried off both daughters, Tomasa and Ramona, aged fifteen and twelve. They were going to kill the mother and her little boy but because of their pleadings the Indians spared them. Instead they stripped them naked and left, taking with them the livestock and other valuables and burning the ranch houses. Several expeditions went out from San Diego to try to recover the girls. Ransoms were offered but refused, and rumors later flourished that the girls had married Indian chiefs.

Later that year, in 1837, other bands of Kumeyaay planned to attack the pueblo of San Diego with the assistance of local servants. The plot was foiled when a loyal Indian told her mistress of the plan. Immediately the military officer in charge, Alférez Macedonio Gonzalez, rounded up the named conspirators, all of whom worked as house servants for the local pueblo families, and forced them to confess. The next day he took them to a nearby cemetery and executed five of them by a firing squad. For the next years, fear of Indian servants and the possibility of revolt from within colored the nightmares of many Californios.

A large and uncounted number of former neophytes lived in quasi-peonage. In Los Angeles, Father Duran noted that two or three hundred Indians lived as virtual slaves, paying off debts that had been advanced to them for food, goods, or liquor. Every Mexican settlement had its floating population of natives who survived on the margins, working as occasional laborers or prostitutes, and sometimes even selling their children in order to eat. The lucky ones worked on the ranchos as servants, farmers, or vaqueros. They too were debt slaves and had to endure the racial pretensions of their masters. These Indians were bound to the land by their indebtedness just as many Mexican peons on the haciendas in Mexico during a later era. By custom the natives had to remain at the rear of the church during mass and they were buried in plots separate from the Californios. The Los Angeles ayuntamiento passed laws to ensure that the local Indians did not live too close to the pueblo or pollute the water of the local irrigation ditches.

At the same time, almost every Californio family could point to a servant who had been raised with their own children and who was considered a member of the family or could, if they chose, remember how cousins and nieces were related to the local Indian tribes by blood. As long as the Hispanicized Indians accepted a Californio paternalism and knew their place, they were accepted within the patriarchal rancho system. There were real friendships and occasional bonds of marriage and *compadrazgo* (godparentage) between some Californios and the Hispanicized Indians. General Mariano Vallejo's Indian ally, Chief Solano, lived with Vallejo's family in his old age, and the two were compadres, sharing their mutual misfortunes well into the American era.

Immigrants and Foreigners

Alta California's population grew slowly, but not nearly enough to challenge the native Indians' demographic dominance. In 1820, at the beginning of the Mexican period, there were perhaps as many as three thousand of Hispano-Indian stock, excluding the mission Indians. By 1848, at the end of the Mexican era, there were probably about seven thousand who considered themselves Californios. At the same time, although the native population was declining due to deaths from diseases, they numbered probably more than one hundred thousand in 1846, most of them not Hispanicized.

As David Weber pointed out in his study of this era, the Mexican government was losing its ability to defend its northern territories because of the lack of northward migration. Political instability in Mexico City made for changing policies regarding the frontier. Mexicans could not be induced to leave family and town for the uncertainties of life on the frontier. Many were economically unable to afford such a journey and many others were peons who were not free to move even if they so desired. Moreover the Spanish administrative mentality had endured, making it difficult for individuals to strike off on their own without governmental approval. And California was isolated from Mexico by the forbidding Sonora and Mojave Deserts, lands inhabited by Indians who had proven their dislike of Spanish and Mexican interlopers.

The Mexican government made one major effort to send new colonists to California, but it ended in disaster and discouraged further attempts. The Mexican government regarded the Russian colony at Fort Ross as a threat to their political control of Alta California and so, in 1833, the government authorized José María Padrés and José María Híjar to recruit 204 settlers to go to California. The plan was for these newcomers to take possession of vacant mission lands. This, of course, antagonized the Californios, who wanted those lands for themselves. The Californios were in luck, however, because en route, a change in the central Mexican government revoked the Padrés-Híjar commission. The expedition continued to California nevertheless and upon arrival, Governor Figueroa, a native Californio, refused to let them have the lands they had been allocated and ordered them to return to Mexico. Most of the colonists ignored this order and settled throughout California, in the pueblos and on some lands in the Sonoma Valley given to them by General Vallejo. Members of the Padrés-Híjar expedition brought much-needed skills to California and were responsible for many improvements in local life, especially in the pueblos.

The Mexican government did not encourage foreign immigration to Alta California. After a decade of encouraging American immigration into Texas in 1836 the foreigners revolted against the national government. This seemed to be ample proof that this was an unwise policy. Nevertheless, foreigners did make their way to this remote territory, many for commercial purposes. By the 1830s the ranchos were developing a thriving trade in hides and tallow with Yankee clipper ships, and hundreds of thousands of hides found their way east to make shoes for the Anglo Americans and the English. Some of the sailors on the American and English ships chose to stay behind. Alfred Robinson, for example, stayed behind and married into the de la Guerra family in Santa Barbara. His book *Life in California* (1846) described the native Californios in a sympathetic light. This was not the case for Richard Henry Dana, who also came on a clipper ship and later wrote his immensely popular account, *Two Years Before the Mast* (1840), in which he deprecated the Californios as an "idle, thriftless people" who were "proud, and extravagant, and very much given to gaming." Dana did, however, praise the lush environment and urged others to come to develop it. He wrote: "In the hands of an enterprising people, what a country this might be!" Dana's views had wide circulation in the East and helped shape sentiments of Manifest Destiny.

The Americans were slow to find their way overland to California and the first ones who came entered illegally. In 1826 the fur trapper Jedediah Smith came overland from Salt Lake into southern California. He was subsequently jailed in San Diego, Mission San José, and Monterey before being expelled for lacking a passport. Smith was the first American to cross the Sierra Nevada mountains and open a trail to Salt Lake. He was also the first American to open the coastal trade route from California to Fort Vancouver on the Columbia River. Among his greatest exploits, Smith blazed a trail across the deserts of the American West—the first American to enter California by crossing the Mojave Desert and the first to traverse the vast Great Basin Desert to return east.

In 1828, Sylvester and James Ohio Pattie, father and son, also fur trappers, arrived in San Diego after an exhausting overland trek from the Colorado River. Governor Echeandía believed them to be spies for Spain and had them imprisoned. The father, Sylvester, died in prison but James, who had brought with him a supply of smallpox vaccine, was allowed to leave the San Diego jail to inoculate the local population. Eventually he traveled up the California coast and vaccinated 22,000 people. He returned home to New Orleans via Mexico in 1830. Later trappers such as Ewing Young and Joseph R. Walker found new ways of entering California from the east, developing trails that later immigrants found useful.

By 1830 fewer than one hundred foreigners were living in California, most of British or American nationality. Under the Mexican Colonization Laws of 1824 and 1828, territorial governors were allowed to grant lands to noncitizens. The regulations governing the procedures were sporadically—and not very effectively—enforced. Despite the availability of free lands, few foreigners took advantage of these laws in California. Most of the best lands were tied up in the missions until the secularization of the mid-1830s. Thereafter, the Californios used their family influence to gain most of the desirable properties.

In spite of their small numbers, the foreigners' influence was felt to a degree that was out of proportion to their numbers. Many had settled in California because of their recognition of the rich opportunities for hunting, trapping, trading, and land acquisition. Others simply sought adventure or had fallen in love with a beautiful Californiana. Most became partially Mexicanized, learning to respect the culture and the language and marrying the daughters of important Californio landholders. As sons-in-law of large extended families they had a stake in California's future. One prominent example is William E. P. Hartnell, an Englishman who came to California as a merchant in 1823, married into the powerful de la Guerra family in Santa Barbara, became a naturalized Mexican citizen, and received a large rancho land grant. In the 1830s he won appointments to a number of official posts as a customs officer, a teacher, and a translator. In the American era he served as the official Spanish-language translator for the California constitutional convention.

Other foreigners participated in rebellions. In 1836, Isaac Graham, an American settler, gathered a company of American riflemen to help Juan Bautista Alvarado in his successful revolt against the government. Later, in 1840, Graham and a few British settlers were arrested by Governor Alvarado on charges of treason but were later sent to Mexico, where they were released. John A. Sutter was a Swiss immigrant who became important in the California Gold Rush. He came to California after having traveled to Santa Fe, Oregon, and Hawai`i. In 1840 he received an eleven-square-league (48,000 acres) grant of land from the Mexican governor, and he set about building a fort at the junction of the Sacramento and American Rivers. He employed local Indians as well as Hawaiian Kanakas and purchased the movable property of Fort Ross from the Russians, including more than forty cannon, to build his fort. Sutter's Fort became a mecca for the foreign community in California, particularly the Americans, who began to enter California in larger numbers. Sutter began developing local industries such as fur trading, wheat farming, and weaving, providing employment to anyone who wanted to work.

In 1837 a merchant named John Marsh immigrated to California from Independence, Missouri, after he had become bankrupt. Marsh claimed to be a medical doctor, having an A.B. degree from Harvard. This was sufficient, however, for him to get a license from the Los Angeles ayuntamiento. Marsh traveled north to San Francisco, and eventually purchased four square leagues of land in what is now Contra Costa County, where he settled down to become a ranchero. Marsh was active in writing letters back home urging more Americans to come to California, suggesting that they could easily "play the Texas game" and take over the Mexican province. As a result of these publicity efforts Marsh's friends in Missouri formed the Western Emigration Society in 1841 and set about encouraging settlers to go to California. One of those who began organizing a wagon train of immigrants was twenty-two-year-old schoolteacher John Bidwell.

Bidwell encouraged some sixty-eight Midwesterners to join the first overland wagon train of Americans to California. They set out from Sapling Grove, Kansas, on May 18, 1841. The elected captain of the group was John Bartleson and the expedition became known as the Bidwell-Bartleson party. They were guided by a Jesuit priest, Father DeSmet, who was going to Oregon, and by an experienced mountain trapper who knew the route. In Idaho about half the group chose to continue on to Oregon instead of to California. One member of the expedition mortally wounded himself with a gun and four others turned back. They had to abandon their wagons in the Sierra mountains, and were reduced to eating mules and coyotes until they reached the California coast. After six months thirty-two men, a woman named Nancy Kelsey, and her baby staggered onto Dr. Marsh's rancho. The Americans in the Bidwell-Bartleson party were illegal immigrants, lacking passports, but Mariano Vallejo, the comandante of the region, was convinced that they did not need this formality and he allowed them to stay. Roughly five years later, some of these same Americans repaid this kindness with insult when they supported Vallejo's imprisonment and backed an American military conquest of California.

The Bidwell-Bartleson expedition opened the door for other overland immigrant wagon trains. The same year, a group of 134 Americans left Santa Fe, New Mexico, under the direction of John Rowland and William Workman. They followed a route called the "Old Spanish Trail" from New Mexico to southern California, a route that had been partially used by the Spanish and Mexican traders and was well known by the 1830s. After reaching Los Angeles, some of the Americans decided to become permanent residents. Workman, Rowland, and several other members of the expedition became rancheros in the Los Angeles region, and they, too, later supported the American acquisition of California.

Bidwell's written account of the 1841 overland trip to California found its way into the papers in the Midwest. Other accounts of California also enjoyed wide circulation, encouraging more immigration. California, however, had to compete with Oregon as a destination, and, until the publication of Bidwell's journal in

1842, California was losing the publicity campaign. This was due to the negative views of Thomas J. Farnham, an American who had briefly visited California in 1840 and whose published letters criticized the Mexican government's efforts to control immigration. Nevertheless, in 1843, several more American wagon trains found their way west to California. Joseph B. Chiles led fifty-nine people into Sacramento via the northern route, and Lansford W. Hastings set out with fifty-three more from Missouri, although most of them decided to go to Oregon instead. In 1844 Andrew and Benjamin Kelsey brought thirty-six settlers overland following the by-then well-known trail, and Elisha Stevens and a large family of Murphys entered California with more than fifty settlers. The latter expedition was notable in that, for the first time, wagons were able to cross the Sierras. The next year, more than 250 Anglo American settlers made the crossing or entered the San Joaquin Valley via Oregon.

The most famous of the overland expeditions to California before the U.S.-Mexican war was the Donner party. In early 1846 eighty-seven men, women, and children left Springfield, Illinois, for California, following the established route. Instead of taking the trail that would have led them north of the Great Salt Lake, they chose a shortcut. This route slowed them down, however, because they had to clear a trail for their wagons and they lost some oxen in the process. Because of this delay they arrived at the California mountains late in the fall and that year the snows came early. Soon the Donner party found themselves caught in the mountains without supplies for the winter. At a lake near the summit (later named Donner Lake), they camped in ten feet of snow, without adequate firewood or food. Faced with sure death, a small group of fifteen set out to try to reach Sutter's Fort to get help. Only seven reached the San Joaquin Valley after having killed and eaten their two Indian guides and several other companions. When the rescue parties finally reached the stranded pioneers, they found more evidence of cannibalism. Only forty-five of the original eighty-seven had survived the ordeal. The Donner expedition became a macabre reminder of the perils of crossing the Sierras in the winter.

The same year as the Donner disaster, another group of immigrants entered California by sea. These were two hundred Mormon settlers led by Sam Brannan. They had been sent by Joseph Smith to colonize the western outposts of Desert, the proposed Mormon national state, which was expected to stretch from the Great Salt Lake to southern California. Earlier settlers had been sent to San Bernardino, near the Mexican settlement of San Salvador, to establish a colony. The Mormon settlers who came in 1846 increased the presence of English-speaking residents, laying the foundation for an eventual American conquest.

Among the foreigners, one of the most influential was Thomas O. Larkin, who came to California in 1832 and established himself as a leading merchant in Monterey. Unlike other Americans who settled before the 1840s, Larkin did not marry into a Californio family and become a ranchero. He married an American woman and remained a U.S. citizen while learning Spanish and slowly amassing a fortune as a merchant. Later he was appointed the U.S. consul general and acted

Costume de la Haute Californie.

Dame de Monterey.

An unidentified French artist with an around-the-world expedition painted these portraits of a Californio man and woman from Monterey in the late 1830s. What evidence is there that these portraits were of the upper classes?

as a confidential agent for President James K. Polk, reporting on British interest in California. Later he secretly worked to convince influential Californios to secede from the Mexican Republic and join the United States.

It is estimated that by 1846, on the eve of the U.S.-Mexican War and the American acquisition of California, there were about thirteen hundred foreign-born settlers in California. About three-fourths of them were Americans, and European nationalities were represented as well. Except for those who had become Mexican citizens in order to receive land grants, most were immigrants who had entered without due authorization from the Mexican government. Local officials were only too glad to have new skilled workers, and they ignored the letter of the law. They did not fully realize that many of the new immigrants had no intention of assimilating into the Californio society. They did not learn Spanish, rejected the Catholic faith, and brought their own families with them instead of intermarrying with the Mexican population. This contrasted with the scores of Mexicanized Americans who had settled prior to the overland migrations of the 1830s, men like Don Abel Stearns in Los Angeles, Henry Delano Fitch in

San Diego, John B. R. Cooper in Monterey, and Alephs B. Thompson in Santa Barbara. These men had married into Californio families, become Mexican citizens, and accepted Mexican society. But these individuals were also of lukewarm loyalty to the Mexican Republic, and most sided with the Americans during the war that resulted in the conquest of California by the United States.

California and the World

Alta California took its first steps toward becoming a participant in the world's economy during the Mexican era, from 1821 through 1848. Trading ships from the United States, England, and France regularly called at California ports. The hide and tallow trade with the eastern United States and Britain increased. Beginning in 1813 and slowly increasing every year, ships plied the California coast laden with merchandise to trade for California hides and tallow. Most of the ships probably avoided paying port duties in Monterey, which amounted to a percentage of the cargo. Southern California led in the production of goods for export and San Diego, because of its port and climate, became the largest trading area in California. Once on board, the tallow was traded in Mexico and Peru and the hides found their way to New England's shoe and boot factories. The British attempted to compete with the Americans, establishing a trading store in Yerba Buena (San Francisco) run by the Hudson's Bay Company. But this outpost could not begin to challenge the Yankees, whose clipper ships regularly pulled into port. Visits by Russian, British, and American whaling ships also added to the Californio economy. These ships visited the California ports in search of food supplies, for which they traded manufactured goods.

Compared with other Mexican frontier regions, such as New Mexico and Texas, California had greater contact with other nations because of the relative ease of ocean communication and trade. Within a generation the Californios had established themselves as a province of private landholders—hacendados and rancheros—where five hundred landowning families dominated the Mexican society. In New Mexico, by contrast, very few private land grants were given during the Mexican era. Most people continued to live on Spanish land grants where title to the land was vested in the community, not in the individual. Alta California's Indian population was a ready source of cheap labor for the development of the thriving cattle industry, whereas the New Mexicans and Texans did not have this benefit. For the most part, the Californios did not have to endure the perils of hostile Indian attacks, which were more common in both Texas and New Mexico. Politically, the Californios enjoyed the same kind of regional democracy as their frontier cousins through the ayuntamiento and alcalde systems; they also had similar internal rivalries and factions based on family and region. Texas had separated from Mexico after the Anglo American immigrant revolution in 1836, and thereafter the English-speaking Americans controlled the former Mexican province. New Mexico and California, while leading successful challenges to Mexican centralism, escaped the violence and racism of the Texas rebellion. They remained part of the Mexican Republic and in control of their own society.

Summary

In 1846, Mexican California was a pastoral society that was rapidly changing because of the changes set in motion by the secularization of the mission lands and the opening of the province to foreign trade and settlement. Few could have foreseen that within a few years even more profound changes were to catapult California into an entirely different era. On the eve of the American conquest, differing cultural traditions and visions competed for control of California's future.

The oldest customs were those of the native peoples. They had been decimated by disease and challenged in their customary territories. Those who lived away from the coastal regions and avoided contact with the Spanish and Mexican colonists continued to live as they had for thousands of years. Even while their physical environment changed, through the introduction of new plants and animals, they continued in their spiritual beliefs about the correct ways to live. Others adapted to Mexican Catholic society by mixing their traditional ways with those of the newcomers. They became acculturated to and dependent on their conquerors.

The Mexican, Spanish-speaking mestizos in California inherited a culture that emphasized family honor, community and regional pride, and ethnic-racial hierarchy. For them the land was less for profit than for possession and dominance, a mark of the prestige of being an hidalgo, or nobleman. The younger Mexican Californians grew up nourished on ideas of popular democracy, free trade, and rationalism, inheriting an ideology of the American and French Revolutions as it was translated through Mexico. Progressive Mexicans believed that they could benefit from political and marital alliances with the Anglo Americans and had a positive view of the Americans' contribution to California.

The English-speaking settlers in California were divided over their views of the future. Mexicanized Americans, like Don Abel Stearns, thought that Mexicans and Americans could and should coexist in harmony for their mutual profit, and that the Californios were willing students in the development of the region. The newer immigrants, those who had come overland by wagon train in the 1840s, considered the Mexicans to be a lazy, thriftless people with few redeeming graces. The Californios who owned the ranchos were obstacles to progress, they thought, and the Californios' Catholic faith was an anathema to these Protestant families. Many of them had absorbed a sense of Manifest Destiny, a belief in the inevitable expansion of the United States across North America, often linked to a faith in the superiority and inevitable triumph of the Anglo American race over native peoples and Mexicans. The future, the Americans thought, belonged to them.

Suggested Readings

- Haas, Lisbeth, *Conquests and Historical Identities in California, 1769–1936* (Berkeley and Los Angeles: University of California Press, 1990). A scholarly yet readable analysis of the changes in ethnic identities among Indians and Californios in southern California.

- Langum, David J., *Law and Community on the Mexican Frontier: Anglo-American Expatriates and the Clash of Legal Traditions, 1821–1846* (London and Norman: University of Oklahoma Press, 1987). The most thorough analysis of the Mexican legal system.

- Monroy, Douglas, *Thrown Among Strangers: The Making of Mexican Culture in Frontier California* (Berkeley and Los Angeles: University of California Press, 1990). A new attempt to synthesize the new social history with California's early history.

- Osio, Antonio María, *The History of Alta California: A Memoir of Mexican California* (Madison: University of Wisconsin Press, 1996). One of the first survey histories of California written by a native Californio, and finally published after more than one hundred years.

- Pico, Pío, *Don Pío Pico's Historical Narrative*, Arthur P. Botello, trans. (Glendale, CA: Arthur Clark Co., 1973). An eyewitness account of many of the major events of Mexican California, written by the last Mexican governor.

- Rosenus, Alan, *General M. G. Vallejo and the Advent of the Americans* (Albuquerque: University of New Mexico Press, 1995). An important study of one of the key Mexican political figures of this era.

- Weber, David J., *The Mexican Frontier, 1821–1846: The American Southwest Under Mexico* (Albuquerque: University of New Mexico Press, 1982). One of the best surveys to place California's Mexican period in the context of Mexican history.

4

War, Conquest, and Gold: The American Era Begins, 1845–1855

Main Topics

▌ The War Between the United States and Mexico

▌ The Gold Rush

▌ California Transformed

▌ A New Direction

In the 1870s Hubert Howe Bancroft, a publisher in San Francisco, set out to write a multivolume history of California and dispatched assistants to interview the Mexican residents of the state, who had important memories of the region's history. Thomas Savage, one of Bancroft's helpers, interviewed Doña Felipa Osuna de Marron. At the time, she had been a widow for twenty-five years. She had lived in California as a Spanish and as a Mexican subject and vividly remembered the American conquest of her native town, San Diego.

In 1846, at the beginning of the war, she was married to Juan María de Marron, a rancher who had been appointed the administrator of Mission San Luis Rey properties. Felipa was at the former mission in the summer of 1846 when General John C. Frémont and the American troops arrived, hoping to capture Californio political leaders. The Americans questioned her about where her husband was and who else was at the mission. Don Matias Moreno, the secretary to the California government, was with Doña Felipa when the Americans appeared. She

CHAPTER 4	War, Conquest, and Gold: The American Era Begins, 1845–1855
1842	Francisco López discovers gold in southern California
MAY 11, 1846	United States declares war on Mexico
JUNE 10, 1846	The Bear Flag Rebellion
JULY 2, 1846	American forces arrive in Monterey
AUGUST 13, 1846	Commodore Stockton occupies Los Angeles
SEPTEMBER 22, 1846	Successful rebellion against American occupation forces in Los Angeles
DECEMBER 8, 1846	Battle of San Pascual; Mexican victory over General Kearny
JANUARY 13, 1847	Surrender of Mexican forces at Cahuenga Pass
JANUARY 24, 1848	John Marshall discovers gold in Coloma
FEBRUARY 2, 1848	Treaty of Guadalupe Hidalgo ends U.S.-Mexican War
JULY 4, 1849	Outbreak of antiforeign violence in mining camps
SEPTEMBER 1, 1849	State Constitutional Convention meets at Colton Hall, Monterey
1850	Mariposa War begins; Humboldt Indians killed
APRIL 1850	California legislature passes the Foreign Miner's Tax law
SEPTEMBER 9, 1850	California admitted as a state to the Union
1851	Joaquín Murrieta is reported killed by the California Rangers
1852	Antonio Garra leads rebellion and is executed in San Diego

quickly disguised him as a sick cousin, fooling the Americans, who then left. Once they had departed, Don Matias, who had recognized his good friend Don Santiago Argüello riding with the Americans, sent a messenger to catch up with Argüello to tell him to return, so that he could join him. So Don Matias changed sides because his friend had done so.

Soon after this incident at the mission Felipa went with her husband to their rancho in the backcountry and then later her husband sent her alone to San Diego for safety. She recounted that in San Diego, Don Miguel de Pedrorena, Don Pedro C. Carrillo, and Argüello, along with others, were allied with the

Americans. The Californios who remained opposed to the Americans asked her husband to join them and he did so. Hoping to be reunited with his family, he joined Felipa and their children in the pueblo of San Diego, which was then occupied by the U.S. Army. Soon they secured a safe conduct pass to leave town and they fled back to their rancho. There they found the Californios "furious" with her husband, accusing him of working as a courier for the Americans. They threatened to shoot him, but instead took the family's horses and took the family as prisoners to another rancho. Almost every day the Californio partisans descended on the rancho to take what they needed, driving Doña Felipa and her family to the verge of starvation.

When the war ended, the Californios continued to accuse Felipa and her husband of being pro-American, though they had never fought with the Americans. Their own countrymen finally forced the Osunas to ask for protection from the American commander of San Diego. Felipa and her husband journeyed from the rancho to town, and when they reached the outskirts her husband raised a white flag. They entered the pueblo, leaving their few remaining livestock outside. Felipa reported that some Americans in San Diego were angry at the return of these Mexicans, whom they regarded as enemies; but the Americans did not punish them.

These episodes, recalled by Felipa Osuna to Thomas Savage in 1878, reveal some of the schisms among the Californios over the American conquest. As evidenced in her testimony the conquest of California was more than a military one, extending to a struggle between friends and families. The real conquest— the transformation of the economy and society—began a few months after the end of the war with the discovery of gold. Within a year thousands of immigrants from the United States, Latin America, Europe, and Asia overwhelmed the native peoples and the Californios. Virtually overnight they created a new society—one that was entirely alien to Felipa Osuna and her family.

Questions to Consider

▎ What was the role that Californios played in the war between the United States and Mexico?

▎ How are we to evaluate the Gold Rush as a social, political, and moral event, given its mixed effect on the traditional cultures of California?

▎ What has been the legacy of the Gold Rush on people of various ethnic and racial backgrounds?

▌ What is the larger meaning for California's history of the economic and social changes brought about by the U.S.-Mexican War and the Gold Rush?

The War Between the United States and Mexico

On the eve of the war between the United States and Mexico, the northern states and the provinces of the Mexican Republic were increasingly being influenced by American commercial interests. The opening of the Santa Fe Trail in the 1820s and the increase in Yankee hide and tallow ships in California created new economic ties with the Mexican upper classes. In 1836 the Anglo Americans in Texas had waged a war of independence from Mexico and declared themselves a sovereign state, the Lone Star Republic. The Texans longed to join the United States but were prevented from doing so until 1845 because of opposition from Northerners, who feared adding another slave state. In the interim, the Texans carried on a thriving trade between their ranches in central Texas and Louisiana. In 1842 they unsuccessfully tried to conquer New Mexico to add its lands to their new republic. Finally in 1845 the United States admitted Texas to the Union as a slave state, with the Texans asserting that their southern boundary was the Rio Grande. Mexico, on the other hand, pointed out that the historic boundary between Texas and the province of Coahuila had always been the Nueces River. The friction between these two claims provided the spark that eventually led to an armed conflict between U.S. and Mexican troops in 1846.

There had been other rebellions in Mexico's northern provinces. In 1837 the lower classes in New Mexico led a rebellion against the Mexican government's centralizing administration, seeking more autonomy for their village governments. The Mexican upper classes soon crushed this rebellion. But they too had their grievances with the Mexican government, primarily its strict trade regulations. The merchants and other wealthy people of northern New Mexico grew to depend on the manufactured goods brought to them over the Santa Fe Trail. The value of goods brought overland from St. Louis increased every year, and Hispano trading families in Santa Fe grew rich. Meanwhile the upper classes knew from past experience that the unstable Mexican government would not be able to preserve their interests.

The Californios were also dissatisfied with the Mexican government (see Chapter 3) and had deposed several Mexican governors, replacing them with their own native-born *hijos de país*. The rebellion of 1836, which placed Juan Bautista Alvarado in power, increased the self-confidence of Californio landholders that they could control their own affairs. They were growing wealthy from the hide and tallow trade, much of it illicitly conducted with American, British, and French ships, and some of them talked openly about separating from Mexico and joining the United States.

Though the upper classes in the Mexican north were growing more and more economically dependent on the Americans, and some of them were contemplating political separation, the vast majority of the more than one hundred thousand Mexican citizens who lived on the frontier, including Hispanicized Indians, were opposed to being forcibly annexed by the United States. They valued their independence and cherished their culture. When the war came, most realized what was being lost, and they fought back.

Manifest Destiny

In May 1846, the United States declared war on Mexico. Though the causes of this conflict were many, perhaps the most important was the spirit of expansionism called Manifest Destiny. Thousands of Anglo Americans believed it was God's will that they move west and north across the entire North American continent, occupying the lands of the Mexicans and Indians and casting them aside in the process. As John O'Sullivan, editor of the *Democratic Review* and popularizer of the term *Manifest Destiny* wrote in 1845, "the Anglo-Americans alone will cover the immense space contained between the polar regions and the tropics." For many, Manifest Destiny had an economic dimension, justifying a more efficient use of natural resources by the industrious Anglo-Saxons. Mixed in with this sentiment of justifiable economic conquest were attitudes of the racial superiority of the Anglo American people. Walt Whitman, the poet, expressed this view in 1846 when he wrote, "What has miserable inefficient Mexico—with her superstition, her burlesque upon freedom, her actual tyranny by the few over the many, what has she to do with the peopling of the new world? With a noble race? Be it ours to achieve that mission." Or, as a writer for the *New York Evening Post* put it in 1845, "The Mexicans are *Aboriginal Indians,* and they must share the destiny of their race."

Beginning with Andrew Jackson's presidency in the 1830s, successive American administrations had offered to purchase California from Mexico in order to give the United States a window on the Pacific and to fulfill the nation's destiny. Mexico had repeatedly refused these offers. In 1845 President James K. Polk sent John Slidell to make yet another offer to purchase California and to settle the Texas boundary dispute. The Mexican government refused. President Polk offered as justification for his declaration of war on Mexico the fact that the Mexican government rejected Slidell's offer of forty million dollars for the purchase of California. There were other more immediate causes as well. Texas had been annexed as a state in 1845, but the Mexican government did not accept the Rio Grande as the southern boundary of Texas. In the spring of 1846, Mexican troops attacked Zachary Taylor's troops on what they believed was their own country's soil. President Polk claimed these skirmishes were proof of a Mexican invasion of the United States. On May 13, 1846, he asked Congress for a declaration of war. In his war message, he recalled the failed attempts at negotiating grievances between the two countries and blamed Mexico for starting the war. "As war exists," he argued, "and, notwithstanding all our efforts to avoid it, exists by the act of Mexico herself, we are called upon by every consideration of duty and patriotism to vindicate with decision the honor, the rights, and the interests of our country." Though the declaration of war passed by a large vote in the Congress, there were opponents. Some Southerners, including John C. Calhoun, feared that a war with Mexico would result in renewed conflict over slavery in the territories and would admit to the Union a new class of nonwhite citizens—a dangerous precedent for the slaveholding South. Some Northerners opposed the war because they viewed it as a conspiracy of slave owners trying to acquire new lands to expand their "peculiar institution." Some of them, including Henry David Thoreau and Abraham Lincoln, also opposed the war on moral grounds, since, in their view, the United States was clearly the aggressor nation.

An important factor in the agitation for war was the desire of many American expansionists to annex California. The value of California harbors for the China trade and the threat of possible British or French occupation of this area combined to heighten interest in acquiring not only California, but all of the territory between California and Texas—the present-day states of New Mexico and Arizona and parts of Nevada, Utah, and Colorado—as well. In 1844 presidential candidate Polk had listed the acquisition of California as one of the objectives of his presidential administration.

The Californios had been aware for some time of the expansionist designs of the Americanos. The mistaken capture of Monterey by Commodore Thomas ap Catesby Jones in 1842 sounded a clear warning of the expansionist objectives of the United States. The U.S. consul in Monterey, Thomas Larkin, had been sending letters to Washington discussing the possibility of annexation with the cooperation of progressive Californios and American émigrés who shared the belief that their political and economic independence would best be guaranteed by the United States. In 1845 President Polk commissioned Larkin as a secret agent to convince the Californio leadership to break away from Mexico and join the United States. Larkin noted that both Mariano Vallejo and General José Castro were predisposed toward independence from Mexico and union with the United States. But, in the spring of 1846, Polk's strategy of acquiring California through peaceful intrigue disintegrated, a casualty of agitation for war and the violent actions of Americans in California.

Frémont and the Bear Flaggers

John Charles Frémont, whose father was a French émigré and whose mother was the daughter of a prominent Virginian family, grew up with a burning desire to be famous. He married Jessie Benton, daughter of Thomas Hart Benton, a powerful U.S. senator. Frémont, like his father-in-law, sought to advance his career by promoting western expansion. In 1842, 1843, and again in 1845 Frémont led expeditions across the Rockies into California and Oregon, earning for himself the name "Pathfinder." In the winter of 1845–46, Frémont, by then commissioned as a lieutenant in the Army Corps of Topographical Engineers, entered California with a group of sixty-two men and a howitzer cannon. They camped near Monterey. Ostensibly he was on a mapping expedition, but even today the real purpose of his mission is unclear. Historians have debated whether Frémont was on a secret presidential mission to accomplish the conquest of California. No hard evidence, however, has ever been found to prove that he was part of a plot to separate California from Mexico. Perhaps his actions in California during the early months of 1846 were his own initiatives and not directed by secret orders. In any case his subsequent actions did assist the American military conquest of California.

When Frémont arrived in California in the spring of 1846, he told General Castro, the military commander of the north, that he was on a scientific expedition. Castro, however, suspected otherwise and ordered Frémont and his men to leave the province. For three days Frémont hesitated. He had his men fortify their positions atop Gavilan Hill near Monterey and defiantly raised the American flag. But after several days of consulting with Oliver Larkin, the U.S. consul in Monterey, and seeing the Mexicans prepare for an attack, Frémont wisely decided to remove his troops from the area and to heed Castro's orders. He and his men slowly withdrew from California, marching toward Oregon. Upon reaching Klamath Lake, Lieutenant Archibald Gillespie arrived from Washington, D.C., bringing letters from Senator Thomas Hart Benton. Some historians suspect that Gillespie may have also brought oral instructions from President Polk himself, namely to assist in the impending conquest of California by arms. We will never know what was said, but soon after Gillespie's arrival Frémont ordered his men to march back to California. In May, he camped near present-day Marysville, a short march from Sutter's Fort. In the days that followed, small groups of Americans came to Frémont's camp and told him of rumors that General Castro was preparing an army to expel all Americans from California.

On June 8, acting on rumors of a possible Californio military action against the American settlers at Sutter's Fort, Frémont sent a message to William Ide, one of their leaders, suggesting that they come to his camp for protection. On June 10, some twelve or fourteen Americans led by Ezekiel Merritt launched a revolt against the Mexican government, capturing approximately 170 horses that were being driven from Sacramento to Santa Clara for use by General Castro's troops. They now had a choice—either be horse thieves or revolutionaries. They chose the latter. They released the Mexicans who were leading the horses, telling them to tell Castro that the Americans were in possession of Sonoma and New Helvetia (Sutter's Fort), and then they returned to Frémont's camp with the horses. Ide remembered that Frémont had encouraged the horse raid and presented to the American settlers a "plan of conquest," which he would support but not participate in directly. The horse thieves then set out for Sonoma, the residence of General Mariano Vallejo, one of the most powerful Californios, and a man who had already voiced his support of American annexation.

In the early morning hours of June 14, 1846, thirty-three rough and dirty men descended on Vallejo's home and forced their way into his parlor, demanding the surrender of his command of the Mexican military forces in the region. Jacob P. Leese, Vallejo's brother-in-law, acted as an interpreter. The mob slowly learned that Vallejo was actually an ally, but they wanted a surrender nevertheless. Negotiations dragged on and Vallejo, with typical Californio hospitality, broke out the *aguardiente* (brandy). The mob proceeded to get drunk, and after a while someone put together a homemade flag, a grizzly bear with a red star on a white field. William Ide declared their intention to break away from Mexican despotism and establish a republic, along the lines of Texas in 1836. With their flag, the proclamation of independence, and a surrender document, the Bear Flaggers marched to Frémont's camp with their prisoners—Vallejo, his brother Salvador, Leese, and Victor Prudon, a French resident of Sonoma. Then, with Frémont's men as an escort, they proceeded to Sutter's Fort, where Frémont assumed responsibility for the prisoners. In the few days after the capture of Sonoma, the Bear Flaggers had also killed three Californios in a skirmish near San Rafael, and the Mexican army had executed two Americans near the Russian River. Frémont, by his words and then through his actions, joined the rebellion. Within a few weeks, his unofficial actions gained the approval of the U.S. government, as news reached California of the declaration of war with Mexico. The Bear Flaggers were then incorporated into the U.S. Army.

Occupation and Resistance

Congress declared war against Mexico on May 13, 1846, but news of the war traveled slowly. Commodore John D. Sloat, in charge of the U.S. Navy's Pacific Squadron, had orders to occupy the California harbors in the event of war. Upon hearing of the war declaration he ordered his ships to sail into Monterey Bay, on July 2. He did not immediately capture the town, however, remembering the earlier embarrassment of Commodore Jones. He waited five days, until learning of the Bear Flag Rebellion. Fearing a British move to seize California, he raised the American flag over the customshouse and announced to the startled populace that "henceforward California will be a portion of the United States." Sloat reassured the Californios that they would benefit from being part of the United States, and he called on General Castro and Governor Pío Pico to surrender. On July 23, because of ill health, Sloat turned over his command to Commodore Robert F. Stockton, a politically ambitious naval officer. Stockton immediately commissioned Frémont and Gillespie as officers in the newly formed California Battalion, composed of Frémont's company of engineers plus a contingent of former Bear Flaggers.

The bulk of the fighting in the conquest of California took place in the south. In the summer of 1846, General Castro and Governor Pico joined forces in Los Angeles to await the American advance but they soon concluded that they were hopelessly outnumbered and outgunned. Both leaders departed for Mexico to seek reinforcements. Meanwhile Frémont and Gillespie sailed for San Diego and, on July 29, after some brief resistance, occupied the town. Californios still controlled the surrounding countryside and continued to harass the occupiers.

Commodore Stockton marched south from Monterey, and following a skirmish his troops occupied Los Angeles, on August 13, 1846. After issuing another proclamation stating that California was now officially part of the United States and promising to respect Mexican political institutions and laws, Stockton and Frémont returned north and left the occupation of Los Angeles in the hands of Gillespie and about fifty soldiers.

What followed was a wave of Mexican Californio resistance against the American invaders. In Los Angeles, the American troops entered private homes and took household goods. Gillespie enforced a strict curfew and forbade Californios to meet in groups. Resentments grew until finally an uprising took place on September 22, 1846, led by José María Flores and Serbulo Varela. Several hundred Californios surrounded the American fortified position and Californio leaders issued El Plan de Los Angeles, calling on all Mexicans to fight against the Americans who were threatening to reduce them to "a condition worse than that of slaves." Gillespie, with only fifty men in his command, saw that his situation was hopeless and on September 29 he signed the Articles of Capitulation. The Americans were then allowed to leave the Los Angeles district and march to San Pedro. Soon after that the new Californio governor, José María Flores, declared California in a state of siege, secured loans to pay for a war, and began to recruit more troops.

For the next four months Los Angeles remained in Californio hands, and their military forces also managed to reoccupy San Diego, Santa Barbara, Santa Inés, and San Luis Obispo. From Los Angeles, Flores sent Francisco Rico, Serbulo Varela, and fifty men to recapture San Diego; this was done without firing a shot in October 1846. They held the town for three weeks until October 24, 1846, when the Americans recaptured the town after a brief battle. According to one eyewitness, the Americans hauled down the Mexican flag, but before it could touch the ground, María Antonia Machado, wife of a local ranchero, rushed into the plaza to save it from being trampled. She clutched it to her bosom and cut the halyards to prevent the American flag from being raised.

In their military forays against the American troops the Californios had the advantage of knowing the terrain and of being superior horsemen. The Americans had superior weapons and formal military training but the Californios used guerrilla tactics and effectively won several victories. The Californio lancers won battles at Chico Rancho (September 26 and 27, 1846), Dominguez Rancho (October 8), Natividad (November 29), and finally at San Pascual (December 8).

The Battle of San Pascual was the bloodiest battle fought in California and was both a victory for the Californio forces and evidence of their determination to resist the American conquest. Early in December, Andrés Pico and a force of 72 Californios lay in wait for the Americans, who were rumored to be approaching from the east. A large body of American troops under General Stephen W. Kearny had, in fact, entered California after marching overland from New Mexico. Kearny's men numbered 179, including several Delaware Indian scouts led by Kit Carson and a few African American servants of the officers and mule drivers.

General Stephen W. Kearny marched overland to California during the U.S.-Mexican War and fought a losing skirmish and was wounded at San Pascual in December 1846. Later, Kearny was the military governor of California until May of 1847. He then was sent to Mexico, where he became the military governor of Vera Cruz and then Mexico City.

Early in the morning of December 6, 1846, the American force attacked the Californio camp in the Indian village of San Pascual. During the charge the Americans became strung out in a long file, with those on stronger mules and horses far outdistancing those on tired mounts. The few gunshots exchanged were in this first charge, as the Californio troops met the early arrivals some distance from their camp. The Californios raced away, allowing themselves to be chased for about three-fourths of a mile. They then turned and charged the Americans with their lances. It had been raining occasionally for several days, and the Americans' gunpowder was damp and unreliable, forcing them to fight with their sabers. The Californios were armed with long lances and were expert at using them to slaughter cattle. In the hand-to-hand combat, the Californios had the advantage of superior mounts, weapons, and battle preparation.

Only about half of the American force was actually involved in the battle. The others were in reserve, guarding the supplies and baggage. The Americans were unfamiliar with their newly issued carbines and had trouble loading these guns in the dark and cold. The two groups fought most of the battle—about half an hour—in the dim light and fog. During the battle the Californios captured one of the American cannons. Finally, the Americans brought up another howitzer, firing at the Californios and causing them to retreat.

Nineteen American soldiers were dead on the field of battle. Two more died later from their wounds. Kearny himself suffered three lance wounds and temporarily relieved himself of command. The Californios had eleven wounded, and one of their group, Pablo Véjar, was taken prisoner. Some of the American deaths may have been from friendly fire in the dim light and confusion. Only one American was killed by a bullet.

General Kearny later wrote that the battle of December 6 had been a "victory" and that the Californios had "fled from the field." One U.S. soldier, however, wrote that the Americans had been saved from decimation by the Californios' capture of the American howitzer—an act that made the Californios "consider themselves victorious, which saved the balance of the command." Later, at the court-martial of General Frémont, Kearny admitted that a rescue party from San Diego had saved them from disaster. Generally the Navy officers, headed by Stockton, considered the Battle of San Pascual a defeat for the U.S. Army. Of course the Californios considered this engagement a victory, and news of it spread throughout the district.

A month later, on January 29, 1847, another overland army arrived in San Diego. This was the Mormon Battalion, commissioned by the U.S. Army to survey a wagon road between Santa Fe and San Diego. The 350 soldiers traveled more than one thousand miles on foot but arrived too late to participate in the final battles of the war in California. Their numbers augmented a small contingent of Mormons who had settled in southern California near San Bernardino.

California Indians and the War

During the Mexican War, some California Indian groups increased their raids on the Californio ranchos, taking advantage of the weakened defense of the Mexican settlements. The Californios thought the Americans were behind the increased Indian depredations, but the majority of the attacks were probably the work of opportunists who took advantage of wartime chaos. In the early months of the war, though, California Indians did join the Americans. When Commodore Stockton organized his march in San Diego to recapture Los Angeles from the Californio insurgents, more than one hundred Indians formed his rear guard to protect the U.S. Army from possible attack. Frémont recruited a small number of local Indians to join his men as he marched from Monterey to San Luis Obispo. And Edward Kern, the American commander at Sutter's Fort, recruited two hundred California and Oregon Indians to help secure the north and to prepare for the reconquest of southern California.

A major tragedy involving the natives and the Californios during the war was the Pauma massacre in southern California. A few days after the Battle of San Pascual, eleven Californio men and youths took refuge in an adobe house on Rancho Pauma, owned by José Antonio Serrano. While they were there they were tricked into allowing themselves to be captured by Luiseño Indians led by Manuelito Cota. The Indians took the men as prisoners to Warner's Ranch. There they consulted with a Mexican named Yguera and William Marshall, an American who had married the daughter of a local Indian chieftain. After a short captivity, the captives were tortured to death by thrusts of red-hot spears. Later rumors strongly implicated Marshall in the murders; he hated one of the prisoners, José María Alvarado, who had successfully courted Doña Lugarda Osuna, once the object of Marshall's affections. Marshall may have suggested that the Indians would be rewarded by the Americans for disposing of the Californios.

Not all Indians supported uprisings against the Mexicans. Within days of the capture of the Californios a force of natives from San Pascual who were loyal to the Mexican cause set out to rescue the captives, but they arrived too late. After learning of the massacre, a punitive force of twenty-two Californios immediately set out with a force of friendly Cahuilla Indians. They ambushed a Luiseño force, killed more than a hundred, and took twenty captives, who were later killed by the Cahuillas. The massacre of the Californios at Rancho Pauma illustrated both the persistence of native animosities toward the Mexicans and the possible manipulation of Indian hatreds by the Americans. News of this massacre, along with memories of previous uprisings and knowledge that the Indians vastly outnumbered the Californios and Mexicans, may have worked to demoralize the Californio resistance movement.

Peace

Despite the Californios' valiant though somewhat hopeless resistance against the American invaders, the American forces had recaptured all of southern California by the winter of 1847. Following the defeat of the last Californio army near Los Angeles, Andrés Pico signed a surrender agreement at Cahuenga Pass on January 13, 1847. Elsewhere in the Southwest, however, resistance continued. In New Mexico, the Taos Indians, in alliance with some of the Hispano families, rebelled against the American occupiers, killed the American military governor, Charles Bent, and recaptured some of the towns in northern New Mexico. On January 24, 1847, a Hispano-Indian army of 1500 met the Americans at La Cañada near Santa Fe, New Mexico, and were defeated. The Americans marched on the town of Mora and destroyed it, then marched south to surround Taos Pueblo, where the

General Andrés Pico, brother of Pío Pico, commanded the Mexican troops at San Pascual. He later signed the Treaty of Cahuenga in 1847 ending the hostilities in California. After the war he became a successful politician serving the California state Senate in 1859. What does this 1855 portrait reveal about Andrés Pico's Mexican identity?

remnants of the resistance had entrenched themselves. In the days that followed, more than 150 defenders were killed and their leaders were captured. Fifteen were tried and convicted of conspiracy, murder, and treason in a display of mock justice. This marked the end of armed resistance in the Southwest.

The Treaty of Guadalupe Hidalgo

In Mexico, the fight against the American invaders killed tens of thousands of soldiers and civilians in massive clashes of armies, at first in the north, near Monterrey, Mexico, and then in the Valley of Mexico. By January 1847, the U.S. Army, commanded by General Winfield Scott, occupied Mexico City and waited to hear the results of peace negotiations. Pressed by European creditors, lacking money to pay their own troops, wracked by internal rebellion, and facing the occupation of their principal cities, the Mexican government had little choice but to sign a treaty of peace, giving in to the Americans' territorial demands in exchange for the removal of troops from their homeland. The Treaty of Guadalupe Hidalgo, ending the war, was signed in a town near Mexico City, across the street from the shrine to the patron saint of Mexico, Our Lady of Guadalupe, on February 2, 1848. Among the provisions in the treaty were those specifying the new boundary between the two nations as starting "one marine league due south of the southernmost point of the Port of San Diego" and running east to the Colorado River, then east following the Gila River and an as yet undefined latitude line to the Rio Grande. The Mexican provinces of California and New Mexico now lay within the United States. Articles VIII and IX of the treaty gave assurances regarding the property and citizenship rights of the Mexicans in the newly conquered territories. Article VIII specifically promised to protect the rights of absentee Mexican landholders and to give U.S. citizenship to all Mexicans who wanted it. Article IX promised that Congress would give citizenship "at the proper time" and that the Mexicans "in the meantime shall be maintained and protected in the free enjoyment of their liberty and property, and secured in the free exercise of their religion without restriction." Finally the treaty transferred more than five hundred thousand square miles of Mexican territory to the United States.

The final ratified version of the treaty omitted Article X, which had contained stronger language protecting land rights, namely that "all grants of land made by the Mexican government or by the competent authorities, in territories previously appertaining to Mexico . . . shall be respected as valid, to the same extent if said territories had remained within the limits of Mexico." The deletion of this article proved fatal to the future of the Mexican landholders in California.

The U.S.-Mexican War awakened new nationalist impulses within Mexico and eventually produced a reform movement led by Benito Juárez in the 1850s. In the United States, the Mexican cession provoked a new and heated debate over slavery in the newly acquired territories. This played a major role in the outbreak of the U.S. Civil War in 1861—the bloodiest conflict in American history.

Within the conquered territories, there were competing visions regarding the future of the territory. The California tribes outnumbered the whites despite the influx of hundreds of American soldiers. Most natives remained unaffected by the war, particularly those living on their traditional homelands away from the settled coastal regions. A few had joined the Americans as scouts and guides during the conflict. Even fewer capitalized on the war to settle old grievances against the Mexicans. Native peoples who had become Hispanicized and who worked on the ranchos and in the pueblos now found themselves with more aggressive masters, the Americans. Indian laborers were still the backbone of the agricultural and ranching industries, and the new American masters inherited a dependence on this labor force.

The Divided Mind of the Californios

On the eve of the American era the Spanish-speaking Mexicans in California were divided in their attitudes about their status as Americans. Some, like Mariano Vallejo or Juan Bandini, were optimistic about their future under an American regime that they thought would bring political stability and increased commercial opportunities for all. It was impossible for them to envision how much their traditional way of life would change. For now, they saw what seemed to be a new opportunity for their enrichment. Others, like Pío Pico, who had been allowed to return to California, or Felipa Osuna de Marron in San Diego, viewed the American occupiers with great suspicion. They felt sure that the conquest meant more than just the transfer of political sovereignty, for they were aware of the differences between the two cultures and knew that they could not coexist easily. Finally, there were the young men who had fought against the Americans in various battles or who almost immediately felt the outrages of racism as the Americans took over their houses and lands. Serbulo Varela, leader of the recapture of Los Angeles in 1847, along with Salomon Pico, Juan Flores, and scores of other ex-soldiers became outlaws rather than submit to the Americans. In subsequent decades their violent actions in response to the American occupation became the source of legend.

It soon became apparent to the Californios that the new American masters believed in their own racial and cultural superiority and that they regarded the mestizo landless classes as little better than Indians. The conflicts between these two groups became evident as thousands of new immigrants began flooding northern California, attracted by the discovery of gold near Sacramento.

The Gold Rush

In 1842, Francisco Lopez discovered gold in San Francisquito canyon in southern California. For several years, hundreds of gold miners trekked north from Sonora to work the mines there. They scoured the riverbanks in a twenty-square-mile area. Mining the deposits depended on water, which diminished in quantity as the number of miners increased. By 1843 about two thousand ounces of gold had been taken out of the canyon. While gold continued to be mined in subsequent years, eventually it played out. This first California Gold Rush paled in comparison to the impact of the discovery of gold on January 24, 1848.

Gold! The Discovery of 1848

James W. Marshall, an employee of John Sutter, was building a sawmill on the American River at a place called Coloma. Sutter had employed about fifty former members of the Mormon Battalion, who had drifted north from San Diego, along with a group of Indian laborers. While they were cutting a ditch to provide water for the mill Marshall noticed a few gold-colored flecks. He collected them over a four-day period, then hurried to Sutter's Fort to consult with Sutter. Together they read an encyclopedia entry on gold and performed primitive tests to confirm whether or not it was the precious metal. Sutter concluded that it was, in fact, gold but he was very anxious that the discovery not disrupt his plans for construction and farming. At the same time, he set about gaining legitimate title to as much land near the discovery as possible. Although Sutter sought to keep his discovery a secret, word leaked out when he sent Charles Bennett to Monterey to

Sunday Morning in the Mines, 1872, is an oil painting by Charles Christian Nahl. This German artist also designed the grizzly bear for the state flag. His chronicle of the Gold Rush echoed European artistic traditions. What strikes you as unlikely about this depiction of Gold Rush life?

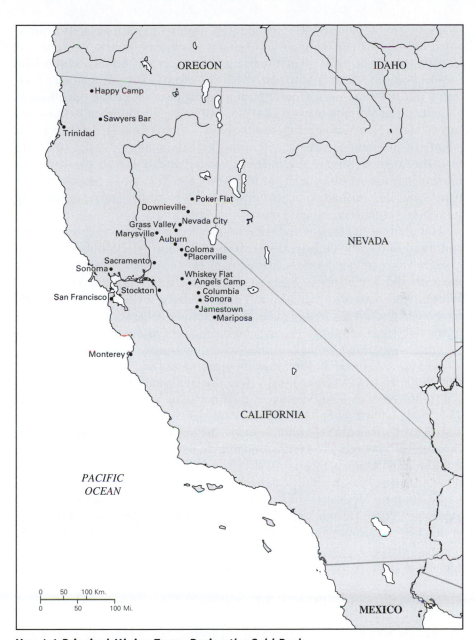

Map 4.1 Principal Mining Towns During the Gold Rush

secure title to the land and its mineral rights. Bennett traveled as far as Benicia, where he bragged about the discovery of gold at a local store. Then in San Francisco he confided with acquaintances who had experience in gold mining. Meanwhile, Samuel Brannan, a former Mormon leader who owned a store near Sutter's Fort, found out that local workers were paying for supplies with small quantities of gold dust. The Mormon workers gave him a tithe in gold and when Brannan returned to San Francisco he publicized the news, running through the streets with a bottle of gold dust in one hand and waving his hat shouting, " Gold! Gold! Gold from the American River." Nevertheless, the importance of this discovery was not immediately appreciated. As late as May 1848, San Francisco newspapers were blasé about the possibility of a gold field somewhere on the American River. By June, however, the fever caught hold.

Hundreds of Californios and American settlers quit their ranchos and jobs and raced to the new diggings. San Francisco, San José, and Monterey became ghost towns overnight. Stores selling pans, picks, shovels, and other mining implements did a tremendous business. Prices rose accordingly. Luzena Stanley Wilson, who came with her husband and family to the Gold Rush country, remembered selling her freshly made biscuits for five dollars each. Soldiers, prisoners, politicians, ministers—young and old—all abandoned their families and occupations to set out for the diggings.

As fate would have it, the Mexican government had ratified the Treaty of Guadalupe Hidalgo a few months before the confirmation of a gold strike in California. News of the discovery reached northern Mexico in the summer of 1848, and hundreds of Sonoran miners immediately headed for Alta California. They had experience in gold mining, unlike the Anglo Americans and foreigners. In the fall of 1848, roughly six thousand miners, many of them Sonorans, entered California and set up mining camps along the American River. The first American miners to arrive knew nothing about gold mining and learned their mining techniques from the Mexicans. At first, life in the diggings was generally orderly and peaceable. Alonzo Delano, one of the so-called forty-eighters, remembered that at that time "property was safer in California than in the older states." Bancroft, the publisher and historian from San Francisco, could only find two cases of robbery in all of the mining camps in 1848. But this soon changed.

The Argonauts

News of the gold strike in California rapidly spread, first to Hawai`i, Oregon, and Utah, and then to South America, Australia, China, the eastern seaboard of the United States, and Europe. By December 1848, President Polk publicly delivered a speech to Congress confirming the gold discovery and interpreting it as a confirmation of God's favor for the war against Mexico. During 1849 about one hundred thousand immigrants from all over the world, but especially from the eastern United States, flooded northern California, forever changing the destiny of the state. Overnight, it seemed, San Francisco was transformed into an international city, a transfer point for miners and mining supplies. The pastoral life of the Californios in the north declined while the rancheros of the south enjoyed a brief flare of prosperity, as their cattle increased in value with the demand for food from the mining camps and the growing population of the north.

By 1850 fully one-quarter of California's population was foreign-born; many were Latin American or Mexican. The Gold Rush was an international affair, attracting people from around the world. Chinese immigrants came, mostly after 1849. They were young men from southeastern China—from big cities like Hong Kong and Canton as well as from the countryside. In order to pay for their trip to the "Gold Mountain," as they called California, these men indentured themselves to Chinese companies that, in turn, sold their labor to Chinese mining operations. Laboring long hours, with very low pay, the Chinese miners were virtual slaves until their debt was repaid, which often took years. By 1852 more than twenty-five thousand Chinese were living in northern California, in the mining camps and in San Francisco.

Two-thirds of the new population attracted to California during the Gold Rush came from the eastern United States and were a multiethnic group of Scottish, French, Irish, German, and British descent. They called themselves the Argonauts, after the mythical Greek adventurers who traveled to the edge of the known world in search of a fabled golden fleece. In 1849 and subsequent years they came to California by boat and wagon, on horseback, and even on foot, enduring grueling and dangerous passages.

This mass migration to California is one of the most documented population movements in world history, with hundreds of letters, diaries, and reminiscences penned along the way and after arrival at the mines. Those who chose to travel by boat had to pick between two routes. One was by ship from New York to Panama, and then by smaller ship up the fever-infested Chagres River, and then by mule over the mountains to the Pacific port of Panama. There they transferred to another ship bound for San Francisco. This voyage could last from two to three months depending on connections. The longest delays were usually on the Pacific side of the Panamanian isthmus, where, in the early years, there were rarely enough ships to carry the numbers who thronged the port seeking passage.

The other route to California by sea involved going around Cape Horn, the stormy southern tip of South America. The demand for travel "around the horn" stimulated a boom in the construction of clipper ships. Built for speed, these remarkable vessels were long and thin and carried huge amounts of sail on three tall masts. Accommodations were small and narrow, with ceilings so low that many had to bend over when moving about. One of the most notable clippers was the *Flying Cloud,* which on its first voyage took only eighty-nine days to sail from New York to San Francisco. Those choosing one of the sea routes had to contend with shipwrecks, shipboard diseases of all kinds, and, if they selected the Panama route, death by yellow fever or malaria.

The overland route was the cheapest way to get to California, costing between $100 and $200. Nevertheless it was still relatively expensive. (For comparison purposes, the daily wage of a New York City laborer in 1850 was less than one dollar.) Anthony Powers of Green Spring, Wisconsin, borrowed $125 to finance an overland journey to the gold fields. Another group from Monroe, Michigan collected $2500 to pay for ten people to make the journey. Though it was the most time-consuming route, it was the one that most of the American migrants chose.

The California immigrants of the 1840s had already blazed several trails, and others had been in use by the Spanish and Mexicans for centuries. The southern route—the Santa Fe Trail—ran from the Missouri River through what is now Kansas, to New Mexico, and then followed the Spanish trail from New Mexico to southern California. This route had the advantage of avoiding the snows of the Sierras. A more direct way was the northern route, the choice of most because it was better known to English speakers due to guidebooks that had been published. An estimated twenty-five thousand immigrants followed the northern route, leaving towns along the Missouri River as soon as the spring grasses were long enough to provide food for their oxen and horses. They followed the Platte River west into what is now southern Wyoming, crossed the Rocky Mountains through a series of passes, and came down in the Great Basin near Salt Lake. From there they went west to the Humboldt River Valley, across the desert to the Sierras, and, once over those forbidding peaks, to Sacramento. The entire journey from Missouri to California lasted from four to five months, depending on the route selected and the luck they encountered.

The dangers faced by the forty-niners going to California on the overland trail included death by cholera and mountain fever and by starvation and dehydration. Very few died from Indian attacks, which were rare. For the most part the native peoples were content to watch in bemusement as wagon after wagon of "white eyes" drove themselves westward with fanatic zeal, abandoning many of their prized possessions in the process, in order to lighten their load. Milus Gay, an overland Argonaut, described one scene: "Such destruction of property as I saw across the Desert I have never seen. I should think I passed the carcasses of 1200 head of cattle and horses and a great many wagons—harnesses—cooking utensils—tools—water casks.... We also saw many men on the point of starvation begging for bread." The phrase "seeing the elephant" described the excitement of new adventure but also referred to the delusional state that many experienced on the trail.

Once in California the forty-niners, as they called themselves, began trying to strike it rich. They labored to separate sand from gold along riverbeds by sloshing gravel in a pan filled with water, knowing that the heavier gold dust settled to the bottom. The miners soon developed more elaborate systems, but all of the techniques still involved washing sand or dirt with water and permitting the heavier gold to settle out. Wooden cradles rocked gravel and water back and forth to separate the gold. Sluices ran a stream of water over a long wooden trough partially filled with gravel. Using such methods, miners took out more than $200 million worth of gold between 1848 and 1852. To put this into perspective, this amount of gold was roughly equal to the total value of all gold and silver money in circulation

An 1852 daguerreotype shows a group of gold miners, including a woman, pausing in their labors near Sacramento. The long sluice box was known as a "long tom." What do the details in this photo tell us about the California Gold Rush?

in the entire nation at the beginning of the Gold Rush, and equivalent to almost $2 billion dollars today.

By mid-1850, the most easily available gold was gone. The miners continued to use pans and long toms (sluices), but they found less and less gold to reward their labor. Some fortune seekers began to return home or to follow the lure of quick riches to new gold strikes elsewhere. Others turned to more elaborate methods of mining. By one estimate, a typical gold seeker averaged twenty dollars of gold in a day in 1848 but only two dollars' worth by 1853. As miners moved farther and farther from streams, and as streams diminished in late summer, miners found they had to expend greater efforts diverting water to their claims. By 1855, miners or water companies had built more than four thousand miles of artificial waterways, mostly wooden channels called flumes.

One technique to get more gold was to use water diverted from rivers and streams for hydraulic mining. Reasoning that the gold dust in the riverbeds had washed there from the mountains, gold seekers began to look for gold in the foothills. Rather than digging through tons of soil and gravel over the prehistoric streambeds, gold seekers began to use water under pressure to blast it away. They developed huge water cannons that could blast away fully grown trees and giant boulders and reduce an entire hillside to bedrock. After bombardment by water cannons, sand and gravel were suspended in water and run through sluices, permitting the gold to settle to the bottom and the tailings (small rocks of no value) to flow into nearby rivers. This hydraulic method was far more expensive than placer mining, but by 1870, 22 percent of all gold produced in California was obtained by hydraulic mining.

As thousands and then tens of thousands of gold seekers converged on the Gold Country, they found a region far removed from traditional structures of law or political authority. The military governor was far away, and Mexican political authority had never extended into the foothills of the Sierras. Gold seekers formed their own political authority, first by developing rough guidelines regarding claims. A gold seeker could preempt a likely spot by "staking a claim," but the consensus was that the claim was valid only if the area it covered could be worked by a single person and only if someone was actually working it. Most mining camps elected someone to arbitrate their differences; this person was often called by the Mexican term, *alcalde.*

Such people functioned as unofficial justices of the peace, trying wrongdoers and prescribing punishment for crimes. Few such magistrates had much training in the law, if any, and many gained reputations for eccentric decisions or for blatant discrimination against foreigners, Californios, or Indians. If someone were accused of a serious crime, most mining camps carried out a semblance of a jury trial, though usually with little reference to established legal principles. Without sheriffs or jails, sentences for theft were usually either banishment (often with a shaved head), flogging, branding, or mutilation (such as cutting off the thief's ears). Murder and horse theft were usually punished by hanging. One of the first such hangings came in January 1849, in a camp thereafter known as Hangtown (later renamed Placerville). Though some punishments resulted from a process much like a jury trial, others were simply a lynching in which a mob, sometimes drunken, acted as judge, jury, and executioner in one.

Though such rough-and-ready justice may have seemed appropriate in the absence of legally constituted political authority, some mining camps continued in such fashion even when a properly authorized judge or sheriff was present. In 1851, in the town of Sonora, for example, a mob overpowered the sheriff and lynched a self-confessed thief. Soon after, the miners formed a vigilance committee. Unlike a lynch mob, which was by definition spontaneous and poorly organized, a vigilance committee was organized, claimed to represent leading citizens of the community, and justified its existence by claiming that the officials responsible for punishing wrongdoers were either corrupt or incompetent or both. Members of such a committee were called *vigilantes.* Led by their committee of vigilance, Sonorans banished an American thief and a French counterfeiter, and flogged and banished four Mexicans (two for counterfeiting, one for horse theft, and one for stealing a pistol) and one Australian (for theft of a mule). Committees of vigilance sprouted in a number of other mining camps in the early and mid-1850s. Lynch mobs also continued to take justice into their own hands. In 1855, for example, in Columbia, a mob took an accused murderer out of the hands of the sheriff and hanged him. Such actions were not limited to mining communities—both Stockton and Sacramento experienced lynchings in 1850.

The new society that was emerging spread outwards from the gold fields of the north, which encompassed an inland area in the San Joaquin Valley, bounded by the Sierra Nevada mountains on the east, and joined by the rivers that drained into the San Francisco Bay. Hundreds of settlements sprang up overnight with names that reflected their cultural tenor: Hangtown, Placerville, Spanish Diggings, Sonora, and El Dorado (see map on page 107). The town of Sacramento grew up to provide food and supplies to the mining district. Similarly, the port city of Stockton, almost one hundred miles from the Pacific Ocean but located on the navigable San Joaquin River, grew to feed the new population. San Francisco, of course, owed its sudden urbanization to the Gold Rush migrants and economy. Overnight its population went from a few hundred souls to more than forty thousand in the last months of 1848. Within a short time it would become the cultural and economic capital of the state.

Camp Life

The rough-and-tumble life in the mining camps that sprang up along the banks of the rivers in northern and central California challenged the morals and standards of living that many miners brought with them from the east. Boredom and homesickness typified the early months in the camps, as the miners began to miss the creature and family comforts of home. Edmund Booth of Iowa wrote in 1850 that "Cal. is a world upside down—nothing like home comforts and home joys." He was referring to the fact that in the gold fields the normal relations between genders, races, and classes were all mixed up: Indians, Africans, and Mexicans shared tents, food, and amusements with Australians, Frenchmen, and Yankees. Men did the cooking and washing, and the boundaries between respectable women and prostitutes seemed irrelevant. Men who had never cooked or done domestic work before found themselves planning their menus around trips to the distant store. They worried about infestations of lice and fleas and feared diseases such as scurvy and dysentery. New Yorker Howard Gardiner recalled that he and his fellow miners "lived more like pigs than human beings." Those few miners who were fortunate to have a woman in their dwelling bragged to the others about their food and comfort.

To relieve the monotony of camp life the miners created leisure activities that they might have avoided back home. Sometimes it seemed that everyone was eager to, in the words of Charles Davis, "join the ranks of Satan and spend their Sabbaths with little or no restraint." Leisure activities associated with sex, liquor, gambling, and other amusements filled the gaps in miners' lives. In these activities— in the fandango hall, the bordello, and the saloon—the mixture of races and classes prevailed. Gold Rush diaries describe the moral anguish miners felt, mostly after the fact, of drunken sprees and of sexual adventures with Indians and prostitutes. In the southern mines where the Latin Americans and Frenchmen worked, the mining camps had a more normal balance of the sexes and morals. Yankees from the northern mines frequently went south for a visit just to see women dancing. Other Sunday amusements included bull and bear fighting, where the two animals were chained together and prodded to fight to the death. Most mining camps had arenas built to accommodate the crowds who assembled for the blood sport. Occasionally, bullfighting took place when a brave individual ventured into the ring. In Sonora Camp, Enos Christian recalled seeing a female matador who turned out to be a man dressed as a woman for the amusement of the crowd.

A few sought out the comforts of religion, although churches were few and far between. In the southern mines rude Catholic churches sprang up in which a diversity of nationalities and classes gathered. For the Protestant miners the occasional preacher and denominational church provided the chance to share the Christian gospel and, perhaps, view a member of the opposite sex.

Historian Susan Lee Johnson called the Gold Rush the "most demographically male event in human history." By 1850 California men outnumbered women by more than ten to one. Two years later the ratio fell to seven to one and by 1860 it was two to one. It was not until the turn of the century that a balance between the sexes was achieved. The first women to live and work in the mining camps were California Indians who worked as prostitutes or held other jobs in the saloons and temporary brothels that sprang up. They were followed by Sonoran Mexicans such as Rosa Feliz, companion of the legendary Joaquín Murrieta, or Latin Americans such as Chilean Rosario Améstica, a prostitute who sailed north with a shipload of men. Some women were reformers. Elizabeth Gunn, who was married to the editor of the *Sonora Herald,* wrote home about the evils of the fandango and prostitution, and soon her husband's paper published criticisms along those lines. Lorena Hays wrote and published under the pen name Lenita, to criticize the immorality of the mining camps, even while identifying with the Mexican and Chilean miners. Wives and prostitutes thus were uneasy companions in the mining camps. Single entrepreneurial women also found their niche. Gold dust acted as a lure to women such as Rose Cartier, a Frenchwoman who owned a saloon in the mining camp of Sonora, where she employed other women who had emigrated from France and Europe.

Married women who traveled to the gold towns and settlements with their husbands endured many hardships and sufferings. Mrs. John Berry arrived in the camps in 1849 with her husband and lived in a wagon and then a tent through the cold wet winter. She wrote: "The rains set in in early November, and continued with little interruption until the latter part of March. . . . Sometimes on a morning I would come out of the wagon (that is & has been our bedroom ever since we left the States) & find my utensils lying in all directions, fire out & it pouring down. . . ." Women tried to set up housekeeping among the dirt, fleas, dust, cold, and wet. Louisa Clappe came to California with her husband in 1850 and then traveled to the mines with him and wrote a series of twenty-three letters to her sister, which she signed "Dame Shirley." These "Shirley Letters" were published serially in 1854 and again in 1933 and are perhaps the most vivid and detailed firsthand description of women's daily life in the diggings. She wrote of the log cabin that they called home and of the few other women who lived nearby. Her detailed observations of the people she met and the mining camps are a classic in Gold Rush literature. Through it all Louisa remained indefatigable and optimistic.

Sometime in 1852 she wrote, "My heart is heavy at the thought of departing forever from this place. I *like* this wild and barbarous life; I leave it with regret."

A characteristic of the gold camps noted by Dame Shirley was the toleration of prostitutes, which she termed "compassionated creatures." Most of the men of the Gold Rush were white men and most of the prostitutes were Mexican, Chinese, Chilean, or Indian. Historian Al Hurtado found that more than three-fourths of the prostitutes in Sacramento were women of color and more than half of them were Chinese. The southern mines, especially, had a multiracial, multinational female population including African Americans and Indians.

One of the most infamous tragedies of the Gold Rush era was the hanging in 1851 of Josefa, the only woman ever lynched in California. Josefa, also known as Juanita (her last name is not known), lived in Downieville with her boyfriend, José, a Mexican gambler. During the night of a Fourth of July celebration a miner named Fred Cannon drunkenly fell into the couple's humble shack and broke the door. The next day when José and Juanita demanded payment for the damage an argument ensued and Cannon called Josefa a prostitute. Soon after, in a rage, she killed him with a bowie knife. That afternoon a mob assembled demanding that she be hanged and voting to execute her at four o'clock. Before she died, Josefa calmly arranged the noose around her neck so that it would not tangle her hair and coolly told the assembled rabble that she would do it all over again. She had defended her honor. Cannon had called her a prostitute.

Women worked for high wages doing domestic chores for the miners, including cooking, sewing, and laundry. Other women owned and operated stores, restaurants, saloons, and gambling and boarding houses. Some unmarried women lived with miners in an attempt to avoid the violence and insecurity that was a constant fact of female life. But respectable women did not stay unmarried for very long. And those who came to the mines as married women were under great temptation to find new husbands among the wealthy, or to seek less-abusive, more-attentive mates.

Because of the scarcity of women, divorce statutes drafted by the California legislature were more liberal than elsewhere. Divorce became more common for women than for men and, beginning in the 1880s, California led all other states in the proportion of divorced to married couples.

Nativism and Racism

One of the negative legacies of the Gold Rush was the wave of antiforeign sentiment that emerged, directed especially toward non-European immigrants. The Latin Americans, especially the Peruvians, Chileans, and Mexicans, along with the French and Chinese, became favorite targets of political agitation and violence in California. Most Mexican and Latin American miners established themselves in the southern mines, including the California counties south of the Sacramento River. Most of the anti-Mexican violence occurred here. Mexican, Californio, and Latin American miners helped teach the newly arrived Americans how to extract the metal from streambeds and ore deposits. But the gratitude they received for these lessons was short-lived. Resentments about the presence of these foreigners soon erupted into violence, especially in 1849, when the Americans arrived in larger numbers. Americans were angry that many of the best claims had been staked out already by the "Sonorans," as they called all Mexican miners. The fact that many of the mining towns, like Sonora, Hornitos, and Stockton, had become multilingual in business dealings grated on the English-speaking Americans, who regarded this development as unpatriotic. On July 4, 1849, acts of violence broke out against the foreigners, beginning with attacks on Chilean merchants and neighborhoods in San Francisco and then spreading to the mining camps. In the camps near Stockton, Yankee miners ousted the Chileans by creating an impromptu code of laws forbidding foreigners from mining. Intimidation and violence followed, and the Anglos confiscated the Chileans' property and sold it at public auction. In November 1849 a vigilante group attacked Mexican miners along the Calaveras River, ousted them from their claims, and "fined" each miner an ounce of gold. A few days later, sixteen Chileans were rounded up and accused of murder. They were given a summary trial, and then three were lynched. Similar acts of violence occurred throughout the diggings during the first few years of the Gold Rush.

Many native-born Mexican Americans, who were now citizens of the United States under the terms of the Treaty of Guadalupe Hidalgo, fell victim to these antiforeign prejudices and laws. One estimate places about thirteen hundred Californios (formerly Mexican citizens, now U.S. citizens) in the gold regions in 1848, with a similar number returning in 1849. In 1849 the military governor of California, General Persifor Smith, responded to nativist fears that foreigners were taking all of the gold out of the mining regions. He announced his "trespass" orders, prohibiting noncitizens from mining gold on public property. He appealed to Americans to help him enforce his policy. Using this order as a pretext and with some protection from the military, Anglo American miners robbed and harassed foreigners. After one riot, French immigrant miners were driven from the gold camps. Irish and Australians became targets of vigilante violence in San Francisco and elsewhere in the diggings. Chinese miners attracted more and more attention by nativists and many were driven out of the gold camps by late 1851.

In April 1850, the California legislature responded to the pressure from the forty-niners and passed the Foreign Miner's Tax, which required all non-U.S. citizens to pay a tax for the privilege of mining gold. The cost was twenty dollars per month—an amount so high as to be prohibitive to all but the most successful. The law applied to all noncitizens, but tax collectors enforced it most consistently for miners whose language or race made them distinctive—Chinese and Latin Americans especially, but also the French and Germans. The tax was repealed the next year, due partly to complaints by gold country merchants that it was destroying their businesses. In 1852 the legislature passed a new Foreign Miner's Tax of four dollars per month, later changed to three dollars. Another amendment, in 1855, exempted from the tax all those who declared their intention to become citizens. This meant that the tax was limited almost entirely to Chinese miners because they alone could not qualify for an exemption—California's constitution limited citizenship to whites only. Until a law in 1870 voided the tax, it provided a major source of state revenue. Of the $5 million collected over twenty years through this tax, Chinese miners paid an estimated $4.9 million. Leaders of the Chinese community voiced their opposition to these discriminatory laws and others that were proposed, but as noncitizens they had little political influence in Sacramento. Nevertheless, members of the Chinese community protested by writing letters to the governor and to San Francisco's newspapers. They also hired a lobbyist, a Presbyterian minister named A. W. Loomis, to fight against discriminatory laws, in particular the one restricting their testimony in court. By hiring lawyers and collectively funding court challenges the Chinese won court victories challenging the Foreign Miner's Tax and other prejudicial laws.

The Legendary Life of Joaquín Murrieta

One of California's first folk legends was Joaquín Murrieta, a person whose life is a subject of controversy, speculation, and myth. According to the story, Murrieta was a Sonoran miner in Murphy's Camp whose brother was lynched and wife raped and murdered. What followed was Joaquín's war of revenge against the Americanos. For a year, Joaquín and a band of Mexicanos and Californios terrorized the state. As a result, the state of California created the California Rangers, a special mounted police force, modeled on the Texas Rangers. The state government placed a price of one thousand dollars on Murrieta's head.

In 1851, after several months of searching the foothills for Murrieta, Captain Harry Love and the Rangers surprised a group of Mexican vaqueros in Cantua Canyon. The Rangers killed several Mexicans, and Captain Love claimed that one of them was Joaquín. To prove his claim, he chopped off Murrieta's head and brought it back for identification. Even though Love gathered a number of testimonials certifying that the head was indeed Joaquín's, some doubted that Murrieta had been killed. To this day many believe that Joaquín escaped and returned to his home in Sonora, Mexico.

Thus, Joaquín Murrieta became one of California's first legendary figures. The first fictional interpretation of his life, based on some historical fact, was *The Life and Adventures of the Celebrated Bandit Joaquín Murrieta,* by John Rollins Ridge, published in 1854. Ridge was a Cherokee Indian whose native name was Yellow Bird. In Ridge's hands, Joaquín became a vicarious avenger, a Robin Hood of the Sierra. Joaquín's adventures soon reappeared in other novels and histories and rapidly became an international legend. As late as the 1960s Joaquín Murrieta's story was an inspiration for resistance against American cultural and economic control. In revolutionary Cuba and Communist Russia, Murrieta appeared in textbooks and in life-size statues as an example of the revolt of the Third World against imperialism. The world-famous Chilean poet Pablo Neruda composed an epic poem in which Murrieta was a Chilean who stood for the struggle of all Latin

American people to be free of North American hegemony. At the same time, however, Anglo American novelists, history buffs, and some academics treated Murrieta as an overly romanticized, bloodthirsty, bandit-murderer, or as a fictitious character whose life is more properly a topic of literary study. This contradictory and ambiguous legacy springs from Gold Rush California.

California Transformed

The military conquest of California took less than six months but the social, economic, and cultural conquest was propelled by the Gold Rush and the subsequent economic development of the state. The cultural and social conquest of California's oldest inhabitants continued over several decades as the newcomers asserted their dominance over the people and the land.

Conquest of the Californios

The Californio landholders also paid a price for the development of California during the Gold Rush. In 1846 roughly ten thousand Mexicans, including Hispanicized Indians, lived in California. Within a few years they were overwhelmed by the sheer numbers of newcomers, most of whom had little love for dark-skinned peoples with their strange language and culture. The Californios swiftly lost control of the courts and the government and soon their land.

Within a generation the Mexican Californians lost political influence and became an impoverished minority, victimized by racist attitudes and laws. In 1855, for example, the state legislature passed laws to control the Mexican population. A Sunday Law imposed fines ranging from fifty to five hundred dollars for engaging in "barbarous or noisy amusements," which were listed as bullfights, cockfights, horseraces, and other traditional Californio amusements. At the same time they passed what was widely called "The Greaser Law" to fine and jail unemployed Mexicans who were considered vagrants.

Conquest of the Indians

The modernization of California's economy came at a cost, largely borne by the native and Mexican peoples whose way of life was seen by the new immigrants as standing in the way of progress. The California Indians, who had been subject to the Spanish and Mexican attempts to change them, now fell victim to the new immigrants, most of whom thought of Indians as laborers, obstacles to settlement, or dangerous savages. During the early years of the Gold Rush, retaliatory massacres occurred when Indians occasionally killed whites—even though such killings may have been provoked by outrages against Indians. At Clear Lake in northern California in 1849, for example, 135 Indians were killed in retaliation for the killing of 2 white men who had enslaved local Pomo Indians. Indian massacres took place sometimes just because the Indians were living in the vicinity. In 1850 more than sixty Humboldt Indians—men, women, and children—were killed as they slept in their village because they occupied property thought to be rich with gold. The state legislature appropriated millions in funds to pay for militia operations against Indians.

When the Indians fought back their resistance was termed *war* by the American settlers. In 1851 the so-called Mariposa War resulted when the Indians of this northern California band fought to preserve their land and succeeded in defeating the local militia until reinforcements arrived from outside the region. That same year a rebellion broke out in southern California. This uprising was the result of an alliance between several Indian bands, perhaps protesting the American taxation of their lands and resenting the treatment of the Cupeño Indians by Juan José Warner. Their leader was Antonio Garra, an ex-neophyte Indian who sought an alliance with disaffected Californios. The Californios did not support his rebellion, however, and the state militia captured Garra with the help of rival Indian bands. He and six of his associates were tried and executed.

Economic Transformation

Without a doubt the Gold Rush was one of the great turning points in California's history, redefining the demographic, economic, and social future of the state. The lure of precious metal drew hundreds of thousands of immigrants to California and assured the rapid domination of the English-speaking peoples. By 1850, the population of California exceeded 150,000, allowing the territory to apply for admission as a state. California gold helped finance the North in the U.S. Civil War, stimulated the construction of the first transcontinental railroad, and encouraged the rapid agricultural and commercial development of the state. It is estimated that in the twenty-five years following the discovery at Coloma, miners extracted more than one billion dollars worth of gold from the mines—the equivalent of more than one hundred billion dollars at the end of the twentieth century.

The mining industry stimulated demand for food and materials, which in turn stimulated home industry and the creation of new cities and towns. Sacramento and Stockton owed their creation to the Gold Rush, and San Francisco became a major international metropolis. The newcomers and their exuberance created a boom mentality within the state. The expectation of quick riches, opulent displays of wealth, a fluid and open society, and colorful and eccentric individuals all became early hallmarks of California's American era. California became the western leader in banking, agriculture, stock raising, industrial development, and trade—a lead that has lengthened over the decades.

The Golden State

During the hectic first two years of the Gold Rush the military governed California, but the American residents protested this situation and held mass meetings to

The Bear Flag was designed by the Americans who took over Sonoma on June 14, 1846. The original was destroyed in the San Francisco fire of 1906. What is the significance of its similarity with the present-day state flag?

demand that a civil government be organized. Bowing to public pressure, military governor General Bennett Riley issued a proclamation calling for the election of delegates from ten districts. These delegates were to assemble in Monterey on September 1, 1849, to work on constructing a state government for California. They were elected by popular vote on August 1, 1848. The result was a group as diverse as the territory. Of the forty-eight men who assembled in Colton Hall that fall, eight of them were native Californios, six were foreign-born European immigrants, and thirteen had been living in California less than a year. Deliberations were in English with translators available for the Spanish-speaking delegates. Votes on many of the issues split along north-south lines. The southern delegates wanted territorial status or, if that were not possible, to split California in two. They lost on both counts. The delegates were unanimous in wanting to exclude slavery from California and also to exclude free African Americans from the state. Many ex-slaves feared the threat of having to work as indentured servants in the mines. Finally, the provision specifically excluding them was deleted in order to get Congress to speedily approve statehood. In dealing with this issue delegates relied on the precedence of free states in the east.

With regard to citizenship rights, native Californios were aware that many Mexican Californios who looked like Indians faced the prospect of racial discrimination. Ultimately they argued for the protection of their people even though it meant endorsing the racist views of their Anglo colleagues toward Indians and persons of African descent. Mexico had granted citizenship to "civilized" Indians and to blacks, and the Treaty of Guadalupe Hidalgo clearly stated that former Mexican citizens were to be given the opportunity to become citizens of the United States. Following the biases of the time, the framers of the state constitution sought wording that would exclude African Americans and Indians while including Mexicans. Eventually the first section of the state constitution limited the suffrage to "every white, male citizen of Mexico who shall have elected to become a citizen of the United States." The convention agreed that Indians and African Americans might at some future date be given the franchise but that, because voting was not an absolute right of citizenship, they could be excluded. The constitution left open the question of Indian citizenship, stating that "nothing herein contained, shall be construed to prevent the Legislature, by a two-thirds concurrent vote, from admitting to the right of suffrage, Indians or the descendants of Indians. . . ."

Ultimately the Mexican Californios became full-fledged citizens, at least in theory, when the Congress of the United States admitted California as a state in 1850. Under the provisions of the treaty those who did not want to become U.S. citizens had a year to declare this intention; they were also free to go to Mexico. No one knows how many Mexican Californios returned, but during the early 1850s there were several colonization expeditions that went south and settled in Sonora and Baja California.

Of course the main issue in California was possession of the land, but the proposed constitution was silent in this regard. The former Mexican citizens had to trust their fate to the courts and their interpretation of the Treaty of Guadalupe Hidalgo. As Chapter 5 explains, their trust was quickly betrayed as the U.S. government established complicated and lengthy procedures for verifying legitimate title to the land. Thus, most Californios had to mortgage or sell their lands to pay for litigation costs. Within a generation most of the Californio rancheros joined the impoverished ranks of their former vaqueros.

The Constitutional Convention also debated where to set the eastern boundary of the state. Mexican maps had never specified an eastern boundary and some argued that California included the present states of Nevada and Utah. The southern delegates argued that this territory would be too difficult to administer and might prevent ratification by Congress. The final agreement established the present eastern boundary, roughly following the Sierra Nevada mountains.

Several sections in the state constitution showed Mexican influence. One provision required that all laws be published in both Spanish and English, in recognition of the Mexican minority. California adopted the concept of community property, wherein married women had joint ownership of property along with their husband, as they had under Mexican laws. Mariano Vallejo, one of the Californio delegates, protested that the state flag and seal should not show a grizzly bear, a reminder of the Bear Flag Rebellion and his own personal humiliation, but his objections did not win a sympathetic hearing.

California's constitution was accepted by the U.S. Congress after a lengthy debate that resulted in the Compromise of 1850. The state government that was established by the admission of California on September 9, 1850, promised to bring some degree of law and order to the politically ambiguous situation created by military government, but the lawlessness engendered by the Gold Rush continued in many areas.

A New Direction

The U.S.-Mexican War and the Gold Rush marked major changes in California's future. Both events were traumatic to the Mexican and Indian populations, who were soon to be overwhelmed by the new immigrants. The conflicts between the old and the new ways of life were sometimes stark, as in the persistence of the adobe barrio houses in the rapidly growing commercial center of Los Angeles. Plastered and painted, and sometimes overlaid with wood, these humble dwellings became the nucleus of Sonora Town, the Mexican section of Los Angeles, where the streets remained of dirt and few newcomers ventured. Visitors to the port town of San Diego found adobe houses, including the large two-story homes of the wealthy rancho owners, but the newcomers quickly built wood-frame homes similar to the homes they had left behind. Not too far from the town, they found Indian rancherías composed of brush huts where transient laborers lived with their families. In the rural regions the old ranchero way of life passed away, to be replaced by large commercial farms owned by banks, railroad companies, and land speculation companies.

The Gold Rush influenced the fortunes of millions of men and women, from the lowly miners who never struck it rich and who abandoned their families back east, to the fabulously wealthy entrepreneurs such as William Ralston, George Hearst, and Leland Stanford, who helped shape the economic future of the state. The Gold Rush changed the world's supply of gold so drastically that silver quickly became devalued as a currency and the gold standard became the norm of industrialized countries into the twentieth century. As can be surmised by the history of this period, the Gold Rush inaugurated a large-scale exploitation of the natural environment in America. As forests were devastated, rivers polluted, and mountains leveled, Americans were slow to realize that they were ravaging a nonrenewable resource. This realization did not come until the last part of the following century. Contemporary historians believe that the Gold Rush was important primarily because of its consequences for families and social values. The tens of thousands of Anglo Americans who left their families in the east created broken homes and, for many, broken lives when their husbands did not return or came back broken and impoverished. In California the Gold Rush had a mixed effect on morality. For some it reinforced values of hard work, democracy, and community. For others it created a "get rich quick" mentality of speculation, lawlessness, and isolation. For the Indians, the Mexicans, and the Chinese, the Gold Rush created an inhospitable society that had to be negotiated with great care.

Ultimately the U.S.-Mexican War and the California Gold Rush were watershed events, not only in the development of the West but in the history of the United States more generally. Coming together, they shaped the future of the nation and created new directions for California. New economic forces and the blending of cultures and peoples begun in these years provided the dynamic energies that would have a worldwide influence.

Suggested Readings

- Griswold del Castillo, Richard, "Joaquín Murrieta: Life and Legend," in *With Badges and Bullets: Lawmen and Outlaws in the Old West,* Richard Etulain and Glenda Riley, eds. (Golden, CO: Fulcrum Press, 1999), pp. 106–123. A review of the many conflicting sources of the Murrieta story along with the legend's contemporary meanings.

- Griswold del Castillo, Richard, *The Treaty of Guadalupe Hidalgo: A Legacy of Conflict* (Norman, OK: University of Oklahoma Press, 1990). The best single-volume study of the political and international importance of the treaty that ended the war with Mexico.

- Harlow, Neal, *California Conquered: War and Peace on the Pacific, 1846–1850* (Berkeley, Los Angeles, and London: University of California Press, 1982). The best single source for studying the U.S.-Mexican War in California.

- Johnson, Susan Lee, *Roaring Camp: The Social World of the California Gold Rush* (New York: W. W. Norton, 2000). An excellent source for understanding the lives of women during the Gold Rush.

- Robinson, Alfred, *Life in California During a Residence of Several Years in That Territory* (New York: Da Capo Press, 1969). A firsthand account of Californio life before the conquest, written by a sympathetic participant.

- Rohrbough, Malcolm I., *Days of Gold: The California Gold Rush and the American Nation* (Berkeley, Los Angeles, and London: University of California Press, 1997). A very thorough study of the social and cultural effect of the Gold Rush on the Anglo American migrants.

- Sanchez, Rosaura, *Telling Identities: The Californio Testimonios* (Minneapolis: University of Minnesota Press, 1995). An analysis of the oral histories of the Californios gathered by Hubert Howe Bancroft in the nineteenth century.

- Starr, Kevin, *Americans and the California Dream, 1850–1915* (New York and Oxford: Oxford University Press, 1973). A sweeping cultural history of this important era written by the official state historian.

5

California and the Crisis of the Union, 1850–1870

Main Topics

▌ Crisis and Conflict in the 1850s

▌ Californians and the Crisis of the Union

▌ Economic Growth in a Time of National Crisis

▌ New Social and Cultural Patterns

▌ Summary

In 1857, Charles Stovall arrived in California from Mississippi. Archy Lee, a slave who belonged to Stovall's father, was with him. Upon arriving in Sacramento, Stovall followed the Southern practice of hiring out Lee to work for others, and he took a job himself. California's state constitution prohibited slavery, however, and by 1857 Californians who opposed slavery, black and white alike, had become practiced in freeing slaves in their state. When Stovall learned of this, he tried to send Lee back to Mississippi, but Lee asserted his freedom and hid in a hotel run by an African American family. Stovall then had him arrested as a fugitive slave. Several white abolitionist lawyers defended Lee. When the judge ordered Lee released, Stovall had him rearrested on a new warrant, issued by David Terry, a state supreme court justice known to support slavery. In an astounding decision, the California Supreme Court ruled that, because Stovall had been ignorant of the law regarding slavery in California, he should not be penalized by the loss of his

CHAPTER 5	California and the Crisis of the Union, 1850–1870
1848	Discovery of gold
1850	California becomes a state
1851	Vigilantes take control in San Francisco
1852–56	Adjudication of claims to land granted by Spain or Mexico
1856	Vigilantes again take control in San Francisco
1859	Senator David Broderick killed in a duel
1861–65	Civil War
1862	Pacific Railroad Act
1869	Joining of Central Pacific and Union Pacific tracks at Promontory Summit, Utah

This woodcut is from the cover of a book about Archy Lee, by Rudolph Lapp, published in 1969. There is, apparently, no photograph of Archy Lee. Why do you think that is?

father's slave. The court ordered Lee to return to Mississippi with Stovall.

When the two arrived in San Francisco en route to Mississippi, black and white abolitionists were prepared. They had Lee arrested to keep him in the state, and they accused Stovall of holding a slave illegally. San Francisco's small African American community sought funds throughout the state, alerting opponents of slavery to the case. Some of the most prominent Republican lawyers in the state, led by Edward D. Baker, represented Lee in his third court hearing. They pointed out the absurdities in the supreme court's ruling and secured a new ruling that Lee was a free man. Stovall, too, was prepared, however, and a federal marshal arrested Lee for violating the Fugitive Slave Law of 1850. Lee went to trial a fourth time, now before a federal commissioner who had come from the South and was presumably proslavery. Crowds of whites and blacks argued over the case on the streets as sidewalk orators harangued the crowds. Lee's lawyers, led by Baker, argued that the 1850 law applied only to slaves who fled from a slave state into a free state, pointing out that Lee had been brought into California with his owner's permission, and concluding that no federal law had been violated. The commissioner agreed and set Lee free. Soon after, Lee moved to British Columbia, out of the jurisdiction of American law. The experience of Archy Lee dramatically indicates that California, separated by a continent from the center of the controversy over slavery, could not escape the political crisis that slavery engendered in the 1850s.

In 1850, however, the delegates who sat in Colton Hall writing a constitution for the new state of California probably had no idea that their request for statehood would contribute significantly to the emerging national crisis. Yet a crisis had long been approaching and was now hastened by the annexation of Texas and the territories acquired under the Treaty of Guadalupe Hidalgo. California's application for statehood compounded that crisis. Many sought to stem the conflict but failed, as the sectional crisis over the extension of slavery into federal territory grew to include the institution of slavery everywhere and eventually raised fundamental questions about the nature of the Union and the meaning of American citizenship. The crisis escalated to civil war, and the war brought the abolition of slavery, the redefinition of American citizenship, and the transformation of the federal Union. Though far removed geographically from the debates in Congress and the battlefields of war, California figured significantly in the crisis of the Union, and that crisis brought important changes to California. At the same time, the state was rapidly changing from a booming mining frontier to an economically and socially diverse society.

Questions to Consider

▌ How did national political issues affect the new state of California?

■ How did federal policy affect Californios and California Indians?

■ How did sectional issues, especially slavery, affect Californians in the 1850s?

■ What changes came to California as a result of the Civil War?

■ How did the state's economy change in the 1850s and 1860s?

■ What role did the federal government play in the development of improved transportation between California and the eastern United States?

■ What was the relation between socially defined gender roles and the creation of new social institutions in the 1850s and 1860s?

■ Why did California acquire a reputation for religious toleration?

■ How did Californians influence national literary development?

Crisis and Conflict in the 1850s

The new state was born in the midst of crisis and conflict—a national political crisis over slavery, a local crisis of political legitimacy, and conflicts within the state over land, labor, race, and ethnicity.

The Compromise of 1850

Some Americans who opposed the extension of slavery saw the annexation of Texas (1845), the war with Mexico (1846–48), and the acquisition of vast new territory under the Treaty of Guadalupe Hidalgo (1848) as part of a slaveholders' conspiracy to expand slavery. From the Missouri Compromise (1820) onward, new states had entered the Union in pairs—one state that banned slavery along with one state that permitted it—so that the numbers of slave states and free states remained equal. Similarly, from the Missouri Compromise onward, slavery had been banned from all of the Louisiana Purchase territory north of 36°30' north latitude (the southern boundary of Missouri). This seemed to cut off any expansion of slavery because nearly all remaining unorganized territory lay north of 36°30'. Opponents of slavery feared that annexation of Texas and the acquisition of territories from Mexico might open new regions to slavery. When Californians requested entry into the Union as a free state, there was no prospect of a slave state being admitted to maintain the balance between free states and slave states in the Senate. Defenders of slavery took alarm, and some prepared to fight against California statehood.

Once the constitutional convention (see Chapter 4) completed its work, California voters approved the new constitution and elected state officials. The legislature met and, amidst other business, elected John C. Frémont and William Gwin to the United States Senate (senators were elected by state legislatures at that time). Frémont and Gwin, along with newly elected members of the House of Representatives, hurried to Washington to press for statehood and to take their congressional seats once that occurred. They found a raging controversy centered in the Senate. Some of the most powerful political leaders of the first half of the century participated in the debate, including Henry Clay, Daniel Webster, and John C. Calhoun.

In the end, a relative newcomer to Congress, Stephen A. Douglas of Illinois, cobbled together a complex compromise based on Clay's proposals. In addition to California statehood, the Compromise of 1850 included separate laws that changed the western boundary of Texas, created territorial governments for New Mexico and Utah, pledged federal authority to return escaped slaves from the North, and abolished the slave trade in the District of Columbia. Most Southerners opposed California statehood, abolition of the slave trade in the District of Columbia, and the change in the Texas boundary. Most northerners voted against the Fugitive Slave Law and territorial status for Utah. All the bills passed, but only because several moderates, led by Douglas, joined sometimes the Northerners and sometimes the southerners to create a majority. California became the thirty-first state, but the Compromise of 1850 failed to ease sectional tensions.

San Francisco's Crisis of Political Legitimacy: Vigilantism in the 1850s

During the 1850s, California experienced a crisis of its own, a crisis of political legitimacy. Political legitimacy in a republic means that a very large majority of the population agrees that the properly elected and appointed governmental officials should exercise the authority specified for them by law. Paying taxes, obeying laws, participating in elections, and accepting a judge's decision are all ways in which individuals denote their acceptance of the political legitimacy of their government. During the 1850s, however, the United States faced a crisis of political legitimacy as abolitionists denied the legitimacy of laws protecting slavery, and defenders of slavery denied that the government had the authority to ban or limit slavery. California in the 1850s also faced a crisis of political legitimacy, as many Californians denied the authority of governmental officials and instead took the law into their own hands. This happened in the gold-mining regions when vigilantes acted as judge, jury, and executioner. But remote mining camps were not the only places where Californians spurned law enforcement officials and turned to vigilantism. San Francisco, the largest American city west of St. Louis, also experienced vigilante versions of justice.

From the raising of the American flag in July 1846 until the first legislature after statehood, San Francisco functioned largely under its Mexican governmental

EXECUTION OF
JAMES P. CASEY & CHARLES CORA,
.... BY THE ....
Vigilance Committee of San Francisco, on Thursday, May 22nd, 1856, from the windows of their Rooms, in
SACRAMENTO STREET, BETWEEN FRONT AND DAVIS.

The execution of James Casey and Charles Cora by the San Francisco Committee of Vigilance, 1856. Notice how the artist has depicted the members of the committee arranged in military order, armed with muskets with fixed bayonets. Why did the vigilantes execute Casey and Cora? Why did they surround themselves with an armed guard when they did so?

structures. The alcalde (mayor) possessed wide powers, both judicial and administrative. Nonetheless, many San Franciscans felt that the city's rapid growth had not been accompanied by corresponding growth in the protection of life and property. In 1849, Sam Brannan and several other businessmen formed a citizens' group to suppress ruffians, who were known as "Hounds." The citizens' group—more than two hundred strong—sought out and held some of the Hounds for trial before a special tribunal consisting of the alcalde and two special judges. This tribunal convicted nine men and, because there was no jail, banished them. This procedure did not circumvent the established authorities—the alcalde was centrally involved—but it was a step toward vigilantism as businessmen took the lead in apprehending those they considered the most flagrant wrongdoers.

The first session of the state legislature created a city government for San Francisco, and the city acquired a full range of public officials to enforce the law and dispense justice. However, a series of robberies, burglaries, and incidents of arson increased San Franciscans' anxiety over the city's growing number of

Australians, most of whom were stereotyped as former convicts. A group of merchants and ship captains, led by Sam Brannan, formed the Committee of Vigilance. Almost immediately, they were presented with an accused burglar—an Australian, purportedly a former convict. Committee members constituted themselves as an impromptu court, convicted the accused man, and—despite rescue efforts by public officials—hanged him. Then, claiming support from five hundred leading merchants and businessmen, the Committee of Vigilance seized more accused criminals, turned some of them over to the legally constituted authorities, banished others, whipped one, and hanged three more, all Australians. The vigilantes could not imprison their victims because the jail was controlled by the legally constituted authorities, whom the vigilantes were ignoring or openly flaunting. The committee functioned from June to September, although it drew opposition from most lawyers, public officials, and political figures.

The fullest development of vigilantism came in 1856, when a gambler named Charles Cora killed William Richardson, a U.S. marshal. Soon after, James Casey, a member of the board of supervisors, shot and killed a popular newspaper editor, who had revealed that Casey had a criminal record in New York and had also announced in his newspaper that he always went about well armed—he seemed almost to be issuing a challenge. Casey claimed self-defense. The Committee of Vigilance was revived with William T. Coleman, a leading merchant, as its president. After hanging Cora and Casey, the committee constituted itself as the civil authority in the city and established a force of nearly six thousand well-armed men, drawn mostly from the city's merchants and businessmen. They hanged two more men, banished about twenty, and disarmed the state militia when it was ordered to restore local officials to power. The 1856 committee provoked a well-organized opposition that included the mayor, the sheriff, the head of the state militia (William T. Sherman), the chief justice of the state (David Terry), and other prominent political figures, most of them Democrats. The governor, thirty-year-old J. Neely Johnson, tried to reestablish the power of law, but the vigilantes simply ignored him. They eventually established a political party and yielded power only after elections in which their candidates won convincing victories. This party and its successors (under various names and with shifting patterns of organization) dominated city politics for most of the next twenty years, institutionalizing government by merchants and businessmen.

California's experience with lynching and vigilantism in the 1850s came at a violent time in the nation's history. Many male Californians routinely armed themselves when in public. An observer noted that more than half the members of the first session of the legislature, in 1850, "appeared in the legislative halls with revolvers and bowie knives fastened to their belts." Chief Justice Terry carried both a gun and a bowie knife. San Francisco experienced sixteen murders in 1850 and fifteen in 1851, not counting the four men hanged by the vigilantes—a murder rate of between fifty and sixty per one hundred thousand inhabitants. (There is little comparative data from other American cities for the 1850s: Boston had seven *arrests* for murder per one hundred thousand inhabitants in the late 1850s, and Philadelphia averaged four *indictments* for murder per one hundred thousand inhabitants in the mid-1850s. San Francisco's homicide rate was less than eight per one hundred thousand between 1997 and 2001.)

The violence of the era provides a necessary context for understanding the lynchings and vigilantism. Even so, the question remains: Are the vigilantes best understood as outraged citizens taking matters into their own hands and cleansing their community, or as an organized effort to overthrow the legally constituted authorities? Josiah Royce, an early historian writing in 1886, called the events of 1856 "a businessmen's revolution"—that is, he considered it an illegal action in defiance of the law. Nearly all subsequent historians have agreed that action outside the law was unnecessary and that the businessmen who made up the Committee of Vigilance scarcely pursued—much less exhausted—legal courses of action. They were too preoccupied with business to bother with politics, and then, when they took action, they took a shortcut. Nonetheless, in the late nineteenth and early twentieth centuries most popular accounts of the vigilantes glorified them, treating them as saviors of the city. And, from 1856 until at least the 1930s, in times of community crisis, there were usually some who invoked the spirit of the vigilantes and urged extralegal action to deal with the situation.

Violence and Displacement: California Indians in the 1850s

For most California Indians, the 1850s and 1860s were years of stark tragedy. Of the estimated 150,000 Native Americans in California in 1848, only 31,000 remained by 1860, after twelve years of the Gold Rush and a decade of statehood. Even so, the censuses of 1860 and 1870 showed California with the largest Indian population of any state.

Long before the Gold Rush, California Indians had become the major part of the work force on the ranchos along the coast between San Francisco and San Diego and inland from San Francisco Bay. Many of them continued some traditional ways, including gathering acorns for food, dancing, and the sweat lodge. At the same time, they adopted practices from their Mexican employers and priests. Some (nearly all women) intermarried with Mexicans, many of whom were themselves *mestizos*—of mixed Spanish, Indian, or African ancestry. Many other Native Americans were familiar with European practices, traded with the ranchos, and occasionally worked for wages. Sometimes they traded with the Californios; other times they raided the Californios, stealing cattle and horses.

John Sutter's settlement near the present site of Sacramento was built largely by Indians hired as laborers. Sutter also maintained a hired Indian army to protect his land and livestock and to wage war on Indian raiders. Other whites who entered the Central Valley in the early 1840s emulated Sutter, and sometimes contracted with Sutter for Indian labor. Thus, on the eve of the American conquest, many whites looked to California Indians as an important source of paid labor. This expectation was a direct outgrowth of the Spanish and Mexican approaches to converting and "civilizing" the Indians and turning them into laborers on the missions and ranchos. By contrast, in the eastern United States, the usual practice in new white settlements was to push Indians further west rather than integrate them into new settlements.

In the earliest stages of the Gold Rush, Mexican patterns prevailed, as Indians were hired to work in mining operations. They learned the value of gold and of their labor and expected to be paid accordingly. However, a flood of Americans who knew the eastern practices but not the Mexican ones soon descended on California, expecting that part of their task in "subduing the wilderness" would be to expel the Indians. Some of the newcomers objected to competing with Indian labor, especially when the Indian laborers worked for Californios. Others, with no real evidence, viewed Indians as dangerous and sought to have them removed from the mining regions because they were considered a threat to white miners.

At the same time, many Native Americans suffered from severely reduced access to traditional food sources. Cattle ate the grass that formerly had produced seeds for food. Large-scale hunting to feed hungry miners decimated the deer and elk herds. Thus, Indians were increasingly barred from wage labor in the mines at the same time that they were deprived of many traditional foods.

Violence soon flared. In a continuation of patterns from Mexican California, some Indians raided white settlements and stole food, cattle, and horses. Others forcibly resisted when white men made advances toward Indian women. Thefts by Indians often brought the burning of the village thought to be responsible. If an Indian killed a white, local militias or volunteers often destroyed the nearest village and killed its adult males and sometimes the women and children too. Undisciplined volunteers often struck out at any Indians they found, whether or not they had any connection to a crime. Some local authorities in the 1850s even offered bounties ranging from fifty cents to five dollars for Indian scalps.

The killing of individual Indians and even the massacre of entire villages were repeated over and over, sometimes by groups of miners, sometimes by local or state authorities. More than one historian has suggested that *genocide* is the only appropriate term for the experience of California Indians during the 1850s and 1860s. Only rarely did anyone seek to punish white men for beating or killing Indians. On the contrary, state power was more often used against the Indians. In 1851, Governor Peter Burnett announced his view that it was inevitable that war be waged against the Indians until they became extinct, and he twice sent state troops against them. His successor, Governor John McDougal, authorized the use of state troops in 1851 in what was called the Mariposa War. In these instances, state troops engaged in the brutal killing of Indians and destruction of Indian villages. When local authorities presented the state with bills for their forays against Indians, the state routinely paid them.

Both the state and federal governments attempted to regulate relations between California Indians and whites. The previous practice of federal authorities, who had exclusive constitutional authority to deal with Indian tribes, had been to negotiate treaties by which Indians yielded their traditional lands in return for other lands, almost always to the west of white settlements. In California, however, it was no longer possible to move Indians west. In California in the 1850s, federal authorities found themselves negotiating with Indians to surrender title to large parts of their lands in return for promises that they could retain small tracts, or reservations. Federal policymakers envisioned the reservations as places where Indian people could be concentrated, protected from the dangers of the surrounding white society, taught to farm, and educated. This new approach owed a good deal to the violence visited upon the California Indians in the Gold Rush regions.

In 1851 federal commissioners began to negotiate with representatives of Indian groups. They eventually drafted eighteen treaties that set aside twelve thousand square miles of land in the Central Valley and the northwestern and southern parts of the state. When the treaties went to the Senate for approval, they were rejected, the chief opposition coming from Californians. New federal agents were then appointed, and the process started over. In the mid-1850s, a few small reservations were finally created, some embracing only a few square miles. Some Indians from the Central Valley were moved north, to live on the new reservations in northern California. Most did not go to the reservations, but continued instead to live in the midst of white settlements, working for wages on ranches and farms and following some traditional practices. A few moved into the mountains, avoiding white settlements as much as possible.

As federal authorities stumbled toward creating reservations within California, state officials also asserted their authority over California Indian peoples. In 1850 the first session of the state legislature approved the Act for the Government and Protection of the Indians. The law permitted Indians to remain in the "homes and villages" that they had long occupied. The law also provided for the indenturing of Indian children, either with consent of their parents or if they were orphans. This law led to the virtual enslavement of many Indian children until age eighteen for boys and fifteen for girls. Adult Indians not employed were subject to arrest for vagrancy and could be hired out by the courts once arrested. Burning of grasslands (see Chapter 1) was made a crime. Penalties were established for anyone who compelled an Indian to work without wages, but Indians were prohibited (under a different law) from offering testimony in court against whites, so violations were difficult to establish. The historian Albert Hurtado concludes that "the 1850 Act for the Government and Protection of the Indians protected them very little and governed them quite a lot."

The Politics of Land and Culture

When the news of gold first became known, Californios were among the first to rush to the gold country. Thousands of immigrants from Mexico, especially Sonora, and others from throughout Latin America, especially Chile, soon joined them. Whether citizens or immigrants, Spanish-speaking miners found themselves derided as "greasers," harassed, assaulted, and sometimes lynched.

Eventually violence and harassment, along with the Foreign Miner's Tax of 1850 (see Chapter 4), drove many Latinos from the gold country. Some of the immigrants returned to their homes, but others took up permanent residence in the existing pueblos, especially San José, Santa Barbara, and Los Angeles.

The Gold Rush, however, was good for some rancheros, who prospered because of the increased demand for cattle to provide food to the massive influx of gold seekers. Cattle prices tripled between 1849 and 1851, and fifty thousand head of cattle from southern California were sent north for slaughter. Los Angeles, still with a Mexican majority, boomed not just from cattle sales but also as a center for the sale and distribution northward of horses and mules brought from northern Mexico to meet the demand for draft animals in the mining regions.

Nearly all Californio landowners struggled to retain their land. Though the Treaty of Guadalupe Hidalgo guaranteed existing landownership, those who poured into California from the eastern United States brought significantly different expectations regarding landownership. In the eastern states, land was carefully surveyed, and each plot was precisely located. There, pioneers sometimes selected a parcel of undeveloped land, built a home on it (called preemption or "squatting"), farmed the land, and then bought the land from the government for $1.25 per acre once the land was surveyed. The intent of federal land policies, though not always the reality, was to encourage family farms and to discourage land speculators. Given widespread expectations of small family farms, land that was apparently not lived on or actively farmed was often considered available for squatting.

In Mexican California, land grants were large and vaguely defined, often based on natural markers (streams or boulders, for example) rather than precise survey lines. For the largest California ranchos, much of the land seemed unused, at least by the standards of the eastern United States. Even before the United States acquired California, some Americans had squatted on land. After the war, many more did the same. Some did so on the assumption that the system they had experienced in the East would be instituted in California. Some did so on the assumption that, having won the war, they could claim what they desired. Some did it with full knowledge that Californios already owned the land.

One of the most important tasks in the transfer of government authority was to verify and record land titles (the official record of landownership). Earlier experiences in Louisiana and Florida suggested that the process invited manipulation, fraud, and litigation. When Frémont and Gwin took their seats in the U.S. Senate in 1850, they immediately proposed federal legislation to clarify land titles. The resulting law, called the Gwin Act (1851), created a board of three commissioners, appointed by the president. Those claiming land presented their evidence of ownership to the commissioners. If others claimed the same land, they too introduced evidence. If the commissioners accepted the evidence of ownership, the title was considered valid. If the commissioners rejected the evidence, the land came under the ownership of the federal government. A federal agent participated in the hearings to challenge dubious evidence. Either the person claiming the land or the federal agent could appeal a decision, first to the federal district court and then to the U.S. Supreme Court. Of several proposals that went before Congress for clarifying land titles, the Gwin Act was probably the most cumbersome, time-consuming, and potentially costly for holders of Spanish and Mexican land titles.

The commissioners began work early in 1852 and continued until 1856, hearing more than eight hundred claims. Some were unquestionably fraudulent. Of the total, more than six hundred were confirmed. Of those confirmed, nearly all were appealed through the courts, and the court proceedings dragged on interminably. Success often came with a high price: travel to San Francisco to present arguments and documents, more travel to court hearings, and attorneys' fees at every step of the way. One historian estimated that the average land-grant holder spent seventeen years before securing final title to the land. Another historian estimated that attorneys' fees involved in defending the Mexican land grants constituted twenty-five to forty percent of the value of the land.

During the hearings, squatters often moved onto the most attractive lands, especially in northern California, and sometimes even barred rancheros from their own homes. The squatters formed a large and influential political group and found many public officials receptive to their pleas. Some rancheros, in desperation, sold their claims for whatever they could receive—but such sales could not be final until after the final court decision on the title. Unscrupulous lawyers sometimes secured powers of attorney from rancheros, then used those powers to saddle their clients with impossible debts, requiring land sales to pay off the mortgages. All in all, most historians who have studied the implementation of the Gwin Act have endorsed the judgment of Henry George, a San Francisco journalist who, in 1871, called it a "history of greed, of perjury, of corruption, of spoliation and high-handed robbery."

If the northern rancheros found themselves flooded with squatters and lawyers, southern rancheros faced devastating tax burdens. South of the Tehachapi mountains, Californios remained in the majority. There, they won elections as local officials and members of the state legislature. One Californio, Pablo de la Guerra, was elected president of the state senate in 1861 and was first in line to succeed the governor.

At the constitutional convention, Californio delegates from the south had raised the possibility of dividing California into a northern section, which would become a state, and a southern section, which would become a territory. Though defeated in the convention, the idea of dividing the state persisted. The 1850 session of the legislature created a tax system based on land and other possessions, including cattle, but not wealth, which included gold. These taxes fell disproportionately on the ranchos of southern California, which provided southerners both a continuing reminder that they were dominated politically by the northern part of the state and a continuing incentive for separation. Though southern Californians' motivation for dividing the state stemmed largely from their desire to separate themselves from the newcomers to the north and regain control over their taxes, the issue was often presented differently in the eastern states, where abolitionists and slaveholders saw it as a way to create a new slave state.

Throughout the 1850s, the state legislature received proposals to divide the state. In 1859, the legislature approved a popular vote in the southern counties on the issue of division. The vote was two to one in favor of division, and the results were forwarded to the federal government for action, but nothing was done in Congress in 1860. The next year found the nation preoccupied with civil war. This effectively ended the possibility for creating a separate state or territory in which Californios and other Latinos might be numerically dominant. And, within a short time, English-speaking Americans soon outnumbered those who spoke Spanish in southern California as well as in the north, and political power slowly passed from the hands of the Californios.

The effort to create a separate state or territory in southern California marked one effort by Spanish-speaking Californians to retain their culture and their political autonomy. Political efforts to secure bilingual schools in Los Angeles (unsuccessful), to insist on implementation of the constitutional provision requiring Spanish translations of official documents (a losing struggle), and to serve on local political bodies represented other efforts. Such efforts came largely from the Californio elite—members of the old, landowning families. Most of them, at least in the south, were accorded a level of respect and even honor by their new, English-speaking neighbors. Some historians have suggested that, in fact, many of them were co-opted into the emerging English-speaking power structure and that, despite their efforts to secure recognition for their language and culture, they made little serious effort to protect the large numbers of landless Mexican laborers and farm workers from economic exploitation.

Californians and the Crisis of the Union

As Californians struggled with issues of land, labor, and ethnicity, national politics moved rapidly toward the ultimate crisis of secession and civil war. Though far removed from Washington, California was never immune from the sectional conflict.

Fighting Slavery in California

Throughout the decade of the 1850s, slaveholders brought enslaved African Americans to live in California—some three hundred in 1852, by one estimate. Some mined gold and others worked as domestic servants. At the same time, the Gold Rush attracted significant numbers of free African Americans, some of whom joined the rush for riches in the hope of gaining enough gold to purchase freedom for their families. By 1860, more than four thousand African Americans lived in California—the largest black population of any western state or territory other than Texas and Indian Territory (now Oklahoma). Just as Southern whites brought their proslavery attitudes, and sometimes their slaves, to California, Northern abolitionists, white and black alike, brought their hatred of slavery.

When slaveholders brought their slaves into California and continued to hold them in slavery, they seldom attracted attention from state or local officials despite the state constitution's prohibition of slavery. Some officials had proslavery attitudes or may have been willing to tolerate slavery. The initiative often fell, instead, to individuals outside government to enforce the state's ban on slavery. As the state's free African American community grew and prospered, its members took the lead in identifying slaves, urging them to claim their freedom, and organizing assistance for them. A German immigrant wrote that "the wealthy California Negroes . . . exhibit a great deal of energy and intelligence in saving their brothers." They could usually count on white abolitionists for financial assistance, political pressure, and legal representation in the courts.

One such court case arose in the Mormon settlement of San Bernardino, in southern California. Robert Smith was a Mormon from Mississippi who brought several slaves first to Utah and then, in 1852, to California. Bridget "Biddy" Mason, one of the slaves, made friends with a free black family in Los Angeles. In 1855, as Smith was preparing to move to Texas, free African Americans persuaded the Los Angeles county sheriff to take Mason and the other slaves into protective custody. Mason then sought freedom through the Los Angeles District Court and succeeded, not just for herself, but for thirteen others as well.

The developing African American community and their white abolitionist allies in California could claim some notable victories through court cases such as those that freed Biddy Mason and Archy Lee (see pp. 124–126). Other times they failed, either because they could not mobilize in time or because they could not persuade a judge. Black Californians had other struggles as well. Though some white Californians strongly opposed slavery and discrimination against free African Americans, the California legislature during the 1850s passed laws that discriminated against African Americans in ways similar to the states of the Midwest and Middle Atlantic regions. Black Californians were prohibited from voting, serving on juries, marrying whites, or testifying in state courts. The prohibition against testifying in court was especially troublesome, as it restricted the ability of African Americans to defend themselves in court in the event of challenges to their property or savings. In 1852, the state legislature passed the California Fugitive Slave Law, designed to assist slave owners in capturing slaves who fled within California, and the law remained in force until 1855.

To organize themselves against such measures and to demonstrate their opposition, black Californians drew upon eastern precedents to hold several statewide conventions, beginning in 1855. Meeting in Sacramento in 1855 and 1856 and in San Francisco in 1857, they demonstrated their continuing connection with events in the East as well as their determination to secure the repeal of discriminatory legislation in California. One convention led to the establishment of the state's first black newspaper. All three conventions called upon white Californians to recognize the contributions of African Americans to the state's economy and its tax rolls and to repeal discriminatory laws. Discouraged by their lack of success, some four hundred black Californians (including Archy Lee) moved to British Columbia in 1858.

Sectional Issues and California Politics

The prospect of a new state, with many elective offices, attracted politically ambitious men who arrived in California with strong political commitments and partisan loyalties. William Gwin, for example, was a slaveholder and a Democrat, from a prosperous and prominent family. He had served one term in the House of Representatives from Mississippi. Stymied in his hope for a U.S. Senate seat, he headed to California. Like Gwin, David Broderick (a Roman Catholic) came to California to pursue a political career when he found his political prospects blocked in New York. Largely self-educated, the son of an Irish immigrant stonecutter, Broderick had entered Democratic Party politics in New York City and aligned himself with the faction that spoke for workers and opposed big business. Gwin arrived in California in time to win election to the constitutional convention, after which he won election to the U.S. Senate. Broderick came to California a bit later, jumped into Democratic Party politics, and won election to the state senate, although his ambition, too, was to sit in the U.S. Senate. Both Broderick and Gwin were Democrats, but the conflict between them came eventually to mirror the nation's conflict over slavery.

This formally posed photograph of David Broderick was probably taken after he had become a member of the United States Senate. How does Broderick's political career in California reflect larger political patterns in the nation?

Within the California Democratic Party, Gwin led a faction called the Chivalry Democrats, many of whom came from the South or border states. Tall, with a shock of gray hair, Gwin moved easily through the corridors of power. Though a slaveholder, he voted in the constitutional convention to ban slavery from California. In the U.S. Senate, he did not criticize slavery and usually voted with the Southern Democrats. As senior senator and close to the administration, Gwin controlled most federal patronage (appointments to federal jobs) in California, and he steered bills through Congress that established important federal agencies in the Bay Area, including the mint and the customshouse. (The customshouse was one of the most important federal agencies in any port city, providing many federal jobs.) Through organization and patronage, Gwin and his Chivalry Democrats dominated the Democratic Party in much of California.

In San Francisco, however, Broderick built a strong Democratic organization using techniques learned in New York City, and he soon dominated the state legislature through his influence over the San Francisco members. As a political leader, he consistently defended the laborers from whom he had sprung and whose votes kept him in office. He opposed the Fugitive Slave Law and defended the rights of free African Americans, becoming an outspoken opponent of slavery.

Just as in California, the sectional conflict over slavery disrupted politics nationwide during the 1850s. When congressional Democrats, led by Stephen Douglas, passed the Kansas-Nebraska Act in 1854, they changed longstanding rules about slavery in the territories. One result was the emergence of a new political party, the Republicans, who opposed any extension of slavery into the territories. The Whig party fragmented over slavery and soon disappeared.

In the mid-1850s, some voters, at least temporarily, chose another new political party, the American Party, which grew out of a secret anti-immigrant society. The American Party appealed to American nationalism and republican ideals and opposed immigrants in general and Catholics in particular. Their opponents called them Know-Nothings because, when asked about the organization, they were supposed to say that they knew nothing about it. In southern California, Californios called them *Ignorantes*. They swept elections in a number of eastern states in 1854 and 1855. In California, divisions within the state Democratic Party led some southern, Protestant Democrats to support the Americans in 1855, and they probably got the votes of many former Whigs as well. They elected the governor and many members of the legislature. However, anti-Catholicism did not play as large a role in the Know-Nothings' victory in California as it did in eastern states, and their ascendancy proved short-lived.

The other new political party of the mid-1850s was the Republican Party. Many of the most outspoken Republicans were abolitionists, who sought to eliminate slavery everywhere. In 1856, the new party chose John C. Frémont, California's first U.S. senator, as its first presidential candidate. But Frémont did not do well in California—he placed third, after both James Buchanan, the Democratic candidate, and former president Millard Fillmore, candidate of the Know-Nothings. Gwin and Broderick had patched over their differences to support the Democratic candidate, James Buchanan, and to regain a Democratic majority in the state legislature. The Republicans did little better in California elections over the next few years.

Gwin and Broderick forged a temporary alliance again in 1857, when Broderick used his control over the state legislature to win election to the U.S. Senate. Promising to relinquish federal patronage to Broderick, Gwin secured Broderick's backing for his own reelection to the Senate. Soon after, however, Gwin and Broderick staked out strongly opposed views over admitting Kansas to the Union as a slave state. Proslavery and antislavery forces had poured into the new territory of Kansas, and they fought with words and with guns to secure the majority there. When proslavery forces met at the town of Lecompton and drafted a slave-state constitution, the Buchanan administration tried to force it through Congress. Gwin led the pro-Lecompton forces in the Senate. Broderick joined Stephen Douglas and a few other Northern Democrats who broke with their party and president and joined the Republicans to defeat the proposal. The bitter dispute between Gwin and Broderick carried over into the California state election of 1859. In communities all around the state, California Democrats divided into two camps. The Broderick faction, calling themselves Douglas Democrats, cooperated with the new Republican Party, but the Gwin faction won most of the state elections.

Shortly after the election, David Terry, a former Texan and former justice of the state supreme court, and a leading member of the Gwin faction, challenged Broderick to a duel, charging that Broderick had insulted him during the campaign. Though illegal in California, dueling was still practiced. Broderick's gun discharged prematurely, permitting Terry to take careful aim and shoot Broderick in the chest. Broderick's death made him a martyr to the antislavery cause, as his supporters widely quoted his supposed dying words: "They have killed me because I was opposed to slavery and a corrupt administration."

Within a year, the national Democratic Party divided into Northern and Southern wings, each of which ran its own candidate in the 1860 presidential election. Gwin supported John Breckinridge, candidate of the Southern Democrats. California's voters, however, chose Abraham Lincoln, the Republican candidate, as did most of the Northern states. Lincoln's election prompted Southerners to secede from a union that they now rightly understood to be in the hands of the enemies of slavery. Gwin and a few other Democrats urged that the South be permitted to leave in peace, but Lincoln and his party considered the Union to be indissoluble. The nation plunged into four years of bloody civil war.

California and Civil War

Far removed from the arena of conflict, Californians nonetheless played a significant role in the conflict. Though the large majority of Californians were loyal to the Union, there were exceptions. David Terry became an officer in the

Confederate army. Though Gwin hoped that the South might be allowed to leave in peace, he did not take up arms against the Union.

When the Union called for volunteers in California, Californians formed eight regiments of infantry, a regiment of cavalry, a battalion of mountaineers, and a battalion of cavalry commanded by Californios and made up of Californios, Mexicans, and other Latinos. The commanders of the Union army ordered these forces to defend the mail and transportation routes between California and the North. When the Confederate army sent troops into New Mexico Territory, the California Volunteers were sent to block its advance. The Californians drove the Confederate troops back into Texas, then spent the remainder of the war in campaigns against the Navajos, Apaches, and other Indian peoples of the Southwest, gaining a reputation as ruthless, even vicious, in their tactics.

In addition to the activities of the California Volunteers, some Californians fought with the Union army in other units. Henry Halleck, a West Point graduate and prominent San Francisco lawyer, led all Union armies from mid-1862 to early 1864, but failed to make much progress against the Confederate forces. William Tecumseh Sherman, another West Point graduate, was more successful. He had passed through California in 1847 while serving in the war with Mexico and returned as a civilian in 1853 and opened a bank. He was appointed major general of the California militia in 1856, shortly before the vigilantes hanged Cora and Casey. Opposed to the vigilantes but unable to use the militia to restore the lawful authorities, he resigned his commission. Sherman left California in 1858. By the end of the Civil War, he stood second among Union generals only to Ulysses S. Grant in his contributions to the Union victory.

Most Californians contributed to the Union in other ways than by bearing arms. Thomas Starr King, pastor of the San Francisco Unitarian Church, undertook grueling speaking campaigns around the state to promote the Union cause. Spurred in part by King's oratory, Californians made their most impressive contribution to the Union in gold, especially as donations for the Sanitary Commission, a voluntary organization formed to channel humanitarian assistance to the Union troops. Medical supplies and personnel were in short supply, and the Sanitary Commission raised funds to care for wounded soldiers. Though only two percent of the Union's population, Californians donated more than a quarter of all funds raised by the Sanitary Commission. California's contributions, furthermore, were in gold, which had greater purchasing power than the depreciated greenbacks that the Lincoln administration was issuing to help cover the cost of the war.

With the Republican victory in the 1860 Republican election, a new group of political leaders emerged in California. Prominent among them was Leland Stanford, a Sacramento merchant who had been the Republicans' unsuccessful candidate for governor in 1859 and who won the governorship in 1861. In California, as elsewhere, Republicans transformed themselves into the Union Party and invited other supporters of the Union to join them. In the 1864 presidential election, Lincoln and his Union Party ticket easily carried California.

Reconstruction and New Understandings of Citizenship

During the war and afterward, events far away in Washington brought important changes in the legal status of African Americans and, ultimately, Asian Americans and others. At the end of the Civil War, the victorious Republicans pushed through three amendments to the U.S. Constitution as a way of making permanent the momentous changes they had created. The Thirteenth Amendment (1865) abolished slavery. The Fourteenth Amendment (1868) defined federal citizenship and the rights of American citizens. The Fifteenth Amendment (1870) specified that the right to vote could not be denied based on race.

The Fourteenth and Fifteenth Amendments meant, immediately, that African Americans could no longer be denied voting rights in California. Even before the Fourteenth Amendment, California Republicans in the state legislature had passed legislation that removed the limits on court testimony for African Americans. There were also some changes in the laws governing education in the late 1860s, requiring school districts to provide schooling for students of color and permitting, though not requiring, students of color to attend the same schools as white children. In 1872, given the language of the Fourteenth Amendment, the legislature repealed the law that prohibited Asians from testifying in court against whites. The Fourteenth Amendment was potentially far-reaching in its provisions and its implications. However, just as was true for the state constitution's prohibition of slavery, the amendment was given meaning only as individuals appealed to the federal courts for protection of "equal protection of the laws."

Economic Growth in a Time of National Crisis

As the hundreds of gold seekers in early 1848 became tens of thousands in 1849 and after, the vast majority hoped to make their fortunes by finding gold. Some, however, sought wealth by selling goods to the miners. Thus, the Gold Rush prompted the rapid development of other aspects of the new state's economy, from merchandising to agriculture to lumbering. Civil war in 1861 did little to slow the state's growth, and the new Republican Party quickly took action to subsidize a railroad to tie California to the Union.

The Transformation of Mining

The first miners found their gold by placer mining—panning or using sluices. The most easily available gold was soon gone, however. After the easy pickings of the early Gold Rush were gone, by 1852 or so, it was often Chinese miners who remained to mine the less productive diggings, rework tailings, and work for wages in the increasingly capital-intensive mining industry. By 1860, thirty-five thousand Chinese immigrants had come to California, most from Guangdong province in southern China, a region that had suffered from war with Great

Britain in the early 1840s, from economic depression and internal strife in the 1850s, then again from war with Britain and France in the late 1850s. By 1860, nearly three-quarters of all Chinese Californians worked in mining, accounting for nearly a third of all those making their living by mining in California. By 1870, more than half of California's miners were Chinese.

At the same time, new forms of mining came into use, including hydraulic mining and quartz mining. By 1870, quartz mining produced forty-two percent of all gold mined in California. Quartz mining involved digging quartz out of rock, often through the sinking of shafts into the face of a mountain, pulverizing the quartz, and then extracting the gold through one of several processes involving chemical reactions. Like hydraulic mining, quartz mining was expensive, involving deep-shaft mines and powerful stamping mills to crush the quartz. By 1858, California's stamping mills alone were estimated to be worth more than three million dollars. Within another ten years, some mine shafts had reached more than one thousand feet in length, requiring elaborate timbering to stabilize the shafts, artificial lighting, cable systems to haul out the ore, and sometimes powerful air pumps to force fresh air to the depths.

Hydraulic mining and quartz mining necessitated capital investment on a massive scale, transforming gold mining from something available to anyone with a pan and patience into a big business. Companies sought to raise necessary capital by selling shares (stock) in the company. In 1862, the San Francisco Stock Exchange opened, to formalize the process of selling stock, nearly all of it in mining companies. Within a year, nearly three thousand mining companies were issuing stock as a way to raise capital. Speculation in mining stocks soon came to rival mining as a source of quick wealth—or financial disaster.

Throughout much of the 1850s, California had produced about $50 million in gold each year, even more in 1851 and 1852, with 1852 reaching the high point of more than $80 million (equivalent in purchasing power to $1.7 billion in 2002). Gold production declined in the 1860s, to about $24 million in 1864 and some $7 million by 1870, but gold continued to be mined for many years afterward. Some gold seekers in the 1880s and 1890s showed great ingenuity. Some built dredging boats that plied the rivers of the Central Valley, scooping up the sand from the bottom and separating out whatever gold it contained. Some even diverted the course of rivers, enabling them to mine the riverbed directly.

By the early 1860s, many miners abandoned the California gold country for the newest mining region—the Washoe region of Nevada, some twenty miles east of the California border. There, in 1859, gold seekers found a silver bonanza. The discovery was called the Comstock Lode, after Henry Comstock, who had established an early claim. Just as the news of gold at Coloma spurred a great rush of prospectors into the Sierra Nevada foothills in 1848 and 1849, so news of silver discoveries brought thousands into the dry mountains east of Lake Tahoe. But the Comstock silver, like gold quartz, required the expensive, up-to-date technology of deep-shaft mining and crushing mills.

Most of the wealth of the Washoe, like that of California mines, flowed as if through a giant funnel to the banks in San Francisco. This made the economic development of California unlike that in almost any part of the United States to that time. As Americans had moved west with dreams of economic development—farming, ranching, lumbering, mining—their enterprises had usually been dependent on capital from the more developed areas to the east and across the Atlantic. Many California enterprises were also dependent on eastern and foreign capital, but the enormous amount of gold and silver meant that California's economic development was different from most other frontier experiences—it soon became, as one historian aptly put it, "a self-financing frontier."

Economic Diversification

The large numbers of gold seekers in 1849 and later stimulated a wide range of other economic developments, for they needed shirts and picks, biscuits and tents, transportation and entertainment. From the beginning, some made their fortunes by mining the miners—trading hardware, dry goods, and food for gold dust. One woman, in 1852, claimed to have earned eleven thousand dollars by baking pies in a skillet over a campfire and selling them to hungry miners. Levi Strauss earned lasting fame when he realized that trousers made of canvas would hold up better than those worn by most miners. By 1870, the durability of Levi's pants—soon dubbed Levis—had made their inventor a millionaire.

The miners were hungry for meat, and the ranchers of southern California rapidly expanded their cattle herds to meet the huge new demand. By 1860, California stood third among the states in the number of cattle being raised for meat. The cattle industry, however, expanded too much, and supply soon exceeded demand. During the extremely wet winter of 1861 to 1862, many cattle drowned when a huge lake appeared in the San Joaquin Valley, and more died during a drought in 1863 and 1864. The number of beef cattle fell by half between 1860 and 1870.

Production of other agricultural goods expanded rapidly. During the early 1850s, flour had been the largest single import into California. By the late 1850s, Californians were producing a surplus of wheat and flour and began to export it. In 1860, California stood second among the states in winemaking and by 1870 held first place, producing well over half of the nation's wine. Sheep raising also boomed, and by 1870 California ranked second among the states in the production of wool.

Much of this early agricultural development was not in the central valleys that eventually became crucial to California agriculture. Instead, most of the leading wheat-growing counties in 1860 were around San Francisco Bay, and the leading wool-producing and cattle-raising counties were mostly along the coast between Monterey and Los Angeles. Los Angeles was the leading wine-producing county in 1860, followed by Santa Barbara. By then, however, Agoston Haraszthy, an immigrant from Hungary, had begun to experiment with viticulture (the growing of grapes for winemaking) in the Sonoma Valley. In 1860, he traveled to Europe and returned with two hundred thousand grapevine cuttings representing more than a thousand varietals, assuring his eventual fame as the father of the California wine industry.

California agriculture was distinctive by the size of its farms and ranches, a holdover in part from the days of the huge ranchos. Throughout the 1850s and 1860s, the average farm in California was over 450 acres, more than double the national average.

The Gold Rush and the expansion of agriculture stimulated the development of manufacturing. Partly through trial and error, partly through careful design, Californians developed new forms of mining equipment, eventually including some of the most technologically sophisticated mining equipment in the world. By the 1860s, foundries and machine shops in the Bay Area, especially in San Francisco, were producing not only technologically advanced mining equipment but also farm machinery, ships, and locomotives. With the expansion of wheat farming came an increase in flour milling. By 1870, flour ranked as the state's most valuable single product. In the early days of the Gold Rush, lumber had been imported from the East. Mining, agriculture, and the growing cities all needed construction material, and lumbering soon became an important industry. Loggers quickly cut the redwoods in the sheltered valleys along the central coast and began to move into the larger stands of trees along the northern coast. By the mid-1850s, Humboldt County was emerging as a major source of lumber.

San Francisco rapidly developed as a commercial center, based on its port and on the federal customshouse and mint. By 1860, the city had become the nation's sixth largest port and a major center for banking and finance.

Transportation

Throughout the 1850s and early 1860s, California remained remote from the eastern half of the nation, accessible only by difficult and dangerous routes. The major overland routes soon became well-beaten roads. By the late 1850s, the firm of Russell, Majors, and Waddell dominated freighting along the Platte River route to Salt Lake City and the Pacific Coast, eventually operating 3,500 wagons drawn by 40,000 oxen. Even so, the overland route could still occupy most of a summer when traveling with oxen. Californians demanded prompter mail service, so Congress offered to subsidize any company that could deliver mail between the Mississippi River and San Francisco in twenty-five days or less. Butterfield Overland Mail secured the subsidy and in 1858 ran its first stagecoaches along the southern route, carrying both mail and as many as nine passengers on a bouncing, three-week-long journey. Though faster, the stage was prohibitively expensive for most. Eventually a few other stage routes were added, also with generous federal subsidies for carrying mail. Freighting operations and stagecoaches required regular stations along the route, staffed by company agents, where stagecoaches could change their teams and travelers could get a meal. In 1860, Russell, Majors, and Waddell launched the Pony Express, a mail delivery system based on relays of individual riders, each of whom was to ride at full speed, with changes of horses every ten miles and changes of riders every seventy miles. The first Pony Express riders left San Francisco and St. Joseph, Missouri, on April 3, 1860, and the mail arrived at the other end ten days later. This fast mail service became obsolete eighteen months later, when the first transcontinental telegraph line was completed.

The other route to California was by sea, either around Cape Horn, at the tip of South America, or to Panama, over the isthmus, and then up the Pacific Coast. Fast clipper ships could make the journey from New York around Cape Horn to San Francisco in 130 days or less. The trip over the isthmus was faster. By the late 1850s, a rickety railroad was completed over the isthmus, and the trip to New York via Panama took about the same time as the Butterfield stage and its rail connections to the Atlantic Coast.

Nearly everyone agreed that only a direct railroad connection could improve transportation between California and the eastern half of the nation. Nearly everyone agreed, too, that the cost of building a rail route was so astronomical that only massive federal subsidies could tempt entrepreneurs to undertake the construction. Such agreement, however, ended over the proper route for the rails. Stephen Douglas, senator from Illinois, led a group who wanted to connect San Francisco to Chicago. Senator Thomas Hart Benton of Missouri, father-in-law of John Frémont, thundered his support for a route west from St. Louis. Southerners pointed to New Orleans as the logical terminus for a route through Texas and New Mexico Territory. Gwin tried to satisfy everyone by proposing a railroad with three eastern branches, for Chicago, St. Louis, and New Orleans, but the costs were prohibitive. The issue remained deadlocked throughout the 1850s.

Tying Together the Union with Iron

When the Republicans took power in Washington in 1861, they faced the crisis of secession and then of war. As Lincoln and his party raised troops and amassed supplies, Republicans also moved quickly to use the power of the federal government to encourage economic growth and development. Among the development measures they passed was the Pacific Railroad Act of 1862.

As the new, Republican Congress assembled late in 1861, Theodore Judah arrived in Washington with a bundle of plans for a railroad over the Sierra Nevadas. Judah, a highly capable engineer, had laid out the route for the first railroad to be built in California, a short line in the Sacramento Valley. His abilities as an engineer combined with his enthusiasm for a transcontinental line to attract support from several Sacramento merchants, all Republicans: Leland Stanford, Collis P. Huntington, Mark Hopkins, and Charles Crocker (whose brother, Edwin, was a prominent abolitionist as well as a leading Republican). As merchants, they may have been persuaded less by a vision of a railroad to the East Coast than by the prospect of a railroad to the silver-mining regions of Nevada. Regardless of their

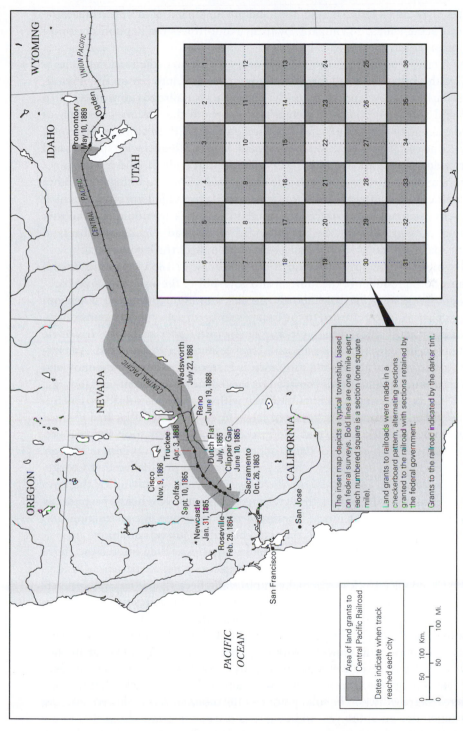

Map 5.1 This map shows the route of the Central Pacific from Sacramento to Promontory Summit, Utah, and also the outer boundaries of the land grant that the company received from the federal government. Land was awarded in a checkerboard pattern, ten square miles (later increased to twenty) for each mile of track completed. Note how long it took for the railroad to be built from Sacramento across the Sierra Nevadas, and then how quickly construction proceeded across Nevada and Utah.

Inset caption: The inset map depicts a typical township, based on federal surveys. Bold lines are one mile apart; each numbered square is a section (one square mile).

Land grants to railroads were made in a checkerboard pattern, alternating sections granted to the railroad with sections retained by the federal government.

Grants to the railroad indicated by the darker tint.

Legend: Area of land grants to Central Pacific Railroad

Dates indicate when track reached each city

motives, they joined Judah in mid-1861 and put up the initial capital to create the Central Pacific Railroad Company. By then, Stanford was the Republican candidate for governor.

With crucial support from members of the California congressional delegation, Judah tirelessly lobbied for federal support. Signed into law on July 1, 1862, the Pacific Railroad Act incorporated the Union Pacific Railroad Company (UP) to build and run a railroad from Nebraska Territory to the western boundary of Nevada, and authorized the Central Pacific Company (CP) to build track to meet the UP. The companies were to receive federal land for their tracks, stations, and other buildings, and, as a subsidy, every other square mile of land for ten miles (later increased to twenty) on each side of the tracks. The remaining land within this checkerboard pattern was to be offered for sale by the federal government at double its usual price, so that the land grant, in the long run, would cost the government nothing. Finally, the act provided for a loan of sixteen thousand dollars—later increased substantially—for every mile of track completed.

A symbolic first shovelful of earth was dug early in 1863 by Stanford, who was now both president of the railroad and governor of the state. Initial preparations got underway that summer. By the fall, however, Judah had fallen out with his partners and returned to the East to seek financial support against them, but he contracted a fever en route and died shortly after reaching New York. Huntington took over as the railroad's chief lobbyist in Washington. Amendments to the original act in 1864 substantially increased both the amount of land and the amount of loan funds provided by the federal government.

The CP faced a range of difficulties even with its generous subsidies. One serious problem was finding a sufficient labor force. The Civil War had drained males from the work force, and the lure of Nevada silver took many more. Charles Crocker—in charge of construction—employed a few Chinese laborers as an experiment. The Chinese crews proved to be so productive that Crocker quickly hired more. From then on, the construction crews, including the foremen, were almost all Chinese, though supervisory jobs were held by whites. By mid-1866, six thousand Chinese laborers were at work on CP construction, and their numbers reached nearly ten thousand before the job was done.

The construction crews faced formidable obstacles as they entered the Sierra Nevadas. The CP was anxious to build as rapidly as possible, because subsidies were awarded once track was actually in place and because the UP was competing for those subsidies. The sooner the CP tracks could reach Nevada and begin to be built across relatively flat regions, the more of the subsidy would go to the CP rather than to the UP. The winters of 1866 to 1867 and 1867 to 1868 were severe, but Crocker pushed his crews to work despite the ice and snow. Eventually they constructed thirty-seven miles of snow sheds—wooden buildings that enclosed the tracks through the areas of greatest snowfall—to keep the tracks clear through the fierce Sierra winters. The solid granite of the mountains also slowed progress; one tunnel took an entire year to build, as construction crews chipped out only eight inches of rock per day. In other places, Chinese laborers were lowered down sheer cliffs in baskets to chip away at the rock or to drill holes for blasting powder. Such work was highly dangerous, and many died in falls, explosions, avalanches, and accidents.

Not until June 1868 did the tracks reach Nevada. Though the UP started well after the CP, its initial construction had been through the flatlands of Nebraska and eastern Wyoming. By June 1868, the UP had built twice as many miles of tracks as the CP. Desperate to push their tracks to eastern Utah to capture the business to and from Salt Lake City, the CP partners pushed their crews even harder. In 1867, the last year of building through the mountains, the crews completed only 40 miles of track. In 1868, building through Nevada, they completed 362 miles. Competition between the CP and UP became ever more intense, as both sought to maximize their tracks as a way to maximize their federal subsidies. UP construction crews, by then, were largely Irish, and ethnic rivalry also became frenzied. In the end, however, Crocker's Chinese crews set the record of ten miles of track in a single day.

A grand ceremony was organized to dramatize the moment when the Union Pacific and Central Pacific rails were joined at Promontory Summit, Utah, just outside the city of Ogden. On May 10, 1869, two giant locomotives from each line moved forward to face each other. Ceremonial spikes of precious metal from several western territories and states were tapped into place, and Stanford used a silver mallet to drive in a final spike of California gold as telegraph lines carried the blows to the nation.

The driving of the golden spike did not unite California with the rest of the nation by rail, as the UP section of the track had some gaps and the Missouri River was still unbridged. Much of the track had been laid so rapidly that it required almost immediate repairs. Nonetheless, the nation celebrated with fireworks and flowery speeches from Boston to San Francisco. The Liberty Bell was rung in Philadelphia. New York City heard a one-hundred-gun salute. The nation, so recently divided by war, seemed determined to celebrate a new symbolic unity. The more-than-three-week-long trip between California and the Missouri valley had been cut to six days.

New Social and Cultural Patterns

During the twenty years following the discovery of gold, the state was transformed in many ways beyond the economic changes. California acquired new social institutions, especially educational and humanitarian institutions, and developed a reputation as a literary center.

Gender Roles and New Social Institutions

The influx of thousands of gold seekers gave the population of the new state a peculiar composition—the state's population in 1850 was composed overwhelmingly of young men. As seen in Figure 5.1, more than half the population was male and aged between fifteen and thirty. But the imbalance between men and women persisted after many gold seekers returned to their homes in the East or left for other mining regions, and it persisted even after flour surpassed gold as the most valuable product of the state. Figure 5.2 presents data for 1870, indicating a continuing, though not so extreme, disproportion between men and women aged twenty to fifty. This ratio between men and women, characteristic of frontier societies, carried implications for other social patterns.

Many Americans in the mid-nineteenth century had sharply defined expectations regarding social roles for men and women. Domesticity was the notion that the proper place for a woman was in the home as wife and mother, and that as wife-mother she was guardian of the family, responsible for its moral, spiritual, and physical well-being. In their role as moral guardians and protectors of children and families, women also assumed important roles in the church and the school and in voluntary organizations devoted to caring for women, children, and the less fortunate. Beyond this, moreover, many Americans believed that women ought not experience much of the world, for fear that business or politics, with their sometimes lax moral standards, might corrupt women. The best choice, it was widely argued, was for women to occupy a separate sphere, immune from such dangers. Though widely advocated in the pulpits and journals of the

Figure 5.1 Numbers of Men and Women by Age, 1850
This figure vividly shows the extreme demographic disproportions by age and sex that were created by the Gold Rush. What do these data suggest regarding the nature of life in the mines?
Source: Statistical view of the United States: being a compendium of the seventh census (Washington, 1854).

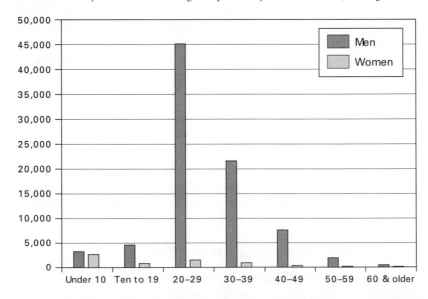

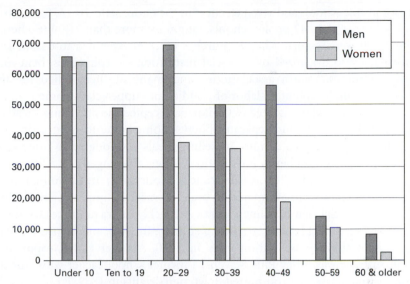

Figure 5.2 Numbers of Men and Women by Age, 1870
Note how men continued to outnumber women long after the initial stages of the Gold Rush had long passed. Such demographic disproportions are typical of frontier economies dependent on the exploitation of raw materials, for example, through mining, lumbering, or ranching. What does this suggest about the California economy?
Source: The statistics of the population of the United States compiled from the ninth census (Washington, 1872).

day, the concepts of domesticity and separate spheres proved most typical of white middle-class and upper-class women in towns and cities, and often held little relevance for farm women, working-class women, and women of color.

Many nineteenth-century Americans also accepted the notion that men naturally tended to be materialistic where women were spiritual and that men tended to be adventurous or even hedonistic where women were restrained and refined. "Nothing is better calculated to preserve a young man from contamination of low pleasures and pursuits," stated one guidebook for young men, than frequent contact "with the more refined and virtuous of the other sex." In California in the 1850s, however, the extreme imbalance between the numbers of men and women made such contact unlikely for many young men. Thus, few Americans were surprised that, without the restraining presence of women, the largely male mining camps seemed to be given over to adolescent-like excesses of vice, violence, and greed.

As women arrived in California during the 1850s and 1860s, many brought with them the middle-class expectations of their day, and they quickly set about constructing social institutions intended to convey morality, educate the young, and care for the unfortunate. They did not do so by themselves, of course, for many men also understood the value of such institutions. In 1850, there were only two public schools and seven teachers in the entire state. By 1870, Californians could boast of 1,342 public schools, taught by more than 2,400 teachers, of whom 1,400 were women. The 28 churches of 1850 expanded to 643 in 1870. Californians also organized other social institutions—orphanages, benevolent societies, libraries, reform associations—and many of them relied for their continuation on the voluntary labor of middle- and upper-class women.

Not all women who migrated to California accepted the prevailing social definitions of domesticity and separate spheres. Some came to California to get rich, a few by panning gold, more by selling meals and lodging to miners, and probably the largest number by prostitution. Others challenged prevailing gender roles in other ways. Ada Clare, a San Francisco journalist, urged women to take advantage of a new gymnasium and to build themselves up physically, to dispel the prevailing social view of women as frail and sickly. Laura de Force Gordon delivered the first public lecture on woman suffrage in 1868, and helped to form a state woman suffrage association early in 1870. Another early proponent of woman suffrage was Emily Pitts Stevens, a former schoolteacher who launched the state's first newspaper committed to women's rights in 1869.

The Growth of Religious Toleration

Though California in the 1850s was rife with ethnic hostility and conflict, it differed little in this regard from other parts of the nation. Discrimination against free African Americans and mistreatment of American Indians could be found nearly everywhere to the east. California and the West were unique, however, in the diversity of their ethnic groups. In the eastern part of the country, racial relations usually involved blacks and whites, or sometimes whites and Indians, or, rarely, blacks and Indians. Racial and ethnic relations in the West, however, involved not just American Indians and Americans of European and African descent, but also Mexican Americans (many of them mestizos) who had become citizens under the Treaty of Guadalupe Hidalgo, and immigrants from Asia, Europe, Australia, the islands of the Pacific, and Latin America. (Table 5.1 presents data on groups included in census tabulations for 1852, 1860, and 1870.)

The Gold Rush attracted many European immigrants, some of whom came from intermediary points including the eastern United States and Australia. The influx included groups subject to discrimination and hostility in the eastern United States. Irish immigrants, for example, were depicted in some eastern newspapers as whiskey-swilling ignoramuses. Anti-Catholicism was as old as the Reformation and anti-Semitism was older. The Know-Nothing movement of the mid-1850s drew support all over the country by criticizing immigrants, especially Catholic immigrants.

Californians, particularly in the gold-mining areas, seem to have displayed an unusual toleration of religious differences. One historian carefully surveyed all available records and found only two clear instances of anti-Semitic discrimination in the mining regions during the entire decade of the 1850s. In 1850 the

TABLE 5.1 RACE, ETHNICITY, OR NATIVITY FOR CALIFORNIA POPULATION, 1852, 1860, 1870

Race, ethnicity, or nativity	1852		1860		1870	
	Number	Percent	Number	Percent	Number	Percent
Asian	not available		34,933	9.2	49,310	8.8
African American (including mulatto)	1,678	0.7	4,086	1.1	4,272	0.8
American Indian*	31,266	12.3	17,798	4.7	7,241	1.3
Foreign-born	54,803	21.4	146,528	38.6	209,831	37.5
• Ireland	not available		33,147	8.7	54,421	9.7
• German states	not available		21,646	5.7	29,699	5.3
• Great Britain	not available		12,227	3.2	17,685	3.2
All others (mostly whites born in the U.S.)	167,375	65.6	176,649	46.5	289,593	51.7
Total	255,122		379,994		560,247	

*Described as "civilized" or "domesticated" by the census, meaning those who lived in the midst of the larger society and followed at least some social and economic patterns of the larger society.
Source: Federal censuses of 1850 (which included a report on the special state census of 1852), 1860, and 1870.

California constitutional convention alternated its daily opening prayer between Protestant and Catholic clergymen. Students in the Catholic school in Los Angeles in 1859 included not just Catholics but also Protestants and Jews. A few years before, Protestants in San Francisco had contributed generously to help build a new Catholic church.

Despite the victory of the Know-Nothings in the state elections of 1855, a similar religious toleration seemed to characterize most of the new state's politics. When he was active in New York Democratic politics, Broderick had understood that the state's Democratic leaders were unwilling to permit Irish Catholics to rise too far. In California, Broderick won a seat in the U.S. Senate in 1857. The Irish-born and Catholic John Downey became governor in 1860 after being elected lieutenant governor the year before. San Franciscans elected an Irish Catholic mayor in 1867, and two Irish Catholics followed Broderick into the U.S. Senate from California before 1870. Catholic Californios were elected to local offices in some parts of northern California as well as in the south, and José Estudillo was elected state treasurer, serving from 1875 to 1880. Jews were also elected to local offices in the mining regions in the 1850s, and Solomon Heydenfeldt, who was Jewish, won election to the state supreme court in 1851.

One key to understanding this toleration of Catholics and Jews may be found in the Gold Rush, when respect went to those who prospered most. By 1870, San Francisco had twenty-seven Irish bankers; at the same time, Philadelphia (much larger in size) had eighteen and Boston (also much larger) had only four. Another part of the reason is undoubtedly the sheer numbers of Catholics—half the churchgoers in the state by one estimate in 1860. Recent historians suggest that the presence of significant numbers of African Americans, American Indians, Chinese, and mestizos may have led whites—whether Protestant, Catholic, or Jewish, Irish, German, British, Californio, or old-stock American—to focus on their "whiteness" rather than their religion or national origin. Whatever the reasons, by 1860 California was developing a reputation for religious toleration. That reputation, however, was limited to religion and failed to extend to race.

Chinese immigrants were barred from American citizenship. Congress approved the first federal law on naturalization in 1790 and, although amended occasionally, the law provided that only white immigrants might become naturalized citizens. State laws also discriminated against immigrants from China. In a court decision in 1854, the law that barred African Americans and American Indians from testifying in court against whites was extended to the Chinese. Though local school boards first created racially separate schools for black students, local officials soon mandated segregated schools for Chinese students as well. The state legislature endorsed and extended these practices in 1863 by directing the state superintendent of instruction to withhold funds from school districts that did not create separate schools for "Negroes, Mongolians and Indians."

Writing the Gold Rush

Among those who came to California in the 1850s and 1860s were an array of young writers, some of whom created new patterns in American literature. The excitement and turbulence of life in the mining districts stimulated the creative imagination of some who mined the local color for a wealth of plots. Writers published articles, poems, essays, and short stories in the new newspapers and literary journals. By the late 1850s, San Francisco could choose among more than ten daily newspapers and a larger number of weekly or monthly publications. Every mining town had at least one, and often two, local papers. Among the many firsthand accounts of the Gold Rush that appeared in such local publications, perhaps the finest were the twenty-three letters written by Louise Clappe under the pseudonym Dame Shirley and published in the San Francisco *Pioneer* in 1854 and 1855.

Bret Harte arrived in California in 1854 and tramped through the mining country before taking a newspaper job in Humboldt County. He scathingly condemned local ruffians for the brutal slaughter of sixty Indians, mostly women and children, then fled when he was apparently threatened with lynching for his story. He made his way to San Francisco and soon became editor of the *Overland Monthly*. In its pages, he presented his and others' accounts of life in the diggings, drawing both on his own experience and on other firsthand accounts like those of Dame Shirley. Through stories such as "The Outcasts of Poker Flat," Harte contributed significantly to the development of local color and realism in American fiction. Other California journalists also began to develop similar themes.

By far the most famous and influential of the Gold Rush authors was Samuel L. Clemens, a Mississippi River steamboat captain who fled from the strife of the Civil War and arrived in Nevada Territory in 1861. There he mined, speculated in mining stock, camped through the Sierra Nevadas, and began to write humorous essays for the Virginia City newspaper. He soon began to use the pen name Mark Twain, and quickly became the most popular humorist writing in Nevada. He moved to San Francisco in May 1864 and pursued his journalism there, developing his humor into satire. His short story "The Celebrated Jumping Frog of Calaveras County" was published in a New York journal in 1865. A San Francisco newspaper, the *Alta California,* commissioned him to travel to the Mediterranean and the Holy Land (then part of the Turkish empire). His book on his travels, *Innocents Abroad* (1869), established his national reputation and he moved to the East.

Ina Coolbrith (see discussion on next page) is shown here as a young woman, probably in her teens. Coolbrith tried to conceal her divorce. She also tried to conceal her family background—that her mother had fled to California from Salt Lake City and that Coolbrith was the niece of Joseph Smith, the founder of the Mormon Church. Why might she have felt it important to conceal these things?

Ina Coolbrith arrived in California with her mother and stepfather in 1851 and grew up in Los Angeles. Her first poetry was published when she was eleven. After a marriage to an abusive husband that ended in divorce, she moved to San Francisco in the early 1860s. There she soon received national attention for her poetry and joined Harte in running the *Overland Monthly* during its glory days. She seems to have dazzled Harte, Twain, and other emerging literary figures with her poetry, literary advice, conversation, and beauty. When Harte, Twain, and the others left California one by one to pursue fame in the East or in Europe— they were all gone by 1870—Coolbrith remained. She worked as city librarian in Oakland for many years, encouraged a new generation of writers, including Jack London, and, in 1915 at the age of seventy-four, was named poet laureate of California.

Summary

California's application for statehood helped to bring about the Compromise of 1850, by which congressional leaders sought to stave off sectional crisis. Sectional issues affected California politics in the 1850s, however, as transplanted Southerners struggled with transplanted Northerners for control of California's two Senate seats. In California, as in the eastern states, the growing sectional crisis precipitated the emergence of a new political party, the Republicans. At the same time that national politics was rupturing over the issue of slavery, California experienced a crisis of political legitimacy with the rise of vigilantism, reaching its apogee when vigilantes overthrew the city government of San Francisco, the state's largest city. The federal government was slow to create reservations for California Indians, many of whom fell victim to violence. Californios who held Spanish or Mexican land grants found it expensive and time-consuming to prove title to their land, and many lost their lands.

Throughout the 1850s, the full meaning of the state constitution's ban on slavery had to be determined through court actions, most initiated by abolitionists, black and white. With the presidential victory of Abraham Lincoln in 1860, the nation plunged into civil war. Far removed from the scene of battle, the war nonetheless affected California in important ways. Some Californians participated in the war itself, and others raised funds for the Union cause. Reconstruction, and especially the Fourteenth Amendment to the Constitution, altered the meaning of citizenship, and California law was amended to remove many laws that discriminated against African Americans.

The economy grew and diversified in the 1850s and 1860s, with growth fueled in major part by the continued development of mining. Throughout the 1850s California remained remote from the eastern United States because of poor transportation, but efforts to connect California to the eastern United States by rail foundered because of the sectional crisis. With the victory of the Republicans, however, came federal subsidies for construction of a railroad to tie California to the North.

With the continued growth of population, sex ratios in California began to move toward a more normal distribution. At the same time, partly through the prompting of women, new social institutions began to emerge. Catholics and Jews in California experienced less religious discrimination than their counterparts in the eastern United States. California, and especially San Francisco, acquired a reputation as a literary center.

Suggested Readings

- Burchell, R. A., *The San Francisco Irish: 1848–1880* (Berkeley and Los Angeles: University of California Press, 1980). Solidly researched and filled with important insights about this important immigrant group.

- Chen, Yong, *Chinese San Francisco, 1850–1943: A Trans-Pacific Community* (Stanford: Stanford University Press, 2000). A recent treatment that emphasizes the continuing contacts between San Francisco's Chinatown and China.

- Clarke, Dwight L., *William Tecumseh Sherman: Gold Rush Banker* (San Francisco: California Historical Society, 1969). Incorporates long excerpts from Sherman's detailed letters.

- Dame Shirley, [Clappe, Louise A. K. S.], *The Shirley Letters* (1854–55; Santa Barbara and Salt Lake City: Peregrine Smith, Inc., 1970). The letters of "Dame Shirley" provide a wealth of information on life in the gold fields.

- Egli, Ida Rae, ed., *No Rooms of Their Own: Women Writers of Early California* (Berkeley: Heyday Books, 1992). An introduction to the leading women writers of the era, with selections of their work.

- Griswold del Castillo, Richard, *The Treaty of Guadalupe Hidalgo* (Norman: University of Oklahoma Press, 1990). The best single treatment of this crucially important document for the history of California and the Southwest.

- Hurtado, Albert L., *Indian Survival on the California Frontier* (New Haven: Yale University Press, 1988). A recent and comprehensive treatment of this important topic.

- Lapp, Rudolph M., *Blacks in Gold Rush California* (New Haven: Yale University Press, 1977). A pioneering work in African American history.

- Lotchin, Roger W., *San Francisco, 1846–1856: From Hamlet to City* (1974; Urbana and Chicago: University of Illinois Press, 1997). An excellent treatment of this crucial decade in the history of the city.

- Rawls, James J., Richard J. Orsi, and Marlene Smith-Baranzini, eds., *A Golden State: Mining and Economic Development in Gold Rush California* (Berkeley:

University of California Press, 1999). Recent and filled with insights into the topic.

■ Rohrbough, Malcolm J., *Days of Gold: The California Gold Rush and the American Nation* (Berkeley and Los Angeles: University of California Press, 1997). A recent, and highly acclaimed, treatment of the Gold Rush itself and its impact on California and the nation.

■ Senkewicz, Robert M., *Vigilantes in Gold Rush San Francisco* (Stanford: Stanford University Press, 1985). An excellent overview of San Francisco vigilantism for the decade of the 1850s.

■ Starr, Kevin, Richard J. Orsi, and Marlene Smith-Baranzini, eds., *Rooted in Barbarous Soil: People, Culture, and Community in Gold Rush California* (Berkeley: University of California Press, 2000). One volume of a series, all of which are excellent, developed by the California Historical Society on the occasion of the state's sesquicentennial.

■ Williams, David A., *David C. Broderick: A Political Portrait* (San Marino: Huntington Library, 1969). A classic, which helped to restore Broderick's reputation as an important leader of the antislavery cause.

6

California in the Gilded Age, 1870–1900

Main Topics

▮ The Economic Transformation of California and the West

▮ New Social Patterns

▮ Politics

▮ Cultural Expression

▮ Summary

Born in Missouri in 1842, Phoebe Apperson began teaching school while still in her late teens. In 1862, however, her life changed dramatically when she married George Hearst, the son of a neighbor, who had gone to California in 1850 to seek his fortune. He turned forty-two in 1862, and she was not yet twenty when they were married. Only when they returned to San Francisco did she learn that Hearst was very wealthy.

Like other wealthy women, Phoebe Apperson Hearst became involved in activities outside the home. She was active in the women's club movement, serving as first president of the Century Club of San Francisco in 1888 and participating in other clubs. She and other women of the clubs championed causes that focused on women and children. She also helped to support an orphanage, a school for female physicians, the earliest kindergartens in San Francisco (kindergartens then provided child care for working-class mothers), and a settlement house (which provided social services for the poor).

CHAPTER 6	California in the Gilded Age, 1870–1900
1859–1880	Most productive period of Comstock silver mining
1864	Ralston opens the Bank of California
1870	Wheat surpasses gold as California's most valuable product
1871	Anti-Chinese riots in Los Angeles
1872–1873	Modoc War
1877	Workingmen's Party of California formed
1878	Constitutional Convention
1879	Publication of Henry George's *Progress and Poverty*
1882	Chinese Exclusion Law approved
1884	Publication of Helen Hunt Jackson's novel *Ramona*
1884	Southern Pacific Corporation chartered in Kentucky
1884	*Woodruff v. North Bloomfield Gravel Mining Company*
1886	George Hearst becomes U.S. Senator
1886	*Yick Wo v. Hopkins*
1887	New state law encourages irrigation
1888	First California fruit travels to New York in refrigerated railroad cars
1897	Phoebe Apperson Hearst becomes Regent of the University of California
1899	Publication of Frank Norris's novel *McTeague*

In 1886 George Hearst became a member of the United States Senate. While in Washington, Phoebe supported kindergartens there, created a training program for kindergarten teachers, endowed a school for girls, and donated funds to help restore Mount Vernon, the home of George Washington. When George died in 1891, Phoebe inherited everything, allowing her to increase her philanthropic endeavors. She helped to organize the Parent Teacher Association and she gave generously to the Young Women's Christian Association (YWCA).

Phoebe Apperson Hearst was also a central figure in the development of the University of California. One of her earliest

This formally posed photograph of Phoebe Apperson Hearst is not dated, but seems to come from the 1890s, when Hearst was taking charge of her late husband's estate and beginning her own career in philanthropy. How could Hearst's philanthropic contributions be seen as reflecting the dominant concepts of domesticity and separate spheres? How could her contributions be seen as undermining those concepts?

biographers reported that she "has an insatiable desire to help girls get an education." She began contributing to the university by endowing its first scholarships for women. In 1897 Governor James Budd—a Democrat, like George Hearst—named her to the University of California Board of Regents, among the most significant political offices held by an American woman up to that time, and she was reappointed until her death in 1919. She gave generously to the university, including funds for buildings, archeological expeditions, an anthropological museum (named in her honor in 1991), and other programs. In her life, Hearst reflected many of the expectations of her day about women's social roles even as she challenged many constraints on women's involvement in the wider sphere of life, beyond the home and the family.

Phoebe Apperson Hearst lived during what historians call the "Gilded Age," the years roughly from 1870 to 1900. A period of rapid industrialization and urbanization, large-scale immigration from Europe, and swift economic development in the West, it was an age of great fortunes and urban poverty, of powerful new technology and rampant child labor. *The Gilded Age* was, in fact, the title of the first novel by one-time Californian Mark Twain, coauthored with his Connecticut neighbor, Charles Dudley Warner. In it, they satirized the materialism and corruption of their day. Although most histories of the Gilded Age focus on the industries, entrepreneurs, cities, immigrants, and workers of the East and Midwest, California shared in all these experiences, although sometimes with unique variations. And Californians were often at the forefront during this era of rapid and far-reaching change.

Questions to Consider

▌ Why were railroads and water so important to the economic development of California during this time?

▌ What made San Francisco the metropolis of the West?

▌ How was education transformed during this period?

▌ In what ways did gender roles change during these years?

▌ How would you compare the experiences of California Indians, Latinos, and immigrants during the late nineteenth century?

▌ What was the significance of third parties in California politics during the 1870s and 1890s?

▌ What were the similarities and differences between the constitutional conventions of 1850 and 1878?

▌ In what ways did writers and artists draw on California as inspiration for their work?

The Economic Transformation of California and the West

Railroad construction was important to economic development in the United States after the Civil War. In California and the West, railroads were even more crucial because of the great distances and the dearth of navigable waterways. Mining continued to be a major element in the western economy. At the same time, agriculture emerged as California's leading industry. And, increasingly, water stood out as indispensable for mining, agriculture, and urban growth.

Railroad Expansion

For a quarter of a century after Leland Stanford placed the golden spike, the Central Pacific Railroad and its successor corporation, the Southern Pacific, dominated rail transportation in California and other parts of the West. Even before 1869, the railroad's "Big Four"—Leland Stanford, Collis Huntington, Mark Hopkins, and Charles Crocker—had begun to buy out potential rivals and block possible competitors.

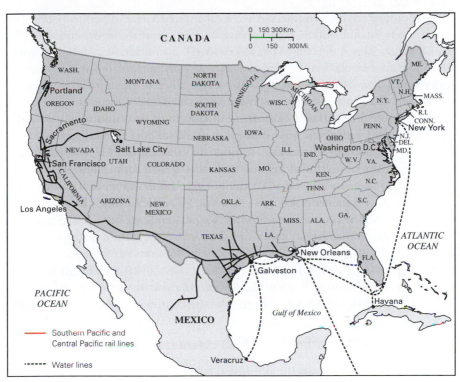

Map 6.1 This map shows the extent of the Southern Pacific's transportation system as of 1894. The Southern Pacific dominated railroad service in California and nearby areas and connected California to New Orleans, the Pacific Northwest, and the Midwest (via the connection in Utah with the Union Pacific). Southern Pacific water routes connected New York and other major eastern cities to New Orleans, making it possible to travel cross-country entirely on Southern Pacific facilities. Does this map help you to understand why the Southern Pacific was sometimes called "the octopus"?

San Francisco entrepreneurs organized the Southern Pacific Railroad to build a line from San Francisco to San Diego, and in 1866 Congress gave the Southern Pacific a generous land grant. The Big Four gained control of the Southern Pacific (SP) and plotted a route through the Santa Clara and San Joaquin Valleys—giving them not only a transportation monopoly there but also a great deal of potentially valuable agricultural land as part of their land grant. The SP reached Los Angeles, a country town with fewer than six thousand people, in 1870.

By the mid-1870s, the Big Four controlled 85 percent of all railroad mileage in California and had ambitious plans for expansion. Eventually, they operated a line across Arizona, New Mexico, and Texas to New Orleans. Another line ran north, through the Sacramento Valley, then to Portland, Oregon. They acquired fleets of ships that carried passengers and freight along the Pacific Coast, between California and Japan, and between New Orleans and New York. In 1884 they merged all these operations into the Southern Pacific Company, a holding company for which Huntington secured a corporate charter in Kentucky after the California legislature balked at approving such a powerful corporation. By 1884 the Big Four claimed that the SP was the largest transportation system in the nation, with more than nine thousand miles of rails, sixteen thousand miles of water lines, and a virtual monopoly within California and other parts of the West.

The SP was also the largest landowner in California. While other land-grant railroads sold much of their lands, the SP held most of its land, arousing opposition from would-be farmers. On occasion, conflict over land erupted into violence. The most famous conflict was the "battle of Mussel Slough," a struggle between the SP and farmers near Hanford, in what is now Kings County. Residents of the area had filed lawsuits over the SP's land grant, and many farmers hoped to purchase land from the federal government for $2.50 per acre, rather than from the SP. The SP prevailed in court, however, and enforced prices of $10 to $25 per acre. In 1880, a federal marshal set out to evict a farm family, but a group of armed farmers blocked his way. Seven men died in the shootout that followed.

Leland Stanford served as president of the Central Pacific and then the SP. A founder of the Republican Party in California and the state's first Republican governor (1863–1865), Stanford won election to the United States Senate in 1885. He and his wife, Jane Lathrop Stanford, had one child, Leland Jr., who died of typhoid at the age of sixteen. They created a magnificent memorial to their son: Stanford University.

Collis P. Huntington was the shrewdest, coldest, and perhaps most ambitious of the Big Four. He represented them in the East and soon considered New York City his home. Huntington invested in other railroads, and by 1884 he could ride in his personal rail car over his own companies' tracks from the Atlantic to the Pacific! He also invested in railroads in Latin America and Africa, urban transit in Brooklyn, land in southern California, shipbuilding in Virginia, and a host of other companies. True to his opposition to slavery in the 1850s, he insisted that his companies pay African Americans the same as white workers and that African Americans be hired on an equal basis with whites. His few charitable contributions included funds for schools for African Americans.

No other railroad challenged the SP's dominance until the 1890s, and the company acquired a reputation for charging "all the traffic will bear," that is, charging for freight and passengers at the very highest possible rate. Such behavior was typical of most railroad companies at the time. More than one entrepreneur reported that, upon complaining about high freight rates, SP officials asked him to produce his account ledgers so that they could determine the highest level of freight rates he could pay without going bankrupt.

Most Californians understood the SP to be the most powerful force in state and local politics. All of the Big Four had taken part in Republican politics in the 1850s, before their investment in the railroad. Stanford served as governor and U.S. senator. Huntington was the SP's lobbyist in Washington, dedicated to preventing political restrictions on the SP and to gaining for it whatever advantages could be realized through the political process. In the early 1880s, the widow of

David Colton, who had been a high-ranking official of the SP, released letters that Huntington had written to her husband in the 1870s. In one of the most notorious, Huntington wrote about one California congressman: "He is a wild hog; don't let him come back to Washington." Another letter dealt with the U.S. Congress: "It costs money to fix things . . . with $200,000 I can pass our bill."

Competition for the SP arrived in 1885 in the form of the Atchison, Topeka, and Santa Fe Railroad, known as the Santa Fe, which completed its line into Los Angeles in 1885. By 1888, passengers could take the Santa Fe from Chicago to San Diego, and a fare war broke out between the Santa Fe and the SP as each tried to undercut the other's fares to southern California. In the meantime, several San Francisco merchants formed the Traffic Association of San Francisco to consider alternatives to the SP and to encourage the legislature to regulate freight rates. Eventually these efforts produced a new railroad company to build a line through the San Joaquin Valley to compete with the SP. Construction began in 1895, and by 1898 a line ran between Stockton and Bakersfield. The Santa Fe then bought the new line, linked it to the Santa Fe in southern California, and, in 1900, completed an extension to San Francisco Bay. The SP's monopoly had finally been broken.

Despite complaints about railroad rates and political influence, rail lines were enormously important to the economic development of the West. Without the railroad, most goods moved by water—up and down the coast and along the few navigable rivers of central California. The railroad permitted mining in remote regions and the shipping of heavy, technologically advanced mining equipment. The railroad encouraged the development of specialized agriculture, especially fruit growing, that required fast trains and refrigeration equipment to carry produce from California to markets on the other side of the nation. By making travel from the eastern United States to California both easy and cheap, railroads also contributed significantly to the growth of the tourist industry and the state's population boom.

Mining and Finance

Mining continued to be centrally important to the state's economy, not only within California, but also for the activities of California's banks and mining entrepreneurs in developing mines throughout the West. Many aspects of mining required a high degree of expertise, technologically advanced equipment, and large amounts of capital. By the 1870s, San Francisco, in particular, and California were providing all three of these elements for mining throughout the West. In the process, the initiative in mining shifted from prospectors and mining engineers toward well-capitalized mining companies and investment bankers.

Nevada's Comstock Lode (see p. 143) made some Californians wealthy. Between 1859 and 1880, a third of a billion dollars in silver (equivalent to five billion dollars today) was taken out of the Comstock Lode. Comstock mining required digging deep shafts and installing complex machinery to move men and equipment thousands of feet into the earth and to keep the tunnels cool and dry. By the mid-1870s, the Comstock mines used some of the most advanced mining equipment in the world.

The career of George Hearst illustrates the role of Californians in western mining. Born in Missouri in 1820, Hearst came overland to California in 1850 and acquired extensive mining experience. In 1859, he bought a one-sixth interest in the Ophir mine in the Comstock. The Ophir proved extraordinarily profitable, permitting him to return to Missouri to wed Phoebe Apperson (see p. 159). Hearst invested his profits in mining and in agricultural and timber lands throughout the West and Mexico. A Democrat, he served in the United States Senate from 1886 until his death in 1891.

Though Hearst became wealthy from his mining investments, his fortune did not place him in the top ranks of San Francisco's financial elite. Those positions were held securely by the Big Four and others who were even more successful than Hearst in coaxing profits from the Comstock. The first Californians to rake in extraordinary profits from the Comstock were William Ralston and William Sharon. Ralston had organized the Bank of California in 1864 and soon set up agencies in the Comstock region. Sharon not only established control over many mines in the region, but he also centralized decision making, financed deeper operations, and discovered new ore bodies. He vertically integrated silver mining, combining ownership of mines with ownership of a mill that separated the silver from the ore, a timber company for shoring up the deep tunnels, water for the mills and for cooling the mines, fuel, and, after 1872, a railroad connection between the Comstock and the Central Pacific. In 1873, he was elected to the United States Senate from Nevada.

Nevada silver earned large profits for Ralston's Bank of California. He invested some of this capital in manufacturing, mostly in San Francisco, including foundries and iron works, a refinery for Hawaiian sugar, and woolen mills to make cloth from the wool of California sheep. Other investments included shipping, hydraulic gold mining, insurance, irrigation canals, and the Palace Hotel, modeled on the great luxury hotels of Europe. He also loaned funds to the Central Pacific. In 1875, however, Ralston faced a financial crisis. Some investments had been hit hard by the nationwide economic depression that began in 1873, and some factories were suffering from competition with the products of eastern factories, now shipped to California over the railroad that Ralston had helped to finance. His back to the wall, Ralston sold his half of the Palace Hotel to Sharon, disposed of other stock as best he could, and resigned from the bank. He died the same day. Sharon took his place as head of a reorganized Bank of California.

By the time Sharon took over the Bank of California, he and the bank had already been displaced as the dominant factors in Nevada silver mining. They lost out to four partners, James G. Fair and John W. Mackay, both experienced mine operators, and James C. Flood and William F. O'Brien, San Francisco saloon keepers turned stockbrokers. These four—all Irish—wrested control of one large mine from Sharon in 1868, and the mine almost immediately began to produce large profits. They soon struck the richest vein of silver ore in American history. Like Sharon before them, they vertically organized operations, investing in a reducing mill and in timber and water companies, all of which profited so long as the mines remained productive. Like others of the era, they invested their profits widely. Flood took the lead in creating the Nevada Bank of San Francisco in 1875 and served as its president. For a brief time, the Nevada Bank claimed to have the largest capitalization of any bank in the world.

San Francisco was the financial center of the Nevada silver boom and of mining throughout the West. The city's merchants sold supplies to the miners, and most stocks in mining companies were bought and sold at San Francisco's Mining Exchange, scene of quick profits and devastating losses. Initially, some San Francisco bankers, like Ralston, relied for capital on California merchants who had prospered during the Gold Rush. San Francisco bankers used their access to capital not just to invest in the Comstock but to centralize economic decision making there and to introduce more productive technologies. San Francisco bankers financed much of the West's mining operations, and the profits helped to develop California industries, as well as to build lavish mansions for the fortunate few. The process not only confirmed San Francisco as the financial capital of a self-financing frontier, but also reinforced the speculative mentality of the Gold Rush.

Agriculture

The 1870 census recorded that wheat had surpassed gold as California's most valuable product. Wheat remained one of California's most valuable products for the next thirty years, a period historians call the Bonanza Wheat Era. This massive expansion in production occurred largely because of the expanding industrial work force of Britain, which required the importation of food. California's weather in the central valleys was conducive to the production of hard, dry wheat suitable for the long sea voyage and highly prized by British and Irish milling companies.

The high demand for California wheat and the relatively flat and dry California terrain led to mass production. Agricultural entrepreneurs carved out huge wheat farms—the largest extending over 103 square miles—and came to rely on machines to a greater extent than wheat farmers anywhere else, particularly on larger and more complex machines. Relatively flat terrain and large fields encouraged California wheat growers to use huge steam-powered tractors and steam-powered combines, which cut the standing wheat and separated the grain from the stalk in one operation. Not for another twenty years or so was such equipment widely used elsewhere.

Such bonanza farms required a large force of laborers, especially at planting and harvesting times. Along with the mammoth cattle ranches of such entrepreneurs as Henry Miller and Charles Lux, the bonanza wheat farms gave a unique character to California agriculture—the farms and ranches were on a scale virtually unknown elsewhere in the country, and they relied on both technologically up-to-date equipment and an army of wage laborers, many of whom could only count on seasonal employment. By 1900 or so, the Bonanza Wheat Era had passed, partly because expansion of wheat growing elsewhere in the world drove down prices.

Viticulture—the growing of grapes—had been well established in southern California by the Spanish missions. In the 1860s and after, grape growing for wine shifted northward, and the valleys around San Francisco Bay—Sonoma, Napa, Livermore, and Santa Clara—became the center of the California wine industry. There the climate, terrain, and soil produced grapes that could be made into high-quality wines. By 1900, California was making more than 80 percent of the nation's wine. Grape growers, especially in the San Joaquin Valley, discovered another market for their products in the form of raisins, and by 1900 almost half of the California grape harvest was used for raisins.

During the 1880s and 1890s, fruit growers began to expand and diversify, especially around San Francisco Bay and in parts of the San Joaquin Valley. Climate and soil conditions gave California fruit growers a great advantage over other parts of the country, and new techniques in preserving fruit meant that dried and canned fruit from California could easily be shipped to the eastern states and elsewhere in the world. The development of refrigerated railroad cars greatly increased the ability of California growers to sell fresh fruit. The first refrigerated shipment of California fruit arrived in New York in 1888, leading to a major increase in demand. Refrigeration technology was soon applied to ships, and by 1892 fresh fruit from California was available in Great Britain. By 1900, Santa Clara County led the state in fruit production by a wide margin, followed by Fresno, Sonoma, and Solano Counties. In the 1870s, the U.S. Department of Agriculture introduced California growers to a navel orange from Brazil that was superior to previous varieties. Orange growing expanded rapidly in southern California once refrigerated railroad cars opened markets in the eastern states. In the 1880s and 1890s, California also became an important producer of vegetables and nuts.

The transition to fruit, nut, and vegetable crops brought important changes in many other aspects of California agriculture. The enormous wheat ranches with their huge machines yielded to smaller farms that relied more on human labor than on machinery. Raisin, peach, plum, and pear growers averaged between ten and seventy-five acres per farm, as opposed to the thousands of acres that had composed some wheat ranches. In many cases, a single family ran these small operations, although harvesting usually required additional labor.

The agricultural work force in central California in the 1880s and 1890s was ethnically diverse, including immigrants from Europe and whites whose families had been in the United States for generations. Cattle raising often employed Latinos, including both descendants of Californios and more recent immigrants from Mexico. Chinese farm workers contributed to the development of specialty crop agriculture out of proportion to their numbers. By the 1890s, there were also increasing numbers of agricultural workers from Japan and India.

Water

Water was key for the success of fruit, nut, and vegetable growing. Miners had developed elaborate water systems almost immediately and continued to require large amounts. Burgeoning urban areas required more and more water. Demands for water came up against legal systems that had been devised for different conditions. As a result, conflict over water often led to protracted legal battles and produced, in the end, new legal definitions of water rights and one of the first court orders protecting the environment.

Hydraulic mining had been used since the early 1850s (see p. 111). By 1880, some hydraulic mining operations operated around the clock, lit by giant electrical floodlights and drawing water from large reservoirs constructed by damming rivers. However, hydraulic mining was highly destructive not only to the terrain where the water cannons were directed but also to the environment downstream. The water from the blasting drained into rivers, carrying with it debris that killed fish and made the water unsuitable for drinking. Mining debris filled river channels and created serious flooding. Floods scattered mining debris over a wide area and damaged agricultural land. Thus, urban residents far downstream from hydraulic mining had to build elaborate dikes to keep rivers from flooding their cities. The mining debris in the river channels also threatened the use of rivers for shipping.

Finally, in 1884, the federal circuit court in San Francisco, in *Woodruff* v. *North Bloomfield Gravel Mining Company,* ordered an end to the dumping of debris in the rivers on the grounds that it was "a public and private nuisance," and inevitably damaged the property and livelihood of farmers. It was, perhaps, the first federal court order restricting a business in order to protect the environment. The SP backed those challenging hydraulic mining because debris caused problems for the railroad too, by fouling its tracks and damaging its land. The court decision in the *Woodruff* case, by limiting mining in the interest of agriculture—and other interests, to be certain—symbolized the transition from mineral extraction to crop production.

The legal system that Californians adapted from the eastern states was ill suited to the West. Eastern water law emphasized riparian rights, that is, the right of all those whose land bordered a stream to have access to the full flow of water from the stream, less small amounts for drinking. Irrigation removed water from the stream permanently, violating the riparian rights of those downstream from the irrigator. A different practice had emerged in the gold country, where the principle of appropriation was used to argue that the first person to take water from a stream gained the rights to that water. Both systems received some legal sanction by the California legislature.

This confusing state of affairs came under increasing challenge as more and more farmers began to use streams for irrigation. Eventually, in 1887, the legislature approved a law that permitted residents in a particular area to form an irrigation district with legal authority to take water for irrigation regardless of downstream claims. By then, California led the nation in the amount of irrigated farmland. By 1889, fourteen thousand California farmers (a quarter of the total), most of them in the San Joaquin Valley, practiced irrigation on more than a million acres, about 8 percent of all improved farmland in the state.

In the 1870s, some companies that had initially been formed to supply water for gold mining began to sell water to cities and for irrigation. To meet the demand for electricity in the late 1880s and after, entrepreneurs in most California cities were building generating plants that burned coal. Some, however, began to adapt the miners' waterways and high-pressure technologies to generate electricity more cheaply and with less pollution. By the early 1890s, there were several hydroelectric generating plants operating in the gold country. Mining towns like Grass Valley were among the first to have lights from hydroelectric power. By 1900, there were twenty-five hydroelectric generating plants in California, most in northern California, and that area was well on its way to becoming the region of the nation with the most intense use of water power to generate electricity.

Rise of Organized Labor

During the Gilded Age, changes in the state's economy resulted in a more complex work force. Figure 6.1 indicates components of the work force, based on the 1900 census. The census data understate the number of women who worked in

Figure 6.1 Major Components of the Wage-Earning Work Force, 1900
This graph suggests how complex the California economy had become by 1900. It also points to the continuing importance of agriculture and lumbering, as well as to the major role of manufacturing.
Source: Occupations at the twelfth census (Washington, 1904).

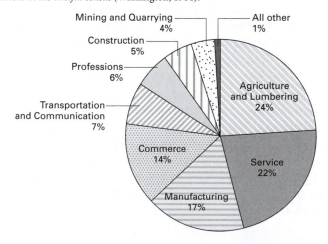

agriculture, so that proportion could be as high as a third. Also, women who ran boarding houses and prostitutes were often undercounted, which would increase the service sector somewhat. Increasing the agriculture and service sectors would, of course, proportionately decrease the others. Otherwise, Figure 6.1 provides a reasonable approximation of the California work force.

As the scale of operations grew in mining, transportation, and some parts of agriculture and manufacturing, and as reliance on technologically sophisticated machinery increased in those areas, fewer people had the necessary capital to enter such fields. Instead, those who worked in these fields were increasingly likely to be wage-earning employees. And, as wage earners, some of them helped to organize unions. In 1910, Lucile Eaves published one of the first scholarly histories of California labor. In it, she wrote that trade union activity appeared so early "that one is tempted to believe that the craftsmen met each other on the way to California and agreed to unite." And, indeed, many immigrants to California brought a concept of trade unionism in their mental baggage.

The first recorded union activity in California came in San Francisco in 1849, when carpenters went on strike for higher wages. Local unions were common in San Francisco and other cities from the Gold Rush onward, though most were short-lived—that is, until the 1880s. The history of early California unions is much like that of their counterparts to the east—workers with a particular skill formed local unions to seek better wages or working conditions, and those organizations often fell apart if they lost a strike.

As in other parts of the country in the 1880s, many local unions in California affiliated with newly formed national trade union organizations and sometimes with the American Federation of Labor (AFL), organized in 1886. Such trade unions typically limited their membership to skilled workers in one particular field, such as carpentry or printing, and many excluded women and people of color. The 1880s also saw the rapid rise of the Knights of Labor, who admitted both skilled and unskilled workers, including women and African Americans, but the Knights were short-lived. All California unions excluded Chinese workers. In fact, most California unions in the 1880s presented themselves as defending white workers against competition with Chinese workers, arguing that employers used Chinese workers to drive down wage levels and working conditions. Most historians agree that opposition to Chinese labor gave California unions what historian Alexander Saxton called "the indispensable enemy." This common enemy proved useful in efforts to organize white workers.

Unions also thrived in the prosperous 1880s because many employers found it to their financial advantage to give in to employee demands for better wages, rather than to face a strike. In 1891, employers formed the Board of Manufacturers and Employers of California, centered in San Francisco and devoted to opposing unions. A major depression that began in 1893 caused many unions to collapse when they lost members due to unemployment or were unable to maintain wage levels. Only with the revival of prosperity in the late 1890s did trade unions revive.

San Francisco: Metropolis of the West

The Southern Pacific, Hearst, Sharon, Flood and Fair, cattle barons, lumber companies, and other entrepreneurs located their corporate headquarters in San Francisco. San Francisco was also the site of the most successful unions. The city was, by any criterion of that day, a major city. In 1880, San Francisco's population reached nearly three hundred thousand, ranking it seventh among the nation's cities—the only large city west of St. Louis. James Bryce, an English visitor, noted in the 1880s that San Francisco "dwarfs" other western cities and "is a commercial and intellectual centre, and source of influence for the surrounding regions, more powerful over them than is any Eastern city over its neighborhood."

Beyond being a commercial and literary center (see pp. 154–156), San Francisco had about it an air of excitement. It boasted technological marvels to be found in few other places within hundreds of miles. Rudyard Kipling, the British author, visited in 1891 and likened the cable cars to a miracle for their ability to climb and descend hills smoothly. The expanding population alone provided opportunities that couldn't exist elsewhere. For example, a group of aspiring women artists formed a sketching club to encourage and critique each other's work, and German immigrants formed German gymnastics societies, singing groups, and other cultural organizations. Seamen the world over knew of the city's storied Barbary Coast, reputed to contain every conceivable form of pleasure and vice. San Francisco's Chinatown was the largest in the United States, and already attracted curious tourists—Oscar Wilde, in 1881, thought it was "the most artistic town I have ever come across."

This photograph of Market Street, 1901, shows the hustle and bustle of the metropolis of the West. Note, on the right, the cable car, filled with well-dressed San Franciscans, and, on the left, the coach carrying hotel clients. Why might newcomers from rural societies, either in the United States or elsewhere, find such a place intimidating?

San Francisco was the metropolis of the West because of its economic prowess. It was a center for finance and held the headquarters of corporations that dominated much of the Pacific Coast and intermountain West. Its dominance also stemmed from its port. In 1880, 99 percent of all imports to the Pacific Coast arrived on its docks, and 83 percent of all Pacific Coast exports were loaded there. Western mining, transportation, and agriculture stimulated San Francisco's manufacturing sector. By 1880, San Francisco's foundries produced advanced mining equipment, large-scale agricultural implements, locomotives, and ships. San Francisco also became a major center for food processing.

San Francisco's entrepreneurs extended their reach throughout the West and into the Pacific. Claus Spreckels, for example, an immigrant from Germany, established a sugar refinery in the city in 1863. In the 1870s, he developed a huge sugar plantation on the Hawaiian island of Maui and soon controlled nearly all of the Hawaiian sugar crop. By the 1890s, Spreckels was one of the three largest sugar producers in the nation, drawing not only upon Hawai`i but also on sugar beet fields in several western states. In the late 1890s, Hawaiian-born sugar planters wrested control from Spreckels, then replicated the chain of vertical integration that Spreckels had pioneered, investing in a steamship company to carry raw sugar to the new C&H (California and Hawaiian) refinery they built at Crockett, northeast of San Francisco.

As the population of California's cities burgeoned, especially San Francisco's, lumberjacks cut the coastal redwoods for use in construction. When timberlands near San Francisco Bay were exhausted, lumbering moved to northern California, Oregon, and Washington. Some lumber companies became vertically integrated, owning lumber mills, schooners that carried rough-cut lumber down the coast, and lumberyards and planing mills in the San Francisco Bay area. Born in Scotland, Robert Dollar grew up in lumber camps and worked his way up to sawmill owner. He purchased a ship in 1895 to carry his lumber to San Francisco, then he added more ships. His Dollar Line eventually became a major oceanic shipping company and the predecessor of today's American President Lines.

Some of California's Gold Rush fortunes were extended and expanded by a second generation. By 1900, George Hearst's former newspaper, the San Francisco *Examiner,* was one of several papers owned by his son, William Randolph Hearst, who became the head of a far-reaching, nationwide publishing empire in the early twentieth century. By the early twentieth century, William H. Crocker, son of Charles Crocker of the Big Four, was president of Crocker Bank and had begun to channel capital into investments throughout the West, including electrical power companies, hydroelectric generating plants, mining, agriculture, shipping, and southern California oil. Claus Spreckels's son John invested heavily in San Diego in commercial properties, banks, newspapers, and the Hotel del Coronado, the city's leading tourist attraction. His investments helped San Diego grow to almost eighteen thousand people by 1900. Henry Huntington—the nephew and heir of Collis Huntington of the SP—created an extensive streetcar system in the Los Angeles basin that both fed upon and contributed to the growth of Los Angeles.

New Social Patterns

California was becoming ever more urban—by 1900, more than 40 percent of Californians lived in its ten largest cities. The growth of cities was just one of the social and cultural changes that were also occurring elsewhere in the United States, including the emergence of new educational institutions, changes in the status of women, and large-scale immigration.

Education

During the late nineteenth century, great changes occurred in education, including the creation of colleges and universities. Religious organizations created California's earliest colleges. Methodists received the state's first college charter, in 1851, for California Wesleyan College, later called the University of the Pacific. In 1851 Joseph Alemany, first bishop of the Catholic diocese of California, gave the Santa Clara mission to Jesuit priests as a college site, and Santa Clara College (later Santa Clara University) obtained its charter in 1855. Southern California lagged in creating colleges. Los Angeles Methodists planned the University of Southern California in the 1870s, but the university opened in 1880 only because of a gift of land by three donors—one Protestant, one Catholic, and one Jewish. Presbyterians founded Occidental College in 1887.

Compared with eastern colleges, more of the early California colleges admitted women. Even so, as was the case in the East, separate women's colleges began to appear, notably Mills College, chartered in 1885 as a private, nondenominational women's college.

Denominational colleges were older than the nation itself. Public universities—nondenominational, tax-supported—appeared in a few places after the American Revolution, but most public universities were created only after 1862, when Congress approved the Morrill Act, giving land to states for use in funding a university. The University of California derived from both traditions. The College of California, founded in 1853 as a private academy, drew upon the traditions of Harvard and Yale. In 1867 the trustees donated their institution to the state. The legislature added to that gift the state's land grant under the Morrill Act, and created the University of California. In 1873 the university acquired a medical college in San Francisco. As was occurring elsewhere, the university moved away from its original classical curriculum and created majors, including engineering, agriculture, and commerce. The university also increased its emphasis on research and service to the state.

The need for better-trained teachers led the legislature to create state-funded, two-year schools called "normal schools." These institutions bore little resemblance to the colleges of the day. Instead of the classical curriculum or the new system of majors, they concentrated on training teachers for grades one through eight. By 1900, state normal schools operated at Chico, Los Angeles, San Diego, San Francisco, San José, and Santa Barbara.

Leland and Jane Stanford spent years planning a university to memorialize their son. They envisioned Stanford University as a nondenominational, "practical" university, whose graduates would be broadly educated and also prepared for a profession. Women were admitted on a basis of equality with men. The first president, David Starr Jordan, sought to mold a modern university, stressing research as well as teaching, providing graduate as well as undergraduate instruction, and permitting students to choose a major.

Throughout the nation at the time, public schooling ended after the eighth grade. This sufficed for those who worked in agriculture or industry but not for college admission. Those who attended college often prepared at private academies. During the Gilded Age, urban parents demanded that local school boards create high schools. High schools prepared students for college, and by 1900 some high schools also offered vocational courses such as bookkeeping or woodworking. By 1900, 32 percent of California men and 39 percent of California women of high school age were in school.

Changing Gender Roles

Increasing participation by women in education was just one indication of the changes in women's status. Another highly visible change was an increase in women throughout the work force—as wage earners, professionals, and self-employed entrepreneurs. These patterns were most pronounced in urban areas and developed even though much of American society, especially the urban, white middle class, still subscribed to notions of domesticity and separate spheres.

Many California women worked outside the home, including in 1880 one-quarter of San Francisco's females over the age of ten. African American women and daughters of immigrants were most likely to work for wages. The largest number of women who worked outside of their own homes were servants and waitresses; the next largest number worked in clothing making, either as factory workers or self-employed dressmakers or milliners. By 1900, women outnumbered men by four to one among stenographers and typists and by three to one among teachers. Though some jobs remained closed to women, California women were working in printing (one in eight were women), medicine (also one in eight), and business (one in four among bookkeepers and accountants). By the late nineteenth century, changes in retailing—especially the appearance of department stores—brought new employment opportunities for women. In 1874, Kate Kennedy, a San Francisco school principal and political activist, persuaded the legislature to require that women teachers be paid the same as male teachers for the same work, but the large majority of women still earned less than their male counterparts.

The majority of California women did not work outside the home, and the social values of domesticity and separate spheres prevailed in many places.

Women continued to be active in church organizations and benevolent societies. By 1894, the 204 charitable organizations in San Francisco dispensed more than $1.3 million, nearly all raised from private sources. Middle- and upper-class women ran most of those charities. They also organized women's clubs devoted to self-education, socializing, and often charitable or reform activities. Throughout the nation, and in much of California, the largest women's organization of the Gilded Age was the Women's Christian Temperance Union (WCTU). Founded in 1874, the WCTU advocated the prohibition of alcoholic beverages and condemned the abuse of wives and children by drunken husbands.

Some California women challenged restrictions on women. Two pioneer female lawyers, Clara Shortridge Foltz of San José and Laura de Force Gordon from San Francisco, promoted a range of women's issues, from admission to law school to changes in laws governing property ownership. (See p. 185, for their accomplishments during the state's second constitutional convention.) Both, at different times, led the California State Woman Suffrage Association. In 1878, California Senator Aaron A. Sargent introduced in the U.S. Congress, for the first time, a proposed constitutional amendment for woman suffrage. A group of California women steadily promoted the cause of woman suffrage, but they could not persuade the state legislature to put the question before the voters until 1896. Susan B. Anthony and other national suffrage leaders then hurried to California to organize the most thorough campaign up to that time. Ellen Clark Sargent, widow of the senator who first introduced the suffrage amendment, led the effort. The cause won support from Jane Lathrop Stanford, the first time that suffrage secured public support from a woman of such high status. Anthony pushed Stanford to make her support public, arguing that "it is cruel for the women of position and power in California not to let the people know they stand with us." As support for woman suffrage grew, liquor industry leaders became alarmed that a suffrage victory might lead to a WCTU victory, and they mounted a strong antisuffrage campaign. Outside San Francisco and Alameda County (Oakland) the suffrage amendment won a small majority, but large majorities against it in those two counties ultimately defeated it statewide.

Urban areas also became the sites for a new type of challenge to accepted gender roles. A few men and somewhat more women changed their dress and behavior, passing for a member of the other sex either briefly or permanently. One famous example was Lillie Hitchcock Coit, a wealthy San Franciscan who occasionally wore men's clothing to attend saloons or nightspots that barred women. Another woman, Charlie Parkhurst, was not famous until years after her death, when Wells Fargo Bank featured her in a television commercial that summarized her twenty years of living and working as a man, much of it as a Wells Fargo stagecoach driver. Elvira Mugarrieta claimed that she wore men's clothing so she could "travel freely, feel protected and find work," and spent much of her life passing as a man, serving as a lieutenant in the Spanish-American War and a male nurse during the San Francisco earthquake.

Though some people passed for the other gender, homosexual behavior was illegal everywhere. Same-sex relationships that involved genital contact violated state laws and social expectations. In the late nineteenth century, however, burgeoning cities provided anonymity for gays and lesbians, who gravitated toward cities and developed distinctive subcultures. By the 1890s, reports of regular meeting places for homosexuals—particular clubs, restaurants, steam baths, parks, and streets—came from most large American cities, including San Francisco.

California Indians

The legal situation of California Indians continued to evolve in unusual ways. In the West during the 1870s and 1880s, federal policy and the army combined to locate Indian people on reservations. Efforts to move the native peoples of California onto reservations in California had been short-circuited before the Civil War (see p. 133), though a few small reservations were established and Indian peoples from several tribes were relocated to them. Most remained outside those reservations, however, living in small villages, called *rancherías,* and working for wages on nearby farms and ranches. Some rancherías existed because local landowners needed the labor of their residents. Sometimes Indian people pooled their resources and bought small plots of land for their rancherías. For most California Indians not living on reservations, however, their legal status remained ambiguous.

The last armed conflict between the U.S. Army and Indian peoples within California was the so-called Modoc War of 1872–1873. The Modocs had traditionally lived in northern California along the Lost River. In 1864, they were assigned to a reservation in southern Oregon along with the Klamath people, traditional adversaries of the Modocs. A group of Modocs led by Kientpoos (also spelled Keintpoos or Kintpuash)—often called Captain Jack—returned to the Lost River region and asked for a reservation there. Sporadic negotiations produced no agreement. U.S. troops arrived in 1872, and ordered the Modocs to return to the reservation in Oregon. Shooting broke out when one Modoc refused to surrender his gun, and the Modocs fled. Several Modocs then killed seventeen white settlers. Ordered to negotiate rather than attack, General Edward Canby opened discussions. Among the Modocs, one faction persuaded the rest that they could improve their bargaining position if they could demonstrate their power by killing the negotiators.

Rumors were rampant about the planned killings. The negotiators knew of the danger but came to the meeting place unarmed on April 11, 1873. Two, including Canby, were killed and another seriously injured. (Canby was the highest-ranking army officer ever killed by Indians.) The Modocs fled into nearby rocky hills (now part of the Lava Beds National Monument). The army ordered the new commander to attack and capture the Modocs. At first, the Modocs eluded the troops, but eventually they had a disagreement and split into two groups. Soldiers captured one group, who then helped locate the other group in return for promises that they would not be put on trial. All of the Modocs were thus captured. The Modocs who had murdered the peace negotiators were tried and found guilty. Four were hanged, and two were sentenced to prison. Meanwhile, Oregon settlers killed several Modocs. Arguing that white settlers were likely to kill the others if they returned to Oregon, federal authorities sent them to Indian Territory (now Oklahoma) and permitted them to return to Oregon only thirty years later.

Changing Patterns of Ethnicity

For the United States, the years between the Civil War and World War I (1865–1917) were a time of large-scale immigration, nearly all from Europe. California received large numbers of European immigrants, but also had its own unique immigration patterns. Streams of immigrants from Europe and Asia significantly affected Californians' understanding of ethnicity.

Table 6.1 summarizes data on immigration, nativity, and race from the U.S. censuses of 1860, 1880, and 1900. The data for 1860 show the influence of the

TABLE 6.1 NATIVITY AND RACE, 1860, 1880, AND 1900

Nativity and Race	1860		1880		1900	
	Number	Percent	Number	Percent	Number	Percent
White, born in U.S. with both parents born in U.S.	176,649	46.5	549,529	63.6	644,428	43.4
White, born in U.S. with one or both parents foreign-born					441,794	29.7
White, foreign-born	146,528	38.6	217,652	25.2	316,505	21.3
Total white	323,177	85.0	767,181	88.7	1,402,727	94.5
Asian, Chinese	34,933	9.2	75,132	8.7	45,753	3.1
Asian, Japanese			86	.0001	10,151	0.7
American Indian	17,798	4.7	16,277	1.9	15,377	1.0
African American	4,086	1.1	6,018	0.7	11,045	0.7
Latino	No reliable data available		No reliable data available		No reliable data available	
TOTAL POPULATION	379,994		864,694		1,485,053	

Source: Population of the United States in 1860 (Washington, 1864); *Statistics of the population of the United States at the tenth census* (Washington, 1883); *Twelfth census of the United States, taken in the year 1900. Population* (Washington, 1901–1902).

Gold Rush, when people from around the world descended on California to strike it rich. Immigration continued afterward, but there also developed a large population born in the United States and, especially, in California.

Table 6.1 shows that half the population of California, as of 1900, consisted of first- or second-generation white immigrants, the vast majority from Europe. As of 1900, the largest numbers of California's immigrants were from Germany and Ireland, each with 19 percent of white immigrants, followed by Britain and English-speaking Canada, with 15 percent. Italy and Scandinavia (Norway, Sweden, Denmark, and Iceland) each provided 6 percent.

In California, some European ethnic groups showed patterns of settlement and occupation that differed in significant ways from those same groups in the Midwest or Northeast. In the Midwest, Scandinavians were among those most likely to be farmers. While some Scandinavians farmed in California, many Scandinavians worked as merchant seamen. A survey by the Sailors Union of the Pacific (SUP) found that 40 percent of its members were born in Scandinavia. Andrew Furuseth, a Norwegian-born seaman, helped to create the SUP and led it for more than forty years. In the northeastern United States, Italians tended to be urban and to work in manufacturing. There were Italians in California who did the same, but there were also many who lived in agricultural areas, especially around San Francisco Bay. Italian farmers around the bay and in the Santa Clara and Sacramento Valleys sent much of their produce to San Francisco, and Italian produce merchants in San Francisco developed long-term relations with Italian farmers. Such contacts helped Amadeo P. Giannini when he made the transition from produce merchant to banker and created the Bank of Italy in 1904. Other Italians moved from selling produce to processing it, including winemaking, pasta making, and the canning of fruits and vegetables.

In many places in California, European immigrants settled into communities defined by language and religion. Most Italians and most Irish were Catholic, so, for both groups, language, religion, and national origin coincided to help create ethnically self-conscious communities. Germans, however, often formed separate ethnic communities by religion—Catholic, Lutheran, Calvinist, and Jewish—although some German ethnic organizations and newspapers crossed religious dividing lines. Most Scandinavians were Lutheran, but the churches they formed in America often differed significantly from the Lutheran organizations created by German immigrants. Many Scandinavian Lutherans, for example, opposed the consumption of alcohol but few Germans saw any sin attached to a glass of beer.

In San Francisco and throughout the West, Chinese immigrants established Chinatowns—relatively autonomous and largely self-contained Chinese communities. Chinese Californians formed kinship organizations and district associations, whose members came from the same part of China, in order to assist and protect each other. A confederation of such associations with headquarters in San Francisco, the Chinese Consolidated Benevolent Association—the "Six Companies"—eventually exercised great power over the social and economic life of Chinese communities throughout the West. Chinese communities were largely male, partly

Shown here is a Chinese vegetable peddler, San Francisco, during the 1890s. Before the era of supermarkets, the women who managed many middle-class and upper-class homes expected to buy many of their fresh produce from door-to-door peddlers, who usually had regular routes in such neighborhoods. In the late nineteenth century, Chinese Californians raised much of the fresh vegetables and caught much of the fresh seafood, and so too Chinese were most prominent in the door-to-door peddling of such produce. Why might such peddlers have avoided working-class neighborhoods?

because of a federal law, the Page Act of 1875, which prohibited "the importation into the United States of women for the purposes of prostitution." This law was often used by immigration officials to exclude Chinese women, thus limiting the possibilities for the creation of families. As in other largely male communities, gambling and prostitution flourished, giving Chinatowns a reputation as vice districts.

Many Chinese immigrants initially came to California for the Gold Rush and railroad construction. During the 1850s and 1860s, four-fifths of Chinese Californians lived in mining regions, and nearly that large a proportion worked in mining. By 1900, however, nearly half of all Chinese Californians lived in the San Francisco Bay area and another quarter in the Central Valley. By then, about one-fifth of Chinese Californians worked in agriculture or fishing, another one-fifth in personal service (barbers, cooks, household servants, and the like), and another fifth as laborers in areas other than agriculture and mining. By 1900, the total number of Chinese Californians had declined significantly, from a high point of some 136,000 in 1883 to fewer than 46,000 by 1900.

These changes in the number and in the regional and occupational distribution of Chinese Californians reflect, in part, general economic changes. As mining declined, agriculture rose. But those changes also reflect the response by Chinese Californians to white mobs who tried to drive the Chinese out of particular occupations and particular communities. A wave of riots took place in the 1870s, accompanying the economic downturn of those years. Some white workers blamed the Chinese for driving down wages and causing unemployment. In 1871, an anti-Chinese riot in Los Angeles erupted when city police, breaking up a fight in the city's Chinatown, were fired upon by Chinese, wounding two policemen and killing a civilian. A white mob surged into Chinatown, burned buildings, looted stores, and attacked Chinese, killing eighteen. San Francisco experienced anti-Chinese rioting in 1877. A second wave of anti-Chinese riots swept communities in the West in 1885. The most serious riot was in Rock Springs, Wyoming, where a mob of white miners burned the local Chinatown and killed twenty-eight Chinese. Anti-Chinese violence led many Chinese to retreat to the agricultural areas of central California and to the larger Chinatowns, especially San Francisco. Declining numbers of Chinese Californians also reflect a return to China by some, the exclusion of new immigrants after 1882, and the limited prospects for forming families.

In parts of California, the Chinese encountered segregation similar to that imposed on blacks in the South, including residential and occupational segregation resulting from local custom rather than law. In 1871 the San Francisco school board barred Chinese students from the public schools, and the ban lasted until 1885, when the parents of Mamie Tape convinced the courts to order the city to provide education for their daughter. The city then opened a segregated Chinese school. Segregated schools for Chinese American children were also established in Sacramento and a few other places.

In places with many Chinese immigrants, merchants often took the lead in establishing a strong economic base. Chinese organizations sometimes succeeded in fighting anti-Chinese legislation. For example, when the San Francisco Board of Supervisors restricted Chinese laundry owners, they went to court. In the case of *Yick Wo* v. *Hopkins* (1886), the U.S. Supreme Court for the first time declared a licensing law unconstitutional because local authorities used it to discriminate on the basis of race.

There was relatively little immigration from Latin America to California between the Gold Rush and about 1900. Many immigrants who came from Latin America to California during the Gold Rush assimilated into Mexican communities that predated the Gold Rush. By 1900, people born in Mexico made up only 3 percent of foreign-born Californians. Most California Latinos, by 1900, had been born in California, and often their parents had been as well. In Los Angeles, only 11 percent of the Latino population had been born in Mexico as of 1880. Research on several southern California communities indicates very little change between 1860 and 1880 in the number of Latinos.

Historians have described a process that Albert Camarillo calls "barrioization"—the creation of *barrios,* or separate Spanish-speaking neighborhoods within the larger cities, often near an old mission church. Such barrios, like neighborhoods of European immigrants, provided their residents with opportunities and institutions to preserve their own cultural heritages even as they adapted to the expectations and opportunities in the larger community. Large barrios, like many large concentrations of immigrants, often had a newspaper, stores run by members of the group where one might buy culturally familiar products, and voluntary organizations including church-related groups, beneficial societies, and political clubs. There was, of course, one glaring difference between immigrant neighborhoods and barrios—European immigrants came to California seeking improved opportunities and a better life, but Mexican Californians went from being the dominant group to a disadvantaged and largely landless minority, with well over half of the males employed as unskilled laborers.

In the late nineteenth century, ethnicity still played a prominent role in the way many Californians identified themselves. Among foreign immigrants to California, most had thought of themselves before they left their homeland as residents of a particular village and perhaps as subjects of a particular monarch. Once in the United States, they began to think of themselves as having much in common with others who spoke their language, worshiped as they did, and shared many of their values and expectations, whether or not they came from the same village. They thought of themselves as members of an ethnic group, different from the ethnic groups around them, whereas before immigrating they were likely to have been members of a more homogeneous society. Not surprisingly, for many Californians of the late nineteenth century, ethnic identities proved to be an important part of their self-identity and affected the way that they related to others.

Politics

During the Gilded Age, American men's ethnicity often influenced their politics. Politics meant political parties, and the large majority of Americans expected that only men would be involved. From the end of the Civil War (1865) to the late 1890s, American men demonstrated the highest degree of party loyalty in the nation's history, and participation in politics was at an all-time high. Political parties nominated candidates for office at party conventions (at local, state, and national levels). The conventions were organized, circus-like campaigns with torchlight parades, free barbecues, and long, arm-waving speeches. The parties distributed ballots on Election Day—a voter had to get the "ticket" with the candidates of his party in order to vote. In most of the country, ethnicity and party were closely linked. In the Northeast and Midwest, Catholics and German Lutherans usually voted Democratic, and most Methodists, Presbyterians, and Scandinavian Lutherans voted Republican. In the South, most whites voted Democratic and nearly all African Americans were Republicans. California differed from these national patterns in several ways: some California males seem to have been less strongly committed to their parties, and ethnicity seems less significantly related to party affiliation in California than elsewhere.

Political Discontent in the 1870s

In the 1871 election, the Republicans of Solano County demonstrated the potential for manipulation that inhered in having political parties print ballots. Normally, parties printed their candidates' names on a sheet of paper and distributed those "tickets" to voters. If a voter wanted to vote for someone else, he had to scratch out the name printed on the ticket and write in the other name. Some candidates distributed "pasters," small strips of paper with the candidate's name on one side and glue on the other, to make "scratching a ticket" easier. Republicans in Solano County devised a ticket only five-eighths of an inch wide and printed in tiny type, making it impossible to write in a name or use a paster. Its long and narrow shape, with dense, tiny printing all over it, was soon labeled the "tapeworm ticket" and was imitated across the state. In 1874, the legislature required that ballots be "uniform in size, color, weight, texture, and appearance"— one of the earliest efforts by any state to regulate political parties. Another law in 1878 regulated the symbols used by parties to distinguish their tickets.

Newton Booth, who won the 1871 election for governor by running as a critic of the Southern Pacific, took office just as the Granger movement began to affect state politics. The Patrons of Husbandry—called the Grange—promoted educational programs and cooperatives among farmers. In several states, farmers formed independent political parties, known by various names but usually called Granger parties. Several states passed "granger laws," creating state railway commissions to investigate, and sometimes regulate, railroad charges. In California in 1873, Grangers combined with opponents of the SP to create a new political party, the People's Independent Party. Governor Booth favored the new party. The People's Independents won a large bloc of legislative seats in 1873 and elected their candidate to the state supreme court (judges were then elected on party tickets). In 1875, the state legislature was faced with filling both U.S. Senate seats, due to the death of one incumbent and the expiration of the other's term. People's Independents combined with Booth's followers and a few Democrats to elect Booth to one Senate seat and a Democrat to the other. When Booth resigned the governorship, Lieutenant Governor Romualdo Pacheco, scion of a prominent Californio family, became governor for the remainder of Booth's term. By 1875, the Granger movement had passed its peak, and the People's Independent Party soon disappeared.

Another third party emerged in San Francisco in 1877. The late 1870s were years of economic depression and high unemployment. In July 1877, a strike by eastern railroad workers, protesting wage cuts, mushroomed into violence in several midwestern and eastern cities. In San Francisco, a meeting to support the railway strikers erupted into a riot aimed at Chinese workers. That fall, Denis Kearney, a drayman whose business had suffered from the depression, attracted a

Beginning in 1877, Denis Kearney attracted large crowds, mostly of working-class San Franciscans, at rallies held on the sandlots near the new City Hall, which was still under construction. His speeches always concluded with the phrase, "The Chinese must go!" From these rallies came the Workingmen's Party of California. How did Kearney attract a strong following among working-class Californians?

wide following when he condemned the monopoly power of the SP and, at the same time, argued that monopolists were using Chinese workers to drive down wages. He formed the Workingmen's Party of California (WPC), and gave it the slogan, "The Chinese Must Go." For a time in the late 1870s, the WPC dominated political life in San Francisco, sweeping elections in 1878 and 1879. WPC candidates also won elections for mayor in Oakland and Sacramento. The Chinese issue differentiated the WPC from labor parties in cities outside of California.

Kearney and the WPC were not the first to attack the Chinese. From the start of Chinese immigration to California, some viewed them as a threat. Beginning with Leland Stanford in 1861, most governors bemoaned the presence of Chinese in California. "Anti-coolie" clubs ("coolie" was a derogatory term for a Chinese laborer) in working-class districts of San Francisco attracted many members. Opponents of the Chinese claimed that they drove down white workers' wages and standard of living. Others portrayed the Chinese as unclean, immoral, clannish, and heathen. State and city laws discriminated against the Chinese from the 1850s onward.

The Second Constitutional Convention, 1878

The WPC's greatest statewide success came in 1878, in elections for a second constitutional convention. In many places, anxious Republicans and Democrats compromised their differences and put up nonpartisan slates to oppose the WPC. In the end, the convention consisted of eighty nonpartisans, fifty-two Workingmen (mostly from San Francisco), ten Republicans, nine Democrats, and one Independent. Of those elected from rural areas, many had been involved with the Granger movement. Together, WPC delegates and Granger delegates comprised a majority.

The convention delegates met in Sacramento in September 1878. The constitution they drafted remains the state constitution—much amended—at the beginning of the twenty-first century. The new constitution set the size of the state senate at forty and the assembly at eighty (both still in force) and specified that the legislature should meet for only sixty days in alternate years (a provision changed in 1966). Statewide officers were to serve four-year terms and be elected in even-numbered years halfway between presidential elections (provisions still in force). The 1849 constitution required publication of all significant public documents in both English and Spanish; the new constitution specified that all public documents were to be in English. The University of California was given autonomy from legislative or executive oversight (still in force). The WPC and the Grangers combined to create an elected railroad commission (still in existence, now called the Public Utilities Commission) empowered to regulate rates. Water was declared to be under state regulation.

Clara Shortridge Foltz and Laura de Force Gordon (see p. 176) set up a well-organized lobbying operation at the convention. Though unable to get woman suffrage, they secured two important constitutional guarantees: equal access for women to any legitimate occupation and to public higher educational institutions.

The convention teemed with proposals for constitutional restrictions on aliens not eligible for citizenship—that is, Chinese and other Asian immigrants. One member of the body spoke against discriminatory legislation but was ignored. In the end, the constitution authorized the legislature to provide for removal from the state of "dangerous or detrimental" aliens, prohibited any corporation or governmental body from employing any "Chinese or Mongolian," directed the legislature to discourage immigration by those not eligible for citizenship, and specified that white foreigners and foreigners of African descent (but with no mention of Asians) had the same property rights as native-born citizens.

The new constitution was highly controversial, mostly because of its restrictions on corporations. Californians voted on it in May 1879. Despite strong opposition, it was approved by a healthy margin. Many of the provisions restricting Asians were later invalidated by the courts.

Politics in the 1880s

Anti-Chinese agitation soon reached national politics. In 1880, President Rutherford B. Hayes sent a representative to China to negotiate a treaty permitting the United States to "regulate, limit, or suspend" the immigration of Chinese laborers, and the treaty was approved in November. That summer, both

Republicans and Democrats promised, in their national platforms, to cut off Chinese immigration.

In 1882, U.S. Senator John Miller, a Republican from California, introduced a bill to exclude Chinese immigration for twenty years and to prohibit Chinese from becoming naturalized citizens. Chinese immigrants, by most legal interpretations, had been barred from naturalization by a federal law from 1790 that limited naturalization to "free, white persons." In 1870, this had been amended to permit persons of African descent to become naturalized citizens. Local courts, however, had permitted a few Chinese immigrants to become citizens. Miller's bill drew strong support from westerners and from Democrats. It passed both houses of Congress by large margins, prohibiting entry to all Chinese except teachers, students, merchants, tourists, and officials. Most opposition came from northeastern Republicans, especially veterans of the abolition movement.

Chester A. Arthur, who had become president in 1881, vetoed Miller's bill, arguing that it violated the 1880 treaty, that twenty years was too long, and that the bill might "drive [Chinese] trade and commerce into more friendly hands." In response, Congress cut exclusion to ten years and stated that the act did not violate the treaty. It now drew even more votes, and Arthur signed the bill into law.

The WPC rose to prominence on the Chinese issue. However, by 1882, the party had broken into factional disarray and disappeared. State politics in the relatively prosperous 1880s involved Republicans and Democrats, with no significant third parties. Republicans and Democrats continued to rotate through the governor's office. Republicans won in 1879, but Democrats swept most state offices in 1882. The Southern Pacific continued to play a prominent part in state politics—symbolized in 1885 when Leland Stanford was elected to the U.S. Senate amid allegations of vote-buying. In 1886, voters elected a Democrat as governor and a Republican as lieutenant governor, and gave a narrow majority in the legislature to the Democrats. This permitted the Democrats, in 1887, to elect George Hearst to a full term in the U.S. Senate; he had been appointed by the Democratic governor to fill a vacancy the year before.

The 1880s marked the peak of power for Christopher A. Buckley, a blind saloon keeper who, around 1880, emerged as the most powerful Democratic leader in San Francisco. Born in Ireland and raised in New York City, Buckley acquired the reputation of being a "boss," a party leader whose organization dominated all access to political office by controlling nominating conventions. As "boss," Buckley used appointive governmental positions to reward his loyal followers. To keep voter support, he kept taxes so low that city government could do very little. Buckley also apparently extracted a price from the many companies who did business with the burgeoning city—when he died, his estate included bonds issued by companies that did business with the city during the 1880s. In the late 1880s, Buckley extended his power to state politics, picking the Democrats who won the governorship in 1882 (George Stoneman) and 1886 (Washington Bartlett).

As of 1890, only one candidate for governor of California had ever been elected to a second term, and the governorship and the state legislature (and therefore the U.S. senatorships filled by the state legislature) changed parties at almost every election. Throughout the 1870s, third parties—first the People's Independents and then the WPC—had attracted large numbers of California voters. Yet during much of the Gilded Age, American voters outside California showed extraordinary loyalty to their political parties. By contrast, enough California voters split their tickets between the two parties or changed party commitments between elections that they produced constant partisan turnover. Theodore Hittell, who published an extensive history of the state in 1897, emphasized that this pattern was virtually without parallel in other states, and he attributed it to the "'thinking-for-itself' character of the people."

Political Realignment in the 1890s

This "thinking-for-itself character" of California voters, producing frequent changes between the two major parties, became even more pronounced in the 1890s. The elections of 1890 provided a catalyst for change. In San Francisco, the usual large Democratic majorities failed to materialize, giving the governorship and control of the legislature to the Republicans. Control of the legislature was important, because Stanford's term in the U.S. Senate was ending, and the legislature was to choose his successor in 1891. Claiming that Buckley had sold out to Stanford, reform-oriented Democrats campaigned to oust the boss. A grand jury investigated Buckley on charges of bribery. Beleaguered, the boss debarked on an extended foreign tour, and his organization fell into disarray.

The legislative session of 1891 reelected Stanford to the Senate, but then exhibited such shameful behavior that it became known as the "legislature of a thousand scandals." For example, when Senator Hearst died and the legislature had to elect someone to complete his term, a wastebasket was found filled with empty currency wrappers and a list of assembly members. Nonetheless, the legislature approved the Australian ballot, a change that drew support from reformers, organized labor, and the WCTU, among others. Henceforth the government printed and distributed ballots that included all candidates, and voters marked their ballots in secret.

During the early 1890s, many Americans questioned existing political and economic systems. In *Looking Backward: 2000–1887*, a novel by Edward Bellamy published in 1887, a young Bostonian named Julian West was mesmerized in 1887 and awakened in 2000 to find that all people were equal, poverty and individual wealth had been eliminated, and everyone shared in a cooperative commonwealth. Bellamy's admirers formed Nationalist Clubs to promote a cooperative commonwealth—an economic system based on producers' and consumers' cooperatives rather than on wage labor and profits. The San Francisco *Examiner* noted in 1890, "California seems to have an especially prolific soil for that sort of product." California claimed sixty-two Nationalist Clubs in 1890, about a third of all those in the entire country, with some 3,500 members. Within a year, however, the movement had virtually disappeared, with many of its adherents swept up in the emergence of the new Populist Party.

Between 1890 and 1892, a new political party emerged in the West and South, taking the name People's Party, or Populists. Growing out of the Farmers' Alliance (an organization similar to the Grange), the new party appealed to hard-pressed farmers in the West and South. In their 1892 national convention, they declared that the old regional lines of division between North and South were healed. The new division, they proclaimed, was between "producers" (farmers and workers) and "capitalists, corporations, national banks, rings [corrupt political organizations], trusts." Among other changes, they called for government ownership of railroads.

Californians organized a state Farmers' Alliance in 1890, later than in the Midwest or South. By late 1891, the California Alliance claimed thirty thousand members and launched a state party. Above all, California Populists campaigned against the railroad, especially the SP, and against railroad influence over politics. In 1892, Populists took 9 percent of the vote in California for president and won one congressional seat and eight seats in the state legislature. They did especially well in rural areas where farmers were suffering from low crop prices, but attracted very few votes in the Democratic stronghold of San Francisco. In the 1893 legislative session, one Populist voted with the Democrats to elect Stephen White to the U.S. Senate. White, a Democrat from Los Angeles, built a political following by his relentless attacks on the SP and on corporate control of politics. Now led by White, California Democrats took the governorship in the elections of 1894, but lost nearly everything else. In 1894, however, the Populist candidate won the office of mayor in San Francisco with his strongest support in working-class parts of the city.

President Grover Cleveland, a Democrat, had grappled with a serious economic depression that began in 1893, but his actions divided and demoralized his own party. He did not seek reelection in 1896. Instead, the Democratic candidate in 1896 was William Jennings Bryan of Nebraska, one of Cleveland's strongest critics. Republicans nominated William McKinley of Ohio, a staunch supporter of the protective tariff as the means of bringing economic recovery. Bryan argued for bringing recovery by counteracting the prevalent deflation (falling prices) through an expanded currency supply. The Populists also endorsed Bryan. On Election Day, Bryan carried nearly all of the West and South, leaving McKinley with the urban, industrial Northeast and the more urban and industrial parts of the Midwest. McKinley also won California, though by the narrowest of margins. Thus, California behaved politically more like the Northeast than like the rest of the West.

Disappointed at Bryan's loss, most California Democrats thought that the close margin put them in a good position for the future. In fact, California and the nation stood at the beginning of a long period of Republican dominance of politics. McKinley's narrow margin of victory in California in 1896 soon widened, as the influx of population from the Midwest into southern California continued to swell Republican majorities there, and as formerly Democratic voters moved toward the Republican Party. Between 1895 and 1938, no Democrat won the California governorship, and Republicans typically controlled the state legislature by large margins. In 1896, California was on the verge of becoming one of the most Republican states in the nation.

California and the World: War with Spain and Acquisition of the Philippines

In April 1898, the United States went to war with Spain. Most Americans—and most Californians—responded enthusiastically to what they understood to be a war undertaken to bring independence and aid to the long-suffering inhabitants of Cuba, the last remaining Spanish colony in the Western Hemisphere. When President William McKinley called for troops, nearly five thousand Californians responded, forming four regiments of California Volunteer Infantry and a battalion of heavy artillery.

Many people were surprised when the first engagement in the war occurred in the Philippine Islands–nearly half-way around the world from Cuba. On May 1, Commodore George Dewey's naval squadron steamed into Manila Bay and quickly destroyed or captured the entire Spanish fleet there. Dewey's victory focused attention on the Philippines and on the Pacific more generally. Troops were needed in the Philippines, and one regiment of the California Volunteer Infantry and part of the California heavy artillery were dispatched there. They encountered not Spanish resistance, but opposition from Filipinos who preferred independence to American control. Several Californians died in action against the Filipino insurgents.

Many Americans now looked to the Hawaiian Islands as a crucial base halfway to the Philippines. Congress approved the annexation of Hawai`i on July 7, 1898. At the war's end, among other settlements, Spain ceded Guam and sold the Philippines to the United States. Soon after, the United States signed the Treaty of Berlin, acquiring part of the Samoan Islands. Some Californians opposed acquisition of the Philippines out of principled opposition to imperialism, and others, especially labor leaders, opposed it out of fear of an influx of Asian labor. Still other Californians, however, embraced the new acquisitions and eagerly anticipated extending their entrepreneurial activities to the new Pacific empire.

Cultural Expression

Though Mark Twain, Bret Harte, and most other literary figures of the Gold Rush era had left California by 1870, a new group of writers had emerged by 1900. One was María Amparo Ruiz de Burton, the state's first published Latina author, whose novel *The Squatter and the Don* (1885) was based, as its subtitle proclaimed, on "contemporary occurrences in California." In her novel, Ruiz de Burton presented a romance set against the conflict between an aristocratic Californio rancho owner and settlers squatting on his lands, and then against the conflict between them and the railroad.

By using contemporary social and economic conflict as the context for her novel, Ruiz de Burton anticipated the work of Frank Norris, the best known of California's new authors. While at Berkeley, Norris discovered the novels of Emile Zola, with their realistic treatment of contemporary life, especially among the working class, and he began to see the people as the stuff for powerful fiction. Of Norris's six novels, *McTeague* (1899), *The Octopus* (1901), and *The Pit* (1903) are the most well-known. He died suddenly in 1902. His final work was a trilogy focused on California wheat. *The Octopus,* the first book of the three, dealt with conflict between wheat growers and the railroad—"the Octopus" was a thinly disguised version of the SP—and included a fictional version of the "battle of Mussel Slough" (see p. 164). In *The Pit,* Norris shifted to Chicago, to treat the financial manipulations in the wholesale buying and selling of wheat. He died before he could write the final novel in the trilogy, *The Wolf*, which was to have been set in Europe, where the wheat that had been produced in the midst of conflict between railroad and farmers and that had bought and sold amidst financial machinations, finally became bread that saved lives during famine.

California also provided the setting for one of the most popular novels of the day, Helen Hunt Jackson's *Ramona* (1884). Jackson was an activist in the movement to change federal policy toward Indians, and *Ramona* was an effort to mold public opinion. Setting *Ramona* in southern California in the 1850s, Jackson used romance as the vehicle to depict the mistreatment of Indians. An instant success, *Ramona* had some influence on federal policies, but its romanticized image of southern California had a great impact in promoting tourism.

Henry George, a San Francisco journalist, also sought to influence politics by his writings. George analyzed the rapid growth and industrialization of California in *Progress and Poverty* (1879), the best known of several works in which he studied the urban, industrial society of his day. George argued that "progress" (economic growth and development) inevitably brought greater poverty, something he attributed to land speculation and land monopolization. He proposed, as the solution, a single tax on the increase in the value of land, which he hoped would create such a tax burden on large landholders as to force them to break up their holdings.

Others also took inspiration from California itself. In his late twenties John Muir set out to witness nature. His travels took him to Yosemite Valley in the Sierra Nevada, and the beauty of that magnificent landscape moved him deeply. "Born again!" he wrote in his journal. For the rest of his long life, he roamed the Sierras in the summers and spent his winters describing their grandeur in magazine articles and books. In 1892, he became the first president of the Sierra Club.

The Sierra Nevada also inspired William Keith, who by 1900 was perhaps the most famous painter in California. His sometimes ethereal paintings of California scenes were popular on both coasts. Carleton Watkins also took inspiration from the California landscape, but his medium was the new one of photography. Considered by many as the most important American photographer of the nineteenth century, Watkins took photographs of Yosemite that made him—and

Yosemite—famous, but his work over nearly a half century included many photographs of urban and farm life as well.

For the first six months of 1894, San Francisco's Golden Gate Park became the site of the California Midwinter International Exposition, one of the era's many celebrations of progress, technology, and culture. The exposition was also intended to proclaim to the world not only that the city and state had attained a high technological and cultural level, but that tourists could bask in California sunshine when their own cities were beset by snow and ice. Great exhibit halls demonstrated accomplishments in manufacturing, liberal arts, fine arts, mechanical arts, and agriculture and horticulture. Electrical lights were strung everywhere in dazzling celebration of that new technology. The fair succeeded, attracting visitors from around the nation and launching San Francisco's reputation as a favorite destination for tourists.

Summary

The "Gilded Age" was an era of rapid industrialization and urbanization and of large-scale immigration from Europe and Asia. In California and the West, railroads were crucial to economic development because of the great distances, and the Southern Pacific (SP) emerged as a powerful corporation, operating with virtually no competition or regulation throughout much of the Gilded Age. Mining continued to be important in the economy of California and the West, especially Nevada, which was an integral part of California's economy. California's bankers played key roles in the economic development of the West. Agriculture emerged as California's leading industry, first with wheat and then specialty crops of fruit and vegetables. Water was indispensable for mining, agriculture, and urban growth. Workers, especially in urban areas, formed unions, but most had little staying power until late in the nineteenth century. In the 1880s and 1890s, San Francisco was one of the largest cities in the nation, and the dominant metropolis of much of the West.

The Gilded Age was a time of significant change in California's social and cultural patterns, including the emergence of new educational institutions, changes in the status of women, and the emergence of a gay and lesbian subculture. California experienced significant immigration from Europe, as did other parts of the United States, but was more unique in some aspects of its ethnic and racial relations, especially those involving Latinos, Asian Californians, and American Indians.

California's voters showed a less pronounced commitment to political parties than was true elsewhere in the country. From the end of the Civil War until 1900, the two major political parties were closely balanced and often alternated in power within state government. Third parties were a recurring feature of state politics, including the Grangers, the Workingmen's Party of California, and the

Populists. The second constitutional convention, in 1878, drafted the constitution still in use, though it has been amended many times. Two recurring political issues were the power of the Southern Pacific and opposition to Chinese immigration. In 1898, the United States went to war with Spain, and acquired an island empire in the Pacific. California became the major route to the new island possessions.

In the Gilded Age, Californians achieved national prominence through their writing, painting, photography, and other forms of cultural expression.

Suggested Readings

▮ Bullough, William A., *The Blind Boss and His City: Christopher Augustine Buckley and Nineteenth-Century San Francisco* (Berkeley and Los Angeles: University of California Press, 1979). A good introduction to urban politics in the Gilded Age.

▮ Chan, Sucheng, *Asian Californians* (San Francisco: MTL/Boyd & Fraser, 1991). Though not limited to the Gilded Age, has a great deal of information about Asian immigrants during that time period.

▮ Deverell, William, *Railroad Crossing: Californians and the Railroad, 1850–1910* (Berkeley and Los Angeles: University of California Press, 1994). An excellent treatment of the sometimes ambivalent view of Californians toward the railroads.

▮ Hundley, Norris, Jr., *The Great Thirst: Californians and Water, 1770s–1990s* (Berkeley and Los Angeles: University of California Press, 1992). Ranges widely over the history of the state, but contains a good treatment of water issues during the Gilded Age.

▮ Igler, David, *Industrial Cowboys: Miller & Lux and the Transformation of the Far West, 1850–1920* (Berkeley and Los Angeles: University of California Press, 2001). An interesting account of a company that played a major role in changing the ecology of the San Joaquin Valley.

▮ Issel, William, and Robert W. Cherny, *San Francisco, 1865–1932: Politics, Power, and Urban Development* (Berkeley and Los Angeles: University of California Press, 1986). Surveys social and economic patterns as well as politics.

▮ Lavender, David, *Nothing Seemed Impossible: William C. Ralston and Early San Francisco* (Palo Alto: American West Publishing Company, 1975). Explores the connections between the gold and silver bonanzas and the urban and industrial development of California.

▮ Levy, Harriet Lane, *920 O'Farrell Street* (1937; reprinted, Berkeley: Heyday Press, 1996). Memoirs of growing up in a Jewish, middle-class family in San Francisco during the Gilded Age.

▮ Monroy, Douglas, *Thrown Among Strangers: The Making of Mexican Culture in Frontier California* (Berkeley and Los Angeles: University of California Press, 1990). An excellent treatment of Mexican Californians during the late nineteenth century.

▮ Shumsky, Neil L., *The Evolution of Political Protest and the Workingmen's Party of California* (Columbus: Ohio State University Press, 1991). Currently the standard treatment of the Workingmen's Party of California.

▮ Vaught, David, *Cultivating California: Growers, Specialty Crops, and Labor, 1875–1920* (Baltimore: Johns Hopkins University Press, 1999). An essential work for understanding changes in California agriculture that accompanied the development of specialty crops.

7

California in the Progressive Era, 1895–1920

Main Topics

▌ The Origins of California Progressivism

▌ Social and Economic Change in the Progressive Era

▌ California Progressivism, 1910–1920

▌ Californians in a World of Revolutions and War

▌ The Meaning of Progressivism for Californians

▌ Summary

"We stand at Armageddon," thundered former president Theodore Roosevelt in 1912, invoking the Biblical prophecy of a final battle between good and evil. "And," he continued, "we battle for the Lord." Roosevelt had been president from 1901 to 1909. A lifelong Republican, he bolted that party in 1912 and ran for president as the candidate of a new party, the Progressives. For his vice-presidential running mate, he chose Hiram Johnson.

Johnson had grown up in Sacramento. His father, Grove Johnson, was active in politics, often serving in the state assembly, where he had a reputation as a staunch conservative and defender of the Southern Pacific. Grove had also been accused of shady political maneuvering. Eventually, Hiram quarreled with his father over politics and moved to San Francisco. While in his father's house, he developed a distaste for politics, and progressive Republicans found it difficult to persuade him

CHAPTER 7	California in the Progressive Era, 1895–1920
1899	Constructions begins on Los Angeles harbor at San Pedro
1901	Teamster and waterfront strike in San Francisco leads to victory of Union Labor Party in municipal elections
1902	National Reclamation Act (Newlands Act)
1905	C. E. Kelsey investigates the situation of California Indians
1906	Earthquake along the San Andreas fault, destroying much of San Francisco
1907	"Gentlemen's Agreement" limits immigration from Japan
1907	Formation of Lincoln-Roosevelt League
1909	Legislature adopts the direct primary
1910	Bombing of the *Los Angeles Times* building
1910	Revolution and civil war in Mexico produce sharp upturn in immigration from Mexico
1910	Hiram Johnson elected governor
1911	Legislature approves long list of progressive reforms
1912	Hiram Johnson nominated for vice president by the new Progressive Party
1913	Legislature approves many more progressive reforms
1913	Owens Valley aqueduct opens
1913	Congress approves damming the Hetch Hetchy Valley
1914	World War I begins in Europe
1916	Preparedness Day bombing in San Francisco
1917	United States enters World War I
1918	World War I ends

to seek the nomination for governor in 1910. Once committed, though, he threw himself into the campaign, going to as many voters as possible, driving the length and breadth of the state, and wearing out his car in the process. Committed and combative, Johnson tirelessly repeated his central message: "The Southern Pacific must keep its dirty hands out of politics." As

Hiram Johnson was alienated from politics by his father, but eventually he seems to have come to enjoy campaign speaking. This photo shows him during the 1914 campaign, when he was seeking reelection as governor. How did Johnson present himself to voters?

governor, Johnson was a whirlwind of action, making good on a long list of campaign promises.

Roosevelt and Johnson lost in 1912, but Johnson remained central in California politics for his entire life. Pugnacious, tenacious, and deeply hostile to corporate influence in government, Johnson defined the meaning of progressivism for a generation of Californians.

Historians give the name the progressive era to the late 1890s and the first fifteen or twenty years of the twentieth century, a time when many individuals and groups sought to change politics and public policy. Though many of the most important changes of this period were in the structure and function of government, there were also important changes in the state's social and economic patterns, including a revival of anti-Asian agitation.

Questions to Consider

▌ How were the experiences of reformers in Los Angeles and San Francisco similar? How do they point up the differences within progressivism?

▌ Do events in California confirm the argument by historians that there was no single progressive *movement* but instead many individuals and groups pursuing separate reforms?

▍ How did the social and economic changes in California sometimes carry international implications? Provide examples.

▍ What was the relation between water and economic growth? How did this sometimes produce conflict?

▍ How did progressive reform change the *structure* of California politics?

▍ How did progressive reform change the *function* of state government?

▍ How did the Mexican Revolution affect Californians?

▍ How did Californians respond to the war that began in Europe in 1914?

▍ What are some of the long-term results of progressivism?

The Origins of California Progressivism

The Roosevelt-Johnson campaign of 1912 marked one high point for progressivism. It took place when reform was "in the air" almost everywhere. This commitment to reform came because many Americans, and probably a majority of Californians, concluded that something had to be done to restrict the new industrial corporations and to remedy the problems of the cities. Many also concluded that traditional politics posed a constraint on reform.

The Many Shapes of Progressivism

Progressivism took form through many individual decisions by voters and political leaders, but a more basic choice loomed behind many of them: Should government play a larger role in people's lives? Time after time, Americans—and Californians—chose a greater role for government. As they gave government more power, Americans also sought to make it more responsive to ordinary citizens by introducing new ways to participate more directly in politics—and nowhere did these reforms reach as far as they did in California. Changes in the structure and function of government during these decades fundamentally altered California's politics, and, at the same time, politics dramatically expanded to embrace a wider range of concerns.

In the 1890s and early twentieth century, new groups organized and entered California's political arena, often sharing an optimism that responsible citizens, acting in concert, assisted by technical know-how, and sometimes drawing on the power of government, could achieve social progress—could improve the human situation. As early as the 1890s, a few Californians began calling themselves "progressive citizens." By 1912, many more called themselves "progressives."

Historians use the term *progressivism* to signify three related developments: (1) the emergence of new concepts of the purposes and functions of government, expressed in a language of reform that many different groups and individuals used to justify their own proposals for change, (2) changes in government policies and institutions, and (3) the political agitation that produced those changes. A *progressive,* then, was a person involved in one or more of these activities. The large number of individuals and organized groups with differing visions of change made progressivism a complex political phenomenon. There was no single progressive movement. Roosevelt's Progressive Party in 1912 probably had more strength in California than in any other state, but even in California it failed to capture the allegiance of all those who called themselves progressives.

There was no single pattern to the development of progressive reform. In some states, most notably Wisconsin, it burst forth initially in state government. In other places, it affected city government first. In California, the first victories for progressive reform came in Los Angeles and San Francisco.

Municipal Reform: Los Angeles

In the 1890s, city boosters in Los Angeles took pride in the city's two railroad connections and its booming population, but worried over the lack of a harbor. When Collis Huntington of the Southern Pacific (SP) sought to develop Santa Monica into a port for oceangoing ships, LA's entrepreneurs and civic leaders organized a Free Harbor League. By "free harbor," they meant one not controlled by the SP. They gained a valuable ally in U.S. Senator Stephen White, the maverick Democrat elected with Populist support (see p. 188). White helped Angelenos secure $2.9 million in federal funds to develop San Pedro as a port. In 1899, the city celebrated a "Free Harbor Jubilee," as construction began on the new breakwater. One of the most significant engineering endeavors on the Pacific Coast, the project made Los Angeles a major port—eventually the largest port in the nation.

Other Angelenos wanted to reform city government through a new charter and to defeat the conservative Republicans who dominated city government. Most of the reformers, though, were also Republicans, so they usually worked within the Republican Party. They also created reform organizations. One of them, the Direct Legislation League, led by Dr. John R. Haynes, persuaded city voters to amend the charter to provide for the initiative, referendum, and recall—reforms that permitted citizens, through petitions, to propose new laws (the initiative), block laws passed by the city council (the referendum), and evict an elected official from office (the recall). Other LA reformers sought municipal ownership of public utilities and the merit system for filling city jobs. Under the merit system, people seeking government jobs would demonstrate their abilities through competitive examinations. Before adoption of this system, people secured appointments to government jobs through loyalty to elected officials. In 1908, reformers promoted charter amendments that made city offices nonpartisan and required city council members to seek election citywide rather than from districts. This change, they argued, was more likely to produce council members who viewed the city as a whole, rather than as a collection of neighborhoods. As that campaign was in progress, reformers found evidence linking the mayor to corruption. They recalled him from office, then elected a progressive mayor.

Municipal Reform: San Francisco

A city's charter defines its structure of government. From 1856 onward, San Francisco's government had been structured by the Consolidation Act, a measure that significantly restricted city government. Several efforts at charter revision had failed. When James D. Phelan was elected mayor in 1896, he made charter reform his first priority. His supporters, some of whom called themselves "progressive citizens," included many of the city's business leaders plus a few representatives of organized labor. The new charter, they argued, was solidly based on progressive and businesslike principles and would create a more centralized city government and increase the mayor's power. These changes, they claimed, would prevent political manipulation by figures like "Boss" Buckley.

The new charter, which took effect in 1900, reflected Phelan's views in providing for eventual city ownership of public utilities. Phelan consistently argued that the city should own and operate utilities including streetcars, water, and electrical power—a position more radical than most other urban reformers, who typically concerned themselves with creating honest and efficient city government. Phelan argued that if city governments regulated private utility companies, those companies would inevitably seek to influence, and corrupt, the officials responsible for the regulation.

In 1901, Phelan's third term as mayor was ending when the city experienced a major battle between unions and employers. The struggle began with a dispute between the new Teamsters' Union and their employers, the Draymen's Association. Teamsters drove teams of horses that pulled freight wagons, delivering goods throughout the city. The strike escalated when the Employers' Association took over the draymen's side of the conflict and refused to bargain with the union. Other unions saw this as a challenge to their own ability to seek improvements in working conditions. Unions on the waterfront, organized into the City Front Federation, went on strike in support of the embattled teamsters, closing down the port. Phelan tried unsuccessfully to bring the two sides together. As the strike dragged on to a second month, events sometimes turned violent, especially when city police began protecting strikebreakers. Father Peter Yorke, a Catholic priest sympathetic to the strikers, had given crucial support to Governor Henry Gage during his campaign for governor in 1898, and Yorke now persuaded Gage to intervene. Gage brought together the teamsters and draymen and got them to agree on a settlement that permitted the teamsters to continue to unionize.

Some angry unionists soon entered city politics as the Union Labor Party (ULP), charging Phelan with having used police to aid the employers. In 1901, the ULP candidate for mayor, Eugene Schmitz, president of the Musicians' Union, won the election. Schmitz won much of the vote in working-class areas and gained some support in middle-class neighborhoods. The Democratic and

Republican candidates divided the other votes. Schmitz was reelected in 1903, and the ULP swept most city offices in 1905. Almost from the beginning, rumors swirled through the city that Abraham Ruef, once a reform Republican, had become the "boss" of the ULP, exacting bribes from businesses that dealt with city government and manipulating Schmitz and ULP members of the Board of Supervisors (San Francisco's equivalent to a city council).

In 1905, Fremont Older, editor of the *San Francisco Bulletin,* published exposés of Ruef's dealings and sought federal assistance in investigating Ruef and Schmitz. He also raised funds from private citizens, including Phelan, and secured the services of the nation's leading private detective firm. As the city suffered through the disastrous earthquake and fire of 1906 and the rebuilding afterward (see pp. 210–212), the "graft prosecution" collected evidence that eventually led to the removal from office of Schmitz and most of the supervisors. A reform mayor was first appointed, and then elected in his own right.

Francis Heney, a former federal prosecutor, was appointed to prosecute Ruef. In the midst of the trial, late in 1908, Heney was shot by a prospective juror whom he had offended by revealing an old criminal record. Heney eventually recovered, but the prosecution of Ruef fell to Hiram Johnson, Heney's assistant. A highly successful trial lawyer, Johnson secured Ruef's conviction and became well known throughout the state.

The ULP survived the embarrassment of the graft prosecution. Without Ruef and Schmitz, the party returned to power in the election of 1909, when Patrick H. McCarthy, head of the Building Trades Council, won the office of mayor. Most recent historians have concluded that the ULP was much more than just a vehicle for Ruef's graft. Instead, it was a labor party much like the emerging labor parties of Great Britain, Australia, and New Zealand—parties formed by labor organizations to prevent governmental power from being used against workers' organizations, and to use government instead to benefit unions and working people more generally.

Thus, by 1910, both of California's largest cities had experienced municipal reform. Both had experimented with structural changes designed to make city government more effective. Both had advocates for the municipal ownership of public utilities. And both had produced successful reform politicians. These campaigns were publicized throughout the state, and were imitated elsewhere.

Organized Labor in the Progressive Era

The political successes of the ULP helped to give San Francisco a reputation as one of the most unionized cities in the nation. After the decline of unions in the early 1890s, San Francisco's unions had revived in the late 1890s and early twentieth century. The San Francisco Building Trades Council (BTC), organized in 1896, won a major strike in 1900 that made it a powerful force within the construction industry, able to require that only union members be hired and that work be limited to eight hours per day. Patrick H. McCarthy, BTC president after

1898, became a significant force in city politics. After a major organizing drive from 1899 to 1901, and encouraged by the strikes of 1900 and 1901, other workers in northern California also joined unions. Within San Francisco, the ULP mayor guaranteed that police would not be used to protect strikebreakers. One journalist described San Francisco as "the city where unionism holds undisputed sway," and, in fact, the city may have been the most unionized major city in the nation. The BTC probably exercised more control over working conditions than any comparable group of workers elsewhere in the country. Workers in foundries and machine shops, organized into the Iron Trades Council, got the eight-hour day after a strike in 1907, at a time when most ironworkers and steelworkers elsewhere in the country were working ten- or twelve-hour days. In general, the unionized workers of San Francisco were better paid and had better working conditions than their nonunion counterparts across the country.

In much of the country then, unions recruited only the most skilled workers. In San Francisco, however, dishwashers, box makers, stable workers, and other unskilled or semiskilled workers all had unions. At a time when some unions resisted efforts to organize women, San Francisco female laundry workers, garment workers, waitresses, and other female wage earners had unions. Women's road to unionization was never easy, however, even in a highly unionized city. But the most important limit on unionization was race. Few unions admitted African Americans, and none admitted Asians. Unions thrived in San Francisco partly because they united white workers by pointing to Asian immigrants as threats to the well-being of white workers. Another important factor was the city's geographic isolation, which made it difficult to bring in strikebreakers. City government—in the hands of the ULP from 1901 to 1906 and from 1909 to 1911—did not intervene on the side of the employers. And San Francisco employers repeatedly failed to organize as effectively as their workers.

If San Francisco was "the city where unionism holds undisputed sway," Los Angeles had a reputation as a stronghold of the *open shop*—the term used to describe employers who refused to bargain with unions. In LA, the chief bulwark against unions was Harrison Gray Otis, publisher of the *Los Angeles Times*, and the moving force behind the Merchants and Manufacturers Association. A conservative Republican and a powerful force in LA, Otis used his newspaper to berate his opponents, including Democrats, and anyone who favored progressivism or unions. The Merchants and Manufacturers Association organized the city's businesses against unions. By keeping out unions, the city's business leaders reasoned, they could attract companies seeking an inexpensive work force. Nonetheless, by 1910, some LA unions were making gains. Mexican workers on the street railways and workers in several industries declared strikes to gain recognition. Pushed by the Merchants and Manufacturers Association and Otis, the city council responded by prohibiting picketing by strikers.

The unions of the Bay Area looked anxiously at LA, for lower wages there tempted companies to relocate. Bay Area unions were also pressured by employers who competed with southern California companies and their lower labor

In the early morning of October 1, a bomb exploded in the *Los Angeles Times* building and ignited highly flammable ink, newsprint, and natural gas, turning the building into a flaming inferno and killing twenty-one people. Why did the LA *Times* attract this form of terror? What was the aftermath?

costs. Extremists in the International Association of Bridge and Structural Iron Workers, including John and James McNamara, had begun to set bombs to terrorize opponents of unions. In 1910, they targeted the *Los Angeles Times* building. In the early morning hours of October 1, an explosion ripped open the building and ignited a roaring fire. Twenty-one people died. William Burns, whose detective agency had aided the San Francisco graft investigation, tracked down the bombers. Most union leaders considered it a "frame-up" and defended the McNamara brothers. When brought to trial in 1911, however, James McNamara confessed and John McNamara pled guilty, cruelly disillusioning their idealistic supporters. Both brothers were sentenced to life imprisonment.

Efforts to Reform State Government before 1910

Several varieties of reform swirled across the nation in the early 1900s. In 1900, Robert M. La Follette, a Republican, won election as governor of Wisconsin and led that state to regulate railroads and reduce the power of political bosses. His success prompted imitators, who began to win state offices across the country by attacking corporations, especially railroads. At the same time, President Theodore Roosevelt secured his reputation as a "trustbuster" by using the Sherman Antitrust Act (1890) to break up giant corporations. He then moved on to railroad regulation. Publishers discovered that their sales boomed when they featured dramatic exposés of political corruption, corporate wrongdoing, or other offenses—for example, Fremont Older's crusade against Ruef. Those who practiced this provocative journalism acquired the name *muckrakers.* Muckraking magazines brought national attention to situations in particular cities or states. In 1904, for example, Ray Stannard Baker profiled San Francisco's unions in *McClure's Magazine,* the most prominent of the muckraking magazines.

Though reform burgeoned across the nation between 1900 and 1910, California state government seemed immune. In 1902, the Republican state convention nominated George C. Pardee—widely considered a reliable conservative and friend of the Southern Pacific—to run for governor. The Democrats ran Franklin K. Lane, who condemned the SP and nearly defeated Pardee. As governor, Pardee slowly separated himself from the SP. When he sought renomination in 1906, the Republican state convention instead chose James Gillett, a member of Congress known to be close to the SP. Journalists accused the SP of brazenly dominating the convention and dumping Pardee. Abraham Ruef, "boss" of San Francisco's Union Labor Party and a Republican in state politics, later admitted that the SP had given him fourteen thousand dollars ($1.00 in 1906 is equivalent to nearly $20 now) to help in nominating Gillett. Theodore Bell, the Democratic candidate, crisscrossed the state demanding railroad regulation and other progressive reforms, but Gillett won.

In 1907, several newspapers charged the SP with blocking reforms in the legislature. In August 1907, a group of Republican reformers, most of them newspaper publishers and lawyers, launched the League of Lincoln-Roosevelt Republican Clubs—usually called the Lincoln-Roosevelt League—and pledged to end SP control of state politics. They scored some victories in the 1908 elections, and the legislative session of 1909 was marked by battles between reformers and conservatives, and between the critics and defenders of the SP—giving Franklin Hichborn material for a muckraking book on the legislature. Most importantly, the legislature passed a direct primary law. In a direct primary, voters registered with a particular party choose that party's candidates for office. Previously, candidates for state offices had been chosen by conventions. At the conventions, reformers charged, political bosses connived with corporations—especially the SP—to nominate candidates agreeable to both of them. Thus, the direct primary was presented as a way to remove corporate influence from the political process.

In 1910, the state stood at a significant crossroads. Progressive Republicans were well organized, and they had the opportunity, for the first time in the state's history, to go directly to the voters for the nomination of candidates for office.

Social and Economic Change in the Progressive Era

While reformers struggled with conservatives over control of state government, the state's social and economic structure was undergoing important changes. Though not as obvious as the dramatic political battles between the opponents of the SP and its defenders, these changes were no less important. And many of them worked their way into the political process.

Immigration and Ethnic Relations

Between 1900 and 1910, California's population grew more rapidly than at any time since the Gold Rush, and this growth was most pronounced in southern California and the San Joaquin Valley. In 1900, California's population ranked twenty-first among the forty-five states. By 1920, it moved up to eighth among forty-eight.

The state's population was becoming racially more homogeneous. In the 1850s, a quarter or more of all Californians were African American, American Indian, Asian, or Latino. However, due to white migration from other countries and from other parts of the United States the state became 95 percent white by 1910. Among white Californians during these years, nearly half were immigrants or children of immigrants, and these foreign-stock Californians came from many different cultural backgrounds. The 1920 census recorded the language of first- and second-generation white immigrants, and those data provide an approximation of their cultural backgrounds. Figure 7.1 indicates the ethnicity, based on language or race, of Californians in 1920. (In Figure 7.1, the percentage for British and Irish are estimated because the census data combined those two groups. Those listed as speaking Spanish include those whose parents were born in Latin America, Spain, and elsewhere.)

Between 1900 and 1908, 55,000 Japanese immigrants came to the United States, and most settled in California. Earlier, a few Japanese students had studied at American universities, including Berkeley and Stanford. However, with the decline in the number of Chinese Californians after the 1880s, California growers sought new sources of labor, including Japan. Smaller numbers of immigrants from Korea and the Punjab area of India (mostly Sikhs) also came to California. And after the United States acquired the Philippines in 1898, Filipino migrants began to arrive.

The Exclusion Act and its extensions significantly limited immigration from China, but those who could prove that they were born in the United States, or were born to American citizens, were citizens, and had the right to enter the country. A brisk trade developed in providing appropriate evidence to would-be immigrants, who became known as "paper sons" or "paper daughters." Sometimes called the "Ellis Island of the West," the Immigration Station on Angel Island, in San Francisco Bay, was opened in 1910. Its major purpose was to detain and interrogate Chinese entering the country, and to seek evidence of fraudulent papers. Most were detained for two to three weeks, some longer.

The rise in immigration from Japan provoked a revival of anti-Asian sentiments. San Francisco union leaders formed the Asiatic Exclusion League. In 1906 the city's school board, dominated by the Union Labor Party, ordered students of Japanese parentage to attend the segregated Chinese school. Newspapers and politicians in Japan denounced the segregation order as a national insult. Most Californians knew that Japanese military and naval forces had recently delivered a stunning defeat to Russia—a white, European nation—in the Russo-Japanese

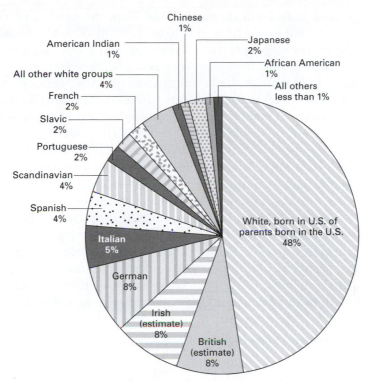

Figure 7.1 Californians in 1920, by Race, Ethnicity, or Mother Tongue of Whites of Foreign Parentage

This figure suggests the ethnic diversity of Californians, even at the same time that it indicates the lack of racial diversity. Though the population of the state was nearly 95 percent white, there was great diversity within the white population in terms of ethnicity. In this figure, the ethnicity of the white population is based on the "mother tongue," i.e., the first language of those who were foreign-born or whose parents were foreign-born. Among the whites who were born in the U.S. of parents born in the U.S., many were also likely to have identified with one of the ethnic groups noted.

Source: Fourteenth census of the United States: . . . California (Washington, 1924).

War. Anxious to maintain good relations with Japan, President Theodore Roosevelt persuaded the San Francisco school board to rescind the segregation order. In return, he promised to try to persuade the Japanese government to cut off the migration of laborers to the United States. This he accomplished through the "Gentlemen's Agreement" (not a formal treaty) of 1907–1908. At the same time, Roosevelt sent the U.S. Navy around the world, painted white as a sign of peaceful intentions—and known therefore as the White Fleet. It was also, however, a strong statement of American ability to carry naval warfare into Japanese waters.

After 1908, immigration from Japan was reduced but not stopped. The large majority of those who arrived before 1908 were males, and many had their relatives in Japan arrange marriages for them. "Picture brides" were permitted to enter the United States until the early 1920s. Thus, the number of Japanese Californians increased from 41,356 in 1910 to 71,952 in 1920. Many made their living as farmers, working small plots—the average was seventy acres in 1920—where they raised labor-intensive crops such as vegetables or berries.

During the early years of the twentieth century, many Mexicans migrated north, most to south Texas and southern California. Though this migration began before 1910, their numbers increased greatly as many Mexicans sought to escape the revolution and civil war that began in 1910—and the serious social and economic dislocations that devastated their nation for years afterward. At the same time, exclusion of Asian immigrants produced a growing demand for Mexican labor in California agriculture. A large Mexican community developed in Los Angeles. Los Angeles County was a major agricultural area, as were surrounding areas. Many Mexican immigrants worked as agricultural field workers or cannery workers, following the crops through the growing, harvesting, and canning seasons, then spending the winter in LA. There they joined a long-standing Mexican community in which many men worked in railroad construction and maintenance (including LA streetcars), construction, or furniture making, and women worked in garment making—all of which, like agricultural field work and canning, were often seasonal in nature. Some Mexican workers formed unions, notably one of streetcar track workers in 1903.

Other Mexican immigrants lived in small *barrios* along the coast or inland. In 1903, Japanese and Mexican sugar beet workers in Oxnard formed a union, conducted their meetings in both languages, went on strike, and won their major objectives. When they petitioned for a union charter from the American Federation of Labor (AFL), however, they were refused because their union admitted Asian workers, a violation of existing AFL rules.

Throughout the late nineteenth and early twentieth centuries, California continued to be home to one of the largest American Indian populations in the nation. Yet California had few reservations, and they were small both in size and in number of residents. Most California Indians continued to live outside the reservations, as they had since the United States acquired California.

Congress, in 1905, authorized an investigation of conditions among California Indians. A special agent, C. E. Kelsey, traveled throughout the state, visiting almost every Indian settlement. He contacted 17,000 California Indians, of whom only 5,200 lived on reservations. Kelsey found that about 3,000 of the nonreservation California Indians owned land, most of which was worthless for farming. More than 1,000 lived in federal forest reserves and national parks, areas that had been their traditional homelands. Nearly 8,000 lived in rural areas, typically in *rancherías* where they preserved some of their traditional ways of life even as they adapted to white society. Men often worked as farm laborers, stock herders, lumber workers, or miners, and many women worked as laundresses, domestic servants, or basket makers. Those not living on reservations usually tried to avoid attention, as they could still occasionally be targets for random violence. Those on the reservations had more protection from random violence, but were constantly pressured by agents of the Bureau of Indian Affairs to give up their traditional ways and send their children to boarding schools.

Kelsey's report led Congress to appropriate funds to create reservations for the landless California Indians. As the Commission of Indian Affairs explained in 1906, by buying land and establishing new reservations, "the Indians of California will be put into a position where they will be protected from the aggression of white people and have a fair chance to make a living." Thereafter, federal authorities began to convert some rancherías into small, but official, reservations. By 1915, they had purchased nearly seven thousand acres for some 3,500 California Indians. Some fifty new reservations were eventually established, many of them based on existing rancherías. For example, the Pinoleville Reservation, comprising about one hundred acres (less than a quarter of a square mile), was established in 1911 on land that a group of Pomo had purchased thirty years before. California's older reservations were also experiencing change. At Round Valley, protests against the federally run school led in 1915 to the creation of a public school on the reservation, with control lodged in a school board elected by reservation residents.

Figure 7.1 illustrates the diversity of languages—and cultures—among Californians classified as white. In fact, the diversity was greater than the chart indicates, for the 49 percent of the population who were white and born in the United States of parents born in the United States included many descendants of immigrants who still identified with an ethnic group.

Immigration in the early twentieth century expanded existing Italian communities, especially in the San Francisco Bay area, where earlier Italian immigrants had established themselves in viticulture, horticulture, and fishing. By the early 1920s, San Francisco had the sixth largest Italian community in the nation, and was second only to New York City, among major cities, in the proportion of its population of Italian parentage.

Other European groups who arrived in California in significant numbers after 1900 included Eastern European Jews, many of them fleeing persecution in Russia; Armenians, many also fleeing persecution, but from the Turkish empire; and Portuguese, including many from Portugal's island possessions in the Atlantic. Eastern European Jews tended to settle in urban areas, especially San Francisco and Los Angeles, which had established Jewish communities, mostly of German origin, dating to Gold Rush days. Many Armenians were drawn to farming in the San Joaquin Valley, especially in the area around Fresno.

From the 1870s through the early twentieth century, some black leaders had promoted the creation of all-black communities as places where African Americans could exercise full political rights and enjoy full economic opportunities—rights and opportunities denied to them in the segregated South. Among these all-black communities was Allensworth, near Bakersfield in the southern San Joaquin Valley. This community was founded in 1908 by Allen Allensworth. Born into slavery, Allensworth spent a career as an army chaplain, reaching the rank of lieutenant colonel, and then retired to Los Angeles in 1906. The inspiration for an all-black town came to him while reading an article in the *California Eagle,* a black newspaper, that advised African Americans: "Get a bank account. Get a home of your own. Get some property." He especially recruited members of the U.S. Army's four all-black units, urging them to live in Allensworth after completing their military service. At its peak, the town included two general stores, a post office, a school, a library, and churches. Allensworth voters elected Oscar Overr as the first African American justice of the peace since the time when California had become a part of the United States. Problems with the water supply contributed to a decline of the town in the 1930s.

Economic Changes

Throughout the early twentieth century, California's economy remained both diverse and highly productive. From 1919 to 1920, the state's farms and ranches yielded produce worth $770 million, and its mines, quarries, and oil wells produced $163 million worth of minerals. At the same time, California manufacturing enterprises produced nearly $2 billion worth of goods. (One dollar in 1920 was equivalent to more than $9.00 now.) Based on the number of employees and the value of the products, food processing was the largest industry. Next came petroleum refining and then shipbuilding; other important manufacturing industries included metal products, lumber, printing, and clothing.

During the early twentieth century, California agriculture continued to diversify through the expansion of specialty crops, especially fruit, nuts, grapes, and vegetables. By 1920, California ranked first among the states in production of many crops. California growers grew 99 percent of all lemons and olives in the United States, 97 percent of apricots, 73 percent of nuts, 69 percent of plums and prunes, 68 percent of table grapes and raisins, and 61 percent of oranges. Citrus crops were concentrated in southern California, other fruits and nuts in the Santa Clara Valley and around San Francisco Bay, and grapes in the winegrowing region north and east of San Francisco Bay and in the raisin-producing region of the San Joaquin Valley.

Expansion of fruit and vegetable growing spurred food processing. As early as 1900, California ranked first among the states in the canning and preserving of fruits and vegetables. The state produced a quarter of the nation's canned and preserved fruits and vegetables in 1900 and half by 1919. The expansion of specialty crops and of canneries necessitated a significant labor force at harvest time, but there was often little work for such employees at other times of the year.

The emergence of large numbers of relatively small-scale fruit, nut, and vegetable growers prompted the development of growers' organizations, initially to influence prices and assist distribution. Orange growers developed an effective marketing cooperative, renamed the California Fruit Growers' Exchange in 1905. It became a powerful force in the industry, organizing nearly all aspects of marketing, and, in 1908, creating its own brand name, Sunkist, which it promoted through extensive advertising. Given this success, other specialty crop growers created their own marketing cooperatives based on the orange growers' model.

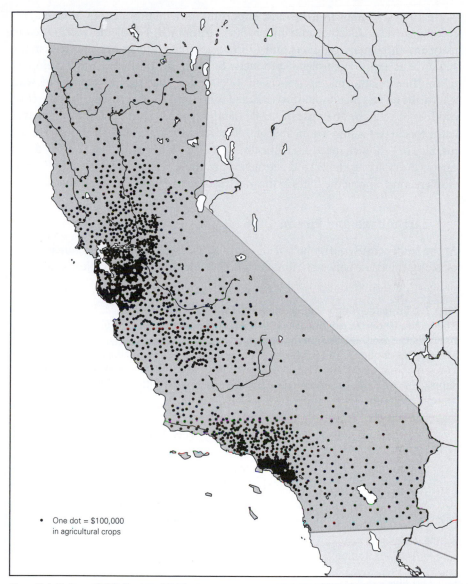

One dot = $100,000
in agricultural crops

Map 7.1 Value of All Crops, 1909

This map shows the distribution of California's agricultural crops, as of 1909. Note, even this late, that irrigation facilities in the Central Valley had still not developed to the point that it could challenge the Bay Area and LA basin as the most productive agricultural regions.

Source: Thirteenth census of the United States taken in the year 1910 (Washington, 1913).

In 1900 gold remained the most important mineral product of California, exceeding in value all other mineral products combined. Petroleum was in second place among mineral products, and California ranked fifth among the states in the value of its refined petroleum products. By then, an oil boom was developing in southern California. Observers in 1899 noted that the only problem with California oil was that it was not well suited for refining into kerosene, then the chief product of refineries because of the demand for home lighting. California petroleum was better suited for making gasoline, for which, in 1899, there was less demand. That soon changed dramatically. By 1920, Californians had registered one car for every six residents, and petroleum production soared. By 1919, California stood second among the states in the making of refined petroleum products.

Earthquake and Fire in 1906

At the 1900 census, nearly half of all Californians lived around San Francisco Bay or along the coast between Monterey and Mendocino Counties. Nearly all those

Map 7.2 Slippage Along the San Andreas Fault in 1906
These maps show the extent of the 1906 earthquake. The map in the upper right indicates the geographic range of damage, from near San Juan Bautista to Cape Mendocino, about 270 miles. The diagram in the lower left shows the amount of horizontal movement of the earth for various locations. Where was the most serious slippage? Why is this earthquake usually closely associated with San Francisco?
Source: United States Geodetic Survey.

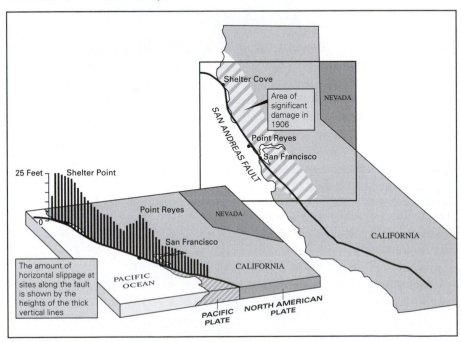

Californians were jolted awake a few minutes after five o'clock in the morning, on April 18, 1906, when a monstrous earthquake rumbled along 270 miles of the San Andreas Fault, from near San Juan Bautista to Cape Mendocino. The epicenter was near San Francisco, but shaking was felt as far away as Los Angeles, Oregon, and Nevada. The earthquake is now estimated to have measured about 7.8 on the Richter scale—one of the most powerful earthquakes on record. Map 7.2 shows the extent of the slippage.

The earthquake toppled centuries-old redwoods, destroyed farms and villages, set church bells ringing wildly, and caused brick walls and chimneys to crash to the ground. One witness in San Francisco said, "I could see it actually coming up Washington Street. The whole street was undulating. It was as if the waves of the ocean were coming toward me." The earthquake destroyed thousands of buildings and killed hundreds of people. It twisted streets, sidewalks, and streetcar tracks, and broke water lines, gas pipes, and electrical power wires.

In San Francisco, broken water mains rendered fire hydrants useless. Fifty or more fires broke out, fed by escaping gas. For the next three days, city residents

Looking down Market Street, from the tower of the Ferry Building, after the earthquake and firestorm of 1906. In this area of older buildings, the devastation was nearly complete. In the distance can be seen the city's first steel-frame office buildings, nearly all of which survived the earthquake, though they were also gutted by fire. Why did San Francisco business leaders rush to rebuild the city rather than engage in a carefully planned reconstruction?

struggled to contain what became a firestorm. General Frederick Funston, commander of the U.S. Army at the Presidio, sent troops to keep order and fight the fires. Without water to battle the flames, firefighters and federal troops dynamited buildings to build firebreaks.

Earthquake, fire, and dynamite destroyed the heart of the city, including 4.11 square miles and 28,000 buildings, including three-quarters of the homes of the city's residents. Destruction was almost universal within the fire zone—corporate headquarters and tenement homes of the poor, churches and brothels, saloons and libraries. The official record listed about five hundred deaths in San Francisco and two hundred outside the city, but subsequent researchers concluded that the number probably reached three thousand or more. Financial help poured in from individuals, organizations, and governments—some $9 million, used for food, temporary housing, and assistance in reestablishing homes and businesses.

Californians rushed to rebuild. San Franciscans feared that any delay in reconstruction would endanger their place as economic leader of the West. Though a few civic leaders urged a careful, planned approach, including wide boulevards and other civic amenities, in the end, the city was rebuilt much as before—although in the current architectural style.

Water Wars

The fire gave new urgency to civic leaders in both San Francisco and Los Angeles who were trying to create water projects. While the danger of fire provided a good talking point, the major concern in both cities was water for growth.

In the late 1890s and early years of the twentieth century, civic leaders in Los Angeles secured their city's control over the Los Angeles River. In 1903 voters approved a charter amendment creating a Board of Water Commissioners to oversee the city's water and remove it from politics. Such commissions were one of the new forms of government that developed during the progressive era. By 1904 the Los Angeles River could not sustain future urban growth. William Mulholland, superintendent of the LA water system, launched an audacious plan to increase the city's water. The city secretly bought up land, including water rights, along the Owens River, 235 miles north of LA. In 1907 city voters approved a bond issue to construct an aqueduct from the Owens Valley to the San Fernando Valley, part of Los Angeles County. Completed in 1913, the project diverted virtually the entire Owens River into the LA water system and permitted rapid development in the San Fernando Valley, which was annexed to LA in 1915. At the time, the Owens Valley aqueduct provided four times as much water as the city needed. Though some Owens Valley residents resisted the water project in court, LA won, and the Owens Valley became a parched area suitable mostly for cattle grazing. By 1920, Los Angeles expanded to nearly 365 square miles and half a million people.

In San Francisco, civic leaders also worried that the water available through the privately owned Spring Valley Water Company was not adequate for growth. Mayor James Phelan, in 1901, chose the Hetch Hetchy Valley for a reservoir. Located

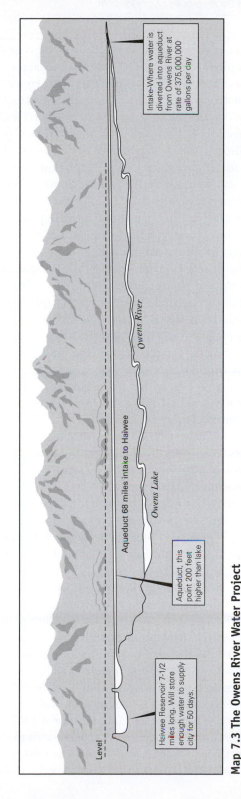

Map 7.3 The Owens River Water Project

This project diverted nearly the entire flow of the Owens River into an aqueduct that ran the length of the Owens Valley and emptied into the Haiwee Reservoir. From there, the water entered an aqueduct which carried it some 150 miles to the San Fernando Valley. Why was the acquisition of large amounts of water crucial to the growth of Los Angeles?

Level

Haiwee Reservoir 7-1/2 miles long. Will store enough water to supply city for 50 days.

Aqueduct, this point 200 feet higher than lake

Aqueduct 68 miles intake to Haiwee

Owens Lake

Owens River

Intake-Where water is diverted into aqueduct from Owens River at rate of 375,000,000 gallons per day

170 miles east of San Francisco, the valley was a canyon with near-perpendicular granite walls—2,500 feet high—and a flat meadow floor, ideal for a reservoir if a dam were built across the canyon entrance. It was part of Yosemite National Park, but uses other than recreation were permitted in national parks at that time. In 1910, city voters approved bonds to construct a water system based on Hetch Hetchy. The city then sought permission from Congress to dam the valley. Opposition came from two sources in addition to the Spring Valley Water Company. John Muir and the Sierra Club argued forcefully against any construction in a national park. Electrical power companies, especially Pacific Gas & Electric, opposed the project because the dam would generate electricity and might lead to public ownership of the city's electrical system. Despite this opposition, Congress passed, and President Woodrow Wilson signed, the necessary legislation in 1913, and construction began in 1914. Hetch Hetchy water finally flowed through the city's faucets in 1934.

Though Muir and the Sierra Club failed to block the damming of Hetch Hetchy, their arguments made a strong impact. Hetch Hetchy, Muir proclaimed, is "one of the greatest of all our natural resources for the uplifting joy and peace and health of the people." "Dam Hetch Hetchy!" he exclaimed angrily. "As well dam for water-tanks the people's cathedrals and churches, for no holier temple has ever been consecrated by the heart of man." The long struggle over Hetch Hetchy revealed divisions within the emerging conservation movement. On one side were those like Muir, who argued for the preservation of wilderness as a place where urban people might find inspiration and recreation. On the other side were progressives like Phelan and Gifford Pinchot, Theodore Roosevelt's chief adviser on conservation, who defined conservation as the careful management of natural resources so as to secure the maximum benefit from them, and who argued that the needs of a half million thirsty San Franciscans should take precedence over the recreation of a few "nature lovers." The preservationists lost the battle over Hetch Hetchy, but helped to shape the nation's awareness of the need to preserve national parks in the future.

As San Francisco, Los Angeles, and other cities began to tap the water of the Sierra Nevada for their own uses, California farmers were also expanding their irrigation facilities. By 1920, over half of California's farms were irrigated. Some irrigation could be found in almost every county but was most common in the San Joaquin and Imperial Valleys and the citrus-growing areas of Los Angeles and Orange Counties.

Many of the initial irrigation projects in California were developed through private enterprise. However, the National Irrigation Association, created in 1899, organized lobbying efforts to secure federal financing of future irrigation projects. Francis Newlands, a member of Congress from Nevada and the son-in-law of William Sharon (p. 166), introduced key legislation. Newlands had extensive investments in California. The National Reclamation Act of 1902, also called the Newlands Act, reserved the funds from the sale of federal lands in sixteen western states for irrigation projects. To promote family farms, the law specified that only farms of 160 acres or less could receive water from its projects. The Newlands Act established a new federal commitment, later expanded many times: The federal government would assume responsibility for constructing western dams, canals, and other facilities that made agriculture possible in areas of slight rainfall. A series of governmental water projects profoundly transformed the western landscape over the course of the twentieth century, and water—perhaps the single most important resource in the arid West—came to be extensively managed.

California in the World Economy

The growth in agriculture, manufacturing, and petroleum production were all reflected in the cargo of the ships that left California's ports, and the importance of those ports was greatly magnified by construction of the Panama Canal. Californians eagerly anticipated the completion of the canal, expecting that it would boost the volume of cargo moving through their ports and significantly reduce the cost of shipping between the West Coast and the East. In both San Francisco and Los Angeles, harbor commissions rushed port improvements to completion.

San Francisco hosted an international exposition to celebrate the opening of the canal. Dominated by a dazzling "Tower of Jewels," the Panama-Pacific International Exposition opened in 1915. Though the exposition presented exhibition halls that displayed the commercial and cultural products of much of the world, San Francisco civic leaders had another purpose as well—they hoped the exposition would provide clear proof of the city's recovery from the devastation of 1906. A similar exposition celebrating the opening of the canal was held in San Diego, and some of its structures, later restored, now stand in Balboa Park.

The opening of the canal in 1914 did bring a significant increase in intercoastal shipping. By the early 1920s, the port of San Francisco was unloading half a million tons of cargo a year from the eastern United States, with metal products and coal the most prominent. Almost as much cargo bound for the East Coast passed over the San Francisco docks, led by canned goods. California's agricultural produce was also shipped all around the Pacific and to Great Britain and Europe, and refined petroleum products were exported throughout the Pacific. California's ports also handled a large volume of Pacific imports—Hawaiian pineapple and sugar, coffee and crude oil from Latin America, silk from Japan and China, coconut products (used in making soap and other toiletries) and sugar from the Philippines and the Pacific islands. California also imported iron, steel, and coal from Great Britain and Europe.

California Progressivism, 1910–1920

Progressivism came late to California state government, but in 1910 Californians elected a governor and a legislature that put their state in the forefront of progressive reform.

Hiram Johnson and the Victory of the Progressives, 1910–1911

The direct primary law of 1909 empowered California voters to choose their party's candidates for state office. For the progressive Republicans of the Lincoln-Roosevelt League, the primary election of 1910 tested their ability to organize a campaign. After considerable discussion, League leaders persuaded Hiram Johnson to seek the Republican nomination for governor.

Johnson easily won the Republican primary, taking nearly half the votes against four opponents. Democratic voters nominated Theodore Bell, their candidate from four years before who had campaigned strongly against the SP. With Johnson and Bell as candidates for governor, Californians were certain to elect an enemy of the SP. Johnson won narrowly, mostly on the basis of his large vote in southern California. Upon winning, Johnson traveled east to talk with Theodore Roosevelt, Robert La Follette, and other leading Republican progressives.

Johnson then wasted no time in announcing the reforms he wanted the legislature to approve. California's progressive tide was rapidly rising. Rarely has a single session of the legislature produced so many new laws as that of 1911. Early in the session, Johnson urged a constitutional amendment for the initiative, referendum, and recall. The initiative and referendum encountered some opposition, but the recall of judges provoked the greatest criticism. Johnson stood firm. When a state judge behaved so irresponsibly that he generated headlines all over the state, the proposal sailed through the legislature and went before the voters in the fall. Johnson also pushed for a measure to permit the voters to elect U.S. senators, another "direct democracy" reform. Other constitutional amendments were also approved by the legislature and submitted to the voters.

Johnson also pushed a drastic overhaul of the state's regulation of railroads by giving the previously ineffective Railroad Commission new power to determine the maximum rates railroads could charge. Another measure gave the commission authority over privately owned public utility companies (companies selling electricity, gas, water, streetcar service, and the like) in addition to railroads.

In extending direct democracy and regulating railroad and utility companies, California progressives followed a path marked out by progressives in other states. When it came to organized labor, however, many California progressives, especially Johnson, showed more sympathy for working people and their unions than was usual elsewhere. Despite some divisions among progressives, the legislature, with Johnson's support, approved laws providing for the eight-hour day for most female workers, restricting child labor, and creating a workmen's compensation program based on employers' liability for injuries caused by industrial accidents.

The legislature passed still more measures. Textbooks were to be provided without charge in the public schools; previously, students had to buy their books. A Board of Control was created to investigate corruption and inefficiency in state government. Elections for judicial and school officials were made nonpartisan—now, candidates for judgeships and school boards or other school positions had to run as individuals rather than as party nominees. Prohibitionists secured a "local option" law that permitted voters in any county supervisorial district to ban the sale of alcohol within the district. Within two years, voters prohibited the sale of alcohol in half the state's supervisorial districts. Other laws prohibited racetrack gambling and slot machines.

Johnson took no position on woman suffrage, but the legislature submitted to the voters an amendment to the state constitution to extend the suffrage to women. In lobbying the legislature and in persuading male voters, a few suffrage advocates made straightforward feminist arguments, that women should have the same rights as men. Most suffragists made more complex arguments, drawing upon some tenets of domesticity to argue that women would bring their moral and nurturing nature to politics, clean up politics, and protect women and children. Still others, especially female unionists, argued that female wage earners needed the ballot to protect themselves from economic exploitation.

Meeting for only three months, the legislature of 1911 passed more than eight hundred bills and sent twenty-three constitutional amendments to the voters. It was an amazing record. The voters approved nearly all of the constitutional changes, including the initiative, referendum, and recall, the changes in the Railroad Commission, and woman suffrage. California now marched in the forefront of progressive reform.

The new laws and constitutional amendments transformed the role of individual voters. The initiative and referendum were extensively used from the beginning: By 1920, Californians had voted on forty-one proposals, including prohibition of alcoholic beverages, the eight-hour day, regulation of dentists and chiropractors, the closing of brothels, and the banning of vivisection. California voters proved to be cautious in using their new power. Of the forty-one proposals, the voters approved only six initiatives and three referenda. California ballots became lengthy as initiatives and referenda joined proposed constitutional amendments and bond issues. In 1914 alone, voters confronted nearly fifty such issues when they entered the voting booth.

California Progressives and the Presidential Election of 1912

In 1912, California progressives, especially Hiram Johnson, moved into the front ranks of national politics. Theodore Roosevelt, during his presidency (1901–1909), had helped to define progressivism by his bold forays against big business—using the antitrust laws to break monopolies and pushing Congress to pass the first meaningful federal regulatory laws. In 1908 he personally picked William Howard Taft as his successor and helped elect him. Taft, however, inherited a Republican Party deeply divided between progressives and conservatives. Lacking Roosevelt's leadership qualities, Taft watched Republican unity rapidly unravel.

As the 1912 presidential election approached, Johnson and other leading California Republican progressives concluded that Taft could not win in

California and probably not in the nation. In January 1912, Roosevelt invited Johnson to discuss the coming election. Johnson quickly boarded an eastbound train, hoping to persuade Roosevelt to seek the Republican nomination. He was not disappointed—Roosevelt announced his candidacy soon after talking with Johnson and several other progressive Republican governors.

In 1912, California was one of only thirteen states that used direct primaries to select delegates to the national nominating convention. Roosevelt easily carried the California primary, winning more votes than his two opponents—Taft and Robert La Follette—combined. In other states with direct primaries, Roosevelt also won the most delegates. Elsewhere, however, Taft supporters controlled the party machinery. At the Republican nominating convention, Taft's supporters dominated the credentials committee and gave contested seats to delegates supporting their man. Johnson led the California delegates out of the convention, claiming that Taft had stolen the nomination. Other Roosevelt delegates followed. The remaining delegates nominated Taft on the first ballot. At the same time, in a hall nearby, Johnson urged the Roosevelt delegates to create a new party and to nominate Roosevelt.

Roosevelt's angry supporters formed the Progressive Party, nicknamed the "Bull Moose Party" after Roosevelt's boast that he was "as fit as a bull moose." The delegates wrote a platform that included regulation of corporations, a national minimum wage, an end to child labor, woman suffrage, tariff reduction, and the initiative, referendum, and recall. Roosevelt was nominated for president without opposition, and Johnson was similarly nominated for vice president.

When the Democratic convention opened, joyful delegates predicted that the Republican split would give them victory. The hotly contested nomination went to Woodrow Wilson, governor of New Jersey, who had a reputation as a progressive.

In much of the nation, the contest was between Roosevelt and Wilson. In California, that was even more the case, because Johnson and his allies kept Taft off the ballot. Johnson campaigned vigorously for Roosevelt in California and across the nation. In California, Wilson's campaign was led by James Phelan, former mayor of San Francisco and the state's leading progressive Democrat. Late in the campaign, Phelan issued a campaign card with a 1906 statement by Roosevelt favoring citizenship rights for Japanese immigrants, and, on the other side, a harshly anti-Asian statement composed by Phelan and signed by Wilson. Johnson thought the card cost Roosevelt ten thousand votes in California, and Phelan agreed that it swayed many voters. Even so, Roosevelt eked out a narrow victory in California, though he lost to Wilson nationwide.

Radicals in a Progressive Era

For the nation as a whole, the 1912 presidential election marked the high point for the new Socialist Party of America (SPA). Before World War I, several radical organizations flourished in California. While many progressive organizations reflected middle-class and upper-class concerns, such as businesslike government, prohibition, and greater reliance on experts, the SPA claimed to be the political voice of workers and farmers. Formed in 1901, the SPA argued that industrial capitalism had produced "an economic slavery which renders intellectual and political tyranny inevitable." Socialists rejected many progressive proposals as inadequate to resolve the nation's problems, and called instead for workers to own and control the means of production, distribution, and exchange.

In California, the SPA scored some local victories. In 1911, amidst the McNamara trial (see p. 202), the citizens of Los Angeles voted in a run-off contest between two candidates for mayor: George Alexander, a progressive Republican, and Job Harriman, a Socialist. The progressive narrowly won. Women had gained the vote between the first election and the run-off, and women voters may have swung the balance against Harriman. Nonetheless, Harriman's strong vote in working-class neighborhoods indicated that many of LA's working people were turning from progressive reformers to a more radical alternative. That same year, J. Stitt Wilson, a Socialist, won election as mayor of Berkeley, and Socialists won a majority on the city board in Daly City. In both places, the Socialists promised little more than municipal ownership of public utilities—proposals not far different from what progressives were implementing in San Francisco (city-owned water and streetcar lines) and Los Angeles (city-owned water and electricity). More radical Socialists dismissed such efforts as mere "gas and water" socialism, and called for public ownership of factories and transportation facilities. Whether of the radical variety or of the gas-and-water persuasion, SPA candidates drew few votes statewide. Nonetheless, in 1912, one Socialist won election to the state assembly, and three were elected to the assembly in 1914.

In 1905 in Chicago, a group of unionists and radicals organized the Industrial Workers of the World (IWW). Often called Wobblies, IWW organizers reached out to the workers at the bottom of the economy—sweatshop workers, migrant and seasonal laborers, and other workers usually ignored by the American Federation of Labor with its emphasis on skilled workers. The Wobblies' objective was simple: when the majority of all workers had joined the IWW, they would call a general strike, labor would refuse to work, and capitalism would collapse.

In California, the IWW organized among timber workers, farm workers, maritime workers, and any others who would listen to their message. One tactic of IWW activists was to stand on a box on a sidewalk and speak about the exploitation of labor. When local authorities in Fresno tried to ban Wobbly speakers from the streets, dozens of Wobblies descended on the town, made speeches, got arrested, and filled the jail. As the costs of maintaining so many prisoners rose, and as more Wobblies kept arriving, the city government gave in and permitted street speaking if the IWW promised to call back the more than one hundred Wobblies on their way to Fresno to continue the fight.

In San Diego, the IWW held frequent street meetings. In 1912, the Merchants and Manufacturers Association pushed the city council to ban street speaking. Wobblies joined AFL unionists, Socialists, and some church groups to form a California Free Speech League, and Wobblies began to pour into San Diego for a "free speech fight." The IWW hoped that the city would back down when they filled the jail and forced the city to feed hundreds of prisoners. Instead, local vigilantes joined San Diego police in beating the demonstrators and running them out of town. Those who were jailed were treated so brutally that one died. The police shot and killed one demonstrator. Governor Johnson sent a personal representative to investigate, and he confirmed the horrors reported by free-speech advocates. Finally the state attorney general arrived and informed local authorities that the state would intervene if they did not handle protests within the law. Vigilante action ceased, but the right to make sidewalk speeches was not restored until 1914.

In 1913, near Wheatland in northern California, violence drew attention to problems afflicting migrant farm labor. The Durst brothers, owners of a ranch that raised hops (used in brewing beer), advertised widely for hoppickers. Some 2,800 men, women, and children responded—double the number needed. The Dursts could name their price for labor and still have enough pickers. There were virtually no sanitary facilities in the camp, and in the blazing hot fields the only drink was watery lemonade, sold by the Dursts for five cents a glass.

Among the pickers were perhaps a hundred IWW members and a few experienced organizers. They called a protest meeting and demanded fresh water, better sanitation, higher wages, and other improvements. Ralph Durst offered some changes but refused others, then discharged the IWW organizers and called in a sheriff's posse. The crowd refused to disperse, so one deputy fired a shotgun in the air, setting off about forty shots, some from the strikers, some from the deputies. Four people were killed, including the district attorney, a deputy, a young striker who had fired on the deputies, and a boy on the edge of the crowd. Others were wounded. Several IWW activists were accused of second-degree murder, convicted, and sentenced to prison—though everyone agreed that they had not fired a gun. They immediately became labor martyrs, imprisoned for no crime other than presenting workers' grievances.

In Los Angeles in 1907, several exiles from Mexico established a branch of the Partido Liberal Mexicano (PLM, or Mexican Liberal Party). Founded in St. Louis by Ricardo Flores Magón in 1905, the PLM opposed the dictatorship of Porfirio Díaz, who ruled Mexico with support from great landholders, the church, and the military. When Magón called for a revolution in 1907, he was arrested as a fugitive and spent nearly two years in the LA jail while his lawyer, Job Harriman (see p. 219), fought to prevent him from being extradited to Mexico. Magón and his followers, called *magonistas,* moved toward a radicalism similar to that of the IWW, advocating the overthrow of Díaz and also a redistribution of property and wealth. When revolution finally came to Mexico, in 1910, the magonistas were ready (see p. 224).

The success of some Socialist candidates and sympathy for the victims of free-speech fights and for miscarriages of justice showed that some Californians were willing to endorse a radical analysis of social problems. Most Californians, however, had no interest in eliminating private property. Most progressive reformers looked aghast at the Socialists and Wobblies and tried to undercut their appeal with reforms that addressed some of their concerns but stopped short of challenging capitalism. Some of the important labor legislation of the 1911 and 1913 legislative sessions may be understood in that light.

A Second Flood of Reform, 1913

After the presidential campaign of 1912, progressives faced some difficult decisions, many of which affected the legislative session of 1913. The session began in controversy, over proposed legislation to prohibit aliens not eligible for citizenship (i.e., immigrants from Asia, especially the Japanese) from owning land in California. Similar proposals had been introduced before, but were blocked by leading Republicans (including Johnson in 1911) to prevent diplomatic problems for Republican presidents Roosevelt and Taft. Now, in 1913, a Democrat, Woodrow Wilson, sat in the White House, and his California supporters had pulled votes away from Governor Johnson's ticket by appealing to anti-Asian sentiments. Johnson signaled legislators, and a bill restricting the property rights of Asian immigrants moved toward passage. The government of Japan protested. Wilson, anxious over relations with Japan, sent his secretary of state to California to urge defeat of the bill. The legislature listened respectfully, then passed the bill.

Johnson signed the Alien Land Act into law, which placed Wilson and the Democrats in the politically embarrassing position of siding with Japan and Japanese immigrants against the California legislature and, probably, a majority of California voters. The law particularly appealed to Central Valley voters, many of whom disliked the Japanese. Some legislators, however, probably understood that the law could be evaded by putting land titles and leases in the names of the American-born children of Japanese immigrants. In retrospect, the Alien Land Act seems little more than a cynical political exercise, as Republican progressives used racial antagonism to benefit their own political standing and create political embarrassment for President Wilson.

The 1913 legislative session accomplished more of lasting significance. Though progressives elsewhere put limits on political parties, California went further than any other state. In 1913, the legislature required all county and local offices to be nonpartisan. When combined with the nonpartisan measures of 1911, this meant that only members of the federal Congress, a half-dozen statewide officers, and members of the state legislature could run for office as party candidates. The 1913 legislature also modified the direct primary law through cross-filing. Under cross-filing, candidates in the primary election could seek the nomination of more than one party, thereby permitting former Republicans who had become Progressives in 1912 to file for the nominations of both parties.

In 1913 the California Federation of Women's Clubs lobbied for a long list of reforms supported by women's groups. Katherine Philips Edson, a clubwoman from Los Angeles who had been active in that city's reform causes, led many of these efforts in Sacramento. With assistance from the nationally prominent

Katherine Philips Edson, seen here in a formally posed photograph, was the most prominent woman in California progressivism. A moving force behind passage of a minimum wage law for women in 1913, she was appointed, by Hiram Johnson, to the new Industrial Welfare Commission and served eighteen years. She also became chief of the Division of Industrial Welfare in 1927. How does her career reflect new patterns of women's involvement in politics during the progressive era?

reformer Florence Kelley, and over the opposition of organized labor, Philips Edson persuaded the legislature to adopt a state minimum wage for female workers. The legislature also created the Industrial Welfare Commission, and Governor Johnson appointed Philips Edson to the new commission. The commission studied and recommended policies regarding the health, safety, and welfare of women and children, and had responsibility for implementing the minimum wage for women. Women's organizations lobbied hard for a law that made property owners responsible if their buildings were used for brothels. Called the Red Light Abatement law, it was challenged in a referendum. Women then took the lead in organizing voter support in the referendum, and voters backed the new law. It led to the closing of the wide-open houses of prostitution that had, until then, flourished in San Francisco and a few other places.

The 1913 legislature approved several new labor laws. One created the Industrial Accident Commission to promote industrial safety and to administer the 1911 workmen's compensation act and a new State Compensation Insurance Fund. Another new commission, the Commission of Immigration and Housing, was to address the needs of migrant farm laborers, whose plight had been so vividly demonstrated at Wheatland. To head the agency, Johnson appointed Simon Lubin, a social worker turned Sacramento businessman. The commission created housing and education programs for migratory farm labor and brought some improvements in sanitation. For these new commissions and other state agencies, Johnson appointed a number of representatives from organized labor—perhaps more than were appointed by any other governor of the progressive era.

The Progressive Tide Recedes, 1914–1920

Late in 1913, Johnson convinced his closest allies to abandon the state Republican Party and form the California Progressive Party. He expected the Progressives to become one of the major parties, and he wanted California to remain in the forefront of progressivism. In 1914, Johnson sought reelection as a Progressive—and received more votes than his Republican and Democratic opponents combined, thus becoming the first governor to win a second term since the 1850s. Republican, Democratic, and Progressive candidates also ran in the state's first direct election for the U.S. Senate, and the winner was James D. Phelan, the progressive Democrat.

The peculiarities of cross-filing became apparent among members elected to the assembly in 1914: twenty-four were elected as Republican, ten as Democrat, seven as Progressive, ten as Republican and Progressive, seven as Republican and Democrat, seven as Democrat and Progressive, six as Republican-Democrat-Progressive, and the other nine had various combinations of Republican, Democratic, Progressive, Prohibitionist, and Socialist nominations. One assembly member, a Socialist, had all five parties' nominations. Thus, from the beginning, cross-filing suggested that party labels had little meaning if one person could simultaneously be the candidate of both the Republican and Socialist parties (despite their contradictory platforms) or of both the Democratic and Prohibitionist parties (which took contrary positions on alcohol) or of the Republican, Democratic, Socialist, and Prohibitionist parties!

By 1914, progressivism seemed to be waning in California. The many new laws adopted in 1911 and 1913 addressed nearly all of the concerns that reformers had voiced before 1910. In 1915 the legislature did little to add to that list of reforms. The next year, in 1916, Theodore Roosevelt urged his followers to return to the Republicans, and most Progressives followed his lead. Johnson was elected to the U.S. Senate in 1916, and his lieutenant governor, William D. Stephens, became governor. Then, in April 1917, the nation went to war, and many Californians turned their attention from reform to mobilizing a war machine. Women continued their political activism, however, and in 1918 four women won seats in the state legislature. And, in 1919, the legislature put significant restrictions on the employment of those under eighteen years of age.

Californians in a World of Revolutions and War

During the early twentieth century, more than ever before, Californians were affected by events elsewhere in the world—the construction of the Panama Canal, revolution in Mexico after 1910, and war that began in Europe in 1914 but engulfed much of the world by 1917.

Californians and the Mexican Revolution

Rebellion broke out in Mexico in 1910, and peasant armies calling for *tierra y libertad* (land and liberty) attacked the mansions of great landowners. A series of governments proved unable to establish stability.

Beginning in 1910, one group of revolutionaries operated from southern California. The leader was Ricardo Flores Magón, who had been jailed for his earlier efforts to use the United States as a base against Mexican dictator Porfirio Díaz (see p. 220). In 1910, Magón moved his headquarters to Los Angeles. Early in 1911, the magonistas joined with some Wobblies on a foray into the Mexican state of Baja California. They first seized the town of Mexicali. Prominent American anarchists, including Emma Goldman, converged on San Diego to build support for the ragtag army of Mexicans, Wobblies, and adventurers. They took Tijuana in early May but developed little following elsewhere. Soon a Mexican army arrived to reestablish control, and the magonistas fled back to the United States Magón, his brother, and a few other leaders were convicted of violating U.S. laws by sending weapons into Mexico.

The growing numbers of Mexican immigrants to southern California combined with the radical agitation of the era to breed what some historians have called a "Brown Scare" during the years from 1913 to 1918—a predecessor of the Red Scare of 1919 and a parallel to the anti-IWW activities in San Diego and elsewhere. The radical speeches and publications of Flores Magón and his followers persuaded some white Californians that the Mexican community of Los Angeles harbored dangerous revolutionaries. In 1915, Texas officials announced that they had found a "Plan de San Diego" for an invasion from Mexico to coincide with an insurrection by Mexican Americans. When Mexican raiders led by the revolutionary Pancho Villa raided Columbus, New Mexico, in 1916, it seemed to confirm rumors of impending insurrection, and intensified the Brown Scare. In Los Angeles, the police chief banned the sale of guns and liquor to Mexicans.

War in Europe and Conflict at Home

In the summer of 1914, assassinations by a Serbian terrorist led to world war. By August, two great alliance systems were attacking each other—the Allies (the British Empire, France, Russia, Belgium, and eventually Italy) versus the Central Powers (Germany, Austria-Hungary, and Turkey).

President Woodrow Wilson proclaimed the United States to be neutral, and urged Americans to be neutral in thought as well as deed. Neutrality proved difficult to maintain, however. From the beginning, some Americans advocated that the United States should join the Allies. Others supported neutrality. By 1916, many Americans had lined up on opposite sides over "preparedness"—a military and naval buildup to prepare the United States for war.

In San Francisco in 1916, the city seemed on the verge of a "labor war," as unions and employers squared off over several issues. In the midst of a strike by longshoremen, the Chamber of Commerce sponsored a mass meeting of the city's business leaders, drew upon the heritage of the vigilantes to create a Law and Order Committee, bankrolled it with a million dollars, and charged it with restoring "peace and quiet" on the waterfront. The Law and Order Committee then launched a wide-ranging offensive against unions. At the same time, a group of business leaders, including many from the Law and Order Committee, organized a parade for July 22 in support of preparedness. Unions urged their members to boycott the parade, as did Socialists, pacifists, and a few leading progressives. About half an hour after the parade began to wend its way down Market Street, as various parade units were still waiting to join the march, a bomb went off at the corner of Market and Steuart Streets, killing nine people and injuring forty. The search for those responsible soon narrowed to a small group of radical unionists.

Authorities arrested five suspects and began to bring them to trial, one at a time. The first, Warren Billings, was convicted and sentenced to life in prison. Next, Tom Mooney was convicted and sentenced to death. By the time of the third trial, of Rena Mooney, the defense had discovered evidence of perjury. Rena Mooney was found not guilty, as was the next defendant, and the prosecution dropped charges against the final defendant. But Billings and Mooney were in prison, Mooney awaiting execution. Radicals and unionists across the country demonstrated for their freedom, but Governor Stephens only commuted Mooney's sentence from death to life imprisonment, guaranteeing the continuation of the struggle to free the two men.

In March 1917, President Wilson began to move toward war with Germany. On March 1, he made public a decoded message from the German foreign minister, Arthur Zimmermann, to the German minister in Mexico. Zimmermann proposed that, if the United States went to war with Germany, Mexico should ally itself with Germany and attack the United States. Further, Mexico should urge Japan to change sides and oppose the United States and the Allies. If the Central Powers won, Mexico would recover its "lost provinces" of Texas, New Mexico, and Arizona. Zimmermann's suggestions created outrage and fear among many Californians as the sensationalist press projected the horrors of a Mexican or Japanese conquest of California. Then, in April 1917, the nation went to war against Germany and the other Central Powers.

Californians Go to War

More than 130,000 Californians served in the war. Nearly all were men who became part of the army or navy. A few women served as army nurses or in the Red Cross or other support organizations. Some 4,000 Californians lost their lives on the battlefield or to disease while serving in the military.

The war produced important changes at home. Historians have called World War I the first "total war" because modern warfare demanded mobilization of an entire society and economy. The State Council of Defense sought to build support for the war effort, usually equating opposition to the war with disloyalty.

German-language newspapers were banned. Radicals came under suspicion, and many were arrested. The war altered nearly every aspect of the economy, as the progressive emphasis on expertise and efficiency produced unprecedented centralization of economic decision making. The railroads and the telephone and telegraph systems came under direct federal management. Mobilization extended beyond war production to the people themselves, their attitudes toward the war, and their response to the need for labor. In the midst of war, in 1918, the nation—and the world—was plunged into a serious influenza epidemic that killed many thousands.

Most Californians' lives were significantly changed by the need for ever more food, clothing, ships and weapons, and other manufactured goods. One crucial American contribution to the Allied victory was through agriculture, for the war disrupted European farming and increased demand for many products. President Wilson chose Herbert Hoover as federal food administrator. Prior to the war, Hoover, a Californian, had a worldwide reputation as a mining engineer. Before the United States entered the war he skillfully directed a relief program in Belgium. Now he promoted increased production and conservation of food. Farmers brought large areas under cultivation for the first time, and food shipments to the Allies tripled. In addition to producing more food, California growers significantly increased their cotton production in response to wartime demands.

Demands for increased production when thousands of men were marching off to war opened up jobs for new workers. Employment of women in factory, office, and retail jobs was increasing before the war, but the war accelerated those trends. The war had a great impact on African American communities. Until the war, about 90 percent of all African Americans lived in the southern states. By 1920, some five hundred thousand had moved out of the South in what has been called the Great Migration. The number of African Americans in Los Angeles more than doubled, and the black community of LA became the state's largest—nearly twice the size of the black communities of the Bay Area—and the state's most important center for black business and politics. In 1918, African Americans in LA helped to elect Frederick Roberts, a Republican, as the first black member of the state legislature. Black voters did not comprise a majority in Roberts's district, however, and he won with support from white as well as black Republicans.

Peace and the Backwash of War

When the war ended on November 11, 1918, church bells pealed and sirens shrieked. Californians thronged into the streets, celebrating the end of the war. One remembered that "it was just like New Year's eve." Huge bonfires were lit on the highest hills in San Francisco, and, on the next day, Catholic, Protestant, and Jewish religious leaders joined in a massive thanksgiving service in San Francisco's Civic Center.

Californians soon found themselves embroiled in economic and social conflicts that spun off from the war. The year 1919 saw not only the return of the troops from Europe, but also raging inflation, massive strikes, fear of subversion, violations of civil liberties, and passage of an unenforceable law to prohibit alcohol.

Inflation—which newspapers called HCL, for "high cost of living"—may have been the most pressing single problem Americans faced after the war. Between late 1914 and the end of the war, the cost of living increased by about half, then continued to climb in 1919. Many unions made wage demands to keep up with the soaring cost of living, but, by 1919, employers were ready for a fight. Some companies were determined to return labor relations to prewar patterns. Others planned to roll back union gains that predated the war.

Against the backdrop of a general strike in Seattle, a police strike in Boston, and a multistate strike by steelworkers—all of which failed—several California unions struck for improved wages and working conditions. In the spring, shipyard workers in Los Angeles went on strike, but lost. Telephone workers struck throughout much of California in June. Telephone companies hired strikebreakers, and by late July most strikers returned to work with no gains. In the fall of 1919, San Francisco longshoremen went on strike; the strike failed, and the longshoremen's union was destroyed. Shipyard workers up and down the Pacific Coast walked out, but their strike, too, was a failure.

Across the country and in California, many companies discredited strikers by claiming that they were motivated not by legitimate desires to improve wages, but by political commitments to Bolshevism—the radical version of socialism that had taken power in Russia in 1917 and that was soon called Communism. The California legislature, like state legislatures across the country, adopted a state criminal syndicalism law, making it a crime to advocate changes in the economy and government of the sort sought by the IWW or the new Communist Party. In May 1919, a group of veterans formed the American Legion, which not only lobbied on behalf of veterans but also condemned radicals and committed itself "to foster and perpetuate a one hundred percent Americanism."

The Meaning of Progressivism for Californians

The progressive era began with efforts at municipal reform in the 1890s, and sputtered to a close during World War I. Some politicians who called themselves progressives, including Hiram Johnson, remained prominent afterward, and progressive concepts of efficiency and expertise continued to guide government decision making. But the war diverted public attention from reform, and by the end of the war political concerns had changed.

The changes of the progressive era transformed California's politics and government. Regulation of railroads and other public utilities continues to be a major function of state government. Protection of particular types of workers—women, children, migrants—has also been a continuing responsibility of state government. The progressives' assault on political parties, through nonpartisan elections, cross-filing, and direct democracy, transformed state politics. As parties declined, organized pressure groups proliferated and gained significant influence in politics. Reliance on the initiative expanded dramatically over the course of the twentieth century. With the decline of political parties came political campaigns based largely on personality and advertising. Hiram Johnson left a far greater personal mark on the state than did any of the governors or senators who preceded him. During the Johnson years, Californians came to expect policy proposals to flow from a forceful governor. Johnson became the standard against which later governors were often measured—often to their disadvantage. Women's participation in politics has continued to increase, especially in the last third of the twentieth century.

Cross-filing remained a feature of California primary elections until 1959. Almost from the beginning, it permitted candidates with large personal followings to lock up all major party nominations in the primary. This gave a strong advantage to incumbents, for they usually had the greatest name recognition among voters. Given the Republican majority among California voters, cross-filing especially benefited Republicans. By the late 1910s and early 1920s, the Republican primary was often the real election, because the winner of the Republican primary won other parties' nominations as well.

Johnson himself became a fixture in state politics, moving from the governorship to the U.S. Senate, and then winning reelection every six years until his death in 1945. Throughout his long career, he remained largely outside the bounds of political parties, though ostensibly a Republican after 1916. But his pugnacious insistence on his own independence meant that his campaigns for office were always *his* campaigns and not party campaigns. In many ways, Johnson set new patterns for state politics.

Summary

California progressivism began with municipal reform in San Francisco and Los Angeles. Efforts to reform state government, especially to regulate the Southern Pacific Railroad, mostly failed before 1910. Organized labor became powerful in San Francisco, but Los Angeles was a stronghold of the open shop. Extremists bombed the *Los Angeles Times* building because of the newspaper's antiunion attitudes.

After 1900, California's population grew rapidly, but the population remained largely white, despite increased immigration from eastern Asia and Mexico. A new federal commitment brought the creation of many new, but small, reservations for California Indians.

California's agricultural economy moved further toward specialty crops including fruit, vegetables, nuts, and grapes. Food processing was the state's largest manufacturing industry, but growing numbers of automobiles stimulated an oil boom and expansion of petroleum refining. In 1906, a massive earthquake caused widespread damage through central California, centered on San Francisco, which was also devastated by fire. Both San Francisco and Los Angeles undertook mammoth water projects to permit further growth. Irrigated agriculture grew in importance. California's agricultural produce and refined petroleum products were sold around the Pacific Rim, and the opening of the Panama Canal in 1914 fostered more shipping between the East and West coasts. To celebrate the opening of the canal, a great exposition was held in San Francisco.

In 1910, the election of Hiram Johnson as governor initiated reform in state government. In 1911, reformers put limits on corporations and political parties and adopted woman suffrage. Johnson became the vice-presidential candidate of the new Progressive Party in 1912. The Socialist Party made a few gains in California, and the IWW tried to organize the most unskilled and exploited workers. In San Diego and Wheatland, IWW demonstrations turned into violent confrontations. The legislature enacted more reforms in 1913, but then progressivism began to recede.

Mexico experienced rebellion and political instability after 1910, and California provided a base for some revolutionaries in Baja California. The unsettled situation in Mexico encouraged migration to the United States, including California. When Europe went to war in 1914, Californians were affected despite American neutrality. An antiwar bombing in San Francisco led to the imprisonment of Tom Mooney and Warren Billings, even though key evidence against them was tainted. When the United States entered the war, it stimulated California agriculture and manufacturing. After the war, several unions were destroyed when strikes failed to improve wages. During the war itself and in 1919, there were efforts to restrict radical groups, including the Socialists, the IWW, and the new Communist Party.

Suggested Readings

■ Brechin, Gray, *Imperial San Francisco: Urban Power, Earthly Ruin* (Berkeley and Los Angeles: University of California Press, 1999). A highly critical account of the growth of the city and its effect on its environment.

■ Deverell, William, and Tom Sitton, eds., *California Progressivism Revisited* (Berkeley and Los Angeles: University of California Press, 1994). An interesting collection of essays focused on class, gender, and ethnicity in California progressivism, intended to supplement and revise earlier treatments.

■ Frost, Richard H., *The Mooney Case* (Stanford: Stanford University Press, 1968). The standard account, filled with interesting information.

■ Kahrl, William L., *Water and Power: The Conflict over Los Angeles' Water Supply in the Owens Valley* (Berkeley and Los Angeles: University of California Press, 1982). The best and most thorough account of the acquisition of the Owens Valley by Los Angeles.

▮ Kazin, Michael, *Barons of Labor: The San Francisco Building Trades and Union Power in the Progressive Era* (Urbana and Chicago: University of Illinois Press, 1987). An outstanding history of one of the most powerful labor organizations in the country, with a good deal of information on the history of the city and state during the early twentieth century.

▮ Lower, Richard Coke, *A Bloc of One: The Political Career of Hiram W. Johnson* (Stanford: Stanford University Press, 1993). A thorough and well-written biography of the most influential progressive leader.

▮ Mowry, George E., *The California Progressives* (Berkeley: University of California Press, 1951). The classic account, still interesting and useful but needs to be read with more recent treatments.

▮ Pisani, Donald J., *From Family Farm to Agribusiness: The Irrigation Crusade in California and the West, 1859–1931* (Berkeley and Los Angeles: University of California Press, 1984). An excellent treatment of this topic.

▮ Olin, Spencer C., *California's Prodigal Sons: Hiram Johnson and the Progressives, 1911–1917* (Berkeley: University of California Press, 1968). A good introduction to events and issues in state politics during the years from Johnson's victory in 1910 until the United States entered World War I.

▮ Walsh, James P., and Timothy J. O'Keefe, *Legacy of a Native Son: James Duval Phelan and Villa Montalvo* (Los Gatos: Forbes Mill Press, 1993). A thoroughly researched and well-written biography of the state's leading Democrat during the early twentieth century.

▮ Walton, John, *Western Times and Water Wars: State, Culture, and Rebellion in California* (Berkeley and Los Angeles: University of California Press, 1992). A good treatment of the many dimensions of the politics of water.

8

California Between the Wars, 1919–1941

Main Topics

▌ The Rise of Los Angeles: Twentieth-Century Metropolis

▌ Prosperity Decade: The 1920s

▌ Depression Decade: The 1930s

▌ Summary

California is a garden of Eden,
A paradise to live in or see,
But believe it or not
You won't find it so hot,
If you ain't got the Do Re Mi.

S o sang Woody Guthrie, who was born in Oklahoma in 1912 and came to California in 1937. Throughout the 1920s, California seemed like a paradise to some. Then the nation's economy turned sour after 1929. A long-lasting drought began in 1931, affecting much of the nation and turning Oklahoma, Kansas, and surrounding areas into a "Dust Bowl." Farm families from the Dust Bowl and farm families displaced from their farms by technology, the Depression, or new governmental policies headed for California, hoping to start over. Guthrie described his trip to California:

I got what you wood call disgursted, busted, and rooled me up a bundel of duds, an' caught a long-tail, frate-train that had a California sign on the side of it. . . . I was headin' out to see

CHAPTER 8	California Between the Wars, 1919–1941
1918	World War I ends
1920–1921	Major oil discoveries in Los Angeles basin
1922	Colorado River Compact
1924	*Piper* v. *Big Pine School District*
1927	First talking movie, *The Jazz Singer*
1929	Great Depression begins
1930	Los Angeles ranks fifth in size among U.S. cities
1930	Bank of Italy renamed as Bank of America
1933	New Deal begins
1934	Coastwide longshore men's strike
1934	San Francisco general strike
1934	Upton Sinclair's unsuccessful EPIC campaign
1935	WPA begins
1937	Woody Guthrie comes to California
1937	Construction completed on Golden Gate Bridge
1938	Culbert Olson elected governor
1939	Publication of John Steinbeck's *The Grapes of Wrath*
1940	Construction completed on first California freeway
1941	United States enters World War II

some relatives, but I didn't know for shore wich r.r. bridge they was a livin' under. . . . I seen about 99 44-100 of California's great senery, from Tia Juana to the Redwood forests, from Reno, an' Lake Tahoe, to the Frisco bay. I finally . . . found my relatives up at Turlock, Calif., and et off of them till we all picked up an' moved down to Lost Angeles—where we've been ever since.

In Los Angeles, Guthrie was one of many Okies—an epithet applied to all those from the Dust Bowl who came to California. Some estimated that as many as two hundred thousand had come. Many found work as seasonal agricultural workers, harvesting

By the time that Woody Guthrie arrived in California in 1937, he had already identified with those most hard hit by the economic and environmental catastrophes of the 1930s, and his politics quickly moved far to the left, in sympathy with the outcast and suffering. After spending a few years in California, he continued to travel around the country, singing his affection for the people and the land, and his criticism of the economic system. What is your reaction to Guthrie's effort to reproduce the language and spelling of someone with little education? What do think the reaction was in the 1930s?

crops up and down the Central Valley. Few Californians greeted them warmly. The LA police chief sent police to the state border to encourage Okies to turn back. Woody sang about that too:

Lots of folks back east, they say,
Leavin' home ev'ry day,
Beatin' the hot old dusty way to the California line.
Cross the desert sands they roll,
Getting out of that old dust bowl,
They think they're going to a sugar bowl
But here is what they find:
Now the police at the port of entry say,
"You're number fourteen thousand for today."
Oh, if you ain't got the do re mi, folks,

If you ain't got the do re mi,
Why, you better go back to beautiful Texas,
Oklahoma, Kansas, Georgia, Tennessee.

Woody found a job singing on radio station KFVD, where he tried many of the songs that later became classics of the Depression and the Dust Bowl. His politics moved left. By 1939 he was writing for the *People's World*, a daily newspaper of the Communist Party in California. As he put it in his first column,

Don't be bashful a bout writing to me if you know of a job. I play the guitar. . . . If you are afraid I woodent go over in your lodge or party, you are possibly right. In such case just mail me $15 and I wont come. When I perform I cut it down to $10. When for a good cause, $5. When for a better cause, I come free. If you can think of a better one still, I'll give you my service, my guitar, my hat and 65¢ cash money.

Woody's songs transformed the folk ballad, making it an instrument of social protest, showing the way for such songwriters as Bob Dylan, Bruce Springsteen, and Tracy Chapman.

The image of California in the 1920s included some of the things Guthrie said about it—a Garden of Eden, a paradise. Many Americans in the prosperous 1920s imagined California by picturing movie stars driving convertibles down palm-lined streets under a sunny sky. During the hard times of the 1930s, that image changed. Now California became a place inhabited, as Woody described it, by "the [Dust Bowl] Refugees a livin' in the various Trailer Cities thet are strung around over the country, the conditions in which the children must live in destitution, want, filth and despair." Both images contained elements of truth, but neither was complete. Nonetheless, everyone who lived through those times drew a sharp distinction between the 1920s and the 1930s.

Economists think in terms of alternating periods of expansion and contraction in the economy. During expansion, the economy grows, demand for products rises, stock market prices rise, unemployment is low, and wages often rise. Expansion phases are periods of prosperity. But every expansion is followed—though not on any easily predictable basis—by contraction, when the economy shrinks, demand for products decline, stock market prices fall, and employers lay off workers or cut wages in response to declining demand. In the 1920s, the economy expanded, based largely on the demand for consumer goods such as automobiles, radios, and electrical appliances. Consumer purchases were encouraged by the introduction of installment buying—making a down payment and paying off the remaining cost (plus interest) in "easy monthly payments."

During the 1930s, the nation experienced the most serious contraction of the twentieth century—the Great Depression. All these national patterns had parallels in California.

Questions to Consider

- What explains the rapid growth of Los Angeles in the early twentieth century?
- How did Los Angeles develop differently from older cities?
- What are the connections between California politics in the 1920s and progressivism?
- What role did the federal government play in the economic and social changes of the 1920s?
- What role did the federal government play in the state's economic and social changes during the 1930s?
- How did the Great Depression change state politics in the 1930s?

The Rise of Los Angeles: Twentieth-Century Metropolis

The 1920 census recorded that Los Angeles had passed San Francisco in population, becoming the tenth largest city in the nation. LA was, in fact, the fastest growing major city in the country during the early twentieth century. Figure 8.1 presents population patterns among the largest cities in California between 1890 and 1940. During the 1920s, LA doubled in size—by 1930 it ranked fifth in the nation in size and continued to grow in the 1930s.

The Economic Basis for Growth

LA's spectacular growth began in the 1880s, when competitive railroad passenger rates from the Midwest and South combined with the warm sunny climate and a romanticized version of California history to attract health seekers and tourists. The development of refrigerated railroad cars and ships in the 1890s contributed to a boom in citrus growing. LA boosters secured massive federal funding to construct a port at San Pedro. The Owens River began to flow into the LA water system in 1913, providing four times as much water as the city then needed, and later projects expanded water supplies in advance of need. The availability of water *permitted* growth, and other factors contributed to the emergence of a diversified economy. During the 1920s and 1930s, three elements contributed to the city's growth: the motion picture industry, oil discoveries, and a variety of manufacturing enterprises.

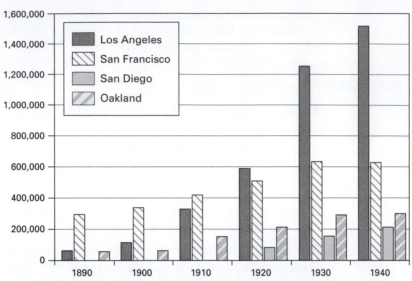

Figure 8.1 Population of Major California Cities, 1890–1940

This graph shows the dramatic surge in the population of Los Angeles over the fifty years between 1890 and 1940. Though the population of San Francisco doubled during those years, the other three cities grew much faster. What factors help to account for the spectacular growth of Los Angeles during this period?

Sources: Report on the social statistics of cities in the United States at the eleventh census, 1890 (Washington, 1895); *Twelfth census of the United States, taken in the year 1900* (Washington, 1901–1902); *Thirteenth census of the United States taken in the year 1910* (Washington, 1913); *Fourteenth census of the United States* (Washington, 1924); *Fifteenth census of the United States, 1930* (Washington, 1932); *Sixteenth census of the United States, 1940* (Washington, 1942–1943).

By World War I, the motion picture industry was the most prominent industry in southern California. Los Angeles was a natural for making movies—the weather was usually sunny, it rarely rained, and a variety of natural scenery existed nearby, including ocean, mountains, and desert. By 1914, Hollywood, a suburb of Los Angeles, had become the center for moviemaking. By the mid-1930s, the industry was dominated by a few large studios, notably Metro-Goldwyn-Mayer (MGM, formed in 1924), RKO (1928), Warner Brothers (1929), 20th Century-Fox (1935), and Paramount (1935). These studios competed to lock up actors and directors in long-term contracts, and to promote their own "stars." Movies became big business, dependent on New York banks for capital to construct huge physical plants and to deploy the latest technology of light and sound. By 1937, moviemaking was the fourth largest industry in the nation. And, by then, eight corporations produced 90 percent of all films and controlled both distribution of the films and many movie theaters.

A second factor in the growth of LA was oil. Major oil discoveries in the LA basin in the early 1920s boosted California to first place among oil-producing states during the 1920s. Discoveries in 1920 and 1921 at Huntington Beach, Long

Beach, and Santa Fe Springs set off a speculative mania—as one observer put it, everyone went "stark, staring oil mad." A geologist called it "the greatest outpouring of mineral wealth the world has ever known." In 1924, oil passed agriculture as the state's leading industry. By 1930, the LA basin held thirty-two refineries employing five thousand people.

A third factor in LA's growth was manufacturing. In the early 1920s, the nation's three largest tire companies all separately concluded that they should build plants in Los Angeles—it was close to newly developed cotton fields (cotton cord was the other major ingredient in making tires), its port was convenient for shipping rubber from Southeast Asia, and it was in the center of the most rapidly growing market for tires. And LA could promise to meet the plants' heavy demands for water. Similar reasoning led Ford to locate an automobile assembly plant in the LA basin and steelmakers to open a plant in Torrance. At the same time, the LA basin remained a major agricultural region, producing crops for food-processing plants. Between 1919 and 1930, LA moved from twenty-eighth to ninth place among American manufacturing cities. However, by 1930, LA ranked fifth in population, so manufacturing did not dominate the city's economy in the same way that it did in Detroit or Pittsburgh, where a third to a half of the work force was in manufacturing. In LA, the proportion was a bit over a quarter.

The Automobile and the Growth of Southern California

The rapid growth of Los Angeles came just as the automobile industry was promoting the notion of a car for every family. By 1925, LA had one automobile for every three residents, twice the national average. The LA basin also had an excellent streetcar system. The auto and the streetcar made it possible for Angelenos to live further from work than ever before. At the same time, real-estate developers busily promoted the ideal of the single-family home. By 1930, 94 percent of residences in Los Angeles were single-family homes—an unprecedented level for a major city—and Los Angeles had the lowest population density by far among the nation's fifteen largest cities.

Life in Los Angeles came to be organized around the automobile to an extent unknown in other major cities, where most growth and construction had taken place in the era of the horse and the streetcar. The experience of LA set the pace for future urban development nearly everywhere else. The first modern supermarket, offering "one-stop shopping," appeared in LA. The "Miracle Mile" along Wilshire Boulevard was the nation's first large shopping district designed for the automobile. The *Los Angeles Times* put it this way in 1926: "Our forefathers . . . set forth 'the pursuit of happiness' as an inalienable right of mankind. And how can one pursue happiness by any swifter and surer means . . . than by the use of the automobile?"

Promoters attracted hundreds of thousands of new residents to southern California by advertising images of perpetual sunshine, tall palm trees lining wide boulevards, gushing fountains, and broad, sandy beaches. The rapid growth of

Grauman's Chinese Theater is perhaps the most famous movie theater in the United States. It opened in 1927, and its architecture and interior décor were even more exotic than most theaters of the day. Why do you think that movie theater owners wanted theaters with unusual, even bizarre, architecture and ornament?

the economy and the population also attracted many who hoped to profit from the unsettled society, and the LA basin acquired a reputation as a center for get-rich-quick schemes, bizarre religious cults, and unusual political groups. Carl Sandburg, in the late 1920s, wrote that "God once took the country by Maine as the handle, gave it a good shake, and all the loose nuts and bolts rolled down to southern California."

Prosperity Decade: The 1920s

Called the "Jazz Age" and the "Roaring Twenties," the 1920s was a period of prosperity that sometimes seems a swirl of conflicting images. Prohibition tried to preserve the values of nineteenth-century America. "Flappers" scandalized many by flaunting their sexuality. The booming stock market and the oil gushers of southern California promised prosperity to all with money to invest. Wage earners endured the destruction of their unions. Technology emerged as an ever-more-potent ingredient in the state's economic growth.

Politics in a Time of Prosperity

During the 1920s, a large majority of California voters registered as Republicans, but the state Republican Party was sharply divided between progressives and conservatives. U.S. Senator Hiram Johnson led the progressive faction. In 1920 he sought the Republican nomination for president, running as a progressive and the heir of Theodore Roosevelt. Another Californian, Herbert Hoover, also ran for the presidency that year. He could claim some commitment to progressive values and pointed to his experience as a highly successful federal administrator during the war. In California, progressives and union leaders lined up behind Johnson, and conservatives and business leaders backed Hoover. In the state's Republican presidential primary, Johnson took about 370,000 votes to Hoover's 209,000. Only about 23,000 Democrats voted in their party's presidential primary. The Republican presidential nomination, however, went to Warren G. Harding, who easily carried California and the nation in the general election. Hoover became secretary of commerce. Johnson turned down the Republican nomination for vice president; had he accepted, he would have become president when Harding died in 1923.

Johnson sought reelection to the U.S. Senate in 1922. He faced strong opposition in the Republican primary but won the election easily. In 1922, there was also a closely contested Republican primary for governor. The incumbent, William Stephens, was a pragmatic progressive, sharing many of Johnson's concerns about big business and willing to extend the role of state government as seemed necessary. Cautious not to move too far in advance of public opinion, he shied away from projects that might prove unpopular or unworkable. Stephens lost in the Republican primary to Friend Richardson, a staunch conservative. When Richardson sought reelection to the governorship in 1926, he was defeated in the Republican primary by a progressive, C. C. Young. In 1928, Johnson sought reelection to the U.S. Senate and again faced a conservative opponent in the Republican primary.

Thus, throughout the 1920s, the Republican Party of California scored victory after victory in statewide and local elections but was deeply divided between progressive and conservative wings. The most important elections were those in the Republican primary. After 1910, many voters seem to have moved to the Republican Party as a way to participate in the important contests that characterized every primary. By 1930, 73 percent of the state's voters called themselves Republicans, making California one of the most Republican states in the nation. Nor was there much variation among major urban areas: San Francisco voters were 81 percent Republican, voters in Alameda County (including Berkeley and Oakland) were 79 percent Republican, those in Los Angeles County were 71 percent

Republican, and voters in San Diego County were 70 percent Republican. California Democrats could not come close to a majority in a single county.

Throughout the 1920s, prohibition also divided voters and affected state politics in sometimes unpredictable ways. The Eighteenth Amendment to the U.S. Constitution, prohibiting the production or sale of alcohol, was, in some ways, the last gasp of the reforming zeal that had generated progressivism. Many Californians simply ignored it from the beginning, and it grew less popular the longer it lasted. Nonetheless, prohibition remained the law from 1920 until 1933, when the Twenty-first Amendment repealed it. Prohibition was most effective among those groups and in those areas—notably southern California—that had provided its greatest support. It was not well enforced in most places, and was largely ignored in most cities, especially in San Francisco. Bootlegging—the production and sale of illegal beverages—flourished.

The administrations of Governors Stephens, Richardson, and Young demonstrated that divisions among Republicans were not mere personality contests; rather, they reflected different approaches to the role of the state in the economy and society. Stephens was a cautious, pragmatic progressive. In 1919, he promoted a huge bond issue to build highways. In 1921, he proposed a number of new programs to regulate business or protect particular groups of consumers or workers. To pay for the new programs, he backed a 35 percent increase in taxes on corporations. At the same time, he tried to reorganize state government to make it more efficient.

Richardson defeated Stephens in the Republican primary in 1922 primarily by condemning Stephens for higher taxes and spending. As governor, Richardson slashed spending for many state programs. In 1925 he set an all-time record by vetoing more than half of all bills passed by the legislature. Young defeated Richardson in the 1926 Republican primary by criticizing his negativity. During Young's administration, state government expanded to assist the disabled and elderly, protect the environment, conserve water, and expand state parks. To pay for these new programs, Young backed a tax on banks and greater efficiency in state government. State budgets had been in the range of $100 million in the early 1920s; by 1930, despite Richardson's budget cutting, the state budget stood at $244 million.

In the early 1920s, California politics continued in the anti-Asian mode set by the progressives through the Alien Land Law in 1913. A wave of anti-Japanese sentiment swept the state beginning in 1919. James D. Phelan, the progressive Democrat elected U.S. senator in 1914, faced reelection in 1920. He based much of his campaign on the slogan, "Keep California White." Though defeated by a large margin, Phelan ran well ahead of other Democrats—due, perhaps, to his anti-Asian campaign but also to his progressive stance on economic issues. Phelan's Republican opponent differed little on racial issues but was more conservative on economic matters. That year, voters approved by a three-to-one margin a second Alien Land Law, designed to close loopholes in the legislation of 1913 by prohibiting aliens who were ineligible for citizenship (those born in Asia) from putting land in the names of their American-born minor children. With this Alien Land Law and with changes in federal immigration policy (see p. 244), anti-Asian rhetoric became more low-key, at least until World War II.

New Economic Patterns

During the 1920s, important changes emerged in the state's economy. Some involved massive construction projects by local, state, or federal government. Others involved innovations in the structure of business or the application of new technologies. And, everywhere in the state, labor organizations found themselves on the defensive.

California's first paved highway opened in 1912, but the 1920s saw a burst of highway construction. The state had 784 miles of concrete-paved roads in 1916 and 2,171 miles in 1930. This construction went far toward realizing a long-term plan for two major highways, one through the Sacramento and San Joaquin Valleys and one along the coast, connecting as many cities and towns as possible and with branches to cities and towns not on one of the highways. The Bayshore Highway, connecting San Francisco and San José, built between 1924 and 1932, represented one of the most advanced highway designs of its day, carrying three lanes of high-speed traffic in each direction. California's first freeway—multilane, divided, with controlled access, patterned after the German *Autobahn*—was in southern California. Planning began in the 1920s for what became the Pasadena Freeway, and it finally opened in 1940.

Highways were crucial for California's transportation infrastructure, but the two most dramatic transportation projects, by far, were the two great bridges that linked San Francisco eastward to Oakland (the San Francisco–Oakland Bay Bridge) and northward to Marin County (the Golden Gate Bridge). Both projects began in the 1920s, but initial progress was slow. When the Golden Gate Bridge opened in 1937, it was the longest and highest single-span suspension bridge in the world, and quickly became a widely recognized symbol of San Francisco. Proposals for a bridge or tunnel connecting San Francisco and Oakland had been discussed for many years before the 1920s, but planning intensified in 1927 and 1928, and the Bay Bridge opened late in 1936. It was, at the time, the largest bridge ever built.

Highway and bridge building created parts of a transportation infrastructure that was crucial to the state's future economic development. Other massive construction projects were intended to develop water and electrical resources by reengineering the landscape. The electrical power companies of California had long been pioneers in the development of hydroelectric power. At the same time, California growers had been at the forefront of developing irrigated agriculture. In the 1920s, state officials began to look beyond privately constructed dams to projects of such size that only the government could possibly undertake them. Throughout the 1920s, Californians debated elaborate plans to dam the Sacramento River and construct canals to carry its water south into the San Joaquin

Valley. Voters rejected three such plans, but the planners persisted, drawing encouragement from Governors Stephens and Young. Eventually, those plans led to the California Water Project after World War II.

Throughout the mid-1920s, Senator Hiram Johnson and Congressman Phil Swing promoted federal legislation to create a dam at Boulder Canyon on the Colorado River, in Nevada. The proposed dam had several purposes: flood control, hydroelectric power, and irrigation. Johnson and Swing first introduced their bill in 1922, but passage came only in 1928, after agreements among the governments of the six states affected by such a drastic change in the river. The first of these, the Colorado River Compact of 1922, was the first compact ever among states under the provisions of Article I, Section 10, of the U.S. Constitution. Negotiations among states and amendments to the original bill limited the amount of water that could be claimed by California. When Boulder Dam was completed in 1935, it was the largest dam in the world. In 1947, it was renamed Hoover Dam, for Herbert Hoover.

Large-scale highway, bridge, and dam construction during the 1920s and 1930s brought the emergence of new business enterprises. Henry Kaiser began in road construction before World War I and built projects throughout much of the West in the 1920s. When the federal government sought contractors for the Boulder Dam project, Kaiser realized that few companies in the entire West could mobilize the resources necessary for such a huge project. He led in the formation of a consortium of six western construction companies that successfully bid on the contract. They emerged from the project as leaders in western construction, and some continued to cooperate on other huge projects in the 1930s. Eventually Kaiser, Warren A. Bechtel, and some of their partners each became the leader of a giant, multinational construction corporation.

When Kaiser needed financing for the Boulder Dam project, he turned to Amadeo Peter Giannini, the San Francisco banker whose Bank of America was transforming Americans' thinking about banking. The son of Italian immigrants, Giannini founded the Bank of Italy in 1904 as a bank for shopkeepers and workers in the Italian neighborhood of San Francisco. Called the greatest innovator in twentieth-century American banking, Giannini created his bank for ordinary people and opened branches near people's homes and workplaces. Until then, most banks had only one location, in the center of town, and most limited their services to businesses and people with hefty accounts. Giannini broadened the base of banking by using advertising to encourage working people to open checking and savings accounts and to borrow for such purposes as car purchases—all virtually unknown before his efforts. By 1920, the Bank of Italy was the largest bank in California, and it became the third largest in the nation in 1927. Giannini renamed it the Bank of America in 1930. Giannini's bank backed entrepreneurs such as Kaiser, and helped to fund the fledgling film industry in southern California. And by 1929 one California farmer in every eleven had a loan from the Bank of Italy. The bank not only made loans to growers, but also provided information on new agricultural techniques and crops.

Between World War I and 1940, cotton emerged as a major crop. In 1909, only eighteen California farms raised cotton; by 1939, more than five thousand farms raised cotton, pushing California to eighth place among the states in cotton production. By then, California cotton growers had become the most productive, on a per acre basis, in the country. Cotton growing was concentrated in the southern San Joaquin Valley, with some production in Imperial and Riverside Counties.

California agriculture was becoming increasingly industrialized during those years. These new patterns can be seen clearly in operations of the California Packing Corporation, or Calpak, whose fruits and vegetables were marketed under the name Del Monte. Throughout the 1920s, Calpak was the largest canning operation in the world. By the 1930s, it not only contracted with thousands of growers to supply its canneries but also raised its own fruit and vegetables on thousands of acres. Another California company, Di Giorgio Fruit Corporation, was the nation's largest seller of fruit, based both on some fifteen thousand acres of irrigated farmland in the San Joaquin Valley and on contracts with other growers. Calpak and Di Giorgio both had storage and distribution facilities in other parts of the nation, and thus represented vertical integration in agriculture—growing crops, processing the fruits and vegetables, and distributing the produce to dealers across the country.

New Social Patterns

California's rapid growth in the 1920s brought changes in some social patterns and intensified some previous patterns. Changes in federal immigration laws altered the ethnic composition of migrants to California, and this, in turn, affected both ethnic and racial relations and ethnic patterns in some sectors of the economy.

Though LA led the state's population growth, other areas also experienced rapid growth. California more than doubled in population between 1920 and 1940, moving from the eighth largest state in 1920 to fifth in 1940. The population growth of the 1920s came largely from other parts of the United States, especially the Midwest, and most of the newcomers located in southern California. Most came for economic opportunities, but some came for other reasons—to establish utopian communities or create new religious organizations, for example.

California, from the time of the Gold Rush, had attracted utopians—those who hoped to create a perfect society. In the early twentieth century a group of artists and writers had created a colony at Carmel, and that area and the nearby Big Sur region attracted artists and writers through the 1920s and after. During the late nineteenth and early twentieth centuries several socialist communities were established, based on cooperative principles, but few lasted very long.

Many utopians had religious inspirations. From 1897 until her death in 1929, Katherine Tingley led the Theosophical Society in America from an elaborate complex at Point Loma, now part of San Diego. They drew upon various religious inspirations, especially those of India, to create a community devoted to "developing a higher type of humanity." A few other Theosophical communities developed along the coast, including a large one at Ojai.

Aimée Semple McPherson preached a different message. She arrived in southern California in 1918 and by 1922 had organized her Four Square Gospel Church in Los Angeles. In her immense Angelus Temple, she preached in white robes, staged spectacular performances complete with a full orchestra that sometimes played jazz, and drew thousands of enthusiastic converts to her version of fundamentalist Protestantism—a call for a return to the Bible and the simplicity of old-time religion. She was also a pioneer in the use of radio. One observer suggested that she was popular because "she made migrants feel at home" and "gave them a chance to meet other people."

Though among the most flamboyant, Sister Aimée was only one of many fundamentalist preachers in California. Fundamentalist Protestantism emerged in the early twentieth century from a conflict between Christian modernism and orthodoxy, and became a powerful force throughout the nation by the 1920s. Whereas modernists tried to reconcile their religious beliefs with modern science, fundamentalists rejected anything incompatible with a literal reading of the Scriptures and argued that the Bible's every word is the revealed word of God.

Migration to California in the 1920s came largely from within the nation rather than from Europe, due partly to changes in federal law. Californians had long been at the forefront of efforts to restrict immigration from Asia, but others also wanted to limit immigration from Europe. The National Origins Act of 1924 limited immigration to 150,000 people each year, with quotas for each European country based on 2 percent of the number of Americans whose ancestors came from that country. Those provisions cut immigration from southern and eastern Europe to a mere trickle. Californians in Congress shaped two provisions of the new law. The author of the law, Albert Johnson, a Republican from Washington State, included no provisions regarding immigration from Asia. Senator Hiram Johnson of California demanded exclusion of all immigrants from Japan, and the final language prohibited entry by any immigrant not eligible for citizenship—meaning those from Asia. Johnson and other Californians failed to persuade Congress to amend the Constitution to deny citizenship to the American-born children of Japanese immigrants. Though the new law excluded Asians, it placed no limits on immigration from Canada and Latin America. Occasional efforts to introduce quotas for the Western Hemisphere were defeated through loud protests from representatives of California and southwestern agriculture and business, who argued that they could not survive without laborers from Mexico.

Though the new law placed no numerical limits on immigration from Latin America, all immigrants entering the United States had to provide birth certificates (and marriage certificates if they were traveling as a family), prove their ability to read and write, undergo health inspections, and pay fees of $18 (equivalent to nearly $194 in 2003) plus $8 for each family member. For poor Mexicans seeking a better life north of the border, these were significant limitations, discouraging many would-be migrants from entering legally. Even so, more than half a million migrants from Mexico did pass through the border patrol check points and secure their papers between 1919 and 1930. The border was long, and much of it was not patrolled, and probably another half million people entered without papers. Most migrants went to Texas, but increasing numbers came to California. By 1930, Mexican Californians (those born in Mexico and those of Mexican descent) made up at least 6.5 percent of the state's population, with larger proportions in the south and the cities. By 1930, the Mexican population of Los Angeles was estimated at 8 to 15 percent, or between 100,000 and 190,000 people. Mexicans also made up some 80 percent of agricultural field labor in southern California, and somewhat less further north.

During the 1920s, in many areas of southern California, the children of Mexican immigrants were increasingly segregated into separate schools as local boards of education established "American Schools." These were separate facilities or classrooms where Mexican students received instruction in English and American culture. Behind this policy there was usually a racial agenda of separating Anglo and Mexican children. The Los Angeles School District, for example, justified segregation by saying that Mexican children "are more interested in action and emotion but grow listless under purely mental effort." Such practices were widespread throughout the Southwest, until the Supreme Court declared them illegal in *Mendez* v. *Westminster* (1947).

Anti-immigrant sentiments, anti-Catholicism, anti-Semitism, and fear of radicalism contributed to the growth of the Ku Klux Klan in the early 1920s. The original Klan, created during Reconstruction to intimidate former slaves, had long since died out. D. W. Griffith's hugely popular film, *The Birth of a Nation*, released in 1915, glorified the old Klan and led to efforts to resurrect it. The new Klan portrayed itself as a patriotic order devoted to America, Protestant Christianity, and white supremacy. It attacked Catholics, Jews, immigrants, and African Americans, along with bootleggers, corrupt politicians, and gamblers. Bob Shuler, a leading fundamentalist preacher in Los Angeles, defended the Klan as helping to keep Los Angeles, as he put it, the only large American city "not dominated by foreigners." Other Protestant ministers also encouraged the Klan, which established strong chapters in Los Angeles and San Diego. There the targets of Klan attacks—verbal and physical—were often Mexicans.

Cultural Expression

The most conspicuous form of cultural expression to come out of California during the 1920s was the movies. The new medium quickly gave birth to a wide variety of genres—comedy, westerns, sentimental dramas, swashbuckling adventure tales, history epics, and romances—all of which were silent. In 1927 Hollywood produced *The Jazz Singer*, the first "talking picture." Many movies derived from earlier forms of cultural expression—novels, vaudeville, and the theater—but they reached much larger audiences than their predecessors could have imagined. The plots of movie westerns and swashbucklers usually bore little resemblance to

This version of the California bungalow is from Santa Ana, in Orange County. Highly popular during the 1920s, the design derived from several architectural sources, but one of its key characteristics was simplicity. The bungalows were usually all on one floor with a large front porch that was offset from the center of the house and which usually had distinctive pillars. One of the great advantages of the simplicity of design was that prices could be kept low. Aside from price, what may have made this design so popular?

historical reality, but they reached so many people that their version of the past was often more widely known than the actual history. *The Mark of Zorro*, for example, a 1920 adventure film, fostered a romantic version of Mexican California. Though some critics dismissed the movies as inherently tasteless and uninspired, some films demonstrated that they were, in fact, a new art form. The comedies of Charlie Chaplin, Buster Keaton, and Harold Lloyd not only provoked laughter—they also frequently provided a moving commentary on the human condition.

Hollywood's productions reached and affected the majority of Americans. Movie attendance doubled from a weekly average of forty million people in 1922 to eighty million in 1929. By then, the equivalent of two-thirds of the nation's population went to the cinema every week! The popularity of movies created a new kind of fame—the movie star. Chaplin, Keaton, and Lloyd, cowboy stars Tom Mix and William S. Hart, and dashing Douglas Fairbanks became as well known as champion baseball sluggers or presidents. Sex, too, sold movie tickets and made stars of Theda Bara, the "vamp," Clara Bow, the "It" girl, and Rudolph Valentino. Through their movies, California's screenwriters, directors, producers, and studios played a significant role in redefining and in homogenizing American culture.

Californians who contributed to literature, the arts, and architecture could not hope to reach the numbers that the movies did, but there was a flowering of cultural expression in the 1920s, especially in architecture. The prosperity of the decade took concrete form as the central business districts in both San Francisco and Los Angeles boomed upward with dramatic new high-rise office buildings. Movie theaters sprouted everywhere; in the cities, especially, architects employed exotic styles for grandiose theaters, drawing inspiration from ancient Egypt, traditional China, and medieval Spain.

The 1920s marked the high point of popularity for the bungalow, a California contribution to residential architecture associated especially with the work of Charles and Henry Greene. The brothers came to Pasadena in 1893 and gradually incorporated architectural elements from Mexican California, Japan, and the Arts and Crafts movement into their work, producing some spectacular residences in the Pasadena area in the early twentieth century. A scaled-down, one-story, inexpensive version, the California bungalow, was widely popular from around 1905 through the 1920s, making it possible for an ever larger number of middle-income Californians to acquire their own single-family home.

The 1920s and 1930s marked the culmination of the careers of two of California's most creative and influential architects. Bernard Maybeck, son of a German immigrant, studied at the École des Beaux-Arts in Paris (the world's leading school for architecture). During the early twentieth century, he adapted the popular Arts and Crafts style to emphasize building materials native to the Pacific Coast and he applied his own vision to the creation of a series of remarkable houses and churches in the Bay Area. The First Church of Christ, Scientist, in Berkeley (1910), is especially notable. He drew upon his Beaux-Arts training to create the majestic Palace of Fine Arts for the Panama-Pacific International Exposition (1915) and to design elegant showrooms for selling automobiles in San Francisco, Oakland, and Los Angeles in the 1920s.

Julia Morgan studied engineering at the University of California at Berkeley, then worked for a time with Maybeck. In 1898, she became the first woman admitted to the École des Beaux-Arts, and completed its demanding requirements in 1902. Upon her return to the Bay Area, she began, like Maybeck, to define a California variant of the Arts and Crafts style with her designs for houses and churches. Morgan also designed larger commercial or public structures, for the YWCA, other women's organizations (the Berkeley Women's City Club is perhaps most notable), the University of California at Berkeley, and Mills College. During the early twentieth century, she was a pioneer in the use of reinforced concrete. She is best known for the creation of William Randolph Hearst's fantastic mansion at San Simeon. When a major earthquake struck San Simeon in 2003, Morgan's sophisticated seismic engineering prevented serious damage to the Hearst castle.

Depression Decade: The 1930s

By 1928 the economy showed signs of slowing, both in California and across the nation. In fact, much of American agriculture had never shared in the prosperity, though California growers had fared relatively better than their counterparts elsewhere in the country. As early as 1926, the southern California construction boom began to level off. The price of stock in Giannini's banks dropped sharply in mid-1928. Then, on October 24, 1929, prices on the New York Stock Exchange fell, and continued to decline over the next weeks, months, and years. Businesses failed. Unemployment mounted, especially for manufacturing workers. Those who kept their jobs often worked fewer hours and at reduced wages. People were evicted from their homes when they could not pay their rent or mortgage payments. Cars and radios bought on the installment plan were repossessed. The economy did not fully recover until World War II.

Impact of the Great Depression

Until the mid-1930s, no governmental agency kept data on unemployment, so there are no reliable statistics on the number of Californians out of work in the early 1930s. Estimates suggest that unemployment reached as high as 30 percent in San Francisco and Los Angeles by late 1932. The number of people employed in the oil industry was about three-fifths of what it had been in the mid-1920s. For lumbering and canning, it was about a third. The Bank of America compiled a monthly business index that, in late 1932, showed the state at 60 percent of normal. New construction slowed to a trickle. Department stores reported a 38 percent decline in sales between 1929 and 1932.

The Depression cruelly affected many individuals and families. In 1930 the Los Angeles Parent Teacher Association (PTA) launched a school milk and lunch program when teachers reported some children coming to school hungry. Some LA schools remained open through the summer to dispense milk and lunch. Even so, in the fall of 1931, some children arrived at school so malnourished they were hospitalized. When the PTA ran out of funds, the county board of supervisors paid for the program. Aimée Semple McPherson's church fed forty thousand people during 1932. On the San Francisco waterfront, Lois Jordan, the "White Angel," fed as many as two thousand men each day using contributed food and financial donations. In 1931, the state created work camps for unemployed, homeless men. They worked on roads and built firebreaks and trails, but received no wages—only food, clothing, and a bed in a barracks. City and county governments mounted work programs in which unemployed men worked for a box of groceries. When San Francisco ran out of money for relief in 1932, the supervisors put a bond issue before the voters, and it was approved by a large margin, permitting the city to borrow funds to provide minimal assistance to the unemployed.

In southern California, some claimed that Mexican immigrants were taking jobs away from whites or driving down wage levels. As unemployment rose, so did agitation to deport undocumented Mexicans, with the loudest voices coming from AFL unions, the Hearst press, and patriotic (and often nativist) groups such as the American Legion. During the presidential administration of Herbert Hoover (1929–1933), the Immigration and Naturalization Service (INS) conducted raids in Mexican neighborhoods. Thousands were deported to Mexico, the large majority for lacking proper papers. Thousands more chose to return to

Mexico to avoid deportation. After the election of Franklin D. Roosevelt (who took office in 1933), the INS took a more humane approach, and the number of deportations fell by half. The Los Angeles county supervisors used county funds for transportation for Mexicans willing to return to Mexico, and more than thirteen thousand did so between 1931 and 1934. Other communities promoted similar programs. Those who were deported and those who returned on their own included some who had lived and worked in the United States for many years, and some left behind their homes, savings, and family members.

As unemployment rates rose, other ethnic groups also felt threatened. After the United States acquired the Philippine Islands in 1898, Filipino immigrants came to California, as growers sought workers for agriculture. Because the Philippines were an American possession, their residents were not considered aliens, but neither were they citizens. The 1940 census recorded more than thirty thousand Filipinos in California, two-thirds of all Filipinos in the United States. Half worked in agriculture or canneries, and some led strikes during the early 1930s. Some white Californians urged that Filipinos be deported, but there was no legal basis for doing so. In 1930, anti-Filipino rioting broke out in Watsonville. Several Filipinos were injured, and two were killed. Other violence followed, spawned by fears that Filipinos were competing for jobs or by anxieties over Filipino men socializing with white women. Eventually anti-Filipino attitudes combined with a long-standing promise of the Democratic Party to bring independence to the Philippines. In 1934, Congress passed and President Roosevelt signed the Tydings-McDuffie Act, which set in motion a process leading to Philippine independence. The same law cut migration from the Philippines to fifty per year.

The plight of migrant farm labor drew less interest. As Mexican farm workers left or were deported, increasing numbers of Dust Bowl migrants took their place. Most Californians at the time thought of the migrants as refugees from drought, but many of them had been uprooted by technological change in agriculture (the transition from small farms to larger units that relied on heavy machinery) or by the impact of federal agricultural programs that favored landowners over tenant farmers. Usually denigrated as Okies, regardless of the state from which they came, they encountered miserable living conditions. The Commission of Immigration and Housing, created in 1913 to supervise migratory labor camps, had its budget cut so much that, by 1933, only four camp inspectors had to cover the entire state. Most migratory labor camps lacked rudimentary sanitation, and most migratory labor families could not afford proper diets or health care. A survey of migratory children in the San Joaquin Valley during 1936 and 1937 found that 80 percent had medical problems, most caused by malnutrition or poor hygiene.

Though some Californians reacted to rising unemployment by seeking scapegoats, others turned to a Marxist analysis and argued that the problem was with capitalism itself. The Socialist Party had declined since its high point before the war. Though it still provided a focal point for a critique of capitalism, it was able to muster less than 4 percent of the vote for governor in 1930, up from 2 percent in the 1928 election for the U.S. Senate.

In the 1930s a different Marxist group began to attract attention. Radicals had formed the Communist Party (CP) of the United States shortly after the war, but it struggled through the 1920s, losing more members than it recruited. The CP defined itself as a revolutionary organization, devoted to ending capitalism and to uniting all the workers of the world. Communists saw the Soviet Union as the only workers' government in the world and committed themselves to its defense. These revolutionary and pro-Soviet attitudes made it difficult to recruit American workers, few of whom wanted to overthrow the government or defend the Soviet Union. At the same time, CP organizers committed themselves to the "class struggle"—to helping workers achieve better wages and working conditions. They saw their special task as organizing the unskilled, African Americans, Mexican Americans, and other workers ignored by existing unions. Throughout the 1920s, they had little success. In California, the CP had 730 dues-paying members in early 1925, recruited 145 new members that year and in early 1926, but had only 438 dues-paying members in mid-1926—a loss of half their members in a year's time.

In the early 1930s the CP grew dramatically, in numbers and visibility. Communists organized Unemployed Councils as protest organizations for the unemployed. Though the CP counted only about 500 members in the entire state in 1930, many more joined the Unemployed Councils. In March 1930, the CP organized marches by the unemployed. A thousand people marched in San Francisco, where Mayor James Rolph met with them and offered them coffee. In LA, the mayor mobilized a thousand police to stand against the marchers and sent police to arrest leaders the night before the march. One LA police commissioner explained his view on dealing with radicals: "The more police beat them up and wreck their headquarters the better." By early 1934, the CP counted 1,800 members in the state, and provided leadership to thousands more.

The Communists were not the only group from the fringes of the political spectrum to attract attention. On the right, remnants of the Ku Klux Klan were still active in some parts of California in the 1930s, and they found new allies in the Silver Shirts, a San Diego branch of a national fascist organization that emulated Nazism. Another right-wing, militaristic group, the California Cavaliers, organized statewide in 1935. These and similar groups usually blamed the state's problems on Jews, immigrants (especially Mexicans and Filipinos), and Communists, and some added President Franklin D. Roosevelt and his New Deal. Most required their members to be proficient with firearms.

Some groups closer to the mainstream, notably the American Legion (the state's largest organization of veterans), also mobilized against what its leaders saw as a Communist menace. Some Legionnaires joined vigilante groups to terrorize radicals and striking workers. The state organization set up a Radical Research Committee to collect information on suspected radicals, sometimes through undercover operatives. The committee cooperated closely with the Industrial

Association and Associated Farmers (see below, this page) and traded information with local and state police and with military and naval intelligence. In Los Angeles, the Better America Federation denounced advocates of publicly owned utilities as Communists, tried to purge liberal books and magazines from the schools, and contributed to the repression of labor unions.

Labor Conflict

During the 1920s, labor organizations were on the defense all across the country, and nowhere more than in California. The powerful Merchants and Manufacturers (M&M) in LA stood ready to block union efforts in southern California. In San Francisco, several failed strikes from 1919 to 1921 led to the decline of once-powerful unions. In 1921, the Chamber of Commerce helped to organize the Industrial Association of San Francisco, a group funded by banks, transportation companies, utility companies—indeed, nearly every company in the city. From the early 1920s until the mid-1930s, the Industrial Association closely governed labor relations in San Francisco, blocking every effort to revive union organizations.

In the early 1930s, California agriculture was wracked by strikes, sometimes violent, usually in response to wage cuts or miserable working conditions. The first came in early 1930, in the Imperial Valley, when Mexican and Filipino farm laborers walked off their jobs in the lettuce fields. The strike spread to five thousand field workers. Communist organizers soon arrived and offered help for the strikers through their union, which was soon after renamed the Cannery and Agricultural Workers Industrial Union (CAWIU). Other strikes broke out elsewhere, most by Mexican and Filipino field and shed workers, and CAWIU organizers always appeared to offer support and seek converts. Whether in the Imperial Valley or Half Moon Bay, the CAWIU seemed unable to win strikes. By 1932, they had begun to target particular areas and to build an organizational base prior to a strike. In 1933, strike after strike hit the state's agricultural regions. By August, an increasing number were successful, pushing average agricultural wages from sixteen cents an hour to twenty-five cents. Growers regrouped, however, and strikes in late 1933 were met by violence against the strikers and threats of lynching against the strike leaders.

Growers and business leaders formed the Associated Farmers in March 1934, with funding from the Industrial Association, banks, railroads, utilities, and other corporations. The Associated Farmers launched a statewide anti-Communist propaganda campaign and sought indictments of CAWIU leaders under criminal syndicalism laws. Seventeen CAWIU leaders, mostly CP members, were brought to trial in 1935. The Associated Farmers paid generously to assist the prosecution, and eight defendants were convicted. The CAWIU was dissolved the next year, but the Associated Farmers remained alert, ready to oppose any new efforts to unionize farm workers.

In May 1934, longshoremen (workers who load and unload ships) went on strike in all Pacific Coast ports. Before World War I, Pacific Coast longshoremen

Longshore strikers parading along San Francisco's Embarcadero, May 10, 1934. City law prohibited picketing, so the strikers held frequent "parades" along the Embarcadero, the wide street that connected nearly all the piers. The banner at the front of the procession calls for teamsters and seamen to honor the strike. How did the 1934 longshoremen's strike come to involve other unions?

had been organized into the International Longshoremen's Association (ILA). By the early 1920s, however, as a result of unsuccessful strikes, California dock-workers had no meaningful union. Dock work was harsh and dangerous, and longshoremen were hired through the "shape-up," in which foremen hired men for a day at a time. In 1933, the ILA launched an organizing drive in Pacific Coast ports. In San Francisco, Harry Bridges, an immigrant from Australia who had worked on the docks since 1922, emerged as a leader of one group of longshoremen—including some Communist Party members—who used the *Waterfront Worker,* a mimeographed newsletter, to advocate militant action.

In 1934, the ILA's Pacific Coast District (California, Oregon, and Washington) sought a union contract. When waterfront employers refused, ten to fifteen thousand longshoremen from northern Washington to San Diego walked out in an attempt to shut down shipping on the Pacific Coast. They demanded a union hiring hall (replacing the hated shape-up), higher wages, and shorter hours. Greeted by picket lines upon entering Pacific Coast ports, ships' crews quickly went on strike with issues of their own, adding six thousand more strikers. In San Pedro on May 15, private guards fired on strikers, killing two of them.

The strike focused on San Francisco, site of the largest ILA local and of many employers' headquarters. Bridges, chairman of the strike committee for the San

Francisco local, became a prominent figure in opposing compromise and insisting on the union's full demands. By late June, the Industrial Association took over the employers' side of the strike and determined to reopen the port using strikebreakers. In a daylong battle on July 5, police killed two union members and injured hundreds more. Governor Frank Merriam dispatched the National Guard in full battle array, armed with machine guns and tanks, to patrol the San Francisco waterfront. Ostensibly deployed to prevent further violence, the Guardsmen also protected the strikebreakers.

On July 9, thousands of silent strikers and strike supporters solemnly marched up Market Street, filling that great thoroughfare as they followed the caskets of those killed on July 5. From July 16 through July 19, the San Francisco Labor Council coordinated a general strike that shut down the city in sympathy with the striking maritime workers and, implicitly, in opposition to the tactics of the police and the governor's use of the National Guard. Never before or since have American unions shut down a city as large as San Francisco through a general strike. At the time, business leaders and politicians discerned in the general strike the seeds of Communist insurrection, but the real moving force was workers' anger over the use of government power to kill workers and protect strikebreakers. By late July, all sides agreed to arbitration, and the longshoremen secured nearly all of their demands.

The strikes by agricultural workers and by longshoremen and seafaring workers were the most prominent California examples of a strike wave that broke over the nation between 1933 and 1937. In 1933, Congress tried to reverse the economic collapse of the nation with the National Industrial Recovery Act. One of its provisions, Section 7-a, encouraged collective bargaining between employers and unions. Section 7-a stimulated union organizing all across the country, as workers turned to unions to stop wage cuts and improve working conditions. The union victory in the 1934 longshoremen's strike inspired other workers to organize. In 1935, Congress passed the Wagner Labor Relations Act, strengthening and extending federal protection of unions and bargaining. Everywhere, workers formed unions. In San Francisco, the number of union members doubled within a few years after 1933.

In Los Angeles, unions challenged the M&M, organizing in many fields, including furniture making, printing, the movie studios, and construction. The newly unionized longshoremen in San Pedro sometimes helped with organizing or with picket duty. The M&M did not give in easily. They hired an army of private guards to protect strikebreakers and counted on city police to work closely with them, but they lost a showdown with the Teamsters' Union in 1937. By 1941, unions claimed that half the workers in LA were union members.

As union membership burgeoned, the labor movement divided between two groups: the American Federation of Labor (AFL), oriented to organizing the more skilled workers into unions that were defined along the lines of skill or craft; and a group led by John L. Lewis of the United Mine Workers, who called for an industrial approach to organizing, in which all workers in an industry would belong to the same union regardless of skill or craft. At first they called themselves the Committee on Industrial Organization (CIO) and worked within the AFL, but in 1937 the AFL expelled the CIO unions.

Lewis and the CIO reorganized themselves into the Congress of Industrial Organizations. The Pacific Coast District of the ILA, now led by Harry Bridges, broke away from the ILA to become the International Longshoremen's and Warehousemen's Union of the CIO, and Bridges became CIO western regional director. The CIO also chartered the United Cannery, Agricultural, Packing, and Allied Workers of America (UCAPAWA), which launched an organizing drive among California agricultural and cannery workers, only to meet strong and often violent opposition from the Associated Farmers. Nonetheless, UCAPAWA organized thousands of cannery workers, the large majority of them women, including many Mexicans. Latinas advanced to leadership in some UCAPAWA locals, and Luisa Moreno, a well-educated immigrant from Guatemala, became a vice president of UCAPAWA, the first Latina to serve in such a post in any American union. Other CIO unions, especially the Auto Workers, Steelworkers, Clothing Workers, and Rubber Workers, organized manufacturing workers in southern California. AFL unions grew too, especially the Teamsters and the Machinists. By 1940, AFL unions in California claimed a half million members and the CIO had 150,000, making California a leading state for union membership.

Federal Politics: The Impact of the New Deal

The revolution in labor relations represents only one of the ways that new federal policies changed life in California during the 1930s. There were many others. The political changes of the 1930s worked a transformation not just in state–federal relations but also in the relationship between individuals and the government at all levels. The stimulus for most of these changes was the Depression. The first changes came during the presidency of Herbert Hoover, but greater changes came after 1933, under President Franklin D. Roosevelt.

Hoover spent much of his four years as president addressing the Depression. He approved programs that went further in establishing state–federal cooperation than ever before. One example was the Hoover-Young Commission to plan the San Francisco–Oakland Bay Bridge. Another was his approval of funding for the bridge construction from the Reconstruction Finance Corporation (RFC), an agency that loaned funds to companies to stabilize the economy. In the case of the Bay Bridge, the loan was to a state agency, for the purpose of constructing a publicly owned bridge—something unprecedented. In the case of the dam project at Boulder Canyon, Hoover's approval helped to promote other massive federal water projects throughout the West. However, Hoover was adamant that the federal government should not directly assist the unemployed or those in need.

When Hoover faced reelection in 1932, he lost in a landslide to the Democratic candidate, Franklin D. Roosevelt, the governor of New York, who promised to do more to address the problems of the Depression. California's voters gave

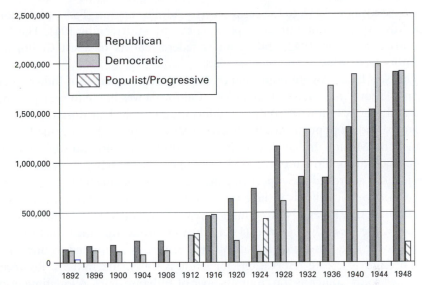

Figure 8.2 Number of Votes Received by Major Party Presidential Candidates in California, 1892–1948

This graph shows the number of votes received by major party presidential candidates in California between 1892 and 1948. Note especially the sharp change from 1928 to 1932 and 1936. What accounts for this dramatic change in voters' support?

Source: Historical Statistics of the United States (Washington, 1975).

1,324,000 votes to Roosevelt, and 848,000 to Hoover. As Figure 8.2 indicates, the election marked the beginning of a new pattern to Californians' voting for president, a move toward the Democratic Party.

As president, Roosevelt conveyed a confidence that something could be done about the Depression, and he called upon Congress to pass legislation for relief, recovery, and reform. The Public Works Administration (PWA) set up an ambitious federal construction program to stimulate the economy. In California, PWA paid for many new federal buildings—post offices, court buildings, and buildings on military posts and naval bases—and also new ships for the navy. Other PWA projects included schools, courthouses, dams, auditoriums, and sewage treatment plants. The Works Progress Administration (WPA), created in 1935, was a work program for the unemployed. WPA projects across the state included public parks, buildings, bridges, and roads. The WPA and PWA together helped to fund the Pasadena Freeway. All in all, the PWA and WPA had a major impact on the state's infrastructure, but the WPA went beyond construction projects to include orchestras (composed of unemployed musicians), murals in public buildings (painted by unemployed artists), a collection of guidebooks (compiled by unemployed writers), and adult education programs (presented by unemployed teachers).

New federal agencies took up the plight of migratory farm workers. In 1935, the Resettlement Administration (RA) set out to construct camps with adequate sanitation and housing that met minimal standards. Two camps were built before the RA gave way, in 1937, to the Farm Security Administration (FSA), which continued the work of building and operating camps—thirteen by 1941. The FSA was closed down in 1942, ending direct federal efforts to assist California's migratory farm workers and their families.

The New Deal brought important changes to the governance of Indian reservations. Throughout the 1920s and 1930s, California was home to nearly twenty thousand American Indians, putting California among the half-dozen states with the largest Indian populations. In the early 1920s, whites and California Indians formed the Mission Indian Federation, to improve the situation of southern California Indians. Similar efforts took place in the north. When the state legislature, in 1921, approved a law specifying that American Indian children could only attend local public schools if there were no Indian school within three miles of their homes, Alice Piper, a Native American, sued to attend her local public school. In *Piper* v. *Big Pine School District* (1924), the California Supreme Court ruled in Piper's favor. The Bureau of Indian Affairs (BIA) also continued to buy small plots of land to create reservations for landless California Indians. Roosevelt appointed John Collier as the commissioner of Indian Affairs. A longtime critic of previous federal Indian policies, Collier closed down programs aimed at forced assimilation, including boarding schools and the suppression of traditional religious practices. His "Indian New Deal" included, as its centerpiece, the Indian Reorganization Act (1934), which encouraged tribal self-government.

State Politics: The Rise of the Democrats

Though California's voters clearly turned to the Democrats in the 1932 presidential election and continued to vote for Democrats through the presidential elections of the 1940s, they showed more ambivalence in state elections. There *was* an increase in support for Democratic candidates, but that increase did not automatically translate to the election of Democrats to state offices.

In the elections of 1930, the real contest, once again, was in the Republican primary. The incumbent progressive governor, C. C. Young, faced two opponents in the Republican primary. One was James C. "Sunny Jim" Rolph, the popular mayor of San Francisco, first elected in 1911 and reelected every four years, usually by large margins. Though Rolph had promoted progressive causes in the 1910s, he became more moderate during the 1920s, and was probably best known, in 1930, for his outspoken opposition to prohibition. Young's other opponent was Buron Fitts, a conservative from LA who was a staunch prohibitionist. Young, too, supported prohibition. Fitts and Young divided the "dry" vote. Rolph took the "wet" vote, won the Republican nomination, and easily defeated his Democratic opponent.

As governor, Rolph spent much of the state's budget surplus on assistance to the victims of the Depression. He also supported the Central Valley Project Act of 1933 to create dams and canals for hydroelectric power and irrigation, and the bill passed despite strong opposition from electrical power companies. With

Rolph's support, the legislature repealed the enforcement of prohibition, which meant that policing the unpopular law was entirely the responsibility of a handful of federal officials. However, Rolph seemed to condone violence against farm strikers, and he publicly approved of the lynching of two men suspected of kidnapping and murder. He died in office, in June 1934, and was succeeded by his lieutenant governor, Frank Merriam.

Democrats hoped to win the governor's office in 1934, for the first time in more than forty years. Voter registrations had shifted from the huge Republican majorities of the late 1920s to a fairly even split by 1934. In 1932 a Democrat captured one of California's U.S. Senate seats. For 1934, Democratic Party leaders chose, as their candidate for governor, George Creel, a moderate liberal. However, the Democratic primary for governor became a battle between Creel and Upton Sinclair. Sinclair had become nationally famous for his novel, *The Jungle,* in 1906. A classic example of progressive muckraking, *The Jungle* revealed in sickening detail the unsanitary conditions and exploitation of workers in Chicago's meatpacking industry. A Pasadena resident after 1915, Sinclair continued to write novels with strong social and political messages. He ran for governor as a Socialist in the 1920s, but changed his party registration to Democrat in 1934 and entered the Democratic primary for governor.

Sinclair's slogan was "End Poverty in California," soon abbreviated to EPIC. He wrote a novel—*I, Candidate for Governor and How I Ended Poverty*—and used it to promote his candidacy. At the center of the EPIC program was "production for use," a plan to let the unemployed raise crops on idle farmland and make goods in idle factories, and then exchange their products using state scrip (by *scrip,* Sinclair meant state-issued certificates that would specify the value of the agricultural and manufacturing products). Thousands of Californians joined EPIC clubs across the state, making them a new force in politics. Sinclair won the nomination for governor by a clear majority in the Democratic primary and his supporters won nominations for other offices. Frank Merriam, the bland conservative who had become governor upon the death of Rolph, won the Republican primary.

In the general election, Sinclair's opponents attacked EPIC as unworkable and Sinclair as incompetent for proposing it. Sinclair's plan reflected a weak grasp of economics but it hardly deserved the abuse heaped on it as dangerously "red." In fact, Socialists and Communists vigorously attacked EPIC. Hollywood studios regularly produced a short news feature that ran in theaters before the main feature; now they created alleged news stories, actually staged, that claimed the state faced a deluge of hobos and Communists attracted by EPIC. Republicans hired press agents Clem Whitaker and Leone Baxter to sort through Sinclair's writings and produce lurid campaign advertisements based on Sinclair's support for free love and contempt for organized religion. In the process, Whitaker and Baxter created a new career—that of the freelance campaign consultant—and their success inspired a host of imitators on both the right and the left. National Democratic leaders abandoned Sinclair, and Roosevelt refused to endorse him. Merriam won, but Sinclair had transformed the California Democratic Party, as twenty-six EPIC candidates were elected to the state assembly, including Augustus Hawkins, the first black Democrat to serve in the legislature. In many places, EPIC clubs began to prepare for the next election.

In the 1934 elections, the Communist Party showed surprising strength. Though their candidate for governor got fewer than 6,000 votes, Anita Whitney, the CP candidate for controller, got 100,000 votes and 5 percent of the total. Leo Gallagher, running for the supreme court without a party label but with support from the CP, received 240,000 votes and 17 percent. The CP was highly critical of the New Deal in 1933 and 1934, but from 1937 to 1939 top CP leaders reversed their position and encouraged party members to support New Deal Democrats.

EPIC was not the only unusual proposal to percolate out of southern California. In 1934, Francis Townsend, a retired physician from Long Beach, launched Old Age Revolving Pensions. He proposed that business transactions be taxed in order to pay two hundred dollars each month to every citizen over the age of sixty (except criminals) on the condition that he or she retire and spend the full amount within each month. The plan had something for nearly everyone: older people could retire; putting money into circulation would stimulate the economy; and retirements would open jobs for younger people. It was enormously popular. Some older people bought goods on credit, expecting to pay for them with their first checks. Townsend's popularity translated to political clout—California candidates hesitated to criticize his plan, and many endorsed it. The adoption of Social Security in 1935, however, took the wind from Townsend's sails. In 1938, grassroots activists put a new panacea on the ballot, nicknamed "Ham and Eggs," which proposed to pay thirty dollars in state "warrants" every Thursday to all unemployed people over fifty. The measure lost in 1938, and a revised version lost in 1939.

The progressive reforms that reduced the power of political parties may have made Californians more likely than before to cross party lines. Thus, they supported Roosevelt in 1932 and elected a Democrat to the U.S. Senate, but in 1934 they elected a conservative Republican as governor. In 1934, Roosevelt endorsed Republican Hiram Johnson for the U.S. Senate, and Johnson used cross-filing to win both the Democratic and Republican nominations. Like other prominent progressive Republicans, Johnson supported Roosevelt in 1932 and endorsed much of the early New Deal. In 1936, California voters gave Roosevelt a large majority and elected a majority of Democrats to the state assembly for the first time in the twentieth century. State senate districts, however, had been drawn to minimize the number of senators from urban districts, where the Democrats were developing much of their support.

After Merriam was elected governor in 1934, he disappointed his most conservative supporters by acting pragmatically to implement some New-Deal-type reforms, to create a state income tax (generally considered a liberal approach to taxation), and to increase taxes on banks and corporations. When he sought re-election in 1938, he faced Culbert Olson, a Democrat who had entered politics through EPIC and now campaigned to "Bring the New Deal to California." In the

Democratic primary, another former EPIC supporter, Sheridan Downey, won the nomination for the U.S. Senate, and still another former EPIC activist won the Democratic nomination for lieutenant governor. Business and conservative groups promoted Proposition 1, an initiative to clamp severe restrictions on unions, and they backed it with the most expensive political campaign for a proposition up to that time. The Republican candidates for governor and senator supported Proposition 1. Despite the bitterness between the AFL and CIO, nearly all the state's unions united to defeat Proposition 1 and support the Democrats. Olson, Downey, and other Democrats won, and the Democrats again won a majority in the state assembly.

A good campaigner, Olson proved less effective as governor. He freed Tom Mooney and Warren Billings (see p. 225), for which he won high praise from labor and the left, but earned the hatred of conservatives. He also supported efforts to unionize farm workers. In 1939 Olson proposed a long list of reform legislation—including medical insurance for most working Californians and the protection of civil rights—but such proposals had no support among the conservative Republicans who dominated the state senate. In 1940, two years into the Olson administration, voters sent a majority of Republicans to the assembly. That same year, Hiram Johnson again won both the Democratic and Republican nominations for U.S. Senate through cross-filing, although, by then, he had become highly critical of the New Deal.

Cultural Expression During the Depression Decade

During the 1920s, many American writers and artists rejected the consumer-oriented society around them. Their novels often seemed exercises in hedonism or escapism. Some artists produced works so abstract that they held different meanings for each viewer. In the 1930s, much of that changed. Some leading novelists of the 1930s portrayed working people and their problems, and others looked for inspiration to leading figures in American history. Artists produced realistic scenes, sometimes motivated by a desire for social change and other times rooted in affection for traditional values. And Californians produced some of the leading examples of these trends.

John Steinbeck defined the social protest novel of the 1930s. Born in Salinas in 1902, Steinbeck attended Stanford briefly. Among his early works, *Tortilla Flat* (1933) portrayed Mexican Californians and *In Dubious Battle* (1936) presented an apple-pickers' strike through the eyes of an idealistic young Communist. *The Grapes of Wrath* (1939), which won the Pulitzer Prize for best novel of the year, presented the story of the Joad family, who lost their farm in Oklahoma and migrated to California. There the family disintegrated under the stresses of transient agricultural work and the violence of a farm-workers' strike. This novel has been likened to *Uncle Tom's Cabin* for its social impact.

Some artists also presented social criticism in their work. Diego Rivera, the great Mexican muralist whose work usually carried a leftist political message,

Dorothea Lange gave this photograph the title "Destitute peapickers in California; a 32 year old mother of seven children. February 1936." In 1960, in an article in *Popular Photography,* Lange explained how she took her famous picture: "I saw and approached the hungry and desperate mother, as if drawn by a magnet. . . . She said that they had been living on frozen vegetables from the surrounding fields, and birds that the children killed. She had just sold the tires from her car to buy food."

painted murals in California and influenced a generation of California mural painters. Other muralists, especially those in the WPA arts projects, often presented the lives of ordinary Californians or themes from the state's history.

Dorothea Lange, a commercial photographer before the Depression, began photographing the victims of the Depression in the early 1930s. Lange became well practiced in photographing these victims, ranging from unemployed men in San Francisco to strikers to migrant workers. In 1935, the California Rural Rehabilitation Administration hired Lange and Paul Taylor (an economics professor at the University of California, Berkeley) to document the plight of agricultural labor, and she continued that work with the Federal Resettlement Administration. Her photograph of a farm-migrant mother and children, later entitled "Migrant Mother," taken in 1936, emerged as perhaps the most famous and most moving photograph of the era. In 1939, Lange and Taylor published *American Exodus,* a documentary counterpart to *The Grapes of Wrath,* vividly depicting the misery of life in the migratory labor camps and in the fields, through photographs, commentary, and statistics.

Hollywood produced a few films of social criticism during this time, most notably an adaptation of *The Grapes of Wrath* (1940), starring Henry Fonda. Charlie Chaplin's leftist politics were apparent in two important works: *Modern Times* (1936), portraying the dehumanizing tendencies of technology, and *The Great Dictator* (1940), which mocked Adolf Hitler. Studio heads were often uncomfortable with social protest films, however, and some barred them entirely, insisting that the public needed entertainment that would take their minds off the Depression. Musical extravaganzas like *Forty-Second Street* (1933) fit the bill. So did some westerns and gangster films, but others probed more deeply into the human condition. *Stagecoach* (1939), directed by John Ford, so defined the western genre that it inspired imitators for years after. Gangster films rose to popularity with *Little Caesar* (1930), which boosted Edward G. Robinson to stardom. Similarly, Hollywood turned the hardboiled detective stories of California writers Dashiell Hammett and Raymond Chandler into immensely successful movies, notably *The Thin Man* (1934) and *The Maltese Falcon* (1941), both based on novels by Hammett. In *The Maltese Falcon,* set in San Francisco, Humphrey Bogart first defined the character he continued to develop in such later films as *Casablanca* (1942), *The Big Sleep* (1946), *Key Largo* (1948), and others.

By the late 1930s, the rise to power of Adolf Hitler in Germany and his Nazi party's attacks on Jews and the Left produced a flood of refugees, and ten thousand of them came to southern California. Hollywood had attracted European immigrants from the beginning. Many of the studio heads and leading directors had been born in Europe, and many studio heads were Jewish. By the late 1930s, southern California had become home to a significant number of displaced European intellectuals, including the German novelist Thomas Mann, the Russian composer Igor Stravinsky, the German writer Bertolt Brecht, and the Austrian director Otto Preminger. Their presence gave the LA basin a more cosmopolitan cultural bent.

Many of these currents came together in 1939 and 1940, when San Francisco hosted the Golden Gate International Exposition, held on Treasure Island, a four-hundred-acre artificial island created in San Francisco Bay with WPA funding. The island was connected to both sides of the bay by the new San Francisco–Oakland Bay Bridge, and had full views of the new Golden Gate Bridge. Much of the exposition's architecture reflected prevailing Art Deco and Moderne styles, but sometimes with Pacific themes. One theme of the exposition was the unity of the Pacific basin, and one of the popular exhibits was the real-life arrival and departure of PanAmerican Airways' Flying Clippers—giant (for the day) airplanes, able to carry forty-eight passengers. They landed and took off from the water of the bay and PanAmerican charged $360 (equivalent to more than $4,700 in 2003) for a one-way ticket to Hawai`i. Another, more mundane, goal of the exposition was to promote the growth of tourism to the Bay Area.

California on the Eve of War

Treasure Island had been constructed with the intent that, after the exposition, it would become San Francisco's airport, and several of the buildings were designed to become airport facilities after the exposition. But the first year of the exposition was marked by war. War was already raging in Asia, as Japan had seized

Manchuria in 1931, and then initiated all-out war against China in 1937. In 1939, Germany marched into Czechoslovakia, then Poland. Britain and France then declared war on Germany. In 1940, German armies rolled into Denmark, Norway, the Low Countries, and France. When the Treasure Island exposition closed, the island became a base for the U.S. Navy.

The creation of a naval base on Treasure Island was just one of many examples of increased federal expenditures in California for the army and navy after World War I. In 1921, the U.S. Navy decided to divide its fleet into Atlantic and Pacific divisions. This decision was due partly to rising concerns about the intentions of Japan in the Pacific and the need to protect the American possessions there. San Francisco, Los Angeles, and San Diego all insisted that they were the best location for a navy base, which was predicted to have as many as 45,000 naval personnel. Members of California's congressional delegation contested with each other over the prize, but in the end the navy decentralized its facilities, scattering elements up and down the Pacific Coast. As international tensions increased in the late 1930s, so too did naval and military expenditures in California.

Despite the headlines of war, despite increasing naval and military preparations all around them, most Californians hoped to stay out of the war. Unlike 1914 through 1917, when advocates of preparedness often hoped openly that the United States would enter the war, few made such arguments during 1939 through 1941. All Californians were shocked when their radios announced, on Sunday morning, December 7, 1941, that Japanese planes and ships had attacked the American naval base at Pearl Harbor, Hawai`i. California was on the verge of one of its greatest transformations.

Summary

The 1920s and 1930s marked very different eras in California's economic history. The 1920s were years of prosperity, the 1930s a time of depression. Still, Los Angeles grew at a rapid pace through both decades. The motion picture industry, oil, and manufacturing all contributed to LA's economic base during the 1920s and 1930s. LA was the first large city to be designed around the automobile and the single-family home.

The large majority of Californians voted Republican during the 1920s, but the Republican Party was divided into progressive and conservative wings. Hiram Johnson served in the U.S. Senate throughout the two decades and beyond, leading the progressive wing of the state Republican Party. The other most prominent California Republican was Herbert Hoover, who was elected president in 1928. Prohibition divided voters during the 1920s, and the early 1920s saw a renewal of anti-Asian actions and laws.

Highway and bridge construction laid the basis for the state's transportation infrastructure in the automobile age. Hoover Dam was a massive hydroelectric and irrigation project promoted largely by Californians, though located in Nevada. Henry Kaiser was one of several construction companies that took on such mammoth projects. A. P. Giannini's Bank of America brought important innovations to banking, especially the concept of branch banking. Cotton became an important crop during the 1920s and 1930s, and agriculture was becoming increasingly industrialized, as large corporations owned farmland, processing plants, and distribution networks.

California's population grew throughout the 1920s and 1930s, with much of the growth concentrated in southern California. Federal immigration policy changed dramatically in 1924. Californians, led by Senator Hiram Johnson, succeeded in writing Asian exclusion into the new law. There were no formal limits placed on immigration from Mexico, but the process for legal immigration was intimidating and expensive.

Movies were California's most conspicuous contribution to cultural expression. They came in a variety of genres and reached large numbers of Americans. Important architectural contributions included the California bungalow, popularized by Greene and Greene. Bernard Maybeck and Julia Morgan helped to create a distinctive California variant of prevailing architectural styles.

During the Great Depression, beginning in 1929, unemployment rose, wage levels fell, and business slowed. Some blamed Mexicans and Filipinos and agitated to have them removed from the state. The Communist Party showed some success in its efforts to organize the unemployed. Migratory farm workers endured labor camps that were unhealthy, as large numbers of Dust Bowl refugees poured into the state seeking work.

Labor conflict broke out among agricultural workers, often led by Communists. Longshoremen struck for three months in 1934 at all Pacific Coast ports and encountered violent opposition, but secured most of their objectives. Changes in federal labor policy encouraged unions, and unions grew rapidly in both the San Francisco Bay area and the Los Angeles basin. The labor movement divided between the AFL and CIO, and both were well represented in California.

New federal laws, especially during the administration of President Franklin D. Roosevelt, redefined federal–state relations. California voters gave large majorities to Roosevelt. PWA and WPA programs resulted in the construction of a wide variety of new buildings and other facilities in California. New federal programs tried to assist migratory farm workers and California Indians.

Democrats hoped to win the governorship in 1934, but Upton Sinclair's EPIC campaign came under heavy attack from both right and left, and the Republican candidate won. Other unusual proposals percolated up from southern California in addition to EPIC, including the Townsend movement and Ham and Eggs. The Democrats won the governorship in 1938, but Governor Culbert Olson proved ineffective.

Californians helped to define the use of cultural expression for social protest, especially through John Steinbeck's *The Grapes of Wrath* and Dorothea Lange's photographs. Hollywood produced some social protest movies, but more movies of the 1930s were escapist. The Treasure Island Exposition of 1939–1940 came just as the world was plunging into a second world war. California, by then, had become a major site for military and naval bases.

Suggested Readings

▪ Bottles, Scott L., *Los Angeles and the Automobile: The Making of the Modern City* (Berkeley and Los Angeles: University of California Press, 1987). A good account of the relation between the expansion of Los Angeles and the automobile.

▪ Daniel, Cletus E., *Bitter Harvest: A History of California Farmworkers, 1870–1941* (Ithaca, NY: Cornell University Press, 1981). A thorough account, focusing especially on efforts to form unions.

▪ Lotchin, Roger W., *Fortress California, 1910–1961: From Warfare to Welfare* (New York: Oxford University Press, 1992). Includes a thorough treatment of the expansion of military and naval spending in California during the 1920s and 1930s.

▪ McWilliams, Carey, *Southern California Country: An Island on the Land* (New York: Duell, Sloane & Pearce, 1946). McWilliams's work is one of the classic works on California; never unbiased, he wrote with a freshness that comes from personal observation.

▪ Sanchez, George J., *Becoming Mexican American: Ethnicity, Culture, and Identity in Chicano Los Angeles, 1900–1945* (New York: Oxford University Press, 1993). Sanchez's work is a major contribution to understanding the experience of Mexican Americans in the early twentieth century.

▪ Selvin, David F., *A Terrible Anger: The 1934 Waterfront and General Strikes in San Francisco* (Detroit: Wayne State University Press, 1996). Thorough and well written, Selvin's book also conveys the intensity of feeling of the strikers.

▪ Shindler, Colin, *Hollywood in Crisis: Cinema and American Society, 1929–1939* (New York: Routledge, 1996). Provides a good introduction to the movies of the 1930s.

▪ Sitton, Tom, and William Deverell, eds., *Metropolis in the Making: Los Angeles in the 1920s* (Berkeley and Los Angeles: University of California Press, 2001). An anthology that treats many of the important elements in the growth of Los Angeles during the 1920s.

▪ Starr, Kevin, *Material Dreams: Southern California Through the 1920s* (New York: Oxford University Press, 1990). The author of a series of books on California history and culture, Starr draws upon a wide range of material to construct a sweeping account of southern California in the 1920s.

■ _____, *Endangered Dreams: The Great Depression in California* (New York: Oxford University Press, 1996). Starr's treatment of the 1930s continues his account of the state's development, with rich details and balanced interpretations.

■ Steinbeck, John, *The Grapes of Wrath* (New York: Viking, 1939). There's nothing quite like this novel for understanding the experience of the Okies and of California farm workers in the 1930s.

■ Tygiel, Jules, *The Great Los Angeles Swindle: Oil, Stocks, and Scandal During the Roaring Twenties* (New York: Oxford University Press, 1994). A lively account of the financial manipulations of C. C. Julian cast against Los Angeles in the 1920s.

World War II and the Great Transformation

Main Topics

▌ Economic Expansion

▌ Japanese Relocation and Internment

▌ Population Growth and Diversity

▌ Daily Life and Culture

▌ Political Transformation

▌ Summary

On October 20, 1943, Theresa Waller stood in the "colored" waiting room in the train station at Houston, Texas. Dressed in her Sunday best, this tall, dignified twenty-four-year-old felt a disquieting mixture of fear, expectation, excitement, and uncertainty. Her strong will and poise—traits that marked her as a person who "wanted to go somewhere and be someone"— had propelled her to this departure point. In a few moments there would be no turning back. A young woman who "wanted to do something good and big, but couldn't name it" was about to leave everything that she had known as a child for the promise of a new life in California.

In Houston, Theresa had worked as a domestic servant. Each morning she left her home in the mostly black Fifth Ward for the rich white neighborhoods in "the heights." As she worked at jobs that "didn't amount to much" and paid only a few dollars a week, she endured the dangers and humiliations

CHAPTER 9	World War II and the Great Transformation
1941	United States enters World War II
1941–1945	Wartime defense production transforms the state's economy Population grows by 1.5 million Women enter the industrial labor force in unprecedented numbers
1941	Executive Order 8802 bans racial discrimination in defense industry
1942	Japanese relocation and internment authorized Earl Warren elected governor Bracero program established Sleepy Lagoon case
1943	Zoot Suit Riots
1944	Port Chicago explosion and "mutiny" Defense industries begin to demobilize
1945	Atomic bombs dropped on Hiroshima and Nagasaki War ends

of life in the segregated South. Struggling to describe her experience, Theresa remarked, "you just don't know what it was like. They [white people] would try to make you feel like you weren't human." Facing a future limited by racial discrimination, she dreamed about leaving Texas.

Early in 1943, Theresa met and fell in love with a man who worked on the Houston waterfront. Through a network of fellow workers, he learned of plentiful, high-paying defense jobs in the San Francisco Bay area. Their relationship flourished on shared dreams of a better life out West, and soon they married. Within weeks, he moved to Oakland, found housing and a job in the shipyards, and sent for his bride. Theresa, about to embark on a journey that would reunite her with her husband and profoundly change her world, felt small and alone on that October day in the Houston train station. But as her journey unfolded, it bore a striking resemblance to the journeys made by countless other California-bound migrants during the war years. While most sought economic opportunity, others—particularly black migrants from the South—sought something more elusive: racial tolerance and greater social and political freedom.

By the early 1940s California had become central to the nation's war effort, and a virtual promised land for migrants like the Wallers. Its aircraft and shipbuilding industries, funded by

Shown here is a shift change of workers at the Kaiser, Richmond Shipyards circa 1942–1944. What does this photograph reveal about wartime changes in the age, gender, and ethnic composition of the industrial labor force?

huge federal defense contracts, dramatically expanded production and provided new employment opportunities for skilled and unskilled workers, women, and ethnic minorities. California's ports and military bases, suddenly bustling with defense-driven activity and thousands of new recruits, also contributed to civilian job growth. The wartime boom spilled over to virtually every sector of the economy. Restaurants, nightclubs, theaters, and other service establishments, responding to a burgeoning clientele of soldiers and round-the-clock defense workers, extended their hours and hired additional employees. The state's growers, attempting to keep pace with wartime demand for agricultural commodities, increased production and expanded their labor force. The defense effort even stimulated the development of new electronics, communications, and aerospace technologies that became the mainstays of the state's postwar economy.

Sadly, the war also ignited long-smoldering anti-Asian prejudice, culminating in the worst mass violation of civil rights in the state's history. In the spring of 1942, California's Japanese American population was deported by government order to a series of internment camps in remote sections of the western United States. In the process, most lost homes, treasured possessions, and businesses, and suffered severe emotional and physical trauma. Wartime prosperity, which partially offset the pain and humiliation of racial discrimination for other ethnic minorities, only added to the raw sense of loss experienced by Japanese Americans.

As this tragedy unfolded, California's economic boom attracted newcomers from a variety of ethnic and class backgrounds, greatly increasing the size and diversity of the state's population. However, growth placed strains on schools, recreation facilities, housing, and transportation systems—strains that heightened existing patterns of racial discrimination and produced tensions between newcomers and established residents. Minority activists and their sympathetic supporters attacked discrimination in housing, employment, and public accommodations with new zeal, creating the foundation for postwar struggles for civil rights and political power. At the same time, state government, under the leadership of Earl Warren, responded to growth-related challenges by taking a more active role in directing the forces of social and economic change.

Questions to Consider

- Did World War II have a significant and lasting impact on the state's economy? How? Discuss why historians have described this era as the "Second Gold Rush."

- Who was responsible for Japanese relocation and internment? Did anti-Asian prejudice, rather than "informed military judgments," contribute to this mass violation of civil rights?

- Excluding Japanese Americans, did Californians benefit equally from the Second Gold Rush? Why or why not?

- How and why did World War II alter the priorities of political activists and leaders, and expand the size and scope of state government?

Economic Expansion

Overview of the War's Economic Impact

By 1939 war in Europe created increased demand for goods produced in the United States. This helped draw California's manufacturing, oil, and agricultural industries out of their Depression-era slump. At the same time, the federal government initiated a rearmament program and the nation's first peacetime draft, leading to an expansion of the state's existing military facilities and the construction of several new training centers, supply depots, and bases. The influx of military personnel, in turn, generated civilian jobs at military installations, and stimulated retail and service sector growth in nearby towns and cities.

When the United States officially entered the war following the Japanese attack on Pearl Harbor in 1941, California's economy, already in recovery, swung into high gear. The war was no longer solely a European conflict, but one waged in the Pacific as well, with personnel, ships, aircraft, food, munitions, and supplies all channeled through California's strategically situated ports and military staging facilities. The federal government, acknowledging California's geographic importance to the Pacific war effort, committed thirty-five billion dollars to the state's defense industries and military installations. And Californians, receiving a windfall that amounted to 40 percent of their total income and 10 percent of the government's entire budget, went from unemployment lines to around-the-clock high-wage production work. Jobs, once scarce, were created faster than workers could fill them. The Second Gold Rush had arrived.

The Aircraft Industry

The southern part of the state, with its mild climate, nonunionized work force, numerous small airstrips, and affordable land prices, began attracting aircraft manufacturers as early as 1912. The industry, however, did not take permanent root until 1920 when Donald Douglas, an aviation engineer for Martin in Ohio, organized his own company in Los Angeles. Two other aircraft entrepreneurs, Ryan in San Diego and Lockheed in Burbank, soon joined Douglas. As the air travel industry expanded during the 1930s, the region attracted other manufacturers, such as Consolidated Aircraft Corporation and American Aviation. By 1940 a majority of the nation's aircraft workers were employed by southern California firms.

With the war, demand for aircraft suddenly increased, and California's fledgling firms, already at the center of aircraft production, came to dominate the industry. Over the course of the conflict, aircraft companies in southern California received nearly 60 percent of all defense contract dollars that flowed into the state from the federal government. Change was sudden and dramatic. In 1939 the region's 20,000 aircraft workers produced only a few thousand planes in modestly sized shops and factories. By 1943, sprawling fabrication facilities employed more than 280,300 workers, who produced one hundred thousand planes in that year alone. Lockheed, whose mostly skilled work force built thirty-seven planes in 1937, employed more than 90,000 workers at the height of the war and mass-produced more than eighteen thousand aircraft between 1941 and 1945, a production record matched by Douglas, Northrup, North American, Convair, and Ryan.

The infusion of federal funds, however, only partially explains the astounding level of productivity. Plant employees, over 40 percent of whom were women, worked around the clock, logged thousands of hours in overtime, and risked serious injury to meet production demands. While rising wages helped motivate workers, many also made wartime sacrifices out of a sense of patriotic duty. Early in the war, Roosevelt called for the production of fifty thousand planes a year. Workers, responding to reports of growing casualties overseas, more than doubled that figure by 1944.

The war left a lasting imprint on southern California's aircraft industry. Federal dollars not only funded plant expansion, they also financed research and development that created the foundation for diversification. Wartime research, funded by the government and conducted in partnership with the California Institute of Technology and UCLA, pushed aircraft manufacturing into the age of aerospace technology. Industry giants like Douglas, Lockheed, and Convair moved confidently into the postwar period as manufacturers of jet propulsion equipment, missiles, missile guidance devices, and electronic tracking systems.

Shipbuilding

California's shipbuilding industry, centered in the San Francisco Bay area, underwent a similar transformation during the war. Existing shipyards expanded their facilities and hired thousands of new workers to fill military contracts. Demand, however, soon exceeded existing capacity and entrepreneurs such as Henry Kaiser constructed new shipyards throughout the region. Prior to the war, Kaiser directed the construction of several large dams and bridges, successfully applying mass production and prefabrication techniques on an enormous scale. When the war started, Kaiser secured government support to build a new shipbuilding facility in Richmond and turned his expertise to the production of supply freighters or "Liberty Ships."

Kaiser's application of assembly-line construction techniques, replicated by other Bay Area shipbuilders including Bechtel in Sausalito, reduced the need for skilled labor and cut production time from 250 days per ship to an average of 25 days. The shipyards were open 7 days a week, twenty-four hours a day. Kaiser Shipyard workers set a record by constructing one ship in 4 days. At peak operation, Kaiser's four Richmond yards employed over 100,000 workers, including large numbers of women and Southern black migrants. To meet ongoing labor demands, Kaiser sent recruiters across the country in search of workers, helped arrange transportation out West, and offered on-the-job training. He also promoted worker retention by funding on-site child care and creating a subsidized, prepaid medical program for his employees, one of the first group health plans in the nation.

During the war shipbuilders employed over 260,000 workers and received more than five billion dollars in federal government contracts. For a brief time, the Bay Area was the country's premier shipbuilding center, producing over one-quarter of the nation's ships, and attracting thousands of newcomers with the promise of high-paying, dignified employment. Wartime shipyards provided unprecedented, though fleeting, economic opportunities to women and ethnic minorities. Most significantly, defense jobs propelled Dust Bowl migrants from the fields into the state's blue-collar work force, removing the stigma of poverty and outsider status that had dogged them throughout the Depression. Their whiteness, now that jobs were plentiful, became the currency of acceptance and assimilation, while other newcomers—particularly African Americans—were branded as undesirable intruders.

Agriculture

Agriculture was one of the first industries to recover from the Great Depression. As domestic and overseas demand increased, labor shortages rather than labor strife became the primary concern of the state's growers. Growers not only fed an expanding civilian labor force, but also supplied troops stationed in California and abroad, and U.S. allies overseas. Between 1939 and 1945, California agriculture grew from a $623 million industry to one netting $1.75 billion—a level of growth that solidified the state's position as the nation's leading agricultural producer and accelerated the trend toward consolidation and corporate ownership of California's farmland.

As the military, defense industries, and forced incarceration of Japanese Americans siphoned workers out of the fields, growers faced severe labor shortages. Defense jobs, in particular, beckoned workers with wages that growers—despite labor shortages—were unwilling to match. Labor shortages also raised the unhappy prospect of unionization; a labor force much in demand could potentially obtain the level of unity and bargaining power that had eluded agricultural workers during the 1930s. In 1942, at growers' urging, Congress approved the "bracero program," a joint agreement between the American and Mexican governments that allowed the importation of Mexican guest workers into California's fields. The program, administered by the United States Department of Agriculture, and monitored by the Mexican government, was intended to provide a steady stream of labor during the wartime emergency, while guaranteeing braceros decent housing, transportation, food, health care, a minimum wage, and unemployment compensation in the unlikely event of work shortages.

The program held several advantages for growers. Transportation, medical, unemployment, and disability expenses were financed by the federal government. The growers were responsible for providing decent housing and working conditions and a minimum wage, but these obligations were easily and repeatedly circumvented. Braceros, as a temporary, contract labor force, undercut the collective bargaining power of other field workers and were frequently used to break strikes. In essence, growers used the federal subsidy to freeze farm wages, to keep all but the most desperate domestic workers from the fields, and to argue that foreign workers were necessary to meet agricultural labor demands. Long after the war ended, growers successfully defended the program on the grounds that the supply of domestic workers was not sufficient to meet demand. Not until 1964 did Congress, bowing to public criticism of the system's abuses, terminate the program.

Other Industry

The war's impact reached beyond aircraft, shipbuilding, and agriculture to several other industries, transforming the state into a powerhouse of heavy industry and creating the foundation for a high-tech postwar economy. Steel, much of it imported from outside the state, was suddenly in huge demand, and Bay Area producers expanded production to meet the needs of local shipbuilders. Kaiser, ever the innovator, further reduced dependence on imports by building a state-of-the-art blast furnace and rolling mill in Fontana. East of Los Angeles, the Kaiser mill produced over 700,000 tons of steel per year, increased the state's production capacity by 70 percent, and created a new blue-collar suburban development to house its work force.

The war also stimulated the growth of the state's fledgling electronics industry. In 1938, Stanford graduate students David Packard and Bill Hewlett began producing electronic devices out of a garage behind their Palo Alto boarding house. One of Hewlett's projects, and the subject of his master's thesis, was a variable frequency oscillator. Hewlett's professor, Fred Terman, was convinced of its commercial potential, and helped the two men secure funding to start a business. Walt Disney Studios made the first large purchase, buying eight oscillators to produce the soundtrack for their full-length animated film, *Fantasia*.

Their real breakthrough, however, came with World War II. By 1942 Hewlett and Packard employed about one hundred workers and grossed around one million dollars in sales of defense-related electronic equipment. More significantly, they pioneered a bottom-up management style that encouraged and rewarded employee creativity and innovation. After the war Hewlett Packard became the nucleus of Silicon Valley and a model for other high-tech firms around the country.

Across the bay, physicists at the University of California, Berkeley, focused their efforts on developing nuclear weapons. During the 1930s, Ernest O. Lawrence created an atom-smashing cyclotron and isolated new radioactive elements and isotopes that soon became integral to weapons production. In 1942 the federal government launched the Manhattan Project and contracted with the university to build atomic weapons. Lawrence's laboratory at Berkeley was expanded, and a second lab, at Los Alamos, New Mexico, was placed under the direction of Lawrence's Berkeley colleague, J. Robert Oppenheimer.

In 1945 the military dropped atomic bombs produced at Los Alamos on the Japanese cities of Hiroshima and Nagasaki, concluding the war in the Pacific and ushering in the "nuclear age." The destructive force of the bombs killed and injured hundreds of thousands of civilians, deeply shocking Lawrence and Oppenheimer, and raising public concern that technological innovation was outstripping the human capacity to ethically judge its impact or control its application. In the meantime, another Los Alamos physicist, Edward Teller, was pioneering the development of a more powerful nuclear weapon: the hydrogen bomb. At his urging in the early 1950s, the Atomic Energy Commission established another weapons lab in Livermore, California, ensuring that the state remained in the forefront of nuclear research for decades to come.

Japanese Relocation and Internment

The war brought Californians out of the Depression and stimulated the growth of new industries that ensured economic vitality for years to come. However, it also generated intense fear and hatred of the "enemy" and fueled long-standing anti-Asian prejudice and hostility. Wartime hysteria, primarily directed toward Japanese Americans, quickly evolved into government policy that deeply wounded many of the state's most loyal citizens.

The Unfolding Tragedy

Immediately following Japan's attack on Pearl Harbor, newspapers and radio commentators across the state began scapegoating Japanese Americans. The *Los Angeles Times* called California a "zone of danger" and warned: "We have thousands of Japanese here. . . . Some, perhaps many, are good Americans. What the rest may be we do not know, nor can we take a chance in light of yesterday's demonstration that treachery and double-dealing are major Japanese weapons." Such reports, found in virtually every California newspaper, were accompanied by Governor Culbert Olson's announcement to the press that he was considering house arrest of all Japanese Americans "to avoid riot and disturbance." In the meantime, the federal Department of Justice took more decisive action, working with local law enforcement to round up and detain "dangerous enemy aliens," including hundreds of Japanese American religious and community leaders. The arrests and detentions, which also involved smaller numbers of German and Italian aliens, deprived many families of their major breadwinners. In some cases authorities failed to notify relatives of the whereabouts of detainees for weeks or even months after their arrest.

Public alarm increased in mid-December when Secretary of the Navy Frank Knox held a press conference in Los Angeles. Detailing the damage in Hawai`i, Knox deflected criticism of the military's incompetence and lack of preparedness by blaming the "treachery" on the island's Japanese American population. Uninformed and frightened Californians speculated that the West Coast was equally vulnerable to alien subversion and attack. By the end of the month the Justice Department authorized the FBI to randomly search the homes and businesses of "enemy aliens" for weapons, explosives, radio transmitters, cameras, and other so-called contraband. Although the FBI later reported that none of the seized "contraband" was used for subversive purposes, the searches contributed to mounting public suspicion and hysteria.

By mid-February, Lieutenant General John L. DeWitt, head of the Western Defense Command in San Francisco, issued a recommendation to the secretary of war for the "Evacuation of Japanese and other Subversive Persons from the Pacific Coast." After outlining how the "enemy" presence threatened West Coast military installations, DeWitt asserted that all persons of Japanese descent, including American-born citizens, were a menace to security: "The Japanese race is an enemy race and while many second and third generation Japanese born on American soil, possessed of United States citizenship, have become 'Americanized,' the racial strains are undiluted." Such a blanket condemnation, issued only in reference to a single ethnic group, betrayed more than DeWitt's personal prejudices.

The press, the general public, the Los Angeles Chamber of Commerce, Los Angeles mayor Fletcher Bowron, Governor Olson, and state Attorney General Earl Warren, all lobbied for Japanese removal. Moreover, the West Coast congressional delegation, led by Leland Ford, John Costello, A. J. Elliot, and Jack Anderson, applied additional political pressure by issuing a unanimous resolution on February 13 that called for the "immediate evacuation of all persons of Japanese lineage and all others, aliens and citizens alike, whose presence shall be deemed dangerous or inimical to the defense of the United States from all strategic areas. . . ." DeWitt was also concerned that failure to take action might result in his removal from command, a disgrace recently suffered by Hawai`i's chief officers, Lieutenant General Short and Admiral Kimmel. Finally, DeWitt's superiors, including Provost General Allen W. Gullion, consistently pressed for the mass evacuation of Japanese Americans.

On February 19, 1942, President Franklin D. Roosevelt signed Executive Order 9066, authorizing the secretary of war to designate military areas from which "any or all persons may be excluded." Although the order never mentioned the words "Japanese" or "Japanese Americans," its executors quickly moved to apply its provisions selectively. Over 93,000 Japanese Americans were forced from their homes in California into internment camps. About two-thirds were American-born citizens, or *Nisei*. The rest, members of the older *Issei* immigrant generation, were "aliens" only in that the law had prevented them from becoming citizens.

Smaller numbers of German and Italian aliens were forced to relocate away from sensitive military installations and were subjected to special curfews and travel restriction. Except for those suspected of enemy connections, none were incarcerated. For an eleven-month period from late 1941 to late 1942, the government also prohibited Italian aliens from leaving port in their fishing boats. This all but decimated San Francisco's fishing industry, and led to fish shortages and higher seafood prices. To be sure, many suffered financial hardship or were wrongly accused of subversive ties, but they were not singled out for internment on a mass scale simply because of their ethnicity. Even on the East Coast, where enemy attack from Europe was more of a direct threat, German and Italian aliens were never subjected to group incarceration.

Prior to the Japanese evacuation, Congress organized a series of hearings to address any lingering public concerns over the plan, including its "military necessity" and constitutionality. State Attorney General Earl Warren, who had recently declared his candidacy for governor, testified that the proposed evacuation was "absolutely constitutional," given the questionable loyalty of the Japanese in California. Warren, in fact, asserted that the American-born Nisei were more dangerous than their noncitizen Issei parents, and that in wartime "every citizen must give up some of his rights."

City and county officials came forward with similar testimony, creating an uncomfortable dilemma for Japanese American leaders: disagreement with the proposal could easily be viewed as un-American or evidence of subversion. Agreement, on the other hand, would be seen as evidence of loyalty, but also as an admission that the public's fears were reasonable. The Nisei-run Japanese American Citizens League filled the leadership vacuum left when the Department of Justice arrested and detained older, Issei community leaders in the weeks following Pearl Harbor. Members of the league adopted a nonconfrontational posture before the hearings, hoping for lenient treatment in exchange for their avowal of loyalty. Others, however, took an opposing stand. James Omura, publisher of a small Japanese American magazine, testified that he was opposed to mass evacuation of American-born citizens. "It is my honest belief that such an action would not solve the question of Nisei loyalty."

Omura and other Japanese American dissenters, along with white supporters from organizations such as the Northern California ACLU and the California CIO, failed to stop the mass evacuation. Just as disappointing, the United States Supreme Court upheld its constitutionality on three separate occasions. In 1942 Gordon Hirabayashi, a student at the University of Washington, refused to comply with the evacuation order and was sentenced in federal court to six months in prison. He and his attorneys appealed on the grounds that the order, to be constitutional, had to apply to all citizens, not just to a select group. In 1943 the Supreme Court upheld his conviction on the grounds that military necessity and the questionable loyalty of persons of Japanese ancestry justified the selective restrictions.

In 1944 the Supreme Court more directly affirmed the constitutionality of the exclusion order by upholding the conviction of Fred Korematsu, a young Californian who refused to report for evacuation. His attorneys asked the court to consider "whether or not a citizen of the United States may, because of his Japanese ancestry, be confined in barbed-wire stockades euphemistically termed Assembly Centers or Relocation Centers—actually concentration camps." The majority opinion, written by Justice Hugo Black, maintained that "the gravest imminent danger to the public safety" and the questionable loyalty of persons of Japanese ancestry justified the order "as of the time it was made and when the petitioner violated it." In both cases, and in another involving Californian Mitsuye Endo, the court refused to challenge the federal government's power to selectively curtail the civil liberties of its citizens—particularly the liberties of nonwhites. The court's failure to act represented a serious breakdown of the system of checks and balances designed to protect the rights of Americans. All levels of government—local, state, federal, legislative, executive, and judicial—abandoned higher moral principles in favor of racist hysteria, undermining the very system that was allegedly threatened by "enemy aliens." It took forty years for the government to acknowledge its mistake and conclude that the exclusion decision was shaped by "race prejudice, war hysteria, and a failure of political leadership," rather than "informed military judgments."

Relocation and Internment

The evacuation process began in early March of 1942 when Lieutenant General DeWitt designated western Washington and Oregon, parts of southern Arizona, and all of California as military areas off-limits to persons of Japanese ancestry. His proclamation created a trickle of voluntary migration out of the zone, but most families either lacked the resources to leave or were discouraged by reports of vigilante violence directed at those who had relocated. By the end of March, DeWitt curtailed even this small option by prohibiting all Japanese Americans from leaving the zone, and issuing the first forced removal order to residents of Bainbridge Island near Seattle. Other removal orders soon followed, giving families only a few days to pack their belongings, vacate their homes, and report to a central receiving station for transport to an assembly center. With an average of six days' notice, and allowed to bring only personal belongings they could carry, families were forced to make major economic and personal decisions under severe time pressure.

This is a view of the desert and camp at Manzanar, east of the Sierra Nevadas. How did the geographic location and physical design of camps like Manzanar shape the daily lives of internees?

The list was endless. Homes and businesses had to be rented or sold, vacated for other tenants, or entrusted to friends and neighbors. Lovingly tended gardens and pets needed new caregivers. Children, infants, the aged, and the ill had to be reassured and prepared for the largely unknown physical and emotional challenges ahead. Possessions accumulated over many years, including family heirlooms, furniture, appliances, automobiles, artwork, clothing, pianos, books, bicycles, and toys, had to be placed in storage or sold at a loss to "human vultures" willing to take advantage of their neighbors' misfortune. All of this and more needed to be accomplished in the context of uncertainty; no one knew how long the war would last, or whether they would ever be allowed to return to their homes. Families also suffered serious financial loss, estimated in the hundreds of millions of dollars for property alone. Added to this were the lost wages and earning power of the period in exile.

While the newly created War Relocation Authority (WRA) constructed permanent camps in remote inland locations, the army converted racetracks, livestock exhibition halls, and fairgrounds into temporary assembly centers. Evacuees—exhausted, frightened, and humiliated by their recent ordeal—now faced a new challenge: living for one to six months in crowded, unsanitary

Shown here is a vegetable garden at Manzanar. Compare this photograph with the one on page 277, and reflect on the ways that internees attempted to soften and humanize their physical surroundings.

barracks or renovated horse stalls. At racetracks like Santa Anita and Tanforan, each family occupied either a twenty-by-nine-foot or a twenty-by-eighteen-foot stall that was only partially partitioned off from neighboring units. A thin veneer of linoleum did little to mask the odor of manure and urine-soaked floorboards, and horsehair, hay, and other debris had been hastily whitewashed into the walls. Latrines and shower facilities, located outside of the barracks and lacking doors or partitions, afforded little privacy and violated the women's sense of modesty. Diarrhea, caused by unsanitary conditions and poor-quality food, afflicted nearly everyone and compounded their embarrassment. Laundry, which had to be done by hand with a limited supply of hot water, created an additional hardship for women, particularly those with babies and small children.

Although they knew that their stay would be temporary, evacuees soon took the initiative to improve their surroundings. Using salvaged lumber and mail-order supplies, they enhanced the comfort and privacy of their quarters. Parents organized day nurseries, schools, scout troops, music classes, arts and crafts programs, and athletic activities for their children, and sought release from their own cares through softball leagues, talent shows, dances, concerts, and gardening. Evacuee vegetable gardeners and chefs even applied their skills to improving camp diets. Soon, however, their remarkable fortitude and resourcefulness were again tested.

Between June and November of 1942, the army moved evacuees to guarded camps outside of the West Coast military zone. These camps, euphemistically called "relocation" or "resettlement" centers, were located on remote, desolate sites that were swelteringly hot in the summer and bitterly cold in the winter. Only two camps, built on Arkansas swampland, were not sited in the desert. These permanent facilities were not much of an improvement over the assembly centers. Barracks containing six one-room units were flimsily constructed of pine and covered with single-thickness tarpaper. Wind and dust constantly swirled in through the cracks and holes in walls and floorboards, making it impossible to keep the barracks warm and clean. Small families crowded into single twenty-by-sixteen-foot units, while larger families of up to seven persons were assigned twenty-by-twenty-five-foot rooms. Each unit was furnished with a single bare light bulb, an army cot for each occupant, and an oil or wood stove. Latrines, showers, and mess halls were depressingly similar to those in the assembly centers.

For a second time, evacuees struggled to create a sense of normalcy in an inhospitable environment by improving their bleak dwellings, planting gardens, and organizing schools, clubs, athletic teams, and cultural events. Their hardships, however, were innumerable. White camp administrators and staff were notoriously unresponsive to the concerns of inmates. As a consequence, schools were understaffed, poorly equipped, and uneven in quality. Camp kitchens were poorly provisioned and frequently pilfered by white staff. Diets were starch-laden, until evacuees took the initiative to raise vegetables and livestock.

Women, while relieved of some of their domestic responsibilities by communal living, continually struggled to keep dwellings clean, preserve domestic harmony in cramped quarters, and care for the young, sick, and aged under crude conditions. Poor medical facilities compounded their burden. Obstetric and gynecological care was woefully inadequate, and many women suffered complications during pregnancy and delivery. Despite crowded, unsanitary living conditions and constant exposure to cold weather, vaccines were in short supply or simply unavailable, as were very basic medical supplies like sutures, lab testing equipment, and sterile infant formula.

Men, normally breadwinners and authority figures, felt their status diminish within their families. Everyone—husbands, wives, sons, and daughters—earned the same low wages for working at various jobs within the camps. And children, spending more time with their peer group in a communal setting, circumvented parental guidance and authority. The loss of jobs and businesses compounded men's pain and humiliation, and led to a high incidence of ulcers, depression, and other stress-related illness among male evacuees.

Nisei teenagers enjoyed greater independence from their more traditional parents, but faced uncertain futures at a time when family stability and support was being undermined. Ties between the generations grew more tenuous when the WRA began to issue leave permits to Nisei who found sponsors outside of the military zone. Beginning in the fall of 1942, the American Friends Service Committee and other church groups helped about 250 young people resume their studies at colleges and universities outside of California. Thousands of other Nisei received permits to take jobs in urban centers like Denver, Chicago, and Salt Lake City. However, most remained in regular contact with their parents, sent money back to the camps, and returned to their families following the internment ordeal.

Nisei received another, more controversial, opportunity to leave in January of 1943 when the War Department announced its intention to enlist recruits from the camps. This decision, coupled with the WRA's desire to relieve pressure in the camps by issuing more leave permits, led the army to prepare and administer a loyalty questionnaire to all inmates over the age of seventeen. Issei and Nisei, who had demonstrated their loyalty by complying with internment orders, were now asked to "swear unqualified allegiance to the United States of America and faithfully defend the United States from any or all attack by foreign or domestic sources, and forswear any form of allegiance or obedience to the Japanese emperor or any other foreign government, power or organization." The Issei, who had been denied citizenship, were particularly distressed by the oath. A "no" answer on their part was an admission of disloyalty, while a "yes" could be interpreted as an admission of prior allegiance to the "enemy." Nisei, on the other hand, risked emotional and physical separation from their families if they chose to answer differently from their parents.

Eventually the questionnaire was reworded, and a majority of both Issei and Nisei answered in the affirmative. Subsequently, thousands of young men served in the segregated 442nd Regimental Combat Team, suffering almost ten thousand casualties, including some six hundred deaths, in seven major Italian and French campaigns. As they fell in battle, and earned the distinction of belonging to the most decorated regiment in army history, their friends and relatives remained behind barbed wire. While the men of the 442nd pondered this contradiction, the army continued to insist that "military necessity" justified internment on the home front.

Camps were closed at the end of the war, and most evacuees gradually returned to the West Coast. Their ordeal, however, was far from over. Many Issei, financially and emotionally broken by the internment experience, were too old to start over and had to rely on their children for support. The Nisei, who before the war had struggled to blend in with their peers by being model students and Americans, continued to be perceived as aliens on their native soil. Business owners posted signs announcing "No Japs Allowed," and refused to sell goods and services to returnees. Property owners refused to rent or sell to Japanese Americans, and evacuees who returned to their own homes and businesses often found them stripped or damaged by looters, vandals, or careless tenants. Employment discrimination was widespread, forcing many Nisei families to rely on more than one breadwinner, settle for menial jobs, or start businesses that required little initial capital, like gardening. Returnees also faced racial violence, often condoned and encouraged by civic leaders and law enforcement. In the first six months of 1945, seventy acts of terrorism and nineteen shootings occurred in California alone. Angry whites in Placer County, for example, fired shots into the home and dynamited the packing shed of a returning Japanese American family. The perpetrators were caught and brought to trial, but a local, all-white jury voted for acquittal.

The violence gradually subsided, but former internees continued to live with deep emotional scars from their ordeal. After years of intense organizing and lobbying by Japanese American activists, organizations, and political leaders, camp survivors obtained a small measure of redress. The Civil Liberties Act of 1988 mandated that each former internee receive twenty thousand dollars, and that the government issue a formal apology for the mass exclusion and detention of Japanese Americans. Representative Robert Matsui, a California Democrat who had been active in the redress movement from its inception in 1970, characterized the victory as "a reaffirmation of the values this country was built on. This is the end of the long ordeal, an arduous national march toward redemption." Though redress could never compensate for the financial and emotional cost of internment, it began, for many, the slow and still-unfinished process of healing.

Population Growth and Diversity

World War II created opportunities as well as challenges for other Californians. Between 1940 and 1944 the defense industry boom attracted over 1.5 million newcomers, making California the fastest-growing state in the nation. Such growth was unprecedented, dwarfing even the Depression-era migration and continuing well into the postwar years. San Diego's population, for example, grew by 110.5 percent between 1940 and 1947. Los Angeles grew by 17.8 percent, and the San Francisco Bay area by nearly 40 percent. Rapid growth, concentrated around aircraft and shipbuilding facilities and military installations, placed heavy strains on surrounding communities. Richmond, home to the massive Kaiser shipyards, grew from 23,642 residents in 1940 to over 93,738 by 1943—a 296.5 percent increase. And like other California boomtowns, Richmond experienced growing pains. Housing, with so many new arrivals, was in short supply, forcing many newcomers to live in trailers, tents, makeshift shanties, or share small units with two or more families. Many of these dwellings, hastily constructed from salvaged materials or subdivided by unscrupulous landlords, lacked basic services like running water, heating, cooking facilities, and electricity. The resulting threat to public health and safety prompted federal authorities to finance temporary war housing developments in Richmond and other defense centers across the state. By the end of the war, Richmond's public housing program, the largest in the nation, sheltered over half of the city's residents in prefabricated, multi-unit developments.

Although still overcrowded, and often racially segregated, public war housing offered several benefits to residents. Most projects were located near defense jobs and public transportation lines. Common laundry and recreation facilities brought newcomers together and fostered friendships, resource sharing, and the growth of permanent community institutions. The projects also provided modern, though modest, amenities that earlier makeshift accommodations frequently lacked. War housing, however, did little to alleviate the strain on municipal services such as garbage collection, police and fire protection, street repair and maintenance, sewers, gas, electricity, and water. Demand simply exceeded supply. Schools, too, could not keep pace with population growth. Between 1940 and 1943, Richmond's student body grew from three thousand to thirty-five thousand, forcing elementary schools to conduct multiple sessions and pack an average of seventy-five pupils into each class. Parks, buses, trains, markets, theaters, and restaurants were equally overcrowded and increasingly "frowzy" from excessive use. Wartime shortages and rationing of essential goods such as gasoline, meat, sugar, and butter added to the overall perception that too many people were crowding into the area.

Established residents, alarmed over deteriorating infrastructure in Richmond and other defense centers, blamed newcomers for "ruining" their cities. Migrants, according to popular stereotypes, were either illiterate, lazy "poor white trash," or ignorant, uncouth "Southern Negroes." Both groups were regarded as morally deficient, criminally inclined, and a threat to public decency. In reality, though, most newcomers came with the skills, education, and work ethic to succeed in an urban, industrial environment. In Richmond and other defense centers, such stereotypes led to municipal law enforcement and moral reform campaigns designed to regulate migrant behavior and access to public space. However, tougher antivice ordinances and police sweeps of "trouble zones," which not surprisingly netted both established residents and newcomers, did little to address the underlying problem of overtaxed, decaying urban infrastructure—a problem that would persist and deepen during the postwar years.

Black Migration

White newcomers gradually gained acceptance as permanent residents, but a large percentage of the established population continued to view black migrants as guest workers who could not be assimilated. Local residents, including many civic leaders, hoped that black migrants would leave California at the end of the war. African Americans, however, came to the state for more than the jobs associated with the booming defense economy. The Wallers and thousands of other black migrants from Texas, Louisiana, Arkansas, Mississippi, and Oklahoma sought freedom from the racial violence and discrimination that cruelly dampened their dreams and expectations in the South. Seeking a better life for themselves and their families, most came to California to stay. Between 1940 and 1950 the state's African American population grew from 124,306 to 462,172, with most of the increase concentrated in the defense centers of Los Angeles, Oakland, Richmond, and San Francisco. In the Bay Area alone, the black population increased 227 percent, from 19,759 in 1940 to 64,680 in 1945. Some communities, with small prewar black populations, saw even more spectacular levels of growth. Richmond's black population, for example, grew from 270 in 1940 to over 10,000 by 1945.

The migration began slowly, but took off after Roosevelt signed Executive Order 8802 in 1941, banning racial discrimination by federal defense contractors. Word of employment opportunities traveled quickly, spread by labor recruiters, word of mouth, and black railroad workers whose jobs took them across the country. The first wave of newcomers, once settled in jobs and housing, encouraged friends and relatives to join them, creating a great chain of migration that continued even after the war ended. Most wartime migrants were young, and contrary to white stereotypes, relatively skilled and well educated. Moreover, they came with high expectations and a long history of battling racial discrimination in the South. Once in California, they joined or formed civil rights organizations, registered to vote, and established churches, fraternal orders, social clubs, and other mutual aid associations.

The determination of the black newcomers to challenge racial barriers and transplant their own cultural institutions alarmed established residents. Whites, who regarded the influx as an "invasion," deeply resented the migrants' sense of entitlement and willingness to violate existing racial boundaries. Established black residents, vastly outnumbered by migrants, feared that hostile whites would reverse what little racial progress had been made, and lump all African Americans together as unwelcome outsiders. California, while not the Jim Crow South, had serious racial problems of its own. Housing discrimination, enforced by restrictive covenants that prohibited property owners from renting or selling to ethnic minorities, confined prewar black residents to specific neighborhoods. Racially biased real estate agents also reinforced residential segregation by steering black clients away from white neighborhoods. When migrants arrived, they were forced into these existing black communities, placing severe strain on already over-crowded, older housing stock. Others secured housing in neighborhoods vacated by Japanese Americans, creating new black enclaves in San Francisco's Fillmore District and Los Angeles's "Little Tokyo." In Richmond and Vallejo, both without distinct prewar black communities, migrants settled in segregated war housing projects, or on vacant land on the outskirts of town. In any case, housing dis-crimination limited their options and set the stage for the emergence of California's postwar urban ghettos.

Despite Roosevelt's executive order, newcomers also encountered widespread job discrimination. Many employers, including large defense contractors, simply ignored the law and refused to hire African Americans. When Boeing, Consoli-dated Vultee, and North American Aviation faced wartime labor shortages, they recruited white women to fill skilled and semiskilled aircraft jobs, rather than integrate their work force. Other employers hired black workers, but channeled them into less skilled, menial, or more strenuous trades. Unions, which con-trolled access to better-paying, highly skilled defense jobs through closed-shop agreements, also created barriers to equal employment. The Boilermakers and the International Association of Machinists, the two largest aviation and ship-building unions and both AFL affiliates, forced black workers into segregated auxiliaries where they had little voice in union affairs, or excluded them from membership altogether. As a consequence, black workers filled the lowest rungs of the occupational ladder, rarely held supervisory positions, and were among the last hired and first fired.

To make matters worse, white coworkers and supervisors subjected black newcomers to verbal abuse, racist "jokes" and "pranks," and physical violence and intimidation. Instead of intervening, unions and employers often justified their own discriminatory policies as necessary to preserve racial harmony. Black workers had few places to turn for support. Even the Fair Employment Practice Committee (FEPC), created by Executive Order 8802 to monitor and curb job dis-crimination, was too swamped with complaints to handle all of them adequately.

One of the most egregious cases of discrimination, occurring entirely outside of the FEPC's jurisdiction, involved black sailors stationed at Port Chicago, a mu-nitions depot near Concord, California. Their ordeal, which underscored the contradiction between fighting a war for democracy and pervasive discrimina-tion on the home front, compounded the sense of betrayal felt by other black workers. On July 17, 1944, 320 men were killed by a massive explosion while load-ing munitions aboard two naval vessels. Of the dead, 200 were black sailors who served in segregated units under the command of white officers.

The survivors, who moved to Mare Island Naval Depot after the blast de-stroyed the Port Chicago facility, refused to resume loading ammunition, citing inadequate training, dangerous working conditions, and residual trauma from the explosion. Charged with mutiny, all fifty black defendants were found guilty, sentenced to fifteen years in prison, and dishonorably discharged. During their twenty-three-day trial, the men testified that their commanding officers held and placed bets on munitions loading contests between crews, punished losing teams, and created a racially hostile working environment. In 1946, with help from the NAACP, most of the sailors returned to active duty with suspended sentences, but they were discharged from the service "under conditions less than honorable," and thus deprived of veterans' benefits. However, Thurgood Marshall, the lead NAACP attorney on the case, linked the tragedy to the wider issue of segregation in the armed forces. As a consequence, the disaster helped generate public and government support for integration of the military. In 1994 the surviving mutineers won a rehearing of their case, but the navy upheld its original decision. In 1999 President Clinton pardoned one of the few remaining survivors, prompting an ongoing campaign for a presidential proclamation that would exonerate all others.

Finally, black servicemen, migrants, and established residents faced discrimination in public accommodations—discrimination that grew worse during the war years, as whites struggled to maintain and strengthen preexisting racial boundaries. The *Oakland Observer*, helping to draw the battle lines, commented that "now we see Negroes all over the place," and accused African Americans of "butting into white civilization instead of keeping in the perfectly orderly and convenient Negro civilization of Oakland." Businesses posted "White Trade Only" signs in shop and restaurant windows, or simply refused to serve black customers. Other businesses instituted various forms of segregation. Ice rinks and nightclubs reserved certain days or hours for white patrons. Bowling alleys prohibited mixed teams and separated lanes by race. Even black servicemen, enlisted in the war for democracy, faced a hostile reception, and were forced to seek recreation at segregated USOs.

Armed with the prodemocracy rhetoric of the war, black Californians fought back. Defense workers took collective action against union and employer discrimination by creating organizations such as the San Francisco Committee Against Segregation and Discrimination and the East Bay Shipyard Workers' Committee. Their effort paid off in 1945 when the state supreme court banned the practice of forcing African Americans into separate Jim Crow auxiliaries as a condition of employment.

Black newcomers swelled the membership of existing NAACP chapters and established new branches in cities like Richmond. They reinvigorated local and state-level campaigns against discrimination in housing, employment, and public accommodations. Newcomers also joined with established civil rights leaders and CIO-affiliated union activists to register voters and run progressive candidates for office. These new "voter leagues" and enlivened NAACP chapters would create the foundation for several major postwar victories: fair employment and housing legislation, a ban on restrictive covenants, and the election of black representatives to state and local office.

Black migrants also asserted their right to remain in California by putting down cultural roots. Instead of turning away from their Southern heritage, they used it to build a positive sense of identity in their largely hostile surroundings. In their homes, churches, social organizations, and mutual aid associations, migrants cultivated their own religious practices, dietary preferences, speech patterns, folklore and crafts, music, and tradition of hospitality, self-help, and reciprocity. Migrants, for example, established hundreds of new churches that reflected and reinforced their black, Southern religious beliefs. In some cases, clusters of migrants from the same Southern town or region even encouraged their ministers to join them in California. At the same time, existing black churches scrambled to adjust their sermons, music, and social service programs to newcomers' needs and preferences in order to reap the financial benefits of an enlarged membership. Newcomers from the same Southern town or city also formed social and mutual aid organizations based on shared geographical ties. In the San Francisco East Bay, for example, migrants from Vicksburg, Mississippi, created a mutual aid and social organization that still provides services for its members. In the process of putting down cultural roots, migrants did more than assert their status as permanent residents. Their gospel and blues music, Creole and soul foods, figures of speech, folklore, modes of worship and recreation, and even celebrations like Juneteenth transformed and enlivened the state's richly textured, ever-changing cultural landscape.

New Challenges and Opportunities

Mexican Americans, long regarded as outsiders who needed to be Americanized through assimilation campaigns, saw the war as an opportunity to prove their loyalty, assert their rights as full-fledged citizens, and uphold their own cultural institutions. In California, over 375,000 Latinos joined the military, choosing the more dangerous Paratroopers and Marine Corps over less risk-intensive branches of the service. Mexican Americans in Los Angeles, for example, made up 10 percent of the city's population, but accounted for 20 percent of its total casualties. Patriotism was also evident on the home front. War ballads, composed in Spanish or translated from English, could be heard in every barrio or *colonia*. The Spanish-language press, including newspapers like San Gabriel Valley's *El Espectador,* Los Angeles's *La Opinión,* and *El Sol de San Bernardino,* not only highlighted Latino contributions to the war effort, but mobilized democratic rhetoric to protest segregation and discrimination in their communities.

Relatives of Latino servicemen, including many who had been locked into low-wage agricultural jobs, found new employment opportunities in the state's defense centers—particularly in southern California. For the first time, large numbers of men moved into relatively high-paying, semiskilled or skilled industrial jobs. Women also found employment in the defense industry, and in the expanding clerical sector. As young men joined the service, and their families moved to urban centers for defense jobs, the state's growers lobbied for the importation of Mexican workers to relieve agricultural labor shortages. The resulting "bracero program" led to a decline in wages and working conditions for domestic workers, and encouraged additional migration out of rural areas well into the postwar years.

Wartime population growth and heightened competition for scarce resources fueled white hostility against perceived outsiders. Mexican Americans, like African Americans, became targets of this intensified animosity, and encountered widespread discrimination in housing, employment, and public accommodations. Southern California's cities, which received the bulk of the rural Mexican American migrants, were the worst offenders. Newcomers, forced into existing barrios, placed strain on already overcrowded and substandard housing and recreation facilities. Their children, even if they lived closer to a white school, were segregated into crowded, poorly equipped "Mexican" schools. Downtown businesses posted "White Trade Only" signs, or in the case of movie theaters, forced Latino patrons into segregated sections. Even public swimming pools operated on a segregated basis, setting aside one or two days a week for nonwhite users.

Two incidents, in particular, illustrate wartime racial prejudice against Mexican Americans: the Sleepy Lagoon case of 1942, and the 1943 Zoot Suit Riots. In August 1942, the Los Angeles police arrested twenty-two members of a Mexican American youth "gang" called the 38th Street Club for murder. The victim, Jose Diaz, had attended a party near an abandoned, water-filled quarry called Sleepy Lagoon—

This is a scene of the Zoot Suit Riot in downtown Los Angeles, June 1943. What does this image reveal about wartime race relations? Why would young sailors, stationed at Los Angeles area bases, engage in unprovoked attacks against local, Mexican American zoot suiters?

a swimming hole used by Latino youth who were excluded from public pools. Some club members crashed the party, and fighting broke out. The police reported that Diaz was killed during this altercation, but his body, found the following morning on a dirt road near the house, showed no signs of injury. A hit-and-run driver could have killed him. Despite the lack of evidence and witnesses, an all-white jury convicted seventeen of the defendants on charges ranging from assault to first-degree murder.

Police Captain Ed Duran Ayers, whose "expert" opinion was widely circulated by the press, maintained that Mexican Americans had an inborn disregard for human life, and an innate desire to use knives and let blood. According to Ayers, they could not change their inborn lust for violence, and would regard lenience as a sign of weakness. Thus, he recommended that all gang members, not just those who belonged to the 38th Street Club, be imprisoned, and that all Latino youth either find jobs or enlist in the military. The defendants did obtain some outside support, especially from the Sleepy Lagoon Defense Committee, which was chaired by noted journalist Carey McWilliams. Its membership included progressive labor leaders, Mexican American activists, and film stars such as Rita Hayworth and Anthony Quinn. The committee helped the defendants secure a new trial. On October 4, 1944, the Second District Court of Appeals unanimously overturned the convictions, ruling that the trial had been conducted in a biased fashion, the defendants' constitutional rights had been violated, and no evidence linked club members to the murder.

Before the case was closed, distorted and inflammatory coverage of the trial fueled anti-Latino prejudice and violence across the state. Throughout the spring of 1943, from San Diego to Oakland, white servicemen invaded Mexican American neighborhoods in search of "hoodlums." Young Latinos, who had adopted a distinctive style of dress called the zoot suit as an expression of cultural pride, were frequent targets. And the police, rather than restraining the marauding servicemen, arrested the victims for disturbing the peace. The "riots" reached a climax in early June, when sailors went on a seven-night rampage through the streets of Los Angeles in search of zoot suiters. Police refused to arrest the perpetrators, who by this time were attacking African Americans and Filipinos as well as Latinos. The press also encouraged the assaults, characterizing the sailors as solid citizens who acted in self-defense or took much-needed initiative against social undesirables.

The riots ended when military authorities, not the police, declared downtown Los Angeles off limits to servicemen. When federal officials, including Eleanor Roosevelt, expressed concern that the violence had been racially motivated, the *Los Angeles Times* came to the city's defense, claiming that Angelenos were proud of their colorful Mexican heritage and that "we like the Mexicans and think they like us." However, an investigative committee, formed by Governor Earl Warren, called for punishment of the perpetrators, a better-educated and better-trained police force, and greater restraint on the part of the press. But these recommendations were virtually ignored, and police harassment, in particular, remained a serious problem within Mexican American communities.

Latinos, like African Americans, fought back, using the prodemocracy rhetoric of the war to attack racial discrimination on the home front. A larger, more stable urban population base enlarged the membership of established organizations like the League of United Latin American Citizens (LULAC), and led to the formation of new civil rights groups like the Unity Leagues, founded by returning veterans. These organizations registered voters, ran Mexican American candidates for political office, and spearheaded legal campaigns against school segregation, housing and employment discrimination, and police brutality.

In 1946, for example, LULAC supported a class action suit against several Orange County school districts, charging that their policy of segregating Mexican students violated the Fourteenth Amendment. One year later, the Ninth Circuit Court of Appeals ruled in their favor, setting a precedent for the historic 1954 *Brown* v. *Board of Education* Supreme Court ruling that ordered schools across the nation to implement integration plans. At the same time, Unity Leagues in Chino and Ontario were registering voters and running Latino candidates for office. In Chino, Andres Morales won election to the city council, and the Ontario candidate lost by only a small margin. *El Espectador,* the region's Mexican American newspaper, proudly announced: "For the first time in the history of these communities candidates of Mexican descent are competing for public office." These small campaigns would later inspire more serious electoral challenges like Edward Roybal's successful 1949 bid for a seat on the Los Angeles City Council.

These organizations and an expanding Mexican American press and radio network also served to transmit and preserve distinct cultural traditions. Latin music, novellas, films, sports, and social clubs created a strong sense of ethnic identity among barrio residents, and added to the growing complexity and richness of California culture. Like African American and white migrants, whose music, foods, humor, and other cultural belongings seeped into the broader social landscape during the war, Mexican Americans exerted a growing cultural influence on their non-Hispanic neighbors. Increasingly, assimilation was not a one-way process.

World War II was also a watershed for California's Chinese American population. Viewed as allies, rather than enemy aliens, women and men moved from low-wage, menial jobs into industrial, clerical, professional, and civil service occupations. Both aircraft plants and shipyards welcomed Chinese Americans. By 1943, for example, they held 15 percent of all shipyard jobs in the Bay Area. The *Mariner,* a Bay Area shipyard publication, foreshadowed the emergence of the model minority stereotype by extolling the virtues of Chinese American defense workers: "We have learned that these Chinese Americans are among the finest workmen. They are skillful, reliable—and inspired with a double allegiance. They know that every blow they strike in building these ships is a blow of freedom for the land of their fathers as well as for the land of their homes."

Chinese Americans, like Latinos, viewed military service as a way to establish their patriotism and loyalty, and they enlisted in large numbers. They were also more likely to be drafted than any other ethnic group. Exclusion acts had created a predominantly male population with few dependents, and thus with one less exemption from military service. Those on the home front supported the troops by participating in War Bond, Red Cross, and Chinese War Relief drives. Organizations like San Francisco's benevolent societies raised thousands of dollars for the war effort, while women's groups rolled bandages, hosted fundraising cultural events, and staffed servicemen's clubs.

Their dedicated war service gave Chinese Americans the moral ammunition to lobby against discriminatory exclusion laws. Congress responded in 1943 by repealing exclusion acts and establishing a new annual quota for Chinese immigrants. The law also allowed resident aliens and newcomers to apply for citizenship, a right long denied under the Naturalization Law of 1790. After the war new legislation, including the War Brides Act, allowed Chinese wives to join their husbands without being counted under the annual quota. Slowly, the male to female ratio balanced out, and California's Chinese American communities became more family centered.

The state's disproportionately male Filipino population also reaped benefits from the war. Prior to 1934, Filipinos were classified as "American nationals" and allowed unrestricted entry into the United States. Most who came settled in California and took jobs in agriculture or domestic service, hoping to work a few years and return home with their savings. The majority were young and male. In 1930 the male to female ratio in California was fourteen to one. The Depression intensified economic competition between white and Filipino workers, and fueled anti-immigrant prejudice and violence. Congress responded in 1934 by reclassifying all resident Filipinos as "aliens" and restricting immigration to fifty persons annually. The same year, the Supreme Court ruled that Filipinos, as nonwhites, were ineligible for citizenship.

Men who returned to the Philippines to visit family or marry then fell under the new quota on attempting reentry, and essentially forfeited their livelihoods. Those who remained in the United States had neither the rights of citizens nor the support of family. California law prohibited racial intermarriage, and the new immigration restrictions prevented wives and children from joining their husbands. Working in California's fields or as "houseboys" in private homes, most Filipinos had little chance of escaping poverty. Labeled as "Malays," "monkeys," and "goo-goos," they also faced discrimination in housing, employment, and public accommodations.

World War II created an abrupt change in status. In 1942, when Roosevelt amended the draft law to include Filipinos, 40 percent of the state's Filipino population volunteered for military service. As members of the armed forces, they became eligible for citizenship. Moreover, their distinguished war record in the Pacific prompted Congress to extend citizenship to all Filipinos in the United States, and to liberalize immigration laws. Finally, the War Brides Act allowed Filipino veterans to bring their wives to the United States, including many who had endured ten or more years of separation. The war also generated new economic opportunities, allowing Filipinos to move out of agricultural and domestic service occupations into industrial, clerical, and technical jobs. For many, these gains would be temporary, but overall the war created an upward trend in occupational mobility.

Shifting Gender Relations

Wartime labor shortages created unprecedented employment opportunities for women. Single, poor, and working-class women exchanged gender-specific service and clerical jobs for higher-paying, traditionally male occupations. Middle-class wives and mothers, previously discouraged from working outside the home, took over production jobs formerly reserved for their husbands. Newspapers, films, magazines, radio, posters, and billboards all glamorized "The Woman Behind the Man Behind the Gun" and "The Janes Who Make the Planes." The Department of Labor and War Production Board proclaimed that women could easily master industrial and technical skills—skills once characterized as too complex and physically demanding for all but the most highly trained male workers.

Women readily responded to the call, filling roughly 25 percent of all shipyard and 40 percent of all aircraft production jobs. Thousands of others worked in the iron and steel industry, machine shops, food-processing plants, munitions factories, warehouses, and military supply depots. Many of these jobs required specialized training, provided either on-site or at public vocational schools. Women often took advantage of these courses beyond entry level training in order to move into more highly skilled, better-paying positions, or to enhance their postwar employment prospects.

Shown here are female defense workers at Douglas Aircraft, Long Beach. Why were women allowed to join the industrial labor force during World War II? If you entered the same factory five years later, would you expect to see similar images? If not, where would you find women workers?

Despite their competence, women met with a mixed reception in the workplace. Employers reserved supervisory and better-paying jobs for men, or reclassified positions and pay scales according to the worker's gender. Male workers often viewed women as unwelcome competitors, or subjected them to sexual harassment. More conservative unions, like the Boilermakers, blamed women for the erosion of skilled trades—a process that actually grew out of Kaiser's pioneering application of mass production and prefabrication techniques to shipbuilding and other large-scale production projects. Other unions, particularly those affiliated with the CIO, were less overtly hostile. They argued, often successfully, that women should earn men's wages for doing men's jobs, fearing that employers would resist returning to higher pay scales when male workers reclaimed their jobs at the end of the war. Thus, their primary concern was to protect men's jobs, rather than the female workers. Black women, burdened with both gender and racial discrimination, fared even worse. Sadly, the hostility of white female coworkers helped ensure that they would be the last hired and the first fired.

Women's increased labor force participation did little to alter traditional gender roles. As "temporary" workers, filling in during a national emergency, women were expected to retain their femininity and primary commitment to home and family. More than half of California's working women were married, forcing many to juggle both workplace demands and domestic responsibilities. This "double burden," largely ignored by employers, was aggravated by wartime food and housing shortages. Migrant women, who had to cook, clean, and do laundry in crowded, poorly equipped surroundings, found domestic duties particularly time consuming.

Child care was a major concern. Some employers and public agencies, alarmed over high rates of female absenteeism and the growing number of latchkey children, stepped in to help. However, demand exceeded supply, and most women were forced to turn to friends and relatives for support. In Los Angeles, for example, the board of education had established twenty-one day care centers, serving 2,000 children by 1943. By this point, over 101,000 women worked in aircraft plants alone, and the existing facilities served only a fraction of their 19,000 children.

As the war ended, women were barraged with propaganda that urged them to voluntarily leave their jobs and return to the home. However, surveys conducted near the end of the war revealed that 80 percent of employed women wished to keep working, most out of economic necessity. Their preferences and needs were largely ignored. As early as 1944, defense industries began to lay off women. Those who needed to work returned to low-wage factory, service, retail, and clerical jobs that offered few opportunities for economic or professional advancement. Other women, willingly or reluctantly, returned to the domestic sphere and helped launch the postwar baby boom.

World War II had a less ambiguous impact on California's gay and lesbian population. Thousands of young men and women from small towns and cities across the United States came to California's defense centers for jobs and military duty. In sex-segregated rooming houses and military barracks, those who were gay readily discovered others like themselves. Men and women who were less certain of their sexual orientation found the freedom to explore same-sex relationships.

Prewar gay communities, relatively small and unstable, benefited from the wartime influx of newcomers. In San Francisco and Los Angeles, gay-owned businesses catered to an expanding clientele. In smaller cities, like San José, gay bars and nightclubs opened for the first time. Gradually, after years of isolation and invisibility, gays and lesbians began to forge a cohesive urban subculture, one that assumed a greater degree of permanence and stability as hundreds of newcomers decided to stay following the end of the war. Having experienced new sexual freedom and a sense of community, many simply could not go back to their small, insular hometowns.

This emerging subculture soon generated organizations dedicated to combating discrimination against lesbians and gays. The Mattachine Society and One Inc. were established in Los Angeles in 1951 and 1953 respectively, and patterned themselves after civil rights organizations like the NAACP. In 1955, two San Francisco lesbians formed the Daughters of Bilitis after hearing about the Mattachine Society's activities. This organization, soon generating new chapters across the country, pledged to improve the public image and self-image of lesbians. Together, these and other gay and lesbian organizations would create the foundation for the much larger, more militant, gay liberation movement of the late 1960s and early 1970s.

Daily Life and Culture

Wartime Challenges

World War II changed the patterns and rhythms of daily life in unpredictable, unsettling ways. Living in a major staging area for the war in the Pacific, Californians witnessed firsthand the departure of thousands of young men and women, many who would not return alive. Moreover, the state served as a rest and relaxation (R&R) center for soldiers on leave or recuperating from injuries. Residents thus had intimate knowledge of the war's brutal toll. Closer to home, numerous Californians sent their own sons and daughters off to war, earning the honor of placing blue stars in their windows. As the war took lives, gold stars, signifying the loss of family members, replaced the blue. Not surprisingly, most families, including children, intently followed radio and newspaper reports on the war's progress, setbacks, and casualties.

The war also demanded greater caution and material sacrifice. Fear of enemy attack, fueled by Japanese submarine operations along the Pacific Coast, prompted military and civil defense planners to institute nightly blackouts. These, however, interfered with round-the-clock defense production and led to a marked increase in traffic accidents when conscientious drivers turned off their headlights. Dim-outs replaced blackouts, except when all-too-frequent air-raid alerts (announced by sirens) demanded total darkness. Police and civil defense patrols enforced these security measures, which were not wholly unwarranted. On December 22, 1941, a Japanese submarine torpedoed an American oil tanker off the central coast. And on February 23, 1942, another submarine attacked a coastal oil storage facility north of Santa Barbara, in Ellwood. These attacks, accompanied by numerous false alarms, heightened public wariness and prompted thousands of residents to enlist as civilian defense volunteers.

Californians registered their cooperation with the war effort in numerous other ways. They purchased war bonds, participated in scrap metal drives, and complied with federal rationing orders. Gasoline, meat, sugar, and butter were strictly rationed in order to provide more fuel and food for troops. Some commodities, like silk stockings and metal toys, disappeared altogether from store shelves. Silk was needed for parachutes, and metal for the manufacture of military hardware. To relieve food shortages, many Californians grew "victory gardens," transforming backyards, empty lots, and schoolyards into vegetable plots. Residents also adapted to fuel shortages by using public transportation and cutting back on recreational travel.

Entertainment

The wartime emergency also had a brighter side. The influx of service personnel and defense workers led to an explosive demand for entertainment. Nightclubs, dance halls, servicemen's clubs, and movie houses geared up to meet the need, providing round-the-clock entertainment to temporary and permanent residents alike. The young, in particular, enjoyed the new diversions and lax supervision associated with rapid expansion. Unfortunately, prostitution, gambling, and trade in black market goods also increased, alarming public health and law enforcement officers, but contributing to the overall excitement of the boomtown atmosphere.

Music, aired on the radio and performed live in clubs and auditoriums, was one of the more popular wartime diversions. Big-name musicians like Count Basie, Tommy Dorsey, Glenn Miller, the Andrews Sisters, Frank Sinatra, and Bing Crosby thrilled California audiences with repertoires that reflected the public's patriotic and nostalgic mood. At the same time, the state's increasingly diverse population broadened and enriched the musical landscape. Black jazz, blues, and bebop artists, arriving as part of the larger wartime migration, packed clubs along Central Avenue in Los Angeles, in West Oakland, and in North Richmond. Blues artists even created a distinct West Coast style, and an even more distinct Oakland blues sound.

White Dust Bowl migrants, who had come a decade earlier, created a thriving subculture with a taste for country or "hillbilly" music. By World War II their music reached a broader audience through "victory barn dances," radio shows, and concerts. Cowboy film stars like Tex Ritter, Roy Rogers, and Gene Autry helped enhance the general public's enthusiasm for all things western. Finally, the growing Mexican American population, particularly in Los Angeles, helped expand the market for Latin music. Playing at smaller clubs as well as larger venues like the Orpheum Theater and Shrine Auditorium, performers introduced the tango, rumba, and Latin-infused swing to Californians. Young Mexican Americans, especially those belonging to the zoot suit subculture, created a unique fusion of jazz, rumba, and swing that later influenced more contemporary artists, such as Carlos Santana.

Even before World War II, motion pictures were an established and highly popular diversion. The war, however, made the movies more attractive than ever. They were cheap, close to home, and offered instant escape from wartime cares. The plush seats and semiprivate darkness of theaters also provided weary service personnel and defense workers with a convenient place to nap, and young lovebirds with an opportunity to escape adult supervision and scrutiny. But Hollywood did more than provide a refuge or diversion; it actively supported the war effort.

Early in the war, the federal government enlisted industry support to produce training and propaganda films, and to make movies that bolstered public unity and patriotism. Content guidelines, issued by the Office of Wartime Information (OWI), encouraged screenwriters to portray America as a harmonious, multiethnic democracy working to overcome the forces of evil and to preserve a unique way of life. Nowhere was this theme more apparent than in war movies where men of different class and ethnic backgrounds pulled together to defeat the German or Japanese enemy. *Bataan,* for example, produced by MGM in 1943, featured a rainbow battalion of Jewish, Anglo, Mexican, Polish, Irish, Italian, and African American characters who set aside personal differences for a common cause. Although it ignored the real segregation and discrimination in the military and on the home front, this and similar films helped to promote a more democratic vision of American society and to erode some of the more offensive ethnic stereotypes that permeated popular culture.

Women, as depicted in wartime films, did not fare as well. Hollywood, following OWI directives, made propaganda and major-release films that encouraged women to take war jobs and courageously accept separation from loved ones. Geared toward middle-class homemakers, rather than the thousands of other women who needed little prodding to enter higher-paying defense work, these films stressed the temporary nature of wartime employment and the inherent femininity of their characters. For example, *Tender Comrade,* released by RKO in 1943, depicted four women who took defense jobs while their husbands were away in the service. Rather than focusing on their on-the-job experiences, the film emphasized the pain of separation, fear for their husbands' lives, and their longing to return to domestic roles. In other films, stars like Betty Grable and Rita Hayworth played sexy, but homespun, girls who gave up glamorous careers or marriage opportunities for average, honest men. Their "cheesecake" photos decorated military barracks, planes, and tanks, and served as a symbol of what awaited servicemen upon their return.

Political Transformation

The war's population boom placed severe strains on California's urban infrastructure and heightened competition for existing resources. Race relations deteriorated as many white residents, attempting to retain control over housing, jobs, and public services, directed their hostility toward ethnic minorities. At the same time, a growing number of Californians—both established residents and newcomers—felt that racial discrimination was incompatible with the prodemocracy thrust of the war. Ethnic groups, they maintained, deserved all of the rights and privileges of citizenship, particularly in light of their wartime service. Moreover, political leaders and governmental institutions had an obligation to ensure that all residents benefited from the war's economic boom and democratic promise. If the state's infrastructure and civic fabric were unraveling, it was the fault of shortsighted, ineffective leadership, not California's newest residents.

Change from the Grassroots

A more liberal political vision took root in the early years of the war with the formation of multiethnic coalitions like the Bay Area Council Against Discrimination, and the Los Angeles–based Council for the Protection of Minority Rights. These coalitions of minority activists, white liberals, and CIO union leadership focused primarily on discrimination in the defense industry and housing. Other coalitions soon followed. Throughout the state, CIO unions, whose membership now included large numbers of African American and Mexican American activists, joined with white liberals to register voters and back pro-labor, liberal candidates for office. In the San Francisco East Bay, for example, the CIO Political Action Committee (PAC) and Democratic Club joined forces to register thousands of new voters, including black migrants. On Election Day in 1944 the East Bay electorate weighed in for Roosevelt and the liberal congressional candidate, George Miller, and helped defeat a right-to-work ballot measure. The PAC then went on to select its own slate of candidates—pro-labor supporters of fair housing and employment legislation—for the municipal elections of 1945. Though its candidates were unsuccessful in 1945, the PAC created a growing interracial alliance that enjoyed greater electoral success in the postwar period.

The efforts of these CIO-led voters leagues were complemented by the activities of civic unity councils, which were multiethnic organizations devoted to ending all forms of discrimination through increased public education and political pressure. For example, in 1944 Mexican Americans, white liberals, and African Americans established the Los Angeles Council for Civic Unity, which attracted membership from a number of labor unions, the NAACP, LULAC, the Church

Federation of Los Angeles, and the Women's Division of the American Jewish Congress. The Los Angeles Council, like another established the same year in the San Francisco Bay area, promoted racial tolerance, equality, and cooperation through public forums, children's summer camps, and social events.

These and other liberal coalitions won small, local victories during the war, but more importantly their efforts helped create the foundation for the civil rights and liberal political advances of the postwar years. Working in concert with various ethnic organizations, larger, more influential coalitions—growing out of this earlier institutional framework—would eventually mobilize large numbers of minority voters, and secure fair employment and housing legislation and the election of African American and Mexican American candidates to local and state office.

Change at the Top

In 1942 state attorney general Earl Warren succeeded Culbert Olson as governor of California. Although a lifelong Republican, Warren secured broad-based, bipartisan support by downplaying his party affiliation and crafting a progressive, even liberal, political image. His pragmatic, nonideological leadership style, mastery of media-based campaign strategy, and exploitation of California's cross-filing system easily won him reelection in 1946 and 1950. Following in the progressive political tradition, Warren believed that government had an obligation to ensure the public good by directing the forces of social and economic change. Entering office during a period of unprecedented growth and upheaval, he had ample opportunity to devise policies that would help the state meet its new challenges.

Warren's first project was to use the tax revenue generated by the booming economy to create a "rainy day fund" in anticipation of defense industry demobilization and mass unemployment at the end of the war. The fund, easing the transition to a peacetime economy, put Californians to work rebuilding existing infrastructure and constructing new schools, hospitals, and other state-run facilities. His massive highway construction program, initiated in 1947, and financed by a gasoline tax that was bitterly opposed by the oil and trucking lobbies, also eased postwar unemployment and created the foundation for future economic and suburban expansion.

Warren's efforts to upgrade the state's infrastructure extended beyond highway and school construction to the development of water resources. He believed that the new Central Valley Project would not be sufficient to meet future demand. Instead, a comprehensive state-funded system was needed to move water from northern California to the more arid agricultural and urban areas in the south. Although Warren did obtain legislative approval to develop the plan, its implementation was blocked until 1959. For more than a decade, northern Californians, conservationists, and organized labor persuasively argued that a state-funded plan would primarily benefit large corporate farmers in the San Joaquin Valley. Indeed, the state, unlike the federal government, imposed no eligibility restrictions on access to subsidized water. If the project were federally funded, farmers cultivating more than 160 acres of land would lose their subsidy and pay higher rates for irrigating their excess acreage. No such limits applied to state-funded projects, and growers would benefit at the taxpayer's expense.

Concerned for the health and welfare of the state's growing population, Warren upgraded the Public Health Service, financed the construction of new mental health facilities, and increased welfare benefits, unemployment insurance, old age pensions, Aid to the Blind, and compensation for disabled workers. In 1945, Warren also proposed a comprehensive health coverage system for all California residents, to be financed by employee and employer contributions. Inspired by an uncle's preventable medical tragedy, Warren's proposal was defeated by the California Medical Association, which characterized the plan as socialized medicine. The powerful agricultural lobby similarly defeated Warren's proposal to include farm workers under the state's unemployment and worker compensation systems. These confrontations with corporate and special-interest groups prompted Warren's vigorous backing of lobby control legislation in 1949 and 1950.

Warren's relationship with organized labor and the state's ethnic groups was more ambiguous. Although he increased worker benefits and opposed antipicketing and right-to-work laws, Warren sided with his fellow Republicans in opposing a CIO-backed initiative to redraw state senate districts so that ethnic and working-class voters would be more fairly represented. As state attorney general and candidate for governor, Warren had helped fuel anti-Japanese hysteria and officially sanctioned relocation and internment. Only at the end of his life did he express regret for his actions. As governor, however, Warren defended the right of internees to return to California and took strong action against perpetrators of anti-Japanese hate crimes.

Throughout his administration, he also lobbied unsuccessfully for state fair employment legislation and the creation of a state Fair Employment Practice Commission. Such legislation would finally pass into law in 1959, during Edmund G. ("Pat") Brown's first term in office. On another race-related issue Warren was less of an advocate. Despite constant pressure from civil rights groups beginning at the end of World War II, Warren refused to integrate the California National Guard until 1949.

Warren, at times inconsistent and always enigmatic, was a transitional political figure. Despite being a lifelong Republican, he often faced challenges with a decidedly liberal outlook—one that was shaped by the expansive optimism and prodemocracy sentiment that grew out of World War II. At many crucial junctures, he failed to take moral or courageous action. At others, he led with remarkable insight and compassion. Over time, however, he would distinguish himself as a leading figure in the civil rights movement and a champion of the poor and disfranchised. In 1953, Warren left office to serve as chief justice of the U.S. Supreme Court, where he wrote the majority opinion for the *Brown* desegregation case of 1954. This, and other decisions made by the "Warren Court," cemented his reputation as one of the most "liberal" justices in American history.

Summary

World War II, like the Gold Rush, was a major turning point in California history. The wartime defense boom lifted the state out of the Depression and led to the growth of new industries that would ensure prosperity for years to come. The war also fueled anti-Japanese hostility, resulting in the relocation and internment of California's Japanese American population. Thousands of newcomers flocked to the state, increasing the size, diversity, and cultural richness of its population. At the same time, declining infrastructure and increased competition for resources fueled racial tensions and intensified discrimination in housing, employment, and public accommodations. Ethnic groups and white liberals, pointing to the contradiction between fighting a war for democracy and racial discrimination on the home front, fought back, creating the institutional framework for postwar civil rights struggles and electoral contestations. Through it all, California's enigmatic governor, Earl Warren, greatly expanded the state's role in directing the forces of social and economic change. Out of this momentous wartime transformation came competing visions of the California "dream" and renewed efforts to extend its promise to all of the state's citizens.

Suggested Readings

▪ Allen, Robert L., *The Port Chicago Mutiny: The Story of the Largest Mass Mutiny Trial in U.S. Naval History* (New York: Warner Books, 1989). This book provides a detailed history of the Port Chicago mutiny in the context of race relations in the military and society at large.

▪ Daniels, Roger, *Concentration Camps U.S.A: Japanese Americans and World War II* (New York: Henry Holt and Company, 1972) and *From Relocation to Redress* (Salt Lake City: University of Utah Press, 1986). These two books provide a comprehensive overview of Japanese relocation and internment, the redress movement, and the personal experiences of internees.

▪ Irons, Peter, *Justice Delayed: The Record of the Japanese American Internment Cases* (Middletown, CT: Wesleyan University Press, 1989). This book provides an overview of the legal challenges to relocation and internment.

▪ Johnson, Marilyn, *The Second Gold Rush: Oakland and the East Bay in World War II* (Berkeley: University of California Press, 1993). This book is a regional study, focusing on the political, economic, cultural, and demographic impact of the war on the San Francisco East Bay area.

▪ Lemke-Santangelo, Gretchen, *Abiding Courage: African American Migrant Women in the East Bay Community* (Chapel Hill: University of North Carolina

Press, 1996). This book, based on oral histories, examines African American migration from the South to the San Francisco East Bay area during World War II.

▌ Lotchin, Roger, ed., *The Way We Really Were: The Golden State in the Second Great War* (Urbana: University of Illinois Press, 2000). This collection of essays details the war's impact on California race relations, politics, industry (including Hollywood), and culture.

▌ Nash, Gerald D., *The American West Transformed: The Impact of the Second World War* (Lincoln: University of Nebraska Press, 1985) and *World War II and the West* (Lincoln: University of Nebraska Press, 1990). These two books provide a good overview of the war's impact on California and the greater American West.

▌ Tateishi, John, *And Justice for All: An Oral History of the Japanese American Detention Camps* (Seattle: University of Washington Press, 1984). This book, based on oral accounts of the internment experience, details the daily lives of camp residents.

▌ Verge, Arthur C., *Paradise Transformed: Los Angeles During the Second World War* (Dubuque: Kendall/Hunt Publishing, 1993). This book, another regional study, focuses on the war's impact on Los Angeles.

▌ White, Edward G., *Earl Warren: A Public Life* (New York: Oxford University Press, 1982). This insightful biography of Earl Warren covers his years as California's governor during and after World War II.

10

Postwar California: Prosperity and Discontent in the Golden State

Main Topics

▎ Unbridled Growth

▎ Postwar Politics

▎ Social and Cultural Dissent

▎ Summary

C esar Chavez, an earnest young navy veteran, rejoined his family in Delano at the end of World War II. After working in the agricultural fields for two years, Chavez married and started a family. He began to search for a way out of the grinding poverty and unrelenting toil that circumscribed the lives of California's migrant farm workers. In 1952 Chavez moved his growing family to the San José barrio of Sal Si Puedes, found work at a lumber mill, and joined a newly formed chapter of the Community Service Organization (CSO). Initially, Chavez worked as a CSO volunteer, registering Mexican American voters in San José. His tireless dedication, however, soon led to a paid position as a statewide organizer, and ultimately to appointment as CSO's national director.

As he rose through CSO's ranks, focusing primarily on increasing the electoral power of urban Latino voters, Chavez became more and more convinced that political and economic justice were entwined—particularly in the state's rural agricultural communities. There, growers used braceros and undocumented

CHAPTER 10	Postwar California: Prosperity and Discontent in the Golden State
1947	Hollywood anti-Communist investigations begin
1949	University of California Regents mandate loyalty oath for faculty
1950	State legislature adopts loyalty oath for state employees
1951	Stanford Research Park, foundation of Silicon Valley, established
1952	Lawrence Livermore Lab established
1953	Goodwin F. Knight takes office as governor after Earl Warren is appointed chief justice of the U.S. Supreme Court
1955	Merger of the AFL and CIO
1956	Allen Ginsberg's "Howl" is published
1957	Students at U.C. Berkeley form SLATE
1958	Edmund G. Brown elected governor
1959	State legislature approves the Fair Employment and Unruh Civil Rights Acts
1960	Anti-HUAC protests in San Francisco Legislature approves Master Plan for Higher Education and California Water Plan Federal Clean Water Act passed
1961	Association of Bay Area Governments formed Save San Francisco Bay Association founded
1962	Rachel Carson's *Silent Spring* published California becomes most populous state in the nation
1963	Federal Clean Air Act passed State legislature adopts the Rumford Fair Housing Act
1964	State Commission on the Status of Women established

immigrants to undercut the wages, working conditions, and bargaining power of domestic workers. In the process, all three groups suffered.

In 1962, at the annual CSO convention, Chavez presented a plan to create a farm workers' union and was voted down. With only nine hundred dollars in savings, eight children, and the support and confidence of his wife, Helen, Chavez resigned from the CSO, moved back to Delano, and began to create the foundation for a new farm labor movement. He, and thousands of other Californians, entered the postwar years with heightened expectations, confident that the state's resources, if more equitably distributed, would provide abundant opportunities for all citizens.

On the surface, Chavez's optimism appeared to have a strong foundation. California's economy, bolstered by Cold War military spending, the growth of new industries, an expanding population, and government investment in transportation, housing, education, and resource development, was booming. Thousands of established residents and newcomers, enjoying their share of the state's wealth, flocked to the burgeoning suburbs and embraced the "California lifestyle"—patterns of consumption that set trends for the rest of the nation.

As rapid growth took a toll on the environment, political leaders, prodded by concerned citizens, took modest steps toward regulating development and controlling pollution. Just as significantly, state legislators supported social programs and antidiscriminatory measures to ensure that all citizens benefited from the postwar economic windfall. By the early 1960s, however, California was still a long way from solving its most pressing problems. Environmental degradation outpaced conservation efforts. Housing and employment discrimination continued to reinforce existing social and economic inequalities, leading to growing frustration and anger within inner-city minority communities. Even middle-class suburbs harbored discontent. Many women and youth, anxious to escape the stifling conformity and isolation of these homogeneous enclaves, launched a quiet protest that soon erupted into more overt forms of social rebellion.

Questions to Consider

▮ How did federal and state government policies contribute to postwar economic expansion and suburban growth?

▮ How would you define liberalism? Which liberal policies or reforms had the most significant impact on Californians during the postwar period?

▮ How did California's Red Scare affect the state's political, social, and cultural landscapes?

▮ Did all Californians benefit from postwar economic expansion and the suburban boom? Why or why not?

Unbridled Growth

After a brief lull immediately following the war, the state, and the nation as a whole, entered one of the longest periods of economic expansion in American history. The war increased industrial capacity, stimulated the growth of new industries, and devastated the economies of our European and Asian competitors. More significantly, the federal government increased defense spending, funneling billions of dollars to private industry in order to wage the Cold War. Federal and state investment in education, transportation, housing, and the development of water resources also helped sustain high levels of economic and population growth. However, growth came with a cost. Industrial expansion and suburbanization took a frightening toll on the state's natural resource base, leading to a gradual awakening of environmental consciousness and tentative efforts to regulate the pace and impact of development.

Industrial Growth and Organized Labor

In northern California, shipbuilding declined only to be replaced with a booming electronics industry. In 1951 Stanford University created a high-technology research park by leasing unused land to private entrepreneurs. Originally intended to generate revenue for the college, the park eventually became a means of translating campus-based research into product development, and attracting star-quality faculty to the university. By 1955 seven companies, including Hewlett Packard and Varian Associates, had signed leases. By 1960 the park had attracted twenty-five more companies, and was drawing numerous other high-tech firms, including Fairchild Semiconductor, to the surrounding region. "Silicon Valley," named after the silicon chips that soon revolutionized the electronics industry, was taking shape. Across the bay, Berkeley's nuclear research was also creating spinoffs. Lawrence Livermore Lab, established in 1952, employed thousands of workers in weapons-related research, while helping, along with the electronics industry, to attract mammoth defense contractors to the Bay Area, including Lockheed, IBM, Westinghouse, and General Electric.

Southern California's industrial growth was no less impressive. Aircraft manufacturers, diversifying into the production of jet engines, radar, supersonic aircraft, rockets, satellites, and missiles, became the center of the nation's aerospace industry by the 1950s. They employed the majority of the manufacturing work force in Los Angeles, Orange, and San Diego Counties. These firms also enjoyed a close partnership with regional research institutions. UCLA, the Jet Propulsion Lab at the California Institute of Technology, and the Rand Corporation received government funding for research and development, and transferred their products to the private aerospace industry.

The expansion of the aerospace and electronics industries was largely a product of the Cold War competition with the Soviet Union. To win this competition, the government transferred billions of dollars to universities and private industry, creating a vast, interlocking university-military-industrial complex. By 1960, California was receiving over 25 percent of the nation's total defense expenditures, and 42 percent of the Defense Department's research contracts.

Other sectors of the state's economy also prospered during the postwar years. Municipal, county, state, and federal government, adjusting to population growth and new demands on infrastructure and public services, generated new bureaucracies and hired scores of additional workers. Minorities, in particular, benefited from the expansion of the public sector. Government, which adopted nondiscriminatory hiring policies more readily than private industry, helped create a growing black and Mexican American middle class. In Oakland, for example, 30 percent of the city's black civilian labor force worked for various branches of government by the early 1960s.

California's apparel, footwear, scientific instruments, frozen foods, cosmetic, chemical, and pharmaceutical industries, benefiting from increased national demand, reached beyond local markets to broaden their consumer base. On a local level, real estate, retail, and financial institutions expanded their services to meet the needs of a growing and increasingly prosperous population. The construction industry, however, received an even more significant boost. Thousands of new residents, many starting families for the first time, demanded housing. The GI Bill, passed by Congress in 1944 to provide benefits for veterans, included the provision of low-interest home loans to veterans. This made home ownership an affordable option for many first-time buyers. Developers met demand by applying mass production and prefabrication techniques to home-building, and by locating new housing "tracts" on cheaper land surrounding the urban core. Across the state, postwar suburban housing tracts, consisting of row upon row of nearly identical dwellings, replaced orchards, truck farms, and open fields.

In contrast, Southern California's film industry faced serious challenges in the postwar period, but it emerged as a stronger, more influential cultural institution. Until 1948, major studios not only produced films, but also monopolized box office profits by screening their movies at their own theater chains. As a result of federal antitrust lawsuits initiated by smaller, independent theaters, the studios had to sell their chains. This seriously eroded profits at a time when production costs and stars' salaries were rising. Simultaneously, studios faced increasing competition both from foreign and independent filmmakers and from the emerging, New York–based television industry. Hollywood adapted by producing more films on location, rather than relying on the costly and elaborate studio sets and lots of the past. It also diversified into recording and television production, reestablishing its dominance in the entertainment industry by the early 1960s.

California's labor unions, enjoying unprecedented power during the postwar years, helped ensure that the benefits of a booming economy were widely distributed. Having taken a "no-strike" pledge during the war, unions—particularly those affiliated with the CIO—focused on expanding their membership, forming political action committees, and creating coalitions with liberal and progressive community organizations. When the war ended, they had not only the numeric strength to obtain wage and benefit concessions from management, but the political clout to influence local and state elections. The anti-Communist crusade, leading to the expulsion of left-wing union leadership, and the 1947 Taft-Hartley Act, which limited the effectiveness of strikes and protected open shops, somewhat muted their new power. But labor rebounded in 1955 when the AFL merged with its more progressive rival, the CIO. Together the two represented over 90 percent of the state's union members. Largely as a result of the decade's rabid anti-Communism, this new entity de-emphasized liberal social activism and rank-and-file participation. Nevertheless, its mostly blue-collar membership obtained substantial material benefits, swelling the state's middle class to a historic high.

Large growers consolidated their dominant position in California agriculture during the postwar years, reaping enormous profits and political influence in the process. Their increasing power partly derived from the "agricultural-industrial complex," a partnership forged by farmers, public research institutions, and private manufacturers of chemicals and farm machinery. For example, the University of California at Davis, the state's premier agricultural institution, obtained private industry funding to develop new high-yield plant varieties, pesticides, fertilizers, herbicides, and farm equipment tailored to the needs of large-scale producers. Industry then secured the patents, and sold their product to large growers. As a consequence, small farmers, unable to afford the new technology or apply it on a reduced scale, fell behind their larger, more competitive counterparts.

Although this partnership predated the war, it grew stronger and more influential in the 1950s and 1960s. Wartime chemical research led to the creation of a new generation of synthetic compounds that could be endlessly combined and modified for agricultural use, even tailored to specific crops, soils, insect pests, and climatic conditions. Plant genetics and farm equipment technology also advanced rapidly during the postwar years.

Postwar agricultural growth, despite this new technology, continued to depend on cheap agricultural labor. Using their considerable political influence, large growers successfully lobbied for the continuation and expansion of the bracero program, ensuring a captive, subsidized labor supply throughout the 1950s. Several hundred thousand undocumented workers and foreigners with temporary work permits also helped keep wages low by maintaining a surplus labor supply. In addition to its labor subsidy, agribusiness received ample cheap water from both state and federally funded sources. The Central Valley Project (CVP), completed in the postwar years with federal funds, diverted water from the Sacramento River to the drier San Joaquin Valley. In accordance with the Reclamation Act of 1902, growers with more than 160 acres of land were not entitled to subsidized water from federally funded projects. Agribusiness used its political influence to obtain significant concessions in the law: additional 160-acre allowances for each child, spouse, joint tenant, and corporate partner; reclassification of

California Aqueduct delivering water to the San Joaquin Valley. Consider the massive scale of the state's water delivery system. Did the benefits to agriculture, industry, and growing urban and suburban areas outweigh its environmental costs?

some CVP water as "natural flow," which was exempt from the federal acreage limit; and suspension of the limitation if local irrigation districts, managed by grower-elected boards, repaid their share of CVP construction costs in a timely fashion. Finally, farmers who leased, rather than owned land, avoided the limit altogether.

The legal costs involved in circumventing federal law prompted growers to back the new state-funded California Water Plan that promised to deliver subsidized, limit-free water from northern California to growers in the San Joaquin Valley and Southern California. Blocked for several years, the plan was finally approved between 1959 and 1960, removing yet another obstacle to agricultural consolidation and corporatization.

Education

Postwar economic growth and Cold War anxieties precipitated changes in the state's educational system. Private industry, government officials, and the scientific community all warned that California's booming economy, increasingly centered on high technology, demanded a more educated, specialized work force.

They also argued that the United States would compromise its ability to wage the Cold War unless it provided the younger generation with adequate scientific and technical training.

At the same time, rapid population growth placed strains on existing educational facilities. Wartime migration, coupled with the postwar baby boom, filled elementary and secondary classrooms beyond capacity. The state's colleges and universities, crowded with veterans who took advantage of the GI Bill's generous education benefits, experienced similar strains. These strains continued as the first baby boomers, attending college at higher rates than any other generation in history, came of age in the 1960s.

With these concerns in mind and with ample support from taxpayers, education policymakers embarked on an ambitious program of school construction, curricular reform, and reformulation of teacher preparation requirements. In keeping with the new curricular emphasis on traditional disciplines, particularly math and science, future elementary and secondary school teachers could no longer major in education. The 1961 Fisher Act instead required teachers to possess a four-year academic degree and a fifth year of professional education training.

Higher education, suffering from uneven academic standards and unnecessary duplication of institutional missions and programs, also needed attention. In 1960 the legislature approved the Master Plan, which created a new three-tiered structure: university, state college, and junior college tiers. Under the plan, the University of California was given sole authority to award doctoral degrees and given exclusive jurisdiction over graduate-level training in law, medicine, dentistry, and veterinary studies. As the premier research and professional institution, the university was to admit students from the top 12.5 percent of the state's high school graduates. Similarly, candidates for advanced degrees were chosen on the basis of high academic and professional promise. State colleges, under the Master Plan, were to provide a liberal arts education to students from the top one-third of high school graduates. Graduate training, with special exceptions, was limited to the master's degree level. Junior colleges, open to all high school graduates, offered a two-year liberal arts curriculum designed to prepare students for transfer to the state college or university system, as well as technical and vocational programs of study leading directly to employment. This system, offering tuition-free education to California's college students, became a model for the rest of the nation.

Population and Suburban Growth

California's population increased dramatically during the war and continued to expand throughout the 1950s and 1960s. From 1951 to 1963 the state's annual growth rate fluctuated between 3.3 and 4.6 percent, with over a million people added every two years. In 1962, California became the most populous state in the nation. During this period the state's population increasingly spilled outside of the urban core into the suburban fringe as developers rushed to meet the demand for new housing. Citrus groves in the Los Angeles basin and orchards and truck farms in the San Francisco Bay area were converted to suburban communities at an astonishing rate. From the early 1950s to the early 1960s, between sixty thousand and ninety thousand acres of prime agricultural land were replaced with tract homes, freeways, and shopping centers. Industry, attracted to ample, cheap land and a less heavily unionized labor force, relocated to the suburbs as well, contributing to the massive, largely unregulated redistribution of the state's population and tax base.

New suburbanites, longing for normalcy after the dislocations of the war years, focused on pursuing the "California lifestyle." Ranch-style homes, and houses built by innovative developer Joseph Eichler with their characteristic flat roofs and open, glass-enclosed interiors, reduced barriers between indoor and outdoor space. Patios, barbecues, outdoor furniture, swimming pools, and casual dinnerware further reduced this separation by facilitating outside entertaining and family activity. Hollywood, television, advertising agencies, and the popular press not only popularized this lifestyle among Californians—they also created a new national trend.

Recreation patterns also shifted. Suburban shopping centers, forerunners of today's malls, framed consumption as a leisure activity. Suburb-based theme parks, following the Disneyland prototype, provided "wholesome" entertainment for the entire family as an alternative to urban, adult-centered cultural institutions. New sports facilities, such as Dodger Stadium and Candlestick Park, built on the urban fringe, also catered to suburban families. Finally, the new emphasis on outdoor living extended to the state's beaches and mountains. Campgrounds, ski lodges, vacation rentals, and summer home developments burgeoned during the 1950s and 1960s, intruding on once-pristine or sparsely populated scenic areas.

The carefree suburban lifestyle came with a price. Its housing tracts, shopping centers, and decentralized industry not only despoiled open space, but also stripped inner cities of their much-needed jobs and tax base. Beginning in the late 1940s, and continuing through the 1960s, white residents left inner cities for the suburbs. Industry soon followed. Black and Mexican American residents, locked out of the suburban exodus because of discriminatory real estate and housing practices, remained behind in the older, decaying urban core. Even after the state adopted fair housing legislation in the mid-1960s, discriminatory lending institutions, homeowners, and real estate agencies continued to block equal access to affordable suburban housing. This process, reinforcing social separation and economic inequality, was repeated in virtually every metropolitan region of the state, setting the stage for the urban revolts of the sixties.

Although idealized in postwar popular culture as safe, untroubled enclaves, suburbs came under criticism in the mid-1960s by a new generation of feminists. The suburb, according to pioneering feminist Betty Friedan, was little more than a "comfortable concentration camp" that fostered depression, a growing sense of isolation, loneliness, and quiet desperation among its female inhabitants.

Many suburban wives, whether they felt trapped or not, did indeed conform to the postwar ideal of the stay-at-home mom. But thousands of others joined the paid labor force in the fifties and sixties. Ironically, the financial demands of maintaining the "California lifestyle" often necessitated more than one wage earner per family, and began to erode the long-held taboo against married women's participation in the labor force. At the same time, increasing numbers of women were attending college—some in search of husbands, but many in preparation for rewarding careers. Young careerists, along with an older generation of professional women, rarely obtained jobs that matched their education and skill levels. Locked into clerical and sales jobs, and a limited number of professional occupations like nursing and teaching, working women earned only sixty cents for every dollar made by their male counterparts.

These inequities, combined with suburban isolation, prompted female activists to press for change. In 1964, after three years of intense lobbying from women's organizations, the California legislature finally agreed to create a state Commission on the Status of Women. The commission's findings on employment discrimination and male/female wage differentials reinvigorated the women's movement and created the foundation for the more radical feminist critiques of the late 1960s and 1970s.

Transportation, Energy, Water Resources, and Environmental Pollution

A massive, postwar freeway construction program, funded with a mix of state and federal dollars, helped facilitate white and industrial flight to the suburbs. In 1947 the state legislature passed the Collier-Burns Act, which approved approximately 12,500 miles of new roads, connecting suburbs to surrounding urban centers and funded with a seven cent per gallon gasoline tax. By the mid-1950s the federal government augmented this expanding network by helping to fund an interstate freeway system that created linkages between each major metropolitan center. Growing dependence on the automobile was further encouraged by the decline of prewar electric rail systems that had connected residential neighborhoods to downtown areas. From San Diego to San Francisco, local governments replaced energy-efficient electric trains and trolleys with diesel-fueled buses. By the late 1950s only isolated remnants of these regional rail systems survived. The automobile—increasingly a symbol of personal freedom and status—reigned supreme.

The new freeway system had several unanticipated drawbacks. It frequently bisected poor, inner-city neighborhoods, cutting them off from surrounding services, wiping out small business districts and large tracts of affordable housing, and contributing to the spatial isolation and "ghettoization" of residents. Declining air quality was yet another problem associated with the postwar transportation boom. By the late 1940s Los Angeles residents faced a human-made atmospheric threat: automobile-generated smog. The city first responded by imposing

San Gabriel Valley in 1938 and in 1959. Reflect on the social, political, and demographic pressures that led to this dramatic transformation, and evaluate the costs and benefits of such rapid growth. How did the uniform nature of postwar subdivisions affect residents' quality of life?

restrictions on factory emissions and backyard waste burning, but failed to address the primary cause—the transportation boom. Part of the problem was that smog came from multiple jurisdictions. Even if city officials imposed regulations in their municipality, pollution from neighboring areas knew no boundaries. By the early 1950s the problem had worsened. Los Angeles County responded by establishing an Air Pollution Control District, which began to monitor air quality and introduce pollution control measures.

Soon after, in 1955, nine counties in the San Francisco Bay area joined forces to create a regional air quality control district, empowered to set emission standards and regulate polluting industries. Although these districts did little to curtail auto emissions, the main source of pollution, they created an important model of regional cooperation that was later adopted by other municipalities. When the federal government passed the Clean Air Act in 1963, regional air quality districts, along with the newly created state Air Resources Board, provided the institutional framework to enforce the act's auto emission standards.

By the early 1960s, declining air quality and increasing traffic congestion on the already overtaxed highway system prompted some cities to reconsider electric transit systems. The Bay Area took the lead in 1962, receiving approval from voters in Alameda, Contra Costa, and San Francisco Counties to build a regional rapid transit system. However, it took another two decades for Los Angeles, Sacramento, San José, and San Diego to follow suit. And even with these systems in place, most Californians continue to prefer private transportation to the cleaner, more fuel-efficient alternatives.

From World War II on, population and economic growth rapidly moved the state from energy self-sufficiency to dependence on imported energy. California's plastics, chemical, and defense-based industries, and its suburban, automobile-centered lifestyle, were fuel intensive, demanding more energy than the state produced. By the early 1960s hydroelectric resources had been exploited to about 80 percent of capacity. And the new California Water Plan, with its extensive network of pumping stations and cross-terrain aqueducts, was expected to use much of the energy it generated. Onshore oil reserves were also limited, leading petroleum companies to search offshore for new deposits during and after World War II, and to supplement domestic supplies with imports. Utility companies followed suit, tapping electricity, gas, and oil from elsewhere in the West, and ultimately turning to foreign suppliers. By 1962, for example, two-thirds of California's natural gas, which was used to generate electricity, heat homes, and produce chemicals and plastics, came from Texas, New Mexico, and Canada.

Long before the energy crisis of the 1970s awakened consumers to their dependence on imported fuel, the state's utility companies searched for alternative sources to meet increasing demand. In 1960 Pacific Gas and Electric (PG&E) became the first private utility in the nation to tap geothermal energy at its Geyserville plant in Sonoma County. Other geothermal plants soon followed, providing a clean, but modest addition to the state's energy mix. More controversially, nuclear power, promoted by the Atomic Energy Commission as a safe, environmentally friendly energy source, was first produced in 1957 on an experimental basis at the Vallecitos plant outside of Livermore. PG&E began operating a commercial facility in 1963 near Eureka, spearheading a ten-year plant construction boom that failed to anticipate growing public concern over seismic hazards, safe disposal of radioactive wastes, and the potentially lethal consequences of human error or reactor malfunction.

By 1964, when PG&E proposed another facility at earthquake-prone Bodega Bay, the public grew more skeptical of industry safety claims and mounted a successful campaign to block the plan. This protest, slowing but not stopping the plant construction boom, set the stage for the more vocal and militant antinuclear protests of the 1970s and 1980s and helped broaden the focus of older environmental organizations. In the meantime, even nuclear energy could not keep pace with demand, and California's utility companies and petroleum industry drew ever more heavily on imported fuel.

Unbridled growth also took its toll on the state's water resources. The Central Valley Project, which became fully operational in the 1950s, diverted vast quantities of water from the Sacramento and San Joaquin Rivers to farmland in the San Joaquin Valley. Its complex network of dams and canals decimated wild fisheries, destroyed thousands of acres of waterfowl habitat, and prevented natural flow from reaching and recharging underground aquifers. The most serious impact of the CVP was the decline of the Sacramento–San Joaquin River Delta water quality. As fresh water was pumped southward, particularly during the dry summer months, salt water from the San Francisco Bay intruded into the delta, damaging fragile ecosystems and reducing freshwater flow into the bay. Salty water, occasionally drawn into canals and used to irrigate farmland, also contributed to the salinization of soils in the San Joaquin.

The California Water Plan, initiated in 1960, eventually diverted additional water from the north to the San Joaquin Valley and up over the Tehachapi Mountains to Southern California. The system tapped the tributaries of the Sacramento River, adding to the problems created by the CVP. North–south competition for water resources intensified, and eventually sparked angry opposition from environmentalists to proposed dams on California's remaining wild rivers.

Postwar growth did more than place strains on the state's water and energy resources; it generated increasing amounts of toxic wastes that poured, virtually unregulated, into the air, water, and soil. New chemical compounds, added to the older mix of heavy metals, solvents, corrosives, paints, and dyes, created an unprecedented threat to California's environment and public health. Produced in increasing quantities by the petrochemical industry following World War II, new substances like DDT, PCBs, and dioxin not only persisted in the environment for long periods of time, but also became more concentrated as they moved up the food chain. By the early 1960s, wildlife biologists began to sound the alarm. More careful study also revealed their potential threat to human health. Despite mounting public concern, mobilized by Rachel Carson's 1962 condemnation of the chemical industry in *Silent Spring,* and by environmental organizations like the Audubon Society and California Tomorrow, effective regulation of toxic chemicals did not occur until the 1970s and 1980s. The federal Clean Water Act of 1960 prompted the state to adopt more stringent sewage treatment standards, but synthetic chemicals and other toxic substances could not be removed by normal processing methods. And the producers and consumers of these compounds, including the state's powerful petrochemical and agricultural industries, vigorously opposed regulation of chemical production, use, and disposal.

As Californians awakened to the growing threat of toxic pollution, a small group of environmental activists launched a path-breaking movement to save one of the state's natural wonders from industrial and suburban development. During the postwar years, the San Francisco Bay lost 2,300 acres each year to accommodate shoreline construction of garbage dumps, airports, housing tracts, and industrial parks. Already reduced by 40 percent of its size from a century earlier, it was in danger of becoming little more than a drainage channel by the year 2000.

Residents of Los Angeles protest the growing smog problem circa the 1960s. Examine the relationship between this photograph and the San Gabriel images. What were the connections between suburban growth and declining air quality?

In an era when limits to growth were inconceivable to most of the state's residents, a small group of Berkeley women, including the wife of university president Clark Kerr, vocally asserted that the public good should prevail over the interests of municipal and private developers. They formed the Save San Francisco Bay Association in 1961, and attracted enough public support over the next four years to secure legislative approval for both a temporary halt to bay fill and the formation of the San Francisco Bay Conservation and Development Commission. This agency, empowered by the state legislature to grant or deny permission for all shoreline construction, established the precedent for government regulation of development. Other commissions, including the California Coastal Commission and the Tahoe Regional Planning Agency, soon followed, along with a host of municipal-level no-growth and controlled growth ordinances and measures.

Postwar Politics

The rapid economic and demographic growth of the postwar period created a host of problems that defied individual and even municipal-level solution. Increasingly, Californians turned to government to regulate and guide the process of change. On the state level, Governor Warren's two successors continued his legacy of support for education, social services, resource development, and highway construction, and enlarged the state's role in protecting environmental quality. On a local level, city governments responded to the negative impact of unbridled growth by forming regional partnerships with their neighbors. Growing numbers of Californians also demanded that local government take a more active role in protecting the rights of working people and ethnic minorities and in bringing the disadvantaged into the economic mainstream through increased social spending. The democratic ideals that fueled support for the war effort, they argued, must now be applied at home.

These general political currents, however, were overshadowed by the anti-Communist hysteria of the early Cold War years. In California and the nation as a whole, fear of internal subversion temporarily limited the pace and extent of political change. Conservative Republicans were alarmed by liberal inroads into state and local politics, the growing power of organized labor, and the new political clout of ethnic minorities. In response, they mounted a counteroffensive by mobilizing the anti-Communist rhetoric of the late 1940s and early 1950s. Accusing their mostly Democratic opponents of being "soft on Communism," they created a political atmosphere charged with fear, intolerance, suspicion, and opportunism. Their attacks not only had a devastating impact on organized labor, civil rights organizations, higher education, and Hollywood, but also convinced many ordinary Californians that "a liberal is only a hop, skip, and a jump from a Communist."

Democrats, however, gradually recovered their political credibility by promoting "responsible liberalism," creating a more effective party structure, and highlighting the excessive conservatism of their opponents. In 1958 Californians elected a Democratic governor, and a Democratic majority to both houses of the state legislature. Locally, liberals also made significant progress in removing Republicans from city office and electing leadership that supported a stronger regulatory and planning role for government. Liberalism, rather than radicalism or conservatism, ultimately prevailed.

California's Red Scare

Although Californians voted overwhelmingly for a liberal Democratic agenda in 1958, many citizens—perhaps a majority—spent the early postwar period suspecting that liberalism amounted to Communism. Governor Earl Warren and his immediate successor, Goodwin Knight, were both Republicans. And although they supported liberal policies that angered their party's conservatives, they escaped direct attack. Democratic candidates, progressive organizations, and any individual or institution supporting liberal causes were not as fortunate.

In 1938 the U.S. Congress established the House Un-American Activities Committee (HUAC) to root out subversives on a national level. HUAC's first major target was the Hollywood film industry, whose writers, directors, and actors were accused of harboring left-wing sympathies. Not coincidentally, industry workers had just concluded a major studio strike, underscoring the growing power of organized labor in the state. Starting in 1947, HUAC held hearings on the "Red Menace in Hollywood" with the full cooperation of many industry leaders, including Ronald Reagan, president of the Screen Actors Guild, and studio owners Louis B. Mayer, Jack Warner, and Walt Disney.

In the course of the hearings several prominent screenwriters, known as the Hollywood Ten, refused to provide testimony about their political beliefs and affiliations, citing their constitutional rights under the First Amendment. The Committee for the First Amendment—whose membership included Lauren Bacall, Humphrey Bogart, John Huston, and Frank Sinatra—attempted to come to their defense and challenge the constitutionality of the hearings. But its efforts were unsuccessful. All ten were sentenced to prison for contempt of Congress, and nine were permanently banned from industry employment. HUAC then went on to compile a list of 324 present and former Hollywood employees with alleged Communist ties. A majority of those on this "blacklist," many with well-established careers, lost their jobs. Equally damaging, those who remained in the industry approached their craft with more caution, avoiding content that might attract negative attention from in-house and external censors. For more than a decade, Hollywood films mirrored the conservatism and moral rigidity that characterized American culture as a whole.

The California Legislative Fact-Finding Committee on Un-American Activities, headed by Senator Jack B. Tenney and emboldened by HUAC's high-profile Hollywood investigation, claimed that it had uncovered evidence of Communist subversion in the state government and educational system. In 1949, fearing a disruptive investigation of its own employees, the University of California, with approval from the Board of Regents, required professors to sign a loyalty oath. The state legislature approved a similar and more exacting oath for all state employees in 1950 when it adopted the Levering Act.

Within the university, the oath generated widespread protest and legal action. Maintaining that the policy violated their constitutional rights and academic freedom, numerous professors refused to sign and were fired for insubordination. Still others resigned in protest, or refused job offers from the university because the oath offended their principles. In 1951 the Third California District Court of Appeals ruled in favor of the dissenting professors, arguing that the oath violated both tenure agreements and the state constitution. The Board of Regents, angered over faculty "insubordination," decided to appeal the decision. After considering the appeal in 1952, the California Supreme Court ordered the reinstatement of the dismissed professors and invalidated the university's oath on the grounds that the state, through the Levering Act, had sole authority to determine employee loyalty. The court, in other words, failed to consider the constitutionality of loyalty tests, and simply ruled that the power to require them belonged to the legislature. The state's loyalty oath, covering all government employees including professors, was not declared unconstitutional until 1967.

The Tenney Commission and its parent organization, HUAC, also launched investigations into subversive infiltration of labor unions and civil rights organizations. Reeling from the negative publicity generated by HUAC allegations and lacking the financial resources to mount a credible defense, numerous organizations expelled leaders and members who fell under suspicion, backed away from more militant strategies and tactics, and avoided building alliances with "subversive"

Lauren Bacall and Humphrey Bogart attend a 1947 protest in Washington, D.C., against the Hollywood HUAC investigation. Why did some members of the film industry, including many high-profile stars, speak out against HUAC's Hollywood investigation? Why did others, including future governor Ronald Reagan, cooperate with efforts to purge the industry of the "Red Menace"?

groups. California's liberal politicians came under attack as well. In a 1946 U.S. congressional race, a young World War II veteran named Richard Nixon defeated his Democratic opponent, Jerry Voorhis, by using red scare tactics. Although Nixon later admitted that he knew "Voorhis wasn't a Communist," he fell short of an apology for his smear tactics. "Nice guys and sissies," he maintained, "didn't win elections." Once in Congress, Nixon advanced his political career by joining HUAC and vigorously pursuing the conviction of Alger Hiss, a State Department official who was accused of spying for the Soviet Union. Although the allegation was never proved, Hiss was convicted of perjury for denying the charges against him. And Nixon received credit for uncovering subversion at high levels of the federal government under the Democrats' watch. On both the state and national level, Republicans used the Hiss case and other allegations of subversion from within to paint the Democrats as either "soft on Communism" or guilty of actual conspiracy.

In the 1950 U.S. Senate race Nixon again turned to red baiting. Mischaracterizing his Democratic opponent, Helen Gahagan Douglas, as "the Pink Lady" with a Communist-like voting record in the U.S. House of Representatives, he handily won the contest. Douglas, like Voorhis, was merely a Democrat with a liberal voting record. Meanwhile, Nixon's political fortunes advanced. Just a year after defeating Douglas, he was rewarded with the vice presidency—a clear indication that the American political process had been deeply influenced by postwar anti-Communist hysteria.

Warren and Knight

Earl Warren and his successor Goodwin J. Knight, both Republicans, held office during the height of California's Red Scare, but unlike Nixon, they refrained from exploiting fear to advance their political careers. Moreover, both men adopted liberal policies that greatly expanded the power of government "over the lives of the people"—policies that were heartily criticized by their more conservative colleagues. Their party affiliation, however, largely protected them from charges of subversion or softness on Communism. Warren, who characterized himself as a progressive, expanded governmental services, upgraded California's infrastructure, and invested heavily in health, welfare, and public education. He also took a principled position on his party's anti-Communist crusade. In 1948, Warren criticized HUAC's Hollywood investigation and refused to support a loyalty oath for state employees. As an ex-officio regent, he attempted to convince his fellow board members that the university's loyalty oath was ineffective and unconstitutional. He also opposed the 1950 Levering Act, which had been drafted by one of his critics, a right-wing Republican assemblyman from Los Angeles. By 1953, when Warren was named chief justice of the U.S. Supreme Court, his foes were heartened that the lieutenant governor, Goodwin J. Knight, a conservative critic of Warren's liberal policies, would take over the office. Knight, having the incumbent's advantage and his party's blessing, then won the governorship in his own right in 1954.

Once firmly in office, however, Knight followed in Warren's footsteps by supporting increased spending on infrastructure, water resource development, workers' benefits, social services, and mental health. Even more troubling to his party's conservatives, Knight expanded the regulatory role of government by endorsing clean air standards and he established himself as a friend of organized labor by opposing right-to-work legislation. As the next election approached, Knight faced serious opposition. Two conservative rivals, Vice President Richard Nixon and Senator William Knowland, saw his office as a step toward the presidency. With proven right-wing credentials, either one could count on the financial backing of the state and national Republican Party in the 1958 election.

In 1957, Knight's fears materialized when Knowland announced that he would run for governor. Making matters worse, Nixon supporters, angry over Knight's refusal to endorse Nixon's 1956 vice-presidential nomination, were sure to back Knowland. Knight's chances of winning the primary were also undercut by a 1952 voter referendum that forced candidates to identify their party affiliation on primary ballots. The old ballot had listed incumbents at the top without revealing their party membership. Knight, as an incumbent with broad, nonpartisan appeal, would have had an advantage over rival Republicans and Democrats under the old system. Cognizant of these liabilities, Knight withdrew from the race and left the field to Knowland.

The state's Democrats, in the meantime, regrouped. Twenty years earlier Republicans had created an efficient, tightly knit organization to raise money and coordinate their campaigns. Having a disproportionate number of incumbents, they were also the primary beneficiaries of the old cross-filing system. And the postwar anti-Communist hysteria provided the Republicans with yet another political advantage. By the election of 1958, however, conditions had changed. The Red Scare tapered off, and many Californians now viewed its main architects as political opportunists and extremists. Moreover, the liberal policies of two Republican governors, although roundly criticized by conservatives, had visibly improved the state's infrastructure, strengthened its economy, and improved the health and welfare of its citizens.

At the same time, election reform gave Democrats a more equal playing field in primary elections, and prompted them to create a vigorous new party organization, the California Democratic Council (CDC), to advance their political agenda. By 1956, the Democrats had ample reason to be hopeful that the tide had turned in their favor. In that year's elections, they eroded the Republican majority in the assembly from 53–27 to 42–38, and in the senate from 29–11 to 20–20. As the 1958 election approached, their prospects seemed even brighter; the Republican incumbent had dropped out of the governor's race, and his replacement had a reputation as a right-wing extremist.

Edmund G. Brown

In 1958, Democrats chose Edmund G. (Pat) Brown, a native San Franciscan and state attorney general, to run for governor. Brown, a New Deal Democrat and active member of the CDC, had impeccable liberal credentials. During the 1940s, as district attorney for San Francisco, Brown transformed a corrupt and inefficient department into a modern, aggressive, crime-fighting unit. While waging legal battles against prostitution, gambling, juvenile delinquency, and political corruption, Brown attacked civil rights violations with equal zeal. Resisting popular opinion, he vocally condemned Japanese relocation and internment, and opposed the anti-Communist crusade against Harry Bridges, the militant leader of the International Longshoremen's and Warehousemen's Union (ILWU). In 1950, with Governor Warren's endorsement, Brown was elected as state attorney general. When probusiness conservatives succeeded in placing a "right-to-work" initiative on the 1958 ballot, Attorney General Brown forced them to change the proposition's title to "Employer and Employee Relations" to avoid misleading voters. This decision bolstered Brown's liberal, pro-labor reputation, and gave him a decisive edge in the upcoming governor's race.

The "right-to-work" initiative, which unions branded as the "right to work for less and less and less," became a major issue of the 1958 campaign. In many workplaces unions secured "closed-shop" agreements from management that made union membership a condition of employment. The "right-to-work" initiative would have prohibited such restrictions, allowing employees to choose whether to join an existing union upon accepting a job. Organized labor feared that the initiative was part of a broader campaign to erode the membership and political power of unions. Knowland, determined to repudiate Warren's and Knight's liberal policies and to secure conservative support for the 1960 Republican presidential nomination, adopted a largely negative, anti-labor platform that highlighted his support of the right-to-work initiative. As a consequence, labor united behind Brown, exercising an unprecedented degree of organizational and political muscle. Brown, assured of union support, moved beyond this single issue to promote a broader, more optimistic agenda that consolidated support within his own party, attracted thousands of new voters, and convinced many independents and moderate Republicans to opt for his "responsible liberalism."

Framing his opposition to the right-to-work initiative as part of a pragmatic, forward-looking plan of action, Brown succeeded in casting Knowland as an ultraconservative, overly pessimistic throwback to a bygone era. With the support of a broad new constituency, Brown won in fifty-four of the state's fifty-six counties, and secured nearly 60 percent of the total vote. Just as significantly, Brown entered office with a Democratic majority in the state senate and assembly. California voters had delivered a strong mandate in favor of governmental advocacy and activism.

Once in office, Brown moved quickly to enact his liberal agenda. Several of his proposals simply expanded existing programs. For example, Brown strengthened the state's social safety net by increasing workers' compensation and unemployment benefits, old age pensions, and welfare entitlements. He also continued government support for mental health benefits, education, and highway construction, and he financed programs through tax increases, much as Warren had done in creating his "rainy-day fund."

Brown, however, was a bold innovator. He overcame opposition to the California Water Plan by stressing that it would create thousands of new jobs, benefit the state as a whole, and include adequate environmental safeguards. In a 1960 special election, preceded by an aggressive media campaign designed to convince voters of the plan's merits, Californians approved a $1.7 billion bond measure to fund this unprecedented expansion of the state's water infrastructure. Although Brown backed policies that accommodated economic and urban development, he strengthened government's role in moderating the impact of rapid growth. Under his leadership, the legislature enacted consumer protection and air quality standards and created the Office of Consumer Affairs and an Air Quality Control Board to enforce the new regulations. These agencies, soon followed by others, greatly expanded the state's regulatory framework, and reflected growing public concern over quality-of-life issues.

Brown acted with a similar degree of boldness in reorganizing the state's system of higher education, supporting both the Master Plan and Fisher Act. He also secured legislative support for a series of political reforms proposed by a fellow Democrat, Assemblyman Jesse Unruh. The cross-filing system, modified in 1952, was abolished completely in 1959, generating more spirited electoral contests and partisan debate. Unruh, with Brown's backing, went on to introduce a series of reforms that greatly improved legislative performance and fairness. In 1965 the legislature abandoned the antiquated system of apportioning senators by county and adopted the more equitable practice of allocating representatives by population-based districts. Finally, Unruh and Brown obtained legislative approval to create a Constitutional Revision Commission, charged with increasing the efficiency and upgrading the quality of state government. Commission reforms and supporting legislative measures streamlined executive and legislative bureaucracies and procedures, increased legislators' salaries and staff, established year-round legislative sessions, enhanced city and county control over local affairs, reduced the qualification requirements for ballot initiatives, and afforded greater constitutional protections to California citizens. By the end of Brown's second term, the state had a national reputation for efficient, professional government—a reputation that prompted the American Good Government Society to honor Jesse Unruh with its George Washington Award in 1967.

Brown, acknowledging the support that he received from the state's growing African American population, placed civil rights at the top of his gubernatorial agenda and lobbied tirelessly for legislative approval. His efforts paid off in 1959 when the legislature banned discrimination in the workplace and created a new regulatory agency, the Division of Fair Employment Practices, to enforce the law. The same year, Brown obtained support for an Unruh-sponsored measure that prohibited racial discrimination in public accommodations, business and real estate transactions, and government-funded housing projects. Brown also supported fair housing legislation introduced by William Byron Rumford, a black assemblyman who was first elected in 1948 by a newly enlarged African American constituency in the San Francisco East Bay. In 1963, with Brown's backing, the legislature approved the Rumford Act, a measure banning racial discrimination in the sale and rental of housing.

Although Brown had succeeded in advancing most of his liberal agenda by the end of his first term, he was exhausted by his own high standards and somewhat dispirited by his few failures. He had repeatedly pushed for an increase in the state's minimum wage, only to meet stubborn and effective resistance from agriculture and private industry. He had also lobbied unsuccessfully against California's death penalty, and received negative publicity for delaying the execution of a violent sex offender, Caryl Chessman. Finally, Brown failed to unite his party's delegation behind John F. Kennedy at the 1960 Democratic National Convention. Although Kennedy won the presidential nomination, California Democrats, still divided on Election Day, could not deliver the necessary votes. Kennedy lost in the state by 36,000 votes, which, much to Brown's embarrassment, almost cost Kennedy the presidency.

Brown decided to run for a second term only after Nixon, who had lost the 1960 presidential race, announced his candidacy for governor in 1962. Nixon revived his old red scare tactics and accused Brown of being "soft on Communism." Brown countered by arguing that Nixon, obviously out of touch with the state's major issues, was intent on using the governorship as a "stepping stone to the presidency." Californians, unmoved by Nixon's tired rhetoric, delivered a second mandate for Brown, returning him to office and preserving the Democratic majority in the legislature. Brown's second term, however, presented greater challenges. By the mid-1960s Californians, either alarmed by the scope of reform or impatient with the slow pace of change, undermined liberalism's fragile foundation.

Liberalism at the Municipal Level

On a municipal level, the problems associated with rapid economic and demographic expansion generated a new level of civic activism. In many communities, citizens elected candidates who promised to increase the professionalism and efficiency of city government and actively direct growth in positive directions. At the same time, minority activists joined with organized labor and progressive whites to forge a broader liberal agenda that called on local government to protect and advance civil rights through fair housing and employment legislation, and increased social spending.

In Berkeley, for example, small businessmen whose primary objective was to keep taxes at a minimum by limiting the expansion of municipal services dominated the government. By the late 1940s liberal Democrats, concerned that the city was failing to meet the needs of its growing population—including large numbers of African American newcomers—began to run their own candidates for office. The conservative incumbents fought back by urging voters to "Keep the Communists and Campus Carpet-Baggers Out of City Hall." Working hard to build a broad-based, multiethnic coalition during the next decade, liberals finally secured a majority on the city council and school board in 1961. Even more significantly, two of their winning candidates were black. Wasting no time, the new city government began to fulfill its platform. In early 1963 the council passed a fair housing ordinance, predating the state-level Rumford Fair Housing Act. The same year, the city became the first in the state to adopt a school integration plan. The council also improved recreation facilities in poorer sections of the city and rezoned the flatlands, which contained Berkeley's largest black neighborhoods, to protect low-income housing from speculation and uncontrolled development.

Just to the south, in Oakland, a labor-initiated coalition mounted a similar, although less successful attack against the city's conservative leadership. In 1947 the Oakland Voters League (OVL), uniting left-wing unions, middle-class white liberals, and black migrants, ran candidates for five seats on the city council. Their platform struck a chord with voters. It called for the construction of public housing and schools; increased funding for recreation facilities, public health, and street improvements; the creation of a fair employment commission; the repeal of anti-labor ordinances; and a more equitable tax structure. Four of their five candidates won, giving the OVL just one seat short of a majority on the nine-member council. But conservative forces mounted a successful campaign against their liberal challengers. In the next two elections three OVL representatives were ousted from office after being smeared as pro-Communist. Soon after, the OVL also collapsed and Oakland's conservative leaders enjoyed the political advantage for several years to come.

In Los Angeles yet another liberal coalition won a modest, but more permanent victory. In 1947 Edward Roybal, a Mexican American army veteran and public health worker, ran unsuccessfully for the city council. Following his defeat, Roybal and his supporters formed the Community Service Organization (CSO) to register Mexican American voters and advocate for community improvements. Soon the CSO attracted the attention of the Chicago-based Industrial Areas Foundation, a group that supported grassroots community organizing efforts across the country. The foundation provided the CSO with financial support and the assistance of Fred Ross, one of its seasoned organizers. In 1949 the CSO supported Roybal's second bid for the ninth-district council seat, a district that housed a growing Mexican American population, but also pockets of Jewish, Asian, African American, and Anglo voters. By focusing on issues that directly impacted all ethnic minorities and appealed to liberal whites—particularly the progressive Jewish community—CSO organizers secured Roybal's victory over the incumbent councilman by a vote of 20,472 to 11,956. Once in office, he not only championed fair housing, employment, and educational opportunities, but also risked his political career by opposing a bill requiring city employees to take a loyalty oath. Roybal, the first Mexican American to serve on the council, remained in office until elected to the U.S. House of Representatives in 1962.

Liberal challenges, like those that took place in Berkeley, Oakland, and Los Angeles, permanently altered municipal politics in other cities throughout the state. In some cases liberal coalitions achieved dramatic results, completely upsetting the local balance of power. But even minor victories produced significant changes. Roybal's campaign, for example, emboldened thousands of new voters to demand the respect of elected officials, and encouraged community organizations to pursue their liberal agendas more aggressively. Despite postwar anti-Communist hysteria, changing demographics, postwar prosperity and optimism, and the problems associated with rapid growth generated an unstoppable tide of popular support for visionary, proactive leadership. Beginning close to home, where the impact of change was more immediate, this tide spread outward, sweeping Pat Brown into office in 1958 and handing him a solid mandate for change.

Social and Cultural Dissent

The postwar period, although an era of relative economic prosperity, social harmony, and political stability, contained the seeds of conflict. While the middle class expanded, largely because of state and federal investment in housing, education, and the military-industrial complex, poverty and racial discrimination remained serious problems. The suburban boom, a symbol of the era's prosperity and stability, bypassed ethnic minorities and the poor, and took—as many were beginning to recognize—a tremendous toll on the environment. Even gender roles were in flux, as increasing numbers of married women entered the work force or confronted what Betty Friedan called the "problem that has no name": the isolation, boredom and lack of status associated with suburban domestic roles. The political arena was also charged with tension, roiling with anti-Communist hysteria, blatant opportunism, and bitter contests between liberal and conservative forces. Only in 1958 did the state approach anything remotely resembling a political consensus.

Diversity and Inequality

The state's black population continued to expand during the postwar period, fueled by the baby boom and a steady stream of opportunity-seeking migrants. By the mid-1960s, reflecting a decade of gradual progress, African Americans held four state assembly seats, representing the 17th District in Alameda County, the 18th District in San Francisco County, and the 53rd and 55th Districts in Los Angeles County. Augustus Hawkins, who had served in the assembly since 1934, became California's first black congressman in 1962. Local gains were also impressive, with African Americans obtaining city council seats in Los Angeles, Compton, and Berkeley; school board seats in Oakland, San Francisco, Los Angeles, and Berkeley; and one seat on the San Francisco Board of Supervisors.

These political advances translated into important civil rights victories, particularly on the state level. In 1959 the legislature banned employment discrimination and created the Division of Fair Employment Practices to enforce the new law. It also passed the Unruh Civil Rights Act prohibiting discrimination in public accommodations, business transactions (including real estate), and public housing. Fair housing legislation, although meeting with greater white resistance, followed in 1963. Finally, several municipalities adopted civil rights measures of their own. San Francisco, for example, created a Fair Employment Practices Commission in 1958, and Berkeley enacted a fair housing law and school integration plan in 1963.

Fair employment legislation, combined with political pressure from civil rights groups, produced the most immediate results. State, county, and local government, which expanded rapidly during the postwar period, adopted nondiscriminatory hiring policies in advance of private industry. As a consequence, increasing numbers of African Americans gained access to civil service employment—jobs that offered relatively high wages and occupational security and contributed to the growth of California's black middle class.

However, the political progress that produced such gains was partly a product of black ghettoization. African Americans won representation not in the booming, prosperous suburbs, but in the urban core and within the confines of well-defined black districts or neighborhoods. Fair employment legislation, all too easily circumvented by private employers, did even less to prevent industry from following whites to the suburbs. And fair housing legislation, which should have allowed minorities to participate in the suburban boom, met with bitter opposition and organized resistance. Even after the courts upheld the law, homeowners and lending and real estate agencies continued to ignore its directives. Most African Americans, regardless of their economic status, were trapped.

As white and industrial flight to the suburbs stripped California's inner cities of their tax and employment base, those who remained behind faced increasingly bleak futures. By the mid-1950s the postwar ghetto had taken shape, characterized by high levels of joblessness, dilapidated housing, inadequate police and fire protection, poor recreation facilities, and limited medical and shopping establishments. The spatial and economic marginalization of ghettos was compounded by government-financed freeway projects that destroyed entire black neighborhoods and business districts, and cut residents off from the rest of the city. By 1960, for example, the Watts section of Los Angeles was effectively Balkanized by the very transportation networks that facilitated white and industrial flight to the suburbs. Although 60 percent of its population was young and full of promise, astonishingly high levels of unemployment created a climate of frustration and despair. Over 40 percent of young adults were unemployed, and most of those who were fortunate enough to find jobs worked part time and for low wages.

De facto school segregation also emerged as a serious problem. Most black children attended predominantly black schools, reflecting their increasing spatial isolation from other inner-city neighborhoods and the surrounding suburbs. Although a few cities adopted school integration plans in the early 1960s, most, including Los Angeles, resisted efforts to ensure educational equity well into the 1970s. Even then, citywide desegregation programs were only partially effective. Many white urbanites either placed their children in private schools or relocated to the suburbs. And predominantly white suburban districts, with a surplus of resources, continued to afford richer academic environments than their urban counterparts.

As conditions in ghettos deteriorated, many municipalities adopted urban renewal plans. These efforts to reclaim "blighted" sections of the inner city frequently entailed the wholesale destruction of entire neighborhoods. At best, older single-family homes were replaced with low-income housing projects that confined the poor to even smaller, more isolated enclaves. At worst, as was said at the time, urban renewal amounted to "Negro removal." In West Oakland, for example, city officials razed block upon block of affordable housing without constructing an equivalent number of low-income units.

Despite the shrinking opportunity structure in California's black ghettos, a majority of black activists embraced a civil rights–oriented agenda. Black advancement, they believed, hinged on full integration into the white mainstream—integration that could be achieved through laws that guaranteed equal access to all the rights and privileges of citizenship. By 1963, however, a new generation of activists realized that legislation alone would not eliminate racial discrimination. Some, retaining the liberal optimism of the older generation, turned to non-violent protest to force compliance with the law. Others, particularly those who had been raised in the inner city, had less faith that whites would willingly relinquish their power, or that civil rights legislation would address the deeper, more tangled form of racism so keenly felt by ghetto residents. Postwar California, despite its booming economy and legislative commitment to racial equality, had fostered and ignored the ghettoization of black citizens. Soon the resulting rage and frustration dispelled any lingering fantasies of social harmony and political stability.

The state's Mexican Americans experienced a similar mixture of hope and despair. During the postwar years the Hispanic population not only increased, but also continued to cluster in urban areas. While most of this growth was concentrated in Southern California, newcomers, mostly Mexican Americans from other southwestern states, settled in northern cities as well. Between 1950 and 1960, the Spanish-surnamed population more than doubled in Los Angeles, San Diego, and San José, and increased by almost 90 percent in Fresno and the San Francisco Bay area. Undocumented immigrants, sharply increasing in number following the war, also contributed to this growth and created a painful dilemma for Mexican American activists.

On one hand, undocumented immigrants exacerbated the problems created by the bracero program. They displaced domestic workers in agriculture and industry, depressed wages, undercut unionization efforts, and were perceived as undermining the efforts of long-term residents to combat negative stereotypes and enter the Anglo American mainstream. Moreover, immigration officials frequently violated the rights of citizens and noncitizens alike during neighborhood and workplace "sweeps" for undocumented residents. These Cold War–era roundups, termed "Operation Wetback" by the federal government, resulted in almost two million deportations between 1953 and 1955 and were partly intended to root out alien dissidents. On the other hand, new immigrants and Mexican Americans shared cultural, linguistic, and often family ties. If unified rather than divided by anti-immigrant hysteria, there was a potential for effective political action against prejudice and discrimination.

Regardless of their nationality, both groups did, in fact, have common concerns. By the mid-1960s, 85 percent of the state's Spanish-surnamed population lived in cities, mostly within segregated enclaves or barrios. Like black ghettos, barrios were products of housing discrimination. And like ghettos, they were increasingly isolated from surrounding areas by freeways, and characterized by older, dilapidated housing, overcrowded and underfunded schools, inadequate recreation facilities, declining infrastructure, and high levels of underemployment and unemployment. Residents who found jobs were limited to low-paying, unskilled occupations by discriminatory hiring practices. Even the public sector, while providing new employment opportunities to other ethnic minorities, extended comparatively few jobs to Mexican Americans. Los Angeles County government, for example, employed 28,584 Anglos and 10,807 African Americans in 1964, but only 1,973 Mexican Americans. As a consequence, one in every five families fell below the poverty line, and a majority earned significantly less than the median white income.

Many city officials, rather than addressing these problems, seemed more intent on harassing residents for petty legal violations, keeping them within the confines of the communities, or erasing barrios altogether through urban renewal. In 1957, for example, Mexican American residents were forced out of Chavez Ravine to make room for the new Los Angeles Dodgers Stadium. Residents rightly suspected that their removal was part of a broader, Cold War–inspired effort to curb the growing political and social power of the Mexican American community. Councilman Edward Roybal, objecting to the treatment of a family that resisted displacement, commented: "The eviction is the kind of thing you might expect in Nazi Germany or during the Spanish Inquisition." Even in communities not threatened by urban renewal, residents lived in a chronic state of insecurity. Immigration sweeps and high levels of police brutality and harassment convinced many that the government was an enemy rather than a friend.

In rural areas conditions were even worse, particularly for migrant farm families. Agricultural workers, lacking the protection of minimum wage laws, earned between forty and seventy cents an hour during the 1950s. Even if a worker was employed for fifty hours a week, thirty-five weeks out of the year, earnings still fell well below the official poverty level. And most workers, given fluctuations in the weather and harvest cycle, averaged fewer than thirty-five weeks of annual labor. To survive, entire families, including children, worked together in the fields and moved repeatedly to find as much employment as possible during the year. Housing, if provided at all by growers, frequently lacked heat, running water, and proper sanitation. Although the state established minimum standards for housing and sanitation, most farm labor camps were not inspected on a regular basis and many growers simply ignored the regulations.

Farm workers also suffered from lack of health care. Even those who could afford medical services often had to travel long distances to the nearest clinic or hospital. As a consequence, they had significantly higher infant mortality rates and lower life expectancies than the general population. The 1962 Migrant Health Act, which provided federal funding for state and local health services, provided some relief, but failed to appropriate sufficient resources to meet even the basic needs of most farm workers. Education was yet another problem. Frequent moves interfered with regular school attendance and forced children to adjust to an ever-changing series of teachers, academic expectations, and learning environments. Rural schools, like those in the barrios, were typically segregated, overcrowded, and underfunded. Spanish-speaking students faced even greater difficulties. Not only was English the language of instruction, but students were often punished or ridiculed for speaking Spanish. Moreover, those who failed to keep up were frequently labeled as slow or retarded, and held back or placed on vocational tracks.

Community activists adopted a variety of strategies to address these problems. In urban areas organizations like LULAC and the CSO attacked discrimination, lobbied for community improvements, and encouraged active political participation. Unlike LULAC, however, the CSO attempted to promote unity among Mexican Americans and immigrants by encouraging noncitizens to join and by helping newcomers obtain U.S. citizenship. Indeed, the CSO's bylaws stated that "residents of the community who are not citizens of the United States shall be encouraged to become citizens and to actively participate in community programs and activities that are for the purpose of improving the general welfare." As the CSO spread from Los Angeles to other cities across the state, its inclusive philosophy produced concrete results. By 1955 the organization operated over 450 citizenship-training classes, which by 1960 had helped over forty thousand immigrants obtain citizenship.

The Asociación Nacional Mexico-Americana (ANMA), formed in 1950, was even more determined to break down the barriers that divided immigrants and Mexican Americans. Like the CSO, ANMA emphasized citizenship and political participation. However, it also recognized that political and economic rights were interconnected. To counter economic exploitation, ANMA advocated unionization, building coalitions with other minority groups, and developing stronger connections with underpaid laborers in Mexico and Latin America. ANMA was also one of the earliest Mexican American organizations to emphasize the beauty and richness of Mexican culture, and vigorously attack negative stereotypes. In 1952, for example, it organized a national boycott against the Colgate-Palmolive-Peet Company, the sponsor of a radio show that contained offensive references to Mexican Americans. In Los Angeles, ANMA criticized Weber's Bread Company for using unflattering caricatures in its advertising, and mounted a similar campaign against Hollywood's exploitation of popular stereotypes. Finally, ANMA, like the CSO, gave its support to the Los Angeles Committee for the Protection of the Foreign Born (LACPFB), founded in 1950 to protest an increasingly aggressive federal immigration policy. ANMA was also an outspoken critic of police brutality against barrio residents.

By 1954 ANMA collapsed after its members and leadership were "identified" as Communists or Communist sympathizers by the FBI, and the U.S. attorney general branded it as a "subversive" organization. However, both ANMA and the CSO had succeeded in building electoral interest and activism among the state's Spanish-speaking population. Just as significantly, both organizations helped foster a more positive sense of ethnic identity based on cultural pride and unity, rather than assimilation into the Anglo mainstream. The Mexican American Political Association (MAPA), founded in 1959, used this foundation to demand entry into the state's Democratic Party structure. MAPA, which militantly promoted ethnic solidarity among Mexican Americans and de-emphasized cultural assimilation, devoted itself almost entirely to running candidates for office, voter registration drives, political lobbying, and get-out-the-vote campaigns.

However, neither MAPA nor the CSO, which unlike ANMA weathered the postwar anti-Communist hysteria, spoke directly to the needs of the state's farm workers. The National Farm Workers Labor Union, crippled by the bracero program and lack of funding, made little progress in organizing agricultural workers during the 1950s. Life in California's fields remained one of sharp contrasts: between worker and employer, the poor and the wealthy, Mexicans and Anglos, the powerless and the powerful. In 1962, after the CSO refused to endorse his plan to create a farm workers' union, Cesar Chavez moved his family to Delano and began to pursue his dream. In a few short years his efforts would shake the nation's conscience and inspire a new level of activism among the state's Mexican Americans.

The postwar baby boom and somewhat more liberal immigration laws contributed to the growth of California's Asian American population between 1950 and 1960. While new immigrants tended to cluster in older ethnic neighborhoods, established residents were more widely dispersed. This was particularly the case with Japanese Americans, whose prewar communities had often been appropriated by other ethnic groups during the war. The Japanese American population grew from 84,956 to 157,317 between 1950 and 1960, Chinese Americans from 58,324 to 95,600, and Filipinos from 40,424 to 65,459. The Korean population, while significantly smaller, almost quadrupled during the same period. Much of this increase grew out of U.S. foreign policy during the Cold War. Chinese immigrants, for example, benefited from the Displaced Persons Act of 1948, which granted entry to political refugees of the Communist Revolution. The Refugee Acts of 1953, 1957, and 1958, passed in the wake of the Korean conflict, extended asylum to both Chinese and Korean dissidents. The Walter McCarren Immigration and Naturalization Act of 1952, supported by Asian American organizations like the Japanese American Citizens League (JACL), had an even greater impact. This act modestly expanded immigration quotas for Asian countries and granted the right of naturalization to Japanese, Chinese, and Korean immigrants. The law, by allowing aliens to apply for citizenship, also invalidated the California Alien Land Act, which had prohibited Asian noncitizens from owning property in the state. However, to remove any remaining ambiguity, California voters formally repealed the Alien Land Act in 1956.

The Walter McCarren Act, while dismantling many anti-Asian policies, contained some troubling provisions. It not only called for the detention and deportation of noncitizens suspected of "acts of espionage or sabotage" but also imposed tougher restrictions on illegal immigration. The postwar sweeps and raids of Mexican American barrios and the systematic deportation of outspoken community activists and union organizers were products of this act. Japanese Americans were particularly alarmed over the provision that authorized the creation of detention camps for suspected subversives, and mounted a twenty-year campaign to repeal that section of the law.

The postwar anti-Communist hysteria exerted a chilling influence on some Asian American political activity. On one hand, the government welcomed refugees from Communist countries. On the other, it mounted an aggressive attack against "subversives" from within. Citizens and noncitizens of Chinese and Korean ancestry were understandably reluctant to engage in political activity that might arouse suspicion of disloyalty. Japanese Americans, still traumatized by the ordeal of internment and struggling to reestablish their livelihoods, were also cautious, but less likely to be confused with the new Communist "enemy." This small measure of immunity emboldened Nisei activists to lobby for Issei citizenship rights and the repeal of the McCarren Act's detention clause.

As the anti-Communist hysteria tapered off in the late 1950s, there was a small but notable increase in Asian American political activism. The JACL joined forces with other civil rights groups to protest housing and employment discrimination and to lobby for equal rights legislation. At the same time, political organizations, including the Los Angeles–based West Jefferson Democratic Club, the Nisei Republican Assembly, and the Chinatown Democratic Club, and San Francisco's Chinese Young Democrats and Nisei Voters League, claimed a role in local and state government. Nonpartisan civic organizations, which promoted mutual aid and community service, also expanded to meet the needs of a growing Asian population. The Chinese American Citizens Alliance, the American-Korean Civic Association, and the Filipino Community all helped to foster interest in civic affairs, maintain cultural traditions, and provide services to their respective ethnic groups.

For California's Indian population the postwar period brought both new opportunities and new challenges. Having made substantial contributions to the war effort on the battlefield and home front, Indians joined other minorities in securing their rights and seeking more equitable treatment. In 1944, after decades of lobbying and litigation, California Indians won an award of $5 million for the illegal seizure of tribal land. This award would have been greater if the federal government had not deducted funds that it had spent on reservation supplies and the administration of the Bureau of Indian Affairs in California. Indians immediately protested these deductions by filing suit against the federal government under the Jurisdictional Act of 1928. In response, the government established the Indian Land Claims Commission in 1946, a federal agency empowered to investigate and settle land claims. The following year, in 1947, Indians established a new organization, the Federated Tribes of California, to press the commission for a more just award than the 1944 ruling. Their efforts failed, and in 1951 the original settlement was distributed in per capita payments of $150 per Indian.

Indians, however, continued to file additional claims. Several claims seeking compensation for land west of the Sierra Nevadas were consolidated into a single case. In 1964 the Indian Land Claims Commission approved a settlement of $29,100,000 for 64,425,000 acres of lost territory in this region. After attorney fees were deducted, the award amounted to about forty-seven cents per acre, or six hundred dollars per eligible claimant. This settlement, like the one issued in 1951, left many Indians bitter and disillusioned.

In the middle of these contentious land claim disputes, the federal government adopted a policy of termination that was designed to abolish government oversight and administration of reservations. In California termination began in earnest with the 1958 California Ranchería Act. Under this act, the federal government identified forty-four Indian rancherías as candidates for termination. In exchange for dividing up tribal landholdings among individual members, giving up their status as federally recognized tribes, and relinquishing all claim to all previously provided federal government services, tribes were promised various improvements to housing, schools, roads, sanitation systems, and water supplies. Over the next twelve years twenty-three rancherías and reservations were terminated. As the policy was implemented the federal government failed to provide the promised improvements to infrastructure. Many Indians, disgusted with poor living conditions or too impoverished to pay taxes on their individual allotments, sold their land. Those who remained often faced serious health threats from poor sanitation, contaminated water, and substandard housing. Finally, in some cases, tribal members did not receive allotments at all. As a result of these problems, most "terminated" tribes filed lawsuits against the government and won reinstatement as rancherías or reservations, but this process would take decades.

While termination was being implemented, the Bureau of Indian Affairs adopted a national program that had an indirect impact on California Indians. In 1951 the bureau instituted a voluntary relocation program designed to entice Indians off reservations and into urban areas with the promise of job training programs and other transitional services. This program drew nearly one hundred thousand non-California Indians—Sioux, Navajo, Chippewa, Apache, Mohawk, Shoshone—to Los Angeles and the Bay Area between 1952 and 1968. Many Indians who made the move arrived without the education, work experience, or life skills to survive in an urban environment. Although they received help finding employment, the federal government provided few other support services. Widely dispersed, far from home, and with no established Indian community to receive them, these newcomers faced isolation, loneliness, and alienation.

In time, however, California Indians and these newcomers came together to establish new organizations that addressed their common concerns. In 1961, with the help of the American Friends Service Committee, Indians of both groups established the Intertribal Friendship House in Oakland. The following year, Friendship House activists formed the United Bay Area Council of American Indians. In Los Angeles, in 1958, urban California Indians and newcomers founded the Federated Indian Tribes to promote social events, and preserve traditional customs and values. These and other organizations provided a foundation for the increased intertribal activism of the late 1960s and 1970s.

Student Activism

During the prosperous postwar period, attending college became the norm for middle-class youth. And a college education, although narrowly conceived by campus administrators as training a new generation of technicians and managers, introduced students to a broad spectrum of issues and problems outside of the comfortable confines of suburban communities. Students' very affluence, far from reinforcing the economic or political status quo, provided the freedom to reflect critically on social values and institutions, and ponder their responsibility to "make a difference" in the world. Raised to believe that capitalism and democracy had created a society free of the poverty, inequality, and political repression that plagued other nations, students soon discovered another, deeply flawed America. This awakening, rather than producing cynicism and despair, gave students a sense of purpose. As the "best and the brightest," they could be instruments of social transformation, forcing America to live up to its values.

Student dissent began in 1957 on the Berkeley campus when a small group of activists formed an organization called SLATE. Its members, impatient with the trivial issues that had long dominated student politics, campaigned against compulsory participation in ROTC and against racial discrimination in sororities, fraternities, and other campus organizations. They also pressed for the creation of a cooperative bookstore and a stronger university policy against housing discrimination within the city of Berkeley. While expanding their influence in student government, SLATE members became increasingly active in the surrounding community. In 1959 the group planned an on-campus rally in support of a citywide fair housing initiative sponsored by a local socialist organization. University administrators, invoking a regulation that prohibited campus groups from supporting outside political causes, ordered SLATE to cancel its demonstration. SLATE refused, and over three hundred students attended the rally.

In 1960 SLATE moved beyond the Berkeley community to organize a protest against the House Un-American Activities Committee hearings in San Francisco. Incensed over HUAC's violation of civil liberties in the "defense" of democracy, students were determined to voice their opposition to its hypocrisy. On Thursday, May 12, Berkeley protestors, joined by San Francisco State College students

Bob Donlin, Neal Cassady, Allen Ginsberg, Robert La Vinge, and Lawrence Ferlinghetti (left to right) outside of Ferlinghetti's City Lights Bookstore in San Francisco. Contrast this image with popular depictions of American life during the 1950s. Does anything in the photograph suggest that its subjects are part of a rebellion against conventional norms and values?

and faculty, gathered for a rally and picket at Union Square, and then marched to city hall to observe the hearings. Once there, however, students were denied entry passes. On Friday, hundreds of other students joined the original contingent in demanding admission to the proceedings. Barred again from the hearing room, the protestors staged a peaceful sit-in at city hall. As they sang "We Shall Not Be Moved," armed police officers forcibly ejected them from the building with clubs and high-powered water hoses. Demonstrators and bystanders alike were shocked by the violence of the police response, watching in horror as the "best and the brightest" were "dragged by their hair, dragged by their arms and legs down the stairs so that their heads were bouncing off the stairs." This show of force, however, only strengthened the students' resolve. The next day five thousand protestors gathered at city hall to picket the hearings.

Although SLATE was prohibited from using university facilities and denied on-campus status following the HUAC demonstrations, activism continued to flower on the Berkeley campus. By 1963 students would find yet another cause to champion—the national and local struggle for civil rights.

Cultural Developments

During the late 1940s and early 1950s the San Francisco Bay area provided a haven for radical writers, artists, playwrights, and actors, many of whom had spent the war in prison or in Civilian Public Service camps for refusing military service. Some, influenced by Gandhian nonviolent philosophy, believed that there were moral alternatives to war. Others, influenced by socialist or anarchist beliefs, saw World War II as a struggle between expansionist nations for global dominance—a struggle that imposed suffering on millions of innocent civilians in the service of corporate and state interests. Their views, highly unpopular during the "Good War," met with equal hostility in the Cold War period. However, by creating an intellectual community in San Francisco they not only escaped isolation and ostracism but also produced a literary and artistic renaissance that stood in stark contrast to the generally barren cultural landscape of the 1950s.

The poets and writers of the San Francisco Renaissance, including William Everson and Kenneth Rexroth, broke new literary ground through their conscious "repudiation of received forms" of composition, and their pointed critiques of militarism, consumer culture, corporate greed, government corruption, and social conformity. Renaissance actors and playwrights, lacking a venue to perform works that "were significant and avant-avant-garde," established the Interplayers, one of San Francisco's first repertory theaters. Others, like Roy Kepler and the poet Lawrence Ferlinghetti, opened bookstores that sold controversial literature, hosted poetry readings, and served as social centers for artists and writers. KPFA, the nation's first listener-supported radio station, also emerged out of this cultural ferment, creating an opening on the airwaves for radical, dissenting voices.

By the mid-1950s, this flourishing subculture helped nourish a new literary and artistic movement. In October 1955, San Francisco's Six Gallery hosted a poetry reading that attracted about 150 participants, including the novelist Jack Kerouac and a young, aspiring poet named Allen Ginsberg. Ginsberg's poem entitled "Howl" attacked the spiritual and emotional sterility of postwar culture, and captured the longing of American youth for more than the "ample rewards" of conforming to "the conventions of the contemporary business society."

The critical edge in "Howl" was made even sharper by its strong language and generated a backlash that propelled the "Beat" poets into the national spotlight. In 1956, Lawrence Ferlinghetti published *Howl and Other Poems* out of City Lights, his North Beach bookstore. The police, charging that the volume was "obscene and indecent," confiscated copies of the book. Ferlinghetti fought back in court, obtaining a much publicized and positive verdict that "Howl" was literature, not pornography. Jack Kerouac's *On the Road,* which celebrated the intentional rejection of the work ethic, material success, emotional reserve, and sexual inhibition, was published in the wake of the "Howl" publicity, and added further stimulus to the movement. By the late 1950s, the Bay Area became a mecca for new writers, including Denise Levertov, Philip Whalen, Gary Snyder, Peter Orlovsky, and Ken Kesey. Artists, including Jay "The Rose" DeFeo and Joan Brown, boldly experimented with color, texture, and new materials, adding to this rich cultural environment.

Alan Watts, a scholar and practitioner of Zen Buddhism, influenced this new literary subculture by introducing Beat writers to Eastern religious traditions that emphasized harmony with nature, renunciation of material possessions, voluntary simplicity, pacifism, and faith in internal rather than external sources of authority. By exalting these values, Beat writers moved beyond mere criticism to create an alternative vision of society that sparked the idealism of young Americans and confirmed their faith that they could make a difference in the world. Just as significantly, the Beats' philosophical orientation helped inform the much broader countercultural movement of the 1960s.

After the war, Southern California became a cultural center of national, even international, importance. This transformation began in the 1940s as hundreds of European refugees, including prominent writers, actors, artists, art collectors, and musicians, found a safe haven in the Los Angeles area. Previously recognized for its Hollywood productions, Los Angeles emerged as a serious contender in theater, symphony, and classical and modern art. Across the state popular culture also flourished. Country music, brought to California by white migrants during the Depression and war years, established Bakersfield as the "Nashville of the West" by the early 1960s. Similarly, black migrants transplanted and later adapted their blues tradition, creating a distinct "California" style of playing. In the suburbs of Los Angeles, the Beach Boys put a southland spin on rock music. Their "California sound," celebrating surf, beaches, sunshine, and young love, introduced the nation's youth to the "California Dream." Finally, Disneyland, McDonald's, and Hollywood's new television industry changed family recreation patterns, and placed Southern California at the forefront of consumer culture.

Summary

During the postwar years, California's booming economy and population propelled the state into the national spotlight. Its industrial base, benefiting from federal defense expenditures, not only broke new technological ground, but also attracted thousands of newcomers with the promise of prosperity. Growth, however, placed severe strains on existing infrastructure, and prompted state and local government to invest heavily in education, social services, transportation, recreation, community health, and public works. At the same time, thousands of Californians abandoned the older urban core for new suburban developments. Industry soon followed. This population shift destroyed millions of acres of open space and valuable agricultural land and transferred urban problems like air and water pollution to relatively unspoiled areas. It also reinforced social and economic inequalities. Nonwhites, shut out of the suburban boom by discriminatory housing practices, were left with a declining urban infrastructure, diminishing tax base, and shrinking job prospects. Despite their "ghettoization," ethnic minorities still had cause for optimism. Many Californians, recalling the democratic rhetoric of the war, were concerned about civil rights. Anti-Communist hysteria, while damaging and distracting, failed to extinguish popular support for liberal reform. Moreover, urban ghettos, by concentrating ethnic groups in specific districts, enhanced minority political power. Thus, by the end of the postwar era, African Americans and Mexican Americans achieved significant legislative and political victories on the state and local levels. By the early 1960s, however, serious questions remained. Was civil rights legislation enough to solve the state's "racial dilemma"? Were middle-class values and the suburban lifestyle stifling women and the young? Was postwar expansion extracting too heavy a toll on the environment? These questions, which arose during the 1950s, would find vocal expression during the tumultuous sixties.

Suggested Readings

■ Broussard, Albert, *Black San Francisco: The Struggle for Racial Equality in the West, 1900–1954* (Lawrence: University Press of Kansas, 1993). This book, while covering a broad span of time, provides good coverage of postwar black activism in the San Francisco Bay area.

■ Ceplair, Larry, and Steven Englund, *The Inquisition in Hollywood* (Urbana: University of Illinois Press, 1983). This book places Hollywood's Red Scare within a larger historical context, describes its human costs, and details its lasting impact on the industry.

▪ Dassman, Raymond F., *The Destruction of California* (Tappan, NJ: Macmillan, 1966). This book, a classic primary source, documents the environmental damage that resulted from rapid growth and development during the postwar period.

▪ Davidson, Michael, *The San Francisco Renaissance* (Cambridge: Cambridge University Press, 1989). This book examines the origins, impact, and legacy of the San Francisco Renaissance, culminating with the rise of the Beat Generation.

▪ Douglas, John A., *The California Idea and American Higher Education, 1850 to the 1960 Master Plan* (Stanford: Stanford University Press, 2000). This book provides a historical overview of higher education in California, including a detailed account of the Master Plan.

▪ Galarza, Ernesto, *Farm Workers and Agri-Business in California, 1947–1960* (Notre Dame, IN: University of Notre Dame Press, 1978). This book exposes the human costs associated with agricultural production, including a thorough critique of the bracero program.

▪ Hundley, Jr., Norris, *The Great Thirst: Californians and Water, 1770s–1990s* (Berkeley: University of California Press, 1992). This book provides an overview of the state's water resources, water exploitation, and local, state, and federal water policy.

▪ Lipset, Seymour, and Sheldon S. Wolin, eds., *The Berkeley Student Revolt* (New York: Doubleday-Anchor, 1965). A classic collection of writings on the Berkeley Free Speech Movement and student activism more generally.

▪ Nash, Gerald D., *The American West Transformed: The Impact of the Second World War* (Lincoln: University of Nebraska Press, 1990). This book details the lasting impact that World War II had on Califorinia's economy, including a discussion of the state's emerging electronics and aerospace industries.

▪ Pincetl, Stephanie, *Transforming California: A Political History of Land Use and Development* (Baltimore: Johns Hopkins University Press, 1999). This book provides a comprehensive history of land use, development, and environmental degradation in California.

▪ Schiesl, Martin, ed., *Responsible Liberalism: Edmund G. "Pat" Brown and Reform Government in California, 1958–1967* (Los Angeles: California State University Los Angeles Institute of Public Affairs, 2003). This recent collection of essays provides a good overview of Brown's political philosophy, agenda, and major accomplishments during his two terms as governor.

▪ Williams, James C., *Energy and the Making of Modern California* (Akron: University of Akron Press, 1997). This book provides a comprehensive overview of the state's energy resources, use patterns, regulatory framework, and policy.

11

Contested Visions: Activism and Politics, 1964–1970

Main Topics

▌ Seeds of Change

▌ The Movement Expands

▌ Politics in the Age of Dissent

▌ Summary

In the fall of 1964, Margot Adler left her home in New York City to attend college at U.C. Berkeley. Raised by left-wing parents during the McCarthy era, Margot was no stranger to political activism. Just before her fourteenth birthday she participated in a demonstration against Woolworth's, a national chain store that discriminated against black customers in Greensboro, North Carolina, and in other Southern cities. While still in high school, Margot joined the Congress of Racial Equality (CORE) and a student peace group that organized protests against civil defense drills, the Cold War practice of forcing children under their desks during mock nuclear attacks. Berkeley, with its outstanding academic reputation and "rich history of student activism," was a logical choice for this bright, idealistic young woman. But just as important, it provided Adler with the opportunity "to find a rich and interesting life" of her own.

When she arrived at Berkeley, administrators had just prohibited on- and off-campus organizations from setting up tables at the south entrance of the campus, an area that had long been used by various groups to distribute their literature,

CHAPTER 11	Contested Visions: Activism and Politics, 1964–1970
1962	Edmund G. Brown reelected as governor National Farm Workers Association (later renamed UFW) formed
1964	Rumford Act repealed by Proposition 14 U.C. Berkeley Free Speech Movement
1965	Delano Grape Strike launched Watts Riot Immigration Act abolishes race-based immigration quotas
1966	Black Panther Party established Ronald Reagan elected governor
1967	The Summer of Love Brown Berets established
1968–1969	Third World Strikes at San Francisco State and U.C. Berkeley
1969	Indians of All Tribes occupy Alcatraz Island Activists create People's Park
1970	Chicano Moratorium march and rally against the war in Vietnam; Ruben Salazar killed by Los Angeles Police Department Reagan elected to second term as governor

recruit members, and engage in spirited political debate and discussion. The ban came during the national struggle for civil rights, when many Berkeley students were protesting the discriminatory hiring practices of local businesses such as Mel's Drive-In, the Sheraton Palace Hotel, and the Lucky supermarket chain. Other students had recently returned from Mississippi, where they had spent the summer volunteering with civil rights organizations like the Student Non-Violent Coordinating Committee to register black voters. For local activists and Mississippi volunteers the tables on Bancroft and Telegraph—mistakenly thought by university administrators to be on campus property—were the primary means of attracting support for the growing civil rights movement.

Not surprisingly, student activists, including some from conservative organizations like the Young Republicans, responded to the ban with anger. The university, they charged, cared more about maintaining good relations with local businesses by controlling campus political activity than about the constitutional right of free speech. The ban also brought other issues to the surface. Many felt that it was a paternalistic policy, designed to shelter students from unwholesome or "subversive" ideas—a policy that reflected the administration's assumption that students were incapable of making informed, independent judgments. To others, the prohibition underscored the university's lack of moral direction. Its officials, students maintained, were mainly interested in "turning out corporate drones for industry" rather than in cultivating critical thought, social responsibility, and civic virtue.

These concerns were broad enough to capture the attention of several thousand students, who, like Adler, believed that "the right to political advocacy seemed obvious." Even conservative student groups, usually at odds with "radical" campus activists, joined the emerging Free Speech Movement (FSM). After a semester-long series of protests, arrests, and fruitless negotiations with the administration, student activists obtained the support of the faculty senate. A week later, the Board of Regents struck down all prohibitions against political activity, affirming that students, like all other citizens, were entitled to the protections of the First and Fourteenth Amendments of the U.S. Constitution. For Adler and other FSM activists, the victory struck a deep chord: "We'd done something to transform the world around us, and we were forever marked by the belief that change was possible. It would affect us for life, making us deep optimists about human possibility and influencing every choice from then on."

In the summer of 1965 Adler went to Mississippi to work on a voter registration project sponsored by the Student Non-Violent Coordinating Committee. Returning to Berkeley as a more sober and seasoned activist, Adler joined the movement against the war in Vietnam—a movement that soon spread across the state, generated often-violent confrontations between police and demonstrators, disrupted "business as usual" on college campuses and in surrounding communities, and deeply polarized Californians.

After graduating from Berkeley in 1968 with a degree in journalism, Adler's desire to change the world—to create a society more rooted in cooperation, spiritual values, and meaningful work—continued to shape her life journey. Reflecting back on her experiences, Adler observed: "For all the limitations of my generation—our unconscious actions, our unexamined ideas, our often silly phrases—we were alive to the deepest spiritual values. We believed that exploration was life-long, that one's life work had to be honorable, creative, and transformative. We seldom thought about consumption, or the eventual need to live the good life. . . . We believed that anything was possible and that everything was open to reexamination."

This "ecstatic sense of possibility" was shared by an entire generation of young Californians during the 1960s, and created the foundation for a broad range of social movements that altered the state's cultural, political, and economic fabric. African Americans, Mexican Americans, Indians, and Asian Americans not only opposed persistent patterns of racial discrimination, but also demanded respect and recognition for their cultural institutions and traditions. At the same time, growing numbers of Californians joined the opposition to the war in Vietnam, and a countercultural rebellion against middle-class norms and values.

Two national tragedies, the assassinations of Martin Luther King and Robert Kennedy in 1968, generated even higher levels of activism and confrontation, and heightened the perception that chaos had replaced law and order as the prevailing social force. To many Californians, particularly those outside the process of change, the state and nation as a whole appeared to be coming apart at the seams. In the presidential election of 1968, Richard Nixon adopted the successful strategy of claiming to speak for "the great majority of Americans, the non-shouters, the non-demonstrators . . . those who do not break the law, people who pay their taxes and go to work, who send their children to school, who go to their churches . . . people who love this country [and] cry out . . . 'that is enough, let's get some new leadership.'"

Just as California had led the way for so many of the decade's social movements, it also provided the foundation for the national assault against "disorder" and "chaos." Two years before Nixon's presidential campaign, Ronald Reagan, the state's Republican candidate for governor, foreshadowed Nixon's conservative appeal by blaming the "mess at Berkeley," urban unrest, and moral decline on Pat Brown's liberal administration. He also promised to cut taxes by reducing government spending on social programs "dreamed up for our supposed betterment," and he attacked the Rumford Fair Housing Act for betraying "sacred" property rights. All of these positions appealed to the "forgotten" voters who believed that government was coddling a vocal, disruptive minority at their expense, and who if not racist, were nonetheless anxious about preserving their political, social, and economic privilege. Although Reagan failed to reduce taxes, quell social unrest, or curb the growth of state government, his conservative rhetoric and his apparent sincerity carried him through two terms as governor, revitalized his party on the state and national level, and eventually won him the presidency.

The sixties, perhaps more than any other era, underscored California's national influence and role as a bellwether state. Moreover, the period's social movements helped extend the democratic promise to a broader cross section of the population, created a greater appreciation of cultural diversity, and enhanced the state's reputation for tolerance, openness, and innovation. This, combined with its burgeoning economy, mild climate, and natural beauty, continued to attract thousands of new residents over the decade.

Questions to Consider

- What caused the shift from nonviolent civil rights protest to Black Power? How did the Black Power movement differ from earlier struggles for civil rights?

- Was the formation of the United Farm Workers union a watershed for California's Mexican Americans? Why or why not?

- How did the youth movements of the 1960s, including the countercultural rebellion, affect California's cultural, social, and political institutions?

- What factors contributed to Ronald Reagan's 1966 electoral victory and his subsequent popularity as governor?

Seeds of Change

The decade's social movements began with the African American and farm worker struggles for social, economic, and political equality; growing opposition to the war in Vietnam; and the emergence of the counterculture. These movements, unfolding almost simultaneously, created the foundation for others that occurred later in the decade, as well as a conservative backlash against perceived chaos and disorder.

From Civil Rights to Civil Unrest

During the early 1960s, California's civil rights activists had reason to be optimistic. In 1959 the state legislature passed laws prohibiting discrimination in employment, public accommodations, and business transactions. The Rumford Fair Housing Act, passed in 1963, banned racial discrimination in housing. Moreover, a few cities had started to address the problem of de facto school segregation by adopting various integration plans like busing students to schools outside of their mostly all-white or all-black neighborhoods. Not all Californians, however, complied with the new legislation or approved of school integration. In response, black activists, white liberals, and idealistic youths joined forces to combat persistent patterns of racial discrimination.

The Congress of Racial Equality (CORE), which had a long history of civil rights activism in the Northeast and South, contributed to the leadership of California's emerging struggle for racial equality. Like their parent organization, the state's first CORE chapters adopted the philosophy and tactics of Gandhian nonviolence and worked closely with older civil rights organizations like the NAACP. In 1963, for example, CORE activists joined the NAACP in a series of protests against housing discrimination and de facto school segregation in Los Angeles. To the north, in the Bay Area, CORE and its supporters focused on employment discrimination, organizing pickets and sit-ins at businesses that refused to hire black workers. Mel's Drive-In chain, the target of an extensive picket campaign in 1963, was forced to revise its hiring policies. The following year, CORE organized protests against Lucky supermarkets, Bank of America, the Sheraton Palace Hotel, and automobile dealerships with similar results.

Berkeley Free Speech demonstration. The 1964 Free Speech Movement on the U.C. Berkeley campus ushered in a decade of political and cultural activism among young Californians. How do you think older residents reacted to images of young, relatively privileged college students challenging the authority of university administrators and the Board of Regents?

The participation of many University of California, Berkeley, students in the Bay Area demonstrations prompted campus administrators to institute the ban on "free speech" described in the beginning of this chapter. In the fall of 1964 the stage was set for confrontation between student activists and university officials. Stung by charges that the campus had become a haven for radical agitators, administrators began to enforce restrictions on student political activity. But students, having gained a sense of their own power and significant organizing experience, mounted a formidable counterattack—one that forced the administration to revoke its ban, and propelled students toward an even higher level of civil rights activism.

These modest and often token victories convinced movement participants that America's democratic promise might soon be extended to all citizens. National events contributed to their euphoria and sense of possibility. The civil rights movement in the South was forcing an entire nation to confront its history of racial discrimination and violence, and generated an unprecedented level of unity among white and black activists. The 1963 March on Washington, where Martin Luther King Jr. delivered his deeply moving "I Have a Dream" speech, attracted a quarter of a million participants and dramatically underscored the seemingly unstoppable momentum of the movement. And a new president, Lyndon B. Johnson, not only responded to the march with federal civil rights legislation, but also promised to wage an all-out "War on Poverty." For the thousands of ghetto residents trapped in poverty, Johnson's economic opportunity bill raised hope that their government had not forgotten them. The Economic Opportunity Act, passed in August of 1964, established the Job Corps to train youths for gainful employment, VISTA (a domestic version of the Peace Corps), and a Community Action Program that provided millions of dollars in federal aid to impoverished areas. To be eligible for Community Action funding, cities had to comply with a "maximum feasible participation" mandate that involved the poor in the allocation and administration of antipoverty monies. This, too, helped convince activists and ghetto residents that change was possible.

By late 1964, however, optimism began to fade. In November, California's voters repealed the Rumford Fair Housing Act by approving Proposition 14, a ballot initiative sponsored by the state's real estate industry. The proponents of the proposition claimed that government had violated the sacred right of citizens to do what they wished with their own property. In reality, however, the initiative's backers wanted to preserve all-white neighborhoods from black encroachment and the perceived threat of declining property values. For civil rights activists and ghetto residents the message was clear: Californians, by a two-to-one margin, had registered—in Pat Brown's words—a "vote for bigotry." Although the state supreme court reinstated the Rumford Act in 1966, a decision upheld by the U.S. Supreme Court in 1967, the damage had been done.

At the same time, the War on Poverty, which had promised relief to the state's ghetto residents, was off to a rocky start. In Oakland, one of the first cities in the nation to receive federal antipoverty funds, the mayor handpicked members of the Economic Development Council, the agency responsible for deciding how federal monies would be allocated. As a consequence, federal funding was diverted into large-scale capital improvement projects that had little impact on living conditions in poor neighborhoods. Even job training programs generated disillusionment. Bobby Seale and Huey Newton, two young participants in the city's War on Poverty program, soon concluded, "employment training programs have become an acknowledged hustle, since few jobs are available at the end of the training program." Like others of their generation, they had observed the negative impact of white and capital flight from their community, and they recognized that jobs, rather than job training, were crucial to their survival.

Nevertheless, Oakland's share of federal funding did provide some relief. Large capital improvement projects, while neglecting the needs of poor neighborhoods, provided much needed jobs for city residents. And young people were paid while enrolled in job training programs. This was not the case in Los Angeles, where War on Poverty funds were held up because city officials refused to comply with the maximum feasible participation mandate of the federal government. By the long, hot summer of 1965, residents of Watts had ample reason to be angry and frustrated. Freeways separated their community from the rest of the city. Urban renewal programs had destroyed black businesses and affordable housing. Jobs and white residents had fled to the suburbs, leaving ghetto residents with few employment opportunities, underfunded all-black schools, deteriorating public facilities, and overcrowded, dilapidated housing stock. Housing discrimination, recently upheld by Proposition 14, and a woefully inadequate public transportation system cut off all avenues of escape. City officials, by failing to obtain federal relief monies, contributed to the growing sense of isolation and despair felt by many Watts residents. Finally, police–community relations had reached an all-time low. Black citizens repeatedly accused officers of ignoring due process, excessive use of force, and being "disrespectful and abusive in their language or manner." Viewed as a brutal, occupying army, the mostly white police department served as a catalyst for mounting discontent.

On Wednesday, August 11, 1965, police patrolling Watts arrested Marquette Frye and his brother for drunken driving. Frye's mother, who arrived at the scene with several other observers, was handcuffed when she protested the arrests. Bystanders reported that the police hit Marquette on the head, placed a gun to his temple, and roughly tossed all three family members into an officer's car. The crowd was further inflamed by a rumor that police had attacked an innocent onlooker. More residents soon gathered as charges of police brutality circulated through the neighborhood. Alarmed officers radioed for backup, but the increased police presence and overreaction provoked the crowd. That evening, violence broke out but was contained within a small area, and largely limited to attacks on police officers, white drivers, and television crews. However, the next day, African American community leaders, fearing the worst, appealed to police to replace white patrols with African American plainclothes officers and convinced the media to allow a respected minister to make a televised plea for peace. Both measures failed. The Los Angeles Police Department refused to assign

African American officers to Watts, and the minister's appeal aired before most viewers had tuned in for the evening.

Beginning on Thursday night and lasting until Monday morning, the Watts uprising took a heavy toll. Crowds moved into the vicinity of the initial altercation, spread out into central Watts, and then moved outward, toward downtown Los Angeles. Venting years of anger and frustration, nearly ten thousand participants looted and burned hundreds of mostly white-owned businesses, resulting in $40 million in property damage. After order was restored by the National Guard, at least thirty-four had died, thirty-one of them black. Hundreds of others were seriously injured, and almost four thousand had been arrested. Although many participants claimed that the riot had forced whites to take note of ghetto conditions, the uprising produced few concrete changes. City officials created a board to administer antipoverty funds immediately after the riot, providing short-term relief to residents. However, little was done to address chronic unemployment, de facto school segregation, housing discrimination, and police brutality. Watts, like the state's other black ghettos, stood in stark contrast to the burgeoning, prosperous suburbs.

The riot, however, marked a transition from nonviolent civil rights activism to more militant assertions of Black Power. Proposition 14, which repealed the Rumford Fair Housing Act, was identified as a contributing cause of the uprising, and it provided tangible evidence of white hostility to racial equality and integration. Moreover, the riot exposed conditions in Watts that clearly defied liberal solutions. African Americans, raised in impoverished inner cities, derived little comfort from Lucky's promise to hire more black workers. Not only did ghettos lack supermarkets where residents could buy fresh, affordable food; they also lacked the public transportation systems that linked workers to jobs. As one black leader observed toward the end of the sixties, the earlier generation of activists "retained their profound faith in America, her institutions, her ideals, and her ability to achieve some day a society reflecting those ideals." Increasingly, however, "there is a growing and seriously held view among some militant Negroes that white people have embedded their own personal flaws so deeply in the institutions that those institutions are beyond redemption."

Black Power

Throughout the nation, from California's inner cities to the Mississippi Delta, young activists embraced more radical solutions to persistent patterns of racial discrimination—solutions that turned on the slogan "Black Power" and included militant assertions of cultural pride, community self-defense and determination, solidarity with Third World peoples, and socialist critiques of capitalism. Stokely Carmichael, who coined the term "Black Power" at a June 1966 civil rights rally in Mississippi, ushered in the change: "The only way we are gonna stop the white men from whuppin' us is to take over. We been saying freedom for six years and we ain't got nothin'. What we gonna start saying now is Black Power!" The shift away from nonviolent civil rights activism to black self-determination alienated many formerly sympathetic whites and moderate black leaders from the emerging movement. For years white and black activists had worked together toward the goal of creating an integrated, color-blind society. Now a new generation of black youths insisted on charting their own course, which in Carmichael's words included "the right for black people to define their own terms, define themselves as they see fit."

Four months after Carmichael's Mississippi speech, Huey Newton and Bobby Seale, two young Merritt College students, founded the Black Panther Party in Oakland, California.

The Panthers' platform demanded full employment, decent housing, an end to police brutality, the "power to determine the destiny of our community," and education that "teaches us our true history and our role in the present day society." It also called on the government to release black people from prison "because they have not received a fair and impartial trial," and demanded exemption from military service because "we will not fight and kill other people of color in the world who, like black people, are being victimized by the white racist government of America." What shocked whites the most, however, was the organization's position on self-defense. Citing the Second Amendment of the Constitution, the Panthers asserted their right to bear arms in defense of "our black community from racist police oppression and brutality."

The Panthers' crusade against police brutality, which emphasized self-defense, placed them in the media spotlight and precipitated a series of violent confrontations with law enforcement. Upon forming the party, Newton and Seale recruited residents of Oakland's ghetto to trail police and ensure that officers did not violate the constitutional rights of those they questioned or arrested. These citizen patrols, armed with guns and legal statutes, captured the media's attention and overshadowed the party's less controversial after-school and free-breakfast programs for children, community clinics, voter registration drives, and concern for education and prison reform. The Panthers, however, often encouraged publicity that emphasized their militancy. In 1967, as the state legislature debated a new gun control measure aimed at curbing militant activism, armed party members converged on the state capitol and demanded access to the proceedings. The confrontation, aired on the national news, contributed to the organization's growing popularity with black inner-city youths and self-described white "revolutionaries," but fueled white fears of black insurrection. The police, sharing this fear, intensified their efforts to suppress the party, leading to a series of violent confrontations where the distinction between victim and perpetrator was often blurred. In 1967, Huey Newton, the party's minister of defense, was arrested following an altercation with the Oakland police that left one officer dead and Newton and another officer injured. Charged and convicted of manslaughter, Newton later won release because of ambiguities in police evidence and testimony. In 1968, the party's minister of education, Eldridge Cleaver, was arrested following another confrontation with the Oakland police in which two officers were wounded and a Panther killed. Cleaver, free on bail, ran as the Peace and Freedom Party's presidential candidate in 1968, but later fled the country to avoid what many activists believed would be a politically charged trial.

Black Panther "Free Huey" demonstration in front of Oakland City Hall. The media, through photographs like this one, often underscored the anger and frustration of Black Power activists. How do you think white Californians reacted to such images? How did the photographer's choices shape and mirror racial attitudes and stereotypes toward African American militants?

As the Black Panther Party spread across the nation, federal, state, and local governments took extreme and sometimes illegal measures to curb militant activity. The FBI, which regarded the Panthers as a threat to internal security, used paid informants both to supply detailed intelligence and to instigate violence where police use of excessive force could be justified. In 1968 alone, local police across the nation killed twenty-eight Panthers and arrested hundreds of others. By the mid-1970s, the party was in disarray, torn apart by bloody confrontations with law enforcement, internal divisions, and the deaths or imprisonment of its leadership. However, it left a significant legacy. The party's emphasis on community empowerment encouraged the black electorate to demand a greater share of political power in the nation's inner cities. In Oakland, for example, the party helped register thirty thousand new voters for the 1972 mayoral election. Stunning the city's political establishment, Bobby Seale, the Panthers' candidate for mayor, came in second, drawing 43,749 votes to the Republican incumbent's 77,634. The Panthers went on to help organize voter support for John George, who became Alameda County's first black supervisor in 1976, and Lionel Wilson, who became Oakland's first black mayor in 1977. Just as significantly, the Panthers' demand for "an educational system that will give our people a knowledge of self" helped ignite the student movement for black and ethnic studies programs and a more general assertion of cultural pride and identity. Rather than basing self-worth on white standards, an entire generation of young minorities reclaimed and celebrated their own history and culture.

Poverty in California's inner cities generated yet another movement of national significance. The welfare rights movement began in Alameda County in 1962 when fire struck the house of a welfare recipient. The welfare office withheld the woman's monthly check because "she was living in unfit housing." With seven young children in her care, the woman desperately turned to other recipients who then began to share similar stories of callous and disrespectful treatment. A permanent organization soon took root, spreading to inner cities throughout California. One of their earliest battles took place in Alameda County. In 1964, the state ended the bracero program, which had transported over five million Mexicans to work in California's fields. Strawberry growers in the northern part of the state complained of labor shortages. Shortly thereafter, the county sent notice to welfare recipients that they would lose their benefits if they failed to take field jobs. However, if recipients took such work they would be identified as "gainfully employed" and would still lose their benefits. Simultaneously, the county began withholding public assistance from new welfare applicants, claiming that agricultural jobs were readily available. The new Welfare Rights Organization (WRO) responded by stating that recipients, many of whom were skilled and semiskilled workers displaced by capital flight to the suburbs, would not be able to find substitute, higher-paying jobs in manufacturing if forced to work in the fields. The WRO then staged a sit-in at the county welfare office and threatened to take similar action in front of the state welfare department in San Francisco. As a consequence, the state allowed those who took agricultural jobs to retain their benefits, but still failed to address the more serious problem of forcing displaced workers into low-wage farm labor.

Emboldened by their partial victory, the WRO went on to lobby successfully for increases in general assistance, an end to waiting periods or residency requirements for benefits, and a complete ban on mandatory farm labor during all but the summer months. Even more significantly, welfare recipients began to challenge the authority of social service providers and the mythology that poor people are responsible for their own condition. As one WRO activist stated, "We are human beings just like everybody else. . . . We don't get the taxpayers' money free. We play the lowest games to get that money. You have to be harassed the whole month to get $200 from the welfare." She went on to enumerate the obstacles women faced in finding gainful employment, including lack of funds for transportation and child care. For her and other welfare recipients, however, the bottom line was the lack of decent-paying employment within inner cities. As the WRO spread across the nation, attracting thousands of members and support from progressive organizations, it successfully lobbied for increased aid and the liberalization of eligibility requirements. While this provided immediate relief to many impoverished families, it failed to stem the continuing economic decline of urban ghettos. By the mid-1970s the movement and its hard-won gains fell victim to the recession and fiscal conservatism of a new federal administration.

The WRO and Black Panther Party, while relatively short-lived, had a more enduring impact on California politics. Early black activism focused on integration and inclusion, revealing a liberal optimism that fair housing and employment legislation, if implemented, would solve persistent patterns of racial inequality. The Black Power movement, growing out of the noticeable toll that white and capital flight had taken on the state's inner cities, abandoned the politics of inclusion in favor of militant contestations over urban political power and economic resources. For example, as War on Poverty funds poured into urban areas in the wake of the Watts riot, residents demanded a greater role in deciding how the money would be spent. In Oakland, poor residents challenged the mayor's policy of handpicking the Economic Development Council. By 1967, they gained control of the council and began redirecting funds to neighborhood-based development projects. Emboldened by their success, Oakland's black community moved on to obtain a greater role in municipal governance, and ultimately became the dominant force in city politics. This pattern of political activism produced concrete results in other cities as well. And gains on the state and federal levels were equally impressive. In 1970, the black vote sent Ronald Dellums to Congress and seated Wilson Riles as the state superintendent of public instruction. In 1972, Yvonne Burke followed Dellums to Washington, and Mervyn Dymally, seated as lieutenant governor, joined a growing contingent of black state legislators in Sacramento.

Municipal power, however, raised a thorny question—one that is still unresolved. According to one observer, cities like Oakland had merely fulfilled "a cynical prediction of the central cities of the future; that as blacks and other minorities gain political office and a voice in governmental affairs, whites' exodus out to the suburbs, and most importantly the major industries which carry a large load of the tax burden follow them. Non-whites gain office to control, but they in effect control nothing because there are no industries and no money. The city becomes yet a larger ghetto, controlled and dependent upon forces from outside." As the Black Power movement waned, California's African American population turned elsewhere for solutions to the state's continuing racial dilemma.

Justice in the Fields

In the midst of growing urban unrest, Cesar Chavez launched a revolution in California's fields. When he returned to Delano in April of 1962, farm workers' living and working conditions were much the same as they had been two decades earlier. Federal and state laws that granted other workers a minimum wage, social security, unemployment insurance, and the right to organize and bargain collectively did not apply to agricultural labor. And the bracero program, providing growers with an unlimited, subsidized work force, kept wages for domestic workers artificially low and made unionization virtually impossible. Against these odds, Chavez began to build a grassroots union that was philosophically committed to participatory democracy, dignity for the common person, nonviolence, and multiethnic unity and cooperation.

With a small team of talented organizers, including Dolores Huerta, Gilbert Padilla, Julio Hernandez, and Jim Drake, Chavez slowly built the organization's

Cesar Chavez in 1965 during the Grape Strike at J. D. Martin Ranch. What does this image convey about Cesar Chavez? What information about his character can you gather from his posture, facial expression, dress, and placement next to other objects in the frame?

membership by going from door to door and town to town, and providing practical services to farm worker families. By September of 1962, the union had built a strong enough base to hold its founding convention. There, delegates voted to name the organization the National Farm Workers Association (NFWA), adopt the black eagle against a white and red background as its emblem, and accept "Viva la Causa" as the union's motto. Delegates also approved monthly membership dues of $3.50, and elected Chavez as president, and Huerta and Padilla as vice presidents.

The new organization, while attracting additional members and volunteers, barely survived the next two years. By 1965, however, the tide had turned. The government finally terminated the bracero program, making it more difficult for growers to use an imported labor force to break strikes and block unionization efforts. The nonviolent civil rights movement in the South had also captured national attention, and created a groundswell of public concern over social and economic inequalities. Liberal Protestant and Catholic clergy and student activists who had championed racial justice in Alabama, Georgia, and Mississippi, now had a compelling cause much closer to home.

The catalyst for liberal support was the Delano Grape Strike, initiated by Filipino farm workers on September 8, 1965. Growers in the San Joaquin Valley, determined to keep wages low, continued to pay domestic workers less than what braceros had received. In response, Filipino members of the Agricultural Workers' Organizing Committee (AWOC), an AFL-CIO affiliate, voted to strike. Their demand was wage parity with braceros, or a modest $1.40 an hour. The growers, including agribusiness giants like the Di Giorgio Corporation, not only refused to meet their demands, but also evicted Filipino workers from labor camps and called in the local police to intimidate strikers. Larry Itliong, the leader of the strike, turned to the fledgling National Farm Workers Association for support. Chavez, in a rousing appeal to his membership, stated: "The strike was begun by Filipinos, but it is not exclusively for them. Tonight we must decide if we are to join our fellow workers in this great labor struggle."

The strike soon gained national attention and support. Student volunteers and clergy flocked to Delano to offer their assistance and helped raise money in college communities and among their congregations. Unions, including the formidable United Auto Workers, pledged their financial support and generated sympathy for "la Causa" among urban blue-collar workers. Luis Valdez, a member of the San Francisco Mime Troupe, returned to his roots in Delano and organized *El Teatro Campesino* (the farm worker theater) to dramatize the unfair treatment of farm labor. El Teatro, which performed to migrant audiences in the fields, helped recruit union members. Its actors, all campesinos, also toured college campuses, urban barrios, and various towns and cities to raise funds for the strike. Finally, Chavez called on the public to support a national boycott of products produced by Delano's largest growers.

Additional support flooded in during and after the union's twenty-five-day procession from Delano to Sacramento in the spring of 1966. Carrying union banners, images of the Virgin of Guadalupe, and Mexican and American flags, striking workers and their supporters made the 250-mile journey in the spirit of a religious pilgrimage, as "an excellent way of training ourselves to endure the long, long struggle." Many who witnessed the march as it aired on the evening news or passed through local communities were deeply moved by the spiritual discipline, humility, and poverty of the participants. The farm workers who made the journey had indeed drawn strength from their Catholic religious traditions to endure the economic hardship of a prolonged strike. Many had lost their homes and were forced to rely on the union's meager resources for food, clothing, and shelter.

The march touched America's moral conscience and placed additional pressure on growers to meet the strikers' demands. Even before the procession reached Sacramento, Schenley Corporation, a producer of wine grapes, gave formal recognition to the union by signing a contract. A rumor that New York bartenders were planning to boycott Schenley products, and the Teamsters' Union's refusal to cross picket lines at the company's San Francisco warehouse, helped convince Schenley to enter into the agreement. Soon after, other major winemakers, including the

Christian Brothers, Almaden, Paul Masson, Gallo, Franzia, and Novitiate, signed contracts. Di Giorgio, whose products were marketed under the S&W and Tree Sweet labels, agreed to allow its workers to vote on whether they wanted union representation.

The Teamsters' Union, which had backed the strike, became increasingly concerned that the NFWA's organizing efforts would disrupt the work schedules of its packers and truckers, and place a drain on union resources. Thus, the Teamsters, in collusion with Di Giorgio, announced that it would compete with the NFWA to represent workers in the upcoming election. Worried that a Teamsters victory might result in a "sweetheart" contract that would fail to improve the wages and working conditions of agricultural labor, the NFWA decided to merge with AWOC to create a united front, affiliated with the AFL-CIO, against their new opposition. Their strategy succeeded. In the August 1966 election, Di Giorgio's workers returned 331 votes in favor of Teamster representation and 530 votes for the newly formed United Farm Workers Organizing Committee (UFWOC-AFL-CIO). However, even after farm workers voted in favor of union representation, Di Giorgio failed to reach an agreement with UFWOC until April 1967.

Despite these major gains, the majority of the state's table grape growers refused to recognize or negotiate with the UFWOC. In 1968 Chavez mounted a national boycott against all table grapes that forced most of the remaining growers to sign contracts with the union by July 1970. The victory, representing the greatest advance for farm labor in American history, came at a high price. In Chavez's words: "Ninety five percent of the strikers lost their homes and cars. But I think that in losing those worldly possessions they found themselves, and they found that only through dedication, through serving mankind, and, in this case, serving the poor, and those who were struggling for justice, only in that way could they really find themselves."

The Antiwar Movement and the Counterculture

The civil rights, Black Power, and farm workers' movements of the sixties paralleled America's growing involvement in the Vietnam War. Although a broad cross section of California's population joined antiwar protests, college students formed the backbone of the movement. By 1965 campus teach-ins on America's role in Vietnam crystallized student opposition to the war. And for the next seven years, activists tried to disrupt "business as usual" on college campuses and in surrounding communities. Their protests, while convincing many citizens and policymakers that unrest at home was too high a price to pay for the war abroad, prompted others to call for the restoration of law and order. Combined with ethnic power movements, the antiwar opposition polarized the state's residents and destroyed the last vestiges of the postwar liberal consensus.

Emboldened by their free speech victory at the end of 1964, Berkeley students embraced a new cause. In the spring of 1965, over twelve thousand students and faculty held a two-day teach-in on the Vietnam War. A series of protests followed, directed at the university's ROTC program, military-related research, and policy of allowing defense industry job recruiters on campus. Their antiwar fervor was also fueled by California's role as a major staging ground for the war in Southeast Asia. Troops, supplies, and military hardware were all deployed from state bases, often along highly visible rail lines and roadways. Teach-ins and protests soon spread to other colleges, creating the foundation for a statewide antiwar movement.

By 1967 many students throughout California had joined the Resistance, an antidraft organization that asserted that "the War in Vietnam is criminal," and "we must act together, at great individual risk to stop it. . . . To cooperate with conscription is to perpetuate its existence, without which the government could not wage war. We have chosen to openly defy the draft and confront the government and its war directly." In addition to providing draft counseling and coordinating antiwar protests, the movement called on its supporters to "move from protest to resistance," to shut down the "war machine." In October of 1967, during "Stop the Draft Week," protestors marched on the Oakland Induction Center, where draftees and recruits were processed for military service. Police in riot gear blocked their attempt to surround and shut down the center. However, the protestors, donning hard hats and homemade shields, regrouped and briefly took control of the facility and surrounding neighborhood following a pitched street battle with the vastly outnumbered police.

Other protests, often violent and confrontational, followed the Tet Offensive in 1968, the U.S. invasion of Cambodia in 1970, and the release of the Pentagon Papers and the U.S. invasion of Laos in 1972. When the war finally ended in 1973, it had taken a frightening toll. Military expenditures had diverted resources from antipoverty programs and plunged the state into economic recession. Thousands of young Californians lost their lives in the war, and those who survived received little assistance in coping with physical and psychological trauma. By 1979, when Congress finally appropriated funds to provide outreach services to veterans, many had already suffered irreversible damage from substance abuse, posttraumatic stress disorder, and exposure to the defoliant known as Agent Orange.

The antiwar movement also exposed deep political rifts. Many old-guard liberals and labor leaders were unwilling to break ranks with Lyndon B. Johnson over his foreign policy. On the other hand, left-wing Democrats called for an end to the conflict and a renewed commitment to ending racism and poverty. By the end of the decade the Democratic Party, on both state and national levels, was deeply divided. Conservative Republicans capitalized on this division and the mounting fears of many ordinary Californians to create a new coalition of "Forgotten Americans"—Americans who were more concerned about curbing government expenditures and militant protest than social and economic reform. This coalition, abandoning the liberal agenda of the postwar era, would shape state and national politics for years to come.

Although many youths retained their commitment to nonviolent social change, they had grown more suspicious of their government. Indeed, some members of the protest generation lost faith in political leaders and institutions and launched violent attacks against the "establishment." For example, the Symbionese Liberation Army, a small fringe group that viewed itself as the revolutionary vanguard, assassinated Oakland School Superintendent Marcus Foster, robbed a series of banks, and kidnapped newspaper heiress Patricia Hearst. After a violent confrontation with police in 1975, the "Army" briefly regrouped, robbing more banks and killing a female bank customer, before its remaining members were arrested or driven into hiding. Four members of the group, who remained in hiding until recently, were finally caught, prosecuted, and sentenced in 2001 and 2002.

By mid-decade growing numbers of young Californians embraced cultural rebellion as well as political protest. The Vietnam War, persistent patterns of racial discrimination, the conservative social values of the older generation, and disillusionment with mainstream political leadership prompted many youths to experiment with alternative lifestyles. Accusing their elders of creating a society based on material greed, competition, violence, and the repression of emotion and sexual desire, these cultural rebels sought liberation through communal living, free love, "mind-expanding" drugs, and psychedelic music. By separating themselves from the world of their parents, they hoped to create a parallel, or counter, culture that would serve as a model to the rest of society. Although some abandoned electoral politics and political protest as an avenue of social change, they nonetheless saw themselves as activists—as pioneers of a new, more peaceful, spiritual, and egalitarian social order.

An earlier generation of cultural rebels, the Beats, played a pivotal role in launching the state's countercultural revolution. In 1963 novelist Ken Kesey used the profits from his book, *One Flew Over the Cuckoo's Nest,* to start a commune in the Santa Cruz Mountains. Its members, calling themselves the Merry Pranksters, toured around the state in a brightly painted bus championing the virtues of psychedelic drugs and flouting middle-class behavioral conventions. Using LSD, a hallucinogenic drug produced by Augustus Owsley Stanley III, the son of a U.S. senator, the Pranksters went on to sponsor a series of "acid tests." Participants, often numbering in the thousands, danced to new bands like the Grateful Dead while under the influence of LSD that had been provided by "test" organizers. From that point on, hallucinogenic drugs became an integral part of the decade's cultural revolt. Following the lead of Kesey and Harvard psychologist-turned-drug-prophet Timothy Leary, young rebels sincerely believed that psychedelic drugs were a gateway to higher consciousness, the key to creating a social order based on cooperation, sensual openness, creative expression, and unity with nature.

By the mid-sixties, San Francisco's Haight Ashbury District became the center of the emerging counterculture. Lined with communal "crash pads," drug paraphernalia and poster shops, hip clothing boutiques, bead stores, and a growing contingent of longhaired, colorfully attired "flower children," its streets attracted national media attention. Much of the publicity emphasized the kooky and seamy side of the hippie lifestyle, portraying its adherents as unkempt, drugged-out hedonists. But this only added to the Haight's mystique among the young who flocked to San Francisco by the tens of thousands. This influx was so significant that it was popularized in a hit song. Musician Scott MacKenzie, in "Are You Going to San Francisco," urged the would-be traveler to "be sure to wear flowers in your hair."

A new form of rock music, often performed in accompaniment with light shows, also helped establish San Francisco as the center of the countercultural revolution. The "San Francisco sound," or acid rock, developed by local bands such as the Grateful Dead, Jefferson Airplane, Country Joe and the Fish, and Big Brother and the Holding Company not only celebrated drug use but also underscored other themes of the movement: peace, open sexual expression, racial unity, cooperation, and alienation from mainstream society. Performed at San Francisco's Fillmore Auditorium, Avalon Ballroom, and outdoor parks and amphitheaters, the music drew thousands of youths together in celebration of their new collective identity. Like drugs, rock music was viewed as an agent of social liberation. In the words of Ralph Gleason, a local music critic, "at no time in American history has youth possessed the strength it possesses now. Trained by music and linked by music, it has the power for good to change the world." Many older Americans saw things differently. Whereas the Beach Boys promoted a wholesome, "fun in the sun" image of California, these bands seemingly encouraged reckless experimentation with sex and drugs, and rebellion against parental authority.

Sexual experimentation now entailed a lower risk of pregnancy because of the development of reliable contraceptives, and thus it became the third cornerstone of the youth culture. Public nudity, casual sex, open displays of affection, and the use of sexually explicit language were viewed as political attacks against "uptight Amerika" as well as expressions of personal liberation. The pursuit of sexual pleasure, however, did not necessarily include the revision of traditional gender roles. Among both political and cultural rebels, men continued to monopolize positions of authority and power and to relegate women to subordinate or supporting roles. Indeed, the antiwar movement, with its emphasis on the heroism and sacrifice of male draft resisters, relegated women's issues and concerns to the back burner. War resistance slogans like "Girls Say Yes to Men Who Say No!" reinforced the notion that sexual availability was a measure of women's political commitment. Within the counterculture this pressure intensified. Women who wanted the emotional security, intimacy, and stability of monogamous relationships were accused of being repressed, uptight, or brainwashed by their puritanical parents.

Within a few years the contradiction between the movement's goal of creating a nonhierarchical, cooperative society and women's lived experience generated a powerful new feminist movement. For the time being, though, youthful rebels continued to elaborate on their counterculture. The underground press, including the *Los Angeles Free Press,* the *Berkeley Barb,* and the *San Francisco Oracle,* promoted both political and cultural defiance. Similarly, underground posters, comics, radio, film, and theater disseminated alternative values and reinforced a shared sense of purpose and unity. Urban and rural communes proliferated throughout the state as hippies or flower children sought to live their vision of a more humane, cooperative, decentralized social order. The Diggers, a San Francisco anarchist group, provided free food on the streets and in parks. People discarded unwanted clothing in "free boxes." And sympathetic health professionals organized free clinics.

By the end of 1969, however, the counterculture was in decline. The "Summer of Love" had attracted thousands of young people to San Francisco, along with drug addicts, dealers, and petty criminals. Idealistic youths, including growing numbers of runaways, were easy targets for more sophisticated criminals, leading one participant to observe: "Everybody knew that the scene had gotten so big that they'd destroyed it. Too many people. Too many runaways. Drugs were getting pretty bad. Heroin was showing up. The street carnivals were crazy." By December, two events marked "The End of the Age of Aquarius": the violence at the Rolling Stones' Altamont concert and the grisly Charles Manson murders. At Altamont, the Stones hired members of the Hollister-based Hell's Angels motorcycle gang to provide "security." The Angels, high on beer and drugs, and armed with clubs, terrorized and assaulted the audience, and stabbed one young man to death. Two other people died when a car ran into a crowd, and another person—high on drugs—drowned in an irrigation ditch. In contrast to the peaceful Woodstock concert earlier in 1969, Altamont exposed a dangerous, violent side to the counterculture. Manson, a self-proclaimed countercultural prophet, attracted a small, but devoted following to his Southern California commune with drugs, free love, and his psychotic preaching. From there, he and his "family" committed a series of brutal murders, including the ritualistic killing of pregnant actress Sharon Tate. Although these two events shocked the public, and contributed to growing skepticism of the "love generation's" values, the counterculture found a final cause before it completely disintegrated in the early 1970s.

Although many cultural rebels withdrew from politics and emphasized building alternative institutions, most were active participants in antiwar protests and other political struggles. Similarly, most political activists crossed over into the counterculture, adopting various aspects of the hippie lifestyle. The convergence of the two took concrete form in the battle over People's Park. In late April of 1969, Berkeley students and community activists took possession of a vacant lot owned by the University of California. After clearing the site of debris, activists planted trees, grass, and flowers, and set up playground equipment, a stage area for musical and street theater performances, and a distribution station for free clothes and food. Political radicals and cultural rebels viewed the seizure as an act of defiance against the university—an institution that devoted its resources to military- and corporate-sponsored research, and to educating a new generation to assume leadership roles in the "establishment." Many activists, however, also viewed their actions in productive or creative terms. Working cooperatively and democratically, they had transformed a barren, trash-strewn lot into a People's Park. If the youth were in charge, they asserted, the world would be a greener, kinder, and more egalitarian place.

University administrators, city officials, and many local business leaders saw things differently. The seizure of university land not only violated private property rights but also revealed the contempt that youths had for adult authority. Moreover, the park threatened to attract an even larger number of hippies and longhaired radicals to the community. On May 15, after the Highway Patrol and Berkeley police cleared the site and constructed a fence around the perimeter, six thousand demonstrators marched down Telegraph Avenue to "liberate" People's Park. Police fired tear gas to disperse the crowd, and protestors retaliated by throwing rocks, breaking store windows, and setting trash containers on fire. As the violence escalated, police sprayed demonstrators with buckshot, blinding one man, killing another, and injuring over one hundred. By evening, Governor Reagan called in the National Guard to restore order.

Protestors, however, continued to gather at the park on a daily basis, in a nonviolent, but uneasy standoff with the "occupying" army. This battle of nerves culminated in more violence on May 20 when the National Guard blocked the southern entrance to the campus and used helicopters to drop tear gas on hundreds of students trapped in the university's Sproul Plaza area. This show of force horrified many Berkeley residents and generated widespread sympathy for the protestors. On May 30, thirty thousand people took part in a march to the park in memory of James Rector, the protestor slain on May 15. Although peaceful, this protest ushered in three years of ongoing conflict over the site. In May 1972, after Nixon announced his intention to mine North Vietnam's main port, demonstrators converged on the park and finally succeeded in tearing down the fence. Shortly after, the Berkeley City Council voted to lease the land from the university and assume responsibility for its upkeep. For the time being, the "people" had won.

The Movement Expands

The Chicano, American Indian, Asian, Feminist, and Gay Pride movements, although rooted in long-standing concerns and grievances, were influenced and informed by the decade's earlier struggles. Civil rights and farm worker advocates, emphasizing political, economic, and social justice, inspired other groups to seek the same opportunities. Similarly, the Black Power movement's call for cultural pride and self-determination resonated with other disfranchised minorities and subcultures.

The Chicano Movement

By 1960 California's Mexican American population was primarily urban. The majority lived in barrios, characterized by underfunded schools, high levels of unemployment, deteriorating housing, and inferior public services. Like black ghettos, barrios were also plagued by police brutality, spatial isolation from more affluent areas, and poorly planned "redevelopment" schemes that destroyed affordable housing and displaced stable neighborhood businesses. Population concentration, however, brought the possibility of greater political power. The Mexican American Political Association (MAPA), recognizing this potential, sought to build on the modest political gains achieved by postwar activists. The Economic Opportunity Act of 1964, the cornerstone of Johnson's War on Poverty, also bolstered the optimism of urban Mexican Americans by promising funds to attack barrio poverty.

Optimism soon turned to disillusionment. In 1962 MAPA helped elect John Moreno and Philip Soto to the state assembly. But both lost in the next election after their political opponents succeeded in reapportioning their districts. During the same period, Los Angeles City Councilman Edward Roybal was elected to Congress, but this major victory left the city's Mexican Americans without representation in city government. The council, instead of calling for an election, appointed Gilbert Lindsay, an African American, to Roybal's seat. Even the state's liberal governor, Pat Brown, seemed to ignore the barrio electorate, appointing fewer than thirty Mexican Americans out of a total of five thousand possible appointments. Finally, the War on Poverty, while raising expectations among Mexican Americans, directed a disproportionate amount of funding to programs in black communities.

These developments, occurring at a time when African Americans were embracing Black Power and the UFW was forcing concessions from growers, inspired young urban Mexican American activists to adopt more militant strategies for social and political change. Rather than emphasizing assimilation into Anglo culture, the Mexican American youth demanded their "right as a people to have their own culture, their own language, their own heritage, and their own way of life." Like Black Power advocates, they argued that self-determination, cultural pride, community self-defense, and Third World solidarity were the true sources of liberation. And like black activists, they believed that recovering their history—a history that had been "distorted" by whites in order to justify exploitation and discrimination—was a crucial first step in forging a new movement.

Their narrative history, which ran counter to most standard textbook accounts, asserted that the Southwest was theirs. The region, they argued, was the original homeland of their indigenous ancestors. After the Spanish conquest, their forebears (now of mixed European and Indian ancestry) created a vast New World empire that extended into the Southwest, an empire inherited by the Mexican Republic following the war for independence. In the late 1840s, Anglos, determined to extend their own empire, then seized Mexican territory in an unprovoked and unjustified war, stripped established residents of their land, and transformed a once proud people into a poorly paid, menial labor force. To a new generation of Mexican American activists who called themselves "Chicanos," this historical equation led to one conclusion: California belonged to *La Raza*—the Mexican Americans. Changing demographics added symbolic weight to their assertion. Between 1960 and 1970, for example, the Hispanic population in

Los Angeles County grew from 576,716 to 1,228,295. This increase, not reflecting large numbers of undocumented immigrants ignored by the census, stood in contrast to a 2 percent decline in the Anglo population. While still in the minority in the county as a whole, the Mexican American population constituted a strong majority within certain communities and districts.

The Mexican American claim to power, based on these shifting demographics and a new sense of cultural pride, took several different forms. In the political arena, some activists abandoned their struggle for recognition and representation within the two parties and established organizations devoted to their empowerment. The La Raza Unida Party (RUP), founded in the late 1960s, enjoyed its greatest success in 1970 and 1972 when it inspired Mexican Americans throughout the Southwest by wresting political control from an Anglo minority in the Crystal City area of Texas. In California, however, the party's political influence was less direct. In 1971, for example, the RUP registered enough voters to dilute the strength of the Democratic Party and cost it the election in the 48th assembly district. The RUP's candidate, Raul Ruiz, a college professor and editor of *La Raza* magazine, took just enough votes away from Democrat Richard Allatorre to hand the election to a non-Hispanic Republican. This prompted state Democrats, who had long taken the Mexican American vote for granted, to run more Hispanic candidates in future elections. However, despite small advances of this nature, the potential political power of Mexican Americans continued to be undermined by language barriers, gerrymandering of political districts, the constant influx of new immigrants, and the low level of voter participation by established residents.

Mexican American activists also sought reform in the educational arena. In March of 1968 thousands of students walked out of their high schools in the Los Angeles area, protesting racial bias among Anglo teachers, the lack of Hispanic administrators and instructors, dilapidated school infrastructure, an uninspiring curriculum that ignored Mexican American culture and history, and the tracking of students into vocational classes. Their action inspired similar protests in high schools across the nation. Similarly, on the state's college campuses students formed organizations like United Mexican American Students (UMAS) and El Movimiento Estudiantil Chicano de Aztlan (MECHA) to press for Chicano or Mexican American studies programs, more financial aid and student services, and the hiring of Mexican American faculty. Their efforts, often supported by students of other ethnicities, led to the establishment of over fifty Chicano studies programs in state colleges and universities across the nation by 1969. Finally, activists launched a long struggle for bilingual education programs in elementary and secondary schools, winning a legislative mandate in 1976.

Heightened appreciation of Mexican American history and culture extended beyond high school and college campuses into the barrios. Activists established cultural centers, organized mural projects, formed theater and dance troupes, and published magazines and journals like *La Raza, Inside Eastside,* and *El Grito: A Journal of Contemporary Mexican American Thought.* Barrio youths, influenced by this cultural renaissance, attacked community problems with a heightened militancy and sense of purpose. The Brown Berets, which grew out of an East Los Angeles youth group called Young Citizens for Community Action, emphasized cultural nationalism, self-determination, and community self-defense. Like the Black Panther Party, the Berets organized citizen patrols to monitor police activity within their communities. And like the Panthers, they soon became targets of law enforcement infiltration, harassment, and intimidation.

Police antagonism toward the Brown Berets and the barrio-based Chicano movement took an ugly turn in the fall of 1970. In 1969 the Berets helped form the National Chicano Moratorium Committee, an organization opposed to the U.S. war in Vietnam and to discriminatory selective service policies. Mexican American youths, less likely to attend college than Anglos, received fewer student deferments. They also lacked the political connections that allowed some of their white counterparts to escape the draft or receive assignment to less risky branches of the military. As a consequence, they were drafted in disproportionate numbers and suffered a disproportionate level of casualties in fighting what many of them regarded as an unjust war against other people of color. On August 29, 1970, the Moratorium Committee sponsored a march and rally in East Los Angeles. Following the march, twenty to thirty thousand participants, including families with small children, gathered peacefully in Laguna Park to listen to music and speakers. Police, in an unprovoked show of force, moved in and disbanded the demonstrators with clubs and tear gas. In the process, hundreds of citizens were arrested, sixty injured, and two killed.

In the late afternoon, after most of the demonstrators had dispersed, Ruben Salazar and two of his coworkers who had been covering the day's events for a Spanish-language television station took a break for a beer in the Silver Dollar Bar. Police, claiming to have seen a man enter with a rifle, surrounded the bar, fired in tear gas canisters, and prevented patrons from leaving. One of the canisters hit Salazar in the head, killing him. His death was not an unfortunate accident or product of police overreaction, charged the Mexican American community. Salazar had earlier exposed Los Angeles Police Department brutality in a case of mistaken identity that led to the shooting deaths of two Mexican nationals. The police had warned Salazar that he would pay the consequences if he did not tone down his coverage. Despite serious evidence of misconduct, no officers were charged for Salazar's death, and police–community relations remained deeply troubled.

Although police brutality, lack of political representation, and poverty continued to plague California's barrios, the Brown Power movement helped promote a more positive sense of identity among urban Mexican Americans. Moreover, it had a lasting impact on higher education. During the 1970s and 1980s state colleges and universities attracted increasing numbers of Mexican American students through affirmative action, financial aid, and ethnic studies programs. This, combined with a greater commitment to affirmative hiring policies in the public and private sectors, led to the growth of the Mexican American middle class, increased representation in professional occupations, and a new, better-educated generation of political leaders.

Indian occupation of Alcatraz Island in 1969. In this photograph young Indian activists are asserting their claim to a physical space, Alcatraz Island. Does this image suggest that they are also asserting a new cultural and political identity?

Taking the Rock

In the late 1960s, the state's American Indian population responded to the pressures and challenges of termination, relocation, poverty, and broken treaties with an assertion of "Red Power," a movement that emphasized cultural pride, intertribal unity, and mutual aid. Indians created the foundation for this movement throughout the 1950s and 1960s by building a new institutional power base. The Intertribal Friendship House in Oakland, the San Francisco Indian Center in San Francisco, the United Bay Area Council of American Indians, and the Intertribal Council of California united "relocates" who came from tribes across the nation with California Indians, and provided them with a forum for articulating shared concerns. Other organizations, devoted to cultural preservation and education, also took root. In 1964 the chairman of the Cahuilla tribe organized the American Indian Historical Society to promote scholarship on Indian life, culture, and history, and the revision of school textbooks. In 1967, the California Indian Education Association was founded to promote Native American studies programs on college campuses and to encourage political activism among the Indian youth.

At the same time, Indian youths were influenced by the Black Power and Chicano Power movements. Impatient with the pace of change, they adopted more militant forms of struggle for cultural recognition and redress. Their protests paid off. By 1969 several college campuses had established Native American studies programs or study groups. In November of 1969 student activists, with the support of Indian organizations and their leadership, planned and carried out the occupation of Alcatraz Island. Launched after a fire destroyed the San Francisco Indian Center—a central gathering place of Bay Area Indians—this action signaled the birth of the Red Power movement. Led by Richard Oakes, a Mohawk Indian and Bay Area student, the "invaders" adopted the name "Indians of All Tribes" to underscore their diverse backgrounds. Other veterans of the occupation included Adam Fortunate Eagle (Anishinabe-Ojibway), John Trudell (Sentee-Sioux), La Nada Boyer (Shoshone-Bannock), Edward Castillo (Cahuilla-Luiseño), Millie Ketcheshawno (Mvskoke), Shirley Guevara (Mono), Luwana Quitiquit (Pomo-Modoc), John Whitefox (Choctaw), and Wilma Mankiller (Cherokee).

The occupation, which began on November 20, 1969, and lasted until June 10, 1971, was not the first attempt by Indians to reclaim "The Rock." On March 9, 1964, Richard McKensie and four other Sioux occupied Alcatraz for four hours, demanding that it be used as an Indian cultural center and university. On November 9, 1969, Richard Oakes and several other Indians staged a preliminary and short-lived invasion after issuing a pointedly humorous "Proclamation to the Great White Father and to All His People":

> We, the Native Americans, re-claim the land known as Alcatraz Island in the name of all American Indians by right of discovery. We wish to be fair and honorable in our dealings with the Caucasian inhabitants of this land, and hereby offer the following treaty: We will purchase said Alcatraz Island for twenty-four dollars (24) in glass beads and red cloth. . . . Our offer of $1.24 per acre is greater than the 47 cents per acre the white men are now paying the California Indians for their land. We will give the inhabitants of this island a portion of the land for their own to be held in trust by the American Indian Affairs and by the Bureau of Caucasian Affairs to hold in perpetuity. . . . We will further guide the inhabitants in the proper way of living. We will offer them our religion, our education, our life-ways, in order to help them achieve our level of civilization and thus raise them and all their white brothers up from their savage and unhappy state.

This preliminary invasion convinced its organizers, including Oakes, that a longer occupation was viable. Just eleven days later approximately one hundred Indians, mostly students, seized the island and issued a series of demands that included permanent title to Alcatraz, and the right to establish a Center for Native American Studies, a Spiritual Center, and an Ecology Center on its soil. They also established an elected council to coordinate day-to-day operations including sanitation, housing, cooking, day care, security, negotiations with government officials, and media relations.

As the months passed occupiers confronted a series of setbacks. The federal government steadfastly refused to concede to their demands. Hundreds of newcomers, including many non-Indians, arrived on the island, placing stress on existing supplies and services. Competing political factions challenged the original elected council. Oakes, distraught over growing political divisions and the accidental death of his daughter in January of 1970, left the island. In the meantime, the government shut off the island's electricity and blocked the transport of water from the mainland. A fire broke out three days after the disruption in water supply, destroying several buildings. Finally, on June 10, 1971, federal marshals and FBI agents invaded the island and removed the remaining occupiers.

The Alcatraz activists, however, left a lasting legacy. In the words of La Nada Boyer, an occupation leader, "Alcatraz was symbolic in the rebirth of Indian people to be recognized as a people, as human beings, whereas before, we were not. We were not recognized, we were not legitimate . . . but we were able to raise, not only the consciousness of other American people, but our own people as well, to reestablish our identity as Indian people, as a culture, as political entities." Even before the occupation ended, President Nixon formally halted the federal policy of termination and restored millions of acres of land to several tribes. He also increased federal spending on Indian education, housing, health care, legal services, and economic development. The occupation inspired Indians across the nation to engage in similar actions, including the occupation of the Bureau of Indian Affairs in Washington, D.C., which forced the agency to hire more Indian employees to administer its programs. Another occupation, of a former army base near Davis, California, led to the establishment of D-Q University, the "first and only indigenous controlled institution of higher learning located outside of a reservation."

Change and Activism Along the Pacific Rim

The 1960s brought massive changes to California's Asian American communities. Immigration reform in 1965 expanded the size and altered the ethnic composition of the state's Asian population. And a new generation, influenced by the militancy of other ethnic groups, reclaimed their heritage, embraced community activism, lobbied for Asian American studies programs, and joined protests against the Vietnam War.

The 1965 Immigration Act, reflecting the more liberal racial attitudes of the postwar, civil rights era, created a new major wave of Asian immigration by abolishing race-based quotas and permitting 170,000 immigrants from the Eastern Hemisphere to enter the United States each year. Spouses, minor children, and parents of U.S. citizens were not counted as part of the quota. Prior to the Immigration Act, Japanese Americans constituted the largest percentage of the Asian American population, followed by Chinese, Filipinos, and Koreans. After 1965, however, Japanese Americans dropped from first place, as immigrants from other groups entered the state in larger numbers.

The Chinese population underwent the greatest transformation. Prior to 1965, a majority of Chinese residents were American-born. With the new immigration, however, the number of foreign-born increased to 63 percent of the total population. About half of the newcomers, lacking professional or technical training, clustered in existing Chinatowns and worked in low-wage menial or service occupations. This population of "Downtown" Chinese stood in contrast to a second group of immigrants: the "Uptown" Chinese, educated professionals and entrepreneurs mostly from Hong Kong and Taiwan. This group either settled outside of existing Chinatowns altogether, following a pattern adopted by American-born Chinese residents, or established new, upscale suburban enclaves. For example, Monterey Park, which was 85 percent white in 1960, was over 50 percent Chinese two decades later, and was known as the "Chinese Beverly Hills."

Filipinos, arriving in even greater numbers, were more widely dispersed and homogeneous in education and training than Chinese immigrants. Most were professional and technical workers fleeing economic hardship and political repression in the Philippines. But although highly skilled, as many as one-half of all newcomers worked in low-wage clerical or manual occupations because American professional associations refused to accept their degrees or grant them licenses to practice. This enormous pool of talent from the Philippines, including doctors, lawyers, dentists, engineers, and professors, was virtually wasted in the United States.

Korean immigrants, although facing greater language barriers than Filipinos, came with similar credentials. A majority were college-educated, middle-class professionals who also faced institutional obstacles in the United States. However, many arrived with the capital to launch small businesses, which in turn fostered the development of ethnic enclaves. Olympic Boulevard in Los Angeles, for example, quickly emerged as a center of entrepreneurial activity, housing churches, grocery stores, insurance companies, restaurants, beauty shops, nightclubs, and travel agencies by 1975. However successful, these business ventures still represented a step down for trained professionals like Kong Mook Lee, who, unable to practice as a pharmacist, opened a sewing factory in Los Angeles. He, and a majority of other highly trained Korean immigrants, never anticipated that their professional skills would be useless in the United States.

As the immigrant population expanded, increasing the size and diversity of the state's Asian population, many sons and daughters of established residents reclaimed their ethnic heritage and launched the Asian American student movement. In the Bay Area, Asian American students joined the 1968 Third World Strike at San Francisco State University, organized by a multiethnic coalition of students and faculty that called for the creation of a Third World College. This, and a second strike that shut down the Berkeley campus in 1969, resulted in the creation of ethnic studies departments on both campuses, and fostered ethnic consciousness among participants. Asian American students, in particular, emerged with a new awareness of their own ethnic heritage, history of oppression, and responsibility to their communities. Vietnam War protests also helped radicalize young Asian Americans. Having experienced anti-Asian prejudice at home, they drew parallels between their own experience and the negative stereotypes used to dehumanize the "enemy."

These experiences encouraged young activists to return to their own roots and recover their culture and history. Cultural organizations, like the Combined

Asian Research Project, encouraged young writers, musicians, and artists to produce works that reflected their ethnic heritage and identity, and to establish an Asian American artistic and literary tradition by locating and documenting the contributions of older generations. Others emphasized political activism within their neighborhoods and communities, focusing on housing conditions, sweatshop labor, and the lack of medical and social services in Chinatowns. For many, however, San Francisco's International Hotel provided the call to action. By the late 1960s the hotel, housing a resident population of older, low-income Filipino and Chinese men, and serving as a home base for activist youth organizations, was threatened with demolition by its owner, Walter Shorenstein. A coalition of tenants, resident activists, and college students persuaded the owner to lease the hotel to the United Filipino Association, and formed a collective to renovate the building and provide services to the residents.

The hotel soon became a symbol of Asian American unity, self-determination, and ethnic pride. However, financial problems and factional struggles among different activist groups undermined the collective experiment, prompting the owner to proceed with eviction and demolition plans. In August of 1977, after activists had exhausted all legal and political options for saving the hotel, they rallied over two thousand supporters to surround the building and block the eviction. Police used force to break through the crowd and remove the tenants from the hotel. The building was eventually demolished, but the site remains vacant because of ongoing political pressure from community activists who insist that low-income housing be part of the development agreement. Of less symbolic— but more lasting—significance was the creation of Asian American studies programs on college and university campuses, increased political participation and representation, and an enduring cultural influence in music, literature, art, film, and theater.

Emerging Feminist and Gay Rights Movements

During the sixties, a relatively quiet, but growing movement went largely unnoticed in the face of more dramatic, noisy protests against the status quo. Just as young women were confronting sexism within the decade's social movements, an older generation of "liberal feminists" began working through legal and political channels to address gender bias in education and employment. In 1964, these mostly white, middle-class professionals convinced the California legislature to establish a State Commission on the Status of Women. Over the next three years, the commission worked to document widespread gender inequities, and sent delegates to the National Conferences of the State Commissions on Women. At the third national conference, held in Washington, D.C., in 1966, delegates criticized the federal Economic Opportunity Commission for failing to investigate complaints of sex discrimination. Following the closing luncheon, several participants formed the National Organization for Women (NOW). NOW's statement of purpose, issued soon after, asserted that "the time has come for a new movement toward true equality for all women in America. . . . We organize to initiate or support action, nationally or in any part of this nation, by individuals or organizations, to break through the silken curtain of prejudice and discrimination against women."

California's liberal feminists returned home determined to organize local and state chapters of NOW. In 1967 the State Commission issued its long-awaited report on the status of women, along with a series of proposed legislative remedies. When Governor Reagan ignored its recommendations, liberal feminists were ready to fight back. By the early 1970s, when they were joined in their struggle by younger activists who had encountered sexism among their "radical" male colleagues, a full-fledged feminist rebellion would emerge.

In a similarly quiet manner, gay and lesbian activists worked diligently throughout the sixties to promote greater acceptance of homosexuality among California's heterosexual majority. Their efforts, emphasizing political engagement, public education, and cooperation with sympathetic liberals, grew out of the same desire for inclusion that informed early civil rights struggles. In 1961, for example, a gay San Franciscan formed the League for Civil Education (LCE), which sought to build a political voting block among the city's homosexual residents. In 1964 the Society for Individual Rights (SIR)—an LCE spinoff—was formed to promote electoral unity and activism as well as "a sense of community; and the establishing of an attractive social atmosphere and constructive outlets for members and friends." By 1967 SIR and the Daughters of Bilitis (1955) began hosting "Candidates Nights," where those seeking political office could meet their gay and lesbian constituents.

Beyond the political arena, organizations like LCE, SIR, the Mattachine Society (1950), and the Daughters of Bilitis created opportunities for social engagement outside of the more closeted confines of gay and lesbian bars. In 1966, for example, SIR established the nation's first gay community center on 6th Street in San Francisco. They had also won a small measure of public tolerance by building coalitions with sympathetic heterosexuals. In 1964 gay and lesbian activists joined with liberal San Francisco clergy to form the Council of Religion and the Homosexual (CRH), an organization that promoted acceptance of homosexuality within mainstream religious denominations. On January 1, 1965, the CRH held a fundraising ball. As guests arrived—both gay and straight—they were harassed and photographed by police. Officers also arrested CRH lawyers who had demanded a search warrant when police attempted to enter the hall. For the first time, heterosexuals experienced the officially sanctioned intimidation and brutality that had long been used to break up gay and lesbian social activity in bars, restaurants, and clubs. The resulting outcry from "respectable" members of the community helped sway public opinion against such routine civil rights abuses.

Liberal activism, however, soon gave way to more militant calls for gay liberation. The shift happened gradually. In 1966, at Compton's Cafeteria on Turk and Taylor Streets in San Francisco, gay patrons fought back when police raided the premises. In 1967, after several police raids of Los Angeles gay bars, several hundred protestors gathered on Sunset Boulevard to demand freedom from harassment. Predating New York's 1969 Stonewall uprising against anti-gay police harassment, usually cited as the catalyst for the gay liberation movement, these two events signaled a radical departure from the old politics of inclusion. A younger generation, influenced by the counterculture's rebellion against "uptight" sexual mores, and minority demands for "power," would soon call for more than acceptance into the mainstream. Asserting that "Gay Is Good," and demanding "complete sexual liberation for all people," they urged gays and lesbians "Out of the Closets and Into the Streets."

Politics in the Age of Dissent

The Decline of Liberalism

Ethnic power struggles, student unrest, and the Vietnam War had a profound and lasting impact on politics. Democrats were deeply divided over foreign and domestic policy. The Right, in the meantime, had formulated a new agenda that included Americans who, in the words of Richard Nixon, believed that "we live in a deeply troubled and profoundly unsettled time. Drugs, crime, campus revolts, racial discord, draft resistance—on every hand we find old standards violated, old values discarded." At the same time, federal expenditures on the war contributed to high levels of inflation. Many Americans, alarmed over a weakening economy, rejected "spendthrift liberalism" in favor of Republican promises to "cut, squeeze, and trim" government spending and to reduce taxes. In contrast to liberals, conservatives argued that government agencies, immune from free market competition, had become inefficient, wasteful of taxpayer money, and bloated. Even worse, many of the public services that they provided undermined individual initiative and responsibility. Private industry, they maintained, would provide ample opportunities for the deserving and hard-working if freed of excessive government regulation. Since California was home to many of the movements that challenged "old standards," the shift from liberalism to a more conservative economic and moral agenda occurred there first, and then rippled over the nation as a whole.

When Edmund "Pat" Brown announced his intention to run for a third term in the gubernatorial election of 1966, he faced serious opposition within his own party. Many antiwar Democrats, disenchanted with Brown's moderate position on the escalating conflict, refused to back his reelection bid. Making matters worse, conservative party members rejected Brown as too liberal and backed Los Angeles mayor Samuel Yorty in the Democratic primary. Although Brown secured his party's nomination, Yorty garnered nearly one million votes—votes that might easily be captured by the Republicans in the upcoming election.

In contrast, Ronald Reagan, who easily won the Republican nomination, enjoyed the full backing of a newly unified, well-funded party organization. He and his advisers had also crafted a campaign strategy designed to capture the support

Ronald Reagan's 1967 inauguration. Reagan won election as governor by pledging to clean up the "mess at Berkeley," curb government spending, reduce taxes, defend free enterprise, and provide moral leadership. How does this image make you feel about his leadership abilities? Does his body language reflect determination and self-confidence or passivity and doubt? What is the impact of the photographer's choice of background, props, and the subject's height and pose?

of conservative white Democrats who were alarmed over student unrest, minority demands for economic and political power, the countercultural assault on traditional morality, and government programs that benefited "cheats" and "spongers" at the taxpayer's expense. Although Reagan denied that race was an issue in his campaign, he did, in fact, exploit the fear and resentment of white voters. His attack on government spending, for example, reinforced white suspicions that liberal social programs encouraged dependence, fraud, and a growing sense of entitlement among minority recipients. Similarly, Reagan repeatedly reminded voters that he had backed Proposition 14, an initiative supported by a majority of white voters, but recently declared unconstitutional by the state supreme court. Brown accused Reagan of exploiting the white backlash against integration, but Reagan deflected criticism by framing his position as a defense of private property rights.

In the 1966 election, Reagan won office by 993,000 votes, nearly the same number that Brown had lost to Yorty in the primary. Republicans also eroded Democratic majorities in the senate and assembly, and captured every other office with the exception of state attorney general. Two years later, another Californian, Richard Nixon, used the Reagan strategy to win the presidency.

Reagan as Governor

During his first term, Reagan attempted to implement his policy of "cut, squeeze, and trim" with disappointing results. Only two areas—higher education and mental health—suffered cuts, and the resulting savings were overshadowed by record-level expenditures elsewhere. In higher education, he reduced funding by several million dollars and urged administrators to make up the shortfall by increasing tuition. This, he maintained, would save the taxpayers money and "help get rid of undesirables"—students who cared more about protesting than their studies. He also vetoed an increase in payments to old age pensioners and implemented sweeping cuts in the mental health budget. The state's mental health system, which the Warren and Brown administrations had expanded, had become a national model of humane and enlightened treatment of the mentally ill. Reagan slashed the staff at state mental hospitals by 3,700, forcing institutions to prematurely discharge patients and reduce the scope and quality of hospital services. He also cut funding for community mental health clinics that provided outpatient treatment for those with less serious mental disabilities. While saving the state over $17 million, these cuts had disastrous and lasting consequences for the mentally ill, their families, and local communities. Reagan also reduced funding for the state's Medi-Cal program, which was created during Brown's last term in office to provide health care to low-income and indigent residents. These cuts, however, were blocked by the state supreme court.

Beyond these relatively modest cost-cutting measures, Reagan met with stiff opposition. Many of the most costly programs were protected by federal and state mandate or vigorously defended by the Democratic majority in the senate and assembly. As a consequence, Reagan's 1967–1968 budget of just over $5 billion was the largest in state history and exceeded the previous year's total by $400 million. To cover the increase he was forced to authorize a record-breaking tax increase of $1 billion. Nevertheless, he remained popular with voters, diverting attention from his larger budgetary failures with folksy references to his smaller cost-saving measures and his "get tough" posture with "campus rioters." His plain-dealing cowboy image, initially honed in Hollywood and ably resurrected by his public relations staff, was also a powerful political asset.

Furthermore, Reagan, like many governors before him, avoided characterization as an extremist by adopting moderate or pragmatic positions on several issues. At the risk of alienating his right-wing colleagues, he failed to support a legislative repeal of the Rumford Fair Housing Act, despite his strong position during the campaign. He also backed the Beilenson Bill, the most liberal abortion law in state history. Finally, conservationists were heartened by his veto of the Round Valley Dam project and his support for legislation that protected the middle fork of the Feather River. In his second term, Reagan improved on his environmental record, signing into law new air and water quality standards and approving legislation that required environmental impact reports for public works projects. Environmentalists, however, were alarmed by his refusal to endorse legislation to regulate development in the Lake Tahoe area, and his belated backing of a watered-down measure to create Redwoods National Park after claiming "a tree is a tree" to a cheering audience at the 1966 meeting of the Western Wood Products Association.

Nevertheless, his blend of personal appeal, pragmatism, and ideological conservatism won Reagan a second term in 1970. Again determined to reduce state spending, he focused on reforming the welfare system. In a compromise with the Democrats, Reagan obtained tougher eligibility requirements for Aid to Families With Dependent Children (AFDC), a work requirement for able-bodied recipients, and a cost reduction in the Medi-Cal program. As part of the compromise, however, the final measure included expensive cost-of-living increases for welfare recipients. Although Reagan claimed that the welfare system fostered dependence and laziness, only 1 percent of recipients were able-bodied males. About three-quarters were blind, aged, or disabled, and the remainder were children in single-parent, female-headed households. Welfare "reform," which appealed to angry taxpayers, completely ignored or misrepresented the plight of the state's most vulnerable citizens. Moreover, the savings that it generated were relatively insignificant because federal mandate protected many programs, and the work requirement was undermined by a weak economy.

Year after year, Reagan signed off on progressively larger budgets, from $6.8 billion in 1971–1972 to $10.2 billion for 1974–1975. At the same time, economic recession produced a decline in state revenue, necessitating additional tax increases. In 1971 Reagan raised $500 million in taxes by introducing a paycheck withholding system and revising capital gains and corporate tax schedules. A year later, Reagan drafted another tax bill with Democratic legislators that raised sales, bank, and corporate taxes. This measure not only generated revenue for education and social welfare programs, but also allowed the state to provide tax relief to homeowners. By the late 1960s rising inflation had increased property valuations and local tax assessments. The new sales tax financed additional state income exemptions for property owners, and temporarily quelled what soon became a statewide campaign to limit local property tax increases—the tax revolt of 1978.

In 1973 Reagan made a final attempt to salvage his reputation as a fiscal conservative. Proposition 1, a Reagan-sponsored ballot measure, was a constitutional amendment that would have prohibited the legislature from raising taxes beyond a certain percentage of a taxpayer's income. Opponents of the initiative argued that local governments and property owners would be forced to compensate for the resulting shortfall in state services. And Reagan admitted that even he did not fully understand the measure's complex provisions and formulas. Voters rejected the proposition by more than three hundred thousand votes, but Reagan had preserved his conservative image by championing fiscal restraint and tax relief. When he left office in 1974, with his eye on a career in national politics, this would be what voters remembered. His basic philosophy of "cut, squeeze, and trim," perfectly in tune with the declining economic fortunes of the Golden State's electorate, was soon to carry the same weight with American voters in the presidential race of 1980.

Summary

The sixties left a lasting impression on the state's culture, politics, and economy. The decade shattered the myth that Californians were one big, happy family. African Americans, Hispanics, Native Americans, and Asian Americans demanded not only equal rights and political power, but also respect for their cultural traditions and historical contributions. As a consequence, the state's residents were forced to acknowledge that they lived in a pluralistic, often contentious society, rather than a melting pot where various ethnic groups blended together by accepting white, middle-class values. At the same time, countercultural rebels and antiwar activists challenged the political and economic priorities of their parents, and created an alternative values system that emphasized cooperation; creative, fulfilling work; sexual and emotional liberation; and environmental awareness.

These challenges to the status quo, however, also produced a backlash. Ronald Reagan, appealing to "forgotten" Californians, attempted to replace the liberal agenda of his Democratic predecessor, Pat Brown, with his own blend of social, fiscal, and political conservatism. Though he failed in the fiscal arena, his conservative philosophy and rhetoric not only revitalized the Republican Party, but also eventually won him the presidency. Change, however, was difficult to suppress. The sixties gave many Californians a new appreciation of cultural diversity, and a broader choice of alternate lifestyle options. In the workplace, emphasis on creativity and shared decision making increased worker productivity and innovation, particularly in the emerging Silicon Valley. In the home, many men and women renegotiated their roles and increasingly chose alternatives to the traditional nuclear family. Colleges and universities gave students more curricular choices and a greater role in governance. Most significantly, they broadened their curricular choices to include non-Western, ethnic, and women's studies.

Finally, the sixties led to the growth of new movements: gay and lesbian liberation, modern feminism, environmentalism, and anti-nuclear activism. What the Right regarded as an abandonment of traditional values, others viewed as a healthy skepticism of authority and a welcome expansion of cultural and political horizons. Rather than reaching a new social consensus in the coming decades, the state's residents would continue to grapple with the sweeping changes introduced during the sixties.

Suggested Readings

▌ Adler, Margot, *Heretic's Heart* (Boston: Beacon Press, 1997). This is a first-person account of student activism on the Berkeley campus during the sixties.

▌ Cannon, Lou, *Governor Reagan: His Rise to Power* (New York: Public Affairs, 2003). This book covers Ronald Reagan's political career from his early years as a New Deal Democrat to his two terms as a conservative governor.

▌ Foner, Philip S., ed., *The Black Panthers Speak* (Cambridge and New York: Da Capo Press, 2002). This collection includes interviews with and writings by Black Panther Party members.

▌ Griswold Del Castillo, Richard, and Richard A. Garcia, *Cesar Chavez, A Triumph of Spirit* (Norman: University of Oklahoma Press, 1995). This is a concise biography of Cesar Chavez that provides ample information about his union activities, fellow organizers, and political opponents.

▌ Johnson, Troy, *The Occupation of Alcatraz* (Urbana: University of Illinois Press, 1996). This is a comprehensive account of the Alcatraz occupation that includes information on organizers, participants, federal government reaction, and the occupation's legacy.

▌ Kerner Commission, *Report of the National Advisory Committee on Civil Disorders* (New York: Bantam, 1968). This report, produced by a federal commission and criticized by many civil rights activists as too superficial, explores the causes and consequences of the Watts uprising.

▌ Muñoz, Carlos, *Youth, Identity, Power: Chicano Movement* (New York: Verso Press, 1989). This book describes the origins, activism, and legacy of the Chicano youth movement.

▌ Perry, Charles, *The Haight-Ashbury* (New York: Vintage, 1984). This book provides a good overview of Haight-Ashbury's counterculture during the sixties.

▌ Rorabaugh W. J., *Berkeley at War: The 1960s* (New York: Oxford, 1989). This book covers the rise of the Free Speech, antiwar, Black Power, and countercultural movements, and describes their impact on American politics and culture.

▌ Seale, Bobby, *Seize the Time: The Story of the Black Panther Party and Huey P. Newton* (Baltimore: Black Classic Press, 1997). This book, written by one of the founders of the Black Panther Party, describes the origins, activities, internal and external problems, and guiding philosophy of the organization.

▌ Wei, William, *The Asian American Movement* (Philadelphia: Temple University Press, 1993). This book details the origins, activities, and legacy of the Asian American youth movement, with particular emphasis on campus activism in California.

▌ Wolfe, Tom, *Electric Kool-Aid Acid Test* (New York: Farrar, Straus and Giroux, 1968). This is an entertaining, journalistic account of the counterculture's founders, philosophy, and alternative lifestyle.

12

Era of Limits

Main Topics

▌ The Legacy of the Sixties

▌ Economic Changes and Environmental Constraints

▌ Politics in the Era of Limits

▌ Summary

Tuyen Ngoc Tran was born in South Vietnam on April 6, 1974, just fifteen months after the United States ended its involvement in one of the longest and most divisive conflicts in American history. Her family lived outside of Saigon (soon to be renamed Ho Chi Minh City), and made a comfortable living raising hogs and distilling rice wine. After Saigon fell to the North Vietnamese army, life became more difficult for the Tran family. Tuyen's father had sympathized with the South Vietnamese government. And he and his parents, as ethnic Chinese, were subject to economic restrictions imposed by the new government in the late 1970s. Fearing for the family's safety and economic future, the Trans fled Vietnam on September 20, 1978. They, like thousands of other South Vietnamese refugees, made their escape on a dangerously overcrowded boat that left them at the mercy of the elements and roving bands of pirates. After surviving this ordeal, the family spent two years in a refugee camp in Pulau Bidong, Malaysia. Although most adults retain vivid impressions of early childhood, Tuyen has no memories of this period.

CHAPTER 12	Era of Limits
1972	Fall of Saigon California ratifies the Equal Rights Amendment Bay Area Rapid Transit System begins operating
1973	Arab oil embargo triggers state energy crisis
1974	*Lau* v. *Nichols* Edmund Brown Jr. elected governor
1975	Agricultural Labor Relations Act signed into law
1978	Harvey Milk elected to the San Francisco Board of Supervisors Proposition 13 approved by voters *Bakke* Supreme Court decision Harvey Milk and San Francisco mayor George Moscone assassinated
1980	AIDS identified by the Centers for Disease Control
1982	George Deukmejian elected governor
1990	Americans with Disabilities Act becomes law

Over five thousand miles away, charitable and religious organizations in the United States enlisted sponsors to assist the federal government in resettling Southeast Asian boat people. In the spring of 1980 a synagogue in Winston-Salem, North Carolina, agreed to help the Tran family. Once there, Tuyen's parents found minimum-wage jobs at a wrecking yard and a French pastry shop, but had difficulty accumulating savings. They also longed for the company of other Vietnamese immigrants.

After three years in North Carolina, the Trans moved to California. Tuyen said, "In the minds of refugees, the other states could not beat the beautiful, mild climate, plentiful jobs, and established Chinese and Vietnamese communities." Indeed, between 1975 and 1985 California was the destination of choice for Southeast Asian refugees. By the end of this period, an estimated 335,000 refugees had moved to the state, giving California the highest refugee density in the world, and increasing the size and diversity of its Asian population.

The Trans, like other immigrants to the state, worked hard to establish a small measure of economic security, and to maintain cultural and familial ties. "My mother worked as a seamstress for nearly ten years and my father was an auto-body mechanic," says Tuyen. Eventually they quit their jobs working for others,

Vietnamese refugees arriving at Camp Pendleton. This photograph shows Vietnamese orphans coming off a plane. What do their ages and dress suggest about their ability to adjust to a new life in California? What barriers might they have faced in their effort to assimilate?

and with the support of family and friends started a small farming business. "It's difficult work from sunrise to sundown and often times I hear them talk of quitting farm work, but this is only talk. The alternatives to farming are not appealing."

Tuyen, who attended a private college on a scholarship, graduated in 1997 and is currently a doctoral student in history at U.C. Berkeley. Her long journey, from a Malaysian refugee camp to life as an American teacher and scholar, gave her a strong sense of identity. "Growing up was a difficult balancing act. I'm realizing now that I can simultaneously be many things—Chinese, Vietnamese, American, refugee, traditional, non-traditional. Each part of my identity has a story behind it. I think that is why I love history so much. My part in this American fabric is to give voice to those who have not been heard in my community."

Whether or not Tuyen realized it, her family's experience was an outgrowth of American foreign policy during the sixties— a foreign policy that gave rise to a contentious antiwar movement and reshaped national and state politics. But Vietnamese immigration was only one legacy of the sixties. New forms of activism, growing out of earlier social movements, flourished during the 1970s and early 1980s, and bolstered California's reputation as a center of experiment and change. As the Trans adapted to their new surroundings, they, like other Californians, entered a shifting economic environment. Throughout the seventies and eighties the state's economy became increasingly tied to the booming trans-Pacific, or Pacific Rim, trade. Although Asian countries provided new markets for California's products, their cheaper exports damaged other industries and contributed to a growing trade deficit.

Even more significantly, the state's economy shifted away from heavy industry to service sector employment. Manufacturing jobs, the most heavily unionized in the state, moved overseas or to lower-wage regions of the United States, while service sector employment accounted for more than three-fourths of all new job growth during the same period. Many Californians, with the education and training to move into higher-wage service employment, benefited from this shift. Others, including new immigrants like the Trans, were forced into low-paying, largely nonunion service jobs that afforded less in terms of security, benefits, and opportunities for advancement than those in heavy industry.

As these economic shifts unfolded, Californians faced unprecedented limits to growth. The state's resource base, undermined by decades of economic and demographic expansion, appeared more fragile than ever. Muted by the upheavals of the sixties, concern resurfaced in often contentious efforts to protect air and water quality, open space, and wilderness areas. During this period of economic change and environmental constraints, a Democratic governor, the son of the great liberal reformer, Pat Brown, entered office. Thirty-seven-year-old Edmund "Jerry" Brown Jr., promising to bring a "new spirit" to Sacramento, defied categorization as a liberal or conservative. He supported the rights of farm workers, opposed the death penalty, and appointed more women and minorities to state office than any of his predecessors. He was also a staunch advocate of environmental protection, resource conservation, and the development of renewable energy sources and sustainable technology. But in fiscal matters, Brown was conservative, asserting that "we are going to cut, squeeze and trim until we reduce the cost of government." His refusal to live in the governor's mansion or use the state limousine and airplane underscored his personal commitment to the "era of limits" philosophy.

By 1982, Brown's popularity had plummeted. A national economic recession and Proposition 13, a property-tax reduction initiative passed by voters in the late 1970s, plunged local and state governments into fiscal crisis. Economic woes prompted worried residents to elect a Republican governor, George Deukmejian. By the mid-1980s, the national and state economy recovered, quelling any lingering concerns that Jerry Brown's cautionary message about learning to live within limits might actually have had substance.

Questions to Consider

- How were the social and political movements described in this chapter connected to those of the sixties? Provide specific examples of the connections.

- To what extent did California's minority groups make significant progress during the seventies and eighties?

- How did the economy change during the "era of limits," and what were the costs associated with its transformation?

- What were the similarities and differences between the Brown and Deukmejian administrations? Can either be easily categorized as liberal or conservative?

The Legacy of the Sixties

During the 1970s and 1980s women, people with disabilities, and gays and lesbians launched new movements for social change. Their quest for equal rights and recognition, inspired by the activists of the sixties, bolstered the state's reputation for diversity and tolerance and ensured that California remained in the forefront of social and cultural change for decades to come. Simultaneously, the state's minority population edged closer to attaining majority status, and reaped concrete benefits from their earlier struggles. Affirmative hiring and admissions policies, which increased employment and educational opportunities, led to the expansion of the middle class. The movement's emphasis on ethnic pride and community self-determination fostered group unity, political awareness, and an artistic and literary renaissance. Most significantly, fair housing and employment legislation afforded some protection against more overt forms of racial discrimination. During the 1970s and 1980s, ethnic minorities sought to consolidate these gains through political action, while simultaneously grappling with a new set of challenges.

Feminism, Disability Rights, and Gay Pride

California's feminist movement, mirroring national trends, took two directions during the "era of limits." Liberal feminists, primarily white, middle-class professionals, worked through existing political channels to address issues like wage equity, reproductive rights, child care, and sex discrimination in government, higher education, and the professions. Radical feminists, younger members of the "protest generation," used more militant tactics to challenge discrimination and alter the cultural values and practices that reinforced women's inequality.

Liberal feminists responded to the lack of political support for gender equity by founding local National Organization for Women (NOW) chapters and joining national efforts to secure passage of the Equal Rights Amendment (ERA). In 1972, California became one of the first states to ratify the amendment, but the battle was far from over. By the 1982 congressional deadline, only thirty-five of the thirty-eight states needed to ensure passage had ratified the ERA.

During the long and ultimately unsuccessful struggle for the ERA, NOW chapters pursued a broader feminist agenda. In 1972 its activists created a statewide organization in California to coordinate the activities of individual chapters and lobby for legislative action. Over the next several years the new organization, located in Sacramento, sponsored assembly and senate bills that addressed inequities in the insurance industry, guaranteed stiffer penalties for repeat sex offenders, and protected the privacy of rape victims. NOW, joined by the California Abortion and Reproductive Rights League (1978), also lobbied for access to abortion and birth control.

During the 1980s NOW and other liberal feminist organizations supported comparable-worth legislation. The number of women in California's labor force had steadily increased during the twentieth century, and by 1970 a majority of women worked for wages. However, most were forced into gender-specific jobs that paid, on the average, only sixty cents for every dollar earned by male workers. Comparable worth, a concept that promoted equal pay for comparable—but not necessarily identical—jobs, was viewed as a solution to these wage disparities. The legislature approved the use of comparable-worth criteria in setting salaries for state employees in 1981. However, Governor George Deukmejian, who opposed government regulation of private industry, vetoed several other bills that would have extended the practice beyond state employment. As late as 1985, a government task force reported that the state's labor market was still segregated by sex, with little change in wage differentials between men and women.

California's women also lagged behind men in holding elected and appointed office. In response, organizations like the California Women's Political Caucus (1973) and the California Elected Women's Association for Education and Research (1974) encouraged women to run for office, lobbied for greater representation in appointed positions, and promoted public education and research on women and the political process. By the mid-1970s, their efforts had produced modest results. Jerry Brown, elected governor in 1974, appointed over 1,600 women to various boards and commissions—more than any previous administration. Women also made gains in the legislature, increasing their representation from six in 1976 to seventeen in 1986. All but four, however, served in the assembly, while the state senate and the congressional delegation remained almost entirely male dominated.

Political gains were even more impressive on the local level. In 1978, following Mayor George Moscone's assassination, Dianne Feinstein was chosen by fellow members of the San Francisco Board of Supervisors to finish his term. In 1979 she won the mayoral contest in her own right, becoming the first woman elected to that post. Subsequently, women were elected as mayors of San Diego, Berkeley, Sacramento, and San José, and to a host of city council and county supervisor offices.

In the meantime, younger, radical feminists argued that "mainstreaming" was not enough. The entire society— its religious and moral beliefs, language, literature, art, media, economy, educational system, and political institutions—undervalued and denigrated women. Throughout the state radical women established small discussion or consciousness-raising groups to share common concerns and come up with strategies for change. Having used direct action to protest racial inequality and the war in Vietnam, many decided to use the same tactics against institutions that they felt degraded women: beauty pageants, the advertising and fashion industries, male-only clubs and professional associations, and the mainstream media.

Similarly, radical feminists followed the countercultural strategy of building alternative institutions: battered women's shelters, rape crisis centers, health clinics, child care cooperatives, bookstores, cultural centers, art galleries, print and publishing collectives, recording and film studios, theater troupes, and urban and rural communes. Within professional associations, women created caucuses to promote feminist research and the hiring and promotion of women. At colleges and universities, feminist students and faculty launched women's studies programs. For example, the women's studies program at San Diego State University, the first in the nation, was established in 1970 by women who had earlier participated in a campus-based consciousness-raising group.

The joint efforts of liberal and radical feminists moved California closer to gender equity, but serious problems remained. Occupational segregation and wage disparities contributed to the "feminization" of poverty in California and the nation as a whole. The women's movement, attracting mostly white, educated, middle-class feminists, was often slow to address such concerns. Women of color also felt isolated by a movement that emphasized sexism, and tended to ignore the impact of racism. In response, African American, Asian American, and Latina feminists often broke away and formed their own organizations, such as Black Women Organized for Action, Asian American Women United, and Mujeres en Marcha.

The disability rights movement, termed the last great civil rights movement and also patterned after the civil rights and ethnic power struggles of the sixties, was founded by a small group of students on the U.C. Berkeley campus. Between

1962 and 1969, the university housed severely disabled students in Cowell Hospital, the campus health center. For the first time, these young people experienced a sense of community, but also faced barriers to full participation in campus and community life—barriers that limited their access to public places, employment, social services, and recreation opportunities. According to one of the students, Phil Draper, "we wanted to be able to control our own destinies—like the philosophies that propelled the civil rights and women's movements."

In 1970, the Berkeley activists, who called themselves the Rolling Quads, formed the Disabled Students' Program on the U.C. campus. A year later they established the Center for Independent Living (CIL) in the city of Berkeley "to give people with disabilities the will and determination to move out of hospitals and institutions," and fully participate in the life of their communities. Over the next several years Berkeley's CIL coordinated independent living arrangements for its clients, and lobbied for increased community access for the disabled. After extensive pressure from the CIL, for example, the Berkeley City Council allocated funds for curb ramps. Activists then lobbied for improved access to buildings, workplaces, recreation facilities, and public transportation.

By the mid-1970s, the disability rights and CIL movements had spread across the nation, and activists focused their efforts on lobbying for federal legislation that advanced their access agenda. In 1973, the Rehabilitation Act was signed into law over President Nixon's veto. Section 504 of the act prohibited any program or agency receiving federal funds from discriminating against handicapped individuals solely on the basis of their disabilities. This was the first time in history that the federal government acknowledged that the exclusion of people with disabilities was a form of discrimination.

The Department of Health, Education and Welfare (HEW) was given the task of drafting guidelines for Section 504's enforcement. However, by 1977, HEW still had not drafted regulations that addressed architectural and communications barriers to access, and reasonable accommodations for people with disabilities. In response, disability rights activists staged sit-ins at HEW offices across the nation. The San Francisco sit-in, lasting twenty-eight days, marked the longest occupation of a federal building in U.S. history. The demonstrations, combined with a lawsuit, letter-writing campaign, and congressional hearings, prompted HEW to act. On May 4, 1977, Section 504 regulations were issued, creating a precedent for the much broader antidiscriminatory protections later provided by the Americans with Disabilities Act (ADA).

During the 1980s, California activists joined the national effort to defend and broaden HEW regulations. Working primarily through the legal system, activists convinced the Supreme Court that Section 504 prohibited employment discrimination and covered people with AIDS and other communicable illnesses. They also obtained federal legislation that allowed the disabled to sue states for violations of Section 504. By 1988 the federal government was ready to introduce a more comprehensive version of the Rehabilitation Act—one that would prohibit all forms of discrimination against people with disabilities, even within organizations and businesses that operated without federal funds. In 1990, the ADA became law, extending to people with disabilities the same protections that the Civil Rights Act of 1964 gave to women and minorities. From its beginnings at Cowell Hospital at U.C. Berkeley, the disability rights movement had become a political force on the local, state, and national levels.

Inspired by the militancy of the sixties, gay and lesbian activists created a host of new organizations to combat discrimination and foster "gay pride." Like radical feminists and disability rights activists, many used direct action to attack homophobic attitudes and institutions. In 1970, for example, gay liberation groups stormed the American Psychiatric Association's annual meeting in San Francisco to protest the profession's characterization of homosexuality as a mental disorder. This and similar protests across the nation prompted the APA in 1973 to delete homosexuality from its *Diagnostic and Statistical Manual of Mental Disorders.*

Like radical feminists, gay liberationists also created alternative institutions and celebrations. Annual gay pride marches in Los Angeles and San Francisco, beginning in 1970, drew ever larger crowds, as did the Gay Games and film festivals. Gay and lesbian community centers, clinics, youth shelters, coffeehouses, restaurants, theaters, sororities, fraternities, choral groups, athletic leagues, and theater companies flourished alongside older gay institutions, adding greater variation and richness to community life.

As these institutions took root, the state became a mecca for those seeking a less-closeted lifestyle. Existing gay and lesbian enclaves, like Venice and West Hollywood, expanded. New communities, like San Diego's Hillcrest neighborhood, sprang to life. And in San Francisco older gay enclaves in the Tenderloin, the South of Market area, and North Beach shifted uptown to the Castro District. In San Francisco alone, the gay population almost doubled between 1972 and 1978, growing from 90,000 to over 150,000.

Growth translated into political power. In 1977 Harvey Milk, a Castro District camera shop owner and community activist, became the first openly gay member of the San Francisco Board of Supervisors. Others soon followed, culminating in the "Lavender Sweep" that brought eleven gays and two lesbians into city office in 1990. Change was even more dramatic in West Hollywood, where, in 1984, voters elected a lesbian mayor and a gay and lesbian majority to the city council. Moreover, by the mid-1980s several cities had included sexual orientation in their nondiscrimination ordinances, banned discrimination against people with AIDS, and acknowledged the validity of domestic partnerships. Such gains, however, were accompanied by a strong, conservative backlash.

The first challenge came in 1977 when state congressman John Briggs sponsored a ballot initiative that would have required school districts "to fire or refuse to hire . . . any teacher, counselor, or aide, or administrator in the public school system . . . who advocates, solicits, imposes, encourages, or promotes private or public homosexual activity . . . that is likely to come to the attention of students or parents." Gay and lesbian activists, working through organizations like the Bay Area Committee Against the Briggs Initiative and the Committee Against the

Briggs Initiative, Los Angeles, convinced voters to reject the measure. However, gay rights advocates soon faced another challenge.

On November 27, 1978, Dan White, a former police officer and member of the Board of Supervisors, murdered San Francisco Supervisor Harvey Milk and Mayor George Moscone. White, who had recently resigned from the board over a series of disagreements with more liberal members, had a change of heart about leaving his post. Moscone, however, was unwilling to reinstate him. Feeling betrayed and defeated by his liberal opponents, White marched into city hall and took his revenge with a gun. Although subject to the death penalty for assassinating public officials, White was only convicted of manslaughter, a charge that carried a sentence of seven years and eight months. The jury, from which gay and lesbian panelists had been excluded, agreed with psychiatrists who testified that White suffered "diminished capacity" from consuming too much junk food—the so-called Twinkie defense.

Following the verdict on May 21, 1979, thousands of protestors converged on city hall, smashing windows and setting police cars on fire. Later that night violence spread to the Castro as angry residents engaged in street battles with what they perceived to be an invading army of police officers. At the end of the "White Night" riots, property damage exceeded $1 million, and hundreds had been injured. Just a few months later another tragedy unfolded.

In 1980 a new disease came to the attention of the Centers for Disease Control. Soon identified as Acquired Immune Deficiency Syndrome (AIDS), it spread rapidly through California's gay male communities and eventually to the general population through blood transfusions, intravenous drug use, and unprotected sex. As the death toll mounted, gay and lesbian activists reacted by creating hospices, food banks, counseling and testing services, shelters, and home care networks. They also rallied to demand increased funding for research, testing, treatment, and prevention. At the same time, the AIDS epidemic gave anti-gay conservatives new ammunition in their moral crusade against homosexuality. Proposition 64, placed on the California ballot in 1986, called for the quarantine of people with AIDS. Another ballot measure, sponsored by Southern California U.S. Representative William Dannemyer in 1988, would have required doctors and clinics to report HIV-positive clients to state authorities. Voters, rejecting attempts to label AIDS a highly contagious "gay disease," defeated both measures. In the meantime, gay and lesbian activists became even more militant. New organizations, like the AIDS Action Coalitions (1987) and ACT-UP (1988), used civil disobedience to counter their conservative critics, demand more funding for treatment and research, and attack the pharmaceutical industry for withholding promising drugs and overcharging consumers.

As older activists met the challenges of the AIDS crisis, a new generation began to broaden the scope of the gay liberation movement. Moving beyond the heterosexual/homosexual paradigm, they created organizations that embraced a wide range of marginalized sexual groups that had often been ignored or excluded by gay and lesbian organizations: bisexuals, transsexuals, transvestites, and those who refused to accept categorization. Queer Nation, representing this new spirit, identified itself as "an informal, multicultural, direct action group committed to the recognition, preservation, expansion, and celebration of queer culture in all its diversity."

Multiethnic Politics, Economics, and Culture

For California's African American population, the 1970s and 1980s brought a higher level of political representation. In 1970 Wilson Riles was elected as the first black superintendent of public instruction. The same year, Marcus Foster became superintendent of the Oakland public schools, the first African American to head a district of that size. Ronald Dellums, elected to the Berkeley City Council in 1967, took a seat in the U.S. Congress in 1970, joining Augustus Hawkins, who had served his Los Angeles district since 1962. Two years later, Yvonne Braithwaite Burke, a former state assemblywoman, also won a seat in the U.S. House of Representatives, raising to three the number of black Californians in Congress. In 1973 Los Angeles City Councilman Thomas Bradley became the city's first African American mayor. Bradley not only served an unprecedented five terms in this office, but also won the Democratic nomination for governor in 1982 and 1986. In 1974 state senator Mervyn Dymally took office as lieutenant governor, and later joined the U.S. Congress. By 1980, black Californians were also well represented in the state legislature, with two senators and six assembly members. Assembly speaker Willie Brown would later become mayor of San Francisco, and assemblywoman Maxine Waters, representing Los Angeles, would join the U.S. Congress.

The state's Hispanic population grew dramatically during the 1970s and 1980s, exceeding 5.7 million by 1985. Constituting nearly 22 percent of the total population by the mid-1980s, Hispanics were California's largest and fastest-growing minority group. Worsening economic conditions in Mexico, combined with an increase in high-tech manufacturing and service sector employment, contributed to some of this growth. However, large numbers of Central Americans and Chileans, fleeing U.S.-sanctioned political repression and violence, also sought refuge in California. As a consequence, the Hispanic population, concentrated primarily in Los Angeles and the San Francisco Bay area, became more diverse. Rapid growth and diversity, in turn, presented challenges to organizations that had long struggled to foster political unity.

In urban areas, middle-class-oriented organizations like LULAC and the GI Forum, which lost membership to more militant groups during the sixties, recovered in the 1970s as strong advocates of political unity, civil rights legislation, and electoral participation. New organizations, such as United Neighborhood Organization (1975) and Communities Organized for Public Services (1974), followed in the footsteps of the Community Service Organization (CSO) by organizing poor and working-class residents to demand political power and better services for their communities. For these and other organizations, the

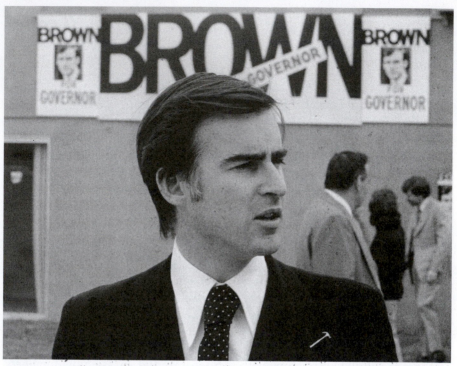

Jerry Brown. How does this image of Governor Jerry Brown contrast with that of Ronald Reagan? Does Brown project the same level of authority, or is his persona more apt to appeal to the increasingly powerful baby boom constituency of the mid-1970s and early 1980s?

primary challenge was how to unify and awaken the "sleeping giant"—the Latino electorate.

During the 1970s, the most striking gains came in the form of political appointments. Governor Jerry Brown, assuming office in 1975, appointed a record number of Hispanics to state agencies and the judiciary, including Secretary of Health, Education and Welfare Mario Obledo. Only a small number of Hispanics held elected office on the local and state levels, despite the fact that the number of eligible voters had dramatically increased. But this was about to change. By the 1980s, the growing influx of undocumented workers, coupled with economic recession, precipitated an anti-immigrant backlash. The Simpson-Mazzolli Immigration Reform and Control Act, passed by Congress in 1986, increased penalties for hiring undocumented workers, and heightened security at the U.S.-Mexico border. The same year, voters approved an amendment to the state constitution establishing that "English is the official language of the State of California," and directing legislators and government officials to "take all steps necessary to ensure that the role of English as the common language of the state is preserved and enhanced." These measures galvanized the Hispanic electorate and led to increased representation in local, state, and national office. The Democratic Party, which took the strongest position in defense of immigrant rights, was the primary beneficiary of this political "awakening."

Within the state's Asian population, Japanese and Chinese Americans made the most striking progress in the political arena. Japanese American activists won a major moral victory in 1980 when Congress agreed to establish the United States Commission on Wartime Relocation and Internment of Civilians. In 1988 the federal government adopted the commission's recommendation to award reparation payments of twenty thousand dollars to each surviving internee, and to issue a formal apology for wartime exclusion and detention. Although Congress failed to appropriate the necessary funds until 1989, and the first payments were not made until 1991, most Japanese Americans felt at least partially vindicated. Significantly, Norman Mineta, one of the state's first Japanese Americans elected to the U.S. House of Representatives, announced the government's decision. In 1976, the year Mineta was initially elected to his post, California voters sent a second Japanese American, Robert Matsui, to Congress, and S. I. Hayakawa to the U.S. Senate. Hayakawa began his controversial political career during the sixties when, as president of San Francisco State University, he took a hard line against student protestors. After his single term in the Senate, he returned to California and spearheaded the campaign for the 1986 "English Only" ballot initiative.

The state's Chinese American residents also made some political progress during the 1970s and 1980s. In 1974, March Fong Eu, elected as secretary of state, became the first Asian American to hold statewide office in California. In 1994, soon after she finished her fourth and final term, her son, Matthew Fong, was elected state treasurer. Chinese Americans also gained representation on the municipal level, holding five elected offices in San Francisco by 1980, and one in Los Angeles by 1985. Reflecting the growing Chinese presence in Monterey Park by the 1980s, voters elected Lily Lee as that city's mayor. In 1974 the state's Chinese Americans won a major legal victory for public school children with limited English language skills. In *Lau* v. *Nichols,* the U.S. Supreme Court ruled that the failure of schools to meet the linguistic needs of children constituted unequal treatment. Two years later, the state legislature mandated bilingual education in California's schools.

The activism of the sixties, including the occupation of Alcatraz Island, reinvigorated the Native American struggle for political visibility and power. In 1983 seventeen terminated tribes were restored to their previous status after winning a class action suit, *Hardwick* v. *United States.* Others were restored through action initiated by California Indian Legal Services. However, the federal government was slow to help these tribes regain their land base and reestablish their tribal governments. During the 1970s the Yuroks fought to protect their fishing rights along the Klamath River and the Achumawis took legal action against Pacific Gas & Electric to reclaim land in northeastern California. In Santa Barbara, Indians occupied a spiritually significant site to prevent construction of an oil tanker terminal. Others, having lost their land and tribal identity, reunified and sought formal recognition from the federal government. For example, the Tolowas of Del Norte County, driven to the brink of extinction in the nineteenth century by disease and white violence, gradually recovered. In the mid-1980s, they applied for tribal status—a status that promised federal funds for education and health care, and the legal standing to assert their land rights. Other groups, however, could ill afford the long and costly process of establishing common ancestral ties among surviving tribal members.

In the economic arena, the state's African American population experienced both gains and persistent barriers to advancement during the 1970s and 1980s. Affirmative hiring policies and fair employment legislation led to the growth of the black middle class. Entrepreneurship also increased, aided in part by minority contract programs. By the 1980s California had more black-owned businesses than any other state in the nation, supporting thousands of workers with a payroll of $217 million. At the same time, stronger enforcement of fair housing legislation allowed more prosperous African Americans to move out of the inner city. As a consequence, the older black enclaves of Los Angeles, San Francisco, and Oakland lost some of their economic diversity. In some cases, middle-class flight also altered the ethnic composition of neighborhoods. Watts, for example, went from being a predominantly black enclave to one that is now mostly Asian and Hispanic.

Economic mobility, however, was offset by an increase in black poverty. During the postwar period, inner cities had steadily lost jobs to the suburbs. In the 1970s and 1980s heavy industry, whether in the urban core or in outlying areas, began to leave the state altogether. Without blue-collar jobs, traditionally a source of upward mobility for those with less education and training, thousands slipped into poverty. State and national cuts in social spending, including Aid to Families with Dependent Children (AFDC), compounded the plight of California's most disadvantaged families. By 1980 nearly three-fourths of all black families lived in poverty. Black workers were twice as likely as whites to be unemployed, and the jobless rate for black youths stood at 40 percent—where it had been just before the Watts riot. Even with the expansion of the black middle class, the average annual income of African American families was only 60 percent of the white average.

Barriers to equal education were part of the problem. Inner-city schools had not only fewer resources than their suburban counterparts, but also a much larger population of disadvantaged youngsters. Recognizing that housing discrimination and income disparities between blacks and whites had contributed to de facto school segregation, many municipalities adopted school integration plans as early as the 1960s. However, Los Angeles, containing the state's largest school district, had long ignored the fact that 90 percent of its black children attended predominantly black schools. In 1970, after the American Civil Liberties Union (ACLU) filed a lawsuit against the district, the state's supreme court judge, Alfred Gitelson, ordered its officials to initiate an integration plan. In 1978, after losing several appeals, the district finally implemented a mandatory busing plan for its students. However, in 1979 California voters approved a constitutional amendment that limited mandatory busing to cases of legal or intentional segregation. As a consequence of this decision, Los Angeles and other cities abandoned mandatory busing. By this time, many affluent parents—most of them white—had simply removed their children from public schools, or relocated to suburban districts. With or without busing, California's public schools would remain highly segregated by race and class.

Affirmative college admission programs, another attempt to ensure educational equity, also came under attack shortly after they were implemented. Beginning in 1969, the U.C. Davis medical school reserved sixteen out of one hundred annual admission slots for minority students. In 1973 and again in 1974 Allan Bakke was turned down for admission. He concluded that Davis rejected him because he was white, and that affirmative action constituted a form of reverse discrimination. After the state supreme court upheld his position, the university appealed to the U.S. Supreme Court. In 1978, the justices ruled five to four in favor of Bakke. However, their decision fell short of a blanket condemnation of affirmative action. Such programs, they maintained, were constitutional as long as race was not the only consideration in evaluating an application. For the time being, racial criteria could still be used to increase the diversity of the student population and ensure equal access to higher education.

For Latinos, economic progress was also mixed with challenges. Throughout the 1970s, agricultural workers continued to benefit from the protections offered by the United Farm Workers. After its successful table grape boycott in the late sixties, the union moved on to organize the state's lettuce workers. This brought renewed conflict with the Teamsters' Union. Claiming to represent field workers in the Salinas Valley, the Teamsters signed contracts with several large lettuce growers that provided few benefits for farm labor. Resenting the UFW's challenge to what they perceived as their jurisdiction, the Teamsters, with growers' support, mounted a campaign of violence and intimidation against their rival union. The UFW responded by launching a lettuce boycott and lobbying for state legislation that would create an Agricultural Labor Relations Board to supervise union elections and recognize only "one industrial bargaining unit per farm." The bill, also allowing legalized strikes and secondary boycotts, passed in 1975. The state gave farm workers the legal right to choose a bargaining agent, and made a commitment to guaranteeing that elections were noncoerced and fair. Moreover, the law mandated that only the union receiving the majority of votes be allowed to represent the workers on any given farm.

A weakness of the Agricultural Labor Relations Act was that it failed to grant organizers the right to enter farms to speak with workers. Growers could legally block the entry of UFW members while allowing free access to the Teamsters. The Labor Relations Board also lacked the funding necessary to follow up on the many violations of the act, particularly election fraud. Cesar Chavez decided to appeal directly to California voters by launching an initiative campaign. Proposition 14, which appeared on the November 1976 ballot, would have given union organizers free access to the state's farms and provided adequate funding for the Labor Relations Board. Growers, using deceptive scare tactics similar to those used to overturn the Rumford Fair Housing Act, convinced voters that the initiative threatened the property rights of all citizens. The measure failed, and the UFW was forced to devote scarce resources to more-labor-intensive efforts to recruit new members.

The Agricultural Labor Relations Act was also weakened when Governor George Deukmejian, who took office in 1983, undermined the regulatory function of its board by stacking it with anti-labor members and staff. The growing number of undocumented workers, jurisdictional disputes with rival unions, and a costly new grape boycott further diluted the strength of the organization and undercut its efforts to recruit new members.

Over the next two decades, the UFW took on new battles: the abolition of the short-handled hoe, protecting workers from excessive exposure to pesticides, preventing growers from using undocumented labor to break strikes, and supporting the rights of immigrant workers. The union's campaign against the short-handled hoe—a tool that crippled thousands of workers—was successful. The other issues, along with the loss of contracts to competing unions and the impact of mechanization on the agricultural labor force, remain on the UFW agenda. With Chavez's death on April 23, 1993, the union suffered a tremendous loss—a loss compounded by financial problems stemming from a series of lawsuits filed by growers against the union.

In the meantime, a majority of Hispanic workers were employed in nonagricultural sectors of the economy, particularly in low-wage service and high-tech assembly occupations. These sectors, although expanding during the 1970s and 1980s, were largely nonunion. Organized labor, focusing its resources on preserving jobs and membership in heavy industry, was only beginning to reassess its role in the new economy. It would be another decade before service workers, like some janitors and home-care providers, organized and enjoyed the benefits of union representation.

California's Asian American population continued to grow throughout the 1970s and 1980s as immigrants from Hong Kong, Taiwan, Korea, and the Philippines benefited from the 1965 abolition of the national-origins quota system. After the fall of Saigon in 1975 the state also received increasing numbers of Southeast Asian refugees. By 1985 about 750,000 Vietnamese, Laotians, Hmong, and Cambodians had resettled in the United States, with roughly 40 percent choosing California as their final destination. Southeast Asians, admitted under a refugee provision in the 1965 Immigration and Nationality Act, arrived with special needs. A majority came with few resources, poor English language skills, little understanding of American culture, and a history of emotional and physical trauma.

By 1985, an estimated 350,000 refugees had resettled in California. Under the Refugee Act of 1980, the federal government agreed to provide thirty-six months of financial support to help newcomers achieve economic self-sufficiency. A year later the Reagan administration reduced support to eighteen months, and decreased funding for refugee assistance programs. As a consequence, state agencies and a growing number of refugee self-help organizations were forced to bear an increasing share of the resettlement burden. The outcome, however, was not entirely negative. Mutual aid organizations, which were given priority in obtaining the remaining federal resettlement funds, were operated by members of the refugee community. Understanding the barriers to assimilation and economic independence, they were able to provide services in a more culturally sensitive manner than state and federal agencies. Moreover, mutual aid societies provided a nucleus for emerging refugee communities, and helped foster the development of internal leadership.

While Southeast Asians put down roots, Chinese and Japanese Americans made strides in education and income. The state's Japanese American residents achieved the most unambiguous measure of success, surpassing the white population in education, representation in professional occupations, life expectancy, family income, and individual earnings. Although Chinese Americans also surpassed whites in high school graduation rates, college attendance, and median family income, their community remained bifurcated. A high proportion had obtained advanced degrees and professional employment, but many lacked the language skills, education, and occupational training to move beyond low-wage service and manufacturing jobs. The experience of Filipino and Korean immigrants also challenged the model minority stereotype. By 1980 Korean Americans were 50 percent more likely than whites to be self-employed or working for a family-owned business. A majority of their businesses, however, were small, requiring the unpaid labor of more than one family member to survive. In addition, Korean entrepreneurship was often the only acceptable substitute for well-educated professionals who faced language and accreditation barriers, and discrimination in their chosen fields.

Filipinos, who displaced Chinese residents as California's largest Asian group in 1980, also found that their education and training did not guarantee professional employment. Consequently, the number entering the United States on professional visas declined from 27 percent of all Filipino immigrants in the early 1970s to 2 percent in 1981. Nor was educational success an Asian American universal. In 1980 through 1981, one-quarter of the state's Filipino high school students, mostly second-generation, failed to graduate. This percentage, far in excess of the 11 percent dropout rate for all Asian Americans, more closely corresponded to the 31 percent average for blacks, and the 35 percent average for Latinos. Finally, while Koreans and Filipinos enjoyed higher median family incomes than whites, they averaged more wage earners per family. When earnings were calculated on a per-person rather than family basis, both groups earned less than whites, even given their higher levels of educational attainment.

Economically, California Indians remained the most disadvantaged of the state's ethnic groups. During the 1980s several tribes introduced bingo on their reservations, raising much-needed revenue from outside patrons. These enterprises, exempt from legal prohibitions against gaming, paved the way for the casino gambling initiatives of the late 1990s, which, while controversial, hold the promise of greater economic autonomy for California's Indian tribes.

Throughout the state, each of these groups made striking contributions in the cultural arena. California's African American population enjoyed greater cultural visibility during the seventies and eighties. Hollywood, responding to criticism from black actors, audiences, filmmakers, and civil rights groups, began to offer more diverse, dramatic portrayals of African American life. Independent filmmakers, benefiting from the cultural awareness that grew out of the social movements of the sixties, reached a wider audience. Marlon Riggs, for example, produced award-winning documentaries on racial stereotypes and black gay identity that aired on public television stations across the nation. Newly established ethnic studies programs and academic associations promoted scholarship on African American history, psychology, politics, health, education, and culture. A new generation of black writers, including poet June Jordan, novelist Ishmael Reed, and social critic Angela Davis, increasingly captured the attention of a multicultural readership. Black dance and theater companies provided new venues for performing artists. And the music world embraced talent as diverse as Tower of Power and the innovative conductor of the Oakland Symphony, Calvin Simmons.

For Latinos, the cultural renaissance launched during the sixties continued into the 1980s. Luis Valdez, founder of El Teatro Campesino, produced a number of plays that reached audiences beyond the farm worker movement. *Zoot Suit, Bandido, Los Corridos,* and *I Don't Have to Show You No Stinkin' Badges,* for example, highlighted Chicano history, folk culture, and political resistance. Muralists continued to decorate public spaces with colorful depictions of historical figures and events, and to commemorate contemporary struggles against immigration restrictions, freeway construction, and urban "renewal" projects. Cultural centers and museums housed and promoted the arts. Mexican American studies programs produced a new generation of scholars, writers, and artists. And barrios, housing a growing number of businesses and cultural institutions, Hispanicized surrounding communities. San Francisco's Mission District, for example, attracted a growing number of outside visitors to its cultural events, restaurants, and markets by the late 1980s. Finally, despite "English Only" legislation, the state maintained and strengthened its commitment to bilingual education, and issued an increasing number of publications, including election materials, in the Spanish language.

In the cultural arena, Asian American scholars, writers, and artists continued to explore their cultural heritage and challenge negative ethnic stereotypes. Maxine Hong Kingston, Jeanne Wakatsuki, Janice Mirikatni, and Yoshiko Uchida enriched and enlivened the state's literary canon. Judy Narita's one-woman show, exploring stereotypes of Asian American women, won the Los Angeles Drama Critics' Circle Award, Drama-Logue Award, and the Association of Asian/Pacific Artists' "Jimmie" Award. Films, including *Farewell to Manzanar,* "*Gam Saan Haak*" (*Guests of Gold Mountain*), *Sewing Woman, The Fall of the I Hotel, Bean Sprouts,* and *China, Land of My Father,* depicted the diversity, strength, and resourcefulness of Asian Americans to broader audiences.

A new generation of Indian activists focused on preserving and reclaiming tribal culture and history. Scholar/writers like Paula Gunn Allen, Greg Sarris, and Gerald Vizenor have devoted their careers to chronicling, interpreting, and establishing the contemporary relevance of traditional myths and cultural practices. Individual tribes, like the Cupeno and Cahuilla, alarmed over the disappearance of their cultural traditions, established cultural centers and museums to preserve their language, history, and tribal artifacts. In 1976 the California Native Heritage Commission was established to help Indians preserve culturally significant sites and artifacts. The Indian Repatriation Act, passed by Congress in 1990, gave tribes across the nation the right to recover cultural artifacts and ancestral remains that had long been held in public museums and institutions. It also prohibited individuals from desecrating or appropriating Indian remains and cultural property.

Economic Changes and Environmental Constraints

In the early 1970s the long era of uninterrupted postwar prosperity came to an abrupt halt. From that point forward, California's economy faced a series of challenges rooted in overseas competition, deindustrialization and capital flight, and shifts in federal spending priorities. As residents entered this new era of economic uncertainty, they also confronted the environmental costs associated with decades of uncontrolled growth. Air and water pollution, diminishing open space, toxic wastes, and resource shortages eroded the quality of life and generated an unprecedented level of public support for regulatory legislation. In the long run, however, it would prove extremely difficult to reconcile ecological constraints with private economic interests and consumer habits. By the mid-1980s, environmental degradation, while slowed by protective measures, was still proceeding with alarming rapidity.

The Economy

Despite periodic downturns, California's economy, by conventional measures of growth, expanded during the 1970s and 1980s. In contrast to its industrial competitors in the East and the Midwest, the state benefited from its competitive edge in the high-tech industry and growing trade with the Pacific Rim, Mexico, and Latin America. As a consequence, the California economy enjoyed an overall increase in corporate profits, gross domestic product, per capita income, and job creation. By the late 1980s, the state's economy outperformed that of most *nations,* ranking sixth in gross domestic product, seventh in the amount of goods and services produced, and twelfth in the value of its international trade.

For large segments of the ever-expanding labor force, however, economic growth did not translate into a higher standard of living. Inflation outpaced wage increases, leading to a decline in real income. Blue-collar jobs in heavy industry increasingly moved overseas or to lower-wage regions of the United States. Many of the newly created jobs were in the service sector, paying lower wages, and affording fewer benefits and opportunities for upward mobility than the industrial jobs that they had replaced. The economic costs of "deindustrialization" were staggering. East Los Angeles, for example, lost ten of its twelve largest manufacturing industries between 1978 and 1982, at a cost of fifty thousand jobs. Fontana, fifty miles to the east, was built around the state's largest steel mill. In 1983 the plant closed, depriving six thousand workers of their jobs and completely destroying the city's industrial base. Oakland and southern Alameda County also felt the impact of deindustrialization and capital flight as businesses closed or relocated where labor and operating costs were lower.

However, California's geographic position on the Pacific Rim and higher levels of economic diversification helped cushion the transition to a service-based economy. By the 1970s, global industrial production shifted from the United States and Europe to developing nations, especially Asian countries. California, situated at the edge of this emerging industrial center, eagerly exploited the economic advantages of foreign trade. By 1984, Pacific Rim nations were buying 78 percent of the state's exports, including agricultural commodities, aircraft, electronics, and military hardware. In turn, they supplied 85 percent of the state's imports, usually at a lower cost to consumers than domestic producers. At the same time, Asian financiers invested in California real estate, financial institutions, hotel and convention facilities, and industry. By 1985, one out of every five jobs in the state was linked directly to trade, with countless others dependent on the influx of investment capital.

Like the rest of the nation, however, California was plagued by a growing trade deficit, spending more on imports than it obtained from its exports. Moreover, more jobs moved overseas than were created by new partnerships with Asian investors. Even California's seemingly invincible electronics industry was in constant danger of losing its competitive edge to overseas manufacturers. Nevertheless, the state's political and business leaders remained convinced that the benefits of Pacific Rim trade would outweigh its short-term disadvantages.

California also had the advantage of a more diverse economic base. Long before most states faced the sudden and traumatic transition to a postindustrial economic order, California had shifted from heavy manufacturing to services. Before World War II, over half of the state's work force was employed in the service sector—jobs including social services, government, education, transportation, retail and wholesale trade, real estate, finance, insurance, and utilities. By 1970 almost 70 percent of the work force held service sector jobs, with only 27 percent employed in manufacturing and construction. During the 1970s and 1980s, the service sector continued to expand, accounting for over three-fourths of all new jobs created in California.

The growth of service sector employment created new job opportunities for many of the state's residents. However, workers who lost their jobs in heavy industry often lacked the education and skills to obtain higher-level service

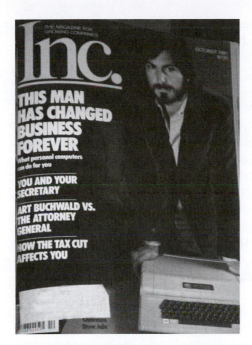

Steve Jobs on *Inc.* cover. Steve Jobs, chairman of Apple Computer and a so-called "Computer Kid" who launched the personal computing revolution, radiates youthful charm and confidence from this 1981 magazine cover. How did images like this one boost the state's reputation as a place of experimentation, innovation, and openness to alternative work and lifestyles?

employment. Instead, they settled for jobs on its lowest rungs: data processing, telemarketing, retail, food service, custodial, customer service, and institutional, home, and child care. Thus, fewer Californians were able to maintain a middle-class lifestyle, and many entered the ranks of the working poor.

Another growth sector of the economy was the high-tech industry. By the late 1950s, Stanford's research park had attracted a growing number of firms that developed transistor-based components for radios, televisions, calculators, missile guidance systems, and other electronic devices. Stanford professor William Shockley, a pioneer of transistor technology, soon pushed the industry in a new direction. Experiments at Shockley Transistor Company and its spinoff, Fairchild Semiconductor, led to the development of the integrated circuit, a silicon-based microprocessor that could transmit electrical signals with greater efficiency and speed, and store huge volumes of information in "memory." The silicon chip, introduced in 1959, led to the development of thousands of new products, including mainframe computers.

Relatively large in size and expensive, most early computers were used by government and private industry. However, by the mid-1970s entrepreneurs were developing computers for personal use. From there the industry boomed. The once pastoral Santa Clara Valley became Silicon Valley, home to high-tech millionaires and 20 percent of the nation's high-tech workers. But while entrepreneurs, engineers, and managers prospered, those who worked on the electronics assembly lines often earned little more than minimum wage. Production workers, mostly immigrant women, were almost exclusively nonunionized, despite their notoriously low wages and dangerous working conditions. Moreover, as housing prices soared, few could afford to live close to their jobs. The industry's golden image was also tarnished by its growing economic vulnerability. By the mid-1980s, foreign competition eroded sales and profits, and produced a wave of layoffs, salary cuts, plant closings, and "downsizings." Although the high-tech industry eventually recovered, Californians came to realize that overreliance on a single industry came with a price.

The state's defense industry, one of its economic mainstays, also had its ups and downs. Dependent on federal contracts, the industry prospered and declined according to Washington's budget priorities. During the late 1960s and early 1970s, as national defense outlays slumped, California's aerospace industry was forced to cut employment by 40 percent. From the mid-1970s to 1980, defense expenditures gradually increased, leading to a modest recovery. When Ronald Reagan assumed the presidency in 1981, federal military spending skyrocketed, bringing unprecedented prosperity to private defense contractors, weapons labs, and military bases. In 1985, for example, Lawrence Livermore Lab received about 35 percent of the Department of Energy's research and development funds, while private industry claimed one-fifth of the nation's total defense budget. This expansion continued until 1989, when the collapse of the Soviet Union ended the Cold War. By the early 1990s, California's defense industries, facing massive reductions in federal funding, were forced to lay off hundreds of thousands of workers.

Environmental Activism and Constraints

Along with these new economic challenges, Californians faced environmental limits to growth. Like other Americans, they had long assumed that natural resources were inexhaustible, or that technological innovation would outpace environmental constraints. However, by the early 1970s a new generation of activists, emerging out of the counterculture and the new Left, sought to redefine America's relationship to the natural environment. Like Thoreau, these young rebels viewed nature as a purifying, spiritually energizing force, a refuge from the violence, competition, and greed of mainstream society. By the late 1960s many began to abandon overcrowded, increasingly crime-ridden hippie enclaves for rural areas. Others, however, stayed behind in urban areas to bring nature back to the city. Whether urban or rural, these back-to-the-land pioneers created a host of countercultural institutions: organic farms, food co-ops, natural food stores and restaurants, recycling and ecology centers, and sustainable living demonstration projects like the Berkeley Integral Urban House and the San Diego Center for Appropriate Technology. An alternative press, disseminating publications like *Laurel's Kitchen Handbook for Vegetarian Cookery and Nutrition* and the *Whole Earth Catalog,* also placed California at the center of this back-to-the-land movement.

Just as significantly, baby boom activists brought new vigor and militancy to the state's environmental movement. Traditional preservationist organizations such as the Sierra Club, National Wildlife Federation, Audubon Society, and Wilderness Society attracted thousands of new members and adopted a less compromising, more militant posture toward their opponents. This included aggressive political lobbying and the use of lawsuits and injunctions to advance their agendas.

Preservationists, however, were only one beneficiary of this new ecological consciousness. Friends of the Earth (1969), League of Conservation Voters (1970), and the Earth Island Institute (1981) attracted young activists by emphasizing a full range of environmental concerns along with more traditional preservationist issues. These three organizations, founded in California but national in scope, addressed resource depletion, overflowing landfills, air and water pollution, species extinction, nuclear contamination, despoliation of wetlands and fisheries, the development of open space and agricultural land, waste dumps, and international environmental issues. Like the older organizations, however, they relied on public education, political lobbying, policy analyses and development, and endorsing or criticizing elected officials.

As environmental concern deepened in the late 1970s and early 1980s, many activists adopted the more militant tactics of the sixties to advance their agenda. In California, organizations like the Abalone Alliance (1977) and Earth First! (1980) engaged in civil disobedience to block the construction of nuclear power plants and the logging of old-growth forests. They also adopted a new philosophical orientation toward nature. Two elements of this philosophy—bioregionalism and ecofeminism—first emerged in California. Bioregionalists argued that humans should establish societies that honor and protect the integrity of natural ecological communities. As a result of their efforts, wetland and creek restoration projects, greenbelt alliances, agricultural and open space land trusts, school and community gardens all proliferated during the late 1970s and 1980s. In some cases, bioregionalism even had an impact on local government, leading cities like Berkeley and Santa Monica to adopt eco-friendly policies like comprehensive recycling programs, municipal greenbelts and organic gardens, and bicycle routes.

Inspired by the work of Berkeley scholars Susan Griffin and Carolyn Merchant, ecofeminism charged that patriarchal values and institutions, deeply rooted in Western tradition, denigrated women as well as nature. Like bioregionalists, ecofeminists called for a shift from anthropocentrism to ecological equality—to a society based on cooperation, diversity, conservation, and stability rather than competition, uniformity, exploitation, and progress. But unlike other radical environmentalists, ecofeminists blended feminism with ecology and gave women the moral authority to claim a leadership role within the contemporary environmental movement.

Although the state's environmental movement broadened its base and adopted new, more militant strategies and tactics during the seventies and eighties, it largely ignored the needs and concerns of economically disadvantaged communities. A majority of organizations attracted a mostly white, middle-class

Santa Barbara oil spill. The 1969 Santa Barbara oil spill contaminated hundreds of square miles of ocean and thirty miles of coastline with oil. How might this and other images of the spill have threatened the state's golden reputation as a place where economic growth and great natural beauty coexisted in perfect harmony?

membership, and focused on preservation, resource management, and pollution control. In the meantime, impoverished inner cities and rural communities lacked the economic and political clout to demand protection from polluting industries and toxic waste dumping. Even more troubling, many were forced to choose between jobs and environmental quality. By the mid-1980s, however, poor communities of color began a movement to tackle "environmental racism." In 1985, Concerned Citizens of South Central Los Angeles, and Mothers of East Los Angeles, representing the city's largest Latino and African American communities, led the way in adding a new dimension to the ethnic power struggles of earlier decades.

Environmental activists only partially succeeded in altering patterns of consumption and resource management—despite their creativity and political clout. Petroleum dependence was a particularly vexing problem. In the early 1970s the Organization of Petroleum Exporting Countries (OPEC) reduced oil exports to the United States, and instituted a series of price increases. The resulting "energy crisis," which fueled inflation and contributed to a nationwide economic recession, was particularly painful for auto-dependent Californians. Several critical industries, including chemicals, plastics, fertilizers, power generation, agriculture, and tourism, also depended on fossil fuels. Offshore oil reserves held some promise of alleviating the crisis, but the disastrous Santa Barbara oil spill of 1969 had produced strong public opposition to coastal drilling. Similarly, the nuclear power industry, which used the crisis to promote atomic energy as a clean, inexhaustible alternative, faced mounting public criticism over safety issues and cost effectiveness.

In Sacramento, the new governor, Jerry Brown, promoted conservation and the development of renewable energy sources as partial solutions to the crisis. Jimmy Carter's administration in Washington followed suit, calling on Americans to fight inflation and unemployment by reducing their consumption of imported oil.

From the 1970s to the early 1980s Californians reduced their energy consumption by purchasing fuel-efficient vehicles and appliances, insulating their homes and water heaters, and more carefully monitoring their use of gas and electricity. The California Energy Commission, created in 1975, promoted such measures by setting energy efficiency standards for new household appliances and commercial and residential construction. The government also promoted the development of energy alternatives. In 1977 the state legislature enacted a tax credit program for consumers who purchased solar energy systems. The following year legislators approved tax incentives for the commercial development of wind energy, giving rise to a series of "wind farms" across the state. Finally, the Public Utilities Commission provided incentives for industries to produce their own electricity through cogeneration.

These measures helped Californians reduce their oil consumption by an astonishing 17 percent between 1979 and 1983. However, this progress was only temporary. When oil prices tumbled in the early 1980s, consumption—particularly in personal transportation—zoomed upward. By 1985 the state was more dependent than ever on imported oil as residents shrugged off their concern and took to the road in a new generation of gas-guzzling vehicles.

At the height of the energy crisis, Californians entered a two-year period of severe drought that necessitated strict water conservation measures and heightened competition over the state's water resources. Agricultural lobbyists and southern residents revived their campaign for a Peripheral Canal that would increase their annual water supply by seven hundred thousand acre-feet by diverting water directly from the Sacramento River into the existing California Aqueduct. Northern Californians and environmentalists countered that the health of the San Francisco Bay and Delta, dependent on regular infusions of fresh water, would be compromised by the proposed project. The California Water Project, they argued, already diverted too much water, endangering fragile delta, bay, and offshore ecosystems. And agribusiness, the largest water consumer of all, had not done its share to conserve resources or safely dispose of salt-, pesticide-, and fertilizer-laden runoff. Instead of diverting more water from the north, the opposition called for conservation, wastewater reclamation, and curbs on suburban growth.

During the late 1970s, the Brown administration worked to forge a compromise between these competing interests. The result, Senate Bill 200, was passed by the legislature in June of 1980. The bill, while appropriating funds for the canal, also called for constitutional amendments that would strengthen protections for the delta and northcoast rivers. Northern Californians and environmentalists quickly mounted a referendum campaign to overturn the legislation. In June of 1982 state voters approved Proposition 9, defeating the proposed canal by a 62 to 38 percent margin. However, the state's water wars were far from over. In 1984, Governor George Deukmejian proposed the construction of a scaled-back version of the Peripheral Canal. When opponents threatened to force "Duke's Ditch" onto the 1986 ballot, the year he would be up for reelection, Deukmejian withdrew the proposal. Meanwhile, new battles erupted over existing water resources. In the early 1980s San Joaquin Valley farmers drained thousands of acre-feet of agricultural wastewater into the Kesterson National Wildlife Refuge. The discharge, contaminated with pesticide residues, selenium, and salts, created frightening abnormalities in the refuge's wildlife population. Growers, facing mounting criticism from environmentalists, argued that the practice protected their land from salt buildup. In 1985 the Interior Department settled the dispute when it ordered farmers to halt discharge into Kesterson. However, the growing problem of agricultural soil contamination still defies solution.

In the north, the wildlife at Mono Lake faced a different threat. The City of Los Angeles had diverted water from the area since the 1940s, but in 1970 began to tap the entire flow of the lake's tributaries. Lake levels dropped precipitously, joining what had once been an island to the shoreline. The California seagull population, which used the island as a breeding ground, was now exposed to predators. Moreover, the increasing salt content of the lake threatened brine shrimp, the major food source of nesting gulls. In 1983, the state supreme court ruled that water rights could be modified or suspended if diversion caused environmental harm. After years of subsequent litigation, Los Angeles was forced to relinquish its water rights, allow the lake to return to pre-diversion levels, and regulate all future diversions to maintain that level.

Yet other conflicts erupted over California's scenic and wild rivers. In 1983 environmentalists lost the long battle to prevent impoundment of the free-flowing Stanislaus River behind the New Melones Dam. However, they succeeded in blocking projects along the Tuolumne, Klamath, Eel, Trinity, Smith, and Lower American Rivers. The Sacramento River Delta also received added protection in 1986 when Congress authorized the release of federal water to preserve the region's fisheries and wildlife habitats.

California's resources, stretched to the limit by population growth, were also threatened by pollution and poor management. State and federal water quality standards, established in the 1960s and 1970s, and enforced by the Water Resources Control Board and nine regional agencies, reduced the amount of organic contaminants flowing into the state's waterways. However, the threat from inorganic substances, including heavy metals, PCBs, dioxin, solvents, fuel, pesticides, and fuel additives, increased during the 1970s and 1980s. Illegal dumping and routine violation of bans on certain chemicals prompted voters to pass an anti-toxics initiative in 1986. This law prohibited the discharge of substances that caused cancer and birth defects into water supplies, held the government more accountable for enforcement, and allowed citizens to file lawsuits against violators. The Deukmejian administration, however, held up implementation of the law until the late 1980s by failing to compile a list of regulated toxics.

The problem continued to grow. By the mid-1980s industry produced over 26.5 million truckloads of toxic substances annually. In Silicon Valley alone, toxic solvents leaking from storage tanks at over 120 different sites had contaminated surrounding soil and water. Defense plants, gas stations, oil refineries, and military bases were also common sources of toxic pollution. Cleanup, even with federal support, could take years and cost billions of dollars. And some contaminated sites, including sediment deposits in the San Francisco Bay, can never be restored to health. Bay fish are so heavily contaminated that the public has been cautioned against consuming them.

Federal and state air quality legislation, requiring automobile and oil companies to produce cleaner vehicles and fuel, led to modest improvements in air quality in the state's older urban centers in the 1970s. However, population growth, concentrated in outlying suburbs, created new smog belts. The Central and Sacramento Valleys, San Bernardino, Orange, East Contra Costa, and San Diego Counties, and the Los Angeles suburbs regularly exceeded federal air quality standards. As smog blew east, it damaged vegetation in Sequoia National Park and the San Bernardino Mountains. Even the Tahoe Basin, suffering from overdevelopment and traffic congestion, faced a growing air pollution problem.

In 1977 the federal government amended the Clean Air Act to require smog inspection programs for states that routinely violated federal air quality standards. After the Environmental Protection Agency (EPA) threatened to withhold funds for highway and sewage treatment projects, California finally adopted a sufficiently rigorous vehicle inspection program. The law, adopted in 1982, required that automobiles pass a smog test every two years. If owners refused to comply, the vehicle's registration would lapse.

Public transportation, the state's long-term solution to its air quality problems, took a step forward in the 1970s. The Bay Area Rapid Transit System, which carried its first passengers in 1972, provided a clean, efficient transportation alternative for East Bay and San Francisco residents. The system, expanded during the 1980s and 1990s, also provided a model for other communities, including San Diego, San José, Sacramento, and most recently, Los Angeles. Still, most Californians preferred private transportation, and increasingly rejected smaller, more fuel-efficient cars in favor of sport-utility vehicles that are not held to the same emissions standards as automobiles.

Growth control measures sponsored by citizens and municipal governments have also met with mixed results. By the mid-1980s at least twenty-five cities and counties passed measures that limited or attached conditions to new construction. But rural areas, eager for the benefits of an expanding tax base, were less willing to limit development. As housing costs increased in established communities, home buyers sought more affordable alternatives in rural areas. To the north, burgeoning suburbs gobbled up fertile farmland in Tracy, Gilroy, Pleasant Hill, Fairfield, Vacaville, Napa, and Santa Rosa. To the south, development pressed into the far reaches of San Diego, Riverside, Los Angeles, and Ventura Counties.

The loss of agricultural land was particularly troubling. In 1965, the state legislature passed the California Agricultural Land Conservation Act to preserve this vital resource. As suburbs spread into rural areas, land values and property taxes increased. Farmers who resisted the temptation to sell to developers faced increasing tax assessments. If farmers signed a ten-year contract agreeing to keep their land in agricultural production, the Land Conservation Act guaranteed that local governments would assess their property at the lower, agricultural level, rather than at subdivided value. However, local governments, wishing to encourage development, frequently allowed farm owners to sell before their contracts had expired. When the courts demanded stricter compliance, developers successfully lobbied for new escape clauses to the Land Conservation Act. By the mid-1980s, legislative efforts to protect agricultural land from suburban development had failed.

Environmentalists' efforts to preserve open space and wilderness areas were also mixed. In 1972 state voters approved Proposition 20, a ballot measure that created a temporary Coastal Commission to regulate development and preserve public access to the shoreline. After vigorous lobbying from conservationists, the legislature voted to create a permanent commission in 1976. With the authority to grant or deny development permits, the commission had jurisdiction over the state's coastline from one thousand yards inland to three miles offshore. During the Brown administration, the commission rejected or called for modification of thousands of development proposals. Deukmejian, more sympathetic to developers, cut the agency's budget and staff, and appointed like-minded commissioners who approved several large hotel and residential projects. The power of the commission was further eroded by a series of budgetary and jurisdictional limits pushed through by pro-development lobbyists.

The Tahoe Regional Planning Agency (TRPA), established by the U.S. Congress in 1969 and jointly managed by California and Nevada, represented another governmental effort to regulate growth and halt environmental degradation. Throughout the 1970s the agency, heavily influenced by developers, did little to advance its own mandate. Construction of casinos, resorts, and housing continued, placing severe strain on the basin's sewage system, roads, air quality, and already limited water supply. Under growing pressure from the federal government and various conservation groups the TRPA finally adopted more stringent environmental protection standards and a new regional plan.

The TRPA's 1984 plan, a compromise between Nevada's pro-development forces and more conservation-minded Californians, allowed for construction of six hundred housing units annually over the next three years, with a case-by-case assessment of environmentally sensitive lots. The League to Save Lake Tahoe and California's attorney general immediately filed legal suits against the agency, charging that the plan violated earlier regional protection compacts. In 1985, the federal court of appeals agreed, suspending the plan and halting all new development in the region. Forced back to the drawing board, the TRPA issued a new plan in 1987 that limited construction to three hundred homes annually, and commercial development to four hundred thousand square feet over the next decade. Amendments also established an environmental ranking system for residential lots, and restricted construction in ecologically sensitive areas such as stream zones. Federal and state legislation, authorizing the use of public funds to purchase environmentally sensitive sites, complemented the TRPA's efforts to restore Tahoe's water quality and wildlife habitat. Critics, however, argued that these measures were too little too late. Sadly, the basin's continuing decline appears to support their contention.

Preservationists' efforts to extend California's park and wilderness areas were more successful. Created in 1972, the Golden Gate National Recreation Area and the San Francisco Bay Wildlife Refuge placed thousands of acres of fragile shoreline, marshland, and tidal areas under protection. In 1978, Congress created the Santa Monica Mountains National Recreation Area, but the Reagan administration held up federal funds to purchase open space from private owners until the mid-1980s. In 1984, Congress designated 1.8 million acres of federally owned land in the state as wilderness or scenic preserves. Two years later, U.S. Senator Allan Cranston introduced the California Desert Protection Act. Passed by Congress in 1994, the act classified 7.5 million acres of public desert land as protected wilderness, and set aside an additional 1.4 million acres as the East Mojave Preserve. Local and state parkland also increased during the 1970s and 1980s, but Proposition 13 forced reductions in maintenance, and necessitated increases in user fees.

Politics in the Era of Limits

Edmund G. Brown Jr.

Edmund G. "Jerry" Brown Jr., like presidential candidate Jimmy Carter, was swept into office on a tide of resurgent liberalism following the Watergate scandal. As secretary of state from 1970 to 1974, Brown established a reputation for honesty by enforcing campaign disclosure laws, exposing election fraud, and uncovering a tax evasion scheme hatched by Richard Nixon. As a principal sponsor of the 1974 Political Reform Act, a ballot initiative that called for the creation of a Fair Campaign Practices Commission, stricter disclosure of candidate spending and assets, and tighter limits on campaign funding, Brown enhanced his standing with disillusioned post-Watergate voters. He also obtained the support of organized labor by opposing Proposition 22, a 1972 ballot measure that restricted union organizing efforts among agricultural workers. By revealing that many of the measure's qualifying signatures had been fraudulently obtained, Brown helped ensure its defeat at the polls.

In the 1974 primary election Brown scored two major political victories: He won the Democratic nomination for governor, and voters endorsed the Political Reform Act. Meanwhile, the Republican favorite, Lieutenant Governor Ed Reinecke, had been indicted for perjury in the Watergate hearings and lost his party's nomination to State Controller Houston Flournoy. The November election was a close contest. Underestimating his opponent, Brown waged a lackluster campaign filled with vague promises to bring a "new spirit" to Sacramento, and barely squeaked by with a 2.9 percent margin of victory. But although he lacked a strong popular mandate, he could count on support from his party. Democrats gained solid majorities in the legislature, dominated the congressional delegation, and secured most statewide offices.

During his first term, Brown adopted policies consistent with California's liberal/progressive tradition. The Agricultural Labor Relations Act of 1975, drafted in collaboration with Rose Bird, whom he appointed secretary of agriculture, was a major breakthrough for farm workers and the UFW. Just as significantly, Brown ensured enforcement of the act by appointing pro-labor advocates to the Agricultural Labor Relations Board. Bird, the first woman to head the Department of Agriculture, and in 1977 the state supreme court, was one of over 1,500 women that Brown appointed to state office during his two terms as governor. He also appointed a record number of minorities, giving both groups unprecedented political visibility and an opportunity to shape public policy.

Consistent with his personal commitment to "voluntary simplicity," Brown established a strong environmental protection record. He created the State Office of Appropriate Technology to promote the development of alternative energy sources, sustainable agriculture, waste recycling, and resource conservation. The solar tax credit and other alternative energy development incentives were other outgrowths of his "era of limits" philosophy. Raising the ire of private industry and developers, Brown appointed conservationists to the Air Resources Board and Energy Commission, advocated more stringent controls on the nuclear power industry, supported the coastal protection initiative, appointed environmentalists to the new coastal commission, and opposed construction of the New Melones Dam. Less controversial was Brown's Civilian Conservation Corps, a public works program that employed young people to improve and maintain public spaces and wilderness areas.

On budget matters, Brown was a fiscal conservative. During his first term he refused to raise taxes, approved only modest increases in the state budget, and held the line on salary raises for state employees. As a consequence, large state agencies like the departments of Health and Welfare and Mental Health, still reeling from Reagan's cost-cutting measures, failed to keep pace with increasing demands for their services. Brown also failed to address the state's recession-driven unemployment problem. Although he initially supported the creation of a public works program, he backed off after the *Oakland Tribune* labeled the proposal as "Brown's Secret Plan for Worker State."

In 1976 Brown decided to seek his party's presidential nomination. Although he won primaries in several states, including California, the Democrats endorsed Jimmy Carter. Determined to try again in 1980, Brown became more attentive to his conservative critics. Announcing that jobs took priority over the environment, Brown supported legislation to simplify the regulatory process for industry wishing to do business in the state. He also made probusiness appointments to several commissions and departments, including Food and Agriculture, Transportation, and the Agricultural Labor Relations Board. To encourage economic development,

Brown traveled to Japan, Canada, Mexico, and England to cultivate new business partnerships, and lobbied the legislature to appropriate funds for a satellite communications system and a new University of California space research facility. Convinced that the state's aerospace and electronics industry could play a leading role in space colonization, Brown vigorously promoted the latter, earning the nickname "Governor Moonbeam."

Brown also responded to charges that he was "soft on crime"—charges that stemmed from his support of legislation that reduced penalties for marijuana possession and the decriminalization of sexual activities between consenting adults. Attempting to placate his critics, he signed a bill authorizing harsher, mandatory penalties for felons convicted of violent crimes. However, he remained steadfastly opposed to the death penalty, vetoing a 1977 bill calling for its reinstatement. In 1978, voters took matters into their own hands, using the initiative process to reinstate the penalty and offset the possibility of another veto from the governor.

Although he succeeded in mending fences with some of his conservative critics, he gained a reputation for inconsistency, flakiness, and political opportunism. Nonetheless, he easily won reelection in 1978, defeating his Republican opponent, Attorney General Evelle Younger, by 1.3 million votes. But at the beginning of the race, Brown's campaign was in serious trouble. Unlike Younger, he had opposed Proposition 13, a tax reduction measure that had appeared on the 1978 primary ballot.

During his first term, Brown gained the respect of voters by refusing to raise taxes. However, he seriously underestimated the impact of inflation. Residents, already forced to shell out more of their income for consumer goods, were also saddled with skyrocketing property values and tax assessments. Wages and salary increases not only failed to keep pace with inflation, but also pushed many into higher income tax brackets. By 1978 inflated sales, property, and income taxes, combined with Brown's tightfisted fiscal policies, generated a state budget surplus of at least $3.5 billion. Taxpayers were outraged.

Two disgruntled property owners, Howard Jarvis and Paul Gann, launched the United Organization of Taxpayers to bring the issue of rising property taxes to voters. Proposition 13, which easily qualified for the 1978 primary ballot, set residential and business property taxes at 1 percent of assessed value, based assessments on 1975 property values, and limited annual increases in assessed value to 2 percent. Reassessments were permitted only when property was bought or improved, and any new taxes required the approval of a two-thirds vote rather than the previously required simple majority.

Brown initially criticized the initiative as skewed in favor of landlords and commercial/industrial property owners, and disadvantageous for renters and future home buyers. But after the measure passed in June with overwhelming public support, his pro-13 Republican opponent gained the advantage in the upcoming gubernatorial election. Brown quickly withdrew his criticism and began to develop plans for distributing the state surplus to local and county governments. He also instituted a state government hiring freeze and created a commission to explore other economizing measures. Brown appeared more inconsistent and opportunistic than ever, but his well-publicized efforts to implement Proposition 13 helped him defeat Evelle Younger in November.

Brown's second term was plagued by financial difficulties, party disunity, humiliating political defeats, and the Medfly controversy. Emboldened by the success of Proposition 13, Paul Gann sponsored a second tax-cutting measure. Proposition 4, approved by voters in 1979, pegged annual government expenditures to the rate of inflation and population growth, and directed local and state governments to return budget surpluses to taxpayers. However, it was the earlier initiative that did the most damage. Within two years, the state's budget surplus had been spent bailing out hard-pressed city and county governments. Across the state, libraries, schools, police, fire, and park departments, and social service providers were forced to cut staff and services. Maintenance on public buildings, roads, and water and sewer systems was also reduced or deferred. The state's public schools, heavily dependent on property taxes, were among the hardest hit. By 1986, California fell from seventeenth to thirty-fifth place in per-pupil spending, and finished last among states in student/teacher ratio. Higher education also suffered. State colleges and universities, among the best in the nation, were forced to eliminate staff, cut course offerings, and consider fee increases to compensate for budget shortfalls.

Brown responded to the growing fiscal crisis by vetoing pay raises for state employees and attempting to hold cost-of-living increases for welfare recipients below federally mandated levels. These and other austerity measures were strongly opposed and ultimately overridden by former Democratic allies in the legislature. Despite growing party disunity, Brown decided to try for the 1980 presidential nomination. Calling for tax cuts and a federal balanced budget amendment to woo conservative voters, Brown further alienated liberal and Left-leaning supporters. His reputation for political opportunism, eccentricity, and inconsistency also damaged his chances.

Returning to California after another humiliating loss to Jimmy Carter in the June primary, Brown faced one of the worst crises of his career. The Mediterranean fruit fly, capable of destroying a wide variety of commercial crops, invaded the Santa Clara Valley. Growers called for aerial spraying with pesticides. Brown, however, sided with suburban residents of the area and approved a less toxic approach: removal of potentially infested fruit, release of sterile fruit flies, and strategic spraying from the ground. The Reagan administration, calling for a quarantine of all California produce, forced Brown to reverse his decision and order aerial spraying. In the end, he lost the support of both constituencies, and provided his critics with more evidence of his indecisiveness and inconsistency.

Deukmejian

In 1982 the combined impact of Proposition 13 and a national economic recession plunged the state into its worst financial crisis since the Depression. Brown, whose popularity had steadily declined, decided to run for the U.S. Senate rather than for a third term as governor. After losing to Pete Wilson, the Republican mayor of San Diego, the outgoing governor wryly announced, "I shall return, but not for awhile."

The gubernatorial race of 1982 was one of the closest in state history. Tom Bradley, who won the Democratic nomination on his strong record of effectiveness as the mayor of Los Angeles, faced the Republican nominee, State Attorney General George Deukmejian. Although Bradley, a former Los Angeles police captain, assured voters that he would be tough on crime, Deukmejian projected a stronger "law and order" image. As a state senator, Deukmejian had pushed through a statute mandating stiffer penalties for gun-related crimes, and authored the state's 1977 initiative reinstating the death penalty. As attorney general from 1978 to 1982, he was a harsh critic of Brown's judicial appointees, accusing Supreme Court Chief Justice Rose Bird and others of being soft on crime. Deukmejian also used the governor's declining popularity against his opponent, claiming "Tom Bradley's administration will be no different than Jerry Brown's." Race, however, was most likely the deciding factor. Deukmejian won the election by a mere 0.68 percent plurality, the smallest margin since 1886. During the campaign 6 percent of polled voters indicated that Bradley's race (African American) had swayed their decision in favor of Deukmejian.

Deukmejian's electoral victory coincided with the state controller's announcement that California faced a huge deficit. Rejecting the legislature's tax increase remedy, Deukmejian proposed massive cuts in social spending and assistance to beleaguered local governments, and rolling over the remaining debt into the following year's budget in hopes that the economy would recover enough to erase the deficit. After weeks of budgetary gridlock, the legislature and governor finally reached a compromise that included spending cuts, debt rollover, and a sales tax increase if the anticipated recovery did not materialize.

Deukmejian, who had promised not to raise taxes, was undoubtedly relieved when the economy began to stabilize. Indeed, by the mid-1980s, the state treasury once again posted a surplus. In the meantime, William Honig, the new superintendent of public instruction, devised a "back to basics" school reform package that called for extending the school day and year, stronger graduation requirements, extra pay for teachers who devoted extra hours to mentoring students, and an overall increase in public school funding. The governor not only backed Honig's plan, but also approved funding increases for the U.C. and C.S.U. systems. Deukmejian took a tougher line with community colleges, insisting that they institute a precedent-shattering fifty dollar enrollment fee. As a consequence, a crucial link in the state's Master Plan for Education was weakened. Between 1980 and 1985, community colleges reported an enrollment decline of 20 percent.

The governor also approved modest funding increases for the state's rapidly deteriorating transportation system, and a pay increase for state employees. More controversially, he pushed through massive appropriations for prison construction, and began the process of reshaping the state's judiciary to reflect his "tough on crime" philosophy. Critics charged that prison construction diverted resources from programs that addressed the root causes of crime. They also pointed to the fact that prisons held growing numbers of petty, nonviolent offenders, while the rate of violent crime continued to climb.

Deukmejian's stance on the environment and welfare reform was equally controversial. Siding with his pro-growth and agribusiness supporters, he angered conservationists by endorsing offshore drilling and a scaled-back version of the Peripheral Canal, and by making pro-development appointments to the California Coastal Commission and other environmental protection agencies. He also raised the ire of liberal Democrats by vetoing welfare pay increases and pushing through a reform package that included a work requirement, or "workfare," for able-bodied recipients.

In the 1984 election, Deukmejian suffered two setbacks. The state legislature, which had the power to reapportion political districts, was firmly controlled by Democrats, stifling Republican efforts to alter the existing balance of power. A ballot initiative, supported by Deukmejian, would have removed reapportionment from the legislature's jurisdiction and placed it in the hands of a panel of retired judges. In the election, voters not only rejected this measure, but also approved another that the governor had opposed, one that established a state-run lottery to help fund public schools. These minor differences of opinion, however, did not translate into voter disapproval of Deukmejian. In 1986, the booming economy—flush with Reagan administration defense contracts—gave the governor a strong advantage in his reelection bid.

In the 1986 race Deukmejian once again faced Democratic opponent Tom Bradley, who had recently won a fourth term as mayor of Los Angeles. The reconfirmation of Supreme Court Chief Justice Rose Bird, a Brown appointee, became a major campaign issue. Conservative politicians accused Bird, a strong opponent of the death penalty, of contributing to the state's growing violent crime problem. Many Californians agreed with this assessment. Deukmejian had long supported Bird's ouster, but Bradley refused to take a position for or against her removal. This helped bolster Deukmejian's reputation as a tough-on-crime victims' advocate. In the election voters registered their approval by handing Deukmejian 4,395,972 votes to Bradley's 2,721,674. They also overwhelmingly rejected Rose Bird's reconfirmation.

Deukmejian's second term was characterized by battles with the Democrat-controlled legislature over his judicial nominations. He retaliated by using the veto to kill or cut their appropriations for social and environmental programs. Republican legislators, although in the minority, united behind Deukmejian to prevent the necessary two-thirds majority from overriding his vetoes. A revived economy, generating surplus state revenue, allowed Deukmejian to keep his promise not to raise taxes. He was even able to issue a $1 billion rebate to taxpayers. He also approved modest increases in education spending and even larger appropriations for prison expansion. Despite these expenditures, California schools continued to decline, while its violent crime rate increased. With a new economic recession in the 1990s, these two problems worsened, igniting explosive public and political debate over the best use of public funds.

Summary

In contrast to the turbulent sixties, the seventies and eighties have been mischaracterized as the period when nothing happened. In reality, California's political, economic, and cultural landscape was richly dynamic and increasingly complex. New movements, often posing a greater challenge to traditional moral and ethical standards than those of the sixties, profoundly altered personal and political relationships. The state's ethnic minorities, soon to be in the majority, made significant progress in consolidating the gains of previous decades, but confronted persistent barriers to full equality. At the same time, California's economy was in flux, increasingly integrated into a system of international trade, and centered on services and information technology rather than heavy industry. While residents grappled with the accompanying economic challenges, they also faced unprecedented limits to growth. In response, many joined the struggle to protect the state's most valuable assets: its natural beauty and resource base. Political leaders, attempting to negotiate rapid change and new limits, escaped easy categorization. Brown, although a fiscal conservative, was a social liberal. Deukmejian, defeating his Democratic opponent by the narrowest of margins in his first bid for governor, often compromised with his liberal critics on fiscal issues. Finally, Californians continued to elect Democratic majorities to the legislature, including growing numbers of women, African Americans, Asian Americans, and Latinos. Perhaps voters, like their leaders, were uncertain how to negotiate the unfamiliar terrain of the postindustrial economic order. In the meantime they tried to strike a balance between liberalism and conservatism.

Suggested Readings

▍ Davis, Mike, *City of Quartz: Excavating the Future of Los Angeles* (New York: Vintage, 1990). This is a critical study of racial and class divisions, political infighting, economic neglect, and poor urban planning in Los Angeles and its suburbs.

▍ D'Emilio, John, *Sexual Politics, Sexual Communities: The Making of a Homosexual Minority in the United States* (Chicago: University of Chicago Press, 1983). This book details the emergence of gay and lesbian communities and organizations, including those in California.

▍ Godfrey, Brian J., *Neighborhoods in Transition: The Making of San Francisco's Ethnic and Nonconformist Communities* (Berkeley: University of California Press, 1988). This book documents the origins and evolution of San Francisco's ethnic, gay, and countercultural communities.

▌ Gutierrez, David, *Walls and Mirrors: Mexican Americans, Mexican Immigrants and the Politics of Ethnicity* (Berkeley: University of California Press, 1995). This book provides a historical overview of Mexican immigration, community and identity formation, and U.S. immigration policy.

▌ Hanson, Dirk, *The New Alchemists: Silicon Valley and the Microelectronics Revolution* (Boston: Little, Brown and Company, 1982). This book details the rise of Silicon Valley and its microelectronics pioneers and entrepreneurs.

▌ Jackson, Bryan, and Michael Preston, *Racial and Ethnic Politics in California* (Berkeley: Institute of Governmental Studies, 1991). This work provides an overview of political contestations among various ethnic constituencies in California.

▌ Kotkin, Joel, and Paul Grabowicz, *California, Inc.* (New York: Rawson, Wade Publishers, 1982). This book discusses the economic development of California, details the economic policies of the Brown and Reagan administrations, and documents the growth of the Pacific Rim economy.

▌ Ong, Paul, Edna Bonacich, and Lucie Cheng, eds., *New Asian Immigration in Los Angeles and Global Restructuring* (Philadelphia: Temple University Press, 1994). This book examines the political and economic factors behind recent Asian immigration, the economic status of immigrant workers, and class and political divisions among various Asian groups.

▌ Palmer, Tim, ed., *California's Threatened Environment: Restoring the Dream* (Washington, D.C.: Island Press, 1993). This is a series of essays exploring diverse threats to California's environment.

▌ Quinones, Juan Gomez, *Chicano Politics: Reality and Promise, 1940–1990* (Albuquerque: University of New Mexico Press, 1990). This book provides a comprehensive political history of Mexican Americans from 1940 to 1990.

▌ Sale, Kirkpatrick, *The Green Revolution* (New York: Hill and Wang, 1993). This book provides a good overview of contemporary environmental movements and activists.

▌ Schrag, Peter, *Paradise Lost: California's Experience, America's Future* (Berkeley: University of California Press, 1999). This book documents the recent decline in California's public education system, infrastructure, and social services network.

▌ Shilts, Randy, *And the Band Played On: Politics, People and the AIDS Epidemic* (New York: St. Martin's Press, 1987). This book examines the impact of the AIDS epidemic on gay communities, efforts to secure resources for prevention and treatment, public response to the crisis, and how AIDS became a political issue.

▌ Wellock, Thomas, *Critical Masses: Opposition to Nuclear Power in California, 1958–1978* (Madison and London: University of Wisconsin Press, 1998). This is a history of anti-nuclear activism in California.

13

California Enters the New Millennium

Main Topics

Richard Rodriguez grew up in Sacramento in the 1950s, the son of immigrant parents from Mexico. He was acutely aware of race and ethnicity from an early age. "In Sacramento, my brown was not halfway between black and white," he wrote. "My family's shades passed as various. We did not pass 'for' white; my family passed among white." He entered first grade speaking about fifty words of English and went on to earn degrees in English at Stanford University and philosophy at Columbia University. His acclaimed memoirs—*Hunger of Memory* (1982), *Days of Obligation* (1992), and *Brown* (2002)—explore American race relations through the lens of his personal experiences. In *Brown,* he considered the contradictions of race

CHAPTER 13	California Enters the New Millennium
1989	Loma Prieta earthquake
1990	Election of Pete Wilson as governor
1992	Publication of Richard Rodriguez's *Days of Obligation*
1992	Los Angeles riots
1993–2000	"Dot-com" boom in the economy
1994	Northridge earthquake
1995	eBay goes online
1995	O.J. Simpson trial
1996	Proposition 209 approved, dismantling state affirmative action programs
1998	Election of Gray Davis as governor
2000	U.S. Census records that California has no ethnic majority group
2000–2001	Energy crisis
2002	Publication of Richard Rodriguez's *Brown*
2003	Davis recalled; Arnold Schwarzenegger elected as governor

from his perspective as a "queer Catholic Indian Spaniard at home in a temperate Chinese city [San Francisco] in a fading blond state in a post-Protestant nation."

Rodriguez embodies several of the contradictions and complexities of contemporary California. His adopted label "brown" speaks to his mixture of ethnic, racial, and cultural heritages. A political nonconformist, Rodriguez has angered many Latinos and liberals for his opposition to affirmative action and bilingual education. He is openly gay and devoutly Catholic. "Of every hue and caste am I," he has written.

In California in the 1990s and early twenty-first century, ethnic and cultural categories blurred and clashed. "The land of golden opportunity is becoming a land of broken promises," proclaimed *Time* magazine in 1991 in an issue devoted to California's "endangered dream." Nonetheless, Americans continued to be fascinated with California. Still associated with

In 1997, Richard Rodriguez said, "After the LA riots in 1992, my sense was not that the city was dying, as the expert opinion had it, but that the city was being formed. What was dying was the idea that LA was a city of separate suburbs and freeway exits. . . . In the LA of the future, no one will need to say, 'Let's celebrate diversity.' Diversity is going to be a fundamental part of our lives. . . . I want to live my life in the center of the world. I want to live my life in Los Angeles."

the glamour of Hollywood and the excitement of cutting-edge industries (especially information technology and aviation), California became increasingly identified, as well, with environmental and social ills and with political dysfunctionality. California remains a land of contradictions but continues to offer opportunities to immigrants from around the world. The state also continues to grow—by more than 18 percent between 1990 and 2002, to thirty-five million people, nearly one-eighth of all Americans. The economy traversed a bust-boom-bust cycle but the state's gross domestic product reached $1.5 trillion in 2003, making California the world's sixth-largest economy, slightly smaller than that of France. Tourism, entertainment, agriculture, and high tech (despite the dot-com bust after 2000) flourish, partly through California's place as the center of Pacific Rim trade. The most populous and productive state in the Union, California is also one of the most ethnically diverse. With its muscular economy, diverse population, urban problems, political divisiveness, and edgy cultural expression, California embodies the hopes—and fears—of the wider nation and world.

Questions to Consider

■ How have California's demographics changed since 1990? What implications do these changes have for the state's future?

■ What are the most important changes in California's economy since 1990? What implications do these changes have for the state's future?

■ What are the most important changes in education, health care, housing, transportation, and the energy situation since 1990? What implications do these changes have for the state's future?

■ What are the most important changes in California's politics and government since 1990? What implications do these changes have for the future?

■ What are the most important changes in California's religious life and cultural expression since the 1990s? What implications do these changes have for the future?

A New Kind of California

Throughout its history, California has constantly been remade as waves of people migrated to the Golden State with dreams for a better life. In the 1990s, the outlines emerged of a California not just being remade but also holding the prospect of being different in major ways.

The Los Angeles Riots and the O.J. Simpson Trial

During the early 1990s, two dramatic events focused attention on race and ethnicity: the so-called Los Angeles riots of 1992 and the O.J. Simpson trial in 1995. Both centered on issues of police interaction with African Americans in Los Angeles, and both focused international attention on California's racial tensions.

The spark that ignited the volatile mix of social, economic, and racial pressures in Southern California was a verdict in a court case involving Rodney King and the Los Angeles Police Department (LAPD). Rodney King, an African American, was savagely beaten by four LAPD officers on March 3, 1991. While nineteen people (mostly other police officers) looked on, the four used police batons to strike King fifty-six times in eighty-one seconds, producing multiple skull fractures, a broken leg, a concussion, and nerve injuries. A nearby resident videotaped the beating, and those images soon played repeatedly on television stations around the world. LA's mayor, Tom Bradley, asked for the resignation of LAPD Chief Daryl Gates, but Gates refused. When indicted by a grand jury, the four officers secured a change of venue for the trial, to suburban and conservative Simi Valley in Ventura County. On April 29, 1992, after hearing the evidence, the jury—ten whites, one Latino, and one Filipino American—acquitted three officers and failed to reach a verdict on the fourth. In South Central Los Angeles, violent protests quickly erupted and swelled into the bloodiest, most costly urban uprising in U.S. history.

The disorders lasted from April 30 to May 5, 1992. As many parts of LA dissolved into chaos, live television documented the tragedy. Motorists were pulled from their cars and beaten, a mob attacked a police station, and arsonists set fires in stores—all on television. The National Guard was mobilized and thousands of highway patrol officers and police were dispatched to Los Angeles. According to police records, 42 percent of the participants were African American, 44 percent Latino, and 9 percent white. The uprising spread from South Central to Korea Town, then to the mid-Wilshire area and Long Beach. In the midst of the violence, television stations repeatedly broadcast a moving appeal by Rodney King to end the violence and to "get along." Given the extensive media coverage, the riots sparked demonstrations—sometimes violent—in other cities as well.

More than fifty people died in the violence, the large majority by gunshot. Twenty-six were African Americans and eighteen were Latinos. No police, sheriffs, national guardsmen, or other officials were killed, though three police officers were wounded. Of all those killed, only two had been carrying weapons. More than two hundred civilians were wounded by gunshots, and more than two thousand were injured. There were fifteen thousand arrests. Police recorded six hundred fires, and estimates of property damage ranged as high as a billion dollars.

Later, analysts pointed to multiple causes for the rioting, including increased ethnic and racial conflict within South Central LA, gang violence, a history of Korean–black conflict, and earlier court verdicts considered unjust. In 1991, for example, a Korean merchant received a suspended sentence after he shot and killed an African American teenager in a dispute over a soft drink. Chronic unemployment of African American youth—more than 50 percent—was related to a high rate of violent crime in the inner city. During the early 1990s, like other large American cities, Los Angeles experienced a significant increase in the number of murders—from 790 per year between 1985 and 1988 to 1,045 between 1990 and 1993. LAPD officials blamed this increase on drugs, guns, and gangs. At the same time, incidents of police violence were well known before the Rodney King case. All these factors contributed to the frustration that exploded in 1992.

Some changes came quickly. On the day after the verdict by the Simi Valley jury, President George Bush announced a federal investigation of the officers for violating the civil rights of Rodney King. Tried on federal charges, two were convicted and sentenced to thirty months in federal correctional camps. The City of Los Angeles passed new ordinances limiting the term of office for the chief of police and increasing the powers of a civilian Board of Police Commissioners. Gates was replaced as police chief by Willie L. Williams, the city's first African American police chief. A special commission investigated the events and proposed reforms, some of which were implemented. The LA "riots" of 1992 may have marked a turning point in California's racial relations, by forcing local and state policymakers to take more seriously the social and economic issues that gave rise to the violence.

Two years later, Southern California was again the site of a trial with potentially explosive racial implications. On June 13, 1994, a neighbor discovered the slashed bodies of Nicole Brown Simpson, former wife of the famous African American football star, Orenthal J. ("O.J.") Simpson, and Ronald Goldman, an employee of a local restaurant. On June 17, Simpson failed to turn himself in when requested to do so, and police announced that he was a fugitive from justice. For the next few hours, Simpson slowly fled south on Interstate 5 in his sport-utility vehicle, with a friend at the wheel and police in pursuit. Ninety-five million people watched the chase on television. Finally, Simpson surrendered to authorities.

Simpson's trial lasted more than eight months, involved more than one hundred witnesses, and featured complex testimony on DNA, charges of planted evidence and racism by the LA police department, and dramatic legal maneuvers. The prosecution presented evidence of Simpson's past history of spousal abuse, blood samples from the crime scene that matched Simpson's, and other physical evidence such as footprints in Simpson's size at the murder site and the discovery of a bloody glove on his property. The defense cast doubt on the DNA evidence, argued that police had mishandled evidence, charged that one lead detective was a racist, and claimed that the LAPD had conspired to frame Simpson.

Across the country, Americans avidly discussed the trial, and it polarized Californians and Americans. The jury announced its verdict, an acquittal of Simpson, on October 3, 1995. The case had put the LA police department on trial as much as it did Simpson, and issues of race and police conduct were as crucial as in the earlier trial of the four police officers. Before and after the verdict, a large proportion of African Americans believed Simpson innocent whereas the majority of whites did not, and some African Americans saw the verdict as evidence that things had finally changed. Other Californians saw the verdict as a miscarriage of justice. Many feminist activists considered Simpson a symbol of domestic violence, and others concluded that the case simply showed how wealthy defendants can manipulate the justice system.

The Brown and Goldman families later initiated a civil trial to determine Simpson's liability in the two deaths. This trial reviewed the same evidence as the previous one but declared Simpson liable for the two deaths and awarded the victims' families $33.5 million in damages.

The Rise of Latino California

The LA riots and the Simpson trial provided dramatic windows into California's racial and ethnic relations, attracting world attention. Less dramatic, but perhaps more important in the long run, are data on California's demographic growth. Figure 13.1 presents data on California's population in 2000 and provides part of the context for understanding its contemporary social and political patterns.

A remarkable growth in the Latino population meant that Latinos constituted almost one-third of California's population in 2000. That year, fully one-third of

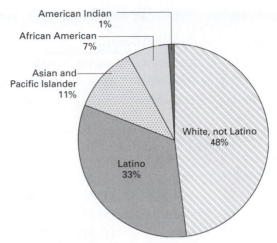

Figure 13.1 Race and Ethnicity of Californians, 2000
This graph summarizes the way that Californians identified themselves for the 2000 census. Compare this graph with Figure 7.1 to see how the state's population has dramatically changed over eighty years. What are the implications for public policy of California's evolving ethnic patterns?
Source: U.S. Census Bureau, "California Quick Facts" <http://quickfacts.census.gov/qfd/states/06000.html>.

Beginning in 1970 community artists and activists created a community park under the Coronado Bay Bridge in the heart of Barrio Logan. Over the years Chicano artists created more than fifty murals reflecting community issues and historical reflections, making the park the largest single Chicano mural display in the United States. Depicted is the mural "Coatlicue" (the Aztec mother of the gods) by Susan Yamagata and Michael Schnorr (1978), and "Chicano Pinto Union" by Tony de Vargas (1978), based on a poster for an organizations dedicated to education for ex-convicts.

TABLE 13.1 CALIFORNIA'S FOREIGN-BORN POPULATION, 1980, 1990, AND 2000

1980 Census		1990 Census		2000 Census	
Mexico	1,277,969	Mexico	2,474,148	Mexico	3,928,701
Philippines	237,713	Philippines	481,837	Philippines	664,935
Canada	163,300	El Salvador	280,781	China	570,487*
Great Britain	133,690	Vietnam	271,061	Vietnam	418,249
China	116,331	China	211,263	El Salvador	359,673
Germany	112,673	Korea	200,194	Korea	268,452
Vietnam	83,277	Canada	150,387	Guatemala	211,458
Korea	83,180	Guatemala	135,875	India	198,613
Japan	79,593	U.K.	135,391	Iran	158,613
El Salvador	67,657	Iran	115,415	Canada	141,181
All Others	1,224,651	All Others	2,002,473	All Others	1,944,305
Total	3,580,033	Total	6,458,825	Total	8,864,255

*2000 data for those born in China includes Hong Kong and Taiwan; earlier years do not.
Source: U.S. Census Bureau.

the country's Latinos lived in California. The largest number of immigrants came from Mexico, accounting for 38 percent of all immigrants in California during the 1990s (see Table 13.1). During that decade, the proportion of Mexican immigrants in California's population was the highest of any state, twice the national level. But the "Latino" category conceals many variations—multi-generation Californians, street-smart kids from Tijuana, Salvadorans who fled the violence in their nation during the 1980s, Portuguese-speaking soccer fans from Brazil, new arrivals from Yucatán who prefer to speak their own Mayan dialect, college professors born in Puerto Rico, and many more.

Despite the many immigrants, only 20 percent of the growth in California's Latino population came through immigration. Most of the increase resulted from a baby boom that led demographers to project that Latinos would become the largest ethnic group in the state by 2025. One study, based on the 1990 census, indicated that among California women older than fifty-four, Latinas had given birth, on average, to 3.55 children, as compared to 2.88 for African American women, 2.26 for white women, and 2.62 for all other women. Latinas' fertility rate was high for a variety of cultural and economic reasons. However, studies consistently found that, among nearly all ethnic groups, the more education a woman had, the fewer children she was likely to have—and Latinas were among those least likely to graduate from high school.

Increased political clout for Latinos accompanied the growth of their numbers. The number of adult Latino citizens nearly doubled in the 1990s, growing from 1.35 million to 2.35 million. By 2000, Latino citizens had registered to vote at a rate similar to non-Latino whites and in higher proportions than African Americans and Asian Americans. In 1998, Cruz Bustamante was elected lieutenant governor, the first Latino elected to statewide office since the 1870s. More than 20 percent of the California legislature was Latino by 2001.

However, among the largest ethnic groups in the 1990s, Latinos had the lowest median family income and remained severely underrepresented in the professional sector. In the mid-1990s, California had one of the lowest rates of high school graduation in the nation, and the dropout rate was highest among Latinos and African Americans. Although a third of the population, Latinos made up only 14 percent of the students in the U.C. system and 25 percent in the C.S.U. system. Forty percent of adult Latinos lacked health insurance. Because many Latinos had limited English proficiency and job skills, they were among those hardest hit by economic downturns. Yet, at the beginning of the twenty-first century, most analysts predicted that Latinos would continue to grow in numbers and political clout. In a *Los Angeles Times* poll in 2001, Latinos were considerably more likely than whites and African Americans to believe that the quality of their lives was improving.

Changing Ethnic Demographics

Figure 13.1 and Table 13.1 indicate not only the dramatic increase in the Latino population of the state but also the growing Asian and Pacific Islander population. Those categorized as "Asians"—including Cambodians, Chinese, Filipinos, Indians, Pacific Islanders, Vietnamese, and others—outnumbered African Americans by 1990. The significant growth in the number of Californians of Asian and Pacific Islander origin came largely from immigration (see Table 13.1). According to the 2000 census, the two largest groups of Asian–Pacific Islander Californians were those who traced their ancestry to China and the Philippines, each of whom accounted for about a quarter of Asian–Pacific Islander Californians.

Monterey Park in Southern California, called the "Chinese Beverly Hills," became the first Asian-majority city in the continental United States, with more than 60 percent of its population Asian, mostly ethnic Chinese. Asian immigrants in Hacienda Heights, also in Southern California, created the majestic Hsi Lai temple, the largest Buddhist temple in the world. During the late 1980s and early 1990s, as the date approached for control of Hong Kong to revert from Britain to China, California experienced an increase in immigrants from that colony, nearly all ethnic Chinese, many with some capital. During the 1990s, earlier immigrants from eastern and southeastern Asia were joined by many engineers and technicians from eastern and southern Asia, especially India, who came for high-tech jobs in Silicon Valley and in Los Angeles.

Table 13.1 points to the significant numbers of immigrants from Vietnam. There were also immigrants from the other countries most affected by the war in

Vietnam in the 1960s and early 1970s. Large numbers of refugees came soon after the United States withdrew its troops from South Vietnam and the government there collapsed in 1975. Many were middle class, well educated, and spoke English. As political refugees, they were exempted from many immigration restrictions. The collapse of U.S.-supported governments in Laos and Cambodia produced refugees from those countries too, including Hmong and other Laotian mountain people. After 1980, more immigrants from Southeast Asia began to arrive, labeled "boat people" by the media because many fled their countries in small boats. Mostly poor and from rural areas, many of them lacked education, English proficiency, or capital, and they remained in low-income service jobs. By 2000, California claimed about half of all Vietnamese, Cambodians, and Laotians in the United States, and half of Vietnamese Californians lived in Los Angeles and Orange Counties, especially in Westminster. San José was also home to many Vietnamese.

As Asian Californians increased in visibility, some of them encountered resentment and discrimination. In Monterey Park in Southern California, the city council required businesses to post their signs in English as well as Chinese. Korean merchants in South Central Los Angeles faced hostility from African American neighbors. Some Californians seemed to resent Asian immigrants as much for their hard work as for their success, an ironic situation in a country that has traditionally taken pride in both.

Contrary to the stereotype of Asians as the model, achieving minority, the average Asian American worker in California earned less than white workers in the 1990s. To be certain, California's Asian youth, regardless of nationality, had high rates of school graduation and college attendance. Nonetheless, due to the immigration of older people from poor countries, Chinese, Filipino, and Southeast Asian groups had fewer high school graduates than whites. Great differences continued both within and among various Asian groups in California in educational attainment and socioeconomic status.

California's Native American population also grew steadily in the 1990s, reaching 179,000 in 2000—a small decline in number from the 1990 census, but possibly due to the mixed-race option available on the 2000 census. Many of the Indians who lived in California in the 1990s were migrants from elsewhere in the nation and not members of local tribes. The state's American Indian population, as a group, remained one of the state's most destitute, according to key indicators of economic and social health. The high school dropout rate among Native Americans in 2000 was 14.2 percent—double that of white students. The Indian unemployment and poverty rates did not significantly change in the 1990s, and many Indians continued to suffer from high rates of alcoholism along with tuberculosis and other communicable diseases.

Some California Indian tribes turned to legalized gambling as a source of economic empowerment, based on a constitutional interpretation that reservations were exempt from state laws regulating or prohibiting gambling. The profits from gaming allowed those tribes to fund a renewal of culture, language, and self-esteem, and to promote Indian education, employment, and economic development. Throughout the 1990s, California's Indian tribes fought governors and courts over gaming, spending more than $100 million on political campaigns to protect their casinos. In 2000, Proposition 1A passed by a large majority and established, without question, the right of California's Indians to provide gaming on their reservations. Within a few decades, gaming had transformed some California Indian tribes from forgotten enclaves of poverty, unemployment, and powerlessness to major political and economic forces. But most Indians did not benefit from gaming. Of the some 180,000 Californians who identified themselves as Indians during the 1990s, only 32,000 were enrolled in tribes eligible to offer legalized gambling. Of these, only about a third belonged to tribes that operated casinos. Several gaming tribes are minuscule in number. Though the gaming tribes shared about $1 million a year with members of non-gaming California tribes, Native Americans not part of federally recognized California tribes—the large majority of Indians in California—did not benefit at all. As of 2000, Indian gaming defined two groups of Indians: the generally affluent members of gaming tribes and the others, many of whom lived in poverty and obscurity in rural areas.

For Californians from lower-income families, education has often been the escalator to move them into the middle class. Among college and university graduates, distinct differences appeared among major ethnic groups. Among high school graduates, proportionately more Asians completed the high school course requirements for admission to the U.C. or C.S.U. systems. And, in every ethnic category, women were more likely to complete the requirements than men. Compared to their proportion of the population, Latinos were the most underrepresented among graduates at every level of higher education. Asians and whites were the most overrepresented among recipients of post-baccalaureate degrees— often the key to entering the professions.

The Economy

During the 1990s, California's economy moved from a serious and long-lasting recession to a spectacular boom, and then back to recession. In the process, changes occurred that may have permanently altered elements of the state's economy.

From Recession to Boom

During the early 1990s, California's economy faltered when a normal, cyclical contraction (a recession) coincided with the collapse of the Soviet Union, the end of the Cold War, and a major reduction in military spending. Figure 13.2 presents employment patterns, and indicates that unemployment in California was more severe and long-lasting than in the nation as a whole—indeed, unemployment in California remained higher than national levels all through the 1990s. Until the early 1990s, many Californians had concluded that the state's economy was "recession-proof" because federal defense spending provided a cushion against large cyclical fluctuations in the economy. Now a normal cyclical fluctuation was magnified and extended as federal military spending declined, producing both

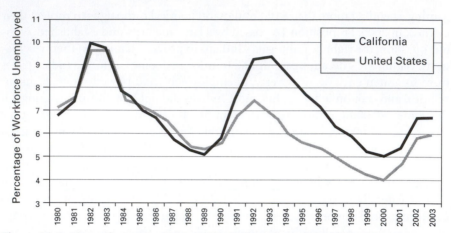

Figure 13.2 Unemployment, 1980–2003, California and the United States
This graph suggests a significant change in the relationship between national patterns of unemployment and those in California. When did the change occur? What may explain this change?
Source: California Department of Finance <http://www.dof.ca.gov/HTML/FS_DATA/LatestEconData/FS_Employment.htm>.

layoffs in defense industries and base closures. Communities with defense-driven economies suffered from unemployment and declining property values, retail sales, and tax revenue.

Natural disasters contributed to the state's economic woes. On October 17, 1989, during the third game of the World Series between the Oakland A's and the San Francisco Giants—the first-ever "Bay Bridge Series"—a devastating earthquake struck the Bay Area. Centered in Loma Prieta, near Santa Cruz, the earthquake caused sixty-three deaths and $6.8 billion of damages. In the fall of 1991, a wildfire destroyed three thousand homes in northern Oakland and Berkeley. On January 14, 1994, an earthquake on the Northridge fault, in the San Fernando Valley, destroyed hundreds of homes and sparked raging fires, causing more than $20 billion in damages. Nearly every building at C.S.U. Northridge was damaged. Elsewhere, Californians in the 1990s experienced major fires, floods, mudslides, and the alternation of droughts with torrential rains, as the El Niño and La Niña effects periodically altered the climate.

Nonethelesss, during the middle to late 1990s, California's economy expanded rapidly. The central elements in the economic expansion included international trade and a growing array of new industries: biotechnology, e-commerce, computer-based entertainment technology, and advanced communications and transportation systems. In the Bay Area especially, information technology (IT) firms were the driving force behind the boom. By the late 1990s, 11 percent of employment and 32 percent of manufacturing and service payrolls in the Bay Area were in IT firms. By contrast, IT made up less than 10 percent of the total payroll in Southern California.

An Economy for the New Millennium?

California's military bases and defense industry suffered serious setbacks in the late 1980s and early 1990s as the federal government reduced military expenditures at the end of the Cold War. Figure 13.3 shows federal defense spending in California, and indicates how both the amount and percentage of total federal defense spending declined throughout the late 1980s and early 1990s, then fell sharply in the mid-1990s, compounding the effects of the recession. Many of the state's military bases were closed, bringing a loss of 82,000 military and civilian jobs. The Base Realignment and Adjustment Commission, created by Congress to ease the transition, sought alternate uses for former military installations, ranging from industrial parks and cultural centers to homeless shelters and new college campuses. A preliminary study found that "while some communities suffered, the outcomes were not catastrophic and not nearly as severe as forecasted." For many individuals, however, military bases had provided a secure, relatively well-paying source of employment. African American and Latino workers especially, benefiting from the federal government's affirmative action policies, filled base jobs in disproportionate numbers. When bases closed, civilian workers of color, and their communities, were often disproportionately affected.

Figure 13.3 Defense Spending in California, 1981–1982 through 2001–2002
This graph shows the dramatic change in federal defense spending in California over twenty years. When did the most significant changes occur? What events in U.S. history or world history might explain the reasons for these changes? What effect did these changes have on the economy of California?
Source: California Department of Finance <http://www.dof.ca.gov/HTML/FS_DATA/LatestEconData/FS_Misc.htm>.

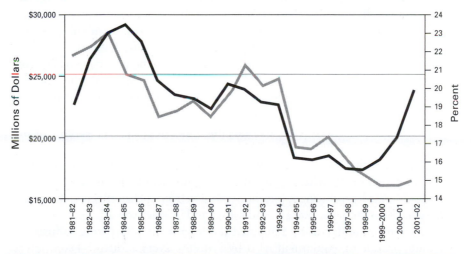

— Defense spending in California, in current dollars (left scale)

— Defense spending in California as a percent of total defense spending (right scale)

The aerospace industry, concentrated in Southern California, also sustained sharp cuts at the end of the Cold War, leading to layoffs and economic stagnation. By the mid-1990s, however, the industry had largely recovered, emerging from its slump less dependent on military contracts. Foreign demand for aircraft and space vehicles contributed to this recovery, along with an expansion of satellite manufacturing buoyed by global telecommunications. By the end of the century, the southern California aerospace industry provided 20 percent of all aerospace jobs in the nation. Still tied to federal defense spending, its one thousand firms had a broader commercial base that provided greater security for its 180,000 workers. However, the aircraft industry experienced another slump following the September 11, 2001, attacks on New York City and Washington, D.C., as many airlines reduced their schedules and cut back on the purchase of new planes.

California's growers maintained their preeminent position within the national economy. The state continued to rank number one in the value of its agricultural produce, which reached $27 billion in 2000. By then, the state was exporting nearly a quarter of its agricultural produce. Six of the state's top ten export markets for agricultural produce were located on the Pacific Rim.

The state's amazing levels of productivity, sustained by a favorable climate, water subsidies, and expanding global markets, received an added boost from a new source in the 1980s and 1990s—biotechnology. In the late 1990s, almost 30 percent of all biotech firms in the nation were headquartered in the state, and California's educational institutions accounted for five of the top ten programs in biochemistry, molecular biology, and molecular and genetic research. One of the world's most sophisticated gene-sequencing laboratories, run by the federal Joint Genome Institute, was located in Walnut Creek. Biotechnology's applications range widely but include genetically engineered agricultural products, drugs and vaccines, gene therapies to prevent or cure diseases, products that detect food-borne microbes and toxins, bacteria that clean up toxic wastes and oil spills, and medical devices that test for and treat genetic and infectious diseases.

One of the state's older industries, entertainment, also benefited from new technology. During the 1990s, the "creative genius" of Hollywood and the "technological genius" of Silicon Valley combined to create new, high-tech entertainment that reshaped the delivery of entertainment as well as its form and content. Visual images could now be transmitted via satellite, telephone, and fiber-optic cable, and the images themselves were enhanced by computer-generated special effects and animation. The state's film and video industry was a prime beneficiary of these advances, accounting for more than half of the nation's employment in that field. Multimedia firms proliferated, producing applications ranging from special effects software and video games to computer systems for distance and interactive learning.

Computer manufacturing remained the largest manufacturing industry in the state, producing equipment used by virtually every industry—computers, storage devices, printers, security devices, semiconductors, peripheral equipment, and more. By 2000 the industry employed 389,000 workers, produced $85 billion worth of equipment, and accounted for a fifth of the nation's total exports of computer hardware. It also branched out beyond Silicon

Valley. Hewlett-Packard, for example, established a new facility in Roseville, helping to transform a once-rural community into the fastest-growing city in the state. The software industry also boomed, connected to advances in Internet and multimedia technology.

The most phenomenal growth occurred in e-commerce. In the late 1990s, thousands of new firms offered consumers a wide variety of goods and services via the Internet. The Bay Area experienced a "dot-com" boom—the creation and rapid expansion of commercial uses of the Internet. New dot-com companies seemed to appear almost daily, offering an amazing variety of goods and services online. At the height of the boom, the initial offering of stock in a new dot-com company attracted eager buyers, and stock prices soared even though most of the new companies were not making a profit and seemed unlikely to do so for the foreseeable future. A clear exception was eBay, with headquarters in San José. eBay first went online in 1995, and soon became the most popular online auction site, claiming more than forty-six million registered users, and selling everything from houses to fine art. Yahoo!, started by two Stanford students in 1994, with headquarters in Sunnyvale, soared to become the leading guide to the Internet, only to yield first place to Google, also the creation of two Stanford students, with headquarters in Mountain View.

By the end of 2000, the dot-com bubble had burst, and many companies closed their doors. Even healthy companies showed a dramatic drop in their stock prices. eBay stock had opened at $7.48 in 1998, soared to over $120 in early 2000, then dropped to $50 in late 2002—and eBay was among the most profitable e-commerce companies. Yahoo! stock opened at $2.62 in 1997, zoomed to over $200 in late 1999, then dropped below $10 in late 2002.

The entire high-tech sector suffered heavy losses. The industry was particularly vulnerable to cyclic declines in consumer demand. This, coupled with rising interest rates and overhead costs, contributed to the crash in late 1999 and early 2000. By mid-2002, the Nasdaq was at its lowest point since May 1997. One New York stock analyst said that the decline was "not like anything we've seen before. . . . The only comparison to Nasdaq you can make is to 1929"—the stock market crash that set off the Great Depression. Even industry-leading companies took a beating. Cisco Systems opened at $47 in 1997, rose above $140 in late 1999, and fell below $10 in 2002. Other industry leaders, such as Apple, Intel, and Sun followed similar patterns.

Nearly all high-tech stocks continued to fall through 2002. Centered in California, the decline sent shock waves through the entire nation, fueling speculation of long-term economic stagnation and underscoring the state's central role in the American and global economies. The terrorist attacks of September 11, 2001, also had an impact on California's economies, as airline companies, hotels, and other businesses dependent on travel and tourism laid off employees, due to significant reductions in travel. The collapse of the dot-com boom, declining demand for IT equipment, and falling stock prices had a major effect on state tax revenues, which had been swollen in the late 1990s by taxes on the sale of stocks at inflated prices, but which now fell drastically, triggering the need for major cuts in state spending in 2002 and 2003.

Together, the adjoining ports of Los Angeles and Long Beach occupy nearly twenty four square miles—about half the size of the entire city of San Francisco—and are the largest and second-largest ports in the nation. Combined, they form the third-largest port in the world, after only Hong Kong and Singapore. How is the expansion of these ports related to economic globalization?

Going Global

The expansion of international trade also fueled the boom of the 1990s. By the late 1980s, California had become the center of Pacific Rim trade, exporting high-tech and agricultural products to Asian countries and importing consumer goods.

Containerization transformed oceanic shipping and allowed California to take full advantage of its position on the Pacific Rim. Containerization is the transportation of cargo in twenty- or forty-foot-long metal boxes, allowing rapid loading and unloading of ships and the quick transfer of containers to trucks or railroad cars. In the late 1950s, California-based Matson Navigation pioneered the use of containers between Hawai`i and the mainland. In 1960, the International Longshoremen's and Warehousemen's Union (ILWU), which represented all Pacific Coast longshore workers, entered into a Mechanization and Modernization (M&M) agreement with the shipping companies. Arguing that "you can't fight the machine," Harry Bridges (see p. 252) and the ILWU traded control of the work process (which they had gained in the mid-1930s) for job security and generous retirement benefits. Under the M&M, containerization of West Coast shipping proceeded rapidly, and longshore work was forever transformed. The container revolution spread rapidly. Between 1980 and 2002, the percentage of worldwide shipping conducted in containers rose from 23 to 70 percent.

Containerization combined with the rise of Pacific Rim trade to transform California's ports. By 2001, Los Angeles and Long Beach were the largest and second-largest ports in the United States (together they made up the third-largest port complex in the world), and Oakland ranked fourth in the United States, but the Port of San Francisco declined into insignificance, due to lack of space for containers.

The state's dependence on Pacific Rim trade deepened during the 1990s, but other global partnerships also developed. The North American Free Trade Agreement (NAFTA) reduced or eliminated trade barriers between the United States, Mexico, and Canada. By 1996, Canada and Mexico ranked as California's second- and third-largest export markets, injecting billions of dollars into the economy and creating thousands of new jobs. The agreement also created incentives for California firms to establish operations in Mexico—which may have reduced the number of California jobs. These companies, however, operating with fewer environmental restrictions, lower labor costs, and minimal trade barriers, not only exported products to California but also used Mexico's free trade links to Central and South American countries to increase exports throughout Latin America.

California's economy also benefited from the creation of a single economic market by the nations of the European Union and economic globalization more generally. In 1997, the state's exports to the European Union totaled $21.1 billion, 19.3 percent of all California exports. Similarly, international free trade agreements generated by the World Trade Organization created additional economic opportunities for California investors and entrepreneurs. By the year 2000, the state's economic fortunes were tied more than ever to foreign trade. That year, the California Trade and Commerce Agency announced that "California's international trade helps drive not only our own economy, but the rest of the nation's as well."

From the start, free trade agreements such as NAFTA attracted criticism from some farmers, unionists, and environmentalists. California's growers voiced concern that cheaper Mexican produce might force them out of business. Organized labor argued that manufacturers would relocate outside the country to take advantage of a cheaper, nonunionized work force. In the end, they maintained, workers in both locations were likely to suffer from reduced bargaining power, low wages, and poor working conditions. Environmentalists argued that existing environmental protection standards, such as those that banned the importation of goods that compromised endangered species, could be undermined by free trade agreements. By the turn of the century, growing numbers of Californians viewed globalization with some suspicion, boycotting companies that produced goods under sweatshop conditions or pressing environmental groups to adopt global agendas.

A Redistribution of Income?

Not all Californians shared in the boom of 1994 to 2000. For many, the high-tech boom generated little more than skyrocketing housing costs and low-wage service jobs, which accounted for two-thirds of all job growth in the 1990s.

Unemployment rates fell significantly (see Figure 13.2), but economic analysts pointed to a 6 percent *decline* in the real adjusted family income for the poorest 20 percent of Californians between 1994 and 2000. Only the wealthiest one-third of California families experienced real income growth in the decade of the 1990s, and they experienced less than 4 percent growth. Economists divide the population into three groups: those of lower income (family incomes no more than double the federal poverty level), a middle-income group (family incomes more than double but less than five times the poverty level), and those of upper income (more than five times the poverty level). Between 1969 and 1998, the middle group shrank from 55 percent of the state's population to 39 percent. Of those who left the middle group, 40 percent moved to the lower-income group, the rest to the upper level. According to a senior analyst for the Federal Reserve Bank of San Francisco, over the course of the 1990s, "a greater number of [California] residents lived in poverty, the middle class was shrinking, and a majority of families had incomes below the level of their counterparts nationwide."

Organized labor joined with church and community activists to attack the growing income disparity by promoting living wage ordinances on the municipal level. In Los Angeles, Oakland, San José, San Francisco, West Hollywood, and Orange County, labor-led coalitions secured higher minimum wage rates for employees of city contractors. San José activists also obtained a companion measure that required city service contractors to adopt union-friendly policies.

At the same time, and perhaps more significantly for many privately employed service sector employees, the largest representative of service workers in the state, the Service Employees International Union (SEIU), launched major organizing drives. In what organizers termed the "largest union victory in decades," SEIU brought seventy-four thousand Los Angeles home-care workers into its union in 1999, highlighting a shift on the part of unions from manufacturing toward the low-paying service sector. Similarly, SEIU janitors carried out successful strikes in Silicon Valley, San Diego, and Los Angeles for higher wages and improved benefits. Responding to the state's shift from an industrial- to a service-based economy, SEIU set the stage for a potential resurgence of labor.

During the 1980s and 1990s, the rate of women's participation in the labor force grew, reaching 55.5 percent by 2000. During the same period, the wage gap between men and women narrowed. By 1997, women's earnings averaged 84.4 percent of men's, the narrowest wage differential in the nation outside of the District of Columbia. This shrinking of the wage gap came in part because of the declining economic fortunes of some male workers rather than a rise in women's earnings, and more women than men continued to live in poverty. Women also continued to be underrepresented at higher corporate levels.

Between 1989 and 1999, two-thirds of the state's new jobs were created at the lower rungs of the service sector. As these jobs replaced ones in such blue-collar, unionized, high-wage industries as manufacturing or transportation, more workers entered nonunion, lower-paying occupations with few opportunities for advancement—the types of jobs long held by women. At the same time, the cost of housing, medical care, and child care rose for most families, further eroding personal and family income. Between 1979 and 1998, those at the bottom 30 percent of the income structure saw their purchasing power decline by 18 percent. Even with women's increased labor force participation, many California families had difficulty making ends meet.

Single women with children, especially those without the education and job skills to move beyond poorly paying service jobs, faced significant obstacles to economic independence. In 1996, single mothers headed one out of every five working poor families, and most of them earned insufficient wages to lift themselves and their children out of poverty. Welfare, the last resort for many poor women with dependent children, was refashioned to reflect changing attitudes toward poverty. A major revision of federal welfare programs took place in 1996, touching off a revision of state programs designed to make welfare "a temporary support in times of crisis rather than a way of life." The new law established a five-year cumulative cap on benefits, after which recipients would have to fend for themselves.

Welfare rolls statewide dropped significantly, but child poverty rates remained high. Before implementation of the welfare reforms, during the 1996–1997 school year, 48 percent of all of California's K–12 students met federal eligibility requirements for free or reduced-price meal programs, and this proportion changed very little thereafter. This concentration of children in need was surpassed only by Louisiana, Mississippi, and the District of Columbia.

The Challenges of Growth

In the 1990s, California's infrastructure strained to provide basic services to its burgeoning, fragmented population. Education, health care, housing, transportation, and energy all seemed on the verge of crisis, and Californians were forced to consider the costs of inadequate planning, the long-term results of the "tax revolt," and the drawbacks of growth.

Education

California's schools in the 1980s and 1990s became more and more diverse. The greatest change in the school-age population was in the percentage of Latino students, which increased from about one-fourth of all public school students in 1985 to almost half by 2000. The proportions of African American students declined slightly, and there were increases in the numbers of proportions of Asian American and Filipino students.

One major challenge for the public schools was their ability to respond to this increasingly diverse student body. By 2000, 42 percent of all California public school

Governors Pete Wilson and Gray Davis targeted overcrowded classrooms as one of the major problems with public education, and both sought to reduce the number of students in elementary classrooms. Their programs showed some success, but came up against serious financial constraints after 2000.

students had a first language other than English. In the Los Angeles Unified School District (LAUSD), the second-largest school system in the nation, 60 percent of students possessed limited English language skills, and more than eighty different languages were spoken in the students' homes. One study concluded that the unusually high proportion of students with limited English proficiency accounted for as much as two-thirds of the gap in math and reading performance between California students and students in other states. In 1996, for example, California placed forty-ninth among the states, tied with Tennessee, in reading scores for fourth graders. In 2001, California students' average scores in mathematics ranked third from the bottom, above only Mississippi and New Mexico. Fewer than 60 percent of all Latinos and African Americans graduated from high school, as compared to nearly 90 percent of Asians and Filipinos and 77 percent of whites.

The problems with schools were not limited to English proficiency among students. California had the largest K–12 classes in the nation. During the 1993–1994 school year, the average elementary school class in California held 29.3 students and the average secondary class was even larger. Many school facilities were in dismal repair, with more than 55 percent classified as being in poor condition. Voters nonetheless rejected a series of construction and repair bond proposals until 1997, when they approved a $2.3 billion omnibus bond issue.

In 1996, Governor Pete Wilson launched a major incentive to reduce K–3 class size to twenty students, and the initiative was later extended to other grades.

By 2002–2003, the average class size for grades K–3 was slightly less than twenty. The sudden reduction in class size combined with increasing numbers of students, growing numbers of teacher retirements, and low salaries for teachers to produce a serious teacher shortage. Of the new teachers hired in the mid-1990s, nearly two-thirds had little or no teaching experience and a quarter even lacked credentials. Soon studies showed that students in classes taught by teachers without credentials failed to learn as effectively as students in classes taught by teachers who had completed the academic coursework to qualify for credentials.

There were other attempts during the decade to improve education by upgrading the requirements for graduation from public schools and using more rigorous textbooks. Governors Wilson and Gray Davis both promoted "accountability" and the implementation of statewide standards. Funding, however, remained problematic for many districts, and some schools sought private funds to supplement their public funding. In 2000, a study by the National Center for Public Policy and Higher Education gave California a grade of C– in its preparation of students for college work, noting that only 12 percent of California high school students scored in the top 20 percent nationally on SAT/ACT college entrance examinations.

Higher education suffered as public funding declined in the early 1990s. When budgets were cut, many temporary and some tenured faculty members were laid off, significantly fewer classes were scheduled, and enrollments fell. Fees to attend public universities more than doubled. In 1990, there were 1.9 million students in the three public higher education systems (California Community Colleges, C.S.U., and U.C.); by 1995 there were 1.7 million. The largest drop was in the community colleges (down 14 percent) and in the C.S.U. (down 13 percent). At the same time, the student–faculty ratio spiked sharply upward. After 1995, college and university enrollments steadily increased, but funding did not keep pace and the student–faculty ratio remained much higher than in the 1980s. Analysts predicted more than a one-third increase in the number of students likely to seek enrollment in higher education between 1998 and 2010, but initial estimates indicated that all three public systems would be at full capacity by 2003. However, the 2003–2004 academic year brought major reductions in state funding, big increases in student fees, and reduced admissions. The first years of the twenty-first century held the portents of a decade of crisis for California's public higher education.

Thus, Californians faced multiple crises in public education. As the state struggled with issues of quality and access, California's voters appeared to be reneging on a social contract they had made decades earlier, as older, affluent, largely white voters seemed to be turning away from young, poor, and largely ethnic Californians.

Health Care and Housing

By the 1990s major changes had occurred in California's health care industry. Previously, much of health care was based on a fee-for-service model, where patients or their insurers paid physicians or clinics directly for medical treatment. A different approach emerged after World War II. In this model, eventually called managed care, patients and/or their employers paid a monthly fee to a health maintenance organization (HMO) in exchange for comprehensive health care benefits. These large-scale organizations, functioning as both insurers and providers, controlled costs by serving large numbers of patients, by accomplishing economies of scale, and in some cases by regulating the types of procedures their practitioners could perform. By the 1990s, more than 90 percent of Californians with employee health coverage were enrolled in managed-care plans—in 2002, Kaiser Permanente alone provided medical care for a third of all Californians with health insurance. Rising health care costs led some facilities to cut staff, reduce or curtail services, and divert indigent and uninsured patients to public hospitals. Even with mergers and managed care, medical costs continued to spiral upward.

At the same time, 7.3 million Californians (as of 1998) under the age of sixty-five—including more than 2 million children—lacked health coverage. More than 80 percent of the uninsured came from families with one or more working adults. For these Californians, cost was the most significant barrier to obtaining health insurance—individual coverage at a major HMO for a couple in their thirties with two children would have cost nearly half the total monthly wages of someone earning the state minimum wage.

The number of uninsured in the state continued to rise, and many of them relied on hospital emergency rooms for basic health care. One study indicated that more than seven million people were using emergency rooms as their primary source of medical care. A study in San Francisco in 2002 suggested that emergency room staff spent 15 percent of their time with non-emergency patients.

Housing also seemed to be approaching a crisis. By the late 1990s there were many more new jobs in California than new housing. For the nation as a whole, there were 1.5 new jobs for every new housing unit in the late 1990s, but in California there were 3.6 new jobs for every new housing unit. This disproportion between new jobs and additional housing pushed California housing prices upward in the late 1990s, especially in the Bay Area. Some people employed in San Francisco or Silicon Valley began to seek housing as far away as Stockton or even Sacramento, where housing prices were significantly lower.

After 2000, even though unemployment was up, pent-up demand for housing coupled with low interest rates to push housing prices even higher. As housing prices moved upward in the late 1990s, residential construction revived. However, the large majority of the new construction was of single-family homes. By early 2002, however, only 29 percent of all households in the state could afford the median-priced family home. Apartment construction, which made up more than half of the new residential units in the mid-1980s, did not revive significantly in the late 1990s. As a result, more and more Californians found themselves priced out of the market for single-family homes at a time when fewer new rental units were coming on the market.

Transportation and Energy

California's emerging global trade relationships, whether involving Europe, Latin America, or Asia, all depended on the state's transportation infrastructure—its airports (including two of the seven busiest in the nation, Los Angeles and San Francisco), ports, rail lines, and trucking routes. Nearly a third of the nation's waterborne international trade came through California in the late 1990s.

During the 1970s and 1980s, per capita government spending on public transportation in California sank to the lowest in the nation. In 1990, the tide began to turn when voters endorsed a gasoline-tax increase and $3 billion in bond issues to fund public transportation systems. Mass transit in many urban areas expanded during the 1990s, including the creation of a light rail and subway system in Los Angeles, and Metrolink, an intracity rail line connecting six southern California counties. The California High Speed Rail Authority, created in 1996, began investigating the feasibility of a seven-hundred-mile "bullet," or magnetic levitation, train running between Sacramento and San Diego at speeds above two hundred miles per hour.

Transporting goods and people made up about half of California's energy consumption. As the state's population continued to soar, so did its energy requirements. By the 1990s, California's power consumption was surpassed only by Texas. In-state sources produced about 16 percent of the natural gas California used, 53 percent of the petroleum, and 75 percent of the electricity—the rest was imported from other states and countries, notably Mexico, Canada, and Indonesia. During the early 1990s, energy prices—especially for electricity—were much higher in California than in neighboring states. The state's three largest privately owned utility companies—Pacific Gas and Electric, San Diego Gas and Electric, and Southern California Edison—constructed very few new power plants during that decade and closed many existing ones for maintenance.

High prices and political pressure from energy companies prompted deregulation. On September 23, 1996, Governor Wilson signed a bill deregulating California's electric utility industry, a measure supported unanimously by state legislators and the major energy companies. Lawmakers optimistically assumed that increased competition would increase supply and keep prices low for consumers. However, demand for electricity rose faster than anticipated, and supply fell due to droughts in the Pacific Northwest and an unexpected shortage of natural gas. Wholesale prices skyrocketed. On July 1, 1999, San Diego Gas and Electric doubled its rates for consumers, causing the legislature to impose a price cap. Later investigations revealed that Texas-based Enron Corporation and other power companies had manipulated the California market to drive prices up. An energy crisis enveloped the state in January 2001 when utility companies, claiming to be unable to buy sufficient energy, instituted a series of hour-long "rolling blackouts" that shut down power to California homes and businesses one grid section at a time.

Policymakers in California and Washington, D.C., responded to the crisis with mixed results. At the peak of the crisis, liberal Democrats in the legislature urged

Governor Davis to call the power companies' bluff—and take them over if necessary. Davis, however, committed $43 billion to long-term contracts with wholesalers—but soon discovered that he had paid too much and sought to renegotiate the contracts. Citing billions of dollars of debts, PG&E filed for bankruptcy in April of 2001—but first awarded large bonuses to its top management. Five different state and federal investigations were launched to determine whether energy companies illegally drove up prices by withholding power and whether power grid officials had manipulated the market. In December 2001, Enron filed for bankruptcy, and subsequent investigations began to reveal the extent of that company's manipulation of the California power market for its own financial advantage. By 2002, the energy crisis had abated but deregulation continued. As gas and electricity bills continued to rise and the threat of future blackouts lurked, Californians had reason to feel less than optimistic about the state's energy future.

California and September 11, 2001

The terrorist attacks on New York City and Washington, D.C., on September 11, 2001, deeply affected California's society and economy. All four of the crashed airliners had been headed to California—three to Los Angeles and one to San Francisco. Forty-three of the 266 people on board the planes were Californians, and more Californians died in the World Trade Center. Governor Gray Davis quickly ordered the closure of all airports and state buildings and bolstered security at the State Water Project, electrical grid, bridges, and nuclear power plants.

California's economy experienced a marked downturn after September 11, mirroring the national economy. Tourism was hit especially hard as air traffic and hotel occupancy fell substantially. The Bay Area suffered the most, as hotel occupancy fell 16.3 percent during the first half of 2002. The California airline industry cut back on flights and laid off thousands of workers, exacerbating the recession that had begun with the bursting of the dot-com bubble in mid-2000.

For Californians of Middle Eastern descent, the months following September 11 brought increased prejudice and threat of violence. "You can feel it in the air," Souleiman Ghali, president of the San Francisco Islamic Society, said on September 12. "All the Arabs and Muslims in this country are beginning to feel suspect—no matter how loyal they are." For a short time, organizations such as the Islamic Network Group in San José received death threats while shops and restaurants owned by Arab Americans throughout California suffered vandalism.

Politics in the New California

As the twentieth century came to a close, Californians faced major questions about crime, immigration, and education. The diversity of racial and ethnic groups in California provided a crucial context for several initiatives that reflected anxieties felt by some Californians about the state's future. The state's restructured economy also carried omens for its politics. However, for the most part, Californians tended toward a centrist mode in their political choices.

Government by Initiative

Some of the state's new demographics and economic patterns found expression in a series of voter initiatives. By the end of the 1990s, political observers were speaking about "government by initiative." This meant the use of voter initiatives, often by well-organized interest groups, to bypass the legislative process and secure public policy. These groups hired agents to solicit the necessary signatures to get a proposal on the ballot and then spent lavishly on political advertising to gain a majority of the votes for the initiative on Election Day. Still, some initiatives also represented genuine voter enterprise and were passed without an elaborate campaign.

Some California initiatives drew national attention and sometimes imitation. In November 1990, California joined Oklahoma as the first states to limit the number of terms for state legislators—California assembly members are restricted to three two-year terms and state senators to two four-year terms, and those who reach the limit are prohibited from ever again running for the legislature. Voters adopted term limits—Proposition 45 of 1990—partly in response to the increasing entrenchment of incumbents. The average tenure of state assembly members had increased from five years in the 1940s to nine years in the 1980s; in the California elections of 1984, 1986, and 1988, 99 percent of incumbents won reelection. However, there were other currents in the term-limits vote as well. Conservatives hoped to open more opportunities for their candidates and to remove long-serving liberals, and some proponents of the measure saw it as a way to end the long tenure of Willie Brown, an African American from San Francisco, as speaker of the assembly.

In 1994, voters used the initiative process to change state policy on the sentencing of repeat offenders. Proposition 184, the so-called "Three Strikes" initiative, was overwhelmingly approved by the electorate (72 percent to 28 percent). Prompted in part by the kidnapping and murder of a twelve-year-old girl by an ex-convict, Proposition 184 required that those convicted of a third felony be given a mandatory sentence of twenty-five years to life. The strong support for this measure was a response, in part, to the previous ten years when drug-related, violent crime rates rose dramatically. The state legislature had passed several laws to increase sentences for crimes, and the number of prison inmates in California exploded to more than 160,000 by 2000. Those who supported Proposition 184 helped to give California the largest prison population in the nation, but, ironically, by 1994 the crime rate had begun to fall.

During the 1990s, several initiatives addressed issues related to race and immigration. Peter Wilson, a Republican, became governor in 1990 and found the state in serious financial difficulty due to a recession. After making major budget cuts, he also pointed to illegal immigrants (most of whom, nearly everyone understood, came from Mexico) as a danger to the state because of the costs of education and social services. In full-page newspaper advertisements in 1993, Wilson argued that illegal immigrants were bankrupting the state, and that "we can no longer allow compassion to override reason." In fact, surveys showed that undocumented immigrants were not using public services in large numbers—fewer than 5 percent of undocumented immigrants who were eligible for welfare actually used it.

In 1994, Wilson supported Proposition 187 to deny undocumented immigrants all state-funded services including public education, social services, and non-emergency health care. Proposition 187 galvanized a coalition of opponents, who focused on such repercussions of the initiative as children being denied education and health care. The Catholic Church, labor unions, and most Democratic leaders, including President Bill Clinton and U.S. Senators Dianne Feinstein and Barbara Boxer, also opposed Proposition 187. Nevertheless, on November 8, 1994, Proposition 187 passed by a large margin. Almost two-thirds of white voters supported it, along with roughly half of black and Asian American voters and nearly a quarter of Latino voters. Opponents immediately filed legal actions challenging the constitutionality of the initiative, and federal courts eventually invalidated most of the proposition. At the same time, as Father Pedro Villarroya, head of the Hispanic ministry for the Catholic Archdiocese of Los Angeles, said: "We need to vote." Perhaps the biggest impact of Proposition 187 was to prompt many Latino immigrants to become citizens and to mobilize a new generation of Latino voters.

In 1995, the Regents of the University of California voted to discontinue affirmative action programs at its campuses, citing growing resentment over the granting of special admissions to minority students. Soon after, in November 1996, Proposition 209, called the "California Civil Rights Initiative," sought to prohibit all gender- and race-based preferences by any state or local "government instrumentalities" in California, thus eliminating all state-mandated affirmative action programs. With strong support from Governor Wilson, Proposition 209 narrowly passed, by 54 to 46 percent. A poll by the *Los Angeles Times* indicated that the vote in favor was heavily Republican, male, and white, and that opposition was strongest among Democrats, liberals, blacks, Latinos, and Asian Americans.

In 1998 Ronald Unz, a multimillionaire, led an effort to restrict bilingual education. Proposition 227 proposed that all instruction in public schools should be conducted in English, except when 25 percent of parents sought and secured a waiver. Unz distanced himself from Pete Wilson and nativist groups and cooperated with several prominent Latino educators. The "English Language Initiative" passed, 61 to 39 percent. Proposition 227 drew support not only from 63 percent of whites but also from 60 percent of Asian Americans and 52 percent of Latinos—who apparently concluded that eliminating bilingual education was the best way for their children to succeed.

Californians further tinkered with the electoral process in 1996 when they approved Proposition 198, creating an "open primary," which allowed voters to choose any candidate in a primary election regardless of party affiliation. Two years later, the open primary seemed to have encouraged candidates to move toward the middle of the political spectrum to win votes from moderate members of the opposite party. However, in June 2000, the U.S. Supreme Court struck down the open primary as unconstitutional on the grounds that it violated political parties' First Amendment rights of association, thereby ending the experiment after only one election.

Another ballot measure supported by California voters in 1996 suffered a similar fate—the "Compassionate Use Act," or Proposition 215, which legalized marijuana use for "seriously ill Californians." The U.S. Supreme Court invalidated the act in May 2001, ruling that the drug had "no medical benefits worthy of an exception." In the meantime, however, voters in several other states had followed the lead of California and passed their own "medical marijuana" initiatives.

In 2000, gays and lesbians became the target of a controversial ballot measure. Proposition 22, the "Limit on Marriages" initiative, stated simply: "Only marriage between a man and a woman is valid or recognized in California." The measure was aimed at the possibility that, through reciprocity arrangements, actions by other states might give legal recognition to same-sex marriages in California. Congress had passed the "Defense of Marriage Act" in 1996, granting states the right to deny the validity of gay and lesbian marriages, and thirty states had done so by 1999. In California, Proposition 22 drew its strongest support from conservative Protestants, Catholics, and Mormons, and it passed by 61 to 39 percent, winning in every county except five in the Bay Area. The measure cut across gender and racial lines, winning support from a majority of men and women as well as every racial group.

In general, however, California remained near the forefront of gay rights issues. Polls in the wake of Prop 22 showed that 81 percent of Californians opposed job or housing discrimination on the basis of sexual orientation. Self-identified gay voters made up 6 percent of the electorate in 2000, and helped elect five gay and lesbian state legislators in 2000. In February 2004, Gavin Newsom, the newly elected mayor of San Francisco, grabbed national headlines when he directed city officials to issue marriage licenses to same-sex couples. Within a few weeks, thousands of people recited their vows, promising to take each other as "spouses for life" rather than as "husband and wife." Newsom argued that Proposition 22 violated the equal rights provision of the state constitution, and his action in ordering the issuance of marriage licenses set up a challenge to the constitutionality of the proposition. A court order halted the same-sex marriages pending a court hearing on the issue of constitutionality, but within a month constitutional challenges were under way in other states as well, and President George W. Bush announced his support for an amendment to the federal constitution to prohibit gays and lesbians from marrying.

With these initiatives and actions, California confirmed its reputation as—in the words of political analyst Michael Barone—"the great laboratory of America."

The Politics of the Center I: The Governorship of Peter Wilson

Just as voter support for initiatives seemed to embrace both social conservatism and social liberalism, the state's politics more generally seemed to alternate between moderate conservatism and moderate liberalism. Attractive and dynamic, Peter Wilson, a former marine, had won election to two terms in the U.S. Senate, where his record combined fiscal conservatism and social moderation, including being generally pro-choice and pro-environment. Republican strategists persuaded Wilson to run for governor because they considered his moderate image most likely to be a winner. At stake in the 1990 election for governor was the redistricting of California's legislative and congressional districts. Republicans knew that they could not win control of the legislature, but by winning the governorship—and the ability to veto legislation—they hoped to keep the Democrats in the legislature from eliminating Republican districts through redistricting.

Wilson narrowly won, but his first term was beset by financial crises. Faced with a sagging economy and a $14.3 billion projected deficit in 1991, Wilson significantly raised taxes and drastically slashed government spending. He also promoted reforms in public K–12 education—reducing class sizes (but not increasing teachers' salaries), promoting statewide curricular standards, and ending "social promotion" of students who did not meet the standards. Wilson also moved steadily to the right—reducing welfare benefits and becoming the first governor since Ronald Reagan to carry out the death penalty. He reduced state expenditures on workers' compensation by 30 percent and convinced the Industrial Welfare Commission to remove restrictions on overtime.

In 1992, Democrats carried the state for their presidential candidate, Bill Clinton. Both of California's U.S. Senate seats were up for election that year: one to fill Wilson's vacated seat and the other due to the expiration of the term of Alan Cranston, who chose not to run again. California made history that year by electing two women to the U.S. Senate: Dianne Feinstein (who won Wilson's former Senate seat) and Barbara Boxer, both Democrats. No other state had ever been represented in the Senate by two women at the same time.

Wilson's tough-on-crime stance and hostility to illegal immigration resonated with many California voters, and he easily won reelection in 1994. Wilson rode a crest of conservatism that year that saw passage of Propositions 184 and 187 and gave Republicans a majority in the state assembly for the first time in twenty-five years. Nonetheless, Democrat Dianne Feinstein won reelection to the U.S. Senate despite a strong challenge. Feinstein, however, had cultivated a centrist posture and managed a close win in the midst of the more general Republican, and conservative, victory.

Despite their victories in 1994, the Republicans failed to control the state assembly throughout most of 1995, even though they started with a tiny majority.

Instead, long-time Assembly Speaker Willie Brown of San Francisco secured re-election as speaker with support from a renegade Republican. When that Republican was recalled in a special election, all the Democratic assembly members then voted for Doris Allen, a Republican, who was dissatisfied with the Republican leadership and who, adding her own vote to the Democrats', became the first female speaker—only to be recalled by the irate Republicans. Maneuverings by Brown and the Republicans kept the assembly in turmoil for months—a turmoil compounded by mean-spiritedness as the new term limits meant that many long-time legislators had to depart and, sometimes, run against each other for other offices. Late in 1995, Brown was elected mayor of San Francisco and resigned from the assembly, having served longer as speaker than anyone else in state history. With term limits in place, it became unlikely that any speaker would serve for more than a few years at most.

Wilson's second term as governor—begun amidst the assembly's partisan intrigues—brought few accomplishments. He sought the Republican nomination for president in 1996 but attracted little support. That year, California's voters gave a large majority to Bill Clinton, the Democratic candidate for president, and returned a Democratic majority to the state assembly. In the end, Wilson's anti-immigrant politics and the passage of Propositions 184, 187, and 209 seem to have triggered a backlash that sent California politics back to Democratic control.

The Politics of the Center II: The Governorship of Gray Davis

In 1998, for the first time in twenty years, Californians elected a Democrat, Joseph "Gray" Davis, as governor. They reelected Barbara Boxer, another Democrat, to the U.S. Senate, elected Democrats as lieutenant governor, attorney general, auditor, and treasurer, sent Democratic majorities to the state senate and state assembly, and elected Democrats to a majority of the state's seats in the U.S. House of Representatives.

This shift to the Democrats came from several sources. Already strongly Democratic, many Latinos were alienated by Republican attacks on immigrants, and more than 70 percent of Latino voters voted Democratic for governor in 1998. Labor unions played an important role, spending more than $33 million in the 1998 election. Wilson's sometimes heavy-handed educational reforms had angered the 290,000-member California Teachers' Association, which gave strong support to the Democrats. Women were also responsible for the Democratic win. During the 1980s, political analysts had drawn public attention to a new phenomenon—a widening gender gap in state and national elections. The gap reflected differences in how men and women regarded political issues, the two major parties, and individual candidates. Women, for example, registered greater concern for child care, family leave, reproductive rights, social security, health care, gun control, and education, while men focused more on fiscal restraint, military preparedness, and limiting the size of government. Female voters were more likely to support Democratic candidates and to show up at the polls in greater numbers.

In 1998, the gender gap was particularly pronounced. Boxer was reelected to the U.S. Senate with a nine-point margin of support from female voters. Gray Davis, the winning Democratic candidate for governor, had liberal views on reproductive rights and social policy, which gave him the commanding lead among female voters. The reelections of Boxer in 1998 and Feinstein in 2000 demonstrated growing support for female candidates, particularly female Democrats. By 2000, women held thirteen (12-D, 1-R) of California's fifty-two seats in the U.S. House of Representatives. In the state legislature, women held eleven of the forty senate seats (10-D, 1-R) and twenty of the eighty assembly seats (15-D, 4-R, 1-I). And, in October 2001, Nancy Pelosi, a Democratic member of Congress from San Francisco, became the first woman to be elected party whip (the second most powerful leadership position for the minority Democrats) in the U.S. House of Representatives.

By the mid-1990s and after, Republican voters, in their primary elections, usually chose candidates opposed to abortion and gun controls. To win a general election, however, it seemed that a candidate could not take those stands. When combined with significant support for the Democrats from Latinos, women, and unions, the result was a series of losses by Republicans in statewide elections. After the 1998 elections, the Republicans held only two of the eight statewide offices; after 2002, they had none.

Though politically tenacious, Davis lacked both charm and charisma. Many Californians came to consider his nickname, "Gray," a description of his personality. As governor, he moved with caution and an eye on the polls. Proudly calling himself a moderate, Davis was often at odds with the liberal Democrats who led the legislature, as he refused to support many of their bills but expected them to follow his lead. Davis alienated some liberals by his approach to filling appointive positions. Rumors spread that most appointive positions required a hefty contribution to Davis's campaign fund, and some positions remained unfilled for many months or even years. Though Davis rejected scores of liberal bills, he and the Democrats in the legislature put through tougher gun control laws, increased health care safeguards, and limited extensions of gay rights, and they spent more than $3.5 billion to improve state highways. Under Republican pressure, the legislature also approved, and Davis signed, measures to reduce taxes. Nevertheless, Davis consistently sought the middle of the road and worked to hold together his complex coalition. His handling of the energy crisis of early 2001 (see pp. 431–432), however, produced a quick drop in his popularity, from nearly 60 percent approval to below 40 percent. In 2002, seeking a second term, Davis faced a very conservative Republican who had virtually no previous experience in electoral politics. Davis won by 47 to 42 percent, with more than 5 percent going to the Green Party candidate. The campaign was so negative that many voters stayed home, producing one of the lowest turnouts in the state's history—and, ironically, significantly reducing the number of signatures needed to launch a recall,

Arnold Schwarzenegger has gone from bodybuilder to Mr. Universe to star of nearly thirty action-hero movies to governor of California. Like Ronald Reagan before him, he understands the power of the media and the importance of his image. However, his election as governor was due to more than just media savvy. What factors explain his election?

because the state constitution provides that the number of signatures necessary to trigger a recall is based on a percentage of the votes cast for that office in the previous election.

The Politics of the Center III: The Governorship of Arnold Schwarzenegger

By early 2003, California faced a monstrous deficit—between $26 and $35 billion—the result of reduced tax revenues due to recession and tax cuts, of spending $43 billion on electricity contracts at the height of the energy crisis, and of the increased cost of state services due to modest inflation. Only a few legislators had any experience in such a situation. Since 1978, Proposition 13 has required that the budget, including any new taxes, be approved by a two-thirds vote of the legislature. Republicans not only refused to support any increase in taxes, but some argued that any Republican who voted for a tax increase should be subject to recall proceedings. Democrats lacked the necessary two-thirds by a few votes in each house, but they refused to slash spending for education and health care. The deadlock continued for months, but was resolved, finally, through a compromise to balance the budget by borrowing—thus putting off the crisis for a year.

In February 2003, just weeks after Davis began his second term, Ted Costa launched a recall campaign. Costa had entered politics as an assistant to Paul Gann, who, with Howard Jarvis, had initiated Proposition 13. Costa's recall campaign sputtered along until Darrell Issa, a conservative Republican member of Congress, pumped two-thirds of a million dollars of his own money into the effort. The additional funds generated additional publicity and put the petition drive over the top. Under provisions adopted in the progressive era, Californians were now to vote on two matters: first, whether Davis should be recalled; second, who should succeed him. Davis was barred from running. The election brought an outpouring of candidates—135 in total—and a media circus that captured national and international headlines.

To the surprise of Issa, who had planned to run, Arnold Schwarzenegger appeared on Jay Leno's *Tonight Show* and announced that he would run to succeed Davis, as a Republican. Born in Austria, Schwarzenegger first achieved fame as a bodybuilder, then became internationally famous as the star of action movies. Other Republicans, including Issa, bowed out under strong pressure from party leaders. Schwarzenegger, like Wilson and Davis, came from the moderate wing of his party—he opposed new taxes but was pro-choice and supported perhaps the most ambitious environmental platform of any major candidate for public office in the country. His wife, Maria Shriver, was a Democrat and part of the politically powerful family of John F. Kennedy.

The vote to recall Davis received 55 percent in favor, as Davis became the second governor in American history to be recalled from office. In the vote for a new governor, Schwarzenegger received 49 percent, easily defeating Lieutenant Governor Cruz Bustamante, the most prominent Democrat on the ballot, who got 32 percent.

In one of his first actions as governor, Schwarzenegger repealed an unpopular motor vehicle license tax, further increasing the state's deficit. Schwarzenegger faced probably the biggest challenge to confront any California governor—many knowledgeable Californians considered that, if the state had been a corporation or a city, it would have had to declare bankruptcy. Schwarzenegger's first major action was to seek a popular vote on a huge bond issue of $15 billion in March 2004, as a way to resolve the state's desperate financial situation. He tied the bond issue to a constitutional amendment to provide for a state reserve fund. He campaigned aggressively around the state on behalf of both measures, and both won by large margins, due primarily to Schwarzenegger's ability to mobilize voters. The approval of the bond issue gave him, at least, a little breathing space in dealing with the state's perilous financial condition.

Religion, Culture, and the Arts

By the beginning of the new century, California, with its growing immigrant population and openness to new belief systems, contained a greater diversity of religious sects and denominations than any other state in the nation. California also came to be seen, more than ever, as a place of innovation and experimentation in self-improvement and spiritual development. And California kept a secure hold on its reputation as a leading site for new developments in cultural expression and the arts.

Spirituality in the Midst of Materialism

By the early 1990s, California was the center for New Age spirituality, a loosely defined and many-centered movement that offered its followers a wide range of strategies for self-improvement and spiritual development. Astrology, meditation, yoga, massage, crystals, channeling (psychic communication with "higher level" spirits), pyramid power, vortexes, numerology, dream work, feng shui (an ancient Chinese practice), interspecies and extraterrestrial communication, runes (ancient Germanic characters used to divine the future), tarot cards, Native American religious traditions, wicca (whose adherents sometimes described their practices as a variety of witchcraft and at other times claimed a linkage to ancient Celtic or even Paleolithic practices), and neo-paganism (groups claiming ties to Druids or other pre-Christian beliefs) were all among the most prominent beliefs or instruments proclaimed or appropriated by various New Age seekers of enlightenment.

The origins of many such groups date to the 1950s and 1960s, when the Beats and other countercultural rebels searched for higher consciousness through experimentation with hallucinogenic drugs, Asian religious practices, and various occult and mystical traditions. Rejecting mainstream religious institutions, which they regarded as upholding the corrupt values of the older generation, they sought a belief system based on cooperation, respect for nature, open sexual expression, egalitarianism, individual creativity, and a life unencumbered by material possessions. By the late 1960s, countercultural astrologers explained that a new age, the Age of Aquarius, was dawning, creating greater receptivity to truth, cooperation, peace, love, and enlightenment. The Aquarian Age, they explained, arrives every two thousand years, with the last coinciding with the birth of Christ.

During the 1970s and 1980s, larger numbers of Californians sought personal and spiritual growth through the Human Potential Movement. Adherents claimed that individuals had greater capacity for spiritual and emotional growth if liberated from traditional social constraints and the everyday stress of modern life. Touting massage, meditation, hot tubs, encounter groups, psychotherapy, rebirthing, and relaxation therapies, the movement attracted a national following. California, however, retained its leadership position by spawning a disproportionate share of self-help programs, gurus, literature, and products. The Esalen Institute, hosting human potential workshops and seminars at its Big Sur retreat facility, played a central role in preserving the state's dominant role in the movement.

By the 1990s, when seekers of spirituality proclaimed a "New Age," they drew upon this heritage and added other beliefs and practices. For some of its adherents, the proliferation of alternatives may have represented a desire for a more spiritual alternative to the prevalent commercialism of daily life and to the rapid technological change that surrounded so many Californians. The search for meaning had its commercial side, too, as some New Age entrepreneurs peddled spiritual goods. Unscrupulous "leaders" proved to be remarkably adept at convincing seekers to part with large sums of money for self-improvement products and programs. Even more ominously, some exercised a dangerous level of control over their flocks. Some religious experiments ended in tragedy. In 1997, thirty-nine members of a group called Heaven's Gate committed suicide in a San Diego suburb when their leader convinced them that a spaceship had come to take them to a higher dimension.

California's spiritual revival also included reform efforts within mainstream religious organizations. Feminists pushed for the ordination of women, more positive representations of female religious figures, and more inclusive language in sacred texts. Others urged their denominations to address contemporary issues and problems. In 1968, the Reverend Troy Perry founded the Metropolitan Community Church (MCC) in Los Angeles as a church for gays and lesbians, and called for greater tolerance within established denominations. More than three hundred MCC churches have since been established throughout the state and around the world. Berkeley Rabbi Michael Lerner attracted a following by emphasizing Judaism's progressive, social justice–oriented tradition. Cecil Williams, pastor of San Francisco's Glide Memorial Methodist Church, spearheaded a similar effort within his denomination by creating a ministry that reflected ethnic and class diversity and provided social services to the needy.

Opposed to the liberalization of mainstream religion, millions of Californians (along with millions of other Americans) embraced Christian fundamentalism, a descendant of the fundamentalism that had shown such strength in the 1920s. These groups typically opposed abortion and any recognition of rights for gays and lesbians, and called for preservation of what they considered "family values." Some constructed huge church buildings, especially in suburbs, and experimented with new forms of worship, including rock music. Many congregations were only loosely tied to denominational structures, and some moved toward charismatic practices, including speaking in tongues and healing. Claiming to speak for a "moral majority," some fundamentalist leaders sought to influence politics by contributing millions of dollars to conservative political action committees and candidates and attempting to create a tightly organized voting bloc.

Fitness, Health, and Entertainment

Physical well-being was an integral part of the Human Potential and New Age movements. During the 1970s, 1980s, and 1990s, Californians became ever more health-conscious, introducing the nation to a wide range of fitness trends, holistic therapies, and food preferences. Jogging, aerobics, personalized training regimens, rock climbing, skateboarding, hang-gliding, rollerblading, sailboarding, snowboarding, and mountain biking provided new physical challenges. Those less inclined to exercise regularly could still project a rugged, outdoor image by wearing fitness fashions or driving a sport-utility vehicle.

A wide range of medical alternatives, first explored by countercultural critics of the medical establishment, gained acceptance among some mainstream consumers. For example, enthusiasts proclaimed that massage, mineral baths, aromatherapy, reflexology, dietary supplements, and herbal remedies helped to ward off stress, recover from strain, and fight disease.

Diet also became a matter of concern for many Californians. Some became vegetarians or vegans (eschewing not only meat but also eggs and dairy products) for health or ethical reasons. Foods bearing the labels "natural" or "organic" also seemed to offer benefits. "California cuisine"—fresh, organically grown food prepared with a minimum of cooking and served in small portions—was developed, especially by Alice Waters, the owner of Berkeley's Chez Panisse restaurant, and became a staple of upscale food establishments across the nation. The popularity of organic foods created new economic opportunities for some entrepreneurs. Although most California growers still used chemical pesticides, fertilizers, and herbicides, some adopted more environmentally conscious agricultural practices in response to consumer demand. They lobbied successfully for the California Organic Foods Act, passed by the legislature in 1990, to ensure that conventional growers could not falsely advertise their produce as "organically" grown. Consumer demand for natural or organic products also affected the food processing industry. By 1990, California-based companies were producing a disproportionate share of the nation's natural or organic cereals, snack foods, beverages, and frozen, baked, and canned goods.

Cultural Expression

Artistic expression in California in the 1990s reflected the state's political and social changes. Music, film, art, and literature produced by Californians spoke to contemporary issues and dug beneath the surface of stereotypes to explore topical problems.

Southern California remained a hotbed of diverse musical activity. Rap and hip-hop artists in particular rose to prominence through their frank portrayals of urban life. N.W.A. (for Niggaz With Attitude) sparked nationwide controversy—and made millions of dollars—with the release of their 1988 album *Straight Outta Compton,* bluntly describing life on the mean streets of South Central Los Angeles. With funky beats and hardcore lyrics, N.W.A. sold millions of records—mostly to white, suburban, male teenagers—and attracted harsh criticism for being misogynistic, violent, and sensationalistic. The group's verbal attacks on police brutality and racism drew upon the same anger that led to the Rodney King "riots" in April 1992. N.W.A. disbanded in 1992 but members Dr. Dre and Ice Cube went on to successful solo careers, inspiring a second generation of West Coast rappers. Formed in 1991, Rage Against the Machine represented another arm of the Los Angeles hip-hop movement. Combining rap and heavy metal,

Rage Against the Machine wrote songs with anti-corporate, anti-war, and anti-globalism lyrics and staged benefits for left-wing causes.

The continuing growth of southern California's Latino population brought Spanish-language music—in a proliferation of styles—into the mainstream. Up-beat, brass-heavy *banda* music made KLAX-FM the highest-rated radio station in Los Angeles. Latino punk bands angrily responded to the nativist political climate fostered by statewide propositions in the 1990s. "Through our music, we can express—we can scream—our thoughts and emotions of all the things that are happening in our communities," said Lina, a vocalist for the LA-based punk band Subsistencia.

The 1980s and 1990s saw Hollywood filmmaking split into mainstream and "independent" camps. Enormous media conglomerates such as Disney and AOL Time Warner bought up not only mainstream movie studios but also television channels, music studios, publishing companies, Internet portals, and theme parks. Such "vertical integration" gave corporate giants multiple opportunities to cross-promote their products, and also encouraged proliferation of homogeneous, blockbuster movies aimed at appealing to the largest possible number of worldwide viewers. So-called independent studios funded more idiosyncratic visions, but by the turn of the century many of these had been absorbed by conglomerates. The arrival of digital technology in the late 1990s promised to democratize moviemaking by dramatically reducing costs, but limited distribution restricted the impact of personal, experimental, and political films.

In the midst of this corporate transformation, some filmmakers produced important works during the late 1980s and 1990s by exploring critical issues in contemporary California society, especially Los Angeles's complex social strata. Ramon Menendez's *Stand and Deliver* (1988) focused upon real-life educator Jaime Escalante's struggles to help his East LA high school math class pass a standardized calculus test, dramatizing class and race inequities in public education. *Boyz N the Hood* (1991), written and directed by twenty-three-year-old LA native John Singleton, followed three African American men growing up in South Central Los Angeles, portraying how economic and familial pressures could erupt into violence. Lawrence Kasdan's *Grand Canyon* (1992), Robert Altman's *Short Cuts* (1993), and Paul Thomas Anderson's *Magnolia* (1999) considered the ways that people from different class and racial backgrounds interact in contemporary LA. Meanwhile, Quentin Tarantino's *Pulp Fiction* (1994), Curtis Hanson's *L.A. Confidential* (1997), and David Lynch's *Mulholland Drive* (2001) reestablished Los Angeles as lurid, mysterious, and quintessentially cool.

California literature enjoyed a renaissance during the 1980s and 1990s as writers emphasized the importance of place. The Central Valley became the center of a dynamic literary movement as diverse as the valley itself. Gerald Haslam celebrated small-town, working-class people in dozens of short stories and novels set in the Central Valley. Gary Soto, son of Mexican American farm laborers, related his experiences growing up in Fresno through poetry and books for young adults. Maxine Hong Kingston, born in Stockton to Chinese immigrant parents, explored Chinese Americans' struggles against prejudice in California past and present in *Woman Warrior* (1976) and *China Men* (1980). Her *Tripmaster Monkey* (1989) centered upon a fifth-generation Californian struggling to strike a balance between tradition and modernity.

The Bay Area maintained its reputation as a literary hub for writers of varied background and inclination. Czeslaw Milosz, born in Lithuania and a Berkeley resident since 1960, won the Nobel Prize in 1980 for his sensitive, often-California-inspired poetry. Oakland native Amy Tan broke onto the bestseller lists with her novels *The Joy Luck Club* (1989) and *The Bonesetter's Daughter* (2001), both centering on relationships between Chinese American mothers and daughters in contemporary San Francisco. Robert Hass, U.S. poet laureate from 1995 to 1997, found much beauty and much pain in the landscapes of his native northern California.

Southern California in the 1980s and 1990s saw a flowering of literature grappling with racial identity. Mystery author Walter Mosley wrote novels and stories examining both pre- and post-civil-rights-era race relations in Los Angeles. Anna Deavere Smith's one-woman play, *Twilight: Los Angeles, 1992,* presented a mosaic of voices from the Rodney King "riots" drawn from more than two hundred interviews she conducted with Angelenos of varying backgrounds. Luis Valdez, a playwright based in LA, wrote *Zoot Suit* (1978), *Bandito!* (1982), and *I Don't Have to Show You No Stinkin' Badges!* (1986), plays focused upon Mexican American identity in California history.

The California Dream in the Twenty-First Century

If demographers are correct, by 2040 California will still be a state without an ethnic majority, though Latinos will be very close, with 48 percent of the total. Whites who are not Latinos will comprise less than a third of the state's population. Asians and Pacific Islanders will make up 15 percent, African Americans 5 percent, and Native Americans 1 percent. These demographic shifts will affect California's society, economy, politics, and cultural expression. So long as its economy remains strong and cutting-edge, the state's prominence in shaping national and world events is likely to increase as its multiethnic population grows. Though the September 11 tragedy serves as a constant reminder that life in California remains inextricably intertwined with national and international events, perhaps the greatest challenge for Californians in the twenty-first century will be learning how to cooperate to manage growth while maintaining equity in a contested, pluralistic society.

"I grew up listening to my Mexican father describe California as *el norte,* even while the lady next door from Minnesota insisted we lived in the West," memoirist Richard Rodriguez has observed. "In twentieth-century California, separate dreams were constructed side by side, as at Walt Disney's Magic Kingdom, where

Tomorrowland was right next door to Frontierland. Disharmony became California's theme and our humor. In this new century, our separate dreams are sliding together." The consequences of "sliding together" are becoming visible in the blurring of racial and gender categories, in heterogeneous political coalitions, and in desegregated neighborhoods. The benefits of California's remarkable cultural richness remain enormous. More contested than ever, the California dream—in its multitude of forms—persists in the twenty-first century.

Summary

At the beginning of the twenty-first century, Latinos and immigrants from Asia swelled California's population and made it more diverse. Two highly publicized court cases, one involving Los Angeles police officers charged with beating Rodney King and the other involving O.J. Simpson, focused attention on issues of race and policing in that city. California's ever increasing ethnic and racial diversity has major implications for other aspects of life in the state.

The state's economy went through a cycle of bust-boom-bust during the 1990s and early 2000s. The recession of the early 1990s was especially serious, but was followed by a major economic expansion fueled especially by information technology and globalization. Many Californians, however, never fully shared in the economic gains of the period.

Throughout the 1990s and early 2000s, California's systems of education, health care, housing, transportation, and energy seemed constantly on the verge of crisis. The public schools faced large classes and also significant numbers of students for whom English was not their first language. The cost of health care excluded significant numbers of Californians from the various systems of managed care that covered a majority of state residents. Construction of housing and public transportation facilities lagged significantly behind the growth of population. And the state's experiment in energy deregulation helped to set off a major crisis in energy.

Many observers described the state's political system as increasingly dysfunctional, partly through repeated use of the initiative to put limits on the ability of state lawmakers to make policy or manage the state's budget. The governors of the period—Peter Wilson, Joseph "Gray" Davis, and Arnold Schwarzenegger—were all more centrist than their parties' leaders. The recall of Davis and election of Schwarzenegger galvanized the state's political system at a time when it faced one of its most significant challenges in the history of the state—the state's near bankruptcy.

During the late twentieth and early twenty-first century, California remained at the forefront of many social and cultural movements, including a variety of spiritual movements that go under the general heading of "New Age." Californians also set national and international trends in diet, exercise and fitness, and cultural expression.

With all of its problems, the California economy at the beginning of the twenty-first century remained the most productive in the nation, and Californians remained at the forefront of many new developments in technology. Other Californians kept the state at the forefront of creativity. Despite its problems, the state continues to attract immigrants from around the world, contributing further to the state's ethnic and racial diversity.

Suggested Readings

- Baldassare, Mark, *California in the New Millennium: The Changing Social and Political Landscape* (Berkeley and Los Angeles: University of California Press, 2002). An overview of social and political change by a leading public policy analyst.

- Barron, Stephanie, Sheri Bernstein, and Ilene Susan Fort, *Made in California: Art, Image, and Identity, 1900–2000* (Berkeley and Los Angeles: University of California Press, 2000). An interesting survey of California's influence on American creativity, including art, film, and fashion.

- Chávez, Lydia, *Color Bind: California's Struggle to End Affirmative Action* (Berkeley and Los Angeles: University of California Press, 1998). A thorough and balanced study of Proposition 209.

- Hayes-Bautista, David E., et al., *No Longer a Minority: Latinos and Social Policy in California* (Los Angeles: UCLA Chicano Studies Research Center Publications, 1992). The economic and social impact of the growth of Latino populations in California, focusing on public policy issues.

- Neale, Steve, and Murray Smith, eds., *Contemporary Hollywood Cinema* (New York: Routledge, 1998). An anthology with essays on virtually every possible aspect of the contemporary California film industry.

- Palmer, Tim, ed., *California's Threatened Environment: Restoring the Dream* (Washington, D.C.: Island Press, 1993). A collection of essays on environmental topics, focusing on damage to the environment.

- Rowland, Wade, *Spirit of the Web: The Age of Information from Telegraph to Internet* (Toronto: Somerville House Pub., 1999). A well-written history of electronic communication.

- Saito, Leland, *Race and Politics: Asian Americans, Latinos, and Whites in a Los Angeles Suburb* (Urbana: University of Illinois Press, 1999). A sociological study of race and ethnicity as related to political mobilization and economic redevelopment in the San Gabriel Valley of Los Angeles County.

- Schrag, Peter, *Paradise Lost: California's Experience, America's Future* (Berkeley and Los Angeles: University of California Press, 1998). Recent California politics, by one of the state's leading political journalists.

▌ Williams, James C., *Energy and the Making of Modern California* (Akron: University of Akron Press, 1997). A thoroughly researched history of energy in California.

▌ Winslow, Ward, *The Making of Silicon Valley* (Palo Alto: Santa Clara Valley Historical Association, 1995). A hundred-year history of the development of technology and industry.

▌ Yáñez-Chávez, Aníbal, ed., *Latino Politics in California* (La Jolla: Center for U.S.-Mexican Studies, University of California, San Diego, 1996). An up-to-date anthology of the impact of the Latino demographic majority on electoral politics in California.

Note: In addition, for state politics since 1990, consult the *California Journal, Los Angeles Times, Sacramento Bee,* and *San Francisco Chronicle.*

Governors of California: 1767 to Present

A. Spanish Period

1767–1771	Gaspar de Portolá		1792–1794	José J. Arrillaga
1771–1774	Felipe de Barri		1794–1800	Diego de Borica
1774–1777	Fernando Rivera y Moncada		1800	Pedro de Alberni
			1800–1814	José J. Arrillaga
1777–1782	Felipe de Neve		1814–1815	José Argüello
1782–1790	Pedro Fajes		1815–1822	Pablo Vincente de Solá
1790–1792	José Antonio Roméu			

B. Mexican Period

1822–1823	Pablo Vincente de Solá		1835–1836	José Castro
1823–1825	Luis Argüello		1836	Nicolas Gutiérrez
1825–1831	José María de Echeandía			Mariano Chico
				Nicolas Gutiérrez
1831–1832	Manuel Victoria		1836–1842	Juan B. Alvarado
1832–1833	Pío Pico		1842–1845	Manuel Micheltorena
1833–1835	José Figueroa		1845–1846	Pío Pico

C. American Military Governors of California, 1846–1849

1846	John Drake Sloat		1847–1849	Richard Barnes Mason (acting)
1846–1847	Robert Field Stockton			
1847	John C. Frémont		1849	Persifor Frazer Smith
1847	Stephen W. Kearny		1849	Bennett Riley

D. Governors of the State of California, 1849–present

1851–1852	John McDougall		1907–1911	James Gillett
1852–1856	John Bigler		1911–1917	Hiram Johnson
1856–1858	J. Neeley Johnson		1917–1923	William Stephens
1858–1860	John Weller		1923–1927	Friend Richardson
1860	Milton Latham		1927–1931	C. C. Young
1860–1862	John Downey		1931–1934	James Rolph
1862–1863	Leland Stanford		1934–1939	Frank Merriam
1863–1867	Frederick Low		1939–1943	Culbert Olson
1867–1871	Henry Haight		1943–1953	Earl Warren
1871–1875	Newton Booth		1953–1959	Goodwin Knight
1875	Romualdo Pacheco		1959–1967	Edmund G. "Pat" Brown
1875–1880	William Irwin			
1880–1883	George Perkins		1967–1975	Ronald Reagan
1883–1887	George Stoneman		1975–1983	Edmund G. "Jerry" Brown
1887	Washington Bartlett			
1887–1891	Robert Waterman		1983–1991	George Deukmejian
1891–1895	Henry Markham		1991–1999	Pete Wilson
1895–1899	James Budd		1999–2003	Gray Davis
1899–1903	Henry Gage		2003–present	Arnold Schwarzenegger
1903–1907	George Pardee			

Glossary of Spanish Terms

alcalde mayor:	district magistrate
alcalde ordinario:	municipal magistrate
alférez:	second lieutenant, subordinate to a commander
ayuntamiento:	city council
castas:	general term for mixed-bloods
casta system:	ordering of Spanish American society according to racial-ethnic characteristics
compadrazgo:	ritual kinship, godparenthood
compadres:	the bond between the father and godparent of a child
comisionado:	commissioner or board member
compromisarios:	electors who vote for the town council
criollo:	American-born Spaniard
diputación:	council for the governor of California
gente de razón:	literally people of reason; term applied to all members of colonial society excepting Indians
hacendado:	the owner of a *hacienda*
hacienda:	large landed estate producing both livestock and crops for market
hijos de país:	native to California
indios bárbaros:	wild Indians, not Christianized
mayordomo:	overseer
mestizaje:	term applied to the process of race mixing among the European, African, and Indian populations of Spanish America
mestizo:	offspring of a Spaniard and an Indian
mulatto:	offspring of an African and a Spaniard
norteños:	northerners; in California those living above Santa Barbara
paisano:	native to California
peninsular:	European-born Spaniard
pobladores:	settlers
pueblo:	village, settlement, people; in New Mexico and Arizona, term applied to the various town-dwelling Indian tribes
rancho:	term for a mixed-use, small to medium rural property that in Texas referred to a large livestock estate
regidor:	alderman, town councilman
sureños:	southerners; in California those living below Santa Barbara
vaquero:	cowboy
vecino:	citizen

Photo Credits

CHAPTER 1: **p. 12:** Florence C. Shipek photograph, courtesy San Diego Museum of Man; **p. 16:** From William H. Emery, Report on the United States and Mexican Boundary Survey, Washington, D.C., 1857; **p. 22:** Oakland Museum of California, Museum Donors Acquisition Fund; **p. 26:** Courtesy M. Edith Coulter, Berkeley

CHAPTER 2: **p. 41:** Courtesy Los Angeles Museum of Natural History; **p. 44:** From San Gabriel Mission Parish, courtesy Los Angeles Museum of Natural History; **p. 45:** Courtesy California Historical Society, North Baker Library, San Francisco, FN-25092; **p. 50:** Courtesy Museo de America, Madrid

CHAPTER 3: **p. 63:** Courtesy Los Angeles Museum of Natural History; **p. 73:** Lithograph based on a watercolor painted in 1842 by a member of Commodore Thomas Catesby Jones's squadron; **p. 77:** Oakland Museum of California, Museum Donors Acquisition Fund; **p. 81:** Courtesy of The Bancroft Library, University of California, Berkeley; **p. 88:** Courtesy of The Bancroft Library, University of California, Berkeley

CHAPTER 4: **p. 101:** © CORBIS; **p. 103:** Courtesy Los Angeles Museum of Natural History; **p. 106:** Crocker Art Museum, E. B. Crocker Collection; **p. 111:** Courtesy Wells Fargo Museum, San Francisco; **p. 120:** The Society of California Pioneers

CHAPTER 5: **p. 125:** Illustration by H. Mallette Dean (1907–1975) from *Archy Lee: A California Fugitive Slave Case* by Dr. Rudolph M. Lapp, 1969, Book Club of California. Courtesy California State Library and Book Club of California; **p. 129:** Courtesy of The Bancroft Library, University of California, Berkeley; **p. 138:** Courtesy of The Bancroft Library, University of California, Berkeley; **p. 155:** Courtesy of The Bancroft Library, University of California, Berkeley

CHAPTER 6: **p. 161:** Courtesy of The Bancroft Library, University of California, Berkeley; **p. 172:** Courtesy of The Bancroft Library, University of California, Berkeley; **p. 180:** Courtesy of The Bancroft Library, University of California, Berkeley; **p. 184:** Courtesy California State Library

CHAPTER 7: **p. 196:** Courtesy of The Bancroft Library, University of California, Berkeley; **p. 202:** Los Angeles Times Photo, TMS Reprints; **p. 211:** Courtesy of The Bancroft Library, University of California, Berkeley; **p. 222:** From California's Magazine, San Francisco, 1915

CHAPTER 8: **p. 233:** © Bettmann/CORBIS; **p. 238:** © Bettmann/CORBIS; **p. 246:** Courtesy Santa Ana History Room, Santa Ana Public Library; **p. 252:** Courtesy of The Bancroft Library, University of California, Berkeley; **p. 260:** © CORBIS

CHAPTER 9: **p. 268:** © Dorothea Lange Collection, Oakland Museum of California, City of Oakland, gift of Paul S. Taylor; **p. 277:** Courtesy of The Bancroft Library, University of California, Berkeley; **p. 278:** Courtesy of The Bancroft Library, University of California, Berkeley; **p. 287:** Los Angeles Times Photo, TMS Reprints; **p. 291:** Brown Brothers

CHAPTER 10: **p. 307:** Courtesy California Department of Water Resources; **p. 311:** UCLA Air Photo Archives, Department of Geography, Spence Air Photo; **p. 314:** Courtesy Los Angeles Public Library; **p. 317:** © Bettmann/CORBIS; **p. 332:** © Allen Ginsberg/CORBIS

CHAPTER 11: **p. 342:** Courtesy of The Bancroft Library, University of California, Berkeley; **p. 347:** © Bettmann/CORBIS; **p. 350:** Walter P. Reuther Library, Wayne State University; **p. 361:** AP/Wide World; **p. 368:** © Bettmann/CORBIS

CHAPTER 12: **p. 375:** © Bettmann/CORBIS; **p. 384:** AP/Wide World; **p. 393:** No credit; **p. 396:** © Bettmann/CORBIS

CHAPTER 13: **p. 411:** © Christine Alcino; **p. 415:** © 2004 Susan Holtz; **p. 424:** © Ed Kashi/CORBIS; **p. 428:** © David Butow/CORBIS SABA; **p. 439:** AP/Wide World

Index